AF624857

BUS 515 Financial Management

Roberts Wesleyan College

M.S. in Strategic Leadership

Eugene F. Brigham | Michael C. Ehrhardt

CENGAGE Learning

Australia • Brazil • Japan • Korea • Mexico • Singapore • Spain • United Kingdom • United States

BUS 515 Financial Management: Roberts Wesleyan College, M.S. in Strategic Leadership

Eugene F. Brigham | Michael C. Ehrhardt

Senior Manager, Student Engagement:

Linda deStefano

Janey Moeller

Manager, Student Engagement:

Julie Dierig

Marketing Manager:

Rachael Kloos

Manager, Production Editorial:

Kim Fry

Manager, Intellectual Property Project Manager:

Brian Methe

Senior Manager, Production and Manufacturing:

Donna M. Brown

Manager, Production:

Terri Daley

Printed in the United States of America

Financial Management: Theory & Practice
Eugene F. Brigham | Michael C. Ehrhardt

© 2013 Cengage Learning. All rights reserved.

ALL RIGHTS RESERVED. No part of this work covered by the copyright herein may be reproduced, transmitted, stored or used in any form or by any means graphic, electronic, or mechanical, including but not limited to photocopying, recording, scanning, digitizing, taping, Web distribution, information networks, or information storage and retrieval systems, except as permitted under Section 107 or 108 of the 1976 United States Copyright Act, without the prior written permission of the publisher.

For product information and technology assistance, contact us at
Cengage Learning Customer & Sales Support, 1-800-354-9706
For permission to use material from this text or product,
submit all requests online at **cengage.com/permissions**
Further permissions questions can be emailed to
permissionrequest@cengage.com

This book contains select works from existing Cengage Learning resources and was produced by Cengage Learning Custom Solutions for collegiate use. As such, those adopting and/or contributing to this work are responsible for editorial content accuracy, continuity and completeness.

Compilation © 2014 Cengage Learning

ISBN-13: 978-1-305-00568-6
ISBN-10: 1-305-00568-6

WCN: 01-100-101

Cengage Learning
5191 Natorp Boulevard
Mason, Ohio 45040
USA

Cengage Learning is a leading provider of customized learning solutions with office locations around the globe, including Singapore, the United Kingdom, Australia, Mexico, Brazil, and Japan. Locate your local office at: **international.cengage.com/region.**

Cengage Learning products are represented in Canada by Nelson Education, Ltd.
For your lifelong learning solutions, visit **www.cengage.com/custom.**
Visit our corporate website at **www.cengage.com.**

Brief Contents

Chapter 1 An Overview of Financial Management and the Financial Environment....... 3

Chapter 2 Financial Statements, Cash Flow, and Taxes....... 51

Chapter 3 Analysis of Financial Statements....... 95

Chapter 4 Time Value of Money....... 133

Chapter 5 Bond, Bond Valuation, and Interest Rates....... 187

Chapter 7 Valuation of Stocks and Corporations....... 289

Chapter 9 The Cost of Capital....... 357

Chapter 10 The Basics of Capital Budgeting: Evaluating Cash Flows....... 397

Chapter 11 Cash Flow Estimation and Risk Analysis....... 437

Appendix 11A Tax Depreciation....... 481

Web Extension 11A Certainty Equivalents and Risk-Adjusted Discount Rates....... 11A-1

Chapter 12 Corporate Valuation and Financial Planning....... 487

Chapter 30 Financial Management in Not-for-Profit Businesses[1]....... 1

Appendix B....... 1067

Appendix c....... 1077

Glossary....... 1093

Name Index....... 1121

Subject Index....... 1127

© lulu/fotolia.com

PART 1 The Company and Its Environment

CHAPTER 1
An Overview of Financial Management and the Financial Environment 3

CHAPTER 2
Financial Statements, Cash Flow, and Taxes 51

CHAPTER 3
Analysis of Financial Statements 95

© Adalberto Rios Szalay/Sexto Sol/Getty Images

CHAPTER 1

An Overview of Financial Management and the Financial Environment

WWW

See **money.cnn.com/magazines/fortune** *for updates on the ranking.*

In a global beauty contest for companies, the winner is . . . Apple Computer. Or at least Apple is the most admired company in the world, according to *Fortune* magazine's annual survey. The others in the global top ten are Google, Berkshire Hathaway, Southwest Airlines, Procter & Gamble, Coca-Cola, Amazon.com, FedEx, Microsoft, and McDonald's. What do these companies have that separates them from the rest of the pack?

According to a survey of executives, directors, and security analysts, these companies have very high average scores across nine attributes: (1) innovativeness, (2) quality of management, (3) long-term investment value, (4) social responsibility, (5) employee talent, (6) quality of products and services, (7) financial soundness, (8) use of corporate assets, and (9) effectiveness in doing business globally. After culling weaker companies, the final rankings are then determined by over 3,700 experts from a wide variety of industries.

What do these companies have in common? First, they have an incredible focus on using technology to understand their customers, reduce costs, reduce inventory, and speed up product delivery. Second, they continually innovate and invest in ways to differentiate their products. Some are known for game-changing products, such as Apple's iPad. Others continually introduce small improvements, such as Southwest Airlines's streamlined boarding procedures.

In addition to their acumen with technology and customers, they are also on the leading edge when it comes to training employees and providing a workplace in which people can thrive.

Prior to the global economic crisis, these companies maintained reasonable debt levels and avoided overpaying for acquisitions. This allowed them to weather the crisis and position themselves for stronger subsequent performance than many of their competitors.

In a nutshell, these companies reduce costs by having innovative production processes, they create value for customers by providing high-quality products and services, and they create value for employees by training and fostering an environment that allows employees to utilize all of their skills and talents. As you will see throughout this book, the resulting cash flow and superior return on capital also create value for investors.

GLOBAL ECONOMIC CRISIS

© uniquely india/Getty Images

The Global Economic Crisis

The global economic crisis is like a guest at a party who has one drink and is very interesting and entertaining but who then has many more drinks, gets sick, and lingers on after everyone else has left. At the risk of oversimplification, this is what happened during the past decade: Many of the world's individuals, financial institutions, and governments borrowed too much money and used those borrowed funds to make speculative investments. Those investments turned out to be worth less than the amounts owed by the borrowers, forcing widespread bankruptcies, buyouts, and restructurings for both borrowers and lenders. This in turn reduced the supply of available funds that financial institutions normally lent to creditworthy individuals, manufacturers, and retailers. Without access to credit, consumers bought less, manufacturers produced less, and retailers sold less—all of which led to layoffs. According to the National Bureau of Economic Research, the resulting recession lasted from December 2007 through June 2009. But as we write this chapter in 2012, the U.S. economy is still not growing very quickly. As we progress through this chapter and the rest of the book, we will discuss different aspects of the crisis. For real-time updates, go to the Global Economic Watch (GEW) Resource Center at **www.cengage.com/thewatch**.

resource

The textbook's Web site has tools for teaching, learning, and conducting financial research.

This chapter should give you an idea of what financial management is all about, including an overview of the financial markets in which corporations operate. Before going into details, let's look at the big picture. You're probably in school because you want an interesting, challenging, and rewarding career. To see where finance fits in, here's a five-minute MBA.

1-1 The Five-Minute MBA

Okay, we realize you can't get an MBA in five minutes. But just as an artist quickly sketches the outline of a picture before filling in the details, we can sketch the key elements of an MBA education. The primary objective of an MBA program is to provide managers with the knowledge and skills they need to run successful companies, so we start our sketch with some common characteristics of successful companies. In particular, all successful companies are able to accomplish two main goals:

1. All successful companies identify, create, and deliver products or services that are highly valued by customers—so highly valued that customers choose to purchase from them rather than from their competitors.
2. All successful companies sell their products/services at prices that are high enough to cover costs and to compensate owners and creditors for the use of their money and their exposure to risk.

It's easy to talk about satisfying customers and investors, but it's not so easy to accomplish these goals. If it were, then all companies would be successful, and you wouldn't need an MBA!

1-1a The Key Attributes of Successful Companies

First, *successful companies have skilled people* at all levels inside the company, including leaders, managers, and a capable workforce.

Second, *successful companies have strong relationships* with groups outside the company. For example, successful companies develop win–win relationships with suppliers and excel in customer relationship management.

Third, *successful companies have enough funding* to execute their plans and support their operations. Most companies need cash to purchase land, buildings, equipment, and materials. Companies can reinvest a portion of their earnings, but most growing companies also must raise additional funds externally by some combination of selling stock and/or borrowing in the financial markets.

Just as a stool needs all three legs to stand, a successful company must have all three attributes: skilled people, strong external relationships, and sufficient capital.

1-1b The MBA, Finance, and Your Career

WWW

Consult **www.careers-in-finance.com** *for an excellent site containing information on a variety of business career areas, listings of current jobs, and other reference materials.*

To be successful, a company must meet its first main goal: identifying, creating, and delivering highly valued products and services to customers. This requires that it possess all three of the key attributes mentioned above. Therefore, it's not surprising that most of your MBA courses are directly related to these attributes. For example, courses in economics, communication, strategy, organizational behavior, and human resources should prepare you for a leadership role and enable you to manage your company's workforce effectively. Other courses, such as marketing, operations management, and information technology, increase your knowledge of specific disciplines, enabling you to develop the efficient business processes and strong external relationships your company needs. Portions of *this* finance course will address raising the capital your company needs to implement its plans. In short, your MBA courses will give you the skills you need to help a company achieve its first goal: producing goods and services that customers want.

Recall, though, that it's not enough just to have highly valued products and satisfied customers. Successful companies must also meet their second main goal, which is generating enough cash to compensate the investors who provided the necessary capital. To help your company accomplish this second goal, you must be able to evaluate any proposal, whether it relates to marketing, production, strategy, or any other area, and implement only the projects that add value for your investors. For this, you must have expertise in finance, no matter your major. Thus, finance is a critical part of an MBA education, and it will help you throughout your career.

SELF-TEST

What are the goals of successful companies?

What are the three key attributes common to all successful companies?

How does expertise in finance help a company become successful?

1-2 The Corporate Life Cycle

Many major corporations, including Apple and Hewlett-Packard, began life in a garage or basement. How is it possible for such companies to grow into the giants we see today? No two companies develop in exactly the same way, but the following sections describe some typical stages in the corporate life cycle.

Columbus Was Wrong—the World Is Flat! And Hot! And Crowded!

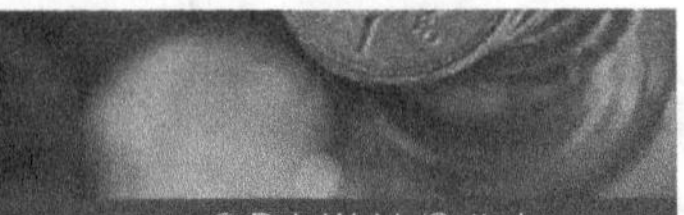
© Rob Webb/Getty Images

In his best-selling book *The World Is Flat*, Thomas L. Friedman argues that many of the barriers that long protected businesses and employees from global competition have been broken down by dramatic improvements in communication and transportation technologies. The result is a level playing field that spans the entire world. As we move into the information age, any work that can be digitized will flow to those able to do it at the lowest cost, whether they live in San Jose's Silicon Valley or Bangalore, India. For physical products, supply chains now span the world. For example, raw materials might be extracted in South America, fabricated into electronic components in Asia, and then used in computers assembled in the United States, with the final product being sold in Europe.

Similar changes are occurring in the financial markets, as capital flows across the globe to those who can best use it. Indeed, China and Hong Kong raised more through initial public offerings in 2011 than both Europe and the United States together.

Unfortunately, a dynamic world can bring runaway growth, which can lead to significant environmental problems and energy shortages. Friedman describes these problems in another bestseller, *Hot, Flat, and Crowded*. In a flat world, the keys to success are knowledge, skills, and a great work ethic. In a flat, hot, and crowded world, these factors must be combined with innovation and creativity to deal with truly global problems.

1-2a Starting Up as a Proprietorship

Many companies begin as a **proprietorship**, which is an unincorporated business owned by one individual. Starting a business as a proprietor is easy—one merely begins business operations after obtaining any required city or state business licenses. The proprietorship has three important advantages: (1) it is easily and inexpensively formed, (2) it is subject to few government regulations, and (3) its income is not subject to corporate taxation but is taxed as part of the proprietor's personal income.

However, the proprietorship also has three important limitations: (1) It may be difficult for a proprietorship to obtain the capital needed for growth. (2) The proprietor has unlimited personal liability for the business's debts, which can result in losses that exceed the money invested in the company (creditors may even be able to seize a proprietor's house or other personal property!). (3) The life of a proprietorship is limited to the life of its founder. For these three reasons, sole proprietorships are used primarily for small businesses. In fact, proprietorships account for only about 13% of all sales, based on dollar values, even though about 80% of all companies are proprietorships.

1-2b More Than One Owner: A Partnership

Some companies start with more than one owner, and some proprietors decide to add a partner as the business grows. A **partnership** exists whenever two or more persons or entities associate to conduct a noncorporate business for profit. Partnerships may operate under different degrees of formality, ranging from informal, oral understandings to formal agreements filed with the secretary of the state in which the partnership was formed. Partnership agreements define the ways any profits and losses are shared between partners. A partnership's advantages and disadvantages are generally similar to those of a proprietorship.

Regarding liability, the partners potentially can lose all of their personal assets, even assets not invested in the business, because under partnership law, each partner is liable for the business's debts. Therefore, in the event the partnership goes bankrupt, if any partner is unable to meet his or her pro rata liability, then the remaining partners must make good on the unsatisfied claims, drawing on their personal assets to the extent necessary. To avoid this, it is possible to limit the liabilities of some of the partners by establishing a **limited partnership**, wherein certain partners are designated **general partners** and others **limited partners**. In a limited partnership, the limited partners can lose only the amount of their investment in the partnership, while the general partners have unlimited liability. However, the limited partners typically have no control—it rests solely with the general partners—and their returns are likewise limited. Limited partnerships are common in real estate, oil, equipment leasing ventures, and venture capital. However, they are not widely used in general business situations because usually no partner is willing to be the general partner and thus accept the majority of the business's risk, and no partners are willing to be limited partners and give up all control.

In both regular and limited partnerships, at least one partner is liable for the debts of the partnership. However, in a **limited liability partnership (LLP)**, sometimes called a **limited liability company (LLC)**, all partners enjoy limited liability with regard to the business's liabilities, and their potential losses are limited to their investment in the LLP. Of course, this arrangement increases the risk faced by an LLP's lenders, customers, and suppliers.

1-2c Many Owners: A Corporation

Most partnerships have difficulty attracting substantial amounts of capital. This is generally not a problem for a slow-growing business, but if a business's products or services really catch on, and if it needs to raise large sums of money to capitalize on its opportunities, then the difficulty in attracting capital becomes a real drawback. Thus, many growth companies, such as Hewlett-Packard and Microsoft, began life as a proprietorship or partnership, and at some point their founders decided to convert to a corporation. On the other hand, some companies, in anticipation of growth, actually begin as corporations. A **corporation** is a legal entity created under state laws, and it is separate and distinct from its owners and managers. This separation gives the corporation three major advantages: (1) *unlimited life*—a corporation can continue after its original owners and managers are deceased; (2) *easy transferability of ownership interest*—ownership interests are divided into shares of stock, which can be transferred far more easily than can proprietorship or partnership interests; and (3) *limited liability*—losses are limited to the actual funds invested.

To illustrate limited liability, suppose you invested $10,000 in a partnership that then went bankrupt and owed $1 million. Because the owners are liable for the debts of a partnership, you could be assessed for a share of the company's debt, and you could be held liable for the entire $1 million if your partners could not pay their shares. On the other hand, if you invested $10,000 in the stock of a corporation that went bankrupt, your potential loss on the investment would be limited to your $10,000 investment.[1] Unlimited life, easy transferability of ownership interest, and limited liability make it much easier for corporations than proprietorships or partnerships to raise money in the financial markets and grow into large companies.

---

[1]In the case of very small corporations, the limited liability may be fiction because lenders frequently require personal guarantees from the stockholders.

The corporate form offers significant advantages over proprietorships and partnerships, but it also has two disadvantages: (1) Corporate earnings may be subject to double taxation—the earnings of the corporation are taxed at the corporate level, and then earnings paid out as dividends are taxed again as income to the stockholders. (2) Setting up a corporation involves preparing a charter, writing a set of bylaws, and filing the many required state and federal reports, which is more complex and time-consuming than creating a proprietorship or a partnership.

The **charter** includes the following information: (1) name of the proposed corporation, (2) types of activities it will pursue, (3) amount of capital stock, (4) number of directors, and (5) names and addresses of directors. The charter is filed with the secretary of the state in which the firm will be incorporated, and when it is approved, the corporation is officially in existence.[2] After the corporation begins operating, quarterly and annual employment, financial, and tax reports must be filed with state and federal authorities.

The **bylaws** are a set of rules drawn up by the founders of the corporation. Included are such points as (1) how directors are to be elected (all elected each year or perhaps one-third each year for 3-year terms); (2) whether the existing stockholders will have the first right to buy any new shares the firm issues; and (3) procedures for changing the bylaws themselves, should conditions require it.

There are several different types of corporations. Professionals such as doctors, lawyers, and accountants often form a **professional corporation (PC)** or a **professional association (PA)**. These types of corporations do not relieve the participants of professional (malpractice) liability. Indeed, the primary motivation behind the professional corporation was to provide a way for groups of professionals to incorporate in order to avoid certain types of unlimited liability yet still be held responsible for professional liability.

Finally, if certain requirements are met, particularly with regard to size and number of stockholders, owners can establish a corporation but elect to be taxed as if the business were a proprietorship or partnership. Such firms, which differ not in organizational form but only in how their owners are taxed, are called **S corporations**.

1-2d Growing and Managing a Corporation

Once a corporation has been established, how does it evolve? When entrepreneurs start a company, they usually provide all the financing from their personal resources, which may include savings, home equity loans, or even credit cards. As the corporation grows, it will need factories, equipment, inventory, and other resources to support its growth. In time, the entrepreneurs usually deplete their own resources and must turn to external financing. Many young companies are too risky for banks, so the founders must sell stock to outsiders, including friends, family, private investors (often called angels), or venture capitalists. If the corporation continues to grow, it may become successful enough to attract lending from banks, or it may even raise additional funds through an **initial public offering (IPO)** by selling stock to the public at large. After an IPO, corporations support their growth by borrowing from banks, issuing debt, or selling additional shares of stock. In short, a corporation's ability to grow depends on its interactions with the financial markets, which we describe in much more detail later in this chapter.

For proprietorships, partnerships, and small corporations, the firm's owners are also its managers. This is usually not true for a large corporation, which means that large firms'

---

[2]More than 60% of major U.S. corporations are chartered in Delaware, which has, over the years, provided a favorable legal environment for corporations. It is not necessary for a firm to be headquartered, or even to conduct operations, in its state of incorporation, or even in its country of incorporation.

stockholders, who are its owners, face a serious problem. What is to prevent managers from acting in their own best interests, rather than in the best interests of the stockholder/owners? This is called an **agency problem**, because managers are hired as agents to act on behalf of the owners. Agency problems can be addressed by a company's **corporate governance**, which is the set of rules that control the company's behavior towards its directors, managers, employees, shareholders, creditors, customers, competitors, and community. We will have much more to say about agency problems and corporate governance throughout the book, especially in Chapters 13, 14, and 15.

SELF-TEST

What are the key differences between proprietorships, partnerships, and corporations?

Describe some special types of partnerships and corporations, and explain the differences among them.

1-3 The Primary Objective of the Corporation: Value Maximization

Shareholders are the owners of a corporation, and they purchase stocks because they want to earn a good return on their investment without undue risk exposure. In most cases, shareholders elect directors, who then hire managers to run the corporation on a day-to-day basis. Because managers are supposed to be working on behalf of shareholders, they should pursue policies that enhance shareholder value. Consequently, throughout this book we operate on the assumption that management's primary objective should be *stockholder wealth maximization.*

The **market price** is the stock price that we observe in the financial markets. We later explain in detail how stock prices are determined, but for now it is enough to say that a company's market price incorporates the information available to investors. If the market price reflects all *relevant* information, then the observed price is the **intrinsic price**, also called the **fundamental price**.

However, investors rarely have all relevant information. Companies report most major decisions, but they may withhold selected information to prevent competitors from gaining strategic advantages. In addition, managers may take actions that boost bonuses linked to higher current earnings yet actually decrease future cash flows, such as reducing scheduled maintenance. As we show in Chapter 7, short-term focus can reduce the intrinsic price but might actually increase the market price if such actions are difficult for investors to discern immediately. Thus, the market price can deviate from the intrinsic price. In this example, the market price initially would go up relative to the intrinsic price, but it would then fall in the future as the company experienced production problems due to poorly maintained equipment.

Therefore, when we say management's objective should be to maximize stockholder wealth, we really mean it is to *maximize the fundamental price of the firm's common stock*, not just the current market price. Firms do, of course, have other objectives; in particular, the managers who make the actual decisions are interested in their own personal satisfaction, in their employees' welfare, and in the good of their communities and society at large. Still, for the reasons set forth in the following sections, *maximizing intrinsic stock value should be the most important objective for most corporations.*

Ethics for Individuals and Businesses

© Rob Webb/Getty Images

A firm's commitment to business ethics can be measured by the tendency of its employees, from the top down, to adhere to laws, regulations, and moral standards relating to product safety and quality, fair employment practices, fair marketing and selling practices, the use of confidential information for personal gain, community involvement, and illegal payments to obtain business.

Ethical Dilemmas

When conflicts arise between profits and ethics, sometimes legal and ethical considerations make the choice obvious. At other times the right choice isn't clear. For example, suppose Norfolk Southern's managers know that its trains are polluting the air, but the amount of pollution is within legal limits and further reduction would be costly, causing harm to their shareholders. Are the managers ethically bound to reduce pollution? Aren't they also ethically bound to act in their shareholders' best interests? This is clearly a dilemma.

Ethical Responsibility

Over the past few years, illegal ethical lapses have led to a number of bankruptcies, which have raised this question: Were the *companies* unethical, or was it just a few of their *employees*? Arthur Andersen, an accounting firm, audited Enron, WorldCom, and several other companies that committed accounting fraud. The U.S. Justice Department concluded that Andersen itself was guilty because it fostered a climate in which unethical behavior was permitted, and it built an incentive system that made such behavior profitable to both the perpetrators and the firm itself. As a result, Andersen went out of business. Andersen was later judged to be not guilty, but by the time the judgment was rendered the company was already out of business. People simply did not want to deal with a tainted accounting firm.

Protecting Ethical Employees

If employees discover questionable activities or are given questionable orders, should they obey their bosses' orders, refuse to obey those orders, or report the situation to a higher authority, such as the company's board of directors, its auditors, or a federal prosecutor? In 2002 Congress passed the Sarbanes-Oxley Act, with a provision designed to protect "whistle-blowers." If an employee reports corporate wrongdoing and later is penalized, he or she can ask the Occupational Safety and Health Administration to investigate the situation. If the employee was improperly penalized, the company can be required to reinstate the person, along with providing back pay and a sizable penalty award. Several big awards have been handed out since the act was passed.

1-3a Intrinsic Stock Value Maximization and Social Welfare

WWW

The Investment Company Institute is a great source of information. For updates on mutual fund ownership, see **www.ici.org/research#fact_books**.

If a firm attempts to maximize its intrinsic stock value, is this good or bad for society? In general, it is good. Aside from such illegal actions as fraudulent accounting, exploiting monopoly power, violating safety codes, and failing to meet environmental standards, *the same actions that maximize intrinsic stock values also benefit society.* Here are some of the reasons:

1. **Most individuals have a stake in the stock market.** Seventy-five years ago this was not true, because most stock ownership was concentrated in the hands of a relatively small segment of society consisting of the wealthiest individuals. More than 44% of all U.S. households now own mutual funds, as compared with only 4.6% in 1980. When direct stock ownership and indirect ownership through pension funds are also considered, many members of society now have an important stake in the stock market, either directly or indirectly. Therefore, when a manager takes actions to maximize the stock price, this improves the quality of life for millions of ordinary citizens.

2. **Consumers benefit.** Stock price maximization requires efficient, low-cost businesses that produce high-quality goods and services at the lowest possible cost. This means that companies must develop products and services that consumers want and need, which leads to new technology and new products. Also, companies that maximize their stock price must generate growth in sales by creating value for customers in the form of efficient and courteous service, adequate stocks of merchandise, and well-located business establishments.

   People sometimes argue that firms, in their efforts to raise profits and stock prices, increase product prices and gouge the public. In a reasonably competitive economy, which we have, prices are constrained by competition and consumer resistance. If a firm raises its prices beyond reasonable levels, it will simply lose market share. Even giant firms such as Dell and Coca-Cola lose business to domestic and foreign competitors if they set prices above the level necessary to cover production costs plus a "normal" profit. Of course, firms *want* to earn more, and they constantly try to cut costs, develop new products, and so on, and thereby earn above-normal profits. Note, though, that if they are indeed successful and do earn above-normal profits, those very profits will attract competition, which will eventually drive prices down. So again, the main long-term beneficiary is the consumer.
3. **Employees benefit.** In some situations a stock increases when a company announces plans to lay off employees, but viewed over time this is the exception rather than the rule. In general, companies that successfully increase stock prices also grow and add more employees, thus benefiting society. Note, too, that many governments across the world, including U.S. federal and state governments, are privatizing some of their state-owned activities by selling these operations to investors. Perhaps not surprisingly, the sales and cash flows of recently privatized companies generally improve. Moreover, studies show that newly privatized companies tend to grow and thus require more employees when they are managed with the goal of stock price maximization.

1-3b Managerial Actions to Maximize Shareholder Wealth

What types of actions can managers take to maximize shareholder wealth? To answer this question, we first need to ask, "What determines a firm's value?" In a nutshell, it is *a company's ability to generate cash flows now and in the future.*

We address different aspects of this in detail throughout the book, but we can lay out three basic facts now: (1) Any financial asset, including a company's stock, is valuable only to the extent that it generates cash flows. (2) The timing of cash flows matters—cash received sooner is better. (3) Investors are averse to risk, so all else equal, they will pay more for a stock whose cash flows are relatively certain than for one whose cash flows are more risky. Therefore, managers can increase their firm's value by increasing the size of the expected cash flows, by speeding up their receipt, and by reducing their risk.

The cash flows that matter are called free cash flows (FCF), not because they are free, but because they are available (or free) for distribution to all of the company's investors, including creditors and stockholders. You will learn how to calculate free cash flows in Chapter 2, but for now you should know that free cash flow is:

$$\text{FCF} = \begin{matrix}\text{Sales}\\\text{revenues}\end{matrix} - \begin{matrix}\text{Operating}\\\text{costs}\end{matrix} - \begin{matrix}\text{Operating}\\\text{taxes}\end{matrix} - \begin{matrix}\text{Required investments}\\\text{in new operating capital}\end{matrix}$$

Corporate Scandals and Maximizing Stock Price

© Rob Webb/Getty Images

The list of corporate scandals seems to go on forever: Sunbeam, Enron, ImClone, WorldCom, Tyco, Adelphia.... At first glance, it's tempting to say, "Look what happens when managers care only about maximizing stock price." But a closer look reveals a much different story. In fact, if these managers were trying to maximize stock price, they failed dismally, given the resulting values of these companies.

Although details vary from company to company, a few common themes emerge. First, managerial compensation was linked to the *short-term* performance of the stock price via poorly designed stock option and stock grant programs. This provided managers with a powerful incentive to drive up the stock price at the option vesting date without worrying about the future. Second, it is virtually impossible to take *legal and ethical* actions that drive up the stock price in the short term without harming it in the long term because the value of a company is based on all of its future free cash flows and not just cash flows in the immediate future. Because legal and ethical actions to quickly drive up the stock price didn't exist (other than the old-fashioned ones, such as increasing sales, cutting costs, or reducing capital requirements), these managers began bending a few rules. Third, as they initially got away with bending rules, it seems that their egos and hubris grew to such an extent that they felt they were above all rules, so they began breaking even more rules.

Stock prices did go up, at least temporarily, but as Abraham Lincoln said, "You can't fool all of the people all of the time." As the scandals became public, the stocks' prices plummeted, and in some cases the companies were ruined.

There are several important lessons to be learned from these examples. First, people respond to incentives, and poorly designed incentives can cause disastrous results. Second, ethical violations usually begin with small steps, so if stockholders want managers to avoid large ethical violations, then they shouldn't let them make the small ones. Third, there is no shortcut to creating lasting value. It takes hard work to increase sales, cut costs, and reduce capital requirements, but this is the formula for success.

Brand managers and marketing managers can increase sales (and prices) by truly understanding their customers and then designing goods and services that customers want. Human resource managers can improve productivity through training and employee retention. Production and logistics managers can improve profit margins, reduce inventory, and improve throughput at factories by implementing supply chain management, just-in-time inventory management, and lean manufacturing. In fact, all managers make decisions that can increase free cash flows.

One of the financial manager's roles is to help others see how their actions affect the company's ability to generate cash flow and, hence, its intrinsic value. Financial managers also must decide *how to finance the firm*. In particular, they must choose the mix of debt and equity to use and the specific types of debt and equity securities to issue. They also must decide what percentage of current earnings to retain and reinvest rather than pay out as dividends. Along with these financing decisions, the general level of interest rates in the economy, the risk of the firm's operations, and stock market investors' overall attitude toward risk determine the rate of return required to satisfy a firm's investors. This rate of return from an investor's perspective is a cost from the company's point of view. Therefore, the rate of return required by investors is called the **weighted average cost of capital (WACC)**.

The following equation defines the relationship between a firm's fundamental value, its free cash flows, and its cost of capital:

$$\text{Value} = \frac{\text{FCF}_1}{(1+\text{WACC})^1} + \frac{\text{FCF}_2}{(1+\text{WACC})^2} + \frac{\text{FCF}_3}{(1+\text{WACC})^3} + \cdots + \frac{\text{FCF}_\infty}{(1+\text{WACC})^\infty} \quad (1\text{-}1)$$

We will explain how to use this equation in later chapters, but for now note that (1) a growing firm often needs to raise external funds in the financial markets, and (2) the actual price of a firm's stock is determined in those markets. The rest of this chapter focuses on financial markets.

SELF-TEST

What should be management's primary objective?

How does maximizing the fundamental stock price benefit society?

Free cash flow depends on what three factors?

How is a firm's fundamental value related to its free cash flows and its cost of capital?

1-4 An Overview of the Capital Allocation Process

Businesses often need capital to implement growth plans; governments require funds to finance building projects; and individuals frequently want loans to purchase cars, homes, and education. Where can they get this money? Fortunately, there are some individuals and firms with incomes greater than their expenditures. In spite of William Shakespeare's advice, most individuals and firms are both borrowers and lenders. For example, an individual might borrow money with a car loan or a home mortgage but might also lend money through a bank savings account. In the aggregate, individuals are net savers and provide most of the funds ultimately used by nonfinancial corporations. Although most nonfinancial corporations own some financial securities, such as short-term Treasury bills, nonfinancial corporations are net borrowers in the aggregate. In the United States federal, state, and local governments are also net borrowers in the aggregate, although many foreign governments, such as those of China and oil-producing countries, are actually net lenders. Banks and other financial corporations raise money with one hand and invest it with the other. For example, a bank might raise money from individuals in the form of a savings account and then lend most of that money to business customers. In the aggregate, financial corporations borrow slightly more than they lend.

Transfers of capital between savers and those who need capital take place in three different ways. Direct transfers of money and securities, as shown in Panel 1 of Figure 1-1, occur when a business (or government) sells its securities directly to savers. The business delivers its securities to savers, who in turn provide the firm with the money it needs. For example, a privately held company might sell shares of stock directly to a new shareholder, or the U.S. government might sell a Treasury bond directly to an individual investor.

As shown in Panel 2, indirect transfers may go through an **investment banking house** such as Goldman Sachs, which *underwrites* the issue. An underwriter serves as a middleman and facilitates the issuance of securities. The company sells its stocks or bonds to the investment bank, which in turn sells these same securities to savers. Because new securities are involved and the corporation receives the proceeds of the sale, this is a "primary" market transaction.

Transfers also can be made through a **financial intermediary** such as a bank or mutual fund, as shown in Panel 3. Here the intermediary obtains funds from savers in exchange for its own securities. The intermediary then uses this money to purchase and then hold businesses' securities. For example, a saver might give dollars to a bank and receive a certificate of deposit, and then the bank might lend the money to a small business, receiving in exchange a signed loan. Thus, intermediaries literally create new types of securities.

FIGURE 1-1

Diagram of the Capital Allocation Process

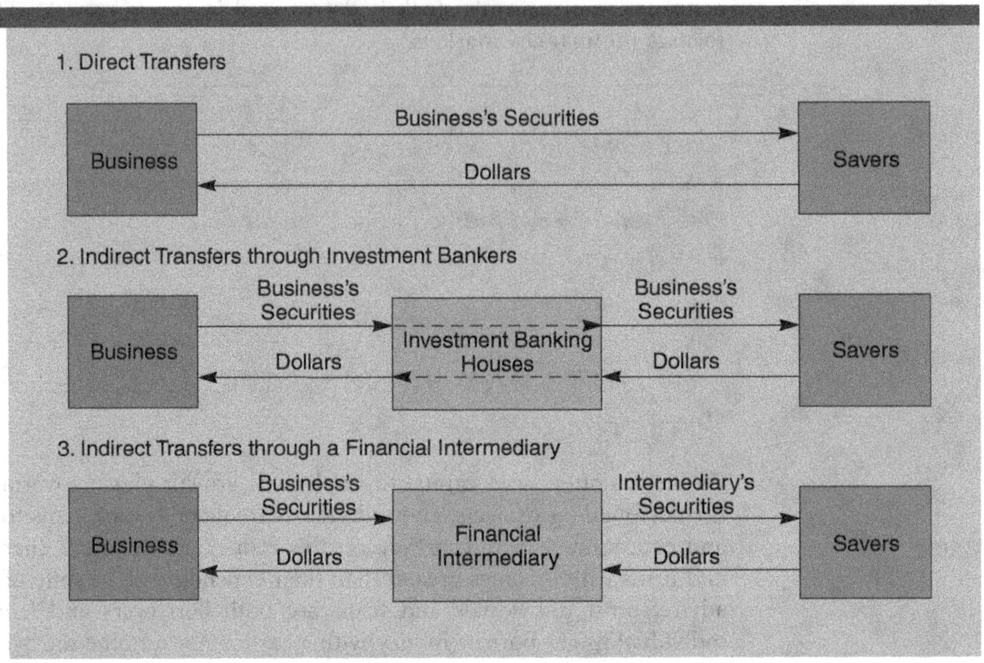

© Cengage Learning 2014

There are three important characteristics of the capital allocation process. First, new financial securities are created. Second, financial institutions are often involved. Third, allocation between providers and users of funds occurs in financial markets. The following sections discuss each of these characteristics.

SELF-TEST

Identify three ways that capital is transferred between savers and borrowers.

Distinguish between the roles played by investment banking houses and financial intermediaries.

1-5 Financial Securities

The variety of financial securities is limited only by human creativity, ingenuity, and governmental regulations. At the risk of oversimplification, we can classify most financial securities by the type of claim and the time until maturity. In addition, some securities actually are created from packages of other securities. We discuss the key aspects of financial securities in this section.

WWW

You can access current and historical interest rates and economic data from the Federal Reserve Economic Data (FRED) site at **www.stls.frb.org/fred.**

1-5a Type of Claim: Debt, Equity, or Derivatives

Financial securities are simply pieces of paper with contractual provisions that entitle their owners to specific rights and claims on specific cash flows or values. Debt instruments typically have specified payments and a specified maturity. For example, an Alcoa bond might promise to pay 10% interest for 30 years, at which time it promises to make a $1,000 principal payment. If debt matures in more than a year, it is called a *capital market security*. Thus, the Alcoa bond in this example is a capital market security.

If the debt matures in less than a year, it is a *money market security*. For example, Home Depot might expect to receive $300,000 in 75 days, but it needs cash now. Home Depot might issue commercial paper, which is essentially an IOU. In this example, Home Depot might agree to pay $300,000 in 75 days in exchange for $297,000 today. Thus, commercial paper is a money market security.

Equity instruments are a claim upon a residual value. For example, Alcoa's stockholders are entitled to the cash flows generated by Alcoa after its bondholders, creditors, and other claimants have been satisfied. Because stock has no maturity date, it is a capital market security.

resource

For an overview of derivatives, see Web Extension 1A on the textbook's Web site.

Notice that debt and equity represent claims upon the cash flows generated by real assets, such as the cash flows generated by Alcoa's factories and operations. In contrast, **derivatives** are securities whose values depend on, or are *derived* from, the values of some other traded assets. For example, options and futures are two important types of derivatives, and their values depend on the prices of other assets. An option on Alcoa stock or a futures contract to buy pork bellies are examples of derivatives. We discuss options in Chapter 8 and in ***Web Extension 1A***, which provides a brief overview of options and other derivatives.

Some securities are a mix of debt, equity, and derivatives. For example, preferred stock has some features like debt and some like equity, while convertible debt has both debt-like and option-like features.

We discuss these and other financial securities in detail later in the book, but Table 1-1 provides a summary of the most important conventional financial securities. We discuss rates of return later in this chapter, but notice now in Table 1-1 that interest rates tend to increase with the maturity and risk of the security.

Some securities are created from packages of other assets, a process called *securitization*. The misuse of securitized assets is one of the primary causes of the global financial crisis, so every manager needs to understand the process of securitization.

1-5b The Process of Securitization

Many types of assets can be securitized, but we will focus on mortgages because they played such an important role in the global financial crisis. At one time, most mortgages were made by **savings and loan associations (S&Ls)**, which took in the vast majority of their deposits from individuals who lived in nearby neighborhoods. The S&Ls pooled these deposits and then lent money to people in the neighborhood in the form of fixed-rate mortgages, which were pieces of paper signed by borrowers promising to make specified payments to the S&L. The new homeowners paid principal and interest to the S&L, which then paid interest to its depositors and reinvested the principal repayments in other mortgages. This was clearly better than having individuals lend directly to aspiring homeowners, because a single individual might not have enough money to finance an entire house or the expertise to know if the borrower was creditworthy. Note that the S&Ls were government-chartered institutions. They obtained money in the form of immediately withdrawable deposits and then invested most of it in the form of mortgages with fixed interest rates and on individual homes. Also, initially the S&Ls were not permitted to have branch operations—they were limited to one office to maintain their local orientation.

These restrictions had important implications. First, in the 1950s there was a massive migration of people to the west, so there was a strong demand for funds

TABLE 1-1
Summary of Major Financial Instruments

Instrument	Major Participants	Risk	Original Maturity	Rates of Return on 1/24/12[a]
U.S. Treasury bills	Sold by U.S. Treasury	Default-free	91 days to 1 year	0.07%
Bankers' acceptances	A firm's promise to pay, guaranteed by a bank	Low if strong bank guarantees	Up to 180 days	0.28%
Commercial paper	Issued by financially secure firms to large investors	Low default risk	Up to 270 days	0.15%
Negotiable certificates of deposit (CDs)	Issued by major banks to large investors	Depends on strength of issuer	Up to 1 year	0.37%
Money market mutual funds	Invest in short-term debt; held by individuals and businesses	Low degree of risk	No specific maturity (instant liquidity)	0.51%
Eurodollar market time deposits	Issued by banks outside the United States	Depends on strength of issuer	Up to 1 year	0.20%
Consumer credit loans	Loans by banks/credit unions/finance companies	Risk is variable	Variable	Variable
Commercial loans	Loans by banks to corporations	Depends on borrower	Up to 7 years	Tied to prime rate (3.25%) or LIBOR (0.56%)[b]
U.S. Treasury notes and bonds	Issued by U.S. government	No default risk, but price falls if interest rates rise	2 to 30 years	3.15%
Mortgages	Loans secured by property	Risk is variable	Up to 30 years	4.11%
Municipal bonds	Issued by state and local governments to individuals and institutions	Riskier than U.S. government bonds, but exempt from most taxes	Up to 30 years	4.08%
Corporate bonds	Issued by corporations to individuals and institutions	Riskier than U.S. government debt; depends on strength of issuer	Up to 40 years[c]	5.33%
Leases	Similar to debt; firms lease assets rather than borrow and then buy them	Risk similar to corporate bonds	Generally 3 to 20 years	Similar to bond yields
Preferred stocks	Issued by corporations to individuals and institutions	Riskier than corporate bonds	Unlimited	6% to 9%
Common stocks[d]	Issued by corporations to individuals and institutions	Riskier than preferred stocks	Unlimited	9% to 15%

[a]Data are from *The Wall Street Journal* (**online.wsj.com**) or the *Federal Reserve Statistical Release* (**www.federalreserve.gov/releases/H15/update**). Bankers' acceptances assume a 3-month maturity. Money market rates are for the Merrill Lynch Ready Assets Trust. The corporate bond rate is for AAA-rated bonds.
[b]The prime rate is the rate U.S. banks charge to good customers. LIBOR (London Interbank Offered Rate) is the rate that U.K. banks charge one another.
[c]A few corporations have issued 100-year bonds; however, most have issued bonds with maturities of less than 40 years.
[d]Common stocks are expected to provide a "return" in the form of dividends and capital gains rather than interest. Of course, if you buy a stock, your *actual* return may be considerably higher or lower than your *expected* return.

© Cengage Learning 2014

in that area. However, the wealthiest savers were in the east. That meant that mortgage interest rates were much higher in California and other western states than in New York and the east. This created disequilibrium in the financial markets, something that can't last forever.

Second, note that the S&Ls' assets consisted mainly of long-term, fixed-rate mortgages, but their liabilities were in the form of deposits that could be withdrawn immediately. The combination of long-term assets and short-term liabilities created another problem. If the overall level of interest rates increased, the S&Ls would have to increase the rates they paid on deposits or else savers would take their money elsewhere. However, the S&Ls couldn't increase the rates on their outstanding mortgages because these mortgages had fixed interest rates. This problem came to a head in the 1960s, when the Vietnam War led to inflation, which pushed up interest rates. At this point, the "money market fund" industry was born, and it literally sucked money out of the S&Ls, forcing many of them into bankruptcy.

The government responded by giving the S&Ls broader lending powers, permitting nationwide branching and allowing them to obtain funds as long-term debt in addition to immediately withdrawable deposits. Unfortunately, these changes had another set of unintended consequences. S&L managers who had previously dealt with a limited array of investments and funding choices in local communities could suddenly expand their scope of operations. Many of these inexperienced S&L managers made poor business decisions and the result was disastrous—virtually the entire S&L industry collapsed, with many S&Ls going bankrupt or being acquired in shotgun mergers with commercial banks.

The demise of the S&Ls created another financial disequilibrium—a higher demand for mortgages than the supply of available funds from the mortgage lending industry. Savings were accumulating in pension funds, insurance companies, and other institutions, not in S&Ls and banks, the traditional mortgage lenders.

This situation led to the development of "mortgage securitization," a process whereby banks, the remaining S&Ls, and specialized mortgage-originating firms would originate mortgages and then sell them to investment banks, which would bundle them into packages and then use these packages as collateral for bonds that could be sold to pension funds, insurance companies, and other institutional investors. Thus, individual loans were bundled and then used to back a bond—a "security"—that could be traded in the financial markets.

Congress facilitated this process by creating two stockholder-owned but government-sponsored entities, the Federal National Mortgage Association (Fannie Mae) and the Federal Home Loan Mortgage Corporation (Freddie Mac). Fannie Mae and Freddie Mac were financed by issuing a relatively small amount of stock and a huge amount of debt.

To illustrate the securitization process, suppose an S&L or bank is paying its depositors 5% but is charging its borrowers 8% on their mortgages. The S&L can take hundreds of these mortgages, put them in a pool, and then sell the pool to Fannie Mae. The mortgagees can still make their payments to the original S&L, which will then forward the payments (less a small handling fee) to Fannie Mae.

Consider the S&L's perspective. First, it can use the cash it receives from selling the mortgages to make additional loans to other aspiring homeowners. Second, the S&L is no longer exposed to the risk of owning mortgages. The risk hasn't disappeared—it has been transferred from the S&L (and its federal deposit insurers) to Fannie Mae. This is clearly a better situation for aspiring homeowners and, perhaps, also for taxpayers.

Fannie Mae can take the mortgages it just bought, put them into a very large pool, and sell bonds backed by the pool to investors. The homeowner will pay the S&L, the S&L will forward the payment to Fannie Mae, and Fannie Mae will use the funds to pay interest on the bonds it issued, to pay dividends on its stock, and to buy additional mortgages from

S&Ls, which can then make additional loans to aspiring homeowners. Notice that the mortgage risk has been shifted from Fannie Mae to the investors who now own the mortgage-backed bonds.

How does the situation look from the perspective of the investors who own the bonds? In theory, they own a share in a large pool of mortgages from all over the country, so a problem in a particular region's real estate market or job market won't affect the whole pool. Therefore, their expected rate of return should be very close to the 8% rate paid by the home-owning mortgagees. (It will be a little less due to handling fees charged by the S&L and Fannie Mae and to the small amount of expected losses from the homeowners who could be expected to default on their mortgages.) These investors could have deposited their money at an S&L and earned a virtually risk-free 5%. Instead, they chose to accept more risk in hopes of the higher 8% return. Note, too, that mortgage-backed bonds are more liquid than individual mortgage loans, so the securitization process increases liquidity, which is desirable. The bottom line is that risk has been reduced by the pooling process and then allocated to those who are willing to accept it in return for a higher rate of return.

Thus, in theory it is a win–win–win situation: More money is available for aspiring homeowners, S&Ls (and taxpayers) have less risk, and there are opportunities for investors who are willing to take on more risk to obtain higher potential returns. Although the securitization process began with mortgages, it is now being used with car loans, student loans, credit card debt, and other loans. The details vary for different assets, but the processes and benefits are similar to those with mortgage securitization: (1) increased supplies of lendable funds; (2) transfer of risk to those who are willing to bear it; and (3) increased liquidity for holders of the debt.

Mortgage securitization was a win–win situation in theory, but as practiced in the last decade it has turned into a lose–lose situation. We will have more to say about securitization and the global economic crisis later in this chapter, but first let's take a look at the cost of money.

1-6 The Cost of Money

In a free economy, capital from those with available funds is allocated through the price system to users who have a need for funds. The interaction of the providers' supply and the users' demand determines the cost (or price) of money, which is the rate users pay to providers. For debt, we call this price the **interest rate**. For equity, we call it the **cost of equity**, and it consists of the dividends and capital gains stockholders expect. Keep in mind that the "price" of money is a cost from a user's perspective but a return from the provider's point of view.

Notice in Table 1-1 that a financial instrument's rate of return generally increases as its maturity and risk increase. We will have much more to say about the relationships among an individual security's features, risk, and return later in the book, but first we will examine some fundamental factors and economic conditions that affect all financial instruments.

1-6a Fundamental Factors That Affect the Cost of Money

The four most fundamental factors affecting the cost of money are (1) **production opportunities,** (2) **time preferences for consumption,** (3) **risk,** and (4) **inflation.** By production opportunities, we mean the ability to turn capital into benefits. If a business raises capital, the benefits are determined by the expected rates of return on its production opportunities. If a student borrows to finance his or her education, the benefits are higher expected future salaries (and, of course, the sheer joy of learning!). If a homeowner borrows, the benefits are the pleasure from living in his or her own home, plus any expected appreciation in the value of the home. Observe that the expected rates of return on these "production opportunities" put an upper limit on how much users can pay to providers.

Providers can use their current funds for consumption or saving. By saving, they give up consumption now in the expectation of having more consumption in the future. If providers have a strong preference for consumption now, then it takes high interest rates to induce them to trade current consumption for future consumption. Therefore, the time preference for consumption has a major impact on the cost of money. Notice that the time preference for consumption varies for different individuals, for different age groups, and for different cultures. For example, people in Japan have a lower time preference for consumption than those in the United States, which partially explains why Japanese families tend to save more than U.S. families even though interest rates are lower in Japan.

If the expected rate of return on an investment is risky, then providers require a higher expected return to induce them to take the extra risk, which drives up the cost of money. As you will see later in this book, the risk of a security is determined by market conditions and the security's particular features.

Inflation also leads to a higher cost of money. For example, suppose you earned 10% one year on your investment but inflation caused prices to increase by 20%. This means you can't consume as much at the end of the year as when you originally invested your money. Obviously, if you had expected 20% inflation, you would have required a higher rate of return than 10%.

1-6b Economic Conditions and Policies That Affect the Cost of Money

WWW

The home page for the Board of Governors of the Federal Reserve System can be found at **www.federalreserve.gov**. *You can access general information about the Federal Reserve, including press releases, speeches, and monetary policy.*

Economic conditions and policies also affect the cost of money. These include: (1) Federal Reserve policy; (2) the federal budget deficit or surplus; (3) the level of business activity; and (4) international factors, including the foreign trade balance, the international business climate, and exchange rates.

Federal Reserve Policy

If the Federal Reserve Board wants to stimulate the economy, it most often uses open market operations to purchase Treasury securities held by banks. Because banks are selling some of their securities, the banks will have more cash, which increases their supply of loanable funds, which in turn makes banks willing to lend more money at lower interest rates. In addition, the Fed's purchases represent an increase in the demand for Treasury securities. As with anything for sale, increased demand causes Treasury securities' prices to go up and interest rates to go down. The net result is a reduction in interest rates, which stimulates the economy by making it less costly for companies to borrow for new projects or for individuals to borrow for major purchases or other expenditures.

When banks sell their holdings of Treasury securities to the Fed, the banks' reserves go up, which increases the money supply. A larger money supply ultimately leads to an increase in expected inflation, which eventually pushes interest rates up. Thus, the Fed can stimulate the economy in the short term by driving down interest rates and increasing the money supply, but this creates longer-term inflationary pressures. This is exactly the dilemma facing the Fed in mid-2012.

On the other hand, if the Fed wishes to slow down the economy and reduce inflation, the Fed reverses the process. Instead of purchasing Treasury securities, the Fed sells Treasury securities to banks, which causes an increase in short-term interest rates but a decrease in long-term inflationary pressures.

Budget Deficits or Surpluses

WWW

For today's cumulative total federal debt (the total public debt), check out the Current Daily Treasury Statement at **www.fms.treas.gov/dts/index.html**.

If the federal government spends more than it takes in from tax revenues, then it runs a deficit, and that deficit must be covered either by borrowing or by printing money (increasing the money supply). The government borrows by issuing new Treasury securities. All else held equal, this creates a greater supply of Treasury securities, which leads to lower security prices and higher interest rates. Other federal government actions that increase the money supply also increase expectations for future inflation, which drives up interest rates. Thus, the larger the federal deficit, other things held constant, the higher the level of interest rates. As shown in Figure 1-2, the federal government has run deficits in 15 of the past 19 years. Annual deficits in the mid-1990s were in the $250 billion range, but they have ballooned to well over a trillion dollars in recent years. These huge deficits have contributed to the cumulative federal debt, which in early 2012 stood at more than $15 trillion.

FIGURE 1-2

Federal Budget Surplus/Deficits and Trade Balances (Billions of Dollars)

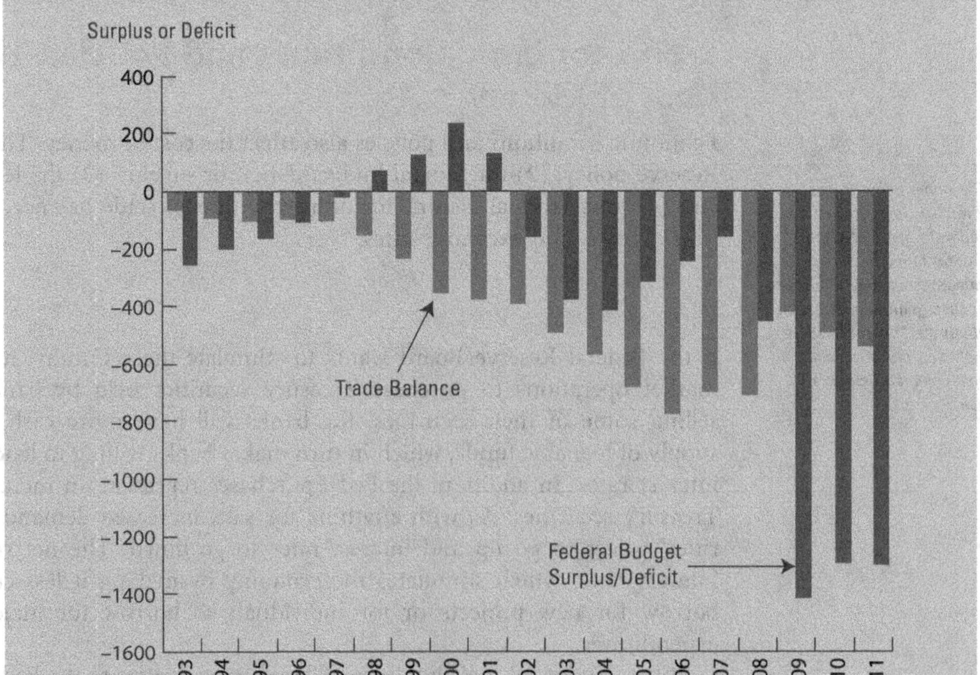

© Cengage Learning 2014

Business Activity

Figure 1-3 shows interest rates, inflation, and recessions. Notice that interest rates and inflation typically rise prior to a recession and fall afterward. There are several reasons for this pattern.

Consumer demand slows during a recession, keeping companies from increasing prices, which reduces price inflation. Companies also cut back on hiring, which reduces wage inflation. Less disposable income causes consumers to reduce their purchases of homes and automobiles, reducing consumer demand for loans. Companies reduce investments in new operations, which reduce their demand for funds. The cumulative effect is downward pressure on inflation and interest rates. The Federal Reserve is also active during recessions, trying to stimulate the economy by driving down interest rates.

International Trade Deficits or Surpluses

Businesses and individuals in the United States buy from and sell to people and firms in other countries. If we buy more than we sell (that is, if we import more than we export), we are said to be running a *foreign trade deficit.* When trade deficits occur, they must be financed, and the main source of financing is debt. In other words, if we

FIGURE 1-3

Business Activity, Interest Rates, and Inflation

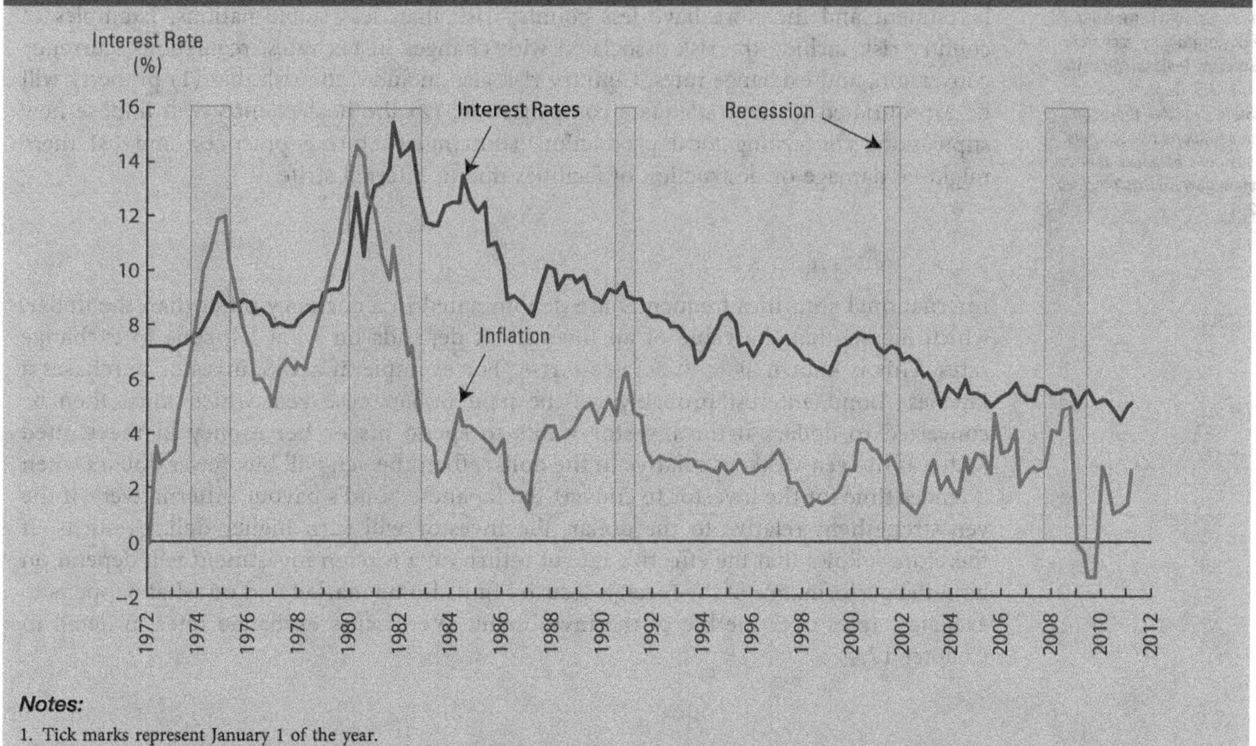

Notes:

1. Tick marks represent January 1 of the year.
2. The shaded areas designate business recessions as defined by the National Bureau of Economic Research; see **www.nber.org/cycles.**
3. Interest rates are for AAA corporate bonds; see the St. Louis Federal Reserve Web site: **http://research.stlouisfed.org/fred.** These rates reflect the average rate during the month ending on the date shown.
4. Inflation is measured by the annual rate of change for the Consumer Price Index (CPI) for the preceding 12 months; see **http://research.stlouisfed.org/fred.**

© Cengage Learning 2014

import $200 billion of goods but export only $90 billion, we run a trade deficit of $110 billion, and we will probably borrow the $110 billion.[3] Therefore, the larger our trade deficit, the more we must borrow, and the increased borrowing drives up interest rates. Also, international investors are willing to hold U.S. debt if and only if the risk-adjusted rate paid on this debt is competitive with interest rates in other countries. Therefore, if the Federal Reserve attempts to lower interest rates in the United States, causing our rates to fall below rates abroad (after adjustments for expected changes in the exchange rate), then international investors will sell U.S. bonds, which will depress bond prices and result in higher U.S. rates. Thus, if the trade deficit is large relative to the size of the overall economy, it will hinder the Fed's ability to reduce interest rates and combat a recession.

The United States has been running annual trade deficits since the mid-1970s; see Figure 1-2 for recent years. The cumulative effect of trade deficits and budget deficits is that the United States has become the largest debtor nation of all time. As noted earlier, this federal debt exceeds *$15 trillion!* As a result, our interest rates are influenced by interest rates in other countries around the world.

International Country Risk

WWW

Transparency International provides a ranking of countries based on their levels of perceived corruption. See **www.transparency.org/policy_research/surveys_indices/cpi/2010.** *The U.S. Department of State provides thorough descriptions of countries' business climates at* **www.state.gov/e/eb/rls/othr/ics/2011.**

International risk factors may increase the cost of money that is invested abroad. **Country risk** is the risk that arises from investing or doing business in a particular country, and it depends on the country's economic, political, and social environment. Countries with stable economic, social, political, and regulatory systems provide a safer climate for investment and therefore have less country risk than less stable nations. Examples of country risk include the risk associated with changes in tax rates, regulations, currency conversion, and exchange rates. Country risk also includes the risk that (1) property will be expropriated without adequate compensation; (2) the host country will impose new stipulations concerning local production, sourcing, or hiring practices; and (3) there might be damage or destruction of facilities due to internal strife.

Exchange Rate Risk

International securities frequently are denominated in a currency other than the dollar, which means that the value of an investment depends on what happens to exchange rates. This is known as **exchange rate risk.** For example, if a U.S. investor purchases a Japanese bond, interest probably will be paid in Japanese yen, which must then be converted to dollars if the investor wants to spend his or her money in the United States. If the yen weakens relative to the dollar, then the yen will buy fewer dollars when it comes time for the investor to convert the Japanese bond's payout. Alternatively, if the yen strengthens relative to the dollar, the investor will earn higher dollar returns. It therefore follows that the effective rate of return on a foreign investment will depend on both the performance of the foreign security in its home market and on what happens to exchange rates over the life of the investment. We discuss exchange rates in detail in Chapter 17.

[3]The deficit could also be financed by selling assets, including gold, corporate stocks, entire companies, and real estate. The United States has financed its massive trade deficits through all of these means in recent years, but the primary method has been by borrowing from foreigners.

SELF-TEST

What four fundamental factors affect the cost of money?
Name some economic conditions that influence interest rates, and explain their effects.

1-7 Financial Institutions

When raising capital, direct transfers of funds from individuals to businesses are most common for small businesses or in economies where financial markets and institutions are not well developed. Businesses in developed economies usually find it more efficient to enlist the services of one or more financial institutions to raise capital. Most financial institutions don't compete in a single line of business but instead provide a wide variety of services and products, both domestically and globally. The following sections describe the major types of financial institutions and services, but keep in mind that the dividing lines among them are often blurred. Also, note that the global financial crisis we are now going through is changing the structure of our financial institutions, and new regulations are certain to affect those that remain. Finance today is dynamic, to say the least!

1-7a Investment Banks and Brokerage Activities

Investment banking houses help companies raise capital. Such organizations underwrite security offerings, which means they (1) advise corporations regarding the design and pricing of new securities, (2) buy these securities from the issuing corporation, and (3) resell them to investors. Although the securities are sold twice, this process is really one primary market transaction, with the investment banker acting as a facilitator to help transfer capital from savers to businesses. An investment bank often is a division or subsidiary of a larger company. For example, JPMorgan Chase & Co. is a very large financial services firm, with over $2 *trillion* in managed assets. One of its holdings is J.P. Morgan, an investment bank.

In addition to security offerings, investment banks also provide consulting and advisory services, such as merger and acquisition (M&A) analysis and investment management for wealthy individuals.

Most investment banks also provide brokerage services for institutions and individuals (called "retail" customers). For example, Merrill Lynch (acquired in 2008 by Bank of America) has a large retail brokerage operation that provides advice and executes trades for its individual clients. Similarly, J.P. Morgan helps execute trades for institutional customers, such as pension funds.

At one time, most investment banks were partnerships, with income generated primarily by fees from their underwriting, M&A consulting, asset management, and brokering activities. When business was good, investment banks generated high fees and paid big bonuses to their partners. When times were tough, investment banks paid no bonuses and often fired employees. In the 1990s, however, most large investment banks were reorganized into publicly traded corporations (or were acquired and then operated as subsidiaries of public companies). For example, in 1994 Lehman Brothers sold some of its own shares of stock to the public via an IPO. Like most corporations, Lehman Brothers was financed by a combination of equity and debt. A relaxation of regulations in the 2000s allowed investment banks to undertake much riskier activities than at any time since the Great Depression. The new regulations allowed investment banks to use an unprecedented amount of debt to finance their activities—Lehman used roughly $30 of debt for every dollar of equity. In addition to their fee-generating activities, most investment banks also began trading securities for their own accounts. In other words, they took the borrowed money and invested it in financial securities. If you are earning 12% on your investments while paying 8% on your borrowings, then the more money you borrow, the more profit you make. But if you are leveraged 30 to 1 and your investments decline in value by even 3.33%, your business will fail. This is exactly what happened to Bear Stearns, Lehman Brothers, and Merrill Lynch in the fall of 2008. In short, they borrowed money, used it to make risky investments, and then failed when the investments turned out to be worth less than the amount they owed. Note that it was not their traditional investment banking activities that caused the failure, but the fact that they borrowed so much and used those funds to speculate in the market.

1-7b Deposit-Taking Financial Intermediaries

Some financial institutions take deposits from savers and then lend most of the deposited money to borrowers. Following is a brief description of such intermediaries.

Savings and Loan Associations (S&Ls)

As we explained in Section 1.5, S&Ls originally accepted deposits from many small savers and then loaned this money to home buyers and consumers. Later, they were allowed to make riskier investments, such as investing in real estate development. **Mutual savings banks (MSBs)** are similar to S&Ls, but they operate primarily in the northeastern states. Today, most S&Ls and MSBs have been acquired by banks.

Credit Unions

Credit unions are cooperative associations whose members have a common bond, such as being employees of the same firm or living in the same geographic area. Members' savings are lent only to other members, generally for auto purchases, home-improvement loans, and home mortgages. Credit unions are often the cheapest source of funds available to individual borrowers.

Commercial Banks

Commercial banks raise funds from depositors and by issuing stock and bonds to investors. For example, someone might deposit money in a checking account. In return, that person can write checks, use a debit card, and even receive interest on the deposits. Those who buy the banks' stocks expect to receive dividends and interest payments. Unlike nonfinancial corporations, most commercial banks are highly leveraged in the sense that they owe much more to their depositors and creditors than they raised from stockholders. For example, a typical bank has about \$90 of debt for every \$10 of stockholders' equity. If the bank's assets are worth \$100, we can calculate its equity capital by subtracting the \$90 of liabilities from the \$100 of assets: Equity capital = \$100 − \$90 = \$10. But if the assets drop in value by 5% to \$95, the equity drops to \$5 = \$95 − \$90, a 50% decline.

Banks are vitally important for a well-functioning economy, and their highly leveraged positions make them risky. As a result, banks are more highly regulated than nonfinancial firms. Given the high risk, banks might have a hard time attracting and retaining deposits unless the deposits were insured, so the Federal Deposit Insurance Corporation (FDIC), which is backed by the U.S. government, insures up to \$250,000 per depositor. As a result of the global economic crisis, this insured amount was increased from \$100,000 in 2008 to reassure depositors.

Without such insurance, if depositors believed that a bank was in trouble, they would rush to withdraw funds. This is called a "bank run," which is exactly what happened in the United States during the Great Depression, causing many bank failures and leading to the creation of the FDIC in an effort to prevent future bank runs. Not all countries have their own versions of the FDIC, so international bank runs are still possible. In fact, a bank run occurred in September 2008 at the U.K. bank Northern Rock, leading to its nationalization by the government.

Most banks are small and locally owned, but the largest banks are parts of giant financial services firms. For example, JPMorgan Chase Bank, commonly called Chase Bank, is owned by JPMorgan Chase & Co., and Citibank is owned by Citicorp (at the time we write this, but perhaps not when you read this—the financial landscape changes daily).

1-7c Investment Funds

At some financial institutions, savers have an ownership interest in a pool of funds rather than owning a deposit account. Examples include mutual funds, hedge funds, and private equity funds.

Mutual Funds

Mutual funds are corporations that accept money from savers and then use these funds to buy financial instruments. These organizations pool funds, which allows them to reduce risks by diversification and achieve economies of scale in analyzing securities, managing portfolios, and buying/selling securities. Different funds are designed to meet the objectives of different types of savers. Hence, there are bond funds for those who desire safety and stock funds for savers who are willing to accept risks in the hope of higher returns. There are literally thousands of different mutual funds with dozens of different goals and purposes. Some funds are actively managed, with their managers trying to find undervalued securities, while other funds are passively managed and simply try to minimize expenses by matching the returns on a particular market index.

Money market funds invest in short-term, low-risk securities, such as Treasury bills and commercial paper. Many of these funds offer interest-bearing checking accounts with rates that are greater than those offered by banks, so many people invest in money market funds as an alternative to depositing money in a bank. Note, though, that money market funds are not required to be insured and so are riskier than bank deposits.[4]

Most traditional mutual funds allow investors to redeem their share of the fund only at the close of business. A special type of mutual fund, the **exchange traded fund (ETF)**, allows investors to sell their share at any time during normal trading hours. ETFs usually have very low management expenses and are rapidly gaining in popularity.

Hedge Funds

Hedge funds raise money from investors and engage in a variety of investment activities. Unlike typical mutual funds, which can have thousands of investors, hedge funds are limited to institutional investors and a relatively small number of high-net-worth individuals. Because these investors are supposed to be sophisticated, hedge funds are much less regulated than mutual funds. The first hedge funds literally tried to hedge their bets by forming portfolios of conventional securities and derivatives in such a way as to limit their potential losses without sacrificing too much of their potential gains. Many hedge funds

[4]The U.S. Treasury sold deposit insurance to eligible money market funds between September 2008 and September 2009 to help stabilize the markets during the height of the financial crisis.

had spectacular rates of return during the 1990s. This success attracted more investors, and thousands of new hedge funds were created. Much of the low-hanging fruit had already been picked, however, so the hedge funds began pursuing much riskier (and unhedged) strategies, including the use of high leverage in unhedged positions. Perhaps not surprisingly (at least in retrospect), some funds have produced spectacular losses. For example, many hedge fund investors suffered huge losses in 2007 and 2008 when large numbers of sub-prime mortgages defaulted.

Private Equity Funds

Private equity funds are similar to hedge funds in that they are limited to a relatively small number of large investors. They differ in that they own stock (equity) in other companies and often control those companies, whereas hedge funds usually own many different types of securities. In contrast to a mutual fund, which might own a small percentage of a publicly traded company's stock, a private equity fund typically owns virtually all of a company's stock. Because the company's stock is not traded in the public markets, it is called "private equity." In fact, private equity funds often take a public company (or subsidiary) and turn it private, such as the 2007 privatization of Chrysler by Cerberus. (Fiat is now the majority owner.) The general partners who manage private equity funds usually sit on the companies' boards and guide their strategies with the goal of later selling the companies for a profit. For example, The Carlyle Group, Clayton Dubilier & Rice, and Merrill Lynch Global Private Equity bought Hertz from Ford on December 22, 2005, and then sold shares of Hertz in an IPO less than a year later.

Many private equity funds experienced high rates of return in the last decade, and those returns attracted enormous sums from investors. A few funds, most notably The Blackstone Group, actually went public themselves through an IPO. Just as with hedge funds, the performance of many private equity funds faltered. For example, shortly after its IPO in June 2007, Blackstone's stock price was over $31 per share; by early 2009, it had fallen to about $4. By early 2012 the stock price was about $15, still well short of its IPO price.

1-7d Life Insurance Companies and Pension Funds

Life insurance companies take premiums, invest these funds in stocks, bonds, real estate, and mortgages, and then make payments to beneficiaries. Life insurance companies also offer a variety of tax-deferred savings plans designed to provide retirement benefits.

Traditional **pension funds** are retirement plans funded by corporations or government agencies. Pension funds invest primarily in bonds, stocks, mortgages, hedge funds, private equity, and real estate. Most companies now offer self-directed retirement plans, such as 401(k) plans, as an addition to or substitute for traditional pension plans. In traditional plans, the plan administrators determine how to invest the funds; in self-directed plans, all individual participants must decide how to invest their own funds. Many companies are switching from traditional plans to self-directed plans, partly because this shifts the risk from the company to the employee.

1-7e Regulation of Financial Institutions

In 1933, the Glass-Steagall Act was passed with the intent of preventing another great depression. In addition to creating the FDIC to insure bank deposits, the law imposed constraints on banking activities and separated investment banking from commercial banking. The regulatory environment of the post-Depression era included a prohibition on nationwide branch banking, restrictions on the types of assets the institutions could buy, ceilings on the interest rates they could pay, and limitations on the types of services they could provide. Arguing that these regulations impeded the free flow of capital and hurt the efficiency of our capital markets, policymakers took several steps from the 1970s to the 1990s to deregulate financial services companies, culminating with the Gramm–Leach–Bliley Act of 1999, which "repealed" Glass-Steagall's separation of commercial and investment banking.

One result of deregulation was the creation of huge financial services corporations, which own commercial banks, S&Ls, mortgage companies, investment-banking houses, insurance companies, pension plan operations, and mutual funds. Many are now global banks with branches and operations across the country and around the world.

WWW

For current bank rankings, go to Global Finance Magazine's Web site, **www.gfmag.com**, *and use the Tools tab.*

For example, Citigroup combined one of the world's largest commercial banks (Citibank), a huge insurance company (Travelers), and a major investment bank (Smith Barney), along with numerous other subsidiaries that operate throughout the world. Bank of America also made numerous acquisitions of many different financial companies, including Merrill Lynch, with its large brokerage and investment banking operations, and mortgage giant Countrywide Financial.

These conglomerate structures are similar to those of major institutions in Europe, Japan, and elsewhere around the globe. Though U.S. banks grew dramatically as a result of recent mergers, they are still relatively small by global standards. Among the world's largest world banks, based upon total assets, only three—Bank of America, Citigroup, and JPMorgan Chase—are headquartered in the United States.

The financial crisis of 2008–2009 and the continuing global economic crisis are causing regulators and financial institutions to rethink the wisdom of deregulating conglomerate financial services corporations. To address some of these concerns, the Dodd-Frank Wall Street Reform and Consumer Protection Act was passed in 2010. We discuss Dodd-Frank and other regulatory changes in Section 1.13, where we explain the events leading up to the global economic crisis.

SELF-TEST

What is the difference between a pure commercial bank and a pure investment bank?

List the major types of financial institutions, and briefly describe the original purpose of each.

What are some important differences between mutual funds and hedge funds? How are they similar?

1-8 Financial Markets

Financial markets bring together people and organizations needing money with those having surplus funds. There are many different financial markets in a developed economy. Each market deals with a somewhat different type of instrument, customer, or geographic location. Here are some ways to classify markets:

1. **Physical asset markets** (also called "tangible" or "real" asset markets) are those for such products as wheat, autos, real estate, computers, and machinery. **Financial asset markets**, on the other hand, deal with stocks, bonds, notes, mortgages, derivatives, and other **financial instruments**.
2. **Spot markets** and **futures markets** are markets where assets are being bought or sold for "on-the-spot" delivery (literally, within a few days) or for delivery at some future date, such as 6 months or a year into the future.

3. **Money markets** are the markets for short-term, highly liquid debt securities, while **capital markets** are the markets for corporate stocks and debt maturing more than a year in the future. The New York Stock Exchange is an example of a capital market. When describing debt markets, "short term" generally means less than 1 year, "intermediate term" means 1 to 5 years, and "long term" means more than 5 years.
4. **Mortgage markets** deal with loans on residential, agricultural, commercial, and industrial real estate, while **consumer credit markets** involve loans for autos, appliances, education, vacations, and so on.
5. **World, national, regional,** and **local markets** also exist. Thus, depending on an organization's size and scope of operations, it may be able to borrow or lend all around the world, or it may be confined to a strictly local, even neighborhood, market.
6. **Primary markets** are the markets in which corporations raise new capital. If Microsoft were to sell a new issue of common stock to raise capital, this would be a primary market transaction. The corporation selling the newly created stock receives the proceeds from such a transaction. The **initial public offering (IPO) market** is a subset of the primary market. Here firms "go public" by offering shares to the public for the first time. For example, Google had its IPO in 2004. Previously, founders Larry Page and Sergey Brin, other insiders, and venture capitalists owned all the shares. In many IPOs, the insiders sell some of their shares and the company sells newly created shares to raise additional capital. **Secondary markets** are markets in which existing, already outstanding securities are traded among investors. Thus, if you decided to buy 1,000 shares of Aeropostale stock, the purchase would occur in the secondary market. The New York Stock Exchange is a secondary market, because it deals in outstanding (as opposed to newly issued) stocks. Secondary markets also exist for bonds, mortgages, and other financial assets. The corporation whose securities are being traded is not involved in a secondary market transaction and, thus, does not receive any funds from such a sale.
7. **Private markets**, where transactions are worked out directly between two parties, are differentiated from **public markets**, where standardized contracts are traded on organized exchanges. Bank loans and private placements of debt with insurance companies are examples of private market transactions. Because these transactions are private, they may be structured in any manner that appeals to the two parties. By contrast, securities that are issued in public markets (for example, common stock and corporate bonds) are ultimately held by a large number of individuals. Public securities must have fairly standardized contractual features because public investors cannot afford the time to study unique, nonstandardized contracts. Hence private market securities are more tailor-made but less liquid, whereas public market securities are more liquid but subject to greater standardization.

You should recognize the big differences among types of markets, but keep in mind that the distinctions are often blurred. For example, it makes little difference if a firm borrows for 11, 12, or 13 months and thus whether such borrowing is a "money" or "capital" market transaction.

SELF-TEST

Distinguish between (1) physical asset markets and financial asset markets, (2) spot and futures markets, (3) money and capital markets, (4) primary and secondary markets, and (5) private and public markets.

1-9 Trading Procedures in Financial Markets

A huge volume of trading occurs in the secondary markets. Although there are many secondary markets for a wide variety of securities, we can classify their trading procedures along two dimensions: location and method of matching orders.

1-9a Physical Location versus Electronic Network

A secondary market can be either a **physical location exchange** or a **computer/telephone network**. For example, the New York Stock Exchange, the American Stock Exchange (AMEX), the Chicago Board of Trade (the CBOT trades futures and options), and the Tokyo Stock Exchange are all physical location exchanges. In other words, the traders actually meet and trade in a specific part of a specific building.

In contrast, NASDAQ, which trades a number of U.S. stocks, is a network of linked computers. Other network examples are the markets for U.S. Treasury bonds and foreign exchange, which operate via telephone and/or computer networks. In these electronic markets, the traders never see one another except maybe for cocktails after work.

By their very nature, networks are less transparent than physical location exchanges. For example, credit default swaps are traded directly between buyers and sellers, and there is no easy mechanism for recording, aggregating, and reporting the transactions or the net positions of the buyers and sellers.

1-9b Matching Orders: Auctions, Dealers, and ECNs

The second dimension is the way orders from sellers and buyers are matched. This can occur through an open outcry **auction** system, through dealers, or by automated order matching. An example of an outcry auction is the CBOT, where traders actually meet in a pit and sellers and buyers communicate with one another through shouts and hand signals.

In a **dealer market**, there are "market makers" who keep an inventory of the stock (or other financial instrument) in much the same way that any merchant keeps an inventory. These dealers list bid quotes and ask quotes, which are the prices at which they are willing to buy or sell. Computerized quotation systems keep track of all bid and asked prices, but they don't actually match buyers and sellers. Instead, traders must contact a specific dealer to complete the transaction. NASDAQ (U.S. stocks) is one such market, as is the London SEAQ (U.K. stocks).

The third method of matching orders is through an **electronic communications network (ECN)**. Participants in an ECN post their orders to buy and sell, and the ECN automatically matches orders. For example, someone might place an order to buy 1,000 shares of IBM stock—this is called a "market order" because it is to buy the stock at the current market price. Suppose another participant had placed an order to sell 1,000 shares of IBM, but only at a price of $91 per share, and this was the lowest price of any "sell" order. The ECN would automatically match these two orders, execute the trade, and notify both participants that the trade has occurred. The $91 sell price was a "limit order" as opposed to a market order because the action was limited by the seller. Note that orders can also be limited with regard to their duration. For example, someone might stipulate that they are willing to buy 1,000 shares of IBM at $90 per share if the price falls that low during the next two hours. In other words, there are limits on the price and/or the duration of the order. The ECN will execute the limit order only if both conditions are met.

Life in the Fast Lane: High-Frequency Trading!

© Rob Webb/Getty Images

In the time it takes to blink an eye, a high-frequency trader's computer could have made hundreds of bids, canceled all but one, purchased shares of stock, and then sold them for a profit of less than a penny. It may sound like a lot of work for such a small profit, but a million similar trades a day add up to big bucks. In fact, high-frequency trading (HFT) firms made about $7.2 billion total profit in 2009.

Who are these traders? First, there are only about 400 HTF firms out of the 20,000 or so institutional traders, so there really aren't very many of them. Second, many of their employees have math and computer science backgrounds rather than trading experience. Third, they have access to the very best computer technology. Their demand for speed is so great that Hibernia Atlantic plans to lay a new underwater cable along a slightly shorter route from the U.K. to Canada in order to cut the transmission time from 65 to 60 milliseconds!

Despite the relatively small number of HFT firms, they have a huge impact on the market, accounting for over 60% of the stock trading volume and over 40% of the foreign exchange volume. But are HFT firms good or bad for markets and other investors? The answer is not clear. On the one hand, other investors can trade much more quickly now, with execution time dropping from 10.1 seconds in 2005 to 0.7 seconds in 2010. The cost of trading, as measured by the spread in bid and ask prices, has also shrunk dramatically. On the other hand, some critics say that high-frequency trading distorts prices and makes markets less stable. As we write this in early 2012, the Securities and Exchange Commission is considering placing restrictions on high-frequency trading. One thing is for sure: Electronic trading will continue to have a big impact on financial markets.

Sources: Doug Cameron and Jacob Bunge, "Underwater Options? Ocean Cable Will Serve High-Frequency Traders," *The Wall Street Journal*, October 1, 2010, p. C-3; and Kambiz Foroohar, "Speed Geeks," *Bloomberg Markets*, November 2010, pp. 111–122.

Two of the largest ECNs for trading U.S. stocks are INET (owned by NASDAQ) and Arca (owned by NYSE Euronext). Other large ECNs include Eurex (an ECN for derivatives, owned by the Deutsche Börse) and SETS (a stock exchange owned by the SIX Swiss Exchange). Notice that most "conventional" exchanges also operate ECNs.

SELF-TEST

What are the major differences between physical location exchanges and computer/telephone networks?

What are the differences among open outcry auctions, dealer markets, and ECNs?

WWW

For updates on IPO activity, see **www.renaissancecapital.com/IPOHome/MarketWatch.aspx**. The Wall Street Journal *also provides IPO data in its Year-End Review of Markets & Finance at* **online.wsj.com**. *See Professor Jay Ritter's Web site for additional IPO data and analysis,* **http://bear.cba.ufl.edu/ritter/ipodata.htm**.

1-10 Types of Stock Market Transactions

Because the primary objectives of financial management are to maximize the firm's intrinsic value and then help ensure that the current stock price equals that value, knowledge of the stock market is important to anyone involved in managing a business. We can classify stock market transactions into three distinct types: (1) initial public offerings, (2) seasoned equity offerings, and (3) secondary market transactions.

Whenever stock is offered to the public for the first time, the company is said to be **going public**. This primary market transaction is called the initial public offering (IPO) market. If a company later decides to sell (i.e., issue) additional shares to raise new equity capital, this is still a primary market, but it is called a **seasoned equity offering**. Trading in the outstanding shares of established, publicly owned companies are secondary market transactions. For example, if the owner of 100 shares of publicly held stock sells his or her stock, the trade is said to have occurred in the secondary market. Thus, the market for outstanding shares, or used shares, is the secondary market. The company receives no new money when sales occur in this market.

resource

For more on issuing stock, see Web Extension 1B on the textbook's Web site.

Here is a brief description of recent IPO activity. There were 1,285 total global IPOs in 2011, with total proceeds of $168 billion. China and Hong Kong together represented over 40% of the total. The biggest IPO was the $10 billion raised by Glencore International, a Swiss mining company.

In the United States, the average first-day return was around 13% in 2011. However, some firms had spectacular first-day price run-ups, such as LinkedIn's 109% gain on its first day of trading. Not all companies fared so well—indeed, FriendFinder fell by over 21% on its first trading day.

For 2011, some IPOs had big gains for the year, such as Imperva's 92.8% return. Others had big annual losses; HCA Holdings fell by over 26%. In fact, the average IPO lost over 13% during 2011.

Even if you are able to identify a "hot" issue, it is often difficult to purchase shares in the initial offering. In strong markets, these deals generally are oversubscribed, which means that the demand for shares at the offering price exceeds the number of shares issued. In such instances, investment bankers favor large institutional investors (who are their best customers), and small investors find it hard, if not impossible, to get in on the ground floor. They can buy the stock in the aftermarket, but evidence suggests that if you do not get in on the ground floor, the average IPO underperforms the overall market over the long run.[5]

Before you conclude that it isn't fair to let only the best customers have the stock in an initial offering, think about what it takes to become a best customer. Best customers are usually investors who have done lots of business in the past with the investment banking firm's brokerage department. In other words, they have paid large sums as commissions in the past, and they are expected to continue doing so in the future. As is so often true, there is no free lunch—most of the investors who get in on the ground floor of an IPO have, in fact, paid for this privilege.

SELF-TEST

Differentiate between an IPO, a seasoned equity offering, and a secondary transaction.

Why is it often difficult for the average investor to make money during an IPO?

1-11 The Secondary Stock Markets

The two leading U.S. stock markets today are the New York Stock Exchange and the NASDAQ stock market.

1-11a The New York Stock Exchange

WWW

You can access the home pages of the major U.S. stock markets at **www.nyse.com** *and* **www.NASDAQ.com**. *These sites provide background information as well as the opportunity to obtain individual stock quotes.*

Before March of 2006, the **New York Stock Exchange (NYSE)** was a privately held firm owned by its members. It then merged with Archipelago, a publicly traded company that was one of the world's largest ECNs. NYSE members received approximately 70% of the shares in the combined firm, with Archipelago shareholders receiving 30%. The combined firm, which also owned the Pacific Exchange, was known as The NYSE Group, Inc., and

[5]See Jay R. Ritter, "The Long-Run Performance of Initial Public Offerings," *Journal of Finance*, March 1991, pp. 3–27.

was traded publicly under the ticker symbol NYX. It continued to operate the New York Stock Exchange (a physical location exchange located on Wall Street) and Arca (comprising the Pacific Exchange and the ECN formerly known as Archipelago). In 2007 the NYSE Group merged with Euronext, a European company that operates stock exchanges (called bourses) in Paris, Amsterdam, Brussels, and Lisbon. The combined company is called NYSE Euronext.

resource

For more on stock markets, see Web Extension 1B on the textbook's Web site.

The NYSE still has over 300 member organizations, which are corporations, partnerships, or LLCs. Membership prices were as high as $4 million in 2005, and the last sale before the Euronext merger was $3.5 million. Member organizations are registered broker-dealers, but they may not conduct trading on the floor of the exchange unless they also hold a trading license issued by the NYSE. Before going public, the equivalent to the trading license was called a "seat," although there was very little sitting on the floor of the exchange. Trading licenses are now leased by member organizations from the exchange, with an annual fee of $40,000 for 2012. The NYSE has leased most of its 1,500 available trading licenses.

Most of the larger investment banking houses operate *brokerage departments* and are members of the NYSE with leased trading rights. The NYSE is open on all normal working days, and members meet in large rooms equipped with electronic equipment that enables each member to communicate with his or her firm's offices throughout the country. For example, Merrill Lynch (now owned by Bank of America) might receive an order in its Atlanta office from a customer who wants to buy shares of Procter & Gamble stock. Simultaneously, Edward Jones' St. Louis office might receive an order from a customer wishing to sell shares of P&G. Each broker communicates electronically with the firm's representative on the NYSE. Other brokers throughout the country also communicate with their own exchange members. The exchange members with *sell orders* offer the shares for sale, and members with *buy orders* bid for them. Thus, the NYSE operates as an *auction market*.[6]

However, trading on the NYSE floor has declined in importance. In addition to the trading of NYSE stocks on its own ECN, Arca, hundreds of private ECNs and brokers trade NYSE stocks. In 2010, about 79% of the trading volume for NYSE-listed stocks occurred on these private networks.

1-11b The NASDAQ Stock Market

The **National Association of Securities Dealers (NASD)** is a self-regulatory body that licenses brokers and oversees trading practices. The computerized network used by the NASD is known as the NASD Automated Quotation System, or NASDAQ. NASDAQ started as a quotation system, but it has grown to become an organized securities market with its own listing requirements. NASDAQ lists about 5,000 stocks, although not all trade through the same NASDAQ system. For example, the NASDAQ National Market

[6]The NYSE is actually a modified auction market, wherein people (through their brokers) bid for stocks. Originally—about 200 years ago—brokers would literally shout, "I have 100 shares of Erie for sale; how much am I offered?" and then sell to the highest bidder. If a broker had a buy order, he or she would shout, "I want to buy 100 shares of Erie; who'll sell at the best price?" The same general situation still exists, although the exchanges now have members known as specialists who facilitate the trading process by keeping an inventory of shares of the stocks in which they specialize. If a buy order comes in at a time when no sell order arrives, the specialist will sell off some inventory. Similarly, if a sell order comes in, the specialist will buy and add to inventory. The specialist sets a bid price (the price the specialist will pay for the stock) and an asked price (the price at which shares will be sold out of inventory). The bid and asked prices are set at levels designed to keep the inventory in balance. If many buy orders start coming in because of favorable developments or sell orders come in because of unfavorable events, the specialist will raise or lower prices to keep supply and demand in balance. Bid prices are somewhat lower than asked prices, with the difference, or spread, representing the specialist's profit margin.

Measuring the Market

© Rob Webb/Getty Images

A *stock index* is designed to show the performance of the stock market. Here we describe some leading indexes.

Dow Jones Industrial Average

Begun in 1896, the Dow Jones Industrial Average (DJIA) now includes 30 widely held stocks that represent almost one-fifth of the market value of all U.S. stocks. See **www.dowjones.com** for more information.

S&P 500 Index

Created in 1926, the S&P 500 Index is widely regarded as the standard for measuring large-cap U.S. stocks' market performance. It is value weighted, so the largest companies (in terms of value) have the greatest influence. The S&P 500 Index is used as a comparison benchmark by 97% of all U.S. money managers and pension plan sponsors. See **www2.standardandpoors.com** for more information.

NASDAQ Composite Index

The NASDAQ Composite Index measures the performance of all common stocks listed on the NASDAQ stock market. Currently, it includes more than 3,200 companies, many of which are in the technology sector. Microsoft, Cisco Systems, and Intel account for a high percentage of the index's value-weighted market capitalization. For this reason, substantial movements in the same direction by these three companies can move the entire index. See **www.NASDAQ.com** for more information.

NYSE Composite Index

The NYSE Composite Index measures the performance of all common stocks listed on the NYSE. It is a value-weighted index and is based on just over 2,000 stocks that represent 77% of the total market capitalization of all publicly traded companies in the United States. See **www.nyse.com** for more information.

Trading the Market

Through the use of exchange traded funds (ETFs), it is now possible to buy and sell the market in much the same way as an individual stock. For example, the Standard & Poor's depository receipt (SPDR) is a share of a fund that holds the stocks of all the companies in the S&P 500. SPDRs trade during regular market hours, making it possible to buy or sell the S&P 500 any time during the day. There are hundreds of other ETFs, including ones for the NASDAQ, the Dow Jones Industrial Average, gold stocks, utilities, and so on.

Recent Performance

Go to the Web site **finance.yahoo.com**. Enter the symbol for any of the indexes (^DJI for the Dow Jones, ^GSPC for the S&P 500, ^IXIC for the NASDAQ, and ^NYA for the NYSE) and then click GO. This will bring up the current value of the index, shown in a table. Click Basic Chart in the panel on the left, which will bring up a chart showing the historical performance of the index. Directly above the chart is a series of buttons that allows you to choose the number of years and to plot the relative performance of several indexes on the same chart. You can even download the historical data in spreadsheet form by clicking Historical Prices in the left panel.

lists the larger NASDAQ stocks, such as Microsoft and Intel, while the NASDAQ Small-Cap Market lists smaller companies with the potential for high growth. NASDAQ also operates the NASDAQ OTC Bulletin Board, which lists quotes for stocks registered with the Securities and Exchange Commission (SEC) but not listed on any exchange, usually because the company is too small or not sufficiently profitable.[7] Finally, NASDAQ

[7]OTC stands for over-the-counter. Before NASDAQ, the quickest way to trade a stock that was not listed at a physical location exchange was to find a brokerage firm that kept shares of that stock in inventory. The stock certificates were kept in a safe and were literally passed over the counter when bought or sold. Today the certificates for almost all listed stocks and bonds in the United States are stored in a vault, beneath Manhattan, that is operated by the Depository Trust and Clearing Corporation (DTCC). Most brokerage firms have an account with the DTCC, and most investors leave their stocks with their brokers. Thus, when stocks are sold, the DTCC simply adjusts the accounts of the brokerage firms that are involved, and no stock certificates are actually moved.

operates the Pink Sheets, which provide quotes on companies that are not registered with the SEC.

"Liquidity" is the ability to trade quickly at a net price (i.e., after any commissions) that is close to the security's recent market price. In a dealer market, such as NASDAQ, a stock's liquidity depends on the number and quality of the dealers who make a market in the stock. NASDAQ has more than 400 dealers, most of whom make markets in a large number of stocks. The typical stock has about 10 market makers, but some stocks have more than 50 market makers. Obviously, there are more market makers, and hence more liquidity, for the NASDAQ National Market than for the SmallCap Market. Stocks listed on the OTC Bulletin Board or the Pink Sheets have much less liquidity.

1-11c Competition in the Secondary Markets

WWW

For updates, see **www.world-exchanges.org/statistics/time-series/market-capitalization** *at the World Federation of Exchanges.*

There is intense competition between the NYSE, NASDAQ, and other international stock exchanges—they all want the larger, more profitable companies to list on their exchange. Because most of the largest U.S. companies trade on the NYSE, the market capitalization of NYSE-traded stocks is much higher than for stocks traded on NASDAQ (about \$13.4 trillion compared with \$3.9 trillion at the end of 2010). However, reported volume (number of shares traded) is often larger on NASDAQ, and more companies are listed on NASDAQ.[8] For comparison, the market capitalizations for global exchanges are \$3.8 trillion in Tokyo, \$3.6 trillion in London, \$2.7 trillion in Shanghai, \$2.7 trillion in Hong Kong, \$1.4 trillion in Germany, and \$1.6 trillion in Bombay.

Interestingly, many high-tech companies such as Microsoft and Intel have remained on NASDAQ even though they easily meet the listing requirements of the NYSE. At the same time, however, other high-tech companies such as Iomega have left NASDAQ for the NYSE. Despite these defections, NASDAQ's growth over the past decade has been impressive. In an effort to become even more competitive with the NYSE and with international markets, NASDAQ acquired one of the leading ECNs, Instinet, in 2005. NASDAQ subsequently acquired the Nordic exchange OMX, giving it an international presence. The combined company is the NASDAQ OMX Group.

Despite the shifting ownerships of exchanges, one thing is clear—there will be a continued consolidation in the securities exchange industry, with a blurring of the lines between physical location exchanges and electronic exchanges.

SELF-TEST

What are some major differences between the NYSE and the NASDAQ stock market?

1-12 Stock Market Returns

During the period 1968–2011, the average annual return for the stock market, as measured by total returns (dividends plus capital gains) on the S&P 500 index, was about 10.9%, but this average does not reflect the considerable annual variation. Notice in Panel A of Figure 1-4 that the market was relatively flat in the 1970s, increased somewhat in the 1980s, and has been a roller coaster ever since. In fact, the market in early 2009 dipped to a level last seen in 1995. Panel B highlights the year-to-year risk by showing annual returns. Notice that stocks have had positive returns in most years, but there have been

---

[8]One transaction on NASDAQ generally shows up as two separate trades (the buy and the sell). This "double counting" makes it difficult to compare the volume between stock markets.

several years with large losses. Stocks lost more than 40% of their value during 1973–1974 and again during 2000–2002, and they lost 37% of their value in 2008 alone. We will examine risk in more detail later in the book, but even a cursory glance at Figure 1-4 shows just how risky investing in stocks can be!

U.S. stocks amount to only about 40% of the world's stocks, and this is prompting many U.S. investors to also hold foreign stocks. Analysts have long touted the benefits of investing overseas, arguing that foreign stocks improve diversification and provide good

FIGURE 1-4

S&P 500 Stock Index Performance

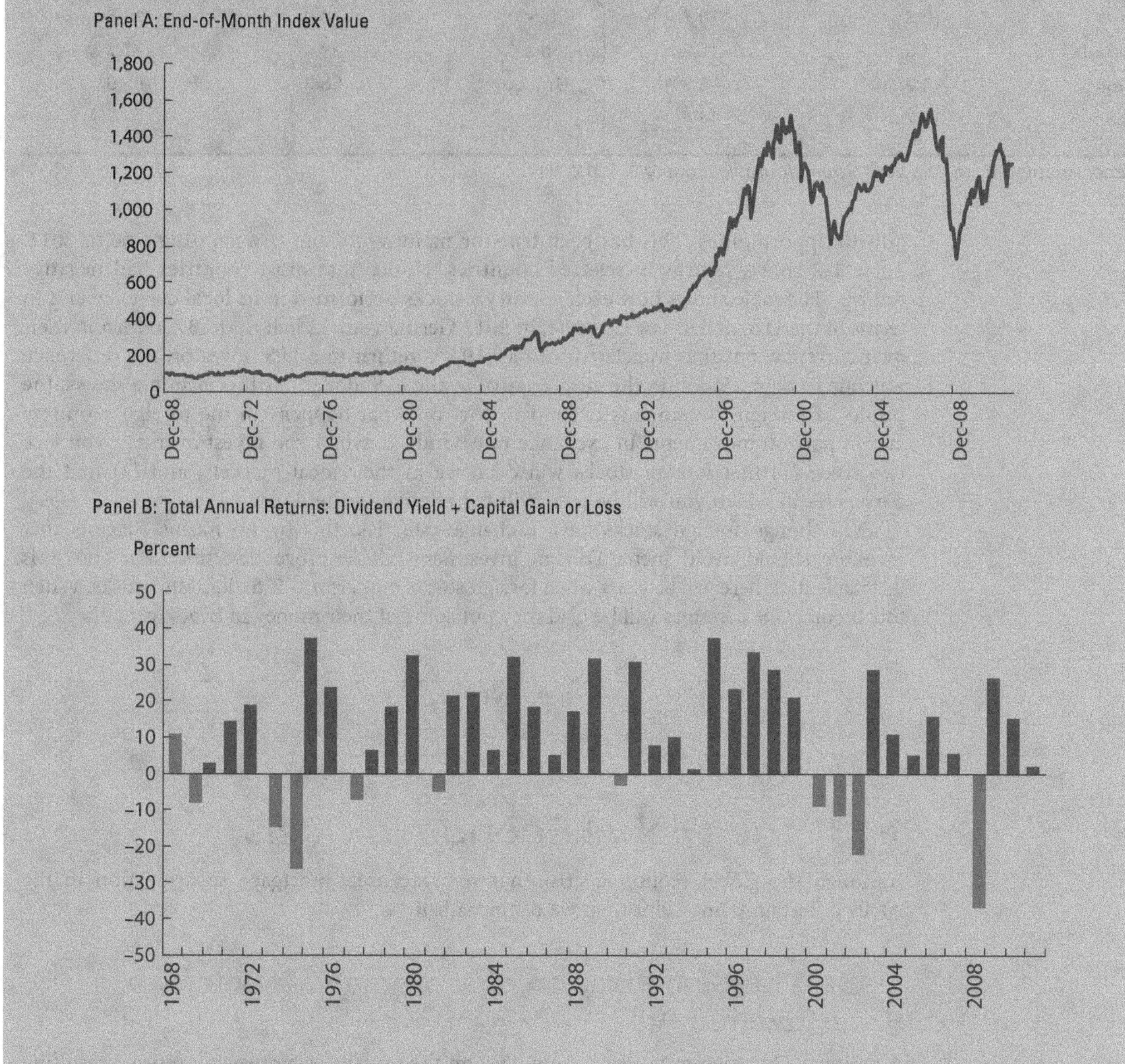

Sources: Returns data are from various issues of *The Wall Street Journal*, "Investment Scoreboard" section; the index level is from **http://finance.yahoo.com**.

TABLE 1-2
2011 Performance of Selected Dow Jones Global Stock Indexes, Ranked Highest to Lowest

Country	U.S. Dollars	Local Currency	Country	U.S. Dollars	Local Currency
Qatar	4.0%	4.0%	France	−19.3%	−16.6%
Iceland	0.6	7.4	Germany	−19.9	−17.3
Ireland	−1.1	2.2	China	−20.2	−20.3
U.K.	−6.7	−6.0	Russia	−21.0	−16.9
Switzerland	−9.0	−8.7	Hong Kong	−23.5	−23.6
South Korea	−11.6	−10.3	Brazil	−24.2	−14.8
Japan	−14.3	−18.7	Chile	−24.9	−16.6
Canada	−14.3	−12.2	India	−39.1	−27.7
Mexico	−14.7	−3.5	Greece	−58.3	−56.9
Spain	−17.2	−14.4			

Source: Adapted from *The Wall Street Journal,* January 3, 2012, R17.

growth opportunities. This has been true for many years, but it wasn't the case in 2011. Table 1-2 shows returns in selected countries. Notice that most countries had negative returns. The table shows how each country's stocks performed in its local currency and in terms of the U.S. dollar. For example, in 2011 German stocks had a −17.3% return in their own currency, but that translated into a −19.9% return to a U.S. investor; the difference was due to depreciation in the euro relative to the U.S. dollar. As this example shows, the results of foreign investments depend in part on what happens in the foreign economy and in part on movements in exchange rates. Indeed, when you invest overseas, you face two risks: (1) that foreign stocks will decrease in their local markets, and (2) that the currencies in which you will be paid will fall relative to the dollar.

Even though foreign stocks have exchange-rate risk, this by no means suggests that investors should avoid them. Foreign investments do improve diversification, and it is inevitable that there will be years when foreign stocks outperform U.S. domestic stocks. When this occurs, U.S. investors will be glad they put some of their money in overseas markets.

SELF-TEST

Explain how exchange rates affect the rate of return on international investments.

1-13 The Global Economic Crisis

Although the global economic crisis has many causes, mortgage securitization in the 2000s is certainly one culprit, so we begin with it.

1-13a The Globalization of Mortgage Market Securitization

A national TV program ran a documentary on the travails of Norwegian retirees resulting from defaults on Florida mortgages. Your first reaction might be to wonder how Norwegian retirees became financially involved with risky Florida mortgages. We will break the answer to that question into two parts. First, we will identify the different links in the financial chain between the retirees and mortgagees. Second, we will explain why there were so many weak links.

In the movie *Jerry Maguire,* Tom Cruise said, "Show me the money!" That's a good way to start identifying the financial links, starting with a single home purchase in Florida.

1. Home Purchase

In exchange for cash, a seller in Florida turned over ownership of a house to a buyer.

2. Mortgage Origination

To get the cash used to purchase the house, the buyer signed a mortgage loan agreement and gave it to an "originator." Years ago the originator would probably have been an S&L or a bank, but more recently the originators have been specialized mortgage brokers, as in this case. The broker gathered and examined the borrower's credit information, arranged for an independent appraisal of the house's value, handled the paperwork, and received a fee for these services.

3. Securitization and Resecuritization

In exchange for cash, the originator sold the mortgage to a securitizing firm. For example, Merrill Lynch's investment banking operation was a major player in securitizing loans. It would bundle large numbers of mortgages into pools and then create new securities that had claims on the pools' cash flows. Some claims were simple, such as a proportional share of a pool; some were more complex, such as a claim on all interest payments during the first 5 years or a claim on only principal payments. More complicated claims were entitled to a fixed payment, while other claims would receive payments only after the "senior" claimants had been paid. These slices of the pool were called "tranches," which comes from a French word for slice.

Some of the tranches were themselves re-combined and then re-divided into securities called collateralized debt obligations (CDOs), some of which were themselves combined and subdivided into other securities, commonly called CDOs-squared. For example, Lehman Brothers often bought different tranches, split them into CDOs of differing risk, and then had the different CDOs rated by an agency like Moody's or Standard & Poor's.

There are three very important points to notice. First, the process didn't change the *total amount of risk* embedded in the mortgages, but it did make it possible to create some securities that were less risky than average and some that were more risky. Second, the complexity of the CDOs spread a little bit of each mortgage's risk to very many different investors, making it difficult for investors to determine the aggregate risk of a particular CDO. Third, each time a new security was created or rated, fees were being earned by the investment banks and rating agencies.

4. The Investors

In exchange for cash, the securitizing firms sold the newly created securities to individual investors, hedge funds, college endowments, insurance companies, and other financial institutions, including a pension fund in Norway. Keep in mind that financial institutions are funded by individuals, so cash begins with individuals and flows through the system until it is eventually received by the seller of the home. If all goes according to plan, payments on the mortgages eventually return to the individuals who originally provided the cash. But in this case, the chain was broken by a wave of mortgage defaults, resulting in problems for Norwegian retirees.

Students and managers often ask, "What happened to all the money?" The short answer is, "It went from investors to home sellers, with fees being skimmed off all along the way."

Although the process is complex, in theory there is nothing inherently wrong with it. In fact, it should, in theory, provide more funding for U.S. home purchasers, and it should allow risk to be shifted to those best able to bear it. Unfortunately, this isn't the end of the story.

1-13b The Dark Side of Securitization: The Sub-Prime Mortgage Meltdown

What caused the financial crisis? Entire books have been written on this subject, but we can identify a few of the culprits.

Regulators Approved Sub-Prime Standards

In the 1980s and early 1990s, regulations did not permit a nonqualifying mortgage to be securitized, so most originators mandated that borrowers meet certain requirements, including having at least a certain minimum level of income relative to the mortgage payments and a minimum down payment relative to the size of the mortgage. But in the mid-1990s, Washington politicians wanted to extend home ownership to groups that traditionally had difficulty obtaining mortgages. To accomplish this, regulations were relaxed so that nonqualifying mortgages could be securitized. Such loans are commonly called sub-prime or Alt-A mortgages. Thus, riskier mortgages were soon being securitized and sold to investors. Again, there was nothing inherently wrong, provided the two following questions were being answered in the affirmative: One, were home buyers making sound decisions regarding their ability to repay the loans? And two, did the ultimate investors recognize the additional risk? We now know that the answer to both questions is a resounding "no." Homeowners were signing mortgages that they could not hope to repay, and investors treated these mortgages as if they were much safer than they actually were.

The Fed Helped Fuel the Real Estate Bubble

With more people able to get a mortgage, including people who should not have obtained one, the demand for homes increased. This alone would have driven up house prices. However, the Fed also slashed interest rates to historic lows after the terrorist attacks of 9/11 to prevent a recession, and it kept them low for a long time. These low rates made mortgage payments lower, which made home ownership seem even more affordable, again contributing to an increase in the demand for housing. Figure 1-5 shows that the combination of lower mortgage qualifications and lower interest rates caused house prices to skyrocket. Thus, the Fed contributed to an artificial bubble in real estate.

Home Buyers Wanted More for Less

Even with low interest rates, how could sub-prime borrowers afford the mortgage payments, especially with house prices rising? First, most sub-prime borrowers chose an adjustable rate mortgage (ARM) with an interest rate based on a short-term rate, such as that on 1-year Treasury bonds, to which the lender added a couple of percentage points. Because the Fed had pushed short-term rates so low, the initial rates on ARMs were very low.

With a traditional fixed-rate mortgage, the payments remain fixed over time. But with an ARM, an increase in market interest rates triggers higher monthly payments, so an ARM is riskier than a fixed-rate mortgage. However, many borrowers chose an *even*

FIGURE 1-5

The Real Estate Boom: Housing Prices and Mortgage Rates

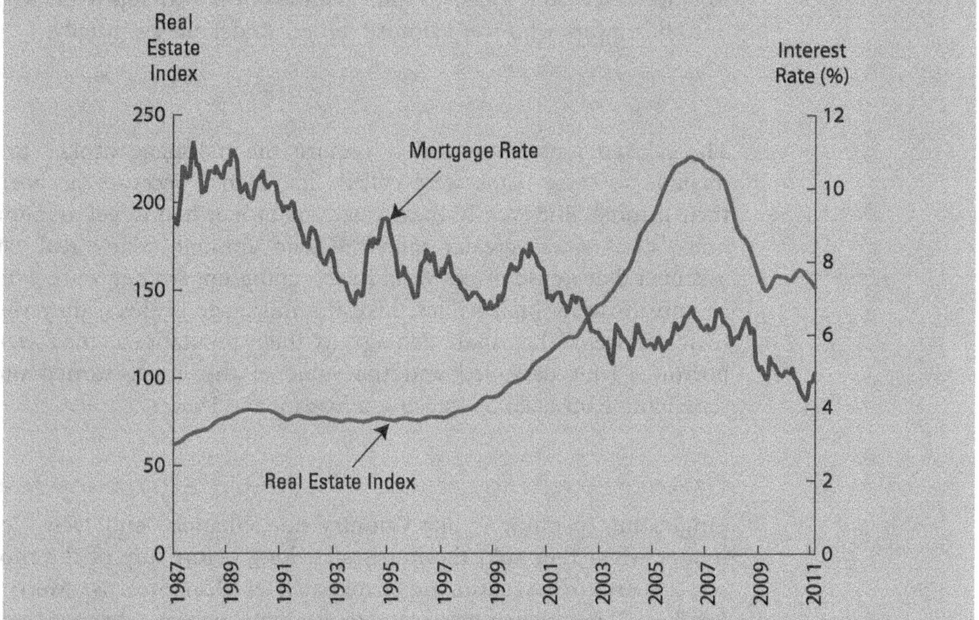

Notes:

1. The real estate index is the Case-Shiller composite index for house prices in 10 real estate markets, not seasonally adjusted, available at **www.standardandpoors.com/indices/sp-case-shiller-home-price-indices/en/us/?indexId=spusa-cashpidff-p-us——**.
2. Interest rates are for 30-year conventional fixed-rate mortgages, available from the St. Louis Federal Reserve: **http://research.stlouisfed.org/fred2/series/MORTG/downloaddata?cid=114**.

© Cengage Learning 2014

riskier mortgage, the "option ARM," where the borrower can choose to make such low payments during the first couple of years that they don't even cover the interest, causing the loan balance to actually increase each month! At a later date, the payments would be reset to reflect both the current market interest rate and the higher loan balance. For example, in some cases a monthly payment of $948 for the first 32 months was reset to $2,454 for the remaining 328 months. (We provide the calculations for this example in Chapter 4.)

Why would anyone who couldn't afford to make a $2,454 monthly payment choose an option ARM? Here are three possible reasons. First, some borrowers simply didn't understand the situation and were victims of predatory lending practices by brokers eager to earn fees regardless of the consequences. Second, some borrowers thought that the home price would go up enough to allow them to sell at a profit or else refinance with another low-payment loan. Third, some people were simply greedy and shortsighted, and they wanted to live in a better home than they could afford.

Mortgage Brokers Didn't Care

Years ago, S&Ls and banks had a vested interest in the mortgages they originated because they held them for the life of the loan—up to 30 years. If a mortgage went bad, the bank or S&L would lose money, so they were careful to verify that the borrower would be able to repay the loan. In the bubble years, though, over 80% of mortgages were arranged by independent mortgage brokers who received a commission. Thus, the broker's incentive was to complete deals even if the borrowers couldn't make the payments after the soon-to-come reset. So it's easy to understand (but not to approve!) why brokers pushed deals onto borrowers who were almost certain to default eventually.

Real Estate Appraisers Were Lax

The relaxed regulations didn't require the mortgage broker to verify the borrower's income, so these loans were called "liar loans" because the borrowers could overstate their income. But even in these cases the broker had to get an appraisal showing that the house's value was greater than the loan amount. Many real estate appraisers simply assumed that house prices would keep going up, so they were willing to appraise houses at unrealistically high values. Like the mortgage brokers, they were paid at the time of their service. Other than damage to their reputations, they weren't concerned if the borrower later defaulted and the value of the house turned out to be less than the remaining loan balance, causing a loss for the lender.

Originators and Securitizers Wanted Quantity, Not Quality

Originating institutions like Countrywide Financial and New Century Mortgage made money when they sold the mortgages, long before any of the mortgages defaulted. The same is true for securitizing firms such as Bear Stearns, Merrill Lynch, and Lehman Brothers. Their incentives were to generate volume through originating loans, not to ensure that the loans were safe investments. This started at the top—CEOs and other top executives received stock options and bonuses based on their firms' profits, and profits depended on volume. Thus, the top officers pushed their subordinates to generate volume, those subordinates pushed the originators to write more mortgages, and the originators pushed the appraisers to come up with high values.

Rating Agencies Were Lax

Investors who purchased the complicated mortgage-backed securities wanted to know how risky they were, so they insisted on seeing the bonds' "ratings." The securitizing firms paid rating agencies to investigate the details of each bond and to assign a rating that reflected the security's risk. For example, Lehman Brothers hired Moody's to rate some of its CDOs. Indeed, the investment banks would actually pay for advice from the rating agencies as they were designing the securities. The rating and consulting activities were extremely lucrative for the agencies, which ignored the obvious conflict of interest: The investment bank wanted a high rating, the rating agency got paid to help design securities that would qualify for a high rating, and high ratings led to continued business for the raters.

Insurance Wasn't Insurance

To provide a higher rating and make these mortgage-backed securities look even more attractive to investors, the issuers would frequently purchase a type of insurance policy on the security called a **credit default swap**. For example, suppose you had wanted to purchase a CDO from Lehman Brothers but worried about the risk. What if Lehman Brothers had agreed to pay an annual fee to an insurance company such as AIG, which would guarantee the CDO's payments if the underlying mortgages defaulted? You probably would have felt confident enough to buy the CDO.

But any similarity to a conventional insurance policy ends here. Unlike home insurance, where there is a single policyholder and a single insurer, totally uninvolved speculators can also make bets on your CDO by either selling or purchasing credit default swaps on the CDO. For example, a hedge fund could buy a credit default swap on your CDO if it thinks the CDO will default; or an investment bank like Bear Stearns could sell a swap, betting that the CDO won't default. In fact, the International Swaps and Derivatives Association estimates that in mid-2008 there was about $54 trillion in credit default swaps. This staggering amount was approximately 7 times the value of all U.S. mortgages, was over 4 times the level of the U.S. national debt, and was over twice the value of the entire U.S. stock market.

Another big difference is that home insurance companies are highly regulated, but there was virtually no regulation in the credit default swap market. The players traded directly among themselves, with no central clearinghouse. It was almost impossible to tell how much risk any of the players had taken on, making it impossible to know whether or not counterparties like AIG would be able to fulfill their obligations in the event of a CDO default. And that made it impossible to know the value of CDOs held by many banks, which in turn made it impossible to judge whether or not those banks were de facto bankrupt.

Rocket Scientists Had Poor Rearview Mirrors and Risk Managers Drove Blind

Brilliant financial experts, often trained in physics and hired from rocket science firms, built elegant models to determine the value of these new securities. Unfortunately, a model is only as good as its inputs. The experts looked at the high growth rates of recent real estate prices (see Figure 1-5) and assumed that future growth rates also would be high. These high growth rates caused models to calculate very high CDO prices. Perhaps more surprisingly, many risk managers simply did not insist on seeing scenarios in which housing prices fell.

Investors Wanted More for Less

In the early 2000s, low-rated debt (including mortgage-backed securities), hedge funds, and private equity funds produced great rates of return. Many investors jumped into this debt to keep up with the Joneses. As shown in Chapter 4 when we discuss bond ratings and bond spreads, investors began lowering the premium they required for taking on extra risk. Thus, investors focused primarily on returns and largely ignored risk. In fairness, some investors assumed the credit ratings were accurate, and they trusted the representatives of the investment banks selling the securities. In retrospect, however, Warren Buffett's maxim that "I only invest in companies I understand" seems wiser than ever.

The Emperor Has No Clothes

In 2006, many of the option ARMs began to reset, borrowers began to default, and home prices first leveled off and then began to fall. Things got worse in 2007 and 2008, and by early 2009, almost 1 out of 10 mortgages was in default or foreclosure, resulting in displaced families and virtual ghost towns of new subdivisions. As homeowners defaulted on their mortgages, so did the CDOs backed by the mortgages. That brought down the counterparties like AIG who had insured the CDOs via credit default swaps. Virtually overnight, investors realized that mortgage-backed security default rates were headed higher and that the houses used as collateral were worth less than the mortgages. Mortgage-backed security prices plummeted, investors quit buying newly securitized mortgages, and liquidity in the secondary market disappeared. Thus, the investors who owned these securities were stuck with pieces of paper that were substantially lower than the values reported on their balance sheets.

1-13c From Sub-Prime Meltdown to Liquidity Crisis to Economic Crisis

Like the Andromeda strain, the sub-prime meltdown went viral, and it ended up infecting almost all aspects of the economy. But why did a burst bubble in one market segment, sub-prime mortgages, spread across the globe?

First, securitization allocated the sub-prime risk to many investors and financial institutions. The huge amount of credit default swaps linked to sub-prime-backed securities spread the risk to even more institutions. Unlike previous downturns in a single market, such as the dot-com bubble in 2002, the decline in the sub-prime mortgage values affected many, if not most, financial institutions.

Second, banks were more vulnerable than at any time since the 1929 Depression. Congress had "repealed" the Glass-Steagall Act in 1999, allowing commercial banks and investment banks to be part of a single financial institution. The SEC compounded the problem in 2004 when it allowed large investment banks' brokerage operations to take on much higher leverage. Some, like Bear Stearns, ended up with $33 of debt for every dollar of its own equity. With such leverage, a small increase in the value of its investments would create enormous gains for the equity holders and large bonuses for the managers; conversely a small decline would ruin the firm.

When the sub-prime market mortgages began defaulting, mortgage companies were the first to fall. Many originating firms had not sold all of their sub-prime mortgages, and they failed. For example, New Century declared bankruptcy in 2007, IndyMac was placed under FDIC control in 2008, and Countrywide was acquired by Bank of America in 2008 to avoid bankruptcy.

Securitizing firms also crashed, partly because they kept some of the new securities they created. For example, Fannie Mae and Freddie Mac had huge losses on their portfolio assets, causing them to be virtually taken over by the Federal Housing Finance Agency in 2008. In addition to big losses on their own sub-prime portfolios, many investment banks also had losses related to their positions in credit default swaps. Thus, Lehman Brothers was forced into bankruptcy, Bear Stearns was sold to JPMorgan Chase, and Merrill Lynch was sold to Bank of America, with huge losses to stockholders.

Because Lehman Brothers defaulted on some of its commercial paper, investors in the Reserve Primary Fund, a big money market mutual fund, saw the value of its investments "break the buck," dropping to less than a dollar per share. To avoid panic and a total lockdown in the money markets, the U.S. Treasury agreed to insure some investments in money market funds.

AIG was the largest backer of credit default swaps, and it operated worldwide. In 2008 it became obvious that AIG could not honor its commitments as a counterparty, so the Fed effectively nationalized AIG to avoid a domino effect in which AIG's failure would topple hundreds of other financial institutions.

In normal times, banks provide liquidity to the economy and funding for creditworthy businesses and individuals. These activities are crucial for a well-functioning economy. However, the financial contagion spread to commercial banks because some owned mortgage-backed securities, some owned commercial paper issued by failing institutions, and some had exposure to credit default swaps. As banks worried about their survival in the fall of 2008, they stopped providing credit to other banks and businesses. The market for commercial paper dried up to such an extent that the Fed began buying new commercial paper from issuing companies.

Prior to the sub-prime meltdown, many nonfinancial corporations had been rolling over short-term financing to take advantage of low interest rates on short-term lending. When the meltdown began, banks began calling in loans rather than renewing them. In

GLOBAL ECONOMIC CRISIS

© uniquely india/Getty Images

Anatomy of a Toxic Asset

Consider the dismal history of one particular toxic asset named "GSAMP TRUST 2006-NC2." This toxic asset began life as 3,949 individual mortgages issued by New Century in 2006 with a total principal of about $881 million. Almost all were adjustable rate mortgages, half were concentrated in just two states (California and Florida), and many of the borrowers had previous credit problems. Goldman Sachs bought the mortgages, pooled them into a trust, and divided the trust into 16 "debt" tranches called mortgage-backed securities (MBS). The tranches had different provisions regarding distribution of payments should there be any defaults, with senior tranches getting paid first and junior tranches getting paid only if funds were available. Despite the mortgages' poor quality and the pool's lack of diversification, Moody's and Standard & Poor's gave most tranches good ratings, with over 79% rated AAA.

Five years later, in July 2011, about 36% of the underlying mortgages were behind in payments, defaulted, or even foreclosed. Not surprisingly, the market prices of the mortgage-backed securities had plummeted. These were very toxic assets indeed!

The story doesn't end here. Fannie Mae and Freddie Mac had purchased some of these toxic assets and taken a beating. In September, 2011, the Federal Housing Finance Agency (now the conservator of Fannie Mae and Freddie Mac) sued Goldman Sachs, alleging that Goldman Sachs had knowingly overstated the value of the securities in the prospectuses. The FHFA also alleges that at the very same time Goldman Sachs was selling these and other mortgage-backed securities to Fannie and Freddie, Goldman was: (1) trying to get rid of the mortgages by "putting" them back to New Century, and (2) was "betting" against the mortgages in the credit default swap market. As of early 2012, this suit has not yet been settled, but it is safe to say that these toxic assets will continue to poison our economy for many more years.

Source: Adam B. Ashcraft and Til Schuermann, *Understanding the Securitization of Subprime Mortgage Credit,* Federal Reserve Bank of New York Staff Reports, no. 318, March 2008; John Cassidy, *How Markets Fail* (New York: Farrar, Straus and Giroux, 2009), pp. 260–272; and the Federal Housing Finance Agency, **www.fhfa.gov/webfiles/22589/FHFA%20v%20Goldman%20Sachs.pdf.**

response, many companies began throttling back their plans. Consumers and small businesses faced a similar situation: With credit harder to obtain, consumers cut back on spending and small businesses cut back on hiring. Plummeting real estate prices caused a major contraction in the construction industry, putting many builders and suppliers out of work.

What began as a slump in housing prices caused enormous distress for commercial banks, not just mortgage companies. Commercial banks cut back on lending, which caused difficulties for nonfinancial business and consumers. Similar scenarios played out all over the world, resulting in the worst recession in the U.S. since 1929.

1-13d Responding to the Economic Crisis

Unlike the beginning of the 1929 Depression, the U.S. government did not take a hands-off approach in the most recent crisis. In late 2008 Congress passed the Troubled Asset Relief Plan (TARP), which authorized the U.S. Treasury to purchase mortgage-related assets from financial institutions. The intent was to simultaneously inject cash into the banking system and get these toxic assets off banks' balance sheets. The Emergency Economic Stabilization Act of 2008 (EESA) allowed the Treasury to purchase preferred stock in banks (whether they wanted the investment or not). Again, this injected cash into the banking system. Several very large banks have already paid back the funding they received from the TARP and EESA financing, although it is doubtful whether all recipients will be able to do so. It is almost certain that some financial institutions, such as AIG, will leave taxpayers bearing the burden of their bailouts.

Although TARP and EESA were originally intended for financial institutions, they were subsequently modified so that the Treasury was able to make loans to GM and Chrylser in 2008 and early 2009 so that they could stave off immediate bankruptcy. Both GM and Chrysler went into bankruptcy in the summer of 2009 despite government loans, but quickly emerged as stronger companies. Although the U.S. government is still a shareholder, there is a possibility that GM and Chrysler will pay back the government's investment.

The government also used traditional measures, such as stimulus spending, tax cuts, and monetary policy: (1) The American Recovery and Reinvestment Act of 2009 provided over $700 billion in direct stimulus spending for a variety of federal projects and aid for state projects. (2) In 2010 the government also temporarily cut Social Security taxes from 6.2% to 4.2%. (3) The Federal Reserve has purchased around $2 trillion in assets, including long-term bonds, from financial institutions, a process called "quantitative easing."

Has the response worked? You will have a better answer at the time you read this than we had when we wrote this in early 2012, but here is our answer: The economy is better now than at the worst of the crisis, with the unemployment rate down to 8.5% from its 2009 high of 10%, and GDP is growing rather than contracting. Whether or not it was due to the government's response, it does not appear likely that the economy will soon fall into another Great Depression, something that we could not write in 2009. On the other hand, it is likely that it will take years, if not a full decade, for the economy and stock markets to fully recover.[9]

1-13e Preventing the Next Crisis

Can the next crisis be prevented? Congress passed the Dodd-Frank Wall Street Reform and Consumer Protection Act in 2010 as an attempt to do just that. As we write this in 2012, many provisions have not yet been enacted. Following is a brief summary of some major elements in the Act.

Protect Consumers from Predators and Themselves

Dodd-Frank established the Consumer Financial Protection Bureau, whose objectives include ensuring that borrowers fully understand the terms and risks of the mortgage contracts, that mortgage originators verify borrower's ability to repay, and that originators maintain an interest in the borrowers by keeping some of the mortgages they originate. The Bureau will also oversee credit cards, debit cards, payday loans, and other areas in which consumers might have been targets of predatory lending practices. As of early 2012, the Bureau has been established, but it has done very little.

Separate Banking from Speculating

The act's "Volker Rule," named after former Fed chairman Paul Volcker, would greatly limit a bank's proprietary trading, such as investing the banks' own funds into hedge funds. The basic idea is to prevent banks from making highly leveraged

[9]For a comparison of this crisis with 15 previous banking crises, see Serge Wind, "A Perspective on 2000's Illiquidity and Capital Crisis: Past Banking Crises and their Relevance to Today's Credit Crisis," *Review of Business*, Volume 31, Number 1, Fall 2010, pp. 68–83. Based on these previous crises, Professor Wind estimates it will take 10 years for equity markets to reach the pre-crisis high.

bets on risky assets. The Volcker Rule has not been implemented as of early 2012, although Goldman Sachs and Morgan Stanley have cut back their proprietary trading operations.

Increase Transparency

The act calls for regulation and transparency in the now-private derivatives markets, including the establishment of a trading exchange. It also provides for more oversight of hedge funds and credit rating agencies in an effort to spot potential landmines before they explode. Not much has been accomplished as of early 2012.

Head Off and Rein In Systemic Failures at Too-Big-to-Fail Banks

When a bank gets extremely large and has business connections with many other companies, it can be very dangerous to the rest of the economy if the institution fails and goes bankrupt, as the 2008 failure of Lehman Brothers illustrates. In other words, a bank or other financial institution can become "too big to fail." Systemic risk is defined as something that affects most companies. When there are a large number of too-big-to-fail institutions and systemic shock hits, the entire world can be dragged into a recession, as we saw in 2008.

Dodd-Frank gives regulators more oversight of too-big-to-fail institutions, including all banks with $50 billion in assets and any other financial institutions that regulators deem systemically important. This oversight includes authority to require additional capital or reductions in leverage if conditions warrant. In addition, these institutions must prepare "transition" plans that would make it easier for regulators to liquidate the institution should it fail. In other words, this provision seeks to reduce the likelihood that a giant financial institution will fail and to minimize the damage if it does fail. Not much has been implemented as of early 2012.

SELF-TEST

Briefly describe some of the mistakes that participants in the sub-prime mortgage process made.

1-14 The Big Picture

Finance has vocabulary and tools that might be new to you. To help you avoid getting bogged down in the trenches, Figure 1-6 presents the big picture. A manager's primary job is to increase the company's intrinsic value, but how exactly does one go about doing that? The equation in the center of Figure 1-6 shows that intrinsic value is the present value of the firm's expected free cash flows, discounted at the weighted average cost of capital. Thus, there are two approaches for increasing intrinsic value: Improve FCF or reduce the WACC. Observe that several factors affect FCF and several factors affect the WACC. In the rest of the book's chapters, we will typically focus on only one of these factors, systematically building the vocabulary and tools that you will use after graduation to improve your company's intrinsic value. It is true that every manager needs to understand financial vocabulary and be able to apply financial tools, but successful managers also understand how their decisions affect the big picture. So as you read this book, keep in mind where each topic fits into the big picture.

FIGURE 1-6

The Determinants of Intrinsic Value: The Big Picture

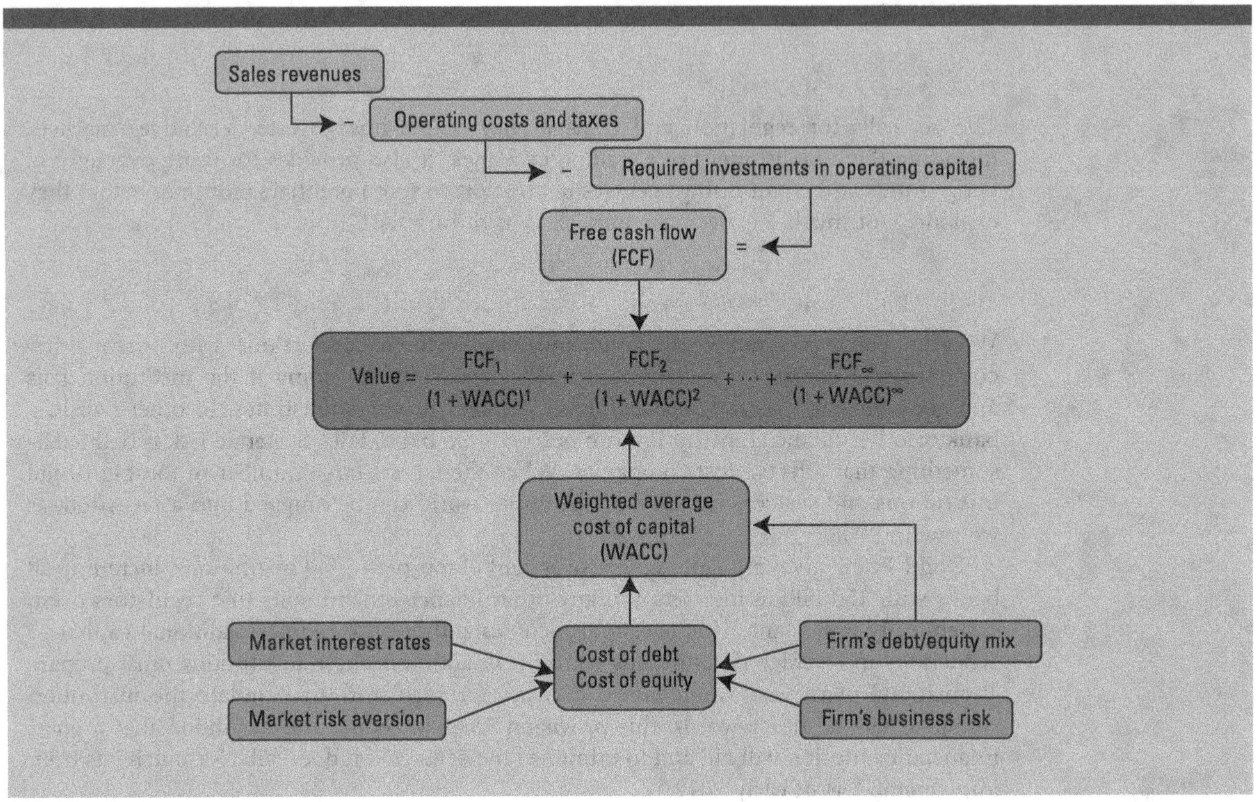

© Cengage Learning 2014

1-15 e-Resources

The textbook's Web site contains several types of files that will be helpful to you:

resource

1. It contains *Excel* files, called ***Tool Kits*** that provide well-documented models for almost all of the text's calculations. Not only will these ***Tool Kits*** help you with this finance course, they also will serve as tool kits for you in other courses and in your career.
2. There are problems at the end of the chapters that require spreadsheets, and the Web site contains the models you will need to begin work on these problems.

www

When we think it might be helpful for you to look at one of the Web site's files, we'll show an icon in the margin like the one shown here.

THOMSON REUTERS

Other resources are also on the Web site, including Cyberproblems and problems that use the Thomson ONE—Business School Edition Web site. The textbook's Web site also contains an electronic library that contains Adobe PDF files for "extensions" to many chapters that cover additional useful material related to the chapter.

SUMMARY

- The three main forms of business organization are the **proprietorship**, the **partnership**, and the **corporation**. Although each form of organization offers advantages and disadvantages, *corporations conduct much more business than the other forms.*

- The primary objective of management should be to *maximize stockholders' wealth,* and this means *maximizing the company's* **fundamental**, or **intrinsic, stock price.** Legal actions that maximize stock prices usually increase social welfare.
- **Free cash flows (FCFs)** are the cash flows available for distribution to all of a firm's investors (shareholders and creditors) after the firm has paid all expenses (including taxes) and has made the required investments in operations to support growth.
- The **weighted average cost of capital (WACC)** is the average return required by all of the firm's investors. It is determined by the firm's *capital structure* (the firm's relative amounts of debt and equity), *interest rates,* the firm's *risk,* and the *market's attitude toward risk.*
- The value of a firm depends on the size of the firm's free cash flows, the timing of those flows, and their risk. A **firm's fundamental,** or **intrinsic, value** is defined by

$$\text{Value} = \frac{FCF_1}{(1 + WACC)^1} + \frac{FCF_2}{(1 + WACC)^2} + \frac{FCF_3}{(1 + WACC)^3} + \dots + \frac{FCF_\infty}{(1 + WACC)^\infty}$$

- Transfers of capital between borrowers and savers take place (1) by **direct transfers** of money and securities; (2) by transfers through **investment banking houses,** which act as go-betweens; and (3) by transfers through **financial intermediaries,** which create new securities.
- Four fundamental factors affect the cost of money: (1) **production opportunities,** (2) **time preferences for consumption,** (3) **risk,** and (4) **inflation.**
- **Derivatives,** such as options, are claims on other financial securities. In **securitization,** new securities are created from claims on packages of other securities.
- Major financial institutions include **commercial banks, savings and loan associations, mutual savings banks, credit unions, pension funds, life insurance companies, mutual funds, money market funds, hedge funds,** and **private equity funds.**
- **Spot markets** and **futures markets** are terms that refer to whether the assets are bought or sold for "on-the-spot" delivery or for delivery at some future date.
- **Money markets** are the markets for debt securities with maturities of less than a year. **Capital markets** are the markets for long-term debt and corporate stocks.
- **Primary markets** are the markets in which corporations raise new capital. **Secondary markets** are markets in which existing, already outstanding securities are traded among investors.
- Orders from buyers and sellers can be matched in one of three ways: (1) in an open outcry **auction,** (2) through **dealers,** and (3) automatically through an **electronic communications network (ECN).**
- There are two basic types of markets—the physical location exchanges (such as the NYSE) and computer/telephone networks (such as NASDAQ).
- ***Web Extension 1A*** discusses derivatives, and ***Web Extension 1B*** provides additional coverage of stock markets.

QUESTIONS

(1-1) Define each of the following terms:

a. Proprietorship; partnership; corporation
b. Limited partnership; limited liability partnership; professional corporation
c. Stockholder wealth maximization
d. Money market; capital market; primary market; secondary market
e. Private markets; public markets; derivatives
f. Investment banker; financial services corporation; financial intermediary

g. Mutual fund; money market fund
h. Physical location exchanges; computer/telephone networks
i. Open outcry auction; dealer market; electronic communications network (ECN)
j. Production opportunities; time preferences for consumption
k. Foreign trade deficit

(1-2) What are the three principal forms of business organization? What are the advantages and disadvantages of each?

(1-3) What is a firm's fundamental, or intrinsic, value? What might cause a firm's intrinsic value to be different from its actual market value?

(1-4) Edmund Enterprises recently made a large investment to upgrade its technology. Although these improvements won't have much of an impact on performance in the short run, they are expected to reduce future costs significantly. What impact will this investment have on Edmund Enterprises's earnings per share this year? What impact might this investment have on the company's intrinsic value and stock price?

(1-5) Describe the ways in which capital can be transferred from suppliers of capital to those who are demanding capital.

(1-6) What are financial intermediaries, and what economic functions do they perform?

(1-7) Is an initial public offering an example of a primary or a secondary market transaction?

(1-8) Differentiate between dealer markets and stock markets that have a physical location.

(1-9) Identify and briefly compare the two leading stock exchanges in the United States today.

MINI CASE

Assume that you recently graduated and have just reported to work as an investment advisor at the brokerage firm of Balik and Kiefer Inc. One of the firm's clients is Michelle DellaTorre, a professional tennis player who has just come to the United States from Chile. DellaTorre is a highly ranked tennis player who would like to start a company to produce and market apparel she designs. She also expects to invest substantial amounts of money through Balik and Kiefer. DellaTorre is very bright, and she would like to understand in general terms what will happen to her money. Your boss has developed the following set of questions you must answer to explain the U.S. financial system to DellaTorre.

a. Why is corporate finance important to all managers?
b. Describe the organizational forms a company might have as it evolves from a start-up to a major corporation. List the advantages and disadvantages of each form.
c. How do corporations go public and continue to grow? What are agency problems? What is corporate governance?
d. What should be the primary objective of managers?
   (1) Do firms have any responsibilities to society at large?
   (2) Is stock price maximization good or bad for society?
   (3) Should firms behave ethically?
e. What three aspects of cash flows affect the value of any investment?
f. What are free cash flows?
g. What is the weighted average cost of capital?
h. How do free cash flows and the weighted average cost of capital interact to determine a firm's value?

i. Who are the providers (savers) and users (borrowers) of capital? How is capital transferred between savers and borrowers?
j. What do we call the price that a borrower must pay for debt capital? What is the price of equity capital? What are the four most fundamental factors that affect the cost of money, or the general level of interest rates, in the economy?
k. What are some economic conditions (including international aspects) that affect the cost of money?
l. What are financial securities? Describe some financial instruments.
m. List some financial institutions.
n. What are some different types of markets?
o. How are secondary markets organized?
   (1) List some physical location markets and some computer/telephone networks.
   (2) Explain the differences between open outcry auctions, dealer markets, and electronic communications networks (ECNs).
p. Briefly explain mortgage securitization and how it contributed to the global economic crisis.

© Adalberto Rios Szalay/Sexto Sol/Getty Images

CHAPTER 2

Financial Statements, Cash Flow, and Taxes

Even in today's era of financial crises, $12.6 billion is a lot of money. This is the amount of cash flow that Hewlett-Packard (HP) generated in 2011. The ability to generate cash flow is the lifeblood of a company and the basis for its fundamental value. How did HP use this cash flow? HP invested for the future by making over $10 billion in acquisitions.

Other companies also generated large cash flows from operations in 2011, but they used the money differently. For example, Walgreens generated over $3.6 billion from its operations and used over $1.2 billion for capital expenditures, much of it on new stores and the purchase of worksite health centers.

Procter & Gamble generated $13.2 billion. The company made relatively small capital expenditures and returned the lion's share (almost $13 billion) to shareholders as dividends or through stock repurchases.

Apple generated over $37 billion but made relatively small capital expenditures, acquisitions, or distributions to shareholders. Instead, it put about $32 billion into short-term financial securities like T-bills.

These four well-managed companies used their operating cash flows in four different ways: HP made acquisitions, Walgreens spent on a mix of internal and external growth, P&G returned cash to shareholders, and Apple saved for a rainy day. Which company made the right choice? Only time will tell, but keep these companies and their different cash flow strategies in mind as you read this chapter.

Intrinsic Value, Free Cash Flow, and Financial Statements

© Rob Webb/Getty Images

In Chapter 1, we told you that managers should strive to make their firms more valuable and that a firm's intrinsic value is determined by the present value of its free cash flows (FCF) discounted at the weighted average cost of capital (WACC). This chapter focuses on FCF, including its calculation from financial statements and its interpretation when evaluating a company and manager.

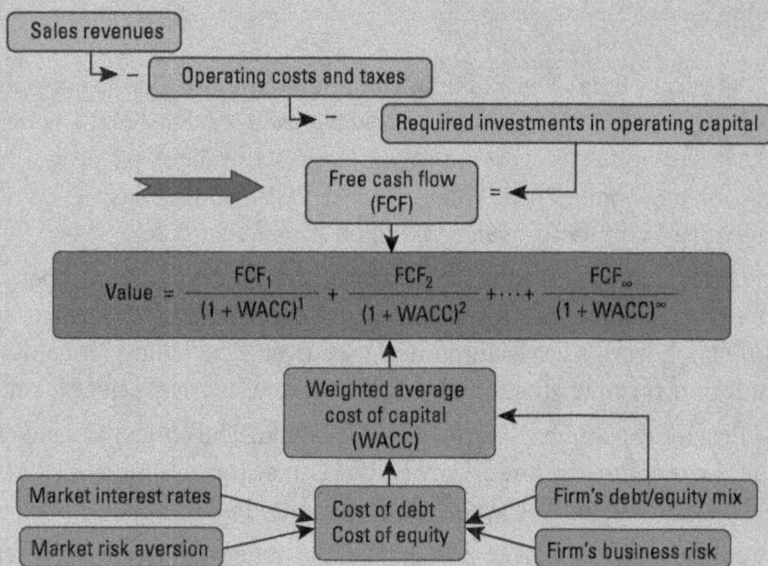

© Cengage Learning 2014

resource

The textbook's Web site contains an Excel file that will guide you through the chapter's calculations. The file for this chapter is ***Ch02 Tool Kit.xls,*** *and we encourage you to open the file and follow along as you read the chapter.*

The stream of cash flows a firm is expected to generate in the future determines its fundamental value (also called intrinsic value). But how does an investor go about estimating future cash flows, and how does a manager decide which actions are most likely to increase cash flows? The first step is to understand the financial statements that publicly traded firms must provide to the public. Thus, we begin with a discussion of financial statements, including how to interpret them and how to use them. Value depends on after-tax cash flows, so we provide an overview of the federal income tax system and highlight differences between accounting income and cash flow.

2-1 Financial Statements and Reports

A company's **annual report** usually begins with the chairperson's description of the firm's operating results during the past year and a discussion of new developments that will affect future operations. The annual report also presents four basic financial statements—the *balance sheet,* the *income statement,* the *statement of stockholders' equity,* and the *statement of cash flows.*

WWW

*See the Securities and Exchange Commission's (SEC) Web site for quarterly reports and more detailed annual reports that provide breakdowns for each major division or subsidiary. These reports, called 10-Q and 10-K reports, are available on the SEC's Web site at **www.sec.gov** under the heading "EDGAR."*

The quantitative and written materials are equally important. The financial statements report *what has actually happened* to assets, earnings, dividends, and cash flows during the past few years, whereas the written materials attempt to explain why things turned out the way they did.

SELF-TEST

What is the annual report, and what two types of information does it present?

What four types of financial statements does the annual report typically include?

2-2 The Balance Sheet

resource

*See **Ch02 Tool Kit.xls** for details.*

For illustrative purposes, we use a hypothetical company, MicroDrive Inc., which produces memory components for computers and smartphones. Figure 2-1 shows MicroDrive's most recent **balance sheets**, which represent "snapshots" of its financial position on the last day of each year. Although most companies report their balance sheets only on the last day of a given period, the "snapshot" actually changes daily as inventories are bought and sold, as fixed assets are added or retired, or as loan balances are increased or paid down. Moreover, a retailer will have larger inventories before Christmas than later in the spring, so balance sheets for the same company can look quite different at different times during the year.

FIGURE 2-1

MicroDrive Inc.: December 31 Balance Sheets (Millions of Dollars)

	A	B	C	D	E	F	G
30	*Assets*					2013	2012
31	Cash and equivalents					$ 50	$ 60
32	Short-term investments					-	40
33	Accounts receivable					500	380
34	Inventories					1,000	820
35	Total current assets					$ 1,550	$ 1,300
36	Net plant and equipment					2,000	1,700
37	Total assets					$ 3,550	$ 3,000
38							
39	*Liabilities and Equity*						
40	Accounts payable					$ 200	$ 190
41	Notes payable					280	130
42	Accruals					300	280
43	Total current liabilities					$ 780	$ 600
44	Long-term bonds					1,200	1,000
45	Total liabilities					$ 1,980	$ 1,600
46	Preferred stock (1,000,000 shares)					100	100
47	Common stock (50,000,000 shares)					500	500
48	Retained earnings					970	800
49	Total common equity					$ 1,470	$ 1,300
50	Total liabilities and equity					$ 3,550	$ 3,000

The balance sheet begins with assets, which are the "things" the company owns. Assets are listed in order of "liquidity," or length of time it typically takes to convert them to cash at fair market values. The balance sheet also lists the claims that various groups have against the company's value; these are listed in the order in which they must be paid. For example, suppliers may have claims called "accounts payable" that are due within 30 days, banks may have claims called "notes payable" that are due within 90 days, and bondholders may have claims that are not due for 20 years or more.

Stockholders' claims represent ownership (or equity) and need never be "paid off." These are residual claims in the sense that stockholders may receive payments only if there is value remaining after other claimants have been paid. The nonstockholder claims are liabilities from the stockholders' perspective. The amounts shown on the balance sheets are called **book values** because they are based on the amounts recorded by bookkeepers when assets are purchased or liabilities are issued. As you will see throughout this textbook, book values may be very different from **market values**, which are the current values as determined in the marketplace.

The following sections provide more information about specific asset, liability, and equity accounts.

2-2a Assets

Cash, short-term investments, accounts receivable, and inventories are listed as current assets because MicroDrive is expected to convert them into cash within a year. All assets are stated in dollars, but only cash represents actual money that can be spent. Some marketable securities mature very soon, and these can be converted quickly into cash at prices close to their book values. Such securities are called "cash equivalents" and are included with cash. Therefore, MicroDrive could write checks for a total of $50 million. Other types of marketable securities have a longer time until maturity, and their market values are less predictable. These securities are classified as "short-term investments."

When MicroDrive sells its products to a customer but doesn't demand immediate payment, the customer then has an obligation called an "account receivable." The $500 million shown in accounts receivable is the amount of sales for which MicroDrive has not yet been paid.

Inventories show the dollars MicroDrive has invested in raw materials, work-in-process, and finished goods available for sale. MicroDrive uses the **FIFO (first-in, first-out)** method to determine the inventory value shown on its balance sheet ($1 billion). It could have used the **LIFO (last-in, first-out)** method. During a period of rising prices, by taking out old, low-cost inventory and leaving in new, high-cost items, FIFO will produce a higher balance sheet inventory value but a lower cost of goods sold on the income statement. (FIFO is used strictly for accounting purposes; companies actually use older items first.) Because MicroDrive uses FIFO and because inflation has been occurring: (1) its balance sheet inventories are higher than they would have been had it used LIFO, (2) its cost of goods sold is lower than it would have been under LIFO, and (3) its reported profits are therefore higher. In MicroDrive's case, if the company had elected to switch to LIFO, then its balance sheet would have had inventories of $850 million rather than $1 billion, and its pre-tax earnings (discussed in the next section) would have been reduced by $50 million. Thus, the inventory valuation method can have a significant effect on financial statements, which is important to know when comparing companies.

Rather than treat the entire purchase price of a long-term asset (such as a factory, plant, or equipment) as an expense in the purchase year, accountants "spread" the purchase cost over the asset's useful life.[1] The amount they charge each year is called the **depreciation** expense. Some companies report an amount called "gross plant and equipment," which is the total cost of the long-term assets they have in place, and another amount called "accumulated depreciation," which is the total amount of depreciation that has been charged on those assets. Some companies, such as MicroDrive, report only net plant and equipment, which is gross plant and equipment less accumulated depreciation. Chapter 11 provides a more detailed explanation of depreciation methods.

2-2b Liabilities and Equity

Accounts payable, notes payable, and accruals are listed as current liabilities because MicroDrive is expected to pay them within a year. When MicroDrive purchases supplies but doesn't immediately pay for them, it takes on an obligation called an account payable. Similarly, when MicroDrive takes out a loan that must be repaid within a year, it signs an IOU called a note payable. MicroDrive doesn't pay its taxes or its employees' wages daily, and the amount it owes on these items at any point in time is called an "accrual" or an "accrued expense." Long-term bonds are also liabilities because they, too, reflect a claim held by someone other than a stockholder.

Preferred stock is a hybrid, or a cross between common stock and debt. In the event of bankruptcy, preferred stock ranks below debt but above common stock. Also, the preferred dividend is fixed, so preferred stockholders do not benefit if the company's earnings grow. Most firms do not use much, if any, preferred stock, so "equity" usually means "common equity" unless the words "total" or "preferred" are included.

When a company sells shares of stock, it records the proceeds in the common stock account.[2] Retained earnings are the cumulative amount of earnings that have not been paid out as dividends. The sum of common stock and retained earnings is called "common equity," or just "equity." If a company could actually sell its assets at their book value, and if the liabilities and preferred stock were actually worth their book values, then a company could sell its assets, pay off its liabilities and preferred stock, and the remaining cash would belong to common stockholders. Therefore, common equity is sometimes called **net worth**—it's the assets minus (or "net of") the liabilities.

SELF-TEST

What is the balance sheet, and what information does it provide?

What determines the order of the information shown on the balance sheet?

Why might a company's December 31 balance sheet differ from its June 30 balance sheet?

A firm has $8 million in total assets. It has $3 million in current liabilities, $2 million in long-term debt, and $1 million in preferred stock. What is the total value of common equity? **($2 million)**

---

[1] This is called *accrual accounting,* which attempts to match revenues to the periods in which they are earned and expenses to the periods in which the effort to generate income occurred.

[2] Companies sometimes break the total proceeds into two parts, one called "par" and the other called "paid-in capital" or "capital surplus." For example, if a company sells shares of stock for $10, it might record $1 of par and $9 of paid-in capital. For most purposes, the distinction between par and paid-in capital is not important, and most companies use no-par stock.

GLOBAL ECONOMIC CRISIS

© uniquely india/Getty Images

The Global Economic Crisis

Let's Play Hide-and-Seek!

In a shameful lapse of regulatory accountability, banks and other financial institutions were allowed to use "structured investment vehicles" (SIVs) to hide assets and liabilities and simply not report them on their balance sheets. Here's how SIVs worked and why they subsequently failed. The SIV was set up as a separate legal entity that the bank owned and managed. The SIV would borrow money in the short-term market (backed by the credit of the bank) and then invest in long-term securities. As you might guess, many SIVs invested in mortgage-backed securities. When the SIV paid only 3% on its borrowings but earned 10% on its investments, the managing bank was able to report fabulous earnings, especially if it also earned fees for creating the mortgage securities that went into the SIV.

But this game of hide-and-seek didn't have a happy ending. Mortgage-backed securities began defaulting in 2007 and 2008, causing the SIVs to pass losses through to the banks. SunTrust, Citigroup, Bank of America, and Northern Rock are just a few of the many banks that reported enormous losses in the SIV game. Investors, depositors, and the government eventually found the hidden assets and liabilities, but by then the assets were worth a lot less than the liabilities.

In a case of too little and too late, regulators are closing these loopholes, and it doesn't look like there will be any more hidden SIVs in the near future. But the damage has been done, and the entire financial system was put at risk in large part because of this high-stakes game of hide-and-seek.

2-3 The Income Statement

Figure 2-2 shows the **income statements** and selected additional information for MicroDrive. Income statements can cover any period of time, but they are usually prepared monthly, quarterly, and annually. Unlike the balance sheet, which is a snapshot of a firm at a point in time, the income statement reflects performance during the period.

resource

*See **Ch02 Tool Kit.xls** for details.*

Net sales are the revenues less any discounts or returns. Depreciation and amortization reflect the estimated costs of the assets that wear out in producing goods and services. To illustrate depreciation, suppose that in 2010 MicroDrive purchased a \$100,000 machine with a life of 5 years and zero expected salvage value. This \$100,000 cost is not expensed in the purchase year but is instead spread out over the machine's 5-year depreciable life. In straight-line depreciation, which we explain in Chapter 11, the depreciation charge for a full year would be \$100,000/5 = \$20,000. The reported depreciation expense on the income statement is the sum of all the assets' annual depreciation charges. Depreciation applies to tangible assets, such as plant and equipment, whereas amortization applies to intangible assets such as patents, copyrights, trademarks, and goodwill.[3]

[3]The accounting treatment of goodwill resulting from mergers has changed in recent years. Rather than an annual charge, companies are required to periodically evaluate the value of goodwill and reduce net income only if the goodwill's value has decreased materially ("become impaired," in the language of accountants). For example, in 2002 AOL Time Warner wrote off almost \$100 billion associated with the AOL merger. It doesn't take too many \$100 billion expenses to really hurt net income!

FIGURE 2-2

MicroDrive Inc.: Income Statements for Years Ending December 31 (Millions of Dollars, Except for Per Share Data)

	A B C D E	F	G
59		**2013**	**2012**
60	**Net sales**	$ 5,000	$ 4,760
61	**Costs of goods sold except depreciation**	3,800	3,560
62	**Depreciation and amortization**	200	170
63	**Other operating expenses**	500	480
64	**Earnings before interest and taxes (EBIT)**	$ 500	$ 550
65	**Less interest**	120	100
66	**Pre-tax earnings**	$ 380	$ 450
67	**Taxes**	152	180
68	**Net Income before preferred dividends**	$ 228	$ 270
69	**Preferred dividends**	8	8
70	**Net Income available to common stockholders**	$ 220	$ 262
71			
72	***Additional Information***		
73	**Common dividends**	$ 50	$ 48
74	**Addition to retained earnings**	$ 170	$ 214
75	**Number of common shares**	50.00	50.00
76	**Stock price per share**	$27.00	$40.00
77			
78	***Per Share Data***		
79	**Earnings per share, EPS**[b]	**$4.40**	**$5.24**
80	**Dividends per share, DPS**[c]	**$1.00**	**$0.96**
81	**Book value per share, BVPS**[d]	**$29.40**	**$26.00**

Notes:

[a]MicroDrive has no amortization charges.

[b] $$\text{EPS} = \frac{\text{Net income available to common stockholders}}{\text{Common shares outstanding}}$$

[c] $$\text{DPS} = \frac{\text{Dividends to common stockholders}}{\text{Common shares outstanding}}$$

[d] $$\text{BVPS} = \frac{\text{Total common equity}}{\text{Common shares outstanding}}$$

The cost of goods sold (COGS) includes labor, raw materials, and other expenses directly related to the production or purchase of the items or services sold in that period. The COGS includes depreciation, but we report depreciation separately so that analysis later in the chapter will be more transparent. Subtracting COGS (including depreciation) and other operating expenses results in earnings before interest and taxes (EBIT).

Many analysts add back depreciation to EBIT to calculate **EBITDA**, which stands for earnings before interest, taxes, depreciation, and amortization. Because neither depreciation nor amortization is paid in cash, some analysts claim that EBITDA is a better measure of financial strength than is net income. MicroDrive's EBITDA is

$$\text{EBITDA} = \text{EBIT} + \text{Depreciation}$$
$$= \$500 + \$200 = \$700 \text{ million}$$

Alternatively, EBITDA's calculation can begin with sales:

$$\text{EBITDA} = \text{Sales} - \text{COGS excluding depreciation} - \text{Other expenses}$$
$$= \$5{,}000 - \$3{,}800 - \$500 = \$700$$

However, as we show later in the chapter, EBITDA is not as useful to managers and analysts as free cash flow, so we usually focus on free cash flow instead of EBITDA.

The net income available to common shareholders, which equals revenues less expenses, taxes, and preferred dividends (but before paying common dividends), is generally referred to as **net income.** Net income is also called **accounting profit, profit,** or **earnings,** particularly in financial news reports. Dividing net income by the number of shares outstanding gives earnings per share (EPS), often called "the bottom line." Throughout this book, unless otherwise indicated, net income means net income available to common stockholders.[4]

SELF-TEST

What is an income statement, and what information does it provide?

What is often called "the bottom line?"

What is EBITDA?

How does the income statement differ from the balance sheet with regard to the time period reported?

A firm has $2 million in earnings before taxes. The firm has an interest expense of $300,000 and depreciation of $200,000; it has no amortization. What is its EBITDA? **($2.5 million)**

2-4 Statement of Stockholders' Equity

resource
See **Ch02 Tool Kit.xls** for details.

Changes in stockholders' equity during the accounting period are reported in the **statement of stockholders' equity.** Figure 2-3 shows that MicroDrive earned $220 million during 2013, paid out $50 million in common dividends, and plowed $150 million back into the business. Thus, the balance sheet item "Retained earnings" increased from $800 million at year-end 2012 to $970 million at year-end 2013.[5] The last column shows the beginning stockholders' equity, any changes, and the end-of-year stockholders' equity.

Note that "retained earnings" does not represent assets but is instead a *claim against assets.* In 2013, MicroDrive's stockholders allowed it to reinvest $170 million instead of distributing the money as dividends, and management spent this money on new assets.

[4]Companies also report "comprehensive income," which is the sum of net income and any "comprehensive" income item, such as the change in market value of a financial asset. For example, a decline in a financial asset's value would be recorded as a loss even though the asset has not been sold. We assume that there are no comprehensive income items in our examples.

Some companies also choose to report "pro forma income." For example, if a company incurs an expense that it doesn't expect to recur, such as the closing of a plant, it might calculate pro forma income as though it had not incurred the one-time expense. There are no hard-and-fast rules for calculating pro forma income, so many companies find ingenious ways to make pro forma income higher than traditional income. The SEC and the Public Company Accounting Oversight Board (PCAOB) are taking steps to reduce deceptive uses of pro forma reporting.

[5]If they had been applicable, then columns would have been used to show "Additional Paid-in Capital" and "Treasury Stock." Also, additional rows would have contained information on such things as new issues of stock, treasury stock acquired or reissued, stock options exercised, and unrealized foreign exchange gains or losses.

FIGURE 2-3

MicroDrive Inc.: Statement of Stockholders' Equity, December 31, 2012

	A B C	D	E	F	G	H
103		Preferred Stock	Common Shares	Common Stock	Retained Earnings	Total Equity
104	Balances, Dec. 31, 2012	$100	50	$500	$800	$1,400
105	Changes during year:					
106	Net income				$220	$220
107	Cash dividends				(50)	(50)
108	Issuance/repurchase of stock	0	0	0		
109	Balances, Dec. 31, 2013	$100	50	$500	$970	$1,570
110						
111	*Note:* In financial statements, parentheses denote a negative number.					

Thus, retained earnings, as reported on the balance sheet, does not represent cash and is not "available" for the payment of dividends or anything else.[6]

SELF-TEST

What is the statement of stockholders' equity, and what information does it provide?

Why do changes in retained earnings occur?

Explain why the following statement is true: "The retained earnings reported on the balance sheet does not represent cash and is not available for the payment of dividends or anything else."

A firm had a retained earnings balance of $3 million in the previous year. In the current year, its net income is $2.5 million. If it pays $1 million in common dividends in the current year, what is its resulting retained earnings balance? **($4.5 million)**

2-5 Statement of Cash Flows

Even if a company reports a large net income during a year, the *amount of cash* reported on its year-end balance sheet may be the same or even lower than its beginning cash. The reason is that the company can use its net income in a variety of ways, not just keep it as cash in the bank. For example, the firm may use its net income to pay dividends, to increase inventories, to finance accounts receivable, to invest in fixed assets, to reduce debt, or to buy back common stock. Indeed, many factors affect a company's *cash position* as reported on its balance sheet. The **statement of cash flows** separates a company's activities into three categories—operating, investing, and financing— and summarizes the resulting cash balance.

[6]The amount reported in the retained earnings account is *not* an indication of the amount of cash the firm has. Cash (as of the balance sheet date) is found in the cash account, an asset account. A positive number in the retained earnings account indicates only that the firm earned some income in the past, but its dividends paid were less than its earnings. Even if a company reports record earnings and shows an increase in its retained earnings account, it still may be short of cash.

The same situation holds for individuals. You might own a new BMW (no loan), lots of clothes, and an expensive stereo and hence have a high net worth. But if you have only 23 cents in your pocket plus $5 in your checking account, you will still be short of cash.

Financial Analysis on the Web

© Rob Webb/Getty Images

A wide range of valuable financial information is available on the Web. With just a couple of clicks, an investor can easily find the key financial statements for most publicly traded companies. Here's a partial (by no means a complete) list of places you can go to get started.

- One of the very best sources of financial information is Thomson Financial. Go to the textbook's Web site and follow the directions to access Thomson ONE—Business School Edition. An especially useful feature is the ability to download up to 10 years of financial statements in spreadsheet form. First, enter the ticker for a company and click Go. From the menu at left (in dark blue), select Financials. A new menu (in light blue) will expand, and selecting Thomson Financials under the Financial Statements heading will reveal Balance Sheets, Income Statements, and Cash Flow Statements items. Select any of these, and a menu item for 5YR and 10YR statements will pop up. Select the 10YR item, and 10 years of the selected financial statements will be displayed. To download the financial statements into a spreadsheet, click on the *Excel* icon toward the right of the light blue row at the top of the Thomson ONE panel. This will bring up a dialog box that lets you download the *Excel* file to your computer.
- Try Yahoo! Finance's Web site, **finance.yahoo.com**. Here you will find updated market information along with links to a variety of interesting research sites. Enter a stock's ticker symbol, click Get Quotes, and you will see the stock's current price along with recent news about the company. The panel on the left has links to key statistics and to the company's income statement, balance sheet, statement of cash flows, and more. The Web site also has a list of insider transactions, so you can tell if a company's CEO and other key insiders are buying or selling their company's stock. In addition, there is a message board where investors share opinions about the company, and there is a link to the company's filings with the SEC. Note that, in most cases, a more complete list of the SEC filings can be found at **www.sec.gov**.
- Other sources for up-to-date market information are **money.cnn.com** and **www.zacks.com**. These sites also provide financial statements in standardized formats.
- Both **www.bloomberg.com** and **www.marketwatch.com** have areas where you can obtain stock quotes along with company financials, links to Wall Street research, and links to SEC filings.
- If you are looking for charts of key accounting variables (for example, sales, inventory, depreciation and amortization, and reported earnings), as well as financial statements, take a look at **www.smartmoney.com**.
- Another good place to look is **www.reuters.com**. Here you can find links to analysts' research reports along with the key financial statements.

In addition to this information, you may be looking for sites that provide opinions regarding the direction of the overall market and views regarding individual stocks. Two popular sites in this category are The Motley Fool's Web site, **www.fool.com**, and the Web site for The Street.com, **www.thestreet.com**.

2-5a Operating Activities

As the name implies, the section for operating activities focuses on the amount of cash generated (or lost) by the firm's operating activities. The section begins with the reported net income before paying preferred dividends and makes several adjustments, beginning with noncash activities.

Noncash Adjustments

Some revenues and expenses reported on the income statement are not received or paid in cash during the year. For example, depreciation and amortization reduce reported net income but are not cash payments.

Reported taxes often differ from the taxes that are paid, resulting in an account called deferred taxes, which is the cumulative difference between the taxes that are reported and those that are paid. Deferred taxes can occur in many ways, including the use of accelerated depreciation for tax purposes but straight-line depreciation for financial reporting. This increases reported taxes relative to actual tax payments in the early years of an asset's life, causing the resulting net income to be lower than the true cash flow. Therefore, increases in deferred taxes are added to net income when calculating cash flow, and decreases are subtracted from net income.

Another example of noncash reporting occurs if a customer purchases services or products that extend beyond the reporting date, such as a 3-year extended warranty for a computer. Even if the company collects the cash at the time of the purchase, it will spread the reported revenues over the life of the purchase. This causes income to be lower than cash flow in the first year and higher in subsequent years, so adjustments must be made when calculating cash flow.

Changes in Working Capital

Increases in current assets other than cash (such as inventories and accounts receivable) decrease cash, whereas decreases in these accounts increase cash. For example, if inventories are to increase, then the firm must use cash to acquire the additional inventory. Conversely, if inventories decrease, this generally means the firm is selling inventories and not replacing all of them, hence generating cash. Here's how we keep track of whether a change in assets increases or decreases cash flow: If the amount we own goes up (like getting a new laptop computer), it means we have spent money and our cash goes down. On the other hand, if something we own goes down (like selling a car), our cash goes up.

Now consider a current liability, such as accounts payable. If accounts payable increase then the firm has received additional credit from its suppliers, which saves cash; but if payables decrease, this means it has used cash to pay off its suppliers. Therefore, increases in current liabilities such as accounts payable increase cash, whereas decreases in current liabilities decrease cash. To keep track of the cash flow's direction, think about the impact of getting a student loan. The amount you owe goes up and your cash goes up. Now think about paying off the loan: The amount you owe goes down, but so does your cash.

2-5b Investing Activities

Investing activities include transactions involving fixed assets or short-term financial investments. For example, if a company buys new IT infrastructure, its cash goes down at the time of the purchase. On the other hand, if it sells a building or T-bill, its cash goes up.

2-5c Financing Activities

Financing activities include raising cash by issuing short-term debt, long-term debt, or stock. Because dividend payments, stock repurchases, and principal payments on debt reduce a company's cash, such transactions are included here.

2-5d Putting the Pieces Together

The statement of cash flows is used to help answer questions such as these: Is the firm generating enough cash to purchase the additional assets required for growth? Is the firm generating any extra cash it can use to repay debt or to invest in new products? Such

resource

See Ch02 Tool Kit.xls for details.

information is useful both for managers and investors, so the statement of cash flows is an important part of the annual report.

Figure 2-4 shows MicroDrive's statement of cash flows as it would appear in the company's annual report. The top section shows cash generated by and used in operations—for MicroDrive, operations provided net cash flows of $158 million. This subtotal is in many respects the most important figure in any of the financial statements. Profits as reported on the income statement can be "doctored" by such tactics as depreciating assets too slowly, not recognizing bad debts promptly, and the like. However, it is far more difficult to simultaneously doctor profits and the working capital accounts. Therefore, it is not

FIGURE 2-4

MicroDrive Inc.: Statement of Cash Flows for 2013 (Millions of Dollars)

	A	B	C	D	E	F
123	*Operating Activities*					2013
124	Net Income before preferred dividends					$ 228
125	*Noncash adjustments*					
126	Depreciation[a]					200
127	*Working capital adjustments*					
128	Increase in accounts receivable[b]					(120)
129	Increase in inventories					(180)
130	Increase in accounts payable					10
131	Increase in accruals					20
132	Net cash provided (used) by operating activities					$ 158
133						
134	*Investing Activities*					
135	Cash used to acquire fixed assets[c]					$ (500)
136	Sale of short-term investments					40
137	Net cash provided (used) by investing activities					$ (460)
138						
139	*Financing Activities*					
140	Increase in notes payable					$ 150
141	Increase in bonds					200
142	Payment of common and preferred dividends					(58)
143	Net cash provided (used) by financing activities					$ 292
144						
145	*Summary*					
146	Net change in cash and equivalents					$ (10)
147	Cash and securities at beginning of the year					60
148	Cash and securities at end of the year					$ 50

Notes:

[a]Depreciation is a noncash expense that was deducted when calculating net income. It must be added back to show the correct cash flow from operations.

[b]An increase in a current asset decreases cash. An increase in a current liability increases cash. For example, inventories increased by $180 million and therefore reduced cash by the same amount.

[c]The net increase in fixed assets is $300 million; however, this net amount is after a deduction for the year's depreciation expense. Depreciation expense must be added back to find the increase in gross fixed assets. From the company's income statement, we see that the year's depreciation expense is $200 million; thus, expenditures on fixed assets were actually $500 million.

Filling in the GAAP

© Rob Webb/Getty Images

While U.S. companies adhere to "generally accepted accounting principles," or GAAP, when preparing financial statements, most other developed countries use "International Financial Reporting Standards," or IFRS. The U.S. GAAP system is rules-based, with thousands of instructions, or "guidances," for how individual transactions should be reported in financial statements. IFRS, on the other hand, is a principles-based system in which detailed instructions are replaced by overall guiding principles.

For example, whereas GAAP provides extensive and detailed rules about when to recognize revenue from any conceivable activity, IFRS provides just four categories of revenue and two overall principles for timing recognition. This means that even the most basic accounting measure, revenue, is different under the two standards—Total Revenue, or Sales, under GAAP won't typically equal Total Revenue under IFRS. Thus, financial statements prepared under GAAP cannot be compared directly to IFRS financial statements, making comparative financial analysis of U.S. and international companies difficult. Perhaps more problematic is that the IFRS principles allow for more company discretion in recording transactions. This means that two different companies may treat an identical transaction differently when using IFRS, which makes company-to-company comparisons more difficult.

The U.S. Financial Accounting Standards Board (FASB) and the International Accounting Standards Board (IASB) have been working to merge the two sets of standards since 2002. If the current timetable holds, the joint standards will be completed by the end of 2013, with adoption by U.S. firms possibly by 2015.

What does this mean for you? There will still be an income statement, a balance sheet, and an equivalent to the statement of cash flows. Line item summary measures may change a bit, and the technical details about how to record individual transactions will certainly change. Accounting systems will be reprogrammed, accounting texts will be rewritten, and CPAs will have to retrain. The end result, though, will be a better ability to compare U.S. and international companies' financial statements.

To keep abreast of developments in IFRS/GAAP convergence, visit the IASB Web site at **www.iasb.org** and the FASB Web site at **www.fasb.org**.

uncommon for a company to report positive net income right up to the day it declares bankruptcy. In such cases, however, the net cash flow from operations almost always began to deteriorate much earlier, and analysts who kept an eye on cash flow could have predicted trouble. Therefore, if you are ever analyzing a company and are pressed for time, look first at the trend in net cash flow provided by operating activities, because it will tell you more than any other single number.

The second section shows investing activities. MicroDrive purchased fixed assets totaling $500 million and sold $40 million of short-term investments, for a net cash flow from investing activities of *minus* $460 million.

The third section, financing activities, includes borrowing from banks (notes payable), selling new bonds, and paying dividends on common and preferred stock. MicroDrive raised $350 million by borrowing, but it paid $58 million in preferred and common dividends. Therefore, its net inflow of funds from financing activities was $292 million.

In the summary, when all of these sources and uses of cash are totaled, we see that MicroDrive's cash outflows exceeded its cash inflows by $10 million during 2013; that is, its net change in cash was a *negative* $10 million.

MicroDrive's statement of cash flows should be worrisome to its managers and to outside analysts. The company had $5 billion in sales but generated only $158 million from operations, not nearly enough to cover the $500 million it spent on fixed assets and the $58 million it paid in dividends. It covered these cash outlays by borrowing heavily and by liquidating short-term investments. Obviously, this situation cannot continue year after year, so MicroDrive managers will have to make changes. We will return to MicroDrive throughout the textbook to see what actions its managers are planning.

SELF-TEST

What types of questions does the statement of cash flows answer?

Identify and briefly explain the three categories of activities in the statement of cash flows.

A firm has inventories of $2 million for the previous year and $1.5 million for the current year. What impact does this have on net cash provided by operations? ***(Increase of $500,000)***

2-6 Net Cash Flow

In addition to the cash flow from operations as defined in the statement of cash flows, many analysts use also calculate **net cash flow**, which is defined as:

$$\text{Net cash flow} = \text{Net income} - \text{Noncash revenues} + \text{Noncash expenses} \quad (2\text{-}1)$$

where net income is the net income available for distribution to common shareholders. Depreciation and amortization usually are the largest noncash items, and in many cases the other noncash items roughly net out to zero. For this reason, many analysts assume that net cash flow equals net income plus depreciation and amortization:

$$\text{Net cash flow} = \text{Net income} + \text{Depreciation and amortization} \quad (2\text{-}2)$$

We will generally assume that Equation 2-2 holds. However, you should remember that Equation 2-2 will not accurately reflect net cash flow when there are significant noncash items other than depreciation and amortization.

We can illustrate Equation 2-2 with 2013 data for MicroDrive taken from Figure 2-2:

$$\text{Net cash flow} = \$220 + \$200 = \$420 \text{ million}$$

You can think of net cash flow as the profit a company would have if it did not have to replace fixed assets as they wear out. This is similar to the net cash flow from operating activities shown on the statement of cash flows, except that the net cash flow from operating activities also includes the impact of working capital. Net income, net cash flow, and net cash flow from operating activities each provide insight into a company's financial health, but none is as useful as the measures we discuss in the next section.

SELF-TEST

Differentiate between net cash flow and accounting profit.

A firm has net income of $5 million. Assuming that depreciation of $1 million is its only noncash expense, what is the firm's net cash flow? ***($6 million)***

2-7 Free Cash Flow: The Cash Flow Available for Distribution to Investors

So far in the chapter we have focused on financial statements as presented in the annual report. When you studied income statements in accounting, the emphasis was probably on the firm's net income. However, the intrinsic value of a company's operations is determined by the stream of cash flows that the operations will generate now and in the future. To be more specific, the value of operations depends on all the future expected **free cash flows (FCF)**, defined as after-tax operating profit minus the amount of new investment in working capital and fixed assets necessary to sustain the business. *Therefore, the way for managers to make their companies more valuable is to increase free cash flow now and in the future.*

Notice that FCF is the cash flow *available for distribution to all the company's investors after the company has made all investments necessary to sustain ongoing operations.* How successful were MicroDrive's managers in generating FCF? In this section, we will calculate MicroDrive's FCF and evaluate the performance of MicroDrive's managers.

Figure 2-5 shows the five steps in calculating free cash flow. As we explain each individual step in the following sections, refer back to Figure 2-1 to keep the big picture in mind.

2-7a Net Operating Profit after Taxes (NOPAT)

If two companies have different amounts of debt, thus different amounts of interest charges, they could have identical operating performances but different net incomes—the one with more debt would have a lower net income. Net income is important, but it

FIGURE 2-5
Calculating Free Cash Flow

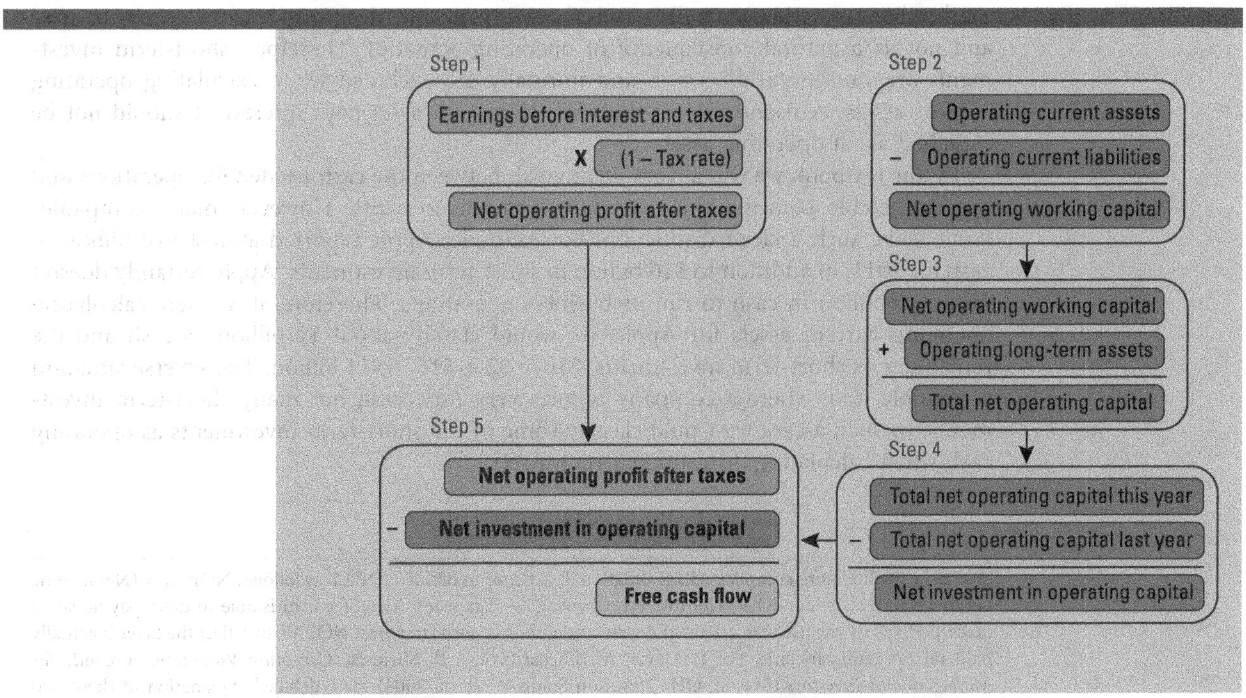

© Cengage Learning 2014

does not always reflect the true performance of a company's operations or the effectiveness of its managers. A better measure for comparing managers' performance is **net operating profit after taxes**, or **NOPAT**, which is the amount of profit a company would generate if it had no debt and held no financial assets. NOPAT is defined as follows:[7]

$$\text{NOPAT} = \text{EBIT}(1 - \text{Tax rate}) \tag{2-3}$$

Using data from the income statements of Figure 2-2, MicroDrive's 2013 NOPAT is

$$\text{NOPAT} = \$500(1 - 0.4) = \$500(0.6) = \$300 \text{ million}$$

This means MicroDrive generated an after-tax operating profit of $300 million, less than its previous NOPAT of $550(0.6) = $330 million.

2-7b Net Operating Working Capital

Most companies need some current assets to support their operating activities. For example, all companies must carry some cash to "grease the wheels" of their operations. Companies continuously receive checks from customers and write checks to suppliers, employees, and so on. Because inflows and outflows do not coincide perfectly, a company must keep some cash in its bank account. In other words, it must have some cash to conduct operations. The same is true for most other current assets, such as inventory and accounts receivable, which are required for normal operations. The short-term assets normally used in a company's operating activities are called **operating current assets.**

Not all current assets are operating current assets. For example, holdings of short-term marketable securities generally result from investment decisions made by the treasurer and not as a natural consequence of operating activities. Therefore, short-term investments are **nonoperating assets** and normally are excluded when calculating operating current assets. A useful rule of thumb is that if an asset pays interest, it should not be classified as an operating asset.

In this textbook we will always distinguish between the cash needed for operations and the marketable securities held as short-term investments. However, many companies don't make such a clean distinction. For example, Apple reported almost $10 billion in cash for 2011, in addition to $16 billion in short-term investments. Apple certainly doesn't need $10 billion in cash to run its business operations. Therefore, if we were calculating operating current assets for Apple, we would classify about $2 billion as cash and the remainder as short-term investments: $10 − $2 + $16 = $24 billion. The reverse situation is possible, too, where a company reports very little cash but many short-term investments. In such a case we would classify some of the short-term investments as operating cash when calculating operating current assets.

[7]For firms with a more complicated tax situation, it is better to define NOPAT as follows: NOPAT = (Net income before preferred dividends) + (Net interest expense)(1 − Tax rate). Also, if a firm is able to defer paying some taxes, perhaps by the use of accelerated depreciation, then it needs to adjust NOPAT to reflect the taxes it actually paid on operating income. See P. Daves, M. Ehrhardt, and R. Shrieves, *Corporate Valuation: A Guide for Managers and Investors* (Mason, OH: Thomson South-Western, 2004) for a detailed explanation of these and other adjustments.

Some current liabilities—especially accounts payable and accruals—arise in the normal course of operations. Such short-term liabilities are called **operating current liabilities.** Not all current liabilities are operating current liabilities. For example, consider the current liability shown as notes payable to banks. The company could have raised an equivalent amount as long-term debt or could have issued stock, so the choice to borrow from the bank was a financing decision and not a consequence of operations. Again, the rule of thumb is that if a liability charges interest, it is not an operating liability.

If you are ever uncertain about whether an item is an operating asset or operating liability, ask yourself whether the item is a natural consequence of operations or if it is a discretionary choice, such as a particular method of financing or an investment in a particular financial asset. If it is discretionary, then the item is not an operating asset or liability.

Notice that each dollar of operating current liabilities is a dollar that the company does not have to raise from investors in order to conduct its short-term operating activities. Therefore, we define **net operating working capital (NOWC)** as operating current assets minus operating current liabilities. In other words, net operating working capital is the working capital acquired with investor-supplied funds. Here is the definition in equation form:

$$\text{Net operating working capital} = \text{Operating current assets} - \text{Operating current liabilities} \tag{2-4}$$

We can apply these definitions to MicroDrive, using the balance sheet data given in Figure 2-1. Here is its net operating working capital at year-end 2013:

$$\begin{aligned} \text{NOWC} &= \text{Operating current assets} - \text{Operating current liabilities} \\ &= (\text{Cash} + \text{Accounts receivable} + \text{Inventories}) \\ &\quad - (\text{Accounts payable} + \text{Accruals}) \\ &= (\$50 + \$500 + \$1,000) - (\$200 + \$300) \\ &= \$1,050 \text{ million} \end{aligned}$$

For the previous year, net operating working capital was

$$\begin{aligned} \text{NOWC} &= (\$60 + \$380 + \$820) - (\$190 + \$280) \\ &= \$790 \text{ million} \end{aligned}$$

2-7c Total Net Operating Capital

In addition to working capital, most companies also use long-term assets to support their operations. These include land, buildings, factories, equipment, and the like. **Total net operating capital** is the sum of NOWC and operating long-term assets:

$$\text{Total net operating capital} = \text{NOWC} + \text{Operating long-term assets} \tag{2-5}$$

Because MicroDrive's operating long-term assets consist only of net plant and equipment, its total net operating capital at year-end 2013 was

$$\begin{aligned} \text{Total net operating capital} &= \$1,050 + \$2,000 \\ &= \$3,050 \text{ million} \end{aligned}$$

For the previous year, its total net operating capital was

$$\text{Total net operating capital} = \$790 + \$1{,}700 = \$2{,}490 \text{ million}$$

Notice that we have defined total net operating capital as the sum of net operating working capital and operating long-term assets. In other words, our definition is in terms of operating assets and liabilities. However, we can also calculate total net operating capital by looking at the sources of funds. **Total investor-supplied capital** is defined as the total of funds provided by investors, such as notes payable, long-term bonds, preferred stock, and common equity. For most companies, total investor-supplied capital is:

$$\text{Total investor-supplied capital} = \text{Notes payable} + \text{Long-term bonds} + \text{Preferred stock} + \text{Common equity} \quad (2\text{-}6)$$

For MicroDrive, the total capital provided by investors at year-end 2012 was \$130 + \$1,000 + \$100 + \$1,300 = \$2,530 million. Of this amount, \$40 million was tied up in short-term investments, which are not directly related to MicroDrive's operations. Therefore, we define **total investor-supplied operating capital** as:

$$\text{Total investor-supplied operating capital} = \text{Total investor-supplied operating capital} - \text{Short-term investments} \quad (2\text{-}7)$$

MicroDrive had \$2,530 − \$40 = \$2,490 million of investor-supplied operating capital. Notice that this is exactly the same value as calculated before. Therefore, we can calculate total net operating capital either from net operating working capital and operating long-term assets or from the investor-supplied funds. We usually base our calculations on operating data because this approach allows us to analyze a division, factory, or work center. In contrast, the approach based on investor-supplied capital is applicable only for the entire company.

The expression "total net operating capital" is a mouthful, so we often call it *operating capital* or even just *capital.* Also, unless we specifically say "investor-supplied capital," we are referring to total net operating capital.

2-7d Net Investment in Operating Capital

As calculated previously, MicroDrive had \$2,490 million of total net operating capital at the end of 2012 and \$3,050 million at the end of 2013. Therefore, during 2013, it made a **net investment in operating capital** of

$$\text{Net investment in operating capital} = \$3{,}050 - \$2{,}490 = \$560 \text{ million}$$

Most of this investment was made in net operating working capital, which rose from \$790 million to \$1,050 million, or by \$260 million. This 33% increase in net operating working capital, in view of a sales increase of only 5% (to \$5 billion from \$4.76 billion), should set off warning bells in your head: Why did MicroDrive tie up so much additional cash in working capital? Is the company gearing up for a big increase in sales, or are inventories not moving and receivables not being collected? We will address these questions in detail in Chapter 3, when we cover ratio analysis.

2-7e Calculating Free Cash Flow

Free cash flow is defined as

$$FCF = NOPAT - \text{Net investment in operating capital} \tag{2-8}$$

MicroDrive's free cash flow in 2013 was

$$\begin{aligned} FCF &= \$300 - (\$3{,}050 - \$2{,}490) \\ &= \$300 - \$560 \\ &= -\$260 \text{ million} \end{aligned}$$

Although we prefer this approach to calculating FCF, sometimes the financial press calculates FCF differently:

$$FCF = \begin{bmatrix} EBIT(1-T) \\ + \text{Depreciation} \end{bmatrix} - \begin{bmatrix} \text{Gross investment} \\ \text{in fixed assets} \end{bmatrix} - \begin{bmatrix} \text{Investment} \\ \text{NOWC} \end{bmatrix} \tag{2-9}$$

For MicroDrive, this calculation is:

$$FCF = (\$300 + \$200) - \$500 - (\$1{,}050 - \$790) = -\$260$$

Notice that the results are the same for either calculation. To see this, substitute NOPAT into the first bracket of Equation 2-9 and substitute the definition for net investment in fixed assets into the second bracket:

$$FCF = \begin{bmatrix} NOPAT \\ + \text{Depreciation} \end{bmatrix} - \begin{bmatrix} \text{Net investment} \\ \text{in fixed assets} \\ + \text{Depreciation} \end{bmatrix} - \begin{bmatrix} \text{Investment} \\ \text{NOWC} \end{bmatrix} \tag{2-9a}$$

Both the first and second brackets have depreciation, so depreciation can be cancelled out, leaving

$$FCF = NOPAT - \begin{bmatrix} \text{Net investment} \\ \text{in fixed assets} \end{bmatrix} - \begin{bmatrix} \text{Investment} \\ \text{NOWC} \end{bmatrix} \tag{2-9b}$$

The last two bracketed terms are equal to the net investment in operating capital, so Equation 2-9b simplifies to Equation 2-8. We usually use Equation 2-8 because it saves us the step of adding depreciation both to NOPAT and to the net investment in fixed assets.

2-7f The Uses of FCF

Recall that free cash flow (FCF) is the amount of cash that is available for distribution to all investors, including shareholders and debtholders. There are five good uses for FCF:

1. Pay interest to debtholders, keeping in mind that the net cost to the company is the after-tax interest expense.
2. Repay debtholders; that is, pay off some of the debt.

Sarbanes-Oxley and Financial Fraud

© Rob Webb/Getty Images

Investors need to be cautious when they review financial statements. Although companies are required to follow generally accepted accounting principles (GAAP), managers still use a lot of discretion in deciding how and when to report certain transactions. Consequently, two firms in the same operating situation may report financial statements that convey different impressions about their financial strength. Some variations may stem from legitimate differences of opinion about the correct way to record transactions. In other cases, managers may choose to report numbers in a way that helps them present either higher earnings or more stable earnings over time. As long as they follow GAAP, such actions are not illegal, but these differences make it harder for investors to compare companies and gauge their true performances.

Unfortunately, there have also been cases in which managers reported fraudulent statements. Indeed, a number of high-profile executives have faced criminal charges because of their misleading accounting practices. For example, in June 2002 it was discovered that WorldCom (now called MCI) had committed the most massive accounting fraud of all time by recording over $7 billion of ordinary operating costs as capital expenditures, thus overstating net income by the same amount.

WorldCom's published financial statements fooled most investors, who bid the stock price up to $64.50; and banks and other lenders provided the company with more than $30 billion of loans. Arthur Andersen, the firm's auditor, was faulted for not detecting the fraud. WorldCom's CFO and CEO were convicted, and Arthur Andersen went bankrupt. But these consequences didn't help the investors who relied on the published financial statements.

In response to these and other abuses, Congress passed the Sarbanes-Oxley Act of 2002. One of its provisions requires both the CEO and the CFO to sign a statement certifying that the "financial statements and disclosures fairly represent, in all material respects, the operations and financial condition" of the company. This will make it easier to haul off in handcuffs a CEO or CFO who has been misleading investors. Whether this will prevent future financial fraud remains to be seen.

3. Pay dividends to shareholders.
4. Repurchase stock from shareholders.
5. Buy short-term investments or other nonoperating assets.

Consider MicroDrive, with its FCF of −$260 million in 2013. How did MicroDrive use the FCF?

MicroDrive's income statement shows an interest expense of $120 million. With a tax rate of 40%, the after-tax interest payment for the year is

$$\text{After-tax interest payment} = \$120(1 - 40\%) = \$72 \text{ million}$$

The net amount of debt that is repaid is equal to the amount at the beginning of the year minus the amount at the end of the year. This includes notes payable and long-term debt. If the amount of ending debt is less than the beginning debt, the company paid down some of its debt. But if the ending debt is greater than the beginning debt, the company actually borrowed additional funds from creditors. In that case, it would be a negative use of FCF. For MicroDrive, the net debt repayment for 2012 is equal to the amount at the beginning of the year minus the amount at the end of the year:

$$\text{Net debt repayment} = (\$130 + \$1{,}000) - (\$280 + \$1{,}200) = -\$350 \text{ million}$$

This is a "negative use" of FCF because it increased the debt balance. This is typical of most companies because growing companies usually add debt each year.

MicroDrive paid \$8 million in preferred dividends and \$50 in common dividends for a total of

$$\text{Dividend payments} = \$8 + \$50 = \$58 \text{ million}$$

The net amount of stock that is repurchased is equal to the amount at the beginning of the year minus the amount at the end of the year. This includes preferred stock and common stock. If the amount of ending stock is less than the beginning stock, then the company made net repurchases. But if the ending stock is greater than the beginning stock, the company actually made net issuances. In that case, it would be a negative use of FCF. Even though MicroDrive neither issued nor repurchased stock during the year, many companies use FCF to repurchase stocks as a replacement for or supplement to dividends, as we discuss in Chapter 14.

The amount of net purchases of short-term investments is equal to the amount at the end of the year minus the amount at the beginning of the year. If the amount of ending investments is greater than the beginning investments, then the company made net purchases. But if the ending investments are less than the beginning investments, the company actually sold investments. In that case, it would be a negative use of FCF. MicroDrive's net purchases of short-term investments in 2013 are:

$$\text{Net purchases of short-term investments} = \$0 - \$40 = -\$40 \text{ million}$$

Notice that this is a "negative use" because MicroDrive sold short-term investments instead of purchasing them.

We combine these individual uses of FCF to find the total uses.

1. After-tax interest:	\$ 72
2. Net debt repayments:	−350
3. Dividends:	58
4. Net stock repurchases:	0
5. Net purchases of ST investments:	−40
Total uses of FCF:	−\$260

As it should be, the −\$260 total for uses of FCF is identical to the value of FCF from operations that we calculated previously.

Observe that a company does not use FCF to acquire operating assets, because the calculation of FCF already takes into account the purchase of operating assets needed to support growth. Unfortunately, there is evidence to suggest that some companies with high FCF tend to make unnecessary investments that don't add value, such as paying too much to acquire another company. Thus, high FCF can cause waste if managers fail to act in the best interests of shareholders. As discussed in Chapter 1, this is called an agency cost, because managers are hired as agents to act on behalf of stockholders. We discuss agency costs and ways to control them in Chapter 13, where we discuss value-based management and corporate governance, and in Chapter 15, where we discuss the choice of capital structure.

2-7g FCF and Corporate Value

Free cash flow is the amount of cash available for distribution to investors; so the fundamental value of a company to its investors depends on the present value of its expected future FCFs, discounted at the company's weighted average cost of capital (WACC). Subsequent chapters will develop the tools needed to forecast FCFs and evaluate their risk. Chapter 12 ties all this together with a model used to calculate the value of a company. Even though you do not yet have all the tools to apply the model, you must understand this basic concept: *FCF is the cash flow available for distribution to investors. Therefore, the fundamental value of a firm depends primarily on its expected future FCF.*

SELF-TEST

What is net operating working capital? Why does it exclude most short-term investments and notes payable?

What is total net operating capital? Why is it important for managers to calculate a company's capital requirements?

Why is NOPAT a better performance measure than net income?

What is free cash flow? Why is it important?

A firm's total net operating capital for the previous year was $2 million. For the current year, its total net operating capital is $2.5 million and its NOPAT is $1.2 million. What is its free cash flow for the current year? **($700,000)**

2-8 Performance Evaluation

Because free cash flow has such a big impact on value, managers and investors can use FCF and its components to measure a company's performance. The following sections explain three performance measures: return on invested capital, market value added, and economic value added.

2-8a The Return on Invested Capital

Even though MicroDrive had a positive NOPAT, its very high investment in operating assets caused a negative FCF. Is a negative free cash flow always bad? The answer is, "Not necessarily; it depends on why the free cash flow is negative." It's a bad sign if FCF is negative because NOPAT is negative, which probably means the company is experiencing operating problems. However, many high-growth companies have positive NOPAT but negative FCF because they are making large investments in operating assets to support growth. For example, Under Armour's sales grew by 38% in 2011 and its NOPAT grew by 42%; however, it made large capital investments to support that growth and ended the year with a FCF of *negative* $148 million.

There is nothing wrong with value-adding growth, even if it causes negative free cash flows, but it is vital to determine whether growth is actually adding value. For this we use the **return on invested capital (ROIC)**, which shows how much NOPAT is generated by each dollar of operating capital:

$$\text{ROIC} = \frac{\text{NOPAT}}{\text{Operating capital}} \quad \text{(2-10)}$$

As shown in Figure 2-6, in 2013 MicroDrive's ROIC is $300/$3,050 = 9.83%. To determine whether this ROIC is high enough to add value, compare it to the weighted average cost of capital (WACC). Chapter 9 explains how to calculate the WACC; for now accept that the WACC considers a company's individual risk as well as overall market conditions. Figure 2-6 shows that MicroDrive's 9.84% ROIC is less than its 11% WACC. Thus, MicroDrive did not generate a sufficient rate of return to compensate its investors for the risk they bore in 2013. This is markedly different from the previous year, in which MicroDrive's 13.25% ROIC was greater than its 10.5% WACC. Not only is the current ROIC too low, but the trend is in the wrong direction.

resource
See Ch02 Tool Kit.xls for details.

Although not the case for MicroDrive, in many situations a negative FCF is not necessarily bad. For example, Under Armour had a negative FCF in 2011, but its ROIC was about 16.2%. Because its WACC was only 12%, Under Armour's growth was adding

FIGURE 2-6
Calculating Performance Measures for MicroDrive Inc. (Millions of Dollars)

	A	B	C	D	E	F	G
349						2013	2012
350	*Calculating NOPAT*						
351	EBIT					$500	$550
352	x (1 – Tax rate)					60%	60%
353	NOPAT = EBIT(1 – T)					$300	$330
354							
355	*Calculating Net Operating Working Capital (NOWC)*						
356	Operating current assets					$1,550	$1,260
357	– Operating current liabilities					$500	$470
358	NOWC					$1,050	$790
359							
360	*Calculating Total Net Operating Capital*						
361	NOWC					$1,050	$790
362	+ Net plant and equipment					$2,000	$1,700
363	Total net operating capital					$3,050	$2,490
364							
365	*Calculating Return on Invested Capital (ROIC)*						
366	NOPAT					$300	$330
367	÷ Total net operating capital					$3,050	$2,490
368	ROIC = NOPAT/Total net operating capital					9.84%	13.25%
369	Weighted average cost of capital (WACC)					11.00%	10.50%
370							
371	*Calculating Market Value Added (MVA)*						
372	Price per share					$27	$40
373	x Number of shares (millions)					50	50
374	Market value of equity = P x (# of shares)					$1,350	$2,000
375	– Book value of equity					$1,470	$1,300
376	MVA = Market value – Book value					–$120	$700
377							
378	*Calculating Economic Value Added (EVA)*						
379	Total net operating capital					$3,050.0	$2,490.0
380	x Weighted average cost of capital (WACC)					11.0%	10.5%
381	Dollar cost of capital					$335.5	$261.5
382							
383	NOPAT					$300.0	$330.0
384	– Dollar cost of capital					$335.5	$261.5
385	EVA = NOPAT – Dollar cost of capital					–$35.5	$68.6

value.[8] At some point Under Armour's growth will slow, and it will not require such large capital investments. If Under Armour maintains a high ROIC, then its FCF will become positive and very large as growth slows.

Neither traditional accounting data nor return on invested capital incorporates stock prices, even though the primary goal of management should be to maximize the firm's intrinsic stock price. In contrast, Market Value Added (MVA) and Economic Value Added (EVA) do attempt to compare intrinsic measures with market measures.[9]

2-8b Market Value Added (MVA)

One measure of shareholder wealth is the *difference* between the market value of the firm's stock and the cumulative amount of equity capital that was supplied by shareholders. This difference is called the **Market Value Added (MVA)**:

$$\begin{aligned} \text{MVA} &= \text{Market value of stock} - \text{Equity capital supplied by shareholders} \\ &= (\text{Shares outstanding})(\text{Stock price}) - \text{Total common equity} \end{aligned} \tag{2-11}$$

W W W

For an updated estimate of Coca-Cola's MVA, go to ***finance.yahoo.com****, enter KO, and click GO. This shows the market value of equity, called Mkt Cap. To get the book value of equity, select Balance Sheet from the left panel.*

To illustrate, consider Coca-Cola. In February 2012, its total market equity value, commonly called market capitalization, was \$157 billion, while its balance sheet showed that stockholders had put up only \$32 billion. Thus, Coca-Cola's MVA was \$157 − \$32 = \$125 billion. This \$125 billion represents the difference between the money that Coca-Cola's stockholders have invested in the corporation since its founding—including indirect investment by retaining earnings—and the cash they could get if they sold the business. The higher its MVA, the better the job management is doing for the firm's shareholders.

Sometimes MVA is defined as the total market value of the company minus the total amount of investor-supplied capital:

$$\begin{aligned} \text{MVA} &= \text{Total market value} - \text{Total investor-supplied capital} \\ &= (\text{Market value of stock} + \text{Market value of debt}) \\ &\quad - \text{Total investor-supplied capital} \end{aligned} \tag{2-11a}$$

For most companies, the total amount of investor-supplied capital is the sum of equity, debt, and preferred stock. We can calculate the total amount of investor-supplied capital directly from their reported values in the financial statements. The total market value of a company is the sum of the market values of common equity, debt, and preferred stock. It is easy to find the market value of equity because stock prices are readily available, but it is not always easy to find the market value of debt. Hence, many analysts use the value of debt reported in the financial statements, which is the debt's book value, as an estimate of the debt's market value.

---

[8]If g is the growth rate in capital, then with a little (or a lot of!) algebra, free cash flow is

$$\text{FCF} = \text{Capital}\left(\text{ROIC} - \frac{g}{1+g}\right)$$

This shows that when the growth rate gets almost as high as ROIC, then FCF will be negative.

[9]The concepts of EVA and MVA were developed by Joel Stern and Bennett Stewart, co-founders of the consulting firm Stern Stewart & Company. Stern Stewart copyrighted the terms "EVA" and "MVA," so other consulting firms have given other names to these values. Still, EVA and MVA are the terms most commonly used in practice.

For Coca-Cola, the total amount of reported debt was about $29 billion; Coca-Cola had no preferred stock. Using the debt's book value as an estimate of the debt's market value, Coke's total market value was $157 + $29 = $186 billion. The total amount of investor-supplied funds was $32 + $29 = $61 billion. Using these total values, the MVA was $186 − $61 = $125 billion. Note that this is the same answer as when we used the previous definition of MVA. Both methods will give the same result if the market value of debt is approximately equal to its book value.

Figure 2-6 shows that MicroDrive has 50 million shares of stock and a stock price of $27, giving it a market value of equity equal to $1,350 million. MicroDrive has $1,470 in book equity, so its MVA is $1,350 − $1,470 = −$120. In other words, MicroDrive's current market value is less than the cumulative amount of equity that its shareholders have invested during the company's life.

2-8c Economic Value Added (EVA)

Whereas MVA measures the effects of managerial actions since the inception of a company, **Economic Value Added (EVA)** focuses on managerial effectiveness in a given year. The EVA formula is:

$$\begin{aligned} \text{EVA} &= \frac{\text{Net operating profit}}{\text{after taxes}} - \frac{\text{After-tax dollar cost of capital}}{\text{used to support operations}} \\ &= \text{NOPAT} - (\text{Total net operating capital})(\text{WACC}) \end{aligned} \tag{2-12}$$

Economic Value Added is an estimate of a business's true economic profit for the year, and it differs sharply from accounting profit.[10] EVA represents the residual income that remains after the cost of *all* capital, including equity capital, has been deducted, whereas accounting profit is determined without imposing a charge for equity capital. As we discuss in Chapter 9, equity capital has a cost because shareholders give up the opportunity to invest and earn returns elsewhere when they provide capital to the firm. This cost is an *opportunity cost* rather than an *accounting cost,* but it is real nonetheless.

Note that when calculating EVA we do not add back depreciation. Although it is not a cash expense, depreciation is a cost because worn-out assets must be replaced, and it is therefore deducted when determining both net income and EVA. Our calculation of EVA assumes that the true economic depreciation of the company's fixed assets exactly equals the depreciation used for accounting and tax purposes. If this were not the case, adjustments would have to be made to obtain a more accurate measure of EVA.

Economic Value Added measures the extent to which the firm has increased shareholder value. Therefore, if managers focus on EVA, they will more likely operate in a manner consistent with maximizing shareholder wealth. Note too that EVA can be determined for divisions as well as for the company as a whole, so it provides a useful basis for determining managerial performance at all levels. Consequently, many firms include EVA as a component of compensation plans.

[10]The most important reason EVA differs from accounting profit is that the cost of equity capital is deducted when EVA is calculated. Other factors that could lead to differences include adjustments that might be made to depreciation, to research and development costs, to inventory valuations, and so on. These other adjustments also can affect the calculation of investor-supplied capital, which affects both EVA and MVA. See G. Bennett Stewart, III, *The Quest for Value,* (New York: HarperCollins Publishers, Inc., 1991).

We can also calculate EVA in terms of ROIC:

$$EVA = (\text{Total net operating capital})(ROIC - WACC) \quad (2\text{-}13)$$

As this equation shows, a firm adds value—that is, has a positive EVA—if its ROIC is greater than its WACC. If WACC exceeds ROIC, then growth can actually reduce a firm's value.

Using Equation 2-12, Figure 2-6 shows that MicroDrive's EVA is

$$EVA = \$300 - (\$3{,}050)(11\%) = \$300 - \$335.5 = -\$35.5 \text{ million}$$

This negative EVA reinforces our earlier conclusions that MicroDrive lost value in 2013 due to an erosion in its operating performance. In Chapter 12 we will determine MicroDrive's intrinsic value and explore ways in which MicroDrive can reverse its downward trend.

2-8d Intrinsic Value, MVA, and EVA

We will have more to say about both MVA and EVA later in the book, but we can close this section with two observations. First, there is a relationship between MVA and EVA, but it is not a direct one. If a company has a history of negative EVAs, then its MVA will probably be negative; conversely, its MVA probably will be positive if the company has a history of positive EVAs. However, the stock price, which is the key ingredient in the MVA calculation, depends more on expected future performance than on historical performance. Therefore, a company with a history of negative EVAs could have a positive MVA, provided investors expect a turnaround in the future.

The second observation is that when EVAs or MVAs are used to evaluate managerial performance as part of an incentive compensation program, EVA is the measure that is typically used. The reasons are: (1) EVA shows the value added during a given year, whereas MVA reflects performance over the company's entire life, perhaps even including times before the current managers were born, and (2) EVA can be applied to individual divisions or other units of a large corporation, whereas MVA must be applied to the entire corporation.

SELF-TEST

A company's NOPAT is $12 million and its total net operating capital is $100 million. What is the ROIC? **(12%)**

Define Market Value Added (MVA) and Economic Value Added (EVA).

How does EVA differ from accounting profit?

A firm has $100 million in total net operating capital. Its return on invested capital is 14%, and its weighted average cost of capital is 10%. What is its EVA? **($4 million)**

2-9 The Federal Income Tax System

The value of any financial asset (including stocks, bonds, and mortgages), as well as most real assets such as plants or even entire firms, depends on the after-tax stream of cash flows produced by the asset. The following sections describe the key features of corporate and individual taxation.

TABLE 2-1
Corporate Tax Rates as of January 2012

If a Corporation's Taxable Income Is	It Pays This Amount on the Base of the Bracket	Plus This Percentage on the Excess Over the Base	Average Tax Rate at Top of Bracket
Up to $50,000	$0	15%	15.0%
$50,000–$75,000	$7,500	25	18.3
$75,000–$100,000	$13,750	34	22.3
$100,000–$335,000	$22,250	39	34.0
$335,000–$10,000,000	$113,900	34	34.0
$10,000,000–$15,000,000	$3,400,000	35	34.3
$15,000,000–$18,333,333	$5,150,000	38	35.0
Over $18,333,333	$6,416,667	35	35.0

© Cengage Learning 2014

2-9a Corporate Income Taxes

The corporate tax structure, shown in Table 2-1, is relatively simple. The **marginal tax rate** is the rate paid on the last dollar of income, while the **average tax rate** is the average rate paid on all income. To illustrate, if a firm had $65,000 of taxable income, its tax bill would be

$$\begin{aligned} \text{Taxes} &= \$7{,}500 + 0.25(\$65{,}000 - \$50{,}000) \\ &= \$7{,}500 + \$3{,}750 = \$11{,}250 \end{aligned}$$

Its marginal rate would be 25%, and its average tax rate would be $11,250/$65,000 = 17.3%. Note that corporate income above $18,333,333 has an average and marginal tax rate of 35%.

Interest and Dividend Income Received by a Corporation

Interest income received by a corporation is taxed as ordinary income at regular corporate tax rates. However, *70% of the dividends received by one corporation from another are excluded from taxable income, while the remaining 30% are taxed at the ordinary tax rate.*[11] Thus, a corporation earning more than $18,333,333 and paying a 35% marginal tax rate would pay only (0.30)(0.35) = 0.105 = 10.5% of its dividend income as taxes, so its effective tax rate on dividends received would be 10.5%. If this firm had $10,000 in pre-tax dividend income, then its after-tax dividend income would be $8,950:

$$\begin{aligned} \text{After-tax income} &= \text{Before-tax income} - \text{Taxes} \\ &= \text{Before-tax income} - (\text{Before-tax income})\ (\text{Effective tax rate}) \\ &= \text{Before-tax income}\ (1 - \text{Effective tax rate}) \\ &= \$10{,}000[1-(0.30)(0.35)] \\ &= \$10{,}000(1-0.105) = \$10{,}000(0.895) = \$8{,}950. \end{aligned}$$

[11]The size of the dividend exclusion actually depends on the degree of ownership. Corporations that own less than 20% of the stock of the dividend-paying company can exclude 70% of the dividends received; firms that own more than 20% but less than 80% can exclude 80% of the dividends; and firms that own more than 80% can exclude the entire dividend payment. We will, in general, assume a 70% dividend exclusion.

If the corporation pays its own after-tax income out to stockholders as dividends, then the income is ultimately subject to *triple taxation:* (1) the original corporation is first taxed, (2) the second corporation is then taxed on the dividends it received, and (3) the individuals who receive the final dividends are taxed again. This is the reason for the 70% exclusion on intercorporate dividends.

If a corporation has surplus funds that can be invested in marketable securities, the tax treatment favors investment in stocks, which pay dividends, rather than in bonds, which pay interest. For example, suppose Home Depot had $100,000 to invest, and suppose it could buy either bonds that paid interest of $8,000 per year or preferred stock that paid dividends of $7,000. Home Depot is in the 35% tax bracket; therefore, its tax on the interest, if it bought bonds, would be 0.35($8,000) = $2,800, and its after-tax income would be $5,200. If it bought preferred (or common) stock, its tax would be 0.35[(0.30)($7,000)] = $735, and its after-tax income would be $6,265. Other factors might lead Home Depot to invest in bonds, but the tax treatment certainly favors stock investments when the investor is a corporation.[12]

INTEREST AND DIVIDENDS PAID BY A CORPORATION

A firm's operations can be financed with either debt or equity capital. If the firm uses debt, then it must pay interest on this debt, but if the firm uses equity, then it is expected to pay dividends to the equity investors (stockholders). The interest *paid* by a corporation is deducted from its operating income to obtain its taxable income, but dividends paid are not deductible. Therefore, a firm needs $1 of pre-tax income to pay $1 of interest, but if it is in the 40% federal-plus-state tax bracket, it must earn $1.67 of pre-tax income to pay $1 of dividends:

$$\begin{matrix}\text{Pre-tax income needed} \\ \text{to pay \$1 of dividends}\end{matrix} = \frac{\$1}{1 - \text{Tax rate}} = \frac{\$1}{0.60} = \$1.67$$

Working backward, if a company has $1.67 in pre-tax income, it must pay $0.67 in taxes: (0.4)($1.67) = $0.67. This leaves the firm with after-tax income of $1.00.

Of course, it is generally not possible to finance exclusively with debt capital, and the risk of doing so would offset the benefits of the higher expected income. Still, *the fact that interest is a deductible expense has a profound effect on the way businesses are financed: Our corporate tax system favors debt financing over equity financing*. This point is discussed in more detail in Chapters 9 and 15.

CORPORATE CAPITAL GAINS

Before 1987 corporate long-term capital gains were taxed at lower rates than corporate ordinary income, so the situation was similar for corporations and individuals. Under current law, however, corporations' capital gains are taxed at the same rates as their operating income.

---

[12]This illustration demonstrates why corporations favor investing in lower-yielding preferred stocks over higher-yielding bonds. When tax consequences are considered, the yield on the preferred stock, [1 – 0.35(0.30)](7.0%) = 6.265%, is higher than the yield on the bond, (1 – 0.35)(8.0%) = 5.2%. Also, note that corporations are restricted in their use of borrowed funds to purchase other firms' preferred or common stocks. Without such restrictions, firms could engage in *tax arbitrage*, whereby the interest on borrowed funds reduces taxable income on a dollar-for-dollar basis while taxable income is increased by only $0.30 per dollar of dividend income. Thus, current tax laws reduce the 70% dividend exclusion in proportion to the amount of borrowed funds used to purchase the stock.

When It Comes to Taxes, History Repeats and Repeals Itself!

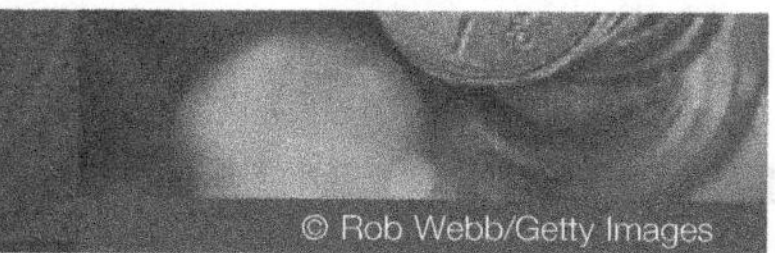

© Rob Webb/Getty Images

Prior to 1987, many large corporations such as General Electric and Boeing paid no federal income taxes even though they reported profits. How could this happen? Some expenses, especially depreciation, were defined differently for calculating taxable income than for reporting earnings to stockholders. So some companies reported positive profits to stockholders but losses—hence no taxes—to the Internal Revenue Service. Also, some companies that otherwise would have paid taxes were able used various tax credits to avoid paying taxes.

The Tax Reform Act of 1986 eliminated many loopholes and tightened up provisions in the corporate Alternative Minimum Tax (AMT) code so that companies would not be able to utilize tax credits and accelerated depreciation to such an extent that their federal taxes fell below a certain minimum level.

Fast forward to the present. According to a report published in late 2011, General Electric and Boeing paid no federal income taxes in 2008, 2009, or 2010 even though they reported profits in each year. In fact, 30 companies with an average profit of over $1.7 billion per year paid no taxes during the 3-year study period. Of the 280 companies in the study, 97 paid 10% or less of their reported profit as federal income taxes. The average effective rate was less than 19%, much lower than the 35% rate shown in the corporate tax table. Only 25% of the companies in the study paid more than 30%. How did history repeat itself?

Over the years Congress gradually repealed many of the 1986 tax reforms and weakened the AMT, adding more and more loopholes and credits. Some of these breaks were for all firms, such as the 2008 acceleration of depreciation intended to stimulate corporate investment in the wake of the global economic crisis. Others were for specific industries, such as tax breaks for ethanol production that might help reduce reliance on imported oil. However, some of the changes appear difficult to justify, such as the 2010 tax breaks given to NASCAR track owners.

The net result is a complicated tax system in which corporations with shrewd accountants and well-connected lobbyists pay substantially less than other companies. As we write this in 2012, President Obama and leaders in Congress are calling for corporate tax reform.

Sources: Adapted from Robert S. McIntyre, Matthew Gardner, Rebecca J. Wilkins, and Richard Phillips "Corporate Taxpayers & Corporate Tax Dodgers 2008–10," *Joint Project of Citizens for Tax Justice & the Institute on Taxation and Economic Policy*, November 2011; see **www.ctj.org/corporatetaxdodgers/CorporateTaxDodgers Report.pdf.**

Corporate Loss Carryback and Carryforward

Ordinary corporate operating losses can be carried back (**carryback**) to each of the preceding 2 years and forward (**carryforward**) for the next 20 years and thus be used to offset taxable income in those years. For example, an operating loss in 2013 could be carried back and used to reduce taxable income in 2011 and 2012 as well as carried forward, if necessary, to reduce taxes in 2014, 2015, and so on, to the year 2033. After carrying back 2 years, any remaining loss is typically carried forward first to the next year, then to the one after that, and so on, until losses have been used up or the 20-year carryforward limit has been reached.

To illustrate, suppose Apex Corporation had $2 million of *pre-tax* profits (taxable income) in 2011 and 2012, and then, in 2013, Apex lost $12 million. Also, assume that Apex's federal-plus-state tax rate is 40%. As shown in Table 2-2, the company would use the carryback feature to recalculate its taxes for 2011, using $2 million of the 2013 operating losses to reduce the 2011 pre-tax profit to zero. This would permit it to recover the taxes paid in 2011. Therefore, in 2013 Apex would receive a refund of its 2011 taxes because of the loss experienced in 2013. Because $10 million of the unrecovered losses would still be available, Apex would repeat this procedure for 2012. Thus, in 2013 the

TABLE 2-2
Apex Corporation: Calculation of $12 Million Loss Carryback and Amount Available for Carryforward

	Past Year 2011	Past Year 2012	Current Year 2013
Original taxable income	$2,000,000	$2,000,000	-$12,000,000
Carryback credit	2,000,000	2,000,000	
Adjusted profit	$ 0	$ 0	
Taxes previously paid (40%)	800,000	800,000	
Difference = Tax refund due	$ 800,000	$ 800,000	
Total tax refund received			$ 1,600,000
Amount of loss carryforward available			
Current loss			-$12,000,000
Carryback losses used			4,000,000
Carryforward losses still available			-$ 8,000,000

© Cengage Learning 2014

company would pay zero taxes for 2013 and also would receive a refund for taxes paid in 2011 and 2012. Apex would still have $8 million of unrecovered losses to carry forward, subject to the 20-year limit. This $8 million could be used to offset future taxable income. The purpose of this loss treatment is to avoid penalizing corporations whose incomes fluctuate substantially from year to year.

resource
See Ch02 Tool Kit.xls for details.

Improper Accumulation to Avoid Payment of Dividends

Corporations could refrain from paying dividends and thus permit their stockholders to avoid personal income taxes on dividends. To prevent this, the Tax Code contains an **improper accumulation** provision that states that earnings accumulated by a corporation are subject to penalty rates *if the purpose of the accumulation is to enable stockholders to avoid personal income taxes.* A cumulative total of $250,000 (the balance sheet item "retained earnings") is by law exempted from the improper accumulation tax for most corporations. This is a benefit primarily to small corporations.

The improper accumulation penalty applies only if the retained earnings in excess of $250,000 are *shown by the IRS to be unnecessary to meet the reasonable needs of the business.* A great many companies do indeed have legitimate reasons for retaining more than $250,000 of earnings. For example, firms may retain and use earnings to pay off debt, finance growth, or provide the corporation with a cushion against possible cash drains caused by losses. How much a firm should be allowed to accumulate for uncertain contingencies is a matter of judgment. We shall consider this matter again in Chapter 14, which deals with corporate dividend policy.

Consolidated Corporate Tax Returns

If a corporation owns 80% or more of another corporation's stock, then it can aggregate income and file one consolidated tax return; thus, the losses of one company can be used to offset the profits of another. (Similarly, one division's losses can be used to offset another division's profits.) No business ever wants to incur losses (you can go broke losing $1 to save 35¢ in taxes), but tax offsets do help make it more feasible for large, multi-divisional corporations to undertake risky new ventures or ventures that will suffer losses during a developmental period.

Taxes on Overseas Income

Many U.S. corporations have overseas subsidiaries, and those subsidiaries must pay taxes in the countries where they operate. Often, foreign tax rates are lower than U.S. rates. As long as foreign earnings are reinvested overseas, no U.S. tax is due on those earnings. However, when foreign earnings are repatriated to the U.S. parent, they are taxed at the applicable U.S. rate, less a credit for taxes paid to the foreign country. As a result, U.S. corporations such as IBM, Coca-Cola, and Microsoft have been able to defer billions of dollars of taxes. This procedure has stimulated overseas investments by U.S. multinational firms—they can continue the deferral indefinitely, but only if they reinvest the earnings in their overseas operations.[13]

2-9b Taxation of Small Businesses: S Corporations

The Tax Code provides that small businesses that meet certain restrictions may be set up as corporations and thus receive the benefits of the corporate form of organization—especially limited liability—yet still be taxed as proprietorships or partnerships rather than as corporations. These corporations are called **S corporations**. ("Regular" corporations are called C corporations.) If a corporation elects S corporation status for tax purposes, then all of the business's income is reported as personal income by its stockholders, on a pro rata basis, and thus is taxed at the rates that apply to individuals. This is an important benefit to the owners of small corporations in which all or most of the income earned each year will be distributed as dividends, because then the income is taxed only once, at the individual level.

2-9c Personal Taxes

Web Extension 2A provides a more detailed treatment of individual taxation, but the key elements are presented here. **Ordinary income** consists primarily of wages or profits from a proprietorship or partnership, plus investment income. For the 2012 tax year, individuals with less than $8,700 of taxable income are subject to a federal income tax rate of 10%. For those with higher income, tax rates increase and go up to 35%, depending on the level of income. This is called a **progressive tax**, because the higher one's income, the larger the percentage paid in taxes.

resource

*See **Web Extension 2A** on the textbook's Web site for details concerning personal taxation.*

As noted before, individuals are taxed on investment income as well as earned income, but with a few exceptions and modifications. For example, interest received from most state and local government bonds, called **municipals** or **munis**, is not subject to federal taxation. However, interest earned on most other bonds or lending is taxed as ordinary income. This means that a lower-yielding muni can provide the same after-tax return as a higher-yielding corporate bond. For a taxpayer in the 35% marginal tax bracket, a muni yielding 5.5% provides the same after-tax return as a corporate bond with a pre-tax yield of 8.46%: 8.46%(1 − 0.35) = 5.5%.

[13]This is a contentious political issue. U.S. corporations argue that our tax system is similar to systems in the rest of the world, and if they were taxed immediately on all overseas earnings then they would be at a competitive disadvantage vis-à-vis their global competitors. Others argue that taxation encourages overseas investments at the expense of domestic investments, contributing to the jobs-outsourcing problem and also to the federal budget deficit.

Assets such as stocks, bonds, and real estate are defined as capital assets. If you own a capital asset and its price goes up, then your wealth increases, but you are not liable for any taxes on your increased wealth until you sell the asset. If you sell the asset for more than you originally paid, the profit is called a **capital gain**; if you sell it for less, then you suffer a **capital loss**. The length of time you owned the asset determines the tax treatment. If held for less than 1 year, then your gain or loss is simply added to your other ordinary income. If held for more than a year, then gains are called *long-term capital gains* and are taxed at a lower rate. See ***Web Extension 2A*** for details, but the long-term capital gains rate is 15% for most situations.

Under the 2003 tax law changes, dividends are now taxed as though they are capital gains. As stated earlier, corporations may deduct interest payments but not dividends when computing their corporate tax liability, which means that dividends are taxed twice, once at the corporate level and again at the personal level. This differential treatment motivates corporations to use debt relatively heavily and to pay small (or even no) dividends. The 2003 tax law did not eliminate the differential treatment of dividends and interest payments from the corporate perspective, but it did make the tax treatment of dividends more similar to that of capital gains from investors' perspectives. To see this, consider a company that doesn't pay a dividend but instead reinvests the cash it could have paid. The company's stock price should increase, leading to a capital gain, which would be taxed at the same rate as the dividend. Of course, the stock price appreciation isn't actually taxed until the stock is sold, whereas the dividend is taxed in the year it is paid, so dividends will still be more costly than capital gains for many investors.

Finally, note that the income of S corporations *and* noncorporate businesses is reported as income by the firms' owners. Because there are far more S corporations, partnerships, and proprietorships than C corporations (which are subject to the corporate tax), individual tax considerations play an important role in business finance.

SELF-TEST

Explain what is meant by this statement: "Our tax rates are progressive."

If a corporation has $85,000 in taxable income, what is its tax liability? **($17,150)**

Explain the difference between marginal tax rates and average tax rates.

What are municipal bonds, and how are these bonds taxed?

What are capital gains and losses, and how are they taxed?

How does the federal income tax system treat dividends received by a corporation versus those received by an individual?

What is the difference in the tax treatment of interest and dividends paid by a corporation? Does this factor favor debt or equity financing?

Briefly explain how tax loss carryback and carryforward procedures work.

SUMMARY

- The four basic statements contained in the **annual report** are the balance sheet, the income statement, the statement of stockholders' equity, and the statement of cash flows.
- The **balance sheet** shows assets and liabilities and equity, or claims against assets. The balance sheet may be thought of as a snapshot of the firm's financial position at a particular point in time.

- The **income statement** reports the results of operations over a period of time, and it shows earnings per share as its "bottom line."
- The **statement of stockholders' equity** shows the change in stockholders' equity, including the change in retained earnings, between balance sheet dates. Retained earnings represent a claim against assets, not assets per se.
- The **statement of cash flows** reports the effect of operating, investing, and financing activities on cash flows over an accounting period.
- **Net cash flow** differs from **accounting profit** because some of the revenues and expenses reflected in accounting profits may not have been received or paid out in cash during the year. Depreciation is typically the largest noncash item, so net cash flow is often expressed as net income plus depreciation.
- **Operating current assets** are the current assets that are used to support operations, such as cash, inventory, and accounts receivable. They do not include short-term investments.
- **Operating current liabilities** are the current liabilities that occur as a natural consequence of operations, such as accounts payable and accruals. They do not include notes payable or any other short-term debts that charge interest.
- **Net operating working capital** is the difference between operating current assets and operating current liabilities. Thus, it is the working capital acquired with investor-supplied funds.
- **Operating long-term assets** are the long-term assets used to support operations, such as net plant and equipment. They do not include any long-term investments that pay interest or dividends.
- **Total net operating capital** (which means the same as **operating capital** and **net operating assets**) is the sum of net operating working capital and operating long-term assets. It is the total amount of capital needed to run the business.
- **NOPAT** is net operating profit after taxes. It is the after-tax profit a company would have if it had no debt and no investments in nonoperating assets. Because NOPAT excludes the effects of financial decisions, it is a better measure of operating performance than is net income.
- **Return on Invested Capital (ROIC)** is equal to NOPAT divided by total net operating capital. It measures the rate of return that the operations are generating. It is the best measure of operating performance.
- **Free cash flow (FCF)** is the amount of cash flow remaining after a company makes the asset investments necessary to support operations. In other words, FCF is the amount of cash flow available for distribution to investors, so *the value of a company is directly related to its ability to generate free cash flow*. FCF is defined as NOPAT minus the net investment in operating capital.
- **Market Value Added (MVA)** represents the difference between the total market value of a firm and the total amount of investor-supplied capital. If the market values of debt and preferred stock equal their values as reported on the financial statements, then MVA is the difference between the market value of a firm's stock and the amount of equity its shareholders have supplied.
- **Economic Value Added (EVA)** is the difference between after-tax operating profit and the total dollar cost of capital, including the cost of equity capital. EVA is an estimate of the value created by management during the year, and it differs substantially from accounting profit because no charge for the use of equity capital is reflected in accounting profit.

- Interest income received by a corporation is taxed as **ordinary income**; however, 70% of the dividends received by one corporation from another are excluded from **taxable income.**
- Because interest paid by a corporation is a **deductible expense** whereas dividends are not, our tax system favors debt over equity financing.
- Ordinary corporate operating losses can be **carried back** to each of the preceding 2 years and **carried forward** for the next 20 years in order to offset taxable income in those years.
- **S corporations** are small businesses that have the limited-liability benefits of the corporate form of organization yet are taxed as partnerships or proprietorships.
- In the United States, tax rates are **progressive**—the higher one's income, the larger the percentage paid in taxes.
- Assets such as stocks, bonds, and real estate are defined as **capital assets.** If a capital asset is sold for more than its cost, the profit is called a **capital gain**; if the asset is sold for a loss, it is called a **capital loss.** Assets held for more than a year provide **long-term gains or losses.**
- Dividends are taxed as though they were capital gains.
- **Personal taxes** are discussed in more detail in ***Web Extension 2A.***

QUESTIONS

(2-1) Define each of the following terms:

a. Annual report; balance sheet; income statement
b. Common stockholders' equity, or net worth; retained earnings
c. Statement of stockholders' equity; statement of cash flows
d. Depreciation; amortization; EBITDA
e. Operating current assets; operating current liabilities; net operating working capital; total net operating capital
f. Accounting profit; net cash flow; NOPAT; free cash flow; return on invested capital
g. Market Value Added; Economic Value Added
h. Progressive tax; taxable income; marginal and average tax rates
i. Capital gain or loss; tax loss carryback and carryforward
j. Improper accumulation; S corporation

(2-2) What four statements are contained in most annual reports?

(2-3) If a "typical" firm reports $20 million of retained earnings on its balance sheet, can the firm definitely pay a $20 million cash dividend?

(2-4) Explain the following statement: "Whereas the balance sheet can be thought of as a snapshot of the firm's financial position *at a point in time,* the income statement reports on operations *over a period of time.*"

(2-5) What is operating capital, and why is it important?

(2-6) Explain the difference between NOPAT and net income. Which is a better measure of the performance of a company's operations?

(2-7) What is free cash flow? Why is it the most important measure of cash flow?

(2-8) If you were starting a business, what tax considerations might cause you to prefer to set it up as a proprietorship or a partnership rather than as a corporation?

SELF-TEST PROBLEM Solution Appears in Appendix A

(ST-1) Net Income, Cash Flow, and EVA

Last year Cole Furnaces had $5 million in operating income (EBIT). The company had a net depreciation expense of $1 million and an interest expense of $1 million; its corporate tax rate was 40%. The company has $14 million in operating current assets and $4 million in operating current liabilities; it has $15 million in net plant and equipment. It estimates that it has an after-tax cost of capital of 10%. Assume that Cole's only noncash item was depreciation.

a. What was the company's net income for the year?
b. What was the company's net cash flow?
c. What was the company's net operating profit after taxes (NOPAT)?
d. Calculate net operating working capital and total net operating capital for the current year.
e. If total net operating capital in the previous year was $24 million, what was the company's free cash flow (FCF) for the year?
f. What was the return on invested capital?
g. What was the company's Economic Value Added (EVA)?

PROBLEMS Answers Appear in Appendix B

Note: By the time this book is published, Congress may have changed rates and/or other provisions of current tax law as noted in the chapter, as such changes occur fairly often. Work all problems on the assumption that the information in the chapter is applicable.

Easy Problems 1–6

(2-1) Personal After-Tax Yield

An investor recently purchased a corporate bond that yields 9%. The investor is in the 36% combined federal and state tax bracket. What is the bond's after-tax yield?

(2-2) Personal After-Tax Yield

Corporate bonds issued by Johnson Corporation currently yield 8%. Municipal bonds of equal risk currently yield 6%. At what tax rate would an investor be indifferent between these two bonds?

(2-3) Income Statement

Molteni Motors Inc. recently reported $6 million of net income. Its EBIT was $13 million, and its tax rate was 40%. What was its interest expense? (*Hint:* Write out the headings for an income statement, and then fill in the known values. Then divide $6 million net income by 1 – T = 0.6 to find the pre-tax income. The difference between EBIT and taxable income must be the interest expense. Use this procedure to work some of the other problems.)

(2-4) Income Statement

Talbot Enterprises recently reported an EBITDA of $8 million and net income of $2.4 million. It had $2.0 million of interest expense, and its corporate tax rate was 40%. What was its charge for depreciation and amortization?

(2-5) Net Cash Flow

Kendall Corners Inc. recently reported net income of $3.1 million and depreciation of $500,000. What was its net cash flow? Assume it had no amortization expense.

(2-6) Statement of Retained Earnings

In its most recent financial statements, Del-Castillo Inc. reported $70 million of net income and $900 million of retained earnings. The previous retained earnings were $855 million. How much in dividends did the firm pay to shareholders during the year?

Intermediate
Problems 7–11

(2-7) Corporate Tax Liability

The Talley Corporation had a taxable income of $365,000 from operations after all operating costs but before (1) interest charges of $50,000, (2) dividends received of $15,000, (3) dividends paid of $25,000, and (4) income taxes. What are the firm's income tax liability and its after-tax income? What are the company's marginal and average tax rates on taxable income?

(2-8) Corporate Tax Liability

The Wendt Corporation had $10.5 million of taxable income.

a. What is the company's federal income tax bill for the year?
b. Assume the firm receives an additional $1 million of interest income from some bonds it owns. What is the tax on this interest income?
c. Now assume that Wendt does not receive the interest income but does receive an additional $1 million as dividends on some stock it owns. What is the tax on this dividend income?

(2-9) Corporate After-Tax Yield

The Shrieves Corporation has $10,000 that it plans to invest in marketable securities. It is choosing among AT&T bonds, which yield 7.5%, state of Florida muni bonds, which yield 5% (but are not taxable), and AT&T preferred stock, with a dividend yield of 6%. Shrieves's corporate tax rate is 35%, and 70% of the dividends received are tax exempt. Find the after-tax rates of return on all three securities.

(2-10) Net Cash Flows

The Moore Corporation has operating income (EBIT) of $750,000. The company's depreciation expense is $200,000. Moore is 100% equity financed, and it faces a 40% tax rate. What is the company's net income? What is its net cash flow?

(2-11) Income and Cash Flow Analysis

The Berndt Corporation expects to have sales of $12 million. Costs other than depreciation are expected to be 75% of sales, and depreciation is expected to be $1.5 million. All sales revenues will be collected in cash, and costs other than depreciation must be paid for during the year. Berndt's federal-plus-state tax rate is 40%. Berndt has no debt.

a. Set up an income statement. What is Berndt's expected net cash flow?
b. Suppose Congress changed the tax laws so that Berndt's depreciation expenses doubled. No changes in operations occurred. What would happen to reported profit and to net cash flow?
c. Now suppose that Congress changed the tax laws such that, instead of doubling Berndt's depreciation, it was reduced by 50%. How would profit and net cash flow be affected?
d. If this were your company, would you prefer Congress to cause your depreciation expense to be doubled or halved? Why?

Challenging
Problems 12–13

(2-12) Free Cash Flows

Using Rhodes Corporation's financial statements (shown below), answer the following questions.

a. What is the net operating profit after taxes (NOPAT) for 2013?
b. What are the amounts of net operating working capital for both years?
c. What are the amounts of total net operating capital for both years?
d. What is the free cash flow for 2013?
e. What is the ROIC for 2013?
f. How much of the FCF did Rhodes use for each of the following purposes: after-tax interest, net debt repayments, dividends, net stock repurchases, and net purchases of short-term investments? (*Hint:* Remember that a net use can be negative.)

Rhodes Corporation: Income Statements for Year Ending December 31 (Millions of Dollars)

	2013	2012
Sales	$11,000	$10,000
Operating costs excluding depreciation	9,360	8,500
Depreciation and amortization	380	360
Earnings before interest and taxes	$ 1,260	$ 1,140
Less interest	120	100
Pre-tax income	$ 1,140	$ 1,040
Taxes (40%)	456	416
Net income available to common stockholders	$ 684	$ 624
Common dividends	$ 220	$ 200

Rhodes Corporation: Balance Sheets as of December 31 (Millions of Dollars)

	2013	2012
Assets		
Cash	$ 550	$ 500
Short-term investments	110	100
Accounts receivable	2,750	2,500
Inventories	1,650	1,500
Total current assets	$5,060	$4,600
Net plant and equipment	3,850	3,500
Total assets	$8,910	$8,100
Liabilities and Equity		
Accounts payable	$1,100	$1,000
Accruals	550	500
Notes payable	384	200
Total current liabilities	$2,034	$1,700
Long-term debt	1,100	1,000
Total liabilities	$3,134	$2,700
Common stock	4,312	4,400
Retained earnings	1,464	1,000
Total common equity	$5,776	$5,400
Total liabilities and equity	$8,910	$8,100

(2-13) Loss Carryback and Carryforward

The Bookbinder Company has made $150,000 before taxes during each of the last 15 years, and it expects to make $150,000 a year before taxes in the future. However, in 2013 the firm incurred a loss of $650,000. The firm will claim a tax credit at the time it files its 2013 income tax return, and it will receive a check from the U.S. Treasury. Show how it calculates this credit, and then indicate the firm's tax liability for each of the next 5 years. Assume a 40% tax rate on *all* income to ease the calculations.

SPREADSHEET PROBLEMS

(2-14) Build a Model: Financial Statements, EVA, and MVA

resource

Begin with the partial model in the file ***Ch02 P14 Build a Model.xls*** *on the textbook's Web site.*

a. The 2013 sales of Cumberland Industries were $455,000,000; operating costs (excluding depreciation) were equal to 85% of sales; net fixed assets were $67,000,000; depreciation amounted to 10% of net fixed assets; interest expenses were $8,550,000; the state-plus-federal corporate tax rate was 40%; and Cumberland paid 25% of its net income out in dividends. Given this information, construct Cumberland's 2013 income statement. Also calculate total dividends and the addition to retained earnings. (*Hint:* Start with the partial model in the file and report all dollar figures in thousands to reduce clutter.)

b. The partial balance sheets of Cumberland Industries are shown below. Cumberland issued $10,000,000 of new common stock in 2013. Using this information and the results from part a, fill in the missing values for common stock, retained earnings, total common equity, and total liabilities and equity.

Cumberland Industries: Balance Sheets as of December 31 (Thousands of Dollars)

	2013	2012
Assets		
Cash	$ 91,450	$ 74,625
Short-term investments	11,400	15,100
Accounts receivable	108,470	85,527
Inventories	38,450	34,982
Total current assets	$249,770	$210,234
Net fixed assets	67,000	42,436
Total assets	$316,770	$252,670
Liabilities and Equity		
Accounts payable	$ 30,761	$ 23,109
Accruals	30,405	22,656
Notes payable	12,717	14,217
Total current liabilities	$ 73,883	$ 59,982
Long-term debt	80,263	63,914
Total liabilities	$154,146	$123,896
Common stock	?	$ 90,000
Retained earnings	?	38,774
Total common equity	?	$128,774
Total liabilities and equity	?	$252,670

c. Construct the statement of cash flows for 2013.

(2-15)
Build a Model: Free Cash Flows, EVA, and MVA

resource

Begin with the partial model in the file ***Ch02 P15 Build a Model.xls*** on the textbook's Web site.

a. Using the financial statements shown below for Lan & Chen Technologies, calculate net operating working capital, total net operating capital, net operating profit after taxes, free cash flow, and return on invested capital for 2013. (*Hint:* Start with the partial model in the file and report all dollar figures in thousands to reduce clutter.)
b. Assume there were 15 million shares outstanding at the end of 2013, the year-end closing stock price was $65 per share, and the after-tax cost of capital was 8%. Calculate EVA and MVA for 2013.

Lan & Chen Technologies: Income Statements for Year Ending December 31 (Thousands of Dollars)

	2013	2012
Sales	$945,000	$900,000
Expenses excluding depreciation and amortization	812,700	774,000
EBITDA	$132,300	$126,000
Depreciation and amortization	33,100	31,500
EBIT	$ 99,200	$ 94,500
Interest expense	10,470	8,600
Pre-tax earnings	$ 88,730	$ 85,900
Taxes (40%)	35,492	34,360
Net income	$ 53,238	$ 51,540
Common dividends	$ 43,300	$ 41,230
Addition to retained earnings	$ 9,938	$ 10,310

Lan & Chen Technologies: December 31 Balance Sheets

	2013	2012
Assets		
Cash and cash equivalents	$ 47,250	$ 45,000
Short-term investments	3,800	3,600
Accounts receivable	283,500	270,000
Inventories	141,750	135,000
Total current assets	$476,300	$453,600
Net fixed assets	330,750	315,000
Total assets	$807,050	$768,600
Liabilities and Equity		
Accounts payable	$ 94,500	$ 90,000
Accruals	47,250	45,000
Notes payable	26,262	9,000
Total current liabilities	$168,012	$144,000
Long-term debt	94,500	90,000
Total liabilities	$262,512	$234,000
Common stock	444,600	444,600
Retained earnings	99,938	90,000
Total common equity	$544,538	$534,600
Total liabilities and equity	$807,050	$768,600

THOMSON ONE Business School Edition Problem

THOMSON REUTERS Use the Thomson ONE—Business School Edition online database to work this chapter's questions.

Exploring Starbucks's Financial Statements with Thomson ONE—Business School Edition

Over the past decade, Starbucks coffee shops have become an increasingly familiar part of the urban landscape. The Thomson ONE—Business School Edition online database can provide a wealth of financial information for companies such as Starbucks. Begin by entering the company's ticker symbol, SBUX, and then selecting GO. The opening screen includes a summary of what Starbucks does, a chart of its recent stock price, EPS estimates, some recent news stories, and a list of key financial data and ratios.

For recent stock price performance, look at the top of the Stock Price Chart and click on the section labeled Interactive Chart. From this point, we are able to obtain a chart of the company's stock price performance relative to the overall market, as measured by the S&P 500. To obtain a 10-year chart, go to Time Frame, click on the down arrow, and select 10 years. Then click on Draw, and a 10-year price chart should appear.

You can also find Starbucks's recent financial statements. On the left side of your screen, click on the Financials tab to find the company's balance sheet, income statement, and statement of cash flows for the past 5 years. Clicking on the Microsoft *Excel* icon downloads these statements directly to a spreadsheet.

Thomson ONE—BSE Discussion Questions

1. Looking at the most recent year available, what is the amount of total assets on Starbucks's balance sheet? What percentage is fixed assets, such as plant and equipment, and what percentage is current assets? How much has the company grown over the years shown?
2. Does Starbucks have a lot of long-term debt? What are Starbucks's primary sources of financing?
3. Looking at the statement of cash flows, what factors can explain the change in the company's cash position over the last couple of years?
4. Looking at the income statement, what are the company's most recent sales and net income? Over the past several years, what has been the sales growth rate? What has been the growth rate in net income?

MINI CASE

Jenny Cochran, a graduate of the University of Tennessee with 4 years of experience as an equities analyst, was recently brought in as assistant to the chairman of the board of Computron Industries, a manufacturer of computer components.

The company doubled its plant capacity, opened new sales offices outside its home territory, and launched an expensive advertising campaign. Computron's results were not satisfactory, to put it mildly. Its board of directors, which consisted of its president and vice president plus its major stockholders (who were all local businesspeople), was most upset when directors learned how the expansion was going. Suppliers were being paid late and were unhappy, and the bank was complaining about the deteriorating situation and threatening to cut off credit. As a result, Robert Edwards, Computron's president, was informed that changes would have to be made—and quickly—or he would be fired. At the board's insistence, Jenny Cochran was given the job of assistant to Gary Meissner, a retired banker who was Computron's chairman and largest stockholder. Meissner agreed to give up a few of his golfing days and to help nurse the company back to health, with Cochran's assistance.

Cochran began by gathering financial statements and other data. Note: these are available in the file ***Ch02 Tool Kit.xls*** in the ***Mini Case*** tab.

	2012	2013
Balance Sheets		
Assets		
Cash	$ 9,000	$ 7,282
Short-term investments	48,600	20,000
Accounts receivable	351,200	632,160
Inventories	715,200	1,287,360
Total current assets	$1,124,000	$1,946,802
Gross fixed assets	491,000	1,202,950
Less: Accumulated depreciation	146,200	263,160
Net fixed assets	$ 344,800	$ 939,790
Total assets	$1,468,800	$2,886,592
Liabilities and Equity		
Accounts payable	$ 145,600	$ 324,000
Notes payable	200,000	720,000
Accruals	136,000	284,960
Total current liabilities	$ 481,600	$1,328,960
Long-term debt	323,432	1,000,000
Common stock (100,000 shares)	460,000	460,000
Retained earnings	203,768	97,632
Total equity	$ 663,768	$ 557,632
Total liabilities and equity	$1,468,800	$2,886,592

	2012	2013
Income Statements		
Sales	$3,432,000	$ 5,834,400
Cost of goods sold	2,864,000	4,980,000
Other expenses	340,000	720,000
Depreciation and amortization	18,900	116,960
Total operating costs	$3,222,900	$ 5,816,960
EBIT	$ 209,100	$ 17,440
Interest expense	62,500	176,000
Pre-tax earnings	$ 146,600	($ 158,560)
Taxes (40%)	58,640	(63,424)
Net income	$ 87,960	($ 95,136)

Other Data	2012	2013
Stock price	$ 8.50	$ 6.00
Shares outstanding	100,000	100,000
EPS	$ 0.880	($ 0.951)
DPS	$ 0.220	$ 0.110
Tax rate	40%	40%

	2013
Statement of Cash Flows	
Operating Activities	
Net income	($ 95,136)
Adjustments:	
Noncash adjustments:	
Depreciation and amortization	116,960
Changes in working capital:	
Change in accounts receivable	(280,960)
Change in inventories	(572,160)
Change in accounts payable	178,400
Change in accruals	148,960
Net cash provided (used) by operating activities	($ 503,936)
Investing Activities	
Cash used to acquire fixed assets	($ 711,950)
Change in short-term investments	28,600
Net cash provided (used) by investing activities	($ 683,350)
Financing Activities	
Change in notes payable	$ 520,000
Change in long-term debt	676,568
Change in common stock	—
Payment of cash dividends	(11,000)
Net cash provided (used) by financing activities	$1,185,568
Summary	
Net change in cash	($ 1,718)
Cash at beginning of year	9,000
Cash at end of year	$ 7,282

Assume that you are Cochran's assistant and that you must help her answer the following questions for Meissner.

a. What effect did the expansion have on sales and net income? What effect did the expansion have on the asset side of the balance sheet? What effect did it have on liabilities and equity?
b. What do you conclude from the statement of cash flows?
c. What is free cash flow? Why is it important? What are the five uses of FCF?

d. What is Computron's net operating profit after taxes (NOPAT)? What are operating current assets? What are operating current liabilities? How much net operating working capital and total net operating capital does Computron have?
e. What is Computron's free cash flow (FCF)? What are Computron's "net uses" of its FCF?
f. Calculate Computron's return on invested capital. Computron has a 10% cost of capital (WACC). Do you think Computron's growth added value?
g. Cochran also has asked you to estimate Computron's EVA. She estimates that the after-tax cost of capital was 10% in both years.
h. What happened to Computron's Market Value Added (MVA)?
i. Assume that a corporation has $100,000 of taxable income from operations plus $5,000 of interest income and $10,000 of dividend income. What is the company's federal tax liability?
j. Assume that you are in the 25% marginal tax bracket and that you have $5,000 to invest. You have narrowed your investment choices down to California bonds with a yield of 7% or equally risky ExxonMobil bonds with a yield of 10%. Which one should you choose and why? At what marginal tax rate would you be indifferent to the choice between California and ExxonMobil bonds?

© Adalberto Rios Szalay/Sexto Sol/Getty Images

CHAPTER 3

Analysis of Financial Statements

Macy's, a large department store retailer, announced its fourth quarter 2011 results of \$1.74 earnings per share (EPS). According to Zacks .com's Earnings Scorecard, Macy's EPS came in a little higher than analysts' estimates of \$1.65. Perhaps not surprisingly, Macy's stock return during the 5-day period centered on its announcement date was positive: Macy's had a 5% return, much greater than the S&P 500's 0.6% return. Macy's announcement also provided guidance for its expected 2012 EPS of \$3.25 to \$3.30.

Should a company provide earnings guidance estimates to investors? Virtually no one disputes that investors need as much information as possible to evaluate a company, and academic studies show that companies with greater transparency have higher valuations. However, greater disclosure often brings the possibility of lawsuits if investors have reason to believe that the disclosure is fraudulent. In addition, the Security and Exchange Commission's Reg FD (Regulation Fair Disclosure) prevents companies from disclosing information only to select groups, such as analysts. Reg FD led many companies to begin providing quarterly earnings forecasts directly to the public. In fact, a survey by the National Investors Relations Institute showed that 95% of respondents in 2006 provided either annual or quarterly earnings forecasts, up from 45% in 1999.

Two trends have emerged. First, the number of companies reporting quarterly earnings forecasts is falling, but the number reporting annual forecasts is increasing. Second, many companies are providing other types of forward-looking information, including key operating ratios plus qualitative information about the company and its industry. Ratio analysis can help investors use such information, so keep that in mind as you read this chapter.

Sources: Adapted from Macy's press release: **http://phx.corporate-ir.net/phoenix.zhtml?c=84477&p=RssLanding&cat=news&id=1663112**; Zacks's Earnings Scorecard: **www.zacks.com/stock/news/70862/Earnings+Scorecard%3A+Macy's**; Joseph McCafferty, "Guidance Lite," *CFO,* June 2006, 16–17; and William F. Coffin and Crocker Coulson, "Is Earnings Guidance Disappearing in 2006?" 2006, White Paper, available at **www.ccgir.com/ccgir/white_papers/pdf/Earnings%20Guidance%202006.pdf.**

Intrinsic Value and Analysis of Financial Statements

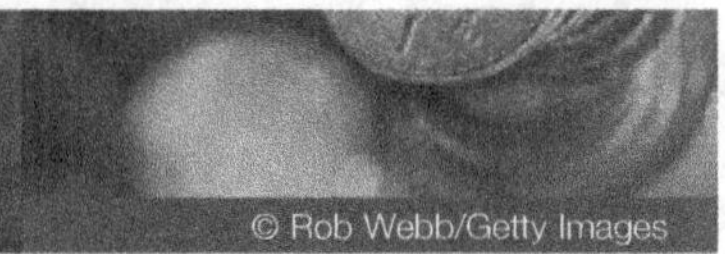

© Rob Webb/Getty Images

The intrinsic value of a firm is determined by the present value of the expected future free cash flows (FCF) when discounted at the weighted average cost of capital (WACC). This chapter explains how to use financial statements to evaluate a company's profitability, required capital investments, business risk, and mix of debt and equity.

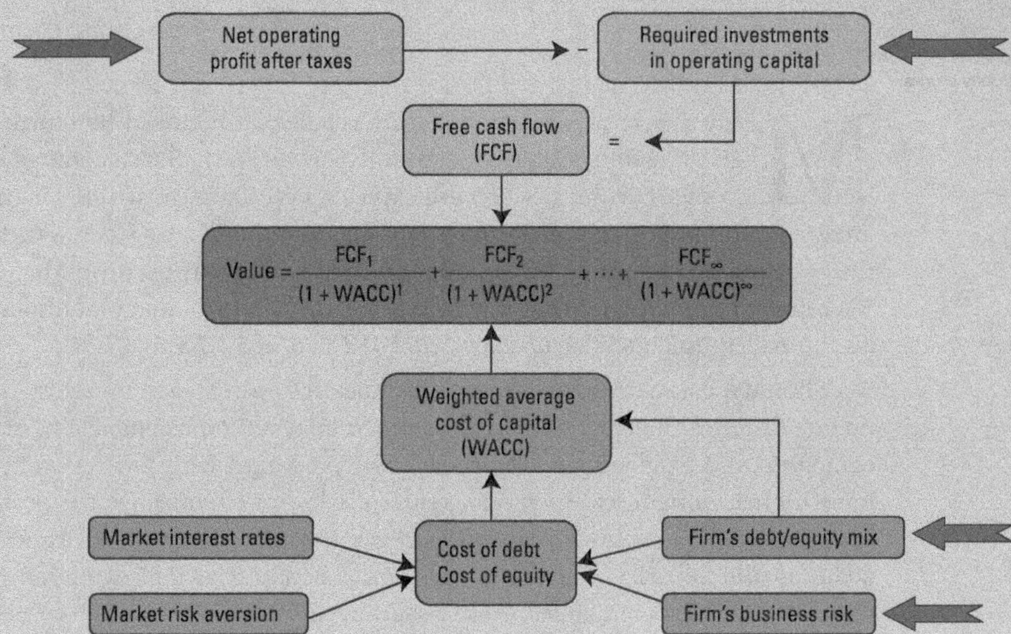

© Cengage Learning 2014

resource

The textbook's Web site contains an Excel *file that will guide you through the chapter's calculations. The file for this chapter is* **Ch03 Tool Kit.xls**, *and we encourage you to open the file and follow along as you read the chapter.*

Financial statement analysis involves (1) comparing a firm's performance with that of other firms in the same industry, and (2) evaluating trends in the firm's financial position over time. Managers use financial analysis to identify situations needing attention, potential lenders use financial analysis to determine whether a company is creditworthy, and stockholders use financial analysis to help predict future earnings, dividends, and free cash flow. This chapter will explain the similarities and differences among these uses.

3-1 Financial Analysis

When we perform a financial analysis, we conduct the following steps.

WWW

See **www.zacks.com** *for a source of standardized financial statements.*

3-1a Gather Data

The first step in financial analysis is to gather data. As discussed in Chapter 2, financial statements can be downloaded from many different Web sites. One of our favorites is Zacks Investment Research, which provides financial statements in a standardized format.

If you cut and paste financial statements from Zacks into a spreadsheet and then perform a financial analysis, you can quickly repeat the analysis on a different company by pasting that company's financial statements into the same cells of the spreadsheet. In other words, you do not need to reinvent the wheel each time you analyze a company.

3-1b Examine the Statement of Cash Flows

Some financial analysis can be done with virtually no calculations. For example, we always look to the statement of cash flows first, particularly the net cash provided by operating activities. Downward trends or negative net cash flow from operations almost always indicate problems. The statement of cash flows section on investing activities shows whether the company has made a big acquisition, especially when compared with the prior years' net cash flows from investing activities. A quick look at the section on financing activities also reveals whether a company is issuing debt or buying back stock; in other words, is the company raising capital from investors or returning it to them?

3-1c Calculate and Examine the Return on Invested Capital and Free Cash Flow

After examining the statement of cash flows, we calculate the free cash flow (FCF) and return on invested capital (ROIC) as described in Chapter 2. The ROIC provides a vital measure of a firm's overall performance. If the ROIC is greater than the company's weighted average cost of capital (WACC), then the company usually is adding value. If the ROIC is less than the WACC, then the company usually has serious problems. No matter what the ROIC tells us about overall performance, it is important to examine specific activities, and to do that we use financial ratios.

3-1d Begin Ratio Analysis

Financial ratios are designed to extract important information that might not be obvious simply from examining a firm's financial statements. For example, suppose Firm A owes \$5 million in debt while Firm B owes \$50 million. Which company is in a stronger financial position? It is impossible to answer this question without first standardizing each firm's debt relative to total assets, earnings, and interest. Such standardized comparisons are provided through *ratio analysis.*

We will calculate the 2013 financial ratios for MicroDrive Inc. using data from the balance sheets and income statements given in Figure 3-1. We will also evaluate the ratios in relation to the industry averages. Note that dollar amounts are in millions.

3-2 Liquidity Ratios

resource
See **Ch03 Tool Kit.xls** *for all calculations.*

As shown in Figure 3-1, MicroDrive has current liabilities of \$780 million that it must pay off within the coming year. Will it have trouble satisfying those obligations? **Liquidity ratios** attempt to answer this type of question. We discuss two commonly used liquidity ratios in this section.

3-2a The Current Ratio

Calculate the **current ratio** by dividing current assets by current liabilities:

$$\text{Current ratio} = \frac{\text{Current assets}}{\text{Current liabilities}}$$

$$= \frac{\$1{,}550}{\$780} = 2.0$$

Industry average = 2.2

FIGURE 3-1

MicroDrive Inc.: Balance Sheets and Income Statements for Years Ending December 31 (Millions of Dollars, Except for Per Share Data)

	A	B	C	D	E
23	*Balance Sheets*			2013	2012
24	*Assets*				
25	Cash and equivalents			$ 50	$ 60
26	Short-term investments			-	40
27	Accounts receivable			500	380
28	Inventories			1,000	820
29	Total current assets			$ 1,550	$ 1,300
30	Net plant and equipment			2,000	1,700
31	Total assets			$ 3,550	$ 3,000
32					
33	*Liabilities and Equity*				
34	Accounts payable			$ 200	$ 190
35	Notes payable			280	130
36	Accruals			300	280
37	Total current liabilities			$ 780	$ 600
38	Long-term bonds			1,200	1,000
39	Total liabilities			$ 1,980	$ 1,600
40	Preferred stock (400,000 shares)			100	100
41	Common stock (50,000,000 shares)			500	500
42	Retained earnings			970	800
43	Total common equity			$ 1,470	$ 1,300
44	Total liabilities and equity			$ 3,550	$ 3,000
45					
46	*Income Statements*			2013	2012
47	Net sales			$ 5,000	$ 4,760
48	Costs of goods sold except depreciation			3,800	3,560
49	Depreciation			200	170
50	Other operating expenses			500	480
51	Earnings before interest and taxes (EBIT)			$ 500	$ 550
52	Less interest			120	100
53	Pretax earnings			$ 380	$ 450
54	Taxes (40%)			152	180
55	Net Income before preferred dividends			$ 228	$ 270
56	Preferred dividends			8	8
57	Net Income available to common stockholders			$ 220	$ 262
58	*Other Data*				
59	Common dividends			$50	$48
60	Addition to retained earnings			$170	$214
61	Lease payments			$28	$28
62	Bonds' required sinking fund payments			$20	$20
63	Common stock price per share			$27	$40

Current assets normally include cash, marketable securities, accounts receivable, and inventories. Current liabilities consist of accounts payable, short-term notes payable, current maturities of long-term debt, accrued taxes, and other accrued expenses.

MicroDrive has a slightly lower current ratio than the average for its industry. Is this good or bad? Sometimes the answer depends on who is asking the question. For example, suppose a supplier is trying to decide whether to extend credit to MicroDrive. In general, creditors like to see a high current ratio. If a company starts to experience financial difficulty, it will begin paying its bills (accounts payable) more slowly and borrowing more from its bank, so its current liabilities will be increasing. If current liabilities are rising faster than current assets, then the current ratio will fall, and this could spell trouble. Because the current ratio provides the best single indicator of the extent to which the claims of short-term creditors are covered by assets that are expected to be converted to cash fairly quickly, it is the most commonly used measure of short-term solvency.

Now consider the current ratio from a shareholder's perspective. A high current ratio could mean that the company has a lot of money tied up in nonproductive assets, such as excess cash or marketable securities. Or perhaps the high current ratio is due to large inventory holdings, which might become obsolete before they can be sold. Thus, shareholders might not want a high current ratio.

An industry average is not a magic number that all firms should strive to maintain—in fact, some well-managed firms will be above the average, while other good firms will be below it. However, if a firm's ratios are far from the averages for its industry, this is a red flag, and analysts should be concerned about why the variance occurs. For example, suppose a low current ratio is traced to low inventories. Is this a competitive advantage resulting from the firm's mastery of just-in-time inventory management, or is it an Achilles' heel that is causing the firm to miss shipments and lose sales? Ratio analysis doesn't answer such questions, but it does point to areas of potential concern.

3-2b The Quick, or Acid Test, Ratio

The **quick ratio**, also called the **acid test ratio**, is calculated by deducting inventories from current assets and then dividing the remainder by current liabilities:

$$\text{Quick ratio} = \frac{\text{Current assets} - \text{Inventories}}{\text{Current liabilities}}$$

$$= \frac{\$1{,}550 - \$1{,}000}{\$780} = 7.0$$

$$\text{Industry average} = 0.8$$

A **liquid asset** is one that trades in an active market, so it can be converted quickly to cash at the going market price. Inventories are typically the least liquid of a firm's current assets; hence they are the current assets on which losses are most likely to occur in a bankruptcy. Therefore, a measure of the firm's ability to pay off short-term obligations without relying on the sale of inventories is important.

MicroDrive's quick ratio is close to the industry average. However, both are below 1.0, which means that inventories would have to be liquidated in order to pay off current liabilities should the need arise.

How does MicroDrive compare to S&P 500 companies? There has been a steady decline in the average liquidity ratios of S&P 500 companies during the past decade. As we write this in 2012, the average current and quick ratios are well below 1.0, so MicroDrive and its industry peers are more liquid than the typical S&P 500 company.

SELF-TEST

Identify two ratios to use to analyze a firm's liquidity position, and write out their equations.

What are the characteristics of a liquid asset? Give some examples.

Which current asset is typically the least liquid?

A company has current liabilities of $800 million, and its current ratio is 2.5. What is its level of current assets? **($2,000 million)** *If this firm's quick ratio is 2, how much inventory does it have?* **($400 million)**

3-3 Asset Management Ratios

Asset management ratios measure how effectively a firm is managing its assets. If a company has excessive investments in assets, then its operating capital is unduly high, which reduces its free cash flow and ultimately its stock price. On the other hand, if a company does not have enough assets, then it may lose sales, which would hurt profitability, free cash flow, and the stock price. Therefore, it is important to have the *right* amount invested in assets. Ratios that analyze the different types of assets are described in this section.

3-3a Evaluating Total Assets: The Total Assets Turnover Ratio

The **total assets turnover ratio** measures the dollars in sales that are generated for each dollar that is tied up in assets:

$$\text{Total assets turnover ratio} = \frac{\text{Sales}}{\text{Total assets}}$$

$$= \frac{\$5{,}000}{\$3{,}550} = 1.4$$

$$\text{Industry average} = 1.8$$

MicroDrive's ratio is somewhat below the industry average, indicating that the company is not generating as much business (relative to its peers) given its total asset investment. In other words, MicroDrive uses its assets relatively inefficiently. The following ratios can be used to identify the specific asset classes that are causing this problem.[1]

[1]Sales occur throughout the year, but assets are reported at end of the period. For a growing company or a company with seasonal variation, it would be better to use *average* assets held during the year when calculating turnover ratios. However, we use year-end values for all turnover ratios so that we are more comparable with most reported industry averages.

3-3b Evaluating Fixed Assets: The Fixed Assets Turnover Ratio

The **fixed assets turnover ratio** measures how effectively the firm uses its plant and equipment. It is the ratio of sales to net fixed assets:

$$\text{Fixed assets turnover ratio} = \frac{\text{Sales}}{\text{Net fixed assets}}$$

$$= \frac{\$5{,}000}{\$2{,}000} = 2.5$$

Industry average = 3.0

MicroDrive's ratio of 2.5 is a little below the industry average, indicating that the firm is not using its fixed assets as intensively as are other firms in its industry.

Inflation can cause problems when interpreting the fixed assets turnover ratio because fixed assets are reported using the historical costs of the assets instead of current replacement costs that may be higher due to inflation. Therefore, a mature firm with fixed assets acquired years ago might well have a higher fixed assets turnover ratio than a younger company with newer fixed assets that are reported at inflated prices relative to the historical prices of the older assets. However, this would reflect the difficulty accountants have in dealing with inflation rather than inefficiency on the part of the new firm. You should be alert to this potential problem when evaluating the fixed assets turnover ratio.

3-3c Evaluating Receivables: The Days Sales Outstanding

Days sales outstanding (DSO), also called the "average collection period" (ACP), is used to appraise accounts receivable, and it is calculated by dividing accounts receivable by average daily sales to find the number of days' sales that are tied up in receivables. Thus, the DSO represents the average length of time that the firm must wait after making a sale before receiving cash, which is the average collection period. MicroDrive's DSO is 37, above the 36-day industry average:

$$\text{DSO} = \frac{\text{Days sales}}{\text{outstanding}} = \frac{\text{Receivables}}{\text{Average sales per day}} = \frac{\text{Receivables}}{\text{Annual sales}/365}$$

$$= \frac{\$500}{\$5{,}000/365} = \frac{\$500}{\$13.7} = 36.5 \text{ days} \approx 37 \text{ days}$$

Industry average = 30 days

MicroDrive's sales terms call for payment within 30 days. The fact that 37 days of sales are outstanding indicates that customers, on average, are not paying their bills on time. As with inventory, high levels of accounts receivable cause high levels of NOWC, which hurts FCF and stock price.

A customer who is paying late may be in financial trouble, which means MicroDrive may have a hard time collecting the receivable. Therefore, if the trend in DSO has been rising unexpectedly, steps should be taken to review credit standards and to expedite the collection of accounts receivable.

3-3d Evaluating Inventories: The Inventory Turnover Ratio

The **inventory turnover ratio** is defined as costs of goods sold (COGS) divided by inventories.[2] The previous ratios use sales instead of COGS. However, sales revenues include costs and profits, whereas inventory usually is reported at cost. Therefore, it is better to compare inventory with costs rather than sales.

The income statement in Figure 3-1 separately reports depreciation and the portion of costs of goods sold that is not comprised of depreciation, which is helpful when calculating cash flows. However, we need the total COGS for calculating the inventory turnover ratio. For MicroDrive, virtually all depreciation is associated with producing its products, so its COGS is:

$$\begin{aligned}\text{COGS} &= \text{Costs of goods sold except depreciation} + \text{Depreciation}\\ &= \$3,800 + \$200 = \$4,000 \text{ million}\end{aligned}$$

We can now calculate the inventory turnover:

$$\text{Inventory turnover ratio} = \frac{\text{COGS}}{\text{Inventories}}$$

$$= \frac{\$3,800 + \$200}{\$1,000} = 4.0$$

$$\text{Industry average} = 5.0$$

As a rough approximation, each item of MicroDrive's inventory is sold out and restocked, or "turned over," 4 times per year.[3]

MicroDrive's turnover of 4 is lower than the industry average of 5. This suggests that MicroDrive is holding too much inventory. High levels of inventory add to net operating working capital (NOWC), which reduces FCF, which leads to lower stock prices. In addition, MicroDrive's low inventory turnover ratio makes us wonder whether the firm is holding obsolete goods not worth their stated value.

In summary, MicroDrive's low fixed asset turnover ratio, high DSO, and low inventory turnover ratio each cause MicroDrive's total assets turnover ratio to be lower than the industry average.

---

[2]In previous editions, we defined the inventory turnover ratio using sales instead of COGS because some compilers of financial ratio statistics, such as Dun & Bradstreet, use the ratio of sales to inventories. However, most sources now report the turnover ratio using COGS, so we have changed our definition to conform to the majority of reporting organizations.

[3]"Turnover" is derived from the old Yankee peddler who would load up his wagon with goods and then go off to peddle his wares. If he made 10 trips per year, stocked 100 pans, and made a gross profit of \$5 per pan, his annual gross profit would be (100)(\$5)(10) = \$5,000. If he "turned over" (i.e., sold) his inventory faster and made 20 trips per year, then his gross profit would double, other things held constant. So, his turnover directly affected his profits.

GLOBAL ECONOMIC CRISIS

© uniquely india/Getty Images

The Global Economic Crisis

The Price Is Right! (Or Wrong!)

How much is an asset worth if no one is buying or selling? The answer to that question matters because an accounting practice called "mark to market" requires that some assets be adjusted on the balance sheet to reflect their "fair market value." The accounting rules are complicated, but the general idea is that if an asset is available for sale, then the balance sheet would be most accurate if it showed the asset's market value. For example, suppose a company purchased $100 million of Treasury bonds and the value of those bonds later fell to $90 million. With mark to market, the company would report the bonds' value on the balance sheet as $90 million, not the original purchase price of $100 million. Notice that marking to market can have a significant impact on financial ratios and thus on investors' perception of a firm's financial health.

But what if the assets are mortgage-backed securities that were originally purchased for $100 million? As defaults increased during 2008, the value of such securities fell rapidly, and then investors virtually stopped trading them. How should the company report them? At the $100 million original price? At a $60 million price that was observed before the market largely dried up? At $25 million when a hedge fund in desperate need for cash to avoid a costly default sold a few of these securities? At $0, because there are no current quotes? Or should they be reported at a price generated by a computer model or in some other manner?

The answer to this is especially important during times of economic stress. Congress, the SEC, FASB, and the U.S. Treasury all are working to find the right answers. If they come up with a price that is too low, it could cause investors mistakenly to believe that some companies are worth much less than their intrinsic values, and this could trigger runs on banks and bankruptcies for companies that might otherwise survive. But if the price is too high, some "walking dead" or "zombie" companies could linger on and later cause even larger losses for investors, including the U.S. government, which is now the largest investor in many financial institutions. Either way, an error in pricing could perhaps trigger a domino effect that might topple the entire financial system. So let's hope the price is right!

SELF-TEST

Identify four ratios that measure how effectively a firm is managing its assets, and write out their equations.

What problem might arise when comparing firms' fixed assets turnover ratios?

A firm has $200 million annual sales, $180 million costs of goods sold, $40 million of inventory, and $60 million of accounts receivable. What is its inventory turnover ratio? **(4.5)** *What is its DSO based on a 365-day year?* **(109.5 days)**

3-4 Debt Management Ratios

The extent to which a firm uses debt financing is called **financial leverage**. Here are three important implications: (1) Stockholders can control a firm with smaller investments of their own equity if they finance part of the firm with debt. (2) If the firm's assets generate a higher pre-tax return than the interest rate on debt, then the shareholders' returns are magnified, or "leveraged." Conversely, shareholders' losses are also magnified if assets generate a pre-tax return less than the interest rate. (3) If a company has high leverage, even a small decline in performance might cause the firm's value to fall below the amount it owes to creditors. Therefore, a creditor's position becomes riskier as leverage increases. Keep these three points in mind as you read the following sections.

3-4a How the Firm Is Financed: Leverage Ratios

MicroDrive's two primary types of debt are notes payable and long-term bonds, but more complicated companies also might report the portion of long-term debt due within a year, the value of capitalized leases, and other types of obligations that charge interest. For MicroDrive, total debt is:

$$\text{Total debt} = \text{Notes payable} + \text{Long-term bonds}$$
$$= \$280 + \$1{,}200 = \$1{,}480 \text{ million}$$

Is this too much debt, not enough, or the right amount? To answer this question, we begin by calculating the percentage of MicroDrive's assets that are financed by debt. The ratio of total debt to total assets is called the **debt-to-assets ratio**. It is sometimes shortened to the **debt ratio**.[4] Total debt is the sum of all short-term debt and long-term debt; it does not include other liabilities. MicroDrive's debt ratio is:

$$\text{Debt-to-assets ratio} = \text{Debt ratio} = \frac{\text{Total debt}}{\text{Total assets}}$$
$$= \frac{\$280 + \$1{,}200}{\$3{,}550} = \frac{\$1{,}480}{\$3{,}550} = 41.7\%$$

$$\text{Industry average} = 25.0\%$$

MicroDrive's debt ratio is 41.7%, which is substantially higher than the 25% industry average.

The debt-to-equity ratio is defined as:[5]

$$\text{Debt-to-equity ratio} = \frac{\text{Total debt}}{\text{Total common equity}}$$
$$= \frac{\$280 + \$1{,}200}{\$1{,}470} = \frac{\$1{,}480}{\$1{,}470} = 1.01$$

$$\text{Industry average} = 0.46$$

The debt-to-equity ratio shows that MicroDrive has $1.01 of debt for every dollar of equity, whereas the debt ratio shows that 41.7% of MicroDrive's assets are financed by debt. We find it more intuitive to think about the percentage of the firm that is financed with debt, so we usually use the debt ratio. However, the debt-to-equity ratio is also widely used, so you should know how to interpret it as well.

Be sure you know how a ratio is defined before you use it. Some sources define the debt ratio using only long-term debt instead of total debt; others use investor-supplied capital instead of total assets. Some sources make similar changes in the debt-to-equity ratio, so be sure to check your source's definition.

---

[4] In previous editions we defined the debt ratio as total liabilities divided by total assets. For better comparability with Web-based reporting sources, we have changed our definition to total debt divided by total assets.

[5] In previous editions we defined the debt-to-equity ratio as total liabilities divided by total common equity. For better comparability with Web-based reporting sources, we have changed our definition to total debt divided by total common equity.

Sometimes it is useful to express debt ratios in terms of market values. It is easy to calculate the market value of equity, which is equal to the stock price multiplied by the number of shares. MicroDrive's market value of equity is $27(50) = $1,350. Often it is difficult to estimate the market value of debt, so many analysts use the debt reported in the financial statements. The market debt ratio is defined as:

$$\text{Market debt ratio} = \frac{\text{Total debt}}{\text{Total debt} + \text{Market value of equity}}$$

$$= \frac{\$280 + \$1{,}200}{(\$280 + \$1{,}200) + (\$27 \times 50)} = \frac{\$1{,}480}{\$1{,}480 + \$1{,}350}$$

$$= 52.3\%$$

$$\text{Industry average} = 20.0\%$$

MicroDrive's market debt ratio in the previous year was 36.1%. The big increase was due to two major factors: Debt increased and the stock price fell. The stock price reflects a company's prospects for generating future cash flows, so a decline in stock price indicates a likely decline in future cash flows. Thus, the market debt ratio reflects a source of risk that is not captured by the conventional debt ratio.

Finally, the ratio of total liabilities to total assets shows the extent to which a firm's assets are not financed by equity. The **liabilities-to-assets ratio** is defined as:

$$\text{Liabilities-to-assets ratio} = \frac{\text{Total liabilities}}{\text{Total assets}}$$

$$= \frac{\$1{,}980}{\$3{,}550} = 55.8\%$$

$$\text{Industry average} = 45.0\%$$

For all the ratios we examined, MicroDrive has more leverage than its industry peers. The next section shows how close MicroDrive might be to serious financial distress.

3-4b Ability to Pay Interest: Times-Interest-Earned Ratio

The **times-interest-earned (TIE) ratio,** also called the **interest coverage ratio,** is determined by dividing earnings before interest and taxes (EBIT in Figure 3-1) by the interest expense:

$$\text{Times-interest-earned (TIE) ratio} = \frac{\text{EBIT}}{\text{Interest expense}}$$

$$= \frac{\$500}{\$120} = 4.2$$

$$\text{Industry average} = 10.0$$

The TIE ratio measures the extent to which operating income can decline before the firm is unable to meet its annual interest costs. Failure to meet this obligation can bring legal action by the firm's creditors, possibly resulting in bankruptcy. Note that earnings before interest and taxes, rather than net income, is used in the numerator. Because interest is paid with pre-tax dollars, the firm's ability to pay current interest is not affected by taxes.

MicroDrive's interest is covered 4.2 times, which is well above 1, the point at which EBIT isn't sufficient to pay interest. The industry average is 10, so even though MicroDrive has enough EBIT to pay interest expenses, it has a relatively low margin of safety compared to its peers. Thus, the TIE ratio reinforces the conclusion from our analysis of the debt ratio that MicroDrive might face difficulties if it attempts to borrow additional funds.

3-4c Ability to Service Debt: EBITDA Coverage Ratio

The TIE ratio is useful for assessing a company's ability to meet interest charges on its debt, but this ratio has two shortcomings: (1) Interest is not the only fixed financial charge—companies must also reduce debt on schedule, and many firms lease assets and thus must make lease payments. Failure to repay debt or meet lease payments may force them into bankruptcy. (2) EBIT (earnings before interest and taxes) does not represent all the cash flow available to service debt, especially if a firm has high depreciation and/or amortization charges. A better coverage ratio would take into account the "cash" earnings and the other financial charges.

MicroDrive had $500 million of EBIT and $200 million in depreciation, for an EBITDA (earnings before interest, taxes, depreciation, and amortization) of $700 million. Also, lease payments of $28 million were deducted while calculating EBIT. That $28 million was available to meet financial charges; hence it must be added back, bringing the total available to cover fixed financial charges to $728 million. Fixed financial charges consisted of $120 million of interest, $20 million of sinking fund payments, and $28 million for lease payments, for a total of $168 million.[6]

MicroDrive's EBITDA coverage ratio is:[7]

$$\text{EBITDA coverage ratio} = \frac{\text{EBITDA} + \text{Lease payments}}{\text{Interest} + \text{Principal payments} + \text{Lease payments}}$$

$$= \frac{(\$500 + 200) + \$28}{\$120 + \$20 + \$28} = \frac{\$728}{\$168} = 4.3$$

$$\text{Industry average} = 12.0$$

MicroDrive covered its fixed financial charges by 4.3 times. MicroDrive's ratio is well below the industry average, so again the company seems to have a relatively high level of debt.

The EBITDA coverage ratio is most useful for relatively short-term lenders such as banks, which rarely make loans (except real estate-backed loans) for longer than about 5 years. Over a relatively short period, depreciation-generated funds can be used to service debt. Over a longer time, those funds must be reinvested to maintain the plant and equipment or else the company cannot remain in business. Therefore, banks and other relatively short-term lenders focus on the EBITDA coverage ratio, whereas long-term bondholders focus on the TIE ratio.

---

[6]A sinking fund is a required annual payment designed to reduce the balance of a bond or preferred stock issue.

[7]Different analysts define the EBITDA coverage ratio in different ways. For example, some omit the lease payment information; others "gross up" principal payments by dividing them by 1 − T because these payments are not tax deductions and so must be made with after-tax cash flows. We included lease payments because for many firms they are quite important, and failing to make them can lead to bankruptcy as surely as can failure to make payments on "regular" debt. We did not gross up principal payments because, if a company is in financial difficulty, then its tax rate will probably be zero; hence the gross up is not necessary whenever the ratio is really important.

SELF-TEST

How does the use of financial leverage affect current stockholders' control position?

Name six ratios that are used to measure the extent to which a firm uses financial leverage, and write out their equations.

A company has EBITDA of $600 million, interest payments of $60 million, lease payments of $40 million, and required principal payments (due this year) of $30 million. What is its EBITDA coverage ratio? **(4.9)**

3-5 Profitability Ratios

Profitability is the net result of a number of policies and decisions. The ratios examined thus far provide useful clues as to the effectiveness of a firm's operations, but the **profitability ratios** go on to show the combined effects of liquidity, asset management, and debt on operating results.

3-5a Net Profit Margin

The **net profit margin**, also called the **profit margin on sales**, is calculated by dividing net income by sales. It gives the profit per dollar of sales:

$$\text{Net profit margin} = \frac{\text{Net income available to common stockholders}}{\text{Sales}}$$

$$= \frac{\$220}{\$5{,}000} = 4.4\%$$

$$\text{Industry average} = 6.2\%$$

MicroDrive's net profit margin is below the industry average of 6.2%, but why is this so? Is it due to inefficient operations, high interest expenses, or both?

Instead of just comparing net income to sales, many analysts also break the income statement into smaller parts to identify the sources of a low net profit margin. For example, the **operating profit margin** is defined as

$$\text{Operating profit margin} = \frac{\text{EBIT}}{\text{Sales}}$$

The operating profit margin identifies how a company is performing with respect to its operations before the impact of interest expenses is considered.

Some analysts drill even deeper by breaking operating costs into their components. For example, the **gross profit margin** is defined as

$$\text{Gross profit margin} = \frac{\text{Sales} - \text{Cost of goods sold}}{\text{Sales}}$$

The gross profit margin identifies the gross profit per dollar of sales before any other expenses are deducted.

Rather than calculate each type of profit margin here, later in the chapter we will use common size analysis and percent change analysis to focus on different parts of the

The World Might Be Flat, but Global Accounting Is Bumpy! The Case of IFRS versus FASB

© Rob Webb/Getty Images

In a flat world, distance is no barrier. Work flows to where it can be done most efficiently, and capital flows to where it can be invested most profitably. If a radiologist in India is more efficient than one in the United States, then images will be e-mailed to India for diagnosis; if rates of return are higher in Brazil, then investors throughout the world will provide funding for Brazilian projects. One key to "flattening" the world is agreement on common standards. For example, there are common Internet standards so that users throughout the world are able to communicate.

A glaring exception to standardization is in accounting. The Securities and Exchange Commission (SEC) in the United States requires firms to comply with standards set by the Financial Accounting Standards Board (FASB). But the European Union requires all EU-listed companies to comply with the International Financial Reporting Standards (IFRS) as defined by the International Accounting Standards Board (IASB).

IFRS tends to rely on general principles, whereas FASB standards are rules-based. As the recent accounting scandals demonstrate, many U.S. companies have been able to comply with U.S. rules while violating the principle, or intent, underlying the rules. The United States is likely to adopt IFRS, or a slightly modified IFRS, but the question is "When?" The SEC estimated that a large company is likely to incur costs of up to $32 million when switching to IFRS. So even though a survey by the accounting firm KPMG indicates that most investors and analysts favor adoption of IFRS, the path to adoption is likely to be bumpy.

Sources: See the Web sites of the IASB and the FASB, **www.iasb.org.uk** and **www.fasb.org**. Also see David M. Katz and Sarah Johnson, "Top Obama Advisers Clash on Global Accounting Standards," January 15, 2009, at **www.cfo.com**; and "Survey Favors IFRS Adoption," February 3, 2009, at **www.webcpa.com**.

income statement. In addition, we will use the DuPont equation to show how the ratios interact with one another.

Sometimes it is confusing to have so many different types of profit margins. To simplify the situation, we will focus primarily on the net profit margin throughout the book and call it the "profit margin."

3-5b Basic Earning Power (BEP) Ratio

The **basic earning power (BEP) ratio** is calculated by dividing earnings before interest and taxes (EBIT) by total assets:

$$\text{Basic earning power (BEP ratio)} = \frac{\text{EBIT}}{\text{Total assets}}$$

$$= \frac{\$500}{\$3{,}550} = 14.1\%$$

$$\text{Industry average} = 20.2\%$$

This ratio shows the earning power of the firm's assets before the influence of taxes and leverage, and it is useful for comparing firms with different tax situations and different degrees of financial leverage. Because of its low turnover ratios and low profit margin on sales, MicroDrive is not getting as high a return on its assets as is the average company in its industry.

3-5c Return on Total Assets

The ratio of net income to total assets measures the **return on total assets (ROA)** after interest and taxes. This ratio is also called the **return on assets** and is defined as follows:

$$\text{Return on total assets} = \text{ROA} = \frac{\text{Net income available to common stockholders}}{\text{Total assets}}$$

$$= \frac{\$220}{\$3{,}550} = 6.2\%$$

$$\text{Industry average} = 11.0\%$$

MicroDrive's 6.2% return is well below the 9% average for the industry. This low return is due to (1) the company's low basic earning power, and (2) high interest costs resulting from its above-average use of debt. Both of these factors cause MicroDrive's net income to be relatively low.

3-5d Return on Common Equity

The ratio of net income to common equity measures the **return on common equity (ROE)**:

$$\text{Return on common equity} = \text{ROE} = \frac{\text{Net income available to common stockholders}}{\text{Common equity}}$$

$$= \frac{\$220}{\$1{,}470} = 15.0\%$$

$$\text{Industry average} = 19.0\%$$

Stockholders invest to earn a return on their money, and this ratio tells how well they are doing in an accounting sense. MicroDrive's 15% return is below the 19% industry average, but not as far below as its return on total assets. This somewhat better result is due to the company's greater use of debt, a point that we explain in detail later in the chapter.

SELF-TEST

Identify and write out the equations for four profitability ratios.

Why is the basic earning power ratio useful?

Why does the use of debt lower ROA?

What does ROE measure?

A company has $200 billion of sales and $10 billion of net income. Its total assets are $100 billion, financed half by debt and half by common equity. What is its profit margin? **(5%)** *What is its ROA?* **(10%)** What is its ROE? **(20%)** *Would ROA increase if the firm used less leverage?* **(Yes)** *Would ROE increase?* **(No)**

3-6 Market Value Ratios

Market value ratios relate a firm's stock price to its earnings, cash flow, and book value per share. Market value ratios are a way to measure the value of a company's stock relative to that of another company.

3-6a Price/Earnings Ratio

The **price/earnings (P/E) ratio** shows how much investors are willing to pay per dollar of reported profits. MicroDrive has $220 million in net income and 50 million shares, so its earnings per share (EPS) is $4.40 = $220/50. MicroDrive's stock sells for $27, so its P/E ratio is:

$$\text{Price/earnings (P/E) ratio} = \frac{\text{Price per share}}{\text{Earnings per share}}$$

$$= \frac{\$27.00}{\$4.40} = 6.1$$

$$\text{Industry average} = 10.5$$

Price/earnings ratios are higher for firms with strong growth prospects, other things held constant, but they are lower for riskier firms. Because MicroDrive's P/E ratio is below the average, this suggests that the company is regarded as being somewhat riskier than most, as having poorer growth prospects, or both. In early 2012, the average P/E ratio for firms in the S&P 500 was 13.4, indicating that investors were willing to pay $13.40 for every dollar of earnings.

3-6b Price/Cash Flow Ratio

Stock prices depend on a company's ability to generate cash flows. Consequently, investors often look at the **price/cash flow ratio**, where cash flow is defined as net income plus depreciation and amortization:

$$\text{Price/cash flow ratio} = \frac{\text{Price per share}}{\text{Cash flow per share}}$$

$$= \frac{\$27.00}{(\$220 + \$200)/50} = 3.2$$

$$\text{Industry average} = 6.8$$

MicroDrive's price/cash flow ratio is also below the industry average, once again suggesting that its growth prospects are below average, its risk is above average, or both.

The **price/EBITDA ratio** is similar to the price/cash flow ratio, except the price/EBITDA ratio measures performance before the impact of interest expenses and taxes, making it a better measure of operating performance. MicroDrive's EBITDA per share is ($500 + $200)/50 = $14, so its price/EBITDA is $27/$14 = 1.9. The industry average price/EBITDA ratio is 4.0, so we see again that MicroDrive is below the industry average.

Note that some analysts look at other multiples as well. For example, depending on the industry, some may look at measures such as price/sales or price/customers. Ultimately, though, value depends on free cash flows, so if these "exotic" ratios do not forecast future free cash flow, they may turn out to be misleading. This was true in the case of the dot-com retailers before they crashed and burned in 2000, costing investors many billions.

3-6c Market/Book Ratio

The ratio of a stock's market price to its book value gives another indication of how investors regard the company. Companies with relatively high rates of return on equity generally sell at higher multiples of book value than those with low returns. First, we find MicroDrive's book value per share:

$$\text{Book value per share} = \frac{\text{Total common equity}}{\text{Shares outstanding}}$$

$$= \frac{\$1.470}{50} = \$29.4$$

Now we divide the market price by the book value to get a **market/book (M/B) ratio:**

$$\text{Market/book ratio} = \text{M/B} = \frac{\text{Market price per share}}{\text{Book value per share}}$$

$$= \frac{\$27.00}{\$29.40} = 0.9$$

$$\text{Industry average} = 1.8$$

Investors are willing to pay relatively little for a dollar of MicroDrive's book value.

The book value is a record of the past, showing the cumulative amount that stockholders have invested, either directly by purchasing newly issued shares or indirectly through retaining earnings. In contrast, the market price is forward-looking, incorporating investors' expectations of future cash flows. For example, in early 2012 Bank of America had a market/book ratio of only 0.4, reflecting the financial services industry's problems, whereas Apple's market/book ratio was 5.6, indicating that investors expected Apple's past successes to continue.

Table 3-1 summarizes selected ratios for MicroDrive. As the table indicates, the company has many problems.

SELF-TEST

Describe three ratios that relate a firm's stock price to its earnings, cash flow, and book value per share, and write out their equations.

What does the price/earnings (P/E) ratio show? If one firm's P/E ratio is lower than that of another, what are some factors that might explain the difference?

How is book value per share calculated? Explain why book values often deviate from market values.

A company has $6 billion of net income, $2 billion of depreciation and amortization, $80 billion of common equity, and 1 billion shares of stock. If its stock price is $96 per share, what is its price/earnings ratio? **(16)** *Its price/cash flow ratio?* **(12)** *Its market/book ratio?* **(1.2)**

TABLE 3-1
MicroDrive Inc.: Summary of Selected Financial Ratios (Millions of Dollars)

Ratio	Formula	Calculation	Ratio	Industry Average	Comment
Liquidity					
Current	Current assets / Current liabilities	$1,550 / $780 =	2.0	2.2	Poor
Quick	(Current assets − Inventories) / Current liabilities	$1,550 / $780 =	0.7	0.8	Poor
Asset Management					
Total assets turnover	Sales / Total assets	$5,000 / $3,550 =	1.4	1.8	Poor
Fixed assets turnover	Sales / Net fixed assets	$5,000 / $2,000 =	2.5	3.0	Poor
Days sales outstanding (DSO)	Receivables / Annual sales/365	$500 / $13.7 =	36.5	30.0	Poor
Inventory turnover	COGS / Inventories	$4,000 / $1,000 =	4.0	5.0	Poor
Debt Management					
Debt-to-assets ratio	Total debt / Total assets	$1,480 / $3,550 =	41.7%	25.0%	High (risky)
Times-interest-earned (TIE)	Earnings before interest and taxes (EBIT) / Interest charges	$500 / $120 =	4.2	10.0	Low (risky)
Profitability					
Profit margin on sales	Net income available to common stockholders / Sales	$220 / $5,000 =	4.4%	6.2%	Poor
Basic earning power (BEP)	Earnings before interest and taxes (EBIT) / Total assets	$500 / $3,550 =	14.1%	20.2%	Poor
Return on total assets (ROA)	Net income available to common stockholders / Total assets	$220 / $3,550 =	6.2%	11.0%	Poor
Return on common equity (ROE)	Net income available to common stockholders / Common equity	$220 / $1,470 =	15.0%	19.0%	Poor
Market Value					
Price/earnings (P/E)	Price per share / Earnings per share	$27.00 / $4.40 =	6.1	10.5	Low
Market/book (M/B)	Market price per share / Book value per share	$27.00 / $29.40 =	0.9	1.8	Low

© Cengage Learning 2014

3-7 Trend Analysis, Common Size Analysis, and Percentage Change Analysis

Trends give clues as to whether a firm's financial condition is likely to improve or deteriorate. To do a **trend analysis**, you examine a ratio over time, as shown in Figure 3-2. This graph shows that MicroDrive's rate of return on common equity has been declining since 2011, in contrast to the industry average. All the other ratios could be analyzed similarly.

In a **common size analysis**, all income statement items are divided by sales, and all balance sheet items are divided by total assets. Thus, a common size income statement shows each item as a percentage of sales, and a common size balance sheet shows each item as a percentage of total assets.[8] The advantage of common size analysis is that it facilitates comparisons of balance sheets and income statements over time and across companies.

Common size statements are easy to generate if the financial statements are in a spreadsheet. In fact, if you obtain your data from a source that uses standardized financial statements, then it is easy to cut and paste the data for a new company over your original company's data, and all of your spreadsheet formulas will be valid for the new company. We generated Figure 3-3 in the *Excel* file ***Ch03 Tool Kit.xls.*** Figure 3-3 shows MicroDrive's 2012 and 2013 common size income statements, along with the composite statement for the industry. (*Note:* Rounding may cause addition/subtraction differences in Figures 3-3, 3-4, and 3-5.) MicroDrive's EBIT is slightly below average, and its interest expenses are slightly above average. The net effect is a relatively low profit margin.

FIGURE 3-2

MicroDrive, Inc.: Trend Analysis of Rate of Return on Common Equity

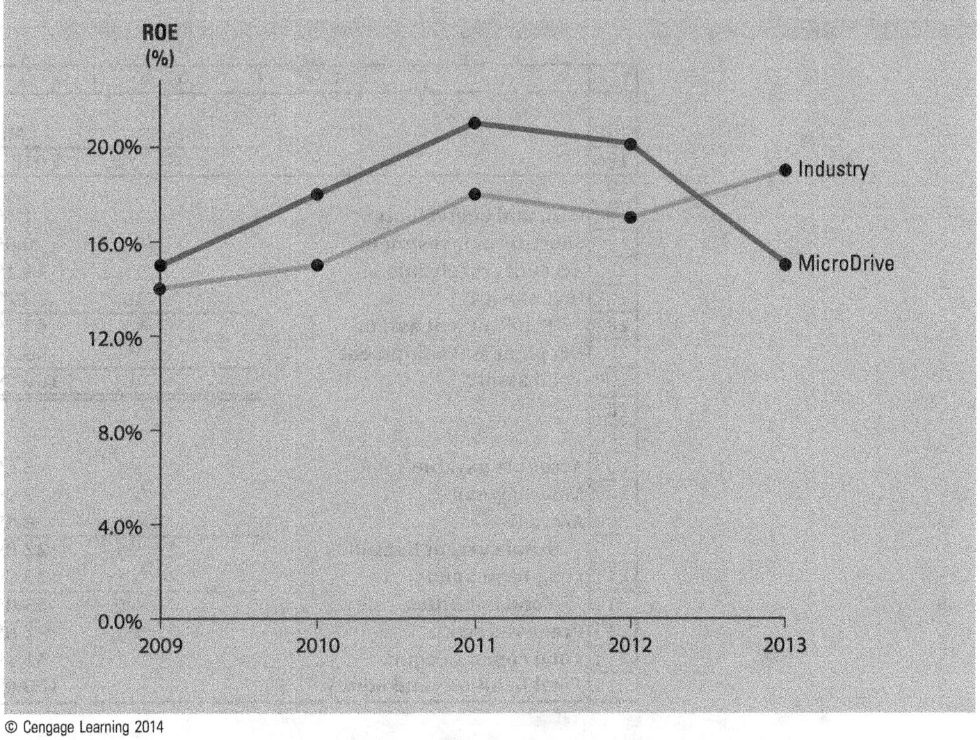

© Cengage Learning 2014

[8]Some sources of industry data, such as Risk Management Associates (formerly known as Robert Morris Associates), are presented exclusively in common size form.

FIGURE 3-3

MicroDrive Inc.: Common Size Income Statement

	A	B	C	D	E	F
175				Industry Composite	MicroDrive	
176				2013	2013	2012
177	Net sales			100.0%	100.0%	100.0%
178	Costs of goods sold except depreciation			75.5%	76.0%	74.8%
179	Depreciation			3.0%	4.0%	3.6%
180	Other operating expenses			10.0%	10.0%	10.1%
181	Earnings before interest and taxes (EBIT)			11.5%	10.0%	11.6%
182	Less interest			1.2%	2.4%	2.1%
183	Pretax earnings			10.4%	7.6%	9.5%
184	Taxes (40%)			4.1%	3.0%	3.8%
185	Net Income before preferred dividends			6.2%	4.6%	5.7%
186	Preferred dividends			0.0%	0.2%	0.2%
187	Net Income available to common stockholders			6.2%	4.4%	5.5%

FIGURE 3-4

MicroDrive Inc.: Common Size Balance Sheet

	A	B	C	D	E
195			Industry Composite	MicroDrive	
196			2013	2013	2012
197	*Assets*				
198	Cash and equivalents		1.8%	1.4%	2.0%
199	Short-term investments		0.0%	0.0%	1.3%
200	Accounts receivable		14.0%	14.1%	12.7%
201	Inventories		26.3%	28.2%	27.3%
202	Total current assets		42.1%	43.7%	43.3%
203	Net plant and equipment		57.9%	56.3%	56.7%
204	Total assets		100.0%	100.0%	100.0%
205					
206	*Liabilities and Equity*				
207	Accounts payable		7.0%	5.6%	6.3%
208	Notes payable		0.0%	7.9%	4.3%
209	Accruals		12.3%	8.5%	9.3%
210	Total current liabilities		19.3%	22.0%	20.0%
211	Long-term bonds		25.4%	33.8%	33.3%
212	Total liabilities		44.7%	55.8%	53.3%
213	Preferred stock		0.0%	2.8%	3.3%
214	Total common equity		55.3%	41.4%	43.3%
215	Total liabilities and equity		100.0%	100.0%	100.0%

FIGURE 3-5

MicroDrive Inc.: Income Statement Percentage Change Analysis

	A	B	C	D
225	Base year = 2012			Percent Change in 2013
226				
227	Net sales			5.0%
228	Costs of goods sold except depreciation			6.7%
229	Depreciation			17.6%
230	Other operating expenses			4.2%
231	Earnings before interest and taxes (EBIT)			(9.1%)
232	Less interest			20.0%
233	Pretax earnings			(15.6%)
234	Taxes (40%)			(15.6%)
235	Net Income before preferred dividends			(15.6%)
236	Preferred dividends			0.0%
237	Net income available to common stockholders			(16.0%)

resource

See *Ch03 Tool Kit.xls* for details.

Figure 3-4 shows MicroDrive's common size balance sheets along with the industry composite. Its accounts receivable are significantly higher than the industry average, its inventories are significantly higher, and it uses much more debt than the average firm.

In **percentage change analysis**, growth rates are calculated for all income statement items and balance sheet accounts relative to a base year. To illustrate, Figure 3-5 contains MicroDrive's income statement percentage change analysis for 2013 relative to 2012. Sales increased at a 5% rate during 2013, but EBIT fell by 9.1%. Part of this decline was due to an increase in depreciation, which is a noncash expense, but the cost of goods sold also increased by a little more than the growth in sales. In addition, interest expenses grew by 20%. We apply the same type of analysis to the balance sheets (see the file ***Ch03 Tool Kit.xls***), which shows that inventories grew at a whopping 22% rate and accounts receivable grew over 31%. With only a 5% growth in sales, the extreme growth in receivables and inventories should be of great concern to MicroDrive's managers.

SELF-TEST

What is a trend analysis, and what information does it provide?

What is common size analysis?

What is percentage change analysis?

3-8 Tying the Ratios Together: The DuPont Equation

In ratio analysis, it is sometimes easy to miss the forest for all the trees. In particular, how do managerial actions affecting a firm's profitability, asset efficiency, and financial leverage interact to determine the return on equity, a performance measure that is important for investors? The extended **DuPont equation** provides just such a framework.

The DuPont equation uses two ratios we covered previously, the profit margin and the total asset turnover ratio, as measures of profitability and asset efficiency. But it also uses a new measure of financial leverage, the *equity multiplier*, which is the ratio of assets to common equity:

$$\text{Equity multiplier} = \frac{\text{Total assets}}{\text{Common equity}} \quad (3\text{-}1)$$

Using this new definition of financial leverage, the extended DuPont equation is:

$$\begin{aligned}\text{ROE} &= \frac{\text{Net income}}{\text{Sales}} = \frac{\text{Net income}}{\text{Sales}} \times \frac{\text{Sales}}{\text{Total assets}} \times \frac{\text{Total assets}}{\text{Common equity}} \\ &= (\text{Profit margin})(\text{Total assets turnover})(\text{Equity multiplier})\end{aligned} \quad (3\text{-}2)$$

As calculated previously, MicroDrive's 2013 profit margin is 4.4% and its total assets turnover ratio is 1.41. MicroDrive's equity multiplier is:

$$\text{Equity multiplier} = \frac{\$3,550}{\$1,470} = 2.415$$

Applying the DuPont equation to MicroDrive, its return on equity is:

$$\text{ROE} = (4.4\%)(1.41)(2.415) = 15\%$$

Sometimes it is useful to focus just on asset profitability and financial leverage. Firms that have a lot of financial leverage (i.e., a lot of liabilities or preferred stock) have a high equity multiplier because the assets are financed with a relatively smaller amount of equity. Therefore, the return on equity (ROE) depends on the ROA and the use of leverage:

$$\begin{aligned}\text{ROE} &= \text{ROA} \times \text{Equity multiplier} \\ &= \frac{\text{Net income}}{\text{Total assets}} \times \frac{\text{Total assets}}{\text{Common equity}}\end{aligned} \quad (3\text{-}3)$$

Using Equation 3-3, we see that MicroDrive's ROE is 15.0%, the same value given by the DuPont equation:

$$\text{ROE} = 6.20\% \times 2.415 = 15\%$$

The insights provided by the DuPont model are valuable, and the model can be used for "quick and dirty" estimates of the impact that operating changes have on returns. For example, holding all else equal, if MicroDrive can implement lean production techniques and increase to 1.8 its ratio of sales to total assets, then its ROE will improve to (4.4%)(1.8)(2.415) = 19.1%.

For a more complete "what if" analysis, most companies use a forecasting model such as the one described in Chapter 12.

SELF-TEST

Explain how the extended, or modified, DuPont equation can be used to reveal the basic determinants of ROE.

What is the equity multiplier?

A company has a profit margin of 6%, a total asset turnover ratio of 2, and an equity multiplier of 1.5. What is its ROE? **(18%)**

3-9 Comparative Ratios and Benchmarking

Ratio analysis involves comparisons. A company's ratios are compared with those of other firms in the same industry—that is, with industry average figures. However, like most firms, MicroDrive's managers go one step further: they also compare their ratios with those of a smaller set of the leading computer companies. This technique is called **benchmarking**, and the companies used for the comparison are called **benchmark companies**. For example, MicroDrive benchmarks against five other firms that its management considers to be the best-managed companies with operations similar to its own.

Many companies also benchmark various parts of their overall operation against top companies, whether they are in the same industry or not. For example, MicroDrive has a division that sells hard drives directly to consumers through catalogs and the Internet. This division's shipping department benchmarks against Amazon, even though they are in different industries, because Amazon's shipping department is one of the best. MicroDrive wants its own shippers to strive to match Amazon's record for on-time shipments.

Comparative ratios are available from a number of sources, including *Value Line*, Dun and Bradstreet (D&B), and the *Annual Statement Studies* published by Risk Management Associates, which is the national association of bank loan officers. Table 3-2 reports selected ratios from Reuters for Apple and its industry, revealing that Apple has a much higher profit margin and lower debt ratio than its peers.

Each data-supplying organization uses a somewhat different set of ratios designed for its own purposes. For example, D&B deals mainly with small firms, many of which are proprietorships, and it sells its services primarily to banks and other lenders. Therefore, D&B is concerned largely with the creditor's viewpoint, and its ratios emphasize current assets and liabilities, not market value ratios. So, when you select a comparative data source, you should be sure that your own emphasis is similar to that of the agency whose ratios you plan to use. Additionally, there are often definitional differences in the ratios presented by different sources, so before using a source, be sure to verify the exact definitions of the ratios to ensure consistency with your own work.

SELF-TEST

Compare and contrast trend analysis and comparative ratio analysis.

Explain benchmarking.

TABLE 3-2
Comparative Ratios for Apple Inc., the Computer Hardware Industry, and the Technology Sector

Ratio	Apple	Computer Hardware Industry[a]	Technology Sector[b]
P/E ratio	15.53	13.69	20.92
Market to book	5.64	2.22	3.6
Net profit margin	21.48	22.48	23.48
Quick ratio	1.55	1.19	1.06
Current ratio	1.58	1.5	2.72
Total debt-to-equity	0.00	56.48	21.7
Interest coverage (TIE)[c]	--	3.38	1.3
Return on assets	29.26	7.06	13.13
Return on equity	35.28	36.28	37.28
Inventory turnover	69.42	15.4	466.83
Asset turnover	1.13	1.45	1.02

[a]The computer hardware industry is composed of 50 firms, including IBM, Dell, Apple, Sun Microsystems, Gateway, and Silicon Graphics.
[b]The technology sector contains 11 industries, including communications equipment, computer hardware, computer networks, semiconductors, and software and programming.
[c]Apple had more interest income than interest expense.

Source: Adapted from **www.reuters.com**, March 10, 2012. Select Market, Stocks, and enter the ticker symbol for Apple, AAPL. Select Financials to see updated data.

3-10 Uses and Limitations of Ratio Analysis

Ratio analysis provides useful information concerning a company's operations and financial condition, but it has limitations that necessitate care and judgment. Some potential problems include the following.

1. Many large firms operate different divisions in different industries, and for such companies it is difficult to develop a meaningful set of industry averages. Therefore, industry averages are more meaningful for small, narrowly focused firms than for large, multidivisional ones.
2. To set goals for high-level performance, it is best to benchmark on the industry *leaders'* ratios rather than the industry *average* ratios.
3. Inflation may badly distort firms' balance sheets—reported values are often substantially different from "true" values. Further, because inflation affects depreciation charges and inventory costs, reported profits are also affected. Thus, inflation can distort a ratio analysis for one firm over time or a comparative analysis of firms of different ages.
4. Seasonal factors can distort a ratio analysis. For example, the inventory turnover ratio for a food processor will be radically different if the balance sheet figure used for inventory is the one just before versus the one just after the close of the canning season. This problem can be minimized by using monthly averages for inventory (and receivables) when calculating turnover ratios.

Ratio Analysis on the Web

© Rob Webb/Getty Images

A great source for comparative ratios is **www.reuters.com**. Enter a company's ticker at the top of the page. This brings up a table with the stock quote, company information, and additional links. Select Financials, which brings up a page with a detailed ratio analysis for the company and includes comparative ratios for other companies in the same sector, the same industry, and the S&P 500. (Note: You may have to register to get extra features, but registration is free.)

5. Firms can employ **"window dressing" techniques** to make their financial statements look stronger. To illustrate, suppose a company takes out a 2-year loan in late December. Because the loan is for more than 1 year, it is not included in current liabilities even though the cash received through the loan is reported as a current asset. This improves the current and quick ratios and makes the year-end balance sheet look stronger. If the company pays the loan back in January, then the transaction was strictly window dressing.
6. Companies' choices of different accounting practices can distort comparisons. For example, choices of inventory valuation and depreciation methods affect financial statements differently, making comparisons among companies less meaningful. As another example, if one firm leases a substantial amount of its productive equipment, then its assets may appear low relative to sales (because leased assets often do not appear on the balance sheet) and its debt may appear low (because the liability associated with the lease obligation may not be shown as debt).[9]

In summary, conducting ratio analysis in a mechanical, unthinking manner is dangerous. But when ratio analysis is used intelligently and with good judgment, it can provide useful insights into a firm's operations and identify the right questions to ask.

SELF-TEST

List several potential problems with ratio analysis.

3-11 Looking Beyond the Numbers

Sound financial analysis involves more than just calculating and comparing ratios—qualitative factors must be considered. Here are some questions suggested by the American Association of Individual Investors (AAII).

1. To what extent are the company's revenues tied to one key customer or to one key product? To what extent does the company rely on a single supplier? Reliance on single customers, products, or suppliers increases risk.
2. What percentage of the company's business is generated overseas? Companies with a large percentage of overseas business are exposed to risk of currency exchange volatility and political instability.
3. What are the probable actions of current competitors and the likelihood of additional new competitors?

[9]This may change when FASB and IASB complete their joint project on leasing. As of mid-2012, the estimated project completion date was not certain. For the current status of the project, go to **www.fasb.org** and select the tab for Projects.

4. Do the company's future prospects depend critically on the success of products currently in the pipeline or on existing products?
5. How does the legal and regulatory environment affect the company?

SELF-TEST

What qualitative factors should analysts consider when evaluating a company's likely future financial performance?

SUMMARY

This chapter explained techniques investors and managers use to analyze financial statements. The key concepts covered are listed below.

- **Liquidity ratios** show the relationship of a firm's current assets to its current liabilities and thus its ability to meet maturing debts. Two commonly used liquidity ratios are the **current ratio** and the **quick, or acid test, ratio.**
- **Asset management ratios** measure how effectively a firm is managing its assets. These ratios include **inventory turnover, days sales outstanding, fixed assets turnover,** and **total assets turnover.**
- **Debt management ratios** reveal (1) the extent to which the firm is financed with debt, and (2) its likelihood of defaulting on its debt obligations. They include the **debt-to-assets ratio** (also called the **debt ratio**), the **debt-to-equity ratio,** the **times-interest-earned ratio,** and the **EBITDA coverage ratio.**
- **Profitability ratios** show the combined effects of liquidity, asset management, and debt management policies on operating results. They include the **net profit margin** (also called the **profit margin on sales**), the **basic earning power ratio,** the **return on total assets,** and the **return on common equity.**
- **Market value ratios** relate the firm's stock price to its earnings, cash flow, and book value per share, thus giving management an indication of what investors think of the company's past performance and future prospects. These include the **price/earnings ratio,** the **price/cash flow ratio,** and the **market/book ratio.**
- **Trend analysis,** in which one plots a ratio over time, is important because it reveals whether the firm's condition has been improving or deteriorating over time.
- The **DuPont system** is designed to show how the profit margin on sales, the assets turnover ratio, and the use of debt all interact to determine the rate of return on equity. The firm's management can use the Du Pont system to analyze ways of improving performance.
- **Benchmarking** is the process of comparing a particular company with a group of similar successful companies.

Ratio analysis has limitations, but when used with care and judgment it can be very helpful.

QUESTIONS

(3-1) Define each of the following terms:

a. *Liquidity ratios:* current ratio; quick, or acid test, ratio
b. Asset management ratios: inventory turnover ratio; days sales outstanding (DSO); fixed assets turnover ratio; total assets turnover ratio

c. *Financial leverage ratios:* debt ratio; times-interest-earned (TIE) ratio; coverage ratio

d. *Profitability ratios:* profit margin on sales; basic earning power (BEP) ratio; return on total assets (ROA); return on common equity (ROE)

e. Market value ratios: price/earnings (P/E) ratio; price/cash flow ratio; market/book (M/B) ratio; book value per share

f. Trend analysis; comparative ratio analysis; benchmarking

g. DuPont equation; window dressing; seasonal effects on ratios

(3-2) Financial ratio analysis is conducted by managers, equity investors, long-term creditors, and short-term creditors. What is the primary emphasis of each of these groups in evaluating ratios?

(3-3) Over the past year, M. D. Ryngaert & Co. has realized an increase in its current ratio and a drop in its total assets turnover ratio. However, the company's sales, quick ratio, and fixed assets turnover ratio have remained constant. What explains these changes?

(3-4) Profit margins and turnover ratios vary from one industry to another. What differences would you expect to find between a grocery chain such as Safeway and a steel company? Think particularly about the turnover ratios, the profit margin, and the Du Pont equation.

(3-5) How might (a) seasonal factors and (b) different growth rates distort a comparative ratio analysis? Give some examples. How might these problems be alleviated?

(3-6) Why is it sometimes misleading to compare a company's financial ratios with those of other firms that operate in the same industry?

SELF-TEST PROBLEMS Solutions Appear in Appendix A

(ST-1) Debt Ratio — Argent Corporation has $60 million in current liabilities, $150 million in total liabilities, and $210 million in total common equity; Argent has no preferred stock. Argent's total debt is $120 million. What is the debt-to-assets ratio? What is the debt-to-equity ratio?

(ST-2) Ratio Analysis — The following data apply to Jacobus and Associates (millions of dollars):

Cash and marketable securities	$ 100.00
Fixed assets	$ 283.50
Sales	$ 1,000.00
Net income	$ 50.00
Quick ratio	2.0
Current ratio	3.0
DSO	40.55 days
ROE	12%

Jacobus has no preferred stock—only common equity, current liabilities, and long-term debt. Find Jacobus's (1) accounts receivable, (2) current liabilities, (3) current assets, (4) total assets, (5) ROA, (6) common equity, and (7) long-term debt.

PROBLEMS Answers Appear in Appendix B

Easy Problems 1–5

(3-1) Days Sales Outstanding Greene Sisters has a DSO of 20 days. The company's average daily sales are $20,000. What is the level of its accounts receivable? Assume there are 365 days in a year.

(3-2) Debt Ratio Vigo Vacations has $200 million in total assets, $5 million in notes payable, and $25 million in long-term debt. What is the debt ratio?

(3-3) Market/Book Ratio Winston Washers's stock price is $75 per share. Winston has $10 billion in total assets. Its balance sheet shows $1 billion in current liabilities, $3 billion in long-term debt, and $6 billion in common equity. It has 800 million shares of common stock outstanding. What is Winston's market/book ratio?

(3-4) Price/Earnings Ratio Reno Revolvers has an EPS of $1.50, a cash flow per share of $3.00, and a price/cash flow ratio of 8.0. What is its P/E ratio?

(3-5) ROE Needham Pharmaceuticals has a profit margin of 3% and an equity multiplier of 2.0. Its sales are $100 million and it has total assets of $50 million. What is its ROE?

Intermediate Problems 6–10

(3-6) Du Pont Analysis Gardial & Son has an ROA of 12%, a 5% profit margin, and a return on equity equal to 20%. What is the company's total assets turnover? What is the firm's equity multiplier?

(3-7) Current and Quick Ratios Ace Industries has current assets equal to $3 million. The company's current ratio is 1.5, and its quick ratio is 1.0. What is the firm's level of current liabilities? What is the firm's level of inventories?

(3-8) Profit Margin and Debt Ratio Assume you are given the following relationships for the Haslam Corporation:

Sales/total assets	1.2
Return on assets (ROA)	4%
Return on equity (ROE)	7%

Calculate Haslam's profit margin and liabilities-to-assets ratio. Suppose half its liabilities are in the form of debt. Calculate the debt-to-assets ratio.

(3-9) Current and Quick Ratios The Nelson Company has $1,312,500 in current assets and $525,000 in current liabilities. Its initial inventory level is $375,000, and it will raise funds as additional notes payable and use them to increase inventory. How much can Nelson's short-term debt (notes payable) increase without pushing its current ratio below 2.0? What will be the firm's quick ratio after Nelson has raised the maximum amount of short-term funds?

(3-10) Times-Interest-Earned Ratio The Morris Corporation has $600,000 of debt outstanding, and it pays an interest rate of 8% annually. Morris's annual sales are $3 million, its average tax rate is 40%, and its net profit margin on sales is 3%. If the company does not maintain a TIE ratio of at least 5 to 1, then its bank will refuse to renew the loan and bankruptcy will result. What is Morris's TIE ratio?

Challenging Problems 11–14

(3-11) Balance Sheet Analysis Complete the balance sheet and sales information in the table that follows for J. White Industries using the following financial data:

Total assets turnover: 1.5
Gross profit margin on sales: (Sales − Cost of goods sold)/Sales = 25%
Total liabilities-to-assets ratio: 40%
Quick ratio: 0.80
Days sales outstanding (based on 365-day year): 36.5 days
Inventory turnover ratio: 3.75

Partial Income	**Statement Information**		
Sales	______		
Cost of goods sold	______		
Balance Sheet			
Cash	______	Accounts payable	______
Accounts receivable	______	Long-term debt	50,000
Inventories	______	Common stock	______
Fixed assets	______	Retained earnings	100,000
Total assets	$400,000	Total liabilities and equity	______

(3-12) Comprehensive Ratio Calculations

The Kretovich Company had a quick ratio of 1.4, a current ratio of 3.0, a days sales outstanding of 36.5 days (based on a 365-day year), total current assets of $810,000, and cash and marketable securities of $120,000. What were Kretovich's annual sales?

(3-13) Comprehensive Ratio Analysis

Data for Lozano Chip Company and its industry averages follow.

a. Calculate the indicated ratios for Lozano.
b. Construct the extended Du Pont equation for both Lozano and the industry.
c. Outline Lozano's strengths and weaknesses as revealed by your analysis.

Lozano Chip Company: Balance Sheet as of December 31, 2013 (Thousands of Dollars)

Cash	$ 225,000	Accounts payable	$ 601,866
Receivables	1,575,000	Notes payable	326,634
Inventories	1,125,000	Other current liabilities	525,000
Total current assets	$2,950,000	Total current liabilities	$1,453,500
Net fixed assets	1,350,000	Long-term debt	1,068,750
		Common equity	1,752,750
Total assets	$4,275,000	Total liabilities and equity	$4,275,000

Lozano Chip Company: Income Statement for Year Ended December 31, 2013 (Thousands of Dollars)

Sales	$ 7,500,000
Cost of goods sold	6,375,000
Selling, general, and administrative expenses	825,000
Earnings before interest and taxes (EBIT)	$ 300,000
Interest expense	111,631
Earnings before taxes (EBT)	$ 188,369
Federal and state income taxes (40%)	75,348
Net income	$ 113,022

Ratio	Lozano	Industry Average
Current assets/Current liabilities	________	2.0
Days sales outstanding (365-day year)	________	35.0 days
COGS/Inventory	________	6.7
Sales/Fixed assets	________	12.1
Sales/Total assets	________	3.0
Net income/Sales	________	1.2%
Net income/Total assets	________	3.6%
Net income/Common equity	________	9.0%
Total debt/Total assets	________	30.0%
Total liabilities/Total assets	________	60.0%

(3-14) Comprehensive Ratio Analysis

The Jimenez Corporation's forecasted 2014 financial statements follow, along with some industry average ratios. Calculate Jimenez's 2014 forecasted ratios, compare them with the industry average data, and comment briefly on Jimenez's projected strengths and weaknesses.

Jimenez Corporation: Forecasted Balance Sheet as of December 31, 2014

Assets	
Cash	$ 72,000
Accounts receivable	439,000
Inventories	894,000
Total current assets	$ 1,405,000
Fixed assets	431,000
Total assets	$ 1,836,000
Liabilities and Equity	
Accounts payable	$ 332,000
Notes payable	100,000
Accruals	170,000
Total current liabilities	$ 602,000
Long-term debt	404,290
Common stock	575,000
Retained earnings	254,710
Total liabilities and equity	$ 1,836,000

Jimenez Corporation: Forecasted Income Statement for 2014

Sales	$4,290,000
Cost of goods sold	3,580,000
Selling, general, and administrative expenses	370,320
Depreciation and amortization	159,000
Earnings before taxes (EBT)	$ 180,680
Taxes (40%)	72,272
Net income	$ 108,408

Per Share Data	
EPS	$ 4.71
Cash dividends per share	$ 0.95
P/E ratio	5.0
Market price (average)	$ 23.57
Number of shares outstanding	23,000
Industry Financial Ratios (2013)[a]	
Quick ratio	1.0
Current ratio	2.7
Inventory turnover[b]	7.0
Days sales outstanding[c]	32.0 days
Fixed assets turnover[b]	13.0
Total assets turnover[b]	2.6
Return on assets	9.1%
Return on equity	18.2%
Profit margin on sales	3.5%
Debt-to-assets ratio	21.0%
Liabilities-to-assets ratio	50.0%
P/E ratio	6.0
Price/Cash flow ratio	3.5
Market/Book ratio	3.5

[a]Industry average ratios have been constant for the past 4 years.
[b]Based on year-end balance sheet figures.
[c]Calculation is based on a 365-day year.

SPREADSHEET PROBLEMS

(3-15) Build a Model: Ratio Analysis

Start with the partial model in the file ***Ch03 P15 Build a Model.xls*** from the textbook's Web site. Joshua & White (J&W) Technologies's financial statements are also shown below. Answer the following questions. (*Note:* Industry average ratios are provided in ***Ch03 P15 Build a Model.xls.)***

resource

a. Has J&W's liquidity position improved or worsened? Explain.
b. Has J&W's ability to manage its assets improved or worsened? Explain.
c. How has J&W's profitability changed during the last year?
d. Perform an extended DuPont analysis for J&W for 2012 and 2013. What do these results tell you?
e. Perform a common size analysis. What has happened to the composition (that is, percentage in each category) of assets and liabilities?
f. Perform a percentage change analysis. What does this tell you about the change in profitability and asset utilization?

Joshua & White Technologies: December 31 Balance Sheets (Thousands of Dollars)

Assets	2013	2012	*Liabilities & Equity*	2013	2012
Cash	$ 21,000	$ 20,000	Accounts payable	$ 33,600	$ 32,000
Short-term investments	3,759	3,240	Accruals	12,600	12,000
Accounts receivable	52,500	48,000	Notes payable	19,929	6,480
Inventories	84,000	56,000	Total current liabilities	$ 66,129	$ 50,480
Total current assets	$161,259	$127,240	Long-term debt	67,662	58,320
Net fixed assets	218,400	200,000	Total liabilities	$133,791	$108,800
Total assets	$379,659	$327,240	Common stock	183,793	178,440
			Retained earnings	62,075	40,000
			Total common equity	$245,868	$218,440
			Total liabilities & equity	$379,659	$327,240

Joshua & White Technologies December 31 Income Statements (Thousands of Dollars)

	2013	2012
Sales	$420,000	$400,000
COGS excluding depr. & amort.	300,000	298,000
Depreciation and amortization	19,660	18,000
Other operating expenses	27,600	22,000
EBIT	$ 72,740	$ 62,000
Interest expense	5,740	4,460
EBT	$ 67,000	$ 57,540
Taxes (40%)	26,800	23,016
Net income	$ 40,200	$ 34,524
Common dividends	$ 18,125	$ 17,262

Other Data	2012	2011
Year-end stock price	$ 90.00	$ 96.00
Number of shares (thousands)	4,052	4,000
Lease payment (thousands of dollars)	$ 20,000	$ 20,000
Sinking fund payment (thousands of dollars)	$ 5,000	$ 5,000

THOMSON ONE Business School Edition Problem

THOMSON REUTERS

Use the Thomson ONE—Business School Edition online database to work this chapter's questions.

Analysis of Ford's Financial Statements with Thomson ONE—Business School Edition

Use Thomson ONE to analyze Ford Motor Company. Enter Ford's ticker symbol (F) and select GO. By selecting the menu at left labeled Financials, you can find Ford's key financial statements for the past several years. Under the Financial Ratios heading, select Thomson Ratios and then Annual Ratios to see an in-depth summary of Ford's various ratios over the past 5 years.

Click on the Comparables menu at left and scroll down to find the submenu items for Key Financials and Key Financial Ratios for Ford and a few of its peers. If you scroll up, still in the Comparables menu, you can select a different list of peer firms to be included in the analysis. The default group is "Peers by SIC code."

Thomson ONE—BSE Discussion Questions

1. What has happened to Ford's liquidity position over the past 3 years? How does Ford's liquidity compare with its peers? (*Hint:* You may use both the peer key financial ratios and liquidity comparison to answer this question.)
2. Look at Ford's inventory turnover ratio. How does this ratio compare with its peers? Have there been any interesting changes over time in this measure? Do you consider Ford's inventory management to be a strength or a weakness?
3. Construct a simple DuPont analysis for Ford and its peers. What are Ford's strengths and weaknesses relative to its competitors?

MINI CASE

The first part of the case, presented in Chapter 2, discussed the situation of Computron Industries after an expansion program. A large loss occurred in 2013, rather than the expected profit. As a result, its managers, directors, and investors are concerned about the firm's survival.

Jenny Cochran was brought in as assistant to Gary Meissner, Computron's chairman, who had the task of getting the company back into a sound financial position. Computron's 2012 and 2013 balance sheets and income statements, together with projections for 2014, are shown in the following tables. The tables also show the 2012 and 2013 financial ratios, along with industry average data. The 2014 projected financial statement data represent Cochran's and Meissner's best guess for 2014 results, assuming that some new financing is arranged to get the company "over the hump."

Balance Sheets

	2012	2013	2014E
Assets			
Cash	$ 9,000	$ 7,282	$ 14,000
Short-term investments	48,600	20,000	71,632
Accounts receivable	351,200	632,160	878,000
Inventories	715,200	1,287,360	1,716,480
Total current assets	$ 1,124,000	$1,946,802	$2,680,112
Gross fixed assets	491,000	1,202,950	1,220,000
Less: Accumulated depreciation	146,200	263,160	383,160
Net fixed assets	$ 344,800	$ 939,790	$ 836,840
Total assets	$ 1,468,800	$2,886,592	$3,516,952
Liabilities and Equity			
Accounts payable	$ 145,600	$ 324,000	$ 359,800
Notes payable	200,000	720,000	300,000
Accruals	136,000	284,960	380,000
Total current liabilities	$ 481,600	$1,328,960	$1,039,800
Long-term debt	323,432	1,000,000	500,000
Common stock (100,000 shares)	460,000	460,000	1,680,936
Retained earnings	203,768	97,632	296,216
Total equity	$ 663,768	$ 557,632	$1,977,152
Total liabilities and equity	$ 1,468,800	$2,886,592	$3,516,952

Note: "E" denotes "estimated"; the 2014 data are forecasts.

Income Statements

	2012	2013	2014E
Sales	$ 3,432,000	$5,834,400	$7,035,600
Cost of goods sold except depr.	2,864,000	4,980,000	5,800,000
Depreciation and amortization	18,900	116,960	120,000
Other expenses	340,000	720,000	612,960
Total operating costs	$ 3,222,900	$5,816,960	$6,532,960
EBIT	$ 209,100	$ 17,440	$ 502,640
Interest expense	62,500	176,000	80,000
EBT	$ 146,600	($ 158,560)	$ 422,640
Taxes (40%)	58,640	(63,424)	169,056
Net income	$ 87,960	($ 95,136)	$ 253,584

Other Data			
Stock price	$ 8.50	$ 6.00	$ 12.17
Shares outstanding	100,000	100,000	250,000
EPS	$ 0.880	($ 0.951)	$ 1.014
DPS	$ 0.220	0.110	0.220
Tax rate	40%	40%	40%
Book value per share	$ 6.638	$ 5.576	$ 7.909
Lease payments	$ 40,000	$ 40,000	$ 40,000

Note: "E" denotes "estimated"; the 2014 data are forecasts.

Ratio Analysis

	2012	2013	2014E	Industry Average
Current	2.3	1.5	______	2.7
Quick	0.8	0.5	______	1.0
Inventory turnover	4.0	4.0	______	6.1
Days sales outstanding	37.3	39.6	______	32.0
Fixed assets turnover	10.0	6.2	______	7.0
Total assets turnover	2.3	2.0	______	2.5
Debt ratio	35.6%	59.6%	______	32.0%
Liabilities-to-assets ratio	54.8%	80.7%	______	50.0%
TIE	3.3	0.1	______	6.2
EBITDA coverage	2.6	0.8	______	8.0
Profit margin	2.6%	−1.6%	______	3.6%
Basic earning power	14.2%	0.6%	______	17.8%
ROA	6.0%	−3.3%	______	9.0%
ROE	13.3%	−17.1%	______	17.9%
Price/Earnings (P/E)	9.7	−6.3	______	16.2
Price/Cash flow	8.0	27.5	______	7.6
Market/Book	1.3	1.1	______	2.9

Note: "E" denotes "estimated."

Cochran must prepare an analysis of where the company is now, what it must do to regain its financial health, and what actions to take. Your assignment is to help her answer the following questions. Provide clear explanations, not yes or no answers.

a. Why are ratios useful? What three groups use ratio analysis and for what reasons?
b. Calculate the 2014 current and quick ratios based on the projected balance sheet and income statement data. What can you say about the company's liquidity position in 2012, 2013, and as projected for 2014? We often think of ratios as being useful (1) to managers to help run the business, (2) to bankers for credit analysis, and (3) to stockholders for stock valuation. Would these different types of analysts have an equal interest in the liquidity ratios?

c. Calculate the 2014 inventory turnover, days sales outstanding (DSO), fixed assets turnover, and total assets turnover. How does Computron's utilization of assets stack up against that of other firms in its industry?
d. Calculate the 2014 debt ratio, liabilities-to-assets ratio, times-interest-earned, and EBITDA coverage ratios. How does Computron compare with the industry with respect to financial leverage? What can you conclude from these ratios?
e. Calculate the 2014 profit margin, basic earning power (BEP), return on assets (ROA), and return on equity (ROE). What can you say about these ratios?
f. Calculate the 2014 price/earnings ratio, price/cash flow ratio, and market/book ratio. Do these ratios indicate that investors are expected to have a high or low opinion of the company?
g. Perform a common size analysis and percentage change analysis. What do these analyses tell you about Computron?
h. Use the extended DuPont equation to provide a summary and overview of Computron's financial condition as projected for 2014. What are the firm's major strengths and weaknesses?
i. What are some potential problems and limitations of financial ratio analysis?
j. What are some qualitative factors that analysts should consider when evaluating a company's likely future financial performance?

SELECTED ADDITIONAL CASES

The following cases from CengageCompose cover many of the concepts discussed in this chapter and are available at **compose.cengage.com**.

Klein-Brigham Series:
Case 35, "Mark X Company (A)," illustrates the use of ratio analysis in the evaluation of a firm's existing and potential financial positions; Case 36, "Garden State Container Corporation," is similar in content to Case 35; Case 51, "Safe Packaging Corporation," updates Case 36; Case 68, "Sweet Dreams Inc.," also updates Case 36; and Case 71, "Swan-Davis, Inc.," illustrates how financial analysis—based on both historical statements and forecasted statements—is used for internal management and lending decisions.

© lulu/fotolia.com

PART 2

Fixed Income Securities

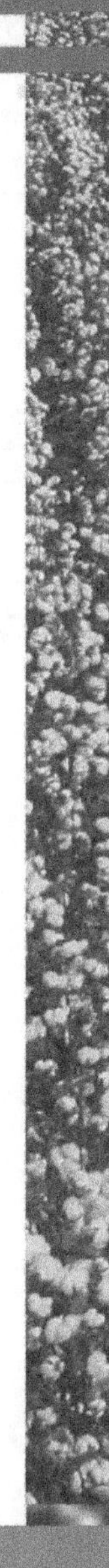

CHAPTER 4
Time Value of Money 133

CHAPTER 5
Bonds, Bond Valuation, and Interest Rates 187

© Adalberto Rios Szalay/Sexto Sol/Getty Images

CHAPTER 4

Time Value of Money

When you graduate and go to work, your compensation package will almost certainly include either a ***defined benefit (DB)*** or a ***defined contribution (DC)*** pension plan. Under a DB plan, the company will put funds for you into its pension fund, which will then invest in stocks, bonds, real estate, and so forth and then use those funds to make the promised payments after you retire. Under a DC plan, the company will put money into your 401(k) plan (which is essentially a mutual fund), you will decide what type of assets to buy, and you will withdraw money after you retire. The analysis required to set up a good retirement program is based on the subject of this chapter, the time value of money (TVM).

How do you suppose a stock market crash like we had in 2008, with the average stock down about 40%, will affect DB and DC retirement plans? If you have a 401(k) plan that holds stocks, as most people do, TVM analysis would show clearly that you will have to work longer than you expected, reduce your post-retirement standard of living, or both.

With a DB plan, a stock market decline reduces the value of the investments set aside for you by the company. If there is also a decline in interest rates, as there was in 2008, TVM analysis shows that the amount of money the company should set aside for you goes up. Thus, the company's pension funding status, which is the difference between the value of the pension plan's investments and the amount the plan should have on hand to cover the future obligations, becomes severely underfunded if the market crashes *and* interest rates fall. This can even lead to bankruptcy, in which case you might end up with retirement payments from the government instead of from the company, with the government's payments a lot lower than those promised by the company's plan. If you don't believe us, ask someone who recently retired from a bankrupt airline or auto company.

Corporate Valuation and the Time Value of Money

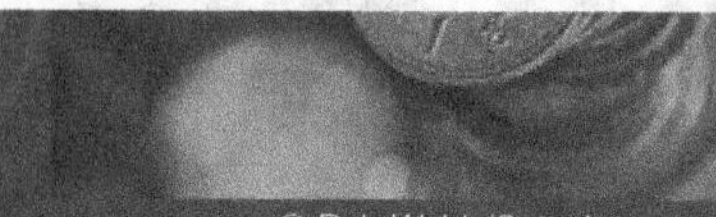

© Rob Webb/Getty Images

In Chapter 1 we explained (1) that managers should strive to make their firms more valuable, and (2) that the value of a firm is determined by the size, timing, and risk of its free cash flows (FCF). Recall from Chapter 2 that free cash flows are the cash flows available for distribution to all of a firm's investors (stockholders and creditors). We explain how to calculate the weighted average cost of capital (WACC) in Chapter 9, but it is enough for now to think of the WACC as the average rate of return required by all of the firm's investors. The intrinsic value of a company is given by the following diagram. Note that central to this value is discounting the free cash flows at the WACC in order to find the value of the firm. This discounting is one aspect of the time value of money. We discuss time value of money techniques in this chapter.

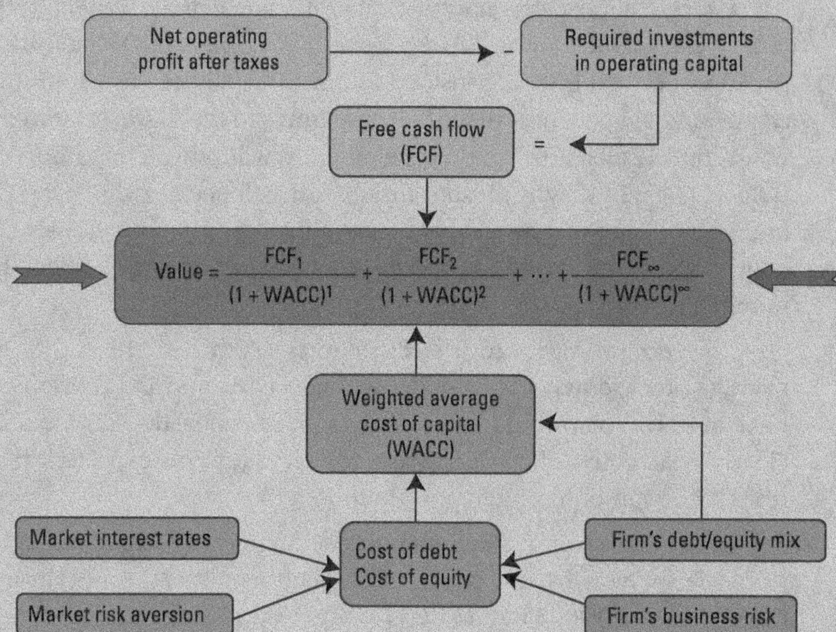

© Cengage Learning 2014

In Chapter 1, we saw that the primary objective of financial management is to maximize the intrinsic value of a firm's stock. We also saw that stock values depend on the timing of the cash flows investors expect from an investment—a dollar expected sooner is worth more than a dollar expected further in the future. Therefore, it is essential for financial managers to understand the time value of money and its impact on stock prices. In this chapter we will explain exactly how the timing of cash flows affects asset values and rates of return.

The principles of time value analysis have many applications, including retirement planning, loan payment schedules, and decisions to invest (or not) in new equipment. *In fact, of all the concepts used in finance, none is more important than the* **time value of money (TVM)**, *also called* **discounted cash flow (DCF) analysis.** Time value concepts are used throughout the remainder of the book, so it is vital that you understand the material in this chapter and be able to work the chapter's problems before you move on to other topics.

4-1 Time Lines

The first step in a time value analysis is to set up a **time line** to help you visualize what's happening in the particular problem. To illustrate, consider the following diagram, where PV represents $100 that is in a bank account today and FV is the value that will be in the account at some future time (3 years from now in this example):

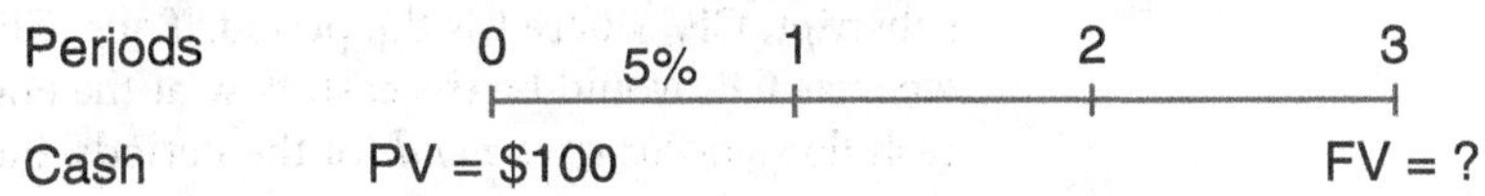

resource

*The textbook's Web site contains an Excel file that will guide you through the chapter's calculations. The file for this chapter is **Ch04 Tool Kit.xls**, and we encourage you to open the file and follow along as you read the chapter.*

The intervals from 0 to 1, 1 to 2, and 2 to 3 are time periods such as years or months. Time 0 is today, and it is the beginning of Period 1; Time 1 is one period from today, and it is both the end of Period 1 and the beginning of Period 2; and so on. In our example, the periods are years, but they could also be quarters or months or even days. Note again that each tick mark corresponds to both the *end* of one period and the *beginning* of the next one. Thus, if the periods are years, the tick mark at Time 2 represents both the end of Year 2 and the beginning of Year 3.

Cash flows are shown directly below the tick marks, and the relevant interest rate is shown just above the time line. Unknown cash flows, which you are trying to find, are indicated by question marks. Here the interest rate is 5%; a single cash outflow, $100, is invested at Time 0; and the Time-3 value is unknown and must be found. In this example, cash flows occur only at Times 0 and 3, with no flows at Times 1 or 2. We will, of course, deal with situations where multiple cash flows occur. Note also that in our example the interest rate is constant for all 3 years. The interest rate is generally held constant, but if it varies, then in the diagram we show different rates for the different periods.

Time lines are especially important when you are first learning time value concepts, but even experts use them to analyze complex problems. Throughout the book, our procedure is to set up a time line to show what's happening, provide an equation that must be solved to find the answer, and then explain how to solve the equation with a regular calculator, a financial calculator, and a computer spreadsheet.

SELF-TEST

Do time lines deal only with years, or could other periods be used?

Set up a time line to illustrate the following situation: You currently have $2,000 in a 3-year certificate of deposit (CD) that pays a guaranteed 4% annually. You want to know the value of the CD after 3 years.

4-2 Future Values

A dollar in hand today is worth more than a dollar to be received in the future—if you had the dollar now you could invest it, earn interest, and end up with more than one dollar in the future. The process of going forward, from **present values (PVs)** to **future values (FVs)**, is called **compounding**. To illustrate, refer back to our 3-year time line and assume that you have $100 in a bank account that pays a guaranteed 5% interest each year. How much would you have at the end of Year 3? We first define some terms, and then we set up a time line and show how the future value is calculated.

PV = Present value, or beginning amount. In our example, PV = \$100.

FV_N = Future value, or ending amount, in the account after N periods. Whereas PV is the value *now*, or the *present value*, FV_N is the value N periods into the *future*, after interest earned has been added to the account.

CF_t = Cash flow. Cash flows can be positive or negative. For a borrower, the first cash flow is positive and the subsequent cash flows are negative, and the reverse holds for a lender. The cash flow for a particular period is often given a subscript, CF_t, where t is the period. Thus, CF_0 = PV = the cash flow at Time 0, whereas CF_3 would be the cash flow at the end of Period 3. In this example the cash flows occur *at the ends* of the periods, but in some problems they occur at the beginning.

I = Interest rate earned per year. (Sometimes a lowercase i is used.) Interest earned is based on the balance at the beginning of each year, and we assume that interest is paid at the end of the year. Here I = 5% or, expressed as a decimal, 0.05. Throughout this chapter, we designate the interest rate as I (or I/YR, for interest rate per year) because that symbol is used on most financial calculators. Note, though, that in later chapters we use the symbol "r" to denote the rate because r (for *rate* of return) is used more often in the finance literature. Also, in this chapter we generally assume that interest payments are guaranteed by the U.S. government and hence are riskless (i.e., certain). In later chapters we will deal with risky investments, where the rate actually earned might be different from its expected level.

INT = Dollars of interest earned during the year = (Beginning amount) × I. In our example, INT = \$100(0.05) = \$5 for Year 1, but it rises in subsequent years as the amount at the beginning of each year increases.

N = Number of periods involved in the analysis. In our example, N = 3. Sometimes the number of periods is designated with a lowercase n, so both N and n indicate number of periods.

We can use four different procedures to solve time value problems.[1] These methods are described next.

4-2a Step-by-Step Approach

The time line itself can be modified and used to find the FV of \$100 compounded for 3 years at 5%, as shown below:

Time	0 (5%)	1	2	3
Amount at beginning of period	\$100.00 →	\$105.00 →	\$110.25 →	\$115.76

[1]A fifth procedure is called the *tabular approach*, which uses tables that provide "interest factors;" this procedure was used before financial calculators and computers became available. Now, though, calculators and spreadsheets such as *Excel* are programmed to calculate the specific factor needed for a given problem, which is then used to find the FV. This is much more efficient than using the tables. Also, calculators and spreadsheets can handle fractional periods and fractional interest rates. For these reasons, tables are not used in business today; hence we do not discuss them in the text. However, because some professors cover the tables for pedagogical purposes, we discuss them in ***Web Extension 4A***, on the textbook's Web site.

We start with \$100 in the account, which is shown at t = 0. We then multiply the initial amount, and each succeeding beginning-of-year amount, by (1 + I) = (1.05).

- You earn \$100(0.05) = \$5 of interest during the first year, so the amount at the end of Year 1 (or at t = 1) is

$$\begin{aligned} FV_1 &= PV + INT \\ &= PV + PV(I) \\ &= PV(1 + I) \\ &= \$100(1 + 0.05) = \$100(1.05) = \$105 \end{aligned}$$

- We begin the second year with \$105, earn 0.05(\$105) = \$5.25 on the now larger beginning-of-period amount, and end the year with \$110.25. Interest during Year 2 is \$5.25, and it is higher than the first year's interest, \$5, because we earned \$5(0.05) = \$0.25 interest on the first year's interest. This is called "compounding," and interest earned on interest is called "compound interest."
- This process continues, and because the beginning balance is higher in each successive year, the interest earned each year increases.
- The total interest earned, \$15.76, is reflected in the final balance, \$115.76.

The step-by-step approach is useful because it shows exactly what is happening. However, this approach is time-consuming, especially if the number of years is large and you are using a calculator rather than *Excel*, so streamlined procedures have been developed.

4-2b Formula Approach

In the step-by-step approach, we multiplied the amount at the beginning of each period by (1 + I) = (1.05). Notice that the value at the end of Year 2 is

$$\begin{aligned} FV_2 &= FV_1(1 + I) \\ &= PV(1 + I)(1 + I) \\ &= PV(1 + I)^2 \\ &= 100(1.05)^2 = \$110.25 \end{aligned}$$

If N = 3, then we multiply PV by (1 + I) three different times, which is the same as multiplying the beginning amount by $(1 + I)^3$. This concept can be extended, and the result is this key equation:

$$FV_N = PV(1 + I)^N \quad (4\text{-}1)$$

We can apply Equation 4-1 to find the FV in our example:

$$FV_3 = \$100(1.05)^3 = \$115.76$$

Equation 4-1 can be used with any calculator, even a nonfinancial calculator that has an exponential function, making it easy to find FVs no matter how many years are involved.

4-2c Financial Calculators

Financial calculators were designed specifically to solve time value problems. First, note that financial calculators have five keys that correspond to the five variables in the basic time value equations. Equation 4-1 has only four variables, but we will shortly deal with situations where a fifth variable (a set of periodic additional payments) is involved. We show the inputs for our example above their keys in the following diagram, and the output, which is the FV, below its key. Because there are no periodic payments in this example, we enter 0 for PMT. We describe the keys in more detail below the diagram.

Inputs	3	5	-100	0	
	N	I/YR	PV	PMT	FV
Output					115.76

N = Number of periods = 3. Some calculators use n rather than N.

I/YR = Interest rate per period = 5. Some calculators use i or I rather than I/YR. Calculators are programmed to automatically convert the 5 to the decimal 0.05 before doing the arithmetic.

PV = Present value = 100. In our example we begin by making a deposit, which is an outflow of 100, so the PV is entered with a negative sign. On most calculators you must enter the 100, then press the +/− key to switch from +100 to −100. If you enter −100 directly, this will subtract 100 from the last number in the calculator, which will give you an incorrect answer unless the last number was zero.

PMT = Payment. This key is used if we have a series of equal, or constant, payments. Because there are no such payments in our current problem, we enter PMT = 0. We will use the PMT key later in this chapter.

FV = Future value. In our example, the calculator automatically shows the FV as a positive number because we entered the PV as a negative number. If we had entered the 100 as a positive number, then the FV would have been negative. Calculators automatically assume that either the PV or the FV must be negative.

As noted in our example, you first enter the four known values (N, I/YR, PV, and PMT) and then press the FV key to get the answer, FV = 115.76.[2]

4-2d Spreadsheets

resource

*See **Ch04 Tool Kit.xls** for all calculations.*

Spreadsheets are ideally suited for solving many financial problems, including those dealing with the time value of money.[2] Spreadsheets are obviously useful for calculations, but they can also be used like a word processor to create exhibits like our Figure 4-1, which includes text, drawings, and calculations. We use this figure to show that four methods can be used to find the FV of $100 after 3 years at an interest rate of 5%. The time line on Rows 36 to 37 is useful for visualizing the problem, after which the spreadsheet calculates the required answer. Note that the letters across the top designate columns, the numbers down the left column designate rows, and the rows and columns jointly designate cells. Thus, cell C32 shows the amount of the investment, $100, and it is given a minus sign because it is an outflow.

[2]The file ***Ch04 Tool Kit.xls*** on the book's Web site does the calculations in the chapter using *Excel.* We *highly recommend* that you study the models in this ***Tool Kit.*** Doing so will give you practice with *Excel,* and that will help you tremendously in later courses, in the job market, and in the workplace. Also, going through the models will improve your understanding of financial concepts.

Hints on Using Financial Calculators

© Rob Webb/Getty Images

When using a financial calculator, make sure your machine is set up as indicated below. Refer to your calculator manual or to our calculator tutorial on the textbook's Web site for information on setting up your calculator.

- **One payment per period.** Many calculators "come out of the box" assuming that 12 payments are made per year; that is, they assume monthly payments. However, in this book we generally deal with problems in which only one payment is made each year. *Therefore, you should set your calculator at one payment per year and leave it there. See our tutorial or your calculator manual if you need assistance.* We will show you how to solve problems with more than 1 payment per year in Section 4-15.
- **End mode.** With most contracts, payments are made at the *end* of each period. However, some contracts call for payments at the *beginning* of each period. You can switch between "End Mode" and "Begin Mode" depending on the problem you are solving. *Because most of the problems in this book call for end-of-period payments, you should return your calculator to End Mode after you work a problem in which payments are made at the beginning of periods.*
- **Negative sign for outflows.** When first learning how to use financial calculators, students often forget that one cash flow must be negative. Mathematically, financial calculators solve a version of this equation:

$$PV(1 + I)^N + FV_N = 0 \tag{4-2}$$

Notice that for reasonable values of I, either PV or FV_N must be negative, and the other one must be positive to make the equation equal 0. This is reasonable because, in all realistic situations, one cash flow is an outflow (which should have a negative sign) and one is an inflow (which should have a positive sign). For example, if you make a deposit (which is an outflow, and hence should have a negative sign) then you will expect to make a later withdrawal (which is an inflow with a positive sign). *The bottom line is that one of your inputs for a cash flow must be negative and one must be positive. This generally means typing the outflow as a positive number and then pressing the +/– key to convert from + to – before hitting the Enter key.*

- **Decimal places.** When doing arithmetic, calculators allow you to show from 0 to 11 decimal places on the display. When working with dollars, we generally specify two decimal places. When dealing with interest rates, we generally specify two places if the rate is expressed as a percentage like 5.25%, but we specify four places if the rate is expressed as a decimal like 0.0525.
- **Interest rates.** *For arithmetic operations with a nonfinancial calculator, the rate 5.25% must be stated as a decimal, .0525. However, with a financial calculator you must enter 5.25, not .0525, because financial calculators are programmed to assume that rates are stated as percentages.*

It is useful to put all inputs in a section of the spreadsheet designated "INPUTS." In Figure 4-1, we put the inputs in the aqua-colored range of cells. Rather than enter fixed numbers into the model's formulas, we enter the cell references for the inputs. This makes it easy to modify the problem by changing the inputs and then automatically use the new data in the calculations.

Time lines are important for solving finance problems because they help us visualize what's happening. When we work a problem by hand we usually draw a time line, and when we work a problem with *Excel*, we set the model up as a time line. For example, in Figure 4-1, Rows 36 to 37 are indeed a time line. It's easy to construct time lines with *Excel*, with each column designating a different period on the time line.

FIGURE 4-1

Alternative Procedures for Calculating Future Values

	A	B	C	D	E	F	G
31	INPUTS:						
32		Investment = CF_0 = PV =	-$100.00				
33		Interest rate = I =	5%				
34		No. of periods = N =	3				
35							
36	Time Line		Periods:	0	1	2	3
37			Cash flow:	-$100.00	0	0	FV = ?
38							
39	1. Step-by-Step: Multiply by (1 + I) each step			$100.00 →	$105.00 →	$110.25 →	$115.76
40							
41	2. Formula: $FV_N = PV(1+I)^N$			FV_3 =	$100(1.05)^3$	=	$115.76
42							
43		Inputs:	3	5	-100	0	
44	3. Financial Calculator:		N	I/YR	PV	PMT	FV
45		Output:					$115.76
46							
47	4. *Excel* Spreadsheet:		FV function:	FV_N =	=FV(I,N,0,PV)		
48			Fixed inputs:	FV_N =	=FV(0.05,3,0,−100) =		$115.76
49			Cell references:	FV_N =	=FV(C33,C34,0,C32) =		$115.76
50–51	In the *Excel* formula, the terms are entered in this sequence: interest, periods, 0 to indicate no periodic cash flows, and then the PV. The data can be entered as fixed numbers or, better yet, as cell references.						

On Row 39, we use *Excel* to go through the step-by-step calculations, multiplying the beginning-of-year values by (1 + I) to find the compounded value at the end of each period. Cell G39 shows the final result of the step-by-step approach.

We illustrate the formula approach in Row 41, using *Excel* to solve Equation 4-1 to find the FV. Cell G41 shows the formula result, $115.76. As it must, it equals the step-by-step result.

Rows 43 to 45 illustrate the financial calculator approach, which again produces the same answer, $115.76.

The last section, in Rows 47 to 49, illustrates *Excel*'s future value (FV) function. You can access the function wizard by clicking the f_x symbol in *Excel*'s formula bar. Then select the category for Financial functions, and then the FV function, which is **=FV(I,N,0,PV)**, as shown in Cell E47.[3] Cell E48 shows how the formula would look with numbers as inputs; the actual function itself is entered in Cell G48, but it shows up in the table as the answer, $115.76. If you access the model and put the pointer on Cell G48,

[3]All functions begin with an equal sign. The third entry is zero in this example, which indicates that there are no periodic payments. Later in this chapter we will use the FV function in situations where we have nonzero periodic payments. Also, for inputs we use our own notation, which is similar but not identical to *Excel*'s notation.

you will see the full formula. Finally, Cell E49 shows how the formula would look with cell references rather than fixed values as inputs, with the actual function again in Cell G49. We generally use cell references as function inputs because this makes it easy to change inputs and see how those changes affect the output. This is called "sensitivity analysis." Many real-world financial applications use sensitivity analysis, so it is useful to form the habit of setting up an input data section and then using cell references rather than fixed numbers in the functions.

When entering interest rates in *Excel,* you can use either actual numbers or percentages, depending on how the cell is formatted. For example, we first formatted Cell C33 to Percentage, and then typed in 5, which showed up as 5%. However, *Excel* uses 0.05 for the arithmetic. Alternatively, we could have formatted C33 as a Number, in which case we would have typed "0.05." If a cell were formatted to Number and you entered 5, then *Excel* would think you meant 500%. Thus, *Excel*'s procedure is different from the convention used in financial calculators.

Sometimes students are confused about the sign of the initial \$100. We used +\$100 in Rows 39 and 41 as the initial investment when calculating the future value using the step-by-step method and the future value formula, but we used −\$100 with a financial calculator and the spreadsheet function in Rows 43 and 48. When must you use a positive value and when must you use a negative value? The answer is that whenever you set up a time line and use either a financial calculator's time value functions or *Excel's* time value functions, you must enter the signs that correspond to the "direction" of the cash flows. Cash flows that go out of your pocket (outflows) are negative, but cash flows that come into your pocket (inflows) are positive. In the case of the FV function in our example, if you invest \$100 (an outflow, and therefore negative) at Time 0 then the bank will make available to you \$115.76 (an inflow, and therefore positive) at Time 3. In essence, the FV function on a financial calculator or *Excel* answers the question "If I invest this much now, how much will be available to me at a time in the future?" The investment is an outflow and negative, and the amount available to you is an inflow and positive. If you use algebraic formulas then you must keep track of whether the value is an outflow or an inflow yourself. When in doubt, refer back to a correctly constructed time line.

4-2e Comparing the Procedures

The first step in solving any time value problem is to understand what is happening and then to diagram it on a time line. Woody Allen said that 90% of success is just showing up. With time value problems, 90% of success is correctly setting up the time line.

After you diagram the problem on a time line, your next step is to pick one of the four approaches shown in Figure 4-1 to solve the problem. Any one approach may be used, but your choice will depend on the particular situation.

All business students should know Equation 4-1 by heart and should also know how to use a financial calculator. So, for simple problems such as finding the future value of a single payment, it is generally easiest and quickest to use either the formula approach or a financial calculator. However, for problems that involve several cash flows, the formula approach usually is time-consuming, so either the calculator or spreadsheet approach would generally be used. Calculators are portable and quick to set up, but if many calculations of the same type must be done, or if you want to see how changes in an input such as the interest rate affect the future value, then the spreadsheet approach is generally more efficient. If the problem has many irregular cash flows, or if you want to analyze alternative scenarios using different cash flows or interest rates, then the spreadsheet approach definitely is the most efficient procedure.

Spreadsheets have two additional advantages over calculators. First, it is easier to check the inputs with a spreadsheet because they are visible; with a calculator the inputs are buried somewhere in the machine. Thus, you are less likely to make a mistake in a complex problem when you use the spreadsheet approach. Second, with a spreadsheet, you can make your analysis much more transparent than you can when using a calculator. This is not necessarily important when all you want is the answer, but if you need to present your calculations to others, like your boss, it helps to be able to show intermediate steps, which enables someone to go through your exhibit and see exactly what you did. Transparency is also important when you must go back, sometime later, and reconstruct what you did.

You should understand the various approaches well enough to make a rational choice, given the nature of the problem and the equipment you have available. In any event, you must understand the concepts behind the calculations, and you also must know how to set up time lines in order to work complex problems. This is true for stock and bond valuation, capital budgeting, lease analysis, and many other types of financial problems.

4-2f Graphic View of the Compounding Process

Figure 4-2 shows how a $100 investment grows (or declines) over time at different interest rates. Interest rates are normally positive, but the "growth" concept is broad enough to include negative rates. We developed the curves by solving Equation 4-1 with different values for N and I. The interest rate is a growth rate: If money is deposited and earns 5% per year, then your funds will grow by 5% per year. Note also that time value concepts can be applied to anything that grows—sales, population, earnings per share, or your future salary. Also, as noted before, the "growth rate" can be negative, as was sales growth for a number of auto companies in recent years.

resource

*See **Ch04 Tool Kit.xls** for all calculations.*

FIGURE 4-2

Growth of $100 at Various Interest Rates and Time Periods

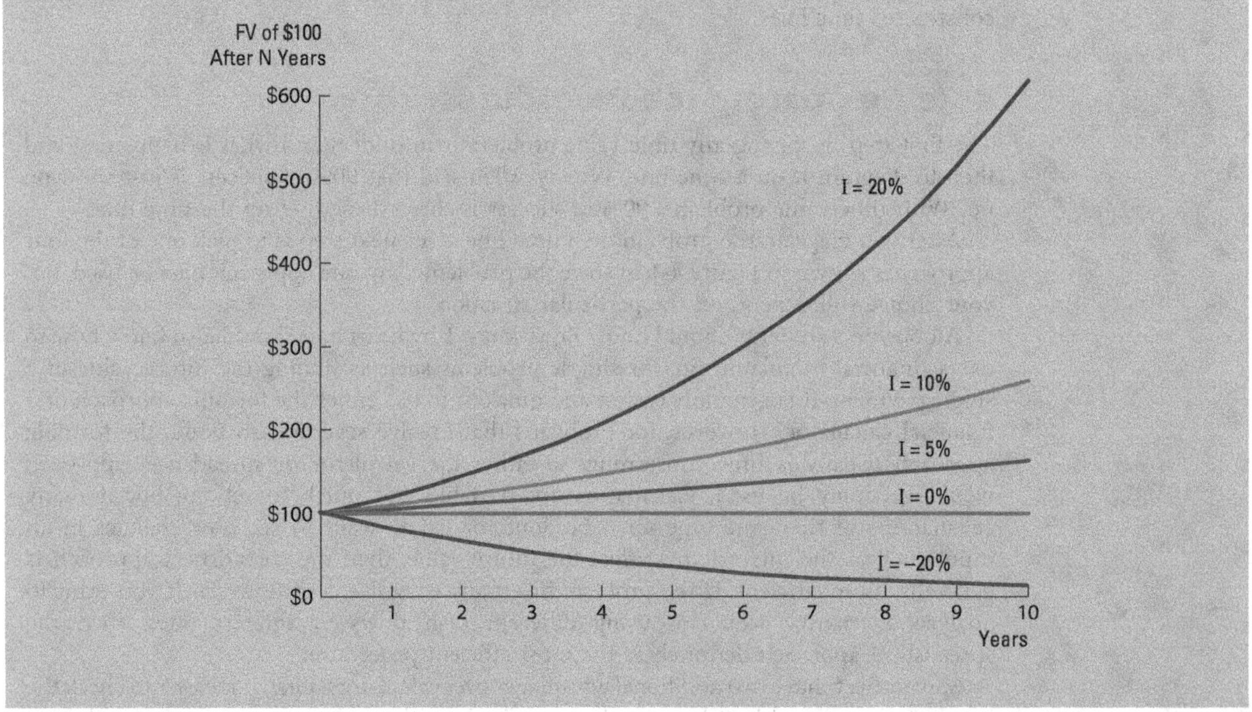

© Cengage Learning 2014

4-2g Simple Interest versus Compound Interest

As explained earlier, when interest is earned on the interest earned in prior periods, we call it **compound interest.** If interest is earned only on the principal, we call it **simple interest.** The total interest earned with simple interest is equal to the principal multiplied by the interest rate times the number of periods: PV(I)(N). The future value is equal to the principal plus the interest: FV = PV + PV(I)(N). For example, suppose you deposit $100 for 3 years and earn simple interest at an annual rate of 5%. Your balance at the end of 3 years would be:

$$\begin{aligned} FV &= PV + PV(I)(N) \\ &= \$100 + \$100(5\%)(3) \\ &= \$100 + \$15 = \$115 \end{aligned}$$

Notice that this is less than the $115.76 we calculated earlier using compound interest. Most applications in finance are based on compound interest, but you should be aware that simple interest is still specified in some legal documents.

SELF-TEST

Explain why this statement is true: "A dollar in hand today is worth more than a dollar to be received next year, assuming interest rates are positive."

What is compounding? What would the future value of $100 be after 5 years at 10% compound *interest?* **($161.05)**

Suppose you currently have $2,000 and plan to purchase a 3-year certificate of deposit (CD) that pays 4% interest, compounded annually. How much will you have when the CD matures? **($2,249.73)** *How would your answer change if the interest rate were 5%, or 6%, or 20%? (*Hint: *With a calculator, enter N = 3, I/YR = 4, PV = −2000, and PMT = 0, then press FV to get 2,249.73. Then, enter I/YR = 5 to override the 4% and press FV again to get the second answer. In general, you can change one input at a time to see how the output changes.)* **($2,315.25; $2,382.03; $3,456.00)**

A company's sales in 2012 were $100 million. If sales grow by 8% annually, what will they be 10 years later? **($215.89 million)** *What would they be if they decline by 8% per year for 10 years?* **($43.44 million)**

How much would $1, growing at 5% per year, be worth after 100 years? **($131.50)** *What would FV be if the growth rate were 10%?* **($13,780.61)**

4-3 Present Values

Suppose you have some extra money and want to make an investment. A broker offers to sell you a bond that will pay a guaranteed $115.76 in 3 years. Banks are currently offering a guaranteed 5% interest on 3-year certificates of deposit (CDs), and if you don't buy the bond you will buy a CD. The 5% rate paid on the CD is defined as your **opportunity cost**, or the rate of return you would earn on an alternative investment of similar risk if you don't invest in the security under consideration. Given these conditions, what's the most you should pay for the bond?

4-3a Discounting a Future Value to Find the Present Value

First, recall from the future value example in the last section that if you invested $100 at 5% in a CD, it would grow to $115.76 in 3 years. You would also have $115.76 after 3 years if you bought the bond. Therefore, the most you should pay for the bond is

It's a Matter of Trust

© Rob Webb/Getty Images

One of our Founding Fathers, Benjamin Franklin, wanted to make a donation to the cities of Boston and Philadelphia, but he didn't want the cities to squander the money before it had grown enough to make a big impact. His solution was the "Methuselah Trust." When Franklin died in 1790, his will left £1,000, at that time about $4,550, to Philadelphia and to Boston, but on the condition that it would be invested for 100 years, after which some the proceeds were to be used for the public projects (primarily trade schools and water works) and the rest invested for another 100 years. Depending on interest rates, this strategy could generate quite a bit of money! For example, if half of his bequest, $2,275, remained invested at 5% compound interest for the entire 200 years, the value in 1990 would be $39.3 million! The ultimate payout, however, was only about $7 million, because substantial amounts were eaten up by trustee fees, taxes, and legal battles. Franklin certainly would have been disappointed!

In 1936 an eccentric investor and New York lawyer, Jonathan Holden, decided to expand on Franklin's idea by donating a series of 500-year and 1,000-year trusts to Hartwick College and several other recipients. By 2008 Hartwick College's trust had grown in value to about $9 million; if invested at 5% for the remaining 928 years of its planned life, its value would grow to ($9 million)$(1.05)^{928}$ = $\$4.15 \times 10^{26}$. That is a lot of dollars by any measure! For example, million-dollar bills (if they existed by then) would paper the earth 10,000 times over, or laid end to end would reach the nearest star, Alpha Centauri, more than 1,000 times. In a move that surely would have disappointed Holden, Hartwick College was able to convert the trust into annual cash flows of about $450,000 a year.

The trusts of Franklin and Holden didn't turn out exactly as they had planned—Franklin's trust didn't grow adequately, and Holden's trust was converted into annual cash flows. This goes to show that you can't always trust a trust!

Sources: Jake Palmateer, "On the Bright Side: Hartwick College Receives $9 million Trust," *The Daily Star, Oneonta, NY*, January 22, 2008, **http://thedailystar.com/local/x112892349/On-The-Bright-Side-Hartwick-College-receives-9M-trust/print**; Lewis H. Lapham, "Trust Issues," *Lapham's Quarterly*, Friday December 2, 2011, **www.laphamsquarterly.org/essays/trust-issues.php?page=1**.

$100—this is its "fair price," which is also its intrinsic, or fundamental, value. If you could buy the bond for *less than* $100, then you should buy it rather than invest in the CD. Conversely, if its price were *more than* $100, you should buy the CD. If the bond's price were exactly $100, you should be indifferent between the bond and the CD.

The $100 is defined as the present value, or PV, of $115.76 due in 3 years when the appropriate interest rate is 5%. In general, *the present value of a cash flow due N years in the future is the amount which, if it were on hand today, would grow to equal the given future amount.* Because $100 would grow to $115.76 in 3 years at a 5% interest rate, $100 is the present value of $115.76 due in 3 years at a 5% rate.

Finding present values is called **discounting**, and as previously noted, it is the reverse of compounding: If you know the PV, you can compound it to find the FV, or if you know the FV, you can discount it to find the PV. Indeed, we simply solve Equation 4-1, the formula for the future value, for the PV to produce the present value equation as follows.

Compounding to find future values: $\text{Future value} = FV_N = PV(1+I)^N$ (4-1)

Discounting to find present values: $\text{Present value} = PV = \dfrac{FV_N}{(1+I)^N}$ (4-3)

The top section of Figure 4-3 shows inputs and a time line for finding the present value of $115.76 discounted back for 3 years. We first calculate the PV using the step-by-step approach. When we found the FV in the previous section, we worked from left to right, *multiplying* the initial amount and each subsequent amount by (1 + I). To find present values, we work backward, or from right to left, *dividing* the future value and each subsequent amount by (1 + I), with the present value of $100 shown in Cell D105. The step-by-step procedure shows exactly what's happening, and that can be quite useful when you are working complex problems or trying to explain a model to others. However, it's inefficient, especially if you are dealing with more than a year or two.

resource
See Ch04 Tool Kit.xls for all calculations.

A more efficient procedure is to use the formula approach in Equation 4-3, simply dividing the future value by $(1 + I)^N$. This gives the same result, as we see in Figure 4-3, Cell G107.

Equation 4-2 is actually programmed into financial calculators. As shown in Figure 4-3, Rows 109 to 111, we can find the PV by entering values for N = 3, I/YR = 5, PMT = 0, and FV = 115.76, and then pressing the PV key to get −100.

FIGURE 4-3
Alternative Procedures for Calculating Present Values

	A	B	C	D	E	F	G
97	INPUTS:						
98		Future payment = CF_N = FV =	$115.76				
99		Interest rate = I =	5.00%				
100		No. of periods = N =	3				
101							
102	Time Line		Periods:	0	1	2	3
103			Cash flow:	PV = ?	0	0	$115.76
104							
105	1. Step-by-Step:			$100.00	← $105.00	← $110.25	← $115.76
106							
107	2. Formula: $PV_N = FV/(1+I)^N$			PV = $115.76/(1.05)^3$		=	$100.00
108							
109		Inputs:	3	5		0	115.76
110	3. Financial Calculator:		N	I/YR	PV	PMT	FV
111		Output:			−$100.00		
112							
113	4. *Excel* Spreadsheet:		PV function:	PV =	=PV(I,N,0,FV)		
114			Fixed inputs:	PV =	=PV(0.05,3,0,115.76) =		−$100.00
115			Cell references:	PV =	=PV(C99,C100,0,C98) =		−$100.00
116	In the *Excel* formula, the terms are entered in this sequence: interest, periods, 0 to indicate no periodic						
117	cash flows, and then the FV. The data can be entered as fixed numbers or, better yet, as cell references.						

Excel also has a function that solves Equation 4-3—this is the PV function, and it is written as **=PV(I,N,0,FV).**[4] Cell E113 shows the inputs to this function. Next, Cell E114 shows the *Excel* function with fixed numbers as inputs, with the actual function and the resulting −$100 in Cell G114. Cell E115 shows the *Excel* function using cell references, with the actual function and the resulting −$100 in Cell G115.

As with the future value calculation, students often wonder why the result of the present value calculation is sometimes positive and sometimes negative. In the algebraic calculations in Rows 105 and 107, the result is +$100, while the result of the calculation using a financial calculator or *Excel's* function in Rows 111 and 114 is −$100. Again, the answer is in the signs of a correctly constructed time line. Outflows are negative and inflows are positive. The PV function for *Excel* and a financial calculator answer the question "How much must I invest today in order to have available to me a certain amount of money in the future?" If you want to have $115.76 available in 3 years (an inflow to you, and therefore positive), then you must invest $100 today (an outflow, and therefore negative). If you use the algebraic functions as in Rows 105 and 107, you must keep track of whether the results of your calculations are inflows or outflows.

The fundamental goal of financial management is to maximize the firm's intrinsic value, and the intrinsic value of a business (or any asset, including stocks and bonds) is the *present value* of its expected future cash flows. Because present value lies at the heart of the valuation process, we will have much more to say about it in the remainder of this chapter and throughout the book.

4-3b Graphic View of the Discounting Process

Figure 4-4 shows that the present value of a sum to be received in the future decreases and approaches zero as the payment date is extended farther and farther into the future; it also shows that, the higher the interest rate, the faster the present value falls. At relatively high rates, funds due in the future are worth very little today, and even at relatively low rates present values of sums due in the very distant future are quite small. For example, at a 20% discount rate, $100 due in 40 years would be worth less than 7 cents today. (However, 1 cent would grow to almost $1 million in 100 years at 20%.)

resource

*See **Ch04 Tool Kit.xls** for all calculations.*

SELF-TEST

What is "discounting," and how is it related to compounding? How is the future value equation (4-1) related to the present value equation (4-3)?

How does the present value of a future payment change as the time to receipt is lengthened? As the interest rate increases?

Suppose a risk-free bond promises to pay $2,249.73 in 3 years. If the going risk-free interest rate is 4%, how much is the bond worth today? **($2,000)** *How much is the bond worth if it matures in 5 rather than 3 years?* **($1,849.11)** *If the risk-free interest rate is 6% rather than 4%, how much is the 5-year bond worth today?* **($1,681.13)**

How much would $1 million due in 100 years be worth today if the discount rate were 5%? **($7,604.49)** *What if the discount rate were 20%?* **($0.0121)**

[4]The third entry in the PV function is zero to indicate that there are no intermediate payments in this example.

FIGURE 4-4

Present Value of $100 at Various Interest Rates and Time Periods

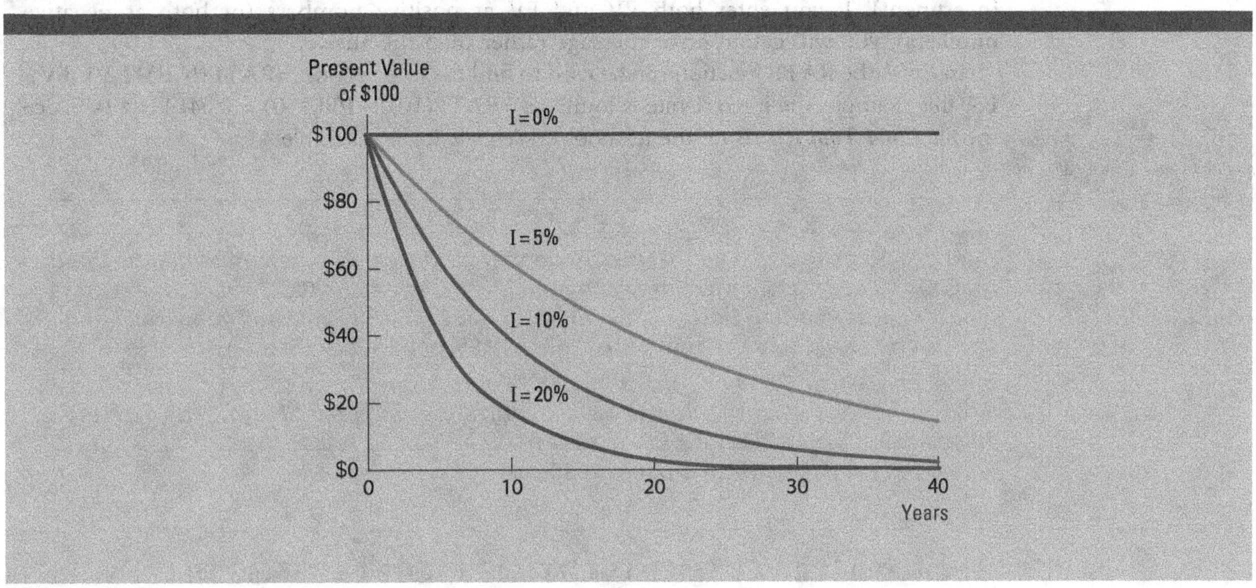

© Cengage Learning 2014

4-4 Finding the Interest Rate, I

We have used Equations 4-1, 4-2, and 4-3 to find future and present values. Those equations have four variables, and if we know three of them, then we (or our calculator or *Excel*) can solve for the fourth. Thus, if we know PV, I, and N, we can solve Equation 4-1 for FV, or if we know FV, I, and N, we can solve Equation 4-3 to find PV. That's what we did in the preceding two sections.

Now suppose we know PV, FV, and N, and we want to find I. For example, suppose we know that a given security has a cost of $100 and that it will return $150 after 10 years. Thus, we know PV, FV, and N, and we want to find the rate of return we will earn if we buy the security. Here's the solution using Equation 4-1 (with FV on the right side of the formula):

$$\begin{aligned} PV(1+I)^N &= FV \\ \$100(1+I)^{10} &= \$150 \\ (1+I)^{10} &= \$150/\$100 \\ (1+I)^{10} &= 1.5 \\ (1+I) &= 1.5^{(1/10)} \\ 1+I &= 1.0414 \\ I &= 0.0414 = 4.14\% \end{aligned}$$

Finding the interest rate by solving the formula takes a little time and thought, but financial calculators and spreadsheets find the answer almost instantly. Here's the calculator setup:

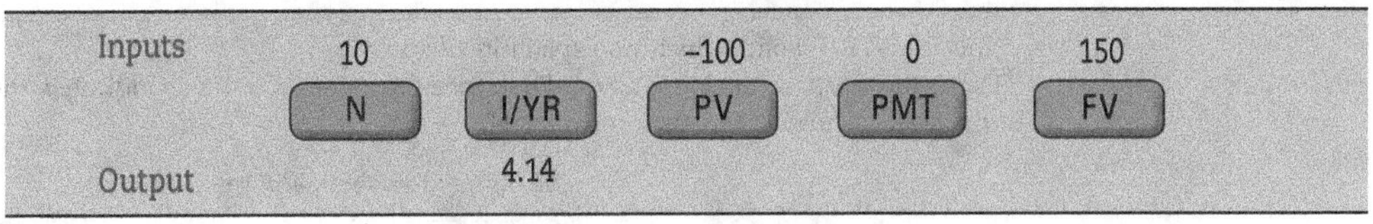

Enter N = 10, PV = −100, PMT = 0 (because there are no payments until the security matures), and FV = 150. Then, when you press the I/YR key, the calculator gives the answer, 4.14%. Notice that the PV is a negative value because it is a cash outflow (an investment) and the FV is positive because it is a cash inflow (a return of the investment). If you enter both PV and FV as positive numbers (or both as negative numbers), you will get an error message rather than the answer.

In *Excel*, the **RATE** function can be used to find the interest rate: **=RATE(N,PMT,PV,FV).** For this example, the interest rate is found as **=RATE(10,0,–100,150)** = 0.0414 = 4.14%. See the file ***Ch04 Tool Kit.xls*** on the textbook's Web site for an example.

resource
*See **Ch04 Tool Kit.xls** for all calculations.*

SELF-TEST

Suppose you can buy a U.S. Treasury bond that makes no payments until the bond matures 10 years from now, at which time it will pay you \$1,000.[5] *What interest rate would you earn if you bought this bond for \$585.43?* **(5.5%)** *What rate would you earn if you could buy the bond for \$550?* **(6.16%)** *For \$600?* **(5.24%)**

Microsoft earned \$0.33 per share in 1997. Fourteen years later, in 2011, it earned \$2.75. What was the growth rate in Microsoft's earnings per share (EPS) over the 14-year period? **(16.35%)** *If EPS in 2011 had been \$2.00 rather than \$2.75, what would the growth rate have been?* **(13.73%)**

4-5 Finding the Number of Years, N

We sometimes need to know how long it will take to accumulate a specific sum of money, given our beginning funds and the rate we will earn. For example, suppose we now have \$500,000 and the interest rate is 4.5%. How long will it be before we have \$1 million?

Here's Equation 4-1, showing all the known variables.

$$\$1{,}000{,}000 = \$500{,}000(1 + 0.045)^N \tag{4-1}$$

We need to solve for N, and we can use three procedures: a financial calculator, *Excel* (or some other spreadsheet), or by working with natural logs. As you might expect, the calculator and spreadsheet approaches are easier.[6] Here's the calculator setup:

Inputs		4.5	-500000	0	1000000
	N	I/YR	PV	PMT	FV
Output	15.7473				

Enter I/YR = 4.5, PV = –500000, PMT = 0, and FV = 1000000. We press the N key to get the answer, 15.7473 years. In *Excel*, we would use the **NPER** function: **=NPER(I,PMT,PV,FV).** Inserting data, we have **=NPER(0.045,0,–500000,1000000)** = 15.7473. The chapter's tool kit, ***Ch04 Tool Kit.xls***, shows this example.

[5] This is a STRIP bond, which we explain in Chapter 5.

[6] Here's the setup for the log solution. First, transform Equation 4-1 as indicated, then find the natural logs using a financial calculator, and then solve for N:

$$\$1{,}000{,}000 = \$500{,}000(1 + 0.045)^N$$
$$2 = (1 + 0.045)^N$$
$$\ln(2) = N[\ln(1.045)]$$
$$N = 0.6931/0.0440 = 15.7473 \text{ years}$$

SELF-TEST

How long would it take \$1,000 to double if it were invested in a bank that pays 6% per year? **(11.9 years)** *How long would it take if the rate were 10%?* **(7.27 years)**

A company's 2013 earnings per share were \$2.75, and its growth rate during the prior 14 years was 16.35% per year. If that growth rate were maintained, how long would it take for EPS to double? **(4.58 years)**

4-6 Perpetuities

The previous sections examined the relationship between the present value and future value of a single payment at a fixed point in time. However, some securities promise to make payments forever. For example, preferred stock, which we discuss in Chapter 7, promises to pay a dividend forever. Another "forever" security originated in the mid-1700s when the British government issued some bonds that never matured and whose proceeds were used to pay off other British bonds. Because this action consolidated the government's debt, the new bonds were called "consols." The term stuck, and now any bond that promises to pay interest perpetually is called a **consol**, or a perpetuity. The interest rate on the consols was 2.5%, so a consol with a face value of £1,000 would pay £25 per year in perpetuity (£ is the currency symbol for a British pound).

A consol, or **perpetuity**, is simply an annuity whose promised payments extend out forever. Since the payments go on forever, you can't apply the step-by-step approach. However, it's easy to find the PV of a perpetuity with the following formula:[7]

$$\text{PV of a perpetuity} = \frac{\text{PMT}}{\text{I}} \tag{4-4}$$

We can use Equation 4-4 to find the value of a British consol with a face value of £1,000 that pays £25 per year in perpetuity. The answer depends on the interest rate being earned on investments of comparable risk at the time the consol is being valued. Originally, the "going rate" as established in the financial marketplace was 2.5%, so originally the consol's value was £1,000:

$$\text{Consol's value}_{\text{Originally}} = £25/0.025 = £1{,}000$$

The annual payment is still £25 today, but the going interest rate has risen to about 5.2%, causing the consol's value to fall to £480.77:

$$\text{Consol's value}_{\text{Today}} = £25/0.052 = £480.77$$

Note, though, that if interest rates decline in the future, say to 2%, then the value of the consol will rise to £1,250.00:

$$\text{Consol's value if rates decline to 2\%} = £25/0.02 = £1{,}250.00$$

[7]Here is an intuitive explanation for Equation 4-4. Suppose you deposit an amount equal to PV in a bank that pays an interest rate of I. Each year you would be able to withdraw an amount equal to I × PV. If you left your deposit in forever, you could withdraw a payment of I × PV forever: PMT = I × PV. Rearranging, we get Equation 4-4. This is only an intuitive explanation, so see ***Web Extension 4B*** on the textbook's Web site for a mathematical derivation of the perpetuity formula.

These examples demonstrate an important point: *When interest rates change, the prices of outstanding bonds also change, but inversely to the change in rates. Thus, bond prices **decline** if rates **rise**, and prices **increase** if rates **fall**. This holds for all bonds, both consols and those with finite maturities.* We discuss this point in more detail in Chapter 5, where we cover bonds in depth.

SELF-TEST

What is the present value of a perpetuity that pays £1,000 per year, beginning 1 year from now, if the appropriate interest rate is 5%? **(£20,000)** *What would the value be if the perpetuity began its payments immediately?* **(£21,000)** *(Hint: Just add the £1,000 to be received immediately to the formula value of the annuity.)*

Do bond prices move directly or inversely with interest rates—that is, what happens to the value of a bond if interest rates increase or decrease?

4-7 Annuities

Thus far, we have dealt with single payments, or "lump sums." However, assets such as bonds provide a series of cash inflows over time, and obligations such as auto loans, student loans, and mortgages call for a series of payments. If the payments are equal and are made at fixed intervals, then we have an **annuity**. For example, $100 paid at the end of each of the next 3 years is a 3-year annuity.

If payments occur at the *end* of each period, then we have an **ordinary** (or **deferred**) **annuity**. Payments on mortgages, car loans, and student loans are generally made at the ends of the periods and thus are ordinary annuities. If the payments are made at the *beginning* of each period, then we have an **annuity due**. Rental lease payments, life insurance premiums, and lottery payoffs (if you are lucky enough to win one!) are examples of annuities due. Ordinary annuities are more common in finance, so when we use the term "annuity" in this book, you may assume that the payments occur at the ends of the periods unless we state otherwise.

Next we show the time lines for a $100, 3-year, 5%, ordinary annuity and for the same annuity on an annuity due basis. With the annuity due, each payment is shifted back (to the left) by 1 year. In our example, we assume that a $100 payment will be made each year, so we show the payments with minus signs.

Ordinary Annuity:

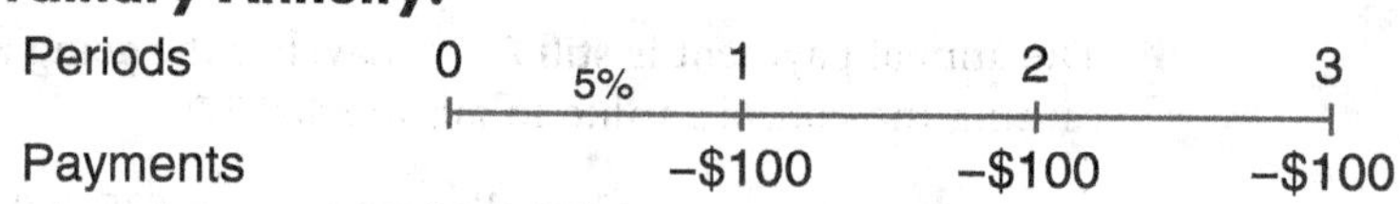

Annuity Due:

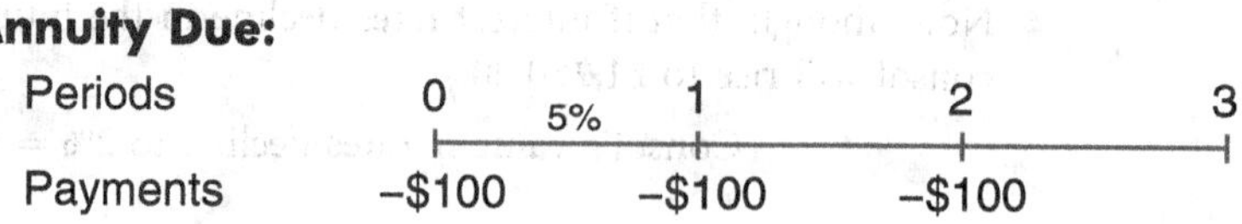

As we demonstrate in the following sections, we can find an annuity's future value, present value, the interest rate built into the contracts, how long it takes to reach a financial goal using the annuity, and, if we know all of those values, the size of the annuity payment. Keep in mind that annuities must have *constant payments* and a *fixed number of periods*. If these conditions don't hold, then the series is not an annuity.

SELF-TEST

What's the difference between an ordinary annuity and an annuity due?

Why should you prefer to receive an annuity due *with payments of $10,000 per year for 10 years than an otherwise similar* ordinary annuity?

4-8 Future Value of an Ordinary Annuity

Consider the ordinary annuity whose time line was shown previously, where you deposit $100 at the *end* of each year for 3 years and earn 5% per year. Figure 4-5 shows how to calculate the **future value of the annuity, FVA_N,** using the same approaches we used for single cash flows.

FIGURE 4-5

Summary: Future Value of an Ordinary Annuity

	A	B	C	D	E	F	G
243	INPUTS:						
244		Payment amount = PMT =	-$100				
245		Interest rate = I =	5.00%				
246		No. of periods = N =	3				
247							
248	1. Step-by-Step:	Periods:	0	1	2	3	
249		Cash flow:		-$100	-$100	-$100	
250				↓	↓	↓	
251				↓	↓	$100.00	
252	Multiply each payment by			↓	↳→→	$105.00	
253	$(1+I)^{N-t}$ and sum these FVs to			↳→→→→→	→→→	$110.25	
254	find FVA_N:					$315.25	
255							
256	2. Formula:						
257							
258		FVA_N	$= PMT \times \left(\frac{(1+I)^N}{I} - \frac{1}{I}\right) =$			$315.25	
259							
260							
261		Inputs:	3	5	0	-100	
262	3. Financial Calculator:		N	I/YR	PV	PMT	FV
263		Output:					$315.25
264							
265	4. *Excel* Spreadsheet:		FV function:	FVA_N =	=FV(I,N,PMT,PV)		
266			Fixed inputs:	FVA_N =	=FV(0.05,3,-100,0)	=	$315.25
267			Cell references:	FVA_N =	=FV(C245,C246,C244,0)	=	$315.25

As shown in the step-by-step section of Figure 4-5, we compound each payment out to Time 3, and then sum those compounded values in Cell F254 to find the annuity's FV, FVA_3 = \$315.25. The first payment earns interest for two periods, the second for one period, and the third earns no interest because it is made at the end of the annuity's life. This approach is straightforward, but if the annuity extends out for many years, it is cumbersome and time-consuming.

As you can see from the time line diagram, with the step-by-step approach we apply the following equation with N = 3 and I = 5%:

$$\begin{aligned} FVA_N &= PMT(1+I)^{N-1} + PMT(1+I)^{N-2} + PMT(1+I)^{N-3} \\ &= \$100(1.05)^2 + \$100(1.05)^1 + \$100(1.05)^0 \\ &= \$315.25 \end{aligned}$$

For the general case, the future value of an annuity is

$$FVA_N = PMT(1+I)^{N-1} + PMT(1+I)^{N-2} + PMT(1+I)^{N-3} + \cdots + PMT(1+I)^0$$

As shown in ***Web Extension 4B*** on the textbook's Web site, the future value of an annuity can be written as follows:[8]

$$FVA_N = PMT\left[\frac{(1+I)^N}{I} - \frac{1}{I}\right] \qquad (4\text{-}5)$$

Using Equation 4-5, the future value of the annuity is found to be \$315.25:

$$FVA_3 = \$100\left[\frac{(1+0.05)^3}{0.05} - \frac{1}{0.05}\right] = \$315.25$$

As you might expect, annuity problems can be solved easily using a financial calculator or a spreadsheet, most of which have the following formula built into them:

$$PV(1+I)^N + PMT\left[\frac{(1+I)^N}{I} - \frac{1}{I}\right] + FV = 0 \qquad (4\text{-}6)$$

The procedure when dealing with annuities is similar to what we have done thus far for single payments, but the presence of recurring payments means that we must use the PMT key. Here's the calculator setup for our illustrative annuity:

						End Mode
Inputs	3	5	0	-100		
	N	I/YR	PV	PMT	FV	
Output					315.25	

[8]Section 4-6 shows that the present value of an infinitely long annuity, called a perpetuity, is equal to PMT/I. The cash flows of an ordinary annuity of N periods are equal to the cash flows of a perpetuity minus the cash flows of a perpetuity that begins at year N+1. Therefore, the future value of an N-period annuity is equal to the future value (as of year N) of a perpetuity minus the value (as of year N) of a perpetuity that begins at year N+1. See ***Web Extension 4B*** on the textbook's Web site for details regarding derivations of Equation 4-5.

The Power of Compound Interest

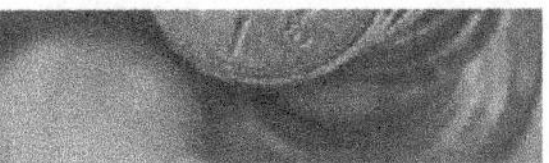

© Rob Webb/Getty Images

Assume that you are 26 and just received your MBA. After reading the introduction to this chapter, you decide to start investing in the stock market for your retirement. Your goal is to have $1 million when you retire at age 65. Assuming you earn 10% annually on your stock investments, how much must you invest at the end of each year in order to reach your goal?

The answer is $2,491, but this amount depends critically on the return your investments earn. If your return drops to 8%, the required annual contribution would rise to $4,185. On the other hand, if the return rises to 12%, you would need to put away only $1,462 per year.

What if you are like most 26-year-olds and wait until later to worry about retirement? If you wait until age 40, you will need to save $10,168 per year to reach your $1 million goal, assuming you can earn 10%, but $13,679 per year if you earn only 8%. If you wait until age 50 and then earn 8%, the required amount will be $36,830 per year!

Although $1 million may seem like a lot of money, it won't be when you get ready to retire. If inflation averages 5% a year over the next 39 years, then your $1 million nest egg would be worth only $149,148 in today's dollars. If you live for 20 years after retirement and earn a real 3% rate of return, your annual retirement income in today's dollars would be only $9,733 before taxes. So, after celebrating your graduation and new job, start saving!

We enter PV = 0 because we start off with nothing, and we enter PMT = −100 because we will deposit this amount in the account at the end of each of the 3 years. The interest rate is 5%, and when we press the FV key we get the answer, FVA_3 = 315.25.

Because this is an ordinary annuity, with payments coming at the *end* of each year, we must set the calculator appropriately. As noted earlier, most calculators "come out of the box" set to assume that payments occur at the end of each period—that is, to deal with ordinary annuities. However, there is a key that enables us to switch between ordinary annuities and annuities due. For ordinary annuities, the designation "End Mode" or something similar is used, while for annuities due the designator is "Begin," "Begin Mode," "Due," or something similar. If you make a mistake and set your calculator on Begin Mode when working with an ordinary annuity, then each payment will earn interest for 1 extra year, which will cause the compounded amounts, and thus the FVA, to be too large.

resource
*See **Ch04 Tool Kit.xls** for all calculations.*

The spreadsheet approach uses *Excel*'s FV function, **=FV(I,N,PMT,PV).** In our example, we have **=FV(0.05,3,−100,0),** and the result is again $315.25.

SELF-TEST

For an ordinary annuity with 5 annual payments of $100 and a 10% interest rate, for how many years will the first payment *earn interest, and what is the compounded value of this payment at the end?* **(4 years, $146.41)** *Answer these questions for the fifth payment.* **(0 years, $100)**

Assume that you plan to buy a condo 5 years from now, and you estimate that you can save $2,500 per year toward a down payment. You plan to deposit the money in a bank that pays 4% interest, and you will make the first deposit at the end of this year. How much will you have after 5 years? **($13,540.81)** *How would your answer change if the bank's interest rate were increased to 6%, or decreased to 3%?* **($14,092.73; $13,272.84)**

4-9 Future Value of an Annuity Due

Because each payment occurs one period earlier with an annuity due, the payments will all earn interest for one additional period. Therefore, the FV of an annuity due will be greater than that of a similar ordinary annuity.

If you followed the step-by-step procedure, you would see that our illustrative annuity due has a FV of $331.01 versus $315.25 for the ordinary annuity. See ***Ch04 Tool Kit.xls*** on the textbook's Web site for a summary of future value calculations.

With the formula approach, we first use Equation 4-5, but because each payment occurs one period earlier, we multiply the Equation 4-5 result by (1 + I):

$$FVA_{due} = FVA_{ordinary}(1 + I) \tag{4-7}$$

Thus, for the annuity due, FVA_{due} = $315.25(1.05) = $331.01, which is the same result as found with the step-by-step approach.

With a calculator, we input the variables just as we did with the ordinary annuity, but we now set the calculator to Begin Mode to get the answer, $331.01.

	N	I/YR	PV	PMT	FV	
Inputs	3	5	0	-100		Begin Mode
Output					331.01	

resource

*See **Ch04 Tool Kit.xls** for all calculations.*

In *Excel*, we still use the FV function, but we must indicate that we have an annuity due. The function is **=FV(I,N,PMT,PV,Type)**, where "Type" indicates the type of annuity. If Type is omitted, then *Excel* assumes that it is 0, which indicates an ordinary annuity. For an annuity due, Type = 1. As shown in ***Ch04 Tool Kit.xls***, the function is **=FV(0.05,3,–100,0,1)** = $331.01.

SELF-TEST

Why does an annuity due always have a higher future value than an ordinary annuity?

If you know the value of an ordinary annuity, explain why you could find the value of the corresponding annuity due by multiplying by (1+I).

Assume that you plan to buy a condo 5 years from now and that you need to save for a down payment. You plan to save $2,500 per year, with the first payment being made immediately *and deposited in a bank that pays 4%. How much will you have after 5 years?* **($14,082.44)** *How much would you have if you made the deposits at the* end *of each year?* **($13,540.81)**

4-10 Present Value of Ordinary Annuities and Annuities Due

The present value of any annuity, $\mathbf{PVA_N}$, can be found using the step-by-step, formula, calculator, or spreadsheet methods. We begin with ordinary annuities.

4-10a Present Value of an Ordinary Annuity

See Figure 4-6 for a summary of the different approaches for calculating the present value of an ordinary annuity.

resource
*See **Ch04 Tool Kit.xls** for all calculations.*

As shown in the step-by-step section of Figure 4-6, we discount each payment back to Time 0, and then sum those discounted values to find the annuity's PV, PVA_3 = \$272.32. This approach is straightforward, but if the annuity extends out for many years, it is cumbersome and time-consuming.

The time line diagram shows that with the step-by-step approach we apply the following equation with N = 3 and I = 5%:

$$PVA_N = PMT/(1+I)^1 + PMT/(1+I)^2 + \cdots + PMT/(1+I)^N$$

FIGURE 4-6

Summary: Present Value of an Ordinary Annuity

	A	B	C	D	E	F	G
313	INPUTS:						
314		Payment amount = PMT =	-\$100				
315		Interest rate = I =	5.00%				
316		No. of periods = N =	3				
317							
318	1. Step-By-Step:	Periods:	0	1	2	3	
319		Cash flow:		-\$100	-\$100	-\$100	
320				↓	↓	↓	
321			\$95.24	←←↲	↓	↓	
322	Divide each payment by		\$90.70	←←←←←←	←←↲	↓	
323	$(1+I)^t$ and sum these PVs to		\$86.38	←←←←←←	←←←←←←	←←↲	
324	find PVA_N:		\$272.32				
325							
326	2. Formula:						
327							
328		PVA_N	$= PMT \times \left(\frac{1}{I} - \frac{1}{I(1+I)^N}\right) =$			\$272.32	
329							
330							
331							
332		Inputs:	3	5		-100	0
333	3. Financial Calculator:		N	I	PV	PMT	FV
334		Output:			272.32		
335							
336	4. *Excel* Spreadsheet:		PV function:	PVA_N =	=PV(I,N,PMT,FV)		
337			Fixed inputs:	PVA_N =	=PV(0.05,3,-100,0)	=	\$272.32
338			Cell references:	PVA_N =	=PV(C315,C316,C314,0)	=	\$272.32

The present value of an annuity can be written as[9]

$$PVA_N = PMT\left[\frac{1}{I} - \frac{1}{I(1+I)^N}\right] \tag{4-8}$$

For our example annuity, the present value is

$$PVA_3 = PMT\left[\frac{1}{0.05} - \frac{1}{0.05(1+0.05)^3}\right] = \$272.32$$

Financial calculators are programmed to solve Equation 4-6, so we input the variables and press the PV key, *first making sure the calculator is set to End Mode*. The calculator setup is shown below:

Inputs	3	5		−100	0	End Mode (Ordinary Annuity)
	N	I/YR	PV	PMT	FV	
Output			272.32			

resource

*See **Ch04 Tool Kit.xls** for all calculations.*

The last section of Figure 4-6 shows the spreadsheet solution using *Excel*'s built-in PV function: **=PV(I,N,PMT,FV)**. In our example, we have **=PV(0.05,3,−100,0)** with a resulting value of $272.32.

4-10b Present Value of Annuities Due

Because each payment for an annuity due occurs one period earlier, the payments will all be discounted for one less period. Therefore, the PV of an annuity due must be greater than that of a similar ordinary annuity.

If you went through the step-by-step procedure, you would see that our example annuity due has a PV of $285.94 versus $272.32 for the ordinary annuity. See ***Ch04 Tool Kit.xls*** for this and the other calculations.

With the formula approach, we first use Equation 4-8 to find the value of the ordinary annuity and then, because each payment now occurs one period earlier, we multiply the Equation 4-8 result by (1 + I):

$$PVA_{due} = PVA_{ordinary}(1+I) \tag{4-9}$$

$$PVA_{due} = \$272.32(1.05) = \$285.94$$

With a financial calculator, the inputs are the same as for an ordinary annuity, except you must set the calculator to Begin Mode:

Inputs	3	5		−100	0	Begin Mode (Annuity Due)
	N	I/YR	PV	PMT	FV	
Output			285.94			

[9]See ***Web Extension 4B*** on the textbook's Web site for details of this derivation.

Variable Annuities: Good or Bad?

© Rob Webb/Getty Images

Retirees appreciate stable, predictable income, so they often buy annuities. Insurance companies have been the traditional suppliers, using the payments they receive to buy high-grade bonds, whose interest is then used to make the promised payments. Such annuities were quite safe and stable and provided returns of around 7.5%. However, returns on stocks (dividends plus capital gains) have historically exceeded bonds' returns (interest). Therefore, some insurance companies in the 1990s began to offer *variable annuities,* which were backed by stocks instead of bonds. If stocks earned in the future as much as they had in the past, then variable annuities could offer returns of about 9%; this is better than the return on fixed-rate annuities. If stock returns turned out to be lower in the future than they had been in the past (or even had negative returns), then the variable annuities promised a *guaranteed minimum payment* of about 6.5%. Variable annuities appealed to many retirees, so companies that offered them had a significant competitive advantage.

The insurance company that pioneered variable annuities, The Hartford Financial Services Group, tried to hedge its position with derivatives that paid off if stocks went down. But like so many other derivatives-based risk management programs, this one went awry in 2008 because stock losses exceeded the assumed worst-case scenario. The Hartford, which was founded in 1810 and was one of the oldest and largest U.S. insurance companies at the beginning of 2008, saw its stock price fall from $85.54 per share to $4.16. Because of the general stock market crash, investors feared that The Hartford would be unable to make good on its variable annuity promises, and this would lead to bankruptcy. The company was bailed out by the economic stimulus package, but this 203-year-old firm will never be the same again.

Source: Leslie Scism and Liam Pleven, "Hartford Aims to Take Risk Out of Annuities," *Online Wall Street Journal,* January 13, 2009.

resource

*See **Ch04 Tool Kit.xls** for all calculations.*

In *Excel,* we again use the PV function, but now we must indicate that we have an annuity due. The function is now **=PV(I,N,PMT,FV,Type)**, where "Type" is the type of annuity. If Type is omitted then *Excel* assumes that it is 0, which indicates an ordinary annuity; for an annuity due, Type = 1. As shown in ***Ch04 Tool Kit.xls***, the function for this example is **=PV(0.05,3,−100,0,1)** = $285.94.

SELF-TEST

Why does an annuity due have a higher present value than an ordinary annuity?

If you know the present value of an ordinary annuity, what's an easy way to find the PV of the corresponding annuity due?

What is the PVA of an ordinary annuity with 10 payments of $100 if the appropriate interest rate is 10%? **($614.46)** *What would the PVA be if the interest rate were 4%?* **($811.09)** *What if the interest rate were 0%?* **($1,000.00)** *What would the PVAs be if we were dealing with annuities due?* **($675.90, $843.53, and $1,000.00)**

Assume that you are offered an annuity that pays $100 at the end of each year for 10 years. You could earn 8% on your money in other equally risky investments. What is the most you should pay for the annuity? **($671.01)** *If the payments began immediately, then how much would the annuity be worth?* **($724.69)**

4-11 Finding Annuity Payments, Periods, and Interest Rates

In the three preceding sections we discussed how to find the FV and PV of ordinary annuities and annuities due, using these four methods: step-by-step, formula, financial calculator, and *Excel*. Five variables are involved—N, I, PMT, FV, and PV—and if you know any four, you can find the fifth by solving either Equation 4-4 (4-6 for annuities due) or 4-7 (4-8 for annuities due). However, a trial-and-error procedure is generally required to find N or I, and that can be quite tedious. Therefore, we discuss only the financial calculator and spreadsheet approaches for finding N and I.

4-11a Finding Annuity Payments, PMT

We need to accumulate $10,000 and have it available 5 years from now. We can earn 6% on our money. Thus, we know that FV = 10,000, PV = 0, N = 5, and I/YR = 6. We can enter these values in a financial calculator and then press the PMT key to find our required deposits. However, the answer depends on whether we make deposits at the end of each year (ordinary annuity) or at the beginning (annuity due), so the mode must be set properly. Here are the results for each type of annuity:

	N	I/YR	PV	PMT	FV	
Inputs	5	6	0		10000	End Mode (Ordinary Annuity)
Output				-1,773.96		

	N	I/YR	PV	PMT	FV	
Inputs	5	6	0		10000	Begin Mode (Annuity Due)
Output				-1,673.55		

Thus, you must put away $1,773.96 per year if you make payments at the *end* of each year, but only $1,673.55 if the payments begin *immediately*. Finally, note that the required payment for the annuity due is the ordinary annuity payment divided by (1 + I): $1,773.96/1.06 = $1,673.55.

Excel can also be used to find annuity payments, as shown below for the two types of annuities. For end-of-year (ordinary) annuities, "Type" can be left blank or a 0 can be inserted. For beginning-of-year annuities (annuities due), the same function is used but now Type is designated as 1. Here is the setup for the two types of annuities.

resource
See ***Ch04 Tool Kit.xls*** for all calculations.

Function: = **PMT(I,N,PV,FV,Type)**

Ordinary annuity: = **PMT(0.06,5,0,10000)** = −$1,773.96

Annuity due: = **PMT(0.06,5,0,10000,1)** = −$1,673.55

4-11b Finding the Number of Periods, N

Suppose you decide to make end-of-year deposits, but you can save only $1,200 per year. Again assuming that you would earn 6%, how long would it take you to reach your $10,000 goal? Here is the calculator setup:

	N	I/YR	PV	PMT	FV	
Inputs		6	0	-1200	10000	End Mode
Output	6.96					

With these smaller deposits, it would take 6.96 years, not 5 years, to reach the $10,000 target. If you began the deposits immediately, then you would have an annuity due and N would be slightly less, 6.63 years.

resource
See ***Ch04 Tool Kit.xls*** for all calculations.

With *Excel*, you can use the NPER function: **=NPER(I,PMT,PV,FV,Type).** For our ordinary annuity example, Type is left blank (or 0 is inserted) and the function is **=NPER(0.06,–1200,0,10000)** = 6.96. If we put in 1 for Type, we would find N = 6.63.

4-11c Finding the Interest Rate, I

Now suppose you can save only $1,200 annually, but you still need to have the $10,000 in 5 years. What rate of return would you have to earn to reach your goal? Here is the calculator setup:

	N	I/YR	PV	PMT	FV	
Inputs	5		0	-1200	10000	End Mode
Output		25.78				

Thus, you would need to earn a whopping 25.78%! About the only way to earn such a high return would be either to invest in speculative stocks or head to a Las Vegas casino. Of course, speculative stocks and gambling aren't like making deposits in a bank with a guaranteed rate of return, so there would be a high probability that you'd end up with nothing. So, you should probably save more, lower your $10,000 target, or extend your time horizon. It might be appropriate to seek a somewhat higher return, but trying to earn 25.78% in a 6% market would involve speculation, not investing.

In *Excel,* you can use the RATE function: **=RATE(N,PMT,PV,FV,Type).** For our example, the function is **=RATE(5,–1200,0,10000)** = 0.2578 = 25.78%. If you decide to make the payments beginning immediately then the required rate of return would decline sharply, to 17.54%.

SELF-TEST

You just inherited $100,000 and invested it at 7% per year. How large a withdrawal could you make at the end of each of the next 10 years and end up with zero? **($14,237.75)** *How would your answer change if you made withdrawals at the beginning of each year?* **($13,306.31)**

If you have $100,000 that is invested at 7% and you wanted to withdraw $10,000 at the end of each year, how long will your funds last? **(17.8 years)** *How long would they last if you earned 0%?* **(10 years)** *How long would they last if you earned the 7% but limited your withdrawals to $7,000 per year?* **(forever)**

Your uncle named you as the beneficiary of his life insurance policy. The insurance company gives you a choice of $100,000 today or a 12-year annuity of $12,000 at the end of each year. What rate of return is the insurance company offering? **(6.11%)**

You just inherited an annuity that will pay you $10,000 per year for 10 years, and you receive the first payment today. A professional investor offers to give you $60,000 for the annuity. If you sell it to him, what rate of return will he earn on the investment? **(13.70%)** *If you think a "fair" rate of return would be 6%, how much should you ask for the annuity?* **($78,016.92)**

Using the Internet for Personal Financial Planning

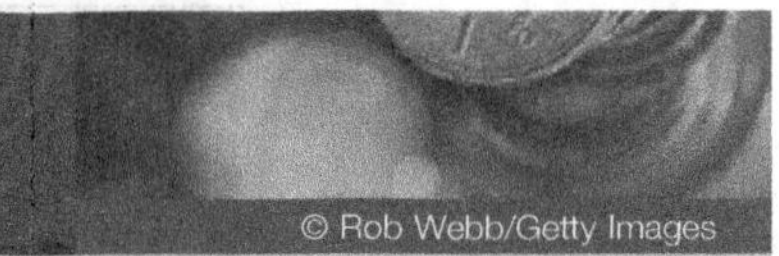

© Rob Webb/Getty Images

How good are your financial planning skills? For example, should you buy or lease a car? How much and how soon should you begin to save for your children's education? How expensive a house can you afford? Should you refinance your home mortgage? How much must you save each year if you are to retire comfortably? The answers to these questions are often complicated and depend on a number of factors, such as projected housing and education costs, interest rates, inflation, expected family income, and stock market returns.

Fortunately, you should be able to use time value of money concepts and online resources to begin developing your financial plan. In addition to the online data sources described in Chapter 2, an excellent source of information is available at **www.smartmoney.com**. *Smartmoney* is a personal finance magazine produced by the publishers of *The Wall Street Journal*. If you go to *Smartmoney*'s Web site, you will find a section entitled "Tools." This section has a number of financial calculators, spreadsheets, and descriptive materials that cover a wide range of personal finance issues.

4-12 Uneven, or Irregular, Cash Flows

The definition of an annuity includes the term *constant payment*, which suggests that annuities involve a set of identical payments over a given number of periods. Although many financial decisions do involve constant payments, many others involve cash flows that are **uneven** or **irregular**. For example, the dividends on common stocks are typically expected to increase over time, and the investments that companies make in new products, expanded production capacity, and replacement machinery almost always generate cash flows that vary from year to year. Throughout the book, we use the term *payment* (PMT) in situations where the cash flows are constant and thus an annuity is involved; if different cash flows occur in different time periods, t, then we use the term CF_t to designate the *cash flow* in period t.

There are two important classes of uneven cash flows: (1) those in which the cash flow stream consists of a series of annuity payments plus an additional final lump sum in Year N, and (2) all other uneven streams. Bonds are an instance of the first type, while stocks and capital investments illustrate the second type. Here's an example of each type.

Stream 1. Annuity plus an additional final payment:

Periods	0 (I = 12%)	1	2	3	4	5
Cash flows	$0	$100	$100	$100	$100	$ 100
						$1,000
						$1,100

Stream 2. Irregular cash flow stream:

Periods	0 (I = 12%)	1	2	3	4	5
Cash flows	$0	$100	$300	$300	$300	$500

Equation 4-10 can be used, following the step-by-step procedure, to find the PV of either stream. However, as we shall see, the solution process differs significantly for the two types.

$$PV = \frac{CF_1}{(1+I)^1} + \frac{CF_2}{(1+I)^2} + \cdots + \frac{CF_N}{(1+I)^N} = \sum_{t=1}^{N} \frac{CF_t}{(1+I)^t} \quad (4\text{-}10)$$

4-12a Annuity Plus Additional Final Payment

First, consider Stream 1 and notice that it is a 5-year, 12%, ordinary annuity plus a final payment of $1,000. We can find the PV of the annuity, find the PV of the final payment, and then sum them to get the PV of the stream. Financial calculators are programmed to do this for us—we use all five time value of money (TVM) keys, entering the data for the four known values as shown below, and then pressing the PV key to get the answer, $927.90:

	N	I/YR	PV	PMT	FV
Inputs	5	12		100	10000
Output			−927.90		

Similarly, we could use *Excel*'s PV function: **=PV(I,N,PMT,FV) = PV(0.12,5,100,1000)** = −$927.90. Note that the process is similar to that for annuities, except we now have a nonzero value for FV.

4-12b Irregular Cash Flow Stream

Now consider the irregular stream, which is analyzed in Figure 4-7. The top section shows the basic time line, which contains the inputs, and we first use the step-by-step approach to find PV = $1,016.35. Note that we show the PV of each cash flow directly below the cash flow, and then we sum these PVs to find the PV of the stream. This setup saves space as compared with showing the individual PVs in a column, and it is also transparent and thus easy to understand.

Now consider the financial calculator approach. The cash flows don't form an annuity, so you can't use the annuity feature on the calculator. You could, of course, use the calculator in the step-by-step procedure, but financial calculators have a feature—the cash flow register—that allows you to find the present value more efficiently. First, you input the individual cash flows, in chronological order, into the cash flow register.[10] Cash flows are designated CF_0, CF_1, CF_2, CF_3, and so on, up to the last cash flow, CF_N. Next, you enter the interest rate, I/YR. At this point, you have substituted in all the known values of Equation 4-10, so when you press the NPV key you get the PV of the stream. The calculator finds the PV of each cash flow and sums them to find the PV of the entire stream. To input the cash flows for this problem, enter 0 (because $CF_0 = 0$), 100, 300, 300, 300, and 500 in that order into the cash flow register, enter I/YR = 12, and then press NPV to obtain the answer, $1,016.35.

resource
*See **Ch04 Tool Kit.xls** for all calculations.*

Two points should be noted. First, when dealing with the cash flow register, the calculator uses the term "NPV" rather than "PV." The N stands for "net," so NPV is the abbreviation for "net present value," which is simply the net present value of a series of positive and negative cash flows, including any cash flow at time zero. The NPV

[10]These instructions are for the HP 10bII+, but most other financial calculators work in a similar manner.

FIGURE 4-7

Present Value of an Irregular Cash Flow Stream

	A	B	C	D	E	F	G
466	INPUTS:						
467		Interest rate = I =	12%				
468							
469	1. Step-by-step:						
470	Periods:	0	1	2	3	4	5
471	Cash Flows:	$0.00	$100.00	$300.00	$300.00	$300.00	$500.00
472	PVs of the CFs:		$89.29	$239.16	$213.53	$190.66	$283.71
473							
474	PV of the Irregular CF Stream = Sum of the Individual PVs =				$1,016.35		
475							
476							
477	2. Calculator:	You could enter the cash flows into the cash flow register of a financial calculator, enter I/YR, and then press the NPV key to find the answer.					$1,016.35
478							
479	3. *Excel* Spreadsheet:		NPV Function:	NPV =	= NPV(I,CFs)		
480			Fixed inputs:	NPV =	=NPV(0.12,100,300,300,300,500)		$1,016.35
481			Cell references:	NPV =	=NPV(C467,C471:G471)		$1,016.35
482–485	The *Excel* formula ignores the initial cash flow (in Year 0). When entering a cash flow range, *Excel* assumes that the first value occurs at the end of the first year. As we will see later, if there is an initial cash flow, it must be added separately to complete the NPV formula result. Notice too that you can enter cash flows one-by-one, but if the cash flows appear in consecutive cells, you can enter the cell range, as we did here.						

function will be used extensively when we get to capital budgeting, where CF_0 is generally the cost of the project.

The second point to note is that repeated cash flows with identical values can be entered into the cash flow register more efficiently on some calculators by using the Nj key. In this illustration, you would enter $CF_0 = 0$, $CF_1 = 100$, $CF_2 = 300$, Nj = 3 (which tells the calculator that the 300 occurs 3 times), and $CF_5 = 500$.[11] Then enter I = 12, press the NPV key, and 1,016.35 will appear in the display. Also, note that numbers entered into the cash flow register remain in the register until they are cleared. Thus, if you previously worked a problem with eight cash flows and then moved to one with only four cash flows, the calculator would simply add the cash flows from the second problem to those of the first problem, and you would get an incorrect answer. Therefore, you must be sure to clear the cash flow register before starting a new problem.

Spreadsheets are especially useful for solving problems with uneven cash flows. You enter the cash flows in the spreadsheet as shown in Figure 4-7 on Row 471. To find the PV of these cash flows without going through the step-by-step process, you would use the NPV function. First put the cursor on the cell where you want the answer to appear, Cell G481, click the function wizard, choose Financial, scroll down to NPV, and click OK to

[11]On some calculators, instead of entering $CF_5 = 500$, you enter $CF_3 = 500$, because this is the next cash flow *different* from 300.

get the dialog box. Then enter C467 (or 0.12) for Rate and enter either the individual cash flows or the range of cells containing the cash flows, C471:G471, for Value 1. Be very careful when entering the range of cash flows. With a financial calculator, you begin by entering the Time-0 cash flow. With *Excel,* you do *not* include the Time-0 cash flow; instead, you begin with the Time-1 cash flow. Now, when you click OK, you get the PV of the stream, $1,016.35. Note that you can use the PV function if the payments are constant, but you must use the NPV function if the cash flows are not constant. Finally, note that *Excel* has a major advantage over financial calculators in that you can see the cash flows, which makes it easy to spot data-entry errors. With a calculator, the numbers are buried in the machine, making it harder to check your work.

SELF-TEST

Could you use Equation 4-3, once for each cash flow, to find the PV of an uneven stream of cash flows?

What is the present value of a 5-year ordinary annuity of $100 plus an additional $500 at the end of Year 5 if the interest rate is 6%? **($794.87)** *What would the PV be if the $100 payments occurred in Years 1 through 10 and the $500 came at the end of Year 10?* **($1,015.21)**

What is the present value of the following uneven cash flow stream: $0 at Time 0, $100 at the end of Year 1 (or at Time 1), $200 at the end of Year 2, $0 at the end of Year 3, and $400 at the end of Year 4—assuming the interest rate is 8%? **($558.07)**

Would a "typical" common stock provide cash flows more like an annuity or more like an uneven cash flow stream?

4-13 Future Value of an Uneven Cash Flow Stream

The future value of an uneven cash flow stream (sometimes called the **terminal,** or **horizon, value**) is found by compounding each payment to the end of the stream and then summing the future values:

$$\begin{aligned} FV &= CF_0(1+I)^N + CF_1(1+I)^{N-1} + CF_2(1+I)^{N-2} + \cdots + CF_{N-1}(1+I) + CF_N \\ &= \sum_{t=0}^{N} CF_t(1+I)^{N-t} \end{aligned} \tag{4-11}$$

The future value of our illustrative uneven cash flow stream is $1,791.15, as shown in Figure 4-8.

Most financial calculators have a net future value (NFV) key, which, after the cash flows and interest rate have been entered, can be used to obtain the future value of an uneven cash flow stream. If your calculator doesn't have the NFV feature, you can first find the net present value of the stream, and then find its net future value as NFV = NPV$(1 + I)^N$. In the illustrative problem, we find PV = 1,016.35 using the cash flow register and I = 12. Then we use the TVM register, entering N = 5, I = 12, PV = −1016.35, and PMT = 0. When we press FV, we find FV = 1,791.15, which is the same as the value shown on the time line in Figure 4-8. As Figure 4-8 also shows, the same procedure can be used with *Excel.*

SELF-TEST

What is the future value of this cash flow stream: $100 at the end of 1 year, $150 after 2 years, and $300 after 3 years, assuming the appropriate interest rate is 15%? **($604.75)**

FIGURE 4-8

Future Value of an Irregular Cash Flow Stream

	A	B	C	D	E	F	G
498	INPUTS:						
499		Interest rate = I =	12%				
500							
501	1. Step-by-step:						
502		Periods:	0	1	2	3	4	5
503		Cash flows:	$0.00	$100.00	$300.00	$300.00	$300.00	$500.00
504		FVs of the CFs:		$157.35	$421.48	$376.32	$336.00	$500.00
505							
506	PV of the Irregular CF Stream = Sum of the Individual PVs =				$1,791.15		
507							
508							
509	2. Calculator:	You could enter the cash flows into the cash flow register of a financial calculator, enter I/YR, and then press the NFV key to find the answer.					$1,791.15
510							
511	3. *Excel* Spreadsheet		Step 1. Find NPV:		=NPV(C499,C503:G503)		$1,016.35
512			Step 2. Compound NPV to find NFV:		=FV(C499,G502,0,-G511)		$1,791.15

4-14 Solving for I with Irregular Cash Flows

Before financial calculators and spreadsheets existed, it was *extremely difficult* to find I if the cash flows were uneven. However, with spreadsheets and financial calculators it's easy to find I. If you have an *annuity plus a final lump sum*, you can input values for N, PV, PMT, and FV into the calculator's TVM registers and then press the I/YR key. Here's the setup for Stream 1 from Section 4-12, assuming we must pay $927.90 to buy the asset:

	N	I/YR	PV	PMT	FV
Inputs	5		-927.90	100	1000
Output		12.00			

The rate of return on the $927.90 investment is 12%.

Finding the interest rate for an *irregular cash flow stream* with a calculator is a bit more complicated. Figure 4-9 shows Stream 2 from Section 4-12, assuming a required investment of $CF_0 = -\$1,000$. First, note that there is no simple step-by-step method for finding the rate of return—finding the rate for this investment requires a trial-and-error process, which is terribly time-consuming. Therefore, we really need a financial calculator or a spreadsheet. With a calculator, we would enter the CFs into the cash flow register and then press the IRR key to get the answer. IRR stands for "internal rate of return," and it is the rate of return the investment provides. The investment is the cash flow at Time 0, and it must be entered as a negative number. When we enter those cash flows in the calculator's cash flow register and press the IRR key, we get the rate of return on the $1,000 investment, 12.55%. Finally, note that once you have entered the cash flows in the calculator's register,

FIGURE 4-9

IRR of an Uneven Cash Flow Stream

	A	B	C	D	E	F	G
545	Periods:	0	1	2	3	4	5
546	Cash flows:	-$1,000	$100	$300	$300	$300	$500
547							
548	1. Calculator:	You could enter the cash flows into the cash flow register of a financial calculator and then press the IRR key to find the answer.					12.55%
549							
550	2. *Excel* IRR Function:		Cell references:	IRR =	=IRR(B546:G546)		12.55%

you can find both the investment's net present value (NPV) and its internal rate of return. For investment decisions, we typically want both of these numbers. Therefore, we generally enter the data once and then find both the NPV and the IRR.

You would get the same answer using *Excel*'s IRR function, as shown in Figure 4-9. Notice that when using the IRR—unlike using the NPV function—you must include all cash flows, including the Time-0 cash flow.

SELF-TEST

An investment costs $465 now and is expected to produce cash flows of $100 at the end of each of the next 4 years, plus an extra lump-sum payment of $200 at the end of the fourth year. What is the expected rate of return on this investment? **(9.05%)**

An investment costs $465 and is expected to produce cash flows of $100 at the end of Year 1, $200 at the end of Year 2, and $300 at the end of Year 3. What is the expected rate of return on this investment? **(11.71%)**

4-15 Semiannual and Other Compounding Periods

In most of our examples thus far, we assumed that interest is compounded once a year, or annually. This is **annual compounding**. Suppose, however, that you put $1,000 into a bank that pays a 6% annual interest rate but credits interest each 6 months. This is **semiannual compounding**. If you leave your funds in the account, how much would you have at the end of 1 year under semiannual compounding? Note that you will receive $60 of interest for the year, but you will receive $30 of it after only 6 months and the other $30 at the end of the year. You will earn interest on the first $30 during the second 6 months, so you will end the year with more than the $60 you would have had under annual compounding. You would be even better off under quarterly, monthly, weekly, or daily compounding. Note also that virtually all bonds pay interest semiannually; most stocks pay dividends quarterly; most mortgages, student loans, and auto loans involve monthly payments; and most money fund accounts pay interest daily. Therefore, it is essential that you understand how to deal with nonannual compounding.

4-15a Types of Interest Rates

When we move beyond annual compounding, we must deal with the following four types of interest rates:

- Nominal annual rates, given the symbol I_{NOM}
- Annual percentage rates, termed **APR** rates
- Periodic rates, denoted as I_{PER}
- Effective annual rates, given the symbol **EAR** or **EFF%**

Nominal (or Quoted) Rate, I_{NOM}[12]

This is the rate quoted by banks, brokers, and other financial institutions. So, if you talk with a banker, broker, mortgage lender, auto finance company, or student loan officer about rates, the nominal rate is the one he or she will normally quote you. However, to be meaningful, the quoted nominal rate must also include the number of compounding periods per year. For example, a bank might offer you a CD at 6% compounded daily, while a credit union might offer 6.1% compounded monthly.

Note that the nominal rate is never shown on a time line, and it is never used as an input in a financial calculator (except when compounding occurs only once a year). If more frequent compounding occurs, you must use periodic rates.

Periodic Rate, I_{PER}

This is the rate charged by a lender or paid by a borrower each period. It can be a rate per year, per 6 months (semiannually), per quarter, per month, per day, or per any other time interval. For example, a bank might charge 1.5% per month on its credit card loans, or a finance company might charge 3% per quarter on installment loans.

We find the periodic rate as follows:

$$\text{Periodic rate } I_{PER} = I_{NOM}/M \quad (4\text{-}12)$$

where I_{NOM} is the nominal annual rate and M is the number of compounding periods per year. Thus, a 6% nominal rate with semiannual payments results in a periodic rate of

$$\text{Periodic rate } I_{PER} = 6\%/2 = 3.00\%$$

If only one payment is made per year then M = 1, in which case the periodic rate would equal the nominal rate: 6%/1 = 6%.

The periodic rate is the rate shown on time lines and used in calculations.[13] To illustrate, suppose you invest $100 in an account that pays a nominal rate of 12%, compounded

---

[12]The term *nominal rate* as used here does not have the same meaning as it did in Chapter 1. There, nominal interest rates referred to stated market rates as opposed to real (zero-inflation) rates. In this chapter, the term *nominal rate* means the stated, or quoted, annual rate as opposed to the effective annual rate, which we explain later. In both cases, though, *nominal* means *stated,* or *quoted,* as opposed to some sort of adjusted rate.

[13]The only exception is in cases where (1) annuities are involved *and* (2) the payment periods do not correspond to the compounding periods. In such cases—for example, if you are making quarterly payments into a bank account to build up a specified future sum but the bank pays interest on a daily basis—then the calculations are more complicated. For such problems, the simplest procedure is to determine the periodic (daily) interest rate by dividing the nominal rate by 365 (or by 360 if the bank uses a 360-day year), then compound each payment over the exact number of days from the payment date to the terminal point, and then sum the compounded payments to find the future value of the annuity. This is a simple process with a computer.

quarterly, or 3% per period. How much would you have after 2 years if you leave the funds on deposit? First, here is the time line for the problem:

Quarters	0	3%	1	2	3	4	5	6	7	8
	-$100									FV=?

To find the FV, we would use this modified version of Equation 4-1:

$$FV_N = PV(1 + I_{PER})^{\text{Number of periods}} = PV\left(1 + \frac{I_{NOM}}{M}\right)^{MN} \quad \text{(4-13)}$$

$$= \$100\left(1 + \frac{0.12}{4}\right)^{4\times 2} = \$100(1 + 0.03)^8 = \$126.68.$$

With a financial calculator, we find the FV using these inputs: N = 4 × 2 = 8, I = 12/4 = 3, PV = −100, and PMT = 0. The result is again FV = $126.68.[14]

	N	I/YR	PV	PMT	FV
Inputs	8	3	-100	0	
Output					126.68

Effective (or Equivalent) Annual Rate (EAR or EFF%)

This is the annual (interest once a year) rate that produces the same final result as compounding at the periodic rate for M times per year. The EAR, also called EFF% (for effective percentage rate), is found as follows:[15]

$$\begin{aligned} EAR = EFF\% &= (1 + I_{PER})^M - 1.0 \\ &= \left(1 + \frac{I_{NOM}}{M}\right)^M - 1.0 \end{aligned} \quad \text{(4-14)}$$

Here I_{NOM}/M is the periodic rate, N is the number of years, and M is the number of periods per year. If a bank would lend you money at a nominal rate of 12%, compounded quarterly, then the EFF% rate would be 12.5509%:

$$\begin{aligned} \textbf{Rate on bank loan: } EFF\% &= (1 + 0.03)^4 - 1.0 = (1.03)^4 - 1.0 \\ &= 1.125509 - 1.0 = 0.125509 = 12.5509\% \end{aligned}$$

[14]Most financial calculators have a feature that allows you to set the number of payments per year and then use the nominal annual interest rate. However, students tend to make fewer errors when using the periodic rate with their calculators set for one payment per year (i.e., per period), so this is what we recommend. Note also that you cannot use a normal time unless you use the periodic rate.

[15]You could also use the "interest conversion feature" of a financial calculator. Most financial calculators are programmed to find the EFF% or, given the EFF%, to find the nominal rate; this is called "interest rate conversion." You enter the nominal rate and the number of compounding periods per year, and then press the EFF% key to find the effective annual rate. However, we generally use Equation 4-14 because it's easy and because using the equation reminds us of what we are really doing. If you do use the interest rate conversion feature on your calculator, don't forget to reset your settings afterward. Interest conversion is discussed in our calculator tutorials.

Truth in Lending: What Loans Really Cost

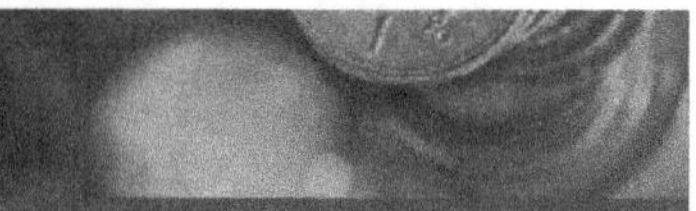

© Rob Webb/Getty Images

Congress passed the Consumer Credit Protection Act in 1968. The Truth in Lending provisions in the Act require banks and other lenders to disclose the **annual percentage rate (APR)** they are charging. For example, suppose you plan to buy a fancy TV set that costs \$3,000, and the store offers you credit for 1 year at an "add-on" quoted rate of 8%. Here we first find the total dollars of interest by multiplying the \$3,000 you are borrowing times 8%, resulting in \$240. Add the interest to the \$3,000 cost of the TV, for a total loan of \$3,240. Then divide the total loan by 12 to get the monthly payments: \$3,240/12 = \$270 per month, with the first payment made at the time of purchase. Therefore, we have a 12-month annuity due with payments of \$270. Is your cost really the 8% that you were quoted?

To find the APR, set your calculator to Begin Mode, then enter N = 12, PV = 3000, PMT = −270, and FV = 0. Then, when you press the I/YR key, you get the periodic rate, 1.4313%. You then multiply by 12 to get the APR, 17.1758%. You could also find the EFF%, which is 18.5945%. We show these calculations using both the calculator and *Excel*, along with a time line that helps us visualize what's happening, in the chapter's *Excel* ***Tool Kit***.

The 17.1758% APR that the dealer is required to report is a much better indicator of the loan's cost than the 8% nominal rate, but it still does not reflect the true cost, which is the 18.5945% effective annual rate. Thus, buying the TV on time would really cost you 18.5945%. If you don't know what's happening when you buy on time or borrow, you may pay a lot more than you think!

To see the importance of the EFF%, suppose that—as an alternative to the bank loan—you could borrow on a credit card that charges 1% per month. Would you be better off using the bank loan or credit card loan? *To answer this question, the cost of each alternative must be expressed as an EFF%.* We just saw that the bank loan's effective cost is 12.5509%. The cost of the credit card loan, with monthly payments, is slightly higher, 12.6825%:

$$\textbf{Credit card loan: } \text{EFF\%} = (1 + 0.01)^{12} - 1.0 = (1.01)^{12} - 1.0$$

$$= 1.126825 - 1.0 = 0.126825 = 12.6825\%$$

This result is logical: Both loans have the same 12% nominal rate, yet you would have to make the first payment after only 1 month on the credit card versus 3 months under the bank loan.

The EFF% rate is rarely used in calculations. *However, it must be used to compare the effective costs of different loans or rates of return on different investments when payment periods differ,* as in our example of the credit card versus a bank loan.

4-15b The Result of Frequent Compounding

What would happen to the future value of an investment if interest were compounded annually, semiannually, quarterly, or some other less-than-annual period? Because interest will be earned on interest more often, you should expect higher future values the more frequently compounding occurs. Similarly, you should expect the effective annual rate to increase with more frequent compounding. As Figure 4-10 shows, these results do occur —the future value and the EFF% do increase as the frequency of compounding increases. Notice that the biggest increase in FV (and in EFF%) occurs when compounding goes from annual to semiannual, and notice also that moving from monthly to daily compounding has a relatively small impact. Although Figure 4-10 shows daily compounding as the smallest interval, it is possible to compound even more frequently. At the limit, compounding can occur **continuously**. This is explained in ***Web Extension 4C*** on the textbook's Web site.

FIGURE 4-10

Effect on $100 of Compounding More Frequently Than Once a Year

	A	B	C	D	E	F	G
568	Frequency of Compounding	Nominal Annual Rate	Number of Periods per Year (M)[a]	Periodic Interest Rate (I_{PER})	Effective Annual Rate (EFF%)[b]	Future Value[c]	Percentage Increase in FV
569	Annual	12%	1	12.0000%	12.0000%	$112.00	
570	Semiannual	12%	2	6.0000%	12.3600%	$112.36	0.32%
571	Quarterly	12%	4	3.0000%	12.5509%	$112.55	0.17%
572	Monthly	12%	12	1.0000%	12.6825%	$112.68	0.12%
573	Daily	12%	365	0.0329%	12.7475%	$112.75	0.06%

Notes:

[a] We used 365 days per year in the calculations.
[b] The EFF% is calculated as $(1 + I_{PER})^M$.
[c] The Future value is calculated as $100(1 + EFF%).

SELF-TEST

Would you rather invest in an account that pays a 7% nominal rate with annual compounding or with monthly compounding? If you borrowed at a nominal rate of 7%, would you rather make annual or monthly payments? Why?

What is the future value of $100 after 3 years if the appropriate interest rate is 8%, compounded annually? **($125.97)** *Compounded monthly?* **($127.02)**

What is the present value of $100 due in 3 years if the appropriate interest rate is 8%, compounded annually? **($79.38)** *Compounded monthly?* **($78.73)**

Define the following terms: annual percentage rate (APR), effective annual rate (EFF%), and nominal interest rate (I_{NOM}).

A bank pays 5% with daily compounding on its savings accounts. Should it advertise the nominal or effective rate if it is seeking to attract new deposits?

Credit card issuers must by law print their annual percentage rate on their monthly statements. A common APR is 18%, with interest paid monthly. What is the EFF% on such a loan? **(19.56%)**

Some years ago banks weren't required to reveal the rate they charged on credit cards. Then Congress passed a "truth in lending" law that required them to publish their APR rate. Is the APR rate really the most truthful rate, or would the EFF% be even more truthful?

4-16 Fractional Time Periods[16]

So far we have assumed that payments occur at either the beginning or the end of periods, but not *within* periods. However, we occasionally encounter situations that require compounding or discounting over fractional periods. For example, suppose you deposited $100 in a bank

[16]This section is interesting and useful, but relatively technical. It can be omitted, at the option of the instructor, without loss of continuity.

that pays a nominal rate of 10%, compounded daily, based on a 365-day year. How much would you have after 9 months? The answer of $107.79 is found as follows:[17]

$$\text{Periodic rate} = I_{PER} = 0.10/365 = 0.000273973 \text{ per day}$$

$$\text{Number of days} = (9/12)(365) = 0.75(365)$$
$$= 273.75 \text{ days, rounded to } 274$$

$$\text{Ending amount} = \$100(1.000273973)^{274} = \$107.79$$

Now suppose that instead you borrow $100 at a nominal rate of 10% per year and are charged *simple interest*, which means that interest is not charged on interest. If the loan is outstanding for 274 days (or 9 months), how much interest would you have to pay? The interest owed is equal to the principal multiplied by the interest rate times the number of periods. In this case, the number of periods is equal to a fraction of a year: N = 274/365 = 0.7506849.

$$\text{Interest owed} = \$100(10\%)(0.7506849) = \$7.51$$

Another approach would be to use the daily rate rather than the annual rate and thus to use the exact number of days rather than the fraction of the year:

$$\text{Interest owed} = \$100(0.000273973)(274) = \$7.51$$

You would owe the bank a total of $107.51 after 274 days. This is the procedure most banks use to calculate interest on loans, except that they generally require borrowers to pay the interest on a monthly basis rather than after 274 days; this more frequent compounding raises the EFF% and thus the total amount of interest paid.

SELF-TEST

Suppose a company borrowed $1 million at a rate of 9%, using simple interest, with interest paid at the end of each month. The bank uses a 360-day year. How much interest would the firm have to pay in a 30-day month? **($7,500.00)** *What would the interest be if the bank used a 365-day year?* **($7,397.26)**

Suppose you deposited $1,000 in a credit union that pays 7% with daily compounding and a 365-day year. What is the EFF%? **(7.250098%)** *How much could you withdraw after 7 months, assuming this is 7/12 of a year?* **($1,041.67)**

4-17 Amortized Loans

An extremely important application of compound interest involves loans that are paid off in installments over time. Included are automobile loans, home mortgage loans, student

---

[17]We assume that these 9 months constitute 9/12 of a year. Also, bank deposit and loan contracts specifically state whether they are based on a 360-day or a 365-day year. If a 360-day year is used, then the daily rate is higher, so the effective rate is also higher. Here we assumed a 365-day year. Finally, note that banks use software with built-in calendars, so they calculate the exact number of days.

Note also that banks often treat such loans as follows: (1) They require monthly payments, and they calculate the interest for the month by multiplying the periodic rate by the beginning-of-month balance times the number of days in the month. This is called "simple interest." (2) The interest for the month is either added to the next beginning of month balance, or the borrower must actually pay the earned interest. In this case, the EFF% is based on 12 compounding periods, not 365 as is assumed in our example.

What You Know Is What You Get: Not in Payday Lending

© Rob Webb/Getty Images

When money runs low toward the end of a month, many individuals turn to payday lenders. If a borrower's application is approved, the payday lender makes a short-term loan, which will be repaid on with the next paycheck. In fact, on the next payday the lender actually transfers the repayment from the borrower's bank account. This repayment consists of the amount borrowed plus a fee.

How costly are payday loans? The lender charges a fee of about $15 to $17 per $100 borrowed. A typical loan is for about $350, so the typical fee is about $56. A typical borrower gets paid about every two weeks, so the loan is for a very short amount of time. With a big fee and a short time until repayment, the typical payday loan has an APR of over 400%.

How informed are borrowers? Two professors at the University of Chicago set out to answer this question. When loans are approved, borrowers receive a form to sign that shows the APR. However, subsequent telephone surveys of borrowers show that over 40% of borrowers thought their APR was around 15%; perhaps not coincidentally, these are similar numerals to the fee schedules that are posted prominently in the lender's office.

The professors then did an experiment (with the agreement of 77 payday loan stores) in which they provided more information than just the APR. One group of borrowers received information about the APR of the payday loan as compared to the APRs of other loans, such as car loans. A second group received information about the dollar cost of the payday loan as compared to the dollar cost of other loans, such as car loans. A third group received information about how long it takes most payday borrowers to repay their loans (which is longer than the next payday; borrowers tend to extend the loan for additional pay periods, accruing additional fees).

Compared to a control group with no additional information, the results show that some borrowers with additional information decided not to take the loan; other borrowers reduced the amount that they borrow. These findings suggest that better information helps borrowers make less costly decisions. The more you know, the less you get, at least when it comes to costly payday loans.

Source: Marianne Bertrand and Adair Morse, "Information Disclosure, Cognitive Biases, and Payday Borrowing," *Journal of Finance*, Vol. 66, No. 6, December 2011, pp. 1865–1893.

loans, and many business loans. A loan that is to be repaid in equal amounts on a monthly, quarterly, or annual basis is called an **amortized loan.**[18]

4-17a Payments

Suppose a company borrows $100,000, with the loan to be repaid in 5 equal payments at the end of each of the next 5 years. The lender charges 6% on the balance at the beginning of each year. Here's a picture of the situation:

Our task is to find the amount of the payment, PMT, such that the sum of their PVs equals the amount of the loan, $100,000:

$$\$100{,}000 = \frac{PMT}{(1.06)^1} + \frac{PMT}{(1.06)^2} + \frac{PMT}{(1.06)^3} + \frac{PMT}{(1.06)^4} + \frac{PMT}{(1.06)^5} = \sum_{t=1}^{5} \frac{PMT}{(1.06)^t}$$

[18]The word *amortized* comes from the Latin *mors*, meaning "death," so an amortized loan is one that is "killed off" over time.

It is possible to solve the annuity formula, Equation 4-8, for PMT, but it is much easier to use a financial calculator or spreadsheet. With a financial calculator, we insert values as shown below to get the required payments, $23,739.64.

	N	I/YR	PV	PMT	FV
Inputs	5	6	100000		0
Output				-23,739.64	

With *Excel*, you would use the PMT function: =PMT(I,N,PV,FV) = PMT(0.06,5,100000,0) = −$23,739.64. Thus, we see that the borrower must pay the lender $23,739.64 per year for the next 5 years.

4-17b Amortization Schedules

Each payment will consist of two parts—part interest and part repayment of principal. This breakdown is shown in the **amortization schedule** given in Figure 4-11. The interest component is relatively high in the first year, but it declines as the loan balance decreases. For tax purposes, the borrower would deduct the interest component while the lender would report the same amount as taxable income. Over the 5 years, the lender will earn 6% on its investment and also recover the amount of its investment.

FIGURE 4-11
Loan Amortization Schedule, $100,000 at 6% for 5 Years

	A	B	C	D	E	F
675	INPUTS:					
676		Amount borrowed:	$100,000			
677		Years:	5			
678		Rate:	6%			
679	Intermediate calculation:					
680		PMT:	$23,739.64 =PMT(C678,C677,−C676)			
681	Year	Beginning Amount (1)	Payment (2)	Interest[a] (3)	Repayment of Principal[b] (2) − (3) = (4)	Ending Balance (1) − (4) = (5)
682	1	$100,000.00	$23,739.64	$6,000.00	$17,739.64	$82,260.36
683	2	$82,260.36	$23,739.64	$4,935.62	$18,804.02	$63,456.34
684	3	$63,456.34	$23,739.64	$3,807.38	$19,932.26	$43,524.08
685	4	$43,524.08	$23,739.64	$2,611.44	$21,128.20	$22,395.89
686	5	$22,395.89	$23,739.64	$1,343.75	$22,395.89	$0.00

Notes:

[a] Interest in each period is calculated by multiplying the loan balance at the beginning of the year by the interest rate. Therefore, interest in Year 1 is $100,000(0.06) = $6,000; in Year 2 it is $82,260.36(0.06) = $4,935.62; and so on.

[b] Repayment of principal is the $23,739.64 annual payment minus the interest charge for the year, $17,739.64 for Year 1.

4-17c Mortgage Interest Payments

Now consider a 30-year home mortgage of $250,000 at an annual rate of 6%. How much interest will the borrower pay over the life of the loan? How much in the first year?

Begin by finding the monthly payment. The financial calculator inputs are shown below (notice that N and I/YR are adjusted to reflect monthly payments):

Inputs	360	0.5%	250000		0
	N	I/YR	PV	PMT	FV
Output				−1,498.8763	

The total amount of payments is 360($1,498.8763) ≈ $539,595. The borrower pays back the borrowed $250,000 over the life of the loan, so the total interest paid is $539,595 − $250,000 = $289,595.

To find the amount of interest paid in the first year, begin by finding the amount the borrower owes at the end of the first year. We know the number of remaining payments (360 − 12 = 348) and the amount of each payment ($1,498.88), so we can solve for the PV:

Inputs	348	0.5%		−1,498.88	0
	N	I/YR	PV	PMT	FV
Output			246,930.58		

The amount of principal repaid in the first year is $250,000 − $246,930.58 = $3,069.42. The total payments during the year are 12($1,498.88) = $17,986.56. So the total interest paid in the year is $17,986.56 − $3,069.42 = $14,917.14. Almost 83% of the payments in the first year go to interest!

Now consider a 15-year mortgage. To compare apples to apples, assume the interest rate stays at 6%, although it probably would be a bit lower. Changing N to 180, the new payment is $2,109.6421. The total amount of payments is 180($2,109.6421) ≈ $379,736 and the total interest paid is $379,736 − $250,000 = $129,736, a big decrease from the $289,595 paid on the 30-year mortgage. As this example shows, increasing the monthly payment can dramatically reduce the total interest paid and the time required to pay off the mortgage.

SELF-TEST

Consider again the example in Figure 4-11. If the loan were amortized over 5 years with 60 equal monthly payments, how much would each payment be, and how would the first payment be divided between interest and principal? **(Each payment would be $1,933.28; the first payment would have $500 of interest and $1,433.28 of principal repayment.)**

Suppose you borrowed $30,000 on a student loan at a rate of 8% and now must repay it in three equal installments at the end of each of the next 3 years. How large would your payments be, how much of the first payment would represent interest and how much would be principal, and what would your ending balance be after the first year? **(PMT = $11,641.01; interest = $2,400; principal = $9,241.01; balance at end of Year 1 = $20,758.99)**

GLOBAL ECONOMIC CRISIS

© uniquely india/Getty Images

An Accident Waiting to Happen: Option Reset Adjustable Rate Mortgages

Option reset adjustable rate mortgages (ARMs) give the borrower some choices regarding the initial monthly payment. One popular option ARM allowed borrowers to make a monthly payment equal to only half of the interest due in the first month. Because the monthly payment was less than the interest charge, the loan balance grew each month. When the loan balance exceeded 110% of the original principal, the monthly payment was reset to fully amortize the now-larger loan at the prevailing market interest rates.

Here's an example. Someone borrows $325,000 for 30 years at an initial rate of 7%. The interest accruing in the first month is (7%/12)($325,000) = $1,895.83. Therefore, the initial monthly payment is 50%($1,895.83) = $947.92. Another $947.92 of deferred interest is added to the loan balance, taking it up to $325,000 + $947.92 = $325,947.82. Because the loan is now larger, interest in the second month is higher, and both interest and the loan balance will continue to rise each month. The first month after the loan balance exceeds 110%($325,000) = $357,500, the contract calls for the payment to be reset so as to fully amortize the loan at the then-prevailing interest rate.

First, how long would it take for the balance to exceed $357,500? Consider this from the lender's perspective: The lender initially pays out $325,000, receives $947.92 each month, and then would receive a payment of $357,500 if the loan were payable when the balance hit that amount, with interest accruing at a 7% annual rate and with monthly compounding. We enter these values into a financial calculator: I = 7%/12, PV = −325000, PMT = 947.92, and FV = 357500. We solve for N = 31.3 months, rounded up to 32 months. Thus, the borrower will make 32 payments of $947.92 before the ARM resets.

The payment after the reset depends upon the terms of the original loan and the market interest rate at the time of the reset. For many borrowers, the initial rate was a lower-than-market "teaser" rate, so a higher-than-market rate would be applied to the remaining balance. For this example, we will assume that the original rate wasn't a teaser and that the rate remains at 7%. Keep in mind, though, that for many borrowers the reset rate was higher than the initial rate. The balance after the 32nd payment can be found as the future value of the original loan and the 32 monthly payments, so we enter these values in the financial calculator: N = 32, I = 7%/12, PMT = 947.92, PV = −325000, and then solve for FV = $358,242.84. The number of remaining payments to amortize the $358,424.84 loan balance is 360 − 32 = 328, so the amount of each payment is found by setting up the calculator as: N = 328, I = 7%/12, PV = 358242.84, and FV = 0. Solving, we find that PMT = $2,453.94.

Even if interest rates don't change, the monthly payment jumps from $947.92 to $2,453.94 and would increase even more if interest rates were higher at the reset. This is exactly what happened to millions of American homeowners who took out option reset ARMS in the early 2000s. When large numbers of resets began in 2007, defaults ballooned. The accident caused by option reset ARMs didn't wait very long to happen!

4-18 Growing Annuities[19]

Normally, an annuity is defined as a series of *constant* payments to be received over a specified number of periods. However, the term **growing annuity** is used to describe a series of payments that grow at a constant rate.

4-18a Example 1: Finding a Constant Real Income

Growing annuities are often used in the area of financial planning, where a prospective retiree wants to determine the maximum constant *real*, or *inflation-adjusted*, withdrawals that he or

[19]This section is interesting and useful, but relatively technical. It can be omitted, at the option of the instructor, without loss of continuity.

she can make over a specified number of years. For example, suppose a 65-year-old is contemplating retirement. The individual expects to live for another 20 years, has a $1 million nest egg, expects the investments to earn a nominal annual rate of 6%, expects inflation to average 3% per year, and wants to withdraw a constant *real* amount annually over the next 20 years so as to maintain a constant standard of living. If the first withdrawal is to be made today, what is the amount of that initial withdrawal?

This problem can be solved in three ways. (1) Set up a spreadsheet model that is similar to an amortization table, where the account earns 6% per year, withdrawals rise at the 3% inflation rate, and *Excel*'s Goal Seek function is used to find the initial inflation-adjusted withdrawal. A zero balance will be shown at the end of the twentieth year. (2) Use a financial calculator, where we first calculate the real rate of return, adjusted for inflation, and use it for I/YR when finding the payment for an annuity due. (3) Use a relatively complicated and obtuse formula to find this same amount.[20] We will focus on the first two approaches.

resource
See ***Ch04 Tool Kit.xls*** *for all calculations.*

We illustrate the spreadsheet approach in the chapter model, ***Ch04 Tool Kit.xls.*** The spreadsheet model provides the most transparent picture, because it shows the value of the retirement portfolio, the portfolio's annual earnings, and each withdrawal over the 20-year planning horizon—especially if you include a graph. A picture is worth a thousand numbers, and graphs make it easy to explain the situation to people who are planning their financial futures.

To implement the calculator approach, we first find the expected *real* rate of return, where r_r is the real rate of return and r_{NOM} the nominal rate of return. The real rate of return is the return that we would see if there were no inflation. We calculate the real rate as:

$$\text{Real rate} = r_r = [(1 + r_{NOM})/(1 + \text{Inflation})] - 1.0 \quad \text{(4-15)}$$

$$= [1.06/1.03] - 1.0 = 0.029126214 = 2.9126214\%$$

Using this real rate of return, we solve the annuity due problem exactly as we did earlier in the chapter. We set the calculator to Begin Mode, after which we input N = 20, I/YR = real rate = 2.9126214, PV = −1000000, and FV = 0; then we press PMT to get $64,786.88. This is the amount of the initial withdrawal at Time 0 (today), and future withdrawals will increase at the inflation rate of 3%. These withdrawals, growing at the inflation rate, will provide the retiree with a constant real income over the next 20 years—provided the inflation rate and the rate of return do not change.

In our example, we assumed that the first withdrawal would be made immediately. The procedure would be slightly different if we wanted to make end-of-year withdrawals. First, we would set the calculator to End Mode. Second, we would enter the same inputs into the calculator as just listed, including the real interest rate for I/YR. The calculated PMT would be $66,673.87. However, that value is in beginning-of-year terms, and because inflation of 3% will occur during the year, we must make the following adjustment to find the inflation-adjusted initial withdrawal:

---

[20]For example, the formula used to find the payment of a growing annuity due is shown below. If g = annuity growth rate and r = nominal rate of return on investment, then

$$\text{PVIF of a growing annuity due} = \text{PVIFGA}_{\text{Due}} = \{1 - [(1+g)/(1+r)]^N\}[(1+r)/(r-g)]$$

$$\text{PMT} = \text{PV}/\text{PVIFGA}_{\text{Due}}$$

where PVIF denotes "present value interest factor." Similar formulas are available for growing ordinary annuities.

$$\text{Initial end-of-year withdrawal} = \$66{,}673.87(1 + \text{Inflation})$$
$$= \$66{,}673.87(1.03)$$
$$= \$68{,}674.09$$

Thus, the first withdrawal at the *end* of the year would be \$68,674.09; it would grow by 3% per year; and after the 20th withdrawal (at the end of the 20th year), the balance in the retirement fund would be zero.

We also demonstrate the solution for this end-of-year payment example in ***Ch04 Tool Kit.xls.*** There we set up a table showing the beginning balance, the annual withdrawals, the annual earnings, and the ending balance for each of the 20 years. This analysis confirms the \$68,674.09 initial end-of-year withdrawal derived previously.

4-18b Example 2: Initial Deposit to Accumulate a Future Sum

As another example of growing annuities, suppose you need to accumulate \$100,000 in 10 years. You plan to make a deposit in a bank now, at Time 0, and then make 9 more deposits at the beginning of each of the following 9 years, for a total of 10 deposits. The bank pays 6% interest, you expect inflation to be 2% per year, and you plan to increase your annual deposits at the inflation rate. How much must you deposit initially? First, we calculate the real rate:

$$\text{Real rate} = r_r = [1.06/1.02] - 1.0 = 0.0392157 = 3.9215686\%$$

Next, because inflation is expected to be 2% per year, in 10 years the target \$100,000 will have a real value of

$$\$100{,}000/(1 + 0.02)^{10} = \$82{,}034.83$$

Now we can find the size of the required initial payment by setting a financial calculator to the Begin Mode and then inputting N = 10, I/YR = 3.9215686, PV = 0, and FV = 82034.83. Then, when we press the PMT key, we get PMT = −6,598.87. Thus, a deposit of \$6,598.87 made at time 0 and growing by 2% per year will accumulate to \$100,000 by Year 10 if the interest rate is 6%. Again, this result is confirmed in the chapter's ***Tool Kit.*** The key to this analysis is to express I/YR, FV, and PMT in real, not nominal, terms.

SELF-TEST

Differentiate between a "regular" and a "growing" annuity.

What three methods can be used to deal with growing annuities?

If the nominal interest rate is 10% and the expected inflation rate is 5%, what is the expected real rate of return? **(4.7619%)**

SUMMARY

Most financial decisions involve situations in which someone makes a payment at one point in time and receives money later. Dollars paid or received at two different points in time are different, and this difference is dealt with using *time value of money (TVM) analysis.*

- **Compounding** is the process of determining the **future value (FV)** of a cash flow or a series of cash flows. The compounded amount, or future value, is equal to the beginning amount plus interest earned.
- Future value of a single payment = $FV_N = PV(1 + I)^N$.
- **Discounting** is the process of finding the **present value (PV)** of a future cash flow or a series of cash flows; discounting is the reciprocal, or reverse, of compounding.
- Present value of a payment received at the end of Time N = PV = $\frac{FV_N}{(1+I)^N}$.
- An **annuity** is defined as a series of equal periodic payments (PMT) for a specified number of periods.
- An annuity whose payments occur at the *end* of each period is called an **ordinary annuity**.
- Future value of an (ordinary) annuity $FVA_N = PMT\left[\frac{(1+I)^N}{I} - \frac{1}{I}\right]$.
- Present value of an (ordinary) annuity $PVA_N = PMT\left[\frac{1}{I} - \frac{1}{I(1+I)^N}\right]$.
- If payments occur at the *beginning* of the periods rather than at the end, then we have an **annuity due**. The PV of each payment is larger, because each payment is discounted back one year less, so the PV of the annuity is also larger. Similarly, the FV of the annuity due is larger because each payment is compounded for an extra year. The following formulas can be used to convert the PV and FV of an ordinary annuity to an annuity due:

$$PVA_{due} = PVA_{ordinary}(1 + I)$$
$$FVA_{due} = FVA_{ordinary}(1 + I)$$

- **A perpetuity** is an annuity with an infinite number of payments.

$$\text{Value of a perpetuity} = \frac{PMT}{I}$$

- To find the PV or FV of an uneven series, find the PV or FV of each individual cash flow and then sum them.
- If you know the cash flows and the PV (or FV) of a cash flow stream, you can **determine its interest rate.**
- When compounding occurs more frequently than once a year, the nominal rate must be converted to a periodic rate, and the number of years must be converted to periods:

$$\text{Periodic rate}(I_{PER}) = \text{Nominal annual rate} \div \text{Periods per year}$$
$$\text{Number of Periods} = \text{Years} \times \text{Periods per year}$$

The periodic rate and number of periods is used for calculations and is shown on time lines.

- If you are comparing the costs of alternative loans that require payments more than once a year, or the rates of return on investments that pay interest more than once a year, then the comparisons should be based on **effective** (or **equivalent**) **rates** of return. Here is the formula:

$$EAR = EFF\% = (1 + I_{PER})^M - 1.0 = \left(1 + \frac{I_{NOM}}{M}\right)^M - 1.0$$

- The general equation for finding the future value of a current cash flow (PV) for any number of compounding periods per year is

$$FV_N = PV(1 + I_{PER})^{\text{Number of periods}} = PV\left(1 + \frac{I_{NOM}}{M}\right)^{MN}$$

where

I_{NOM} = Nominal quoted interest rate
M = Number of compounding periods per year
N = Number of years

- An **amortized loan** is paid off with equal payments over a specified period. An **amortization schedule** shows how much of each payment constitutes interest, how much is used to reduce the principal, and the unpaid balance at the end of each period. The unpaid balance at Time N must be zero.
- A "**growing annuity**" is a stream of cash flows that grows at a constant rate for a specified number of years. The present and future values of growing annuities can be found with relatively complicated formulas or, more easily, with an *Excel* model.
- ***Web Extension 4A*** explains the **tabular approach.**
- ***Web Extension 4B*** provides derivations of the annuity formulas.
- ***Web Extension 4C*** explains **continuous compounding.**

QUESTIONS

(4-1) Define each of the following terms:

a. PV; I; INT; FV_N; PVA_N; FVA_N; PMT; M; I_{NOM}
b. Opportunity cost rate
c. Annuity; lump-sum payment; cash flow; uneven cash flow stream
d. Ordinary (or deferred) annuity; annuity due
e. Perpetuity; consol
f. Outflow; inflow; time line; terminal value
g. Compounding; discounting
h. Annual, semiannual, quarterly, monthly, and daily compounding
i. Effective annual rate (EAR or EFF%); nominal (quoted) interest rate; APR; periodic rate
j. Amortization schedule; principal versus interest component of a payment; amortized loan

(4-2) What is an *opportunity cost rate?* How is this rate used in discounted cash flow analysis, and where is it shown on a time line? Is the opportunity rate a single number that is used to evaluate all potential investments?

(4-3) An *annuity* is defined as a series of payments of a fixed amount for a specific number of periods. Thus, \$100 a year for 10 years is an annuity, but \$100 in Year 1, \$200 in Year 2, and \$400 in Years 3 through 10 does *not* constitute an annuity. However, the entire series *does contain* an annuity. Is this statement true or false?

(4-4) If a firm's earnings per share grew from \$1 to \$2 over a 10-year period, the *total growth* would be 100%, but the *annual growth rate* would be *less than* 10%. True or false? Explain.

(4-5) Would you rather have a savings account that pays 5% interest compounded semiannually or one that pays 5% interest compounded daily? Explain.

SELF-TEST PROBLEMS Solutions Appear in Appendix A

(ST-1) Future Value

Assume that 1 year from now you plan to deposit $1,000 in a savings account that pays a nominal rate of 8%.

a. If the bank compounds interest annually, how much will you have in your account 4 years from now?
b. What would your balance be 4 years from now if the bank used quarterly compounding rather than annual compounding?
c. Suppose you deposited the $1,000 in 4 payments of $250 each at the end of Years 1, 2, 3, and 4. How much would you have in your account at the end of Year 4, based on 8% annual compounding?
d. Suppose you deposited 4 equal payments in your account at the end of Years 1, 2, 3, and 4. Assuming an 8% interest rate, how large would each of your payments have to be for you to obtain the same ending balance as you calculated in part a?

(ST-2) Time Value of Money

Assume that 4 years from now you will need $1,000. Your bank compounds interest at an 8% annual rate.

a. How much must you deposit 1 year from now to have a balance of $1,000 at Year 4?
b. If you want to make equal payments at the end of Years 1 through 4 to accumulate the $1,000, how large must each of the 4 payments be?
c. If your father were to offer either to make the payments calculated in part b ($221.92) or to give you a lump sum of $750 one year from now, which would you choose?
d. If you will have only $750 at the end of Year 1, what interest rate, compounded annually, would you have to earn to have the necessary $1,000 at Year 4?
e. Suppose you can deposit only $186.29 each at the end of Years 1 through 4, but you still need $1,000 at the end of Year 4. What interest rate, with annual compounding, is required to achieve your goal?
f. To help you reach your $1,000 goal, your father offers to give you $400 one year from now. You will get a part-time job and make 6 additional deposits of equal amounts each 6 months thereafter. If all of this money is deposited in a bank that pays 8%, compounded semiannually, how large must each of the 6 deposits be?
g. What is the effective annual rate being paid by the bank in part f?

(ST-3) Effective Annual Rates

Bank A pays 8% interest, compounded quarterly, on its money market account. The managers of Bank B want its money market account's effective annual rate to equal that of Bank A, but Bank B will compound interest on a monthly basis. What nominal, or quoted, rate must Bank B set?

PROBLEMS Answers Appear in Appendix B

Easy Problems 1–8

(4-1) Future Value of a Single Payment

If you deposit $10,000 in a bank account that pays 10% interest annually, how much will be in your account after 5 years?

(4-2) Present Value of a Single Payment

What is the present value of a security that will pay $5,000 in 20 years if securities of equal risk pay 7% annually?

(4-3) Interest Rate on a Single Payment

Your parents will retire in 18 years. They currently have $250,000, and they think they will need $1 million at retirement. What annual interest rate must they earn to reach their goal, assuming they don't save any additional funds?

(4-4) **Number of Periods of a Single Payment**

If you deposit money today in an account that pays 6.5% annual interest, how long will it take to double your money?

(4-5) **Number of Periods for an Annuity**

You have $42,180.53 in a brokerage account, and you plan to deposit an additional $5,000 at the end of every future year until your account totals $250,000. You expect to earn 12% annually on the account. How many years will it take to reach your goal?

(4-6) **Future Value: Ordinary Annuity versus Annuity Due**

What is the future value of a 7%, 5-year ordinary annuity that pays $300 each year? If this were an annuity due, what would its future value be?

(4-7) **Present and Future Value of an Uneven Cash Flow Stream**

An investment will pay $100 at the end of each of the next 3 years, $200 at the end of Year 4, $300 at the end of Year 5, and $500 at the end of Year 6. If other investments of equal risk earn 8% annually, what is this investment's present value? Its future value?

(4-8) **Annuity Payment and EAR**

You want to buy a car, and a local bank will lend you $20,000. The loan would be fully amortized over 5 years (60 months), and the nominal interest rate would be 12%, with interest paid monthly. What is the monthly loan payment? What is the loan's EFF%?

Intermediate Problems 9–29

(4-9) **Present and Future Values of Single Cash Flows for Different Periods**

Find the following values, *using the equations*, and then work the problems using a financial calculator to check your answers. Disregard rounding differences. (*Hint:* If you are using a financial calculator, you can enter the known values and then press the appropriate key to find the unknown variable. Then, without clearing the TVM register, you can "override" the variable that changes by simply entering a new value for it and then pressing the key for the unknown variable to obtain the second answer. This procedure can be used in parts b and d, and in many other situations, to see how changes in input variables affect the output variable.)

a. An initial $500 compounded for 1 year at 6%
b. An initial $500 compounded for 2 years at 6%
c. The present value of $500 due in 1 year at a discount rate of 6%
d. The present value of $500 due in 2 years at a discount rate of 6%

(4-10) **Present and Future Values of Single Cash Flows for Different Interest Rates**

Use both the TVM equations and a financial calculator to find the following values. See the Hint for Problem 4-9.

a. An initial $500 compounded for 10 years at 6%
b. An initial $500 compounded for 10 years at 12%
c. The present value of $500 due in 10 years at a 6% discount rate
d. The present value of $500 due in 10 years at a 12% discount rate

(4-11) **Time for a Lump Sum to Double**

To the closest year, how long will it take $200 to double if it is deposited and earns the following rates? [*Notes:* (1) See the Hint for Problem 4-9. (2) This problem cannot be solved exactly with some financial calculators. For example, if you enter PV = −200, PMT = 0, FV = 400, and I = 7 in an HP-12C and then press the N key, you will get 11 years for part a. The correct answer is 10.2448 years, which rounds to 10, but the calculator rounds up. However, the HP10BII gives the exact answer.]

a. 7%
b. 10%
c. 18%
d. 100%

(4-12) Future Value of an Annuity

Find the *future value* of the following annuities. The first payment in these annuities is made at the *end* of Year 1, so they are *ordinary annuities.* (*Notes:* See the Hint to Problem 4-9. Also, note that you can leave values in the TVM register, switch to Begin Mode, press FV, and find the FV of the annuity due.)

a. $400 per year for 10 years at 10%
b. $200 per year for 5 years at 5%
c. $400 per year for 5 years at 0%
d. Now rework parts a, b, and c assuming that payments are made at the *beginning* of each year; that is, they are *annuities due.*

(4-13) Present Value of an Annuity

Find the *present value* of the following *ordinary annuities* (see the *Notes* to Problem 4-12).

a. $400 per year for 10 years at 10%
b. $200 per year for 5 years at 5%
c. $400 per year for 5 years at 0%
d. Now rework parts a, b, and c assuming that payments are made at the *beginning* of each year; that is, they are *annuities due.*

(4-14) Uneven Cash Flow Stream

a. Find the present values of the following cash flow streams. The appropriate interest rate is 8%. (*Hint:* It is fairly easy to work this problem dealing with the individual cash flows. However, if you have a financial calculator, read the section of the manual that describes how to enter cash flows such as the ones in this problem. This will take a little time, but the investment will pay huge dividends throughout the course. Note that, when working with the calculator's cash flow register, you must enter CF0 = 0. Note also that it is quite easy to work the problem with *Excel*, using procedures described in the Chapter 4 ***Tool Kit.***)

Year	Cash Stream A	Cash Stream B
1	$100	$300
2	400	400
3	400	400
4	400	400
5	300	100

b. What is the value of each cash flow stream at a 0% interest rate?

(4-15) Effective Rate of Interest

Find the interest rate (or rates of return) in each of the following situations.

a. You *borrow* $700 and promise to pay back $749 at the end of 1 year.
b. You *lend* $700 and receive a promise to be paid $749 at the end of 1 year.
c. You borrow $85,000 and promise to pay back $201,229 at the end of 10 years.
d. You borrow $9,000 and promise to make payments of $2,684.80 at the end of each of the next 5 years.

(4-16) Future Value for Various Compounding Periods

Find the amount to which $500 will grow under each of the following conditions.

a. 12% compounded annually for 5 years
b. 12% compounded semiannually for 5 years
c. 12% compounded quarterly for 5 years
d. 12% compounded monthly for 5 years

(4-17) **Present Value for Various Compounding Periods**

Find the present value of $500 due in the future under each of the following conditions.

a. 12% nominal rate, semiannual compounding, discounted back 5 years
b. 12% nominal rate, quarterly compounding, discounted back 5 years
c. 12% nominal rate, monthly compounding, discounted back 1 year

(4-18) **Future Value of an Annuity for Various Compounding Periods**

Find the future values of the following ordinary annuities.

a. FV of $400 each 6 months for 5 years at a nominal rate of 12%, compounded semiannually
b. FV of $200 each 3 months for 5 years at a nominal rate of 12%, compounded quarterly
c. The annuities described in parts a and b have the same total amount of money paid into them during the 5-year period, and both earn interest at the same nominal rate, yet the annuity in part b earns $101.75 more than the one in part a over the 5 years. Why does this occur?

(4-19) **Effective versus Nominal Interest Rates**

Universal Bank pays 7% interest, compounded annually, on time deposits. Regional Bank pays 6% interest, compounded quarterly.

a. Based on effective interest rates, in which bank would you prefer to deposit your money?
b. Could your choice of banks be influenced by the fact that you might want to withdraw your funds during the year as opposed to at the end of the year? In answering this question, assume that funds must be left on deposit during an entire compounding period in order for you to receive any interest.

(4-20) **Amortization Schedule**

a. Set up an amortization schedule for a $25,000 loan to be repaid in equal installments at the end of each of the next 5 years. The interest rate is 10%.
b. How large must each annual payment be if the loan is for $50,000? Assume that the interest rate remains at 10% and that the loan is still paid off over 5 years.
c. How large must each payment be if the loan is for $50,000, the interest rate is 10%, and the loan is paid off in equal installments at the end of each of the next 10 years? This loan is for the same amount as the loan in part b, but the payments are spread out over twice as many periods. Why are these payments not half as large as the payments on the loan in part b?

(4-21) **Growth Rates**

Sales for Hanebury Corporation's just-ended year were $12 million. Sales were $6 million 5 years earlier.

a. At what rate did sales grow?
b. Suppose someone calculated the sales growth for Hanebury in part a as follows: "Sales doubled in 5 years. This represents a growth of 100% in 5 years; dividing 100% by 5 results in an estimated growth rate of 20% per year." Explain what is wrong with this calculation.

(4-22) **Expected Rate of Return**

Washington-Pacific invested $4 million to buy a tract of land and plant some young pine trees. The trees can be harvested in 10 years, at which time W-P plans to sell the forest at an expected price of $8 million. What is W-P's expected rate of return?

(4-23) **Effective Rate of Interest**

A mortgage company offers to lend you $85,000; the loan calls for payments of $8,273.59 at the end of each year for 30 years. What interest rate is the mortgage company charging you?

(4-24) **Required Lump-Sum Payment**

To complete your last year in business school and then go through law school, you will need $10,000 per year for 4 years, starting next year (that is, you will need to withdraw the first $10,000 one year from today). Your uncle offers to put you through school, and he will deposit in a bank paying 7% interest a sum of money that is sufficient to provide the 4 payments of $10,000 each. His deposit will be made today.

a. How large must the deposit be?
b. How much will be in the account immediately after you make the first withdrawal? After the last withdrawal?

(4-25) Repaying a Loan

While Mary Corens was a student at the University of Tennessee, she borrowed $12,000 in student loans at an annual interest rate of 9%. If Mary repays $1,500 per year, then how long (to the nearest year) will it take her to repay the loan?

(4-26) Reaching a Financial Goal

You need to accumulate $10,000. To do so, you plan to make deposits of $1,250 per year—with the first payment being made a year from today—into a bank account that pays 12% annual interest. Your last deposit will be less than $1,250 if less is needed to round out to $10,000. How many years will it take you to reach your $10,000 goal, and how large will the last deposit be?

(4-27) Present Value of a Perpetuity

What is the present value of a perpetuity of $100 per year if the appropriate discount rate is 7%? If interest rates in general were to double and the appropriate discount rate rose to 14%, what would happen to the present value of the perpetuity?

(4-28) PV and Effective Annual Rate

Assume that you inherited some money. A friend of yours is working as an unpaid intern at a local brokerage firm, and her boss is selling securities that call for 4 payments of $50 (1 payment at the end of each of the next 4 years) plus an extra payment of $1,000 at the end of Year 4. Your friend says she can get you some of these securities at a cost of $900 each. Your money is now invested in a bank that pays an 8% nominal (quoted) interest rate but with quarterly compounding. You regard the securities as being just as safe, and as liquid, as your bank deposit, so your required effective annual rate of return on the securities is the same as that on your bank deposit. You must calculate the value of the securities to decide whether they are a good investment. What is their present value to you?

(4-29) Loan Amortization

Assume that your aunt sold her house on December 31, and to help close the sale she took a second mortgage in the amount of $10,000 as part of the payment. The mortgage has a quoted (or nominal) interest rate of 10%; it calls for payments every 6 months, beginning on June 30, and is to be amortized over 10 years. Now, 1 year later, your aunt must inform the IRS and the person who bought the house about the interest that was included in the two payments made during the year. (This interest will be income to your aunt and a deduction to the buyer of the house.) To the closest dollar, what is the total amount of interest that was paid during the first year?

Challenging Problems 30–34

(4-30) Loan Amortization

Your company is planning to borrow $1 million on a 5-year, 15%, annual payment, fully amortized term loan. What fraction of the payment made at the end of the second year will represent repayment of principal?

(4-31) Nonannual Compounding

a. It is now January 1. You plan to make a total of 5 deposits of $100 each, one every 6 months, with the first payment being made *today.* The bank pays a nominal interest rate of 12% but uses *semiannual* compounding. You plan to leave the money in the bank for 10 years. How much will be in your account after 10 years?
b. You must make a payment of $1,432.02 in 10 years. To get the money for this payment, you will make 5 equal deposits, beginning today and for the following 4 quarters, in a bank that pays a nominal interest rate of 12% with *quarterly compounding.* How large must each of the 5 payments be?

(4-32) Nominal Rate of Return

Anne Lockwood, manager of Oaks Mall Jewelry, wants to sell on credit, giving customers 3 months to pay. However, Anne will have to borrow from her bank to carry the accounts receivable. The bank will charge a nominal rate of 15% and will compound monthly.

Anne wants to quote a nominal rate to her customers (all of whom are expected to pay on time) that will exactly offset her financing costs. What nominal annual rate should she quote to her credit customers?

(4-33) Required Annuity Payments Assume that your father is now 50 years old, plans to retire in 10 years, and expects to live for 25 years after he retires—that is, until age 85. He wants his first retirement payment to have the same purchasing power at the time he retires as $40,000 has today. He wants all of his subsequent retirement payments to be equal to his first retirement payment. (Do not let the retirement payments grow with inflation: Your father realizes that if inflation occurs the real value of his retirement income will decline year by year after he retires.) His retirement income will begin the day he retires, 10 years from today, and he will then receive 24 additional annual payments. Inflation is expected to be 5% per year from today forward. He currently has $100,000 saved and expects to earn a return on his savings of 8% per year with annual compounding. To the nearest dollar, how much must he save during each of the next 10 years (with equal deposits being made at the end of each year, beginning a year from today) to meet his retirement goal? (*Note:* Neither the amount he saves nor the amount he withdraws upon retirement is a growing annuity.)

(4-34) Growing Annuity Payments You want to accumulate $1 million by your retirement date, which is 25 years from now. You will make 25 deposits in your bank, with the first occurring *today.* The bank pays 8% interest, compounded annually. You expect to receive annual raises of 3%, which will offset inflation, and you will let the amount you deposit each year also grow by 3% (i.e., your second deposit will be 3% greater than your first, the third will be 3% greater than the second, etc.). How much must your first deposit be if you are to meet your goal?

SPREADSHEET PROBLEM

(4-35) Build a Model: The Time Value of Money

resource

1. Start with the partial model in the file ***Ch04 P35 Build a Model.xls*** from the textbook's Web site. Answer the following questions, using a spreadsheet model to do the calculations.
   a. Find the FV of $1,000 invested to earn 10% annually 5 years from now. Answer this question first by using a math formula and then by using the *Excel* function wizard.
   b. Now create a table that shows the FV at 0%, 5%, and 20% for 0, 1, 2, 3, 4, and 5 years. Then create a graph with years on the horizontal axis and FV on the vertical axis to display your results.
   c. Find the PV of $1,000 due in 5 years if the discount rate is 10% per year. Again, first work the problem with a formula and then by using the function wizard.
   d. A security has a cost of $1,000 and will return $2,000 after 5 years. What rate of return does the security provide?
   e. Suppose California's population is 30 million people and its population is expected to grow by 2% per year. How long would it take for the population to double?
   f. Find the PV of an ordinary annuity that pays $1,000 at the end of each of the next 5 years if the interest rate is 15%. Then find the FV of that same annuity.
   g. How would the PV and FV of the above annuity change if it were an annuity due rather than an ordinary annuity?
   h. What would the FV and PV for parts a and c be if the interest rate were 10% with *semiannual* compounding rather than 10% with *annual* compounding?

i. Find the PV and FV of an investment that makes the following end-of-year payments. The interest rate is 8%.

Year	Payment
1	$100
2	200
3	400

j. Suppose you bought a house and took out a mortgage for $50,000. The interest rate is 8%, and you must amortize the loan over 10 years with equal end-of-year payments. Set up an amortization schedule that shows the annual payments and the amount of each payment that repays the principal and the amount that constitutes interest expense to the borrower and interest income to the lender.

(1) Create a graph that shows how the payments are divided between interest and principal repayment over time.

(2) Suppose the loan called for 10 years of monthly payments, 120 payments in all, with the same original amount and the same nominal interest rate. What would the amortization schedule show now?

MINI CASE

Assume that you are nearing graduation and have applied for a job with a local bank. The bank's evaluation process requires you to take an examination that covers several financial analysis techniques. The first section of the test addresses discounted cash flow analysis. See how you would do by answering the following questions.

a. Draw time lines for (1) a $100 lump sum cash flow at the end of Year 2, (2) an ordinary annuity of $100 per year for 3 years, and (3) an uneven cash flow stream of –$50, $100, $75, and $50 at the end of Years 0 through 3.

b. (1) What's the *future value* of an initial $100 after 3 years if it is invested in an account paying 10% annual interest?

(2) What's the *present value* of $100 to be received in 3 years if the appropriate interest rate is 10%?

c. We sometimes need to find out how long it will take a sum of money (or something else, such as earnings, population, or prices) to grow to some specified amount. For example, if a company's sales are growing at a rate of 20% per year, how long will it take sales to double?

d. If you want an investment to double in 3 years, what interest rate must it earn?

e. What's the difference between an ordinary annuity and an annuity due? What type of annuity is shown below? How would you change the time line to show the other type of annuity?

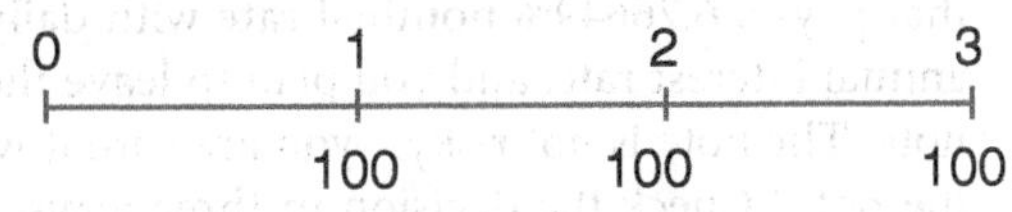

f. (1) What's the future value of a 3-year ordinary annuity of $100 if the appropriate interest rate is 10%?

(2) What's the present value of the annuity?

(3) What would the future and present values be if the annuity were an annuity due?

g. What is the present value of the following uneven cash flow stream? The appropriate interest rate is 10%, compounded annually.

0	1	2	3	4
0	100	300	300	–50

h. (1) Define the stated (quoted) or nominal rate I_{NOM} as well as the periodic rate I_{PER}.
(2) Will the future value be larger or smaller if we compound an initial amount more often than annually—for example, every 6 months, or *semiannually*—holding the stated interest rate constant? Why?
(3) What is the future value of $100 after 5 years under 12% annual compounding? Semiannual compounding? Quarterly compounding? Monthly compounding? Daily compounding?
(4) What is the effective annual rate (EAR or EFF%)? What is the EFF% for a nominal rate of 12%, compounded semiannually? Compounded quarterly? Compounded monthly? Compounded daily?

i. Will the effective annual rate ever be equal to the nominal (quoted) rate?

j. (1) Construct an amortization schedule for a $1,000, 10% annual rate loan with 3 equal installments.
(2) During Year 2, what is the annual interest expense for the borrower, and what is the annual interest income for the lender?

k. Suppose that on January 1 you deposit $100 in an account that pays a nominal (or quoted) interest rate of 11.33463%, with interest added (compounded) daily. How much will you have in your account on October 1, or 9 months later?

l. (1) What is the value at the end of Year 3 of the following cash flow stream if the quoted interest rate is 10%, compounded semiannually?

0		1		2		3 Years
		100		100		100

(2) What is the PV of the same stream?
(3) Is the stream an annuity?
(4) An important rule is that you should never show a nominal rate on a time line or use it in calculations unless what condition holds? (*Hint:* Think of annual compounding, when I_{NOM} = EFF% = I_{PER}.) What would be wrong with your answers to parts (1) and (2) if you used the nominal rate of 10% rather than the periodic rate, $I_{NOM}/2$ = 10%/2 = 5%?

m. Suppose someone offered to sell you a note calling for the payment of $1,000 in 15 months. They offer to sell it to you for $850. You have $850 in a bank time deposit that pays a 6.76649% nominal rate with daily compounding, which is a 7% effective annual interest rate, and you plan to leave the money in the bank unless you buy the note. The note is not risky—you are sure it will be paid on schedule. Should you buy the note? Check the decision in three ways: (1) by comparing your future value if you buy the note versus leaving your money in the bank; (2) by comparing the PV of the note with your current bank account; and (3) by comparing the EFF% on the note with that of the bank account.

© Adalberto Rios Szalay/Sexto Sol/Getty Images

CHAPTER 5

Bond, Bond Valuation, and Interest Rates

A lot of bonds have been issued in the United States, and we mean a *lot!* According to the Federal Reserve, at the beginning of 2012 there were about $10.4 trillion of outstanding U.S. Treasury securities, more than $3.7 trillion of municipal securities, $4.9 trillion of corporate bonds, and more than $1.7 trillion of foreign bonds held in the United States. Not only is the dollar amount mind-boggling, but so is the variety.

Bonds aren't the only way to borrow. In addition to their bonds, corporations owe $2.9 trillion in short-term debt. Noncorporate businesses, which include small businesses, owe $3.8 trillion. Interestingly, small business borrowing is down from $4.1 trillion from the beginning of 2009, reflecting the reluctance of many banks to make loans during the financial crisis.

Let's not ignore households, which owe $2.5 trillion in consumer debt, such as car loans and credit cards. This works out to about $22,000 per household, and this doesn't even include the $10.3 trillion (about $90,000 per household) in federal debt.

Given the enormous amount of debt in the modern world, it is vital for everyone to understand debt and interest rates.

Sources: **"Flow of Funds Accounts of the United States, Section L.2, Credit Market Debt Owed by Nonfinancial Sectors," www.federalreserve.gov/releases/Z1/current/; http://quickfacts.census.gov/qfd/states/00000.html.**

Intrinsic Value and the Cost of Debt

© Rob Webb/Getty Images

This chapter explains bond pricing and bond risk, which affect the return demanded by a firm's bondholders. A bondholder's return is a cost from the company's point of view. This cost of debt affects the firm's weighted average cost of capital (WACC), which in turn affects the company's intrinsic value. Therefore, it is important for all managers to understand the cost of debt, which we explain in this chapter.

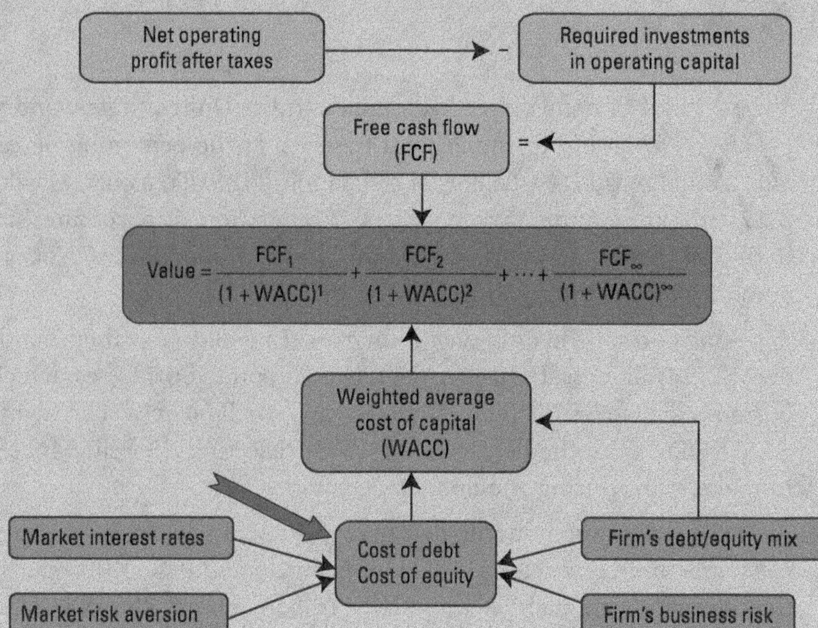

© Cengage Learning 2014

Growing companies must acquire land, buildings, equipment, inventory, and other operating assets. The debt markets are a major source of funding for such purchases. Therefore, every manager should have a working knowledge of the types of bonds that companies and government agencies issue, the terms that are contained in bond contracts, the types of risks to which both bond investors and issuers are exposed, and procedures for determining the values of and rates of return on bonds.

resource

The textbook's Web site contains an Excel file that will guide you through the chapter's calculations. The file for this chapter is ***Ch05 Tool Kit.xls,*** *and we encourage you to open the file and follow along as you read the chapter.*

5-1 Who Issues Bonds?

A **bond** is a long-term contract under which a borrower agrees to make payments of interest and principal, on specific dates, to the holders of the bond. For example, on January 5, 2013, MicroDrive Inc. issued $200 million of bonds. For convenience, we assume that MicroDrive sold 200,000 individual bonds for $1,000 each. Actually, it could have sold one $200 million bond, 10 bonds with a $20 million face value, or any other combination that totals to $200 million. In exchange for $200 million, MicroDrive promised to make annual interest payments and to repay the $200 million on a specified maturity date.

Investors have many choices when investing in bonds, but bonds are classified into four main types: Treasury, corporate, municipal, and foreign. Each type differs with respect to expected return and degree of risk.

Treasury bonds, sometimes referred to as *government bonds,* are issued by the U.S. federal government.[1] It is reasonable to assume that the federal government will make good on its promised payments, so these bonds have almost no default risk. However, Treasury bond prices decline when interest rates rise, so they are not free of all risks.

Federal agencies and other government-sponsored entities (GSEs) include the Tennessee Valley Authority, the Small Business Administration, Fannie Mae, Freddie Mac, and the Federal Home Loan Bank System, among others. **Agency debt** and **GSE debt** are not officially backed by the full faith and credit of the U.S. government, but investors assume that the government implicitly guarantees this debt, so these bonds carry interest rates only slightly higher than Treasury bonds. In 2008, the implicit guarantee became much more explicit as the government placed several GSEs into conservatorship, including Fannie Mae and Freddie Mac.

Corporate bonds, as the name implies, are issued by corporations. Unlike Treasury bonds, corporate bonds are exposed to default risk—if the issuing company gets into trouble, it may be unable to make the promised interest and principal payments. Different corporate bonds have different levels of default risk, depending on the issuing company's characteristics and the terms of the specific bond. Default risk is often referred to as "credit risk," and the larger the credit risk, the higher the interest rate the issuer must pay.

Municipal bonds, or "munis," are issued by state and local governments. Like corporate bonds, munis have default risk. However, munis offer one major advantage: The interest earned on most municipal bonds is exempt from federal taxes and also from state taxes if the holder is a resident of the issuing state. Consequently, municipal bonds carry interest rates that are considerably lower than those on corporate bonds with the same default risk.

Foreign bonds are issued by foreign governments or foreign corporations. Foreign corporate bonds are, of course, exposed to default risk, and so are some foreign government bonds. An additional risk exists if the bonds are denominated in a currency other than that of the investor's home currency. For example, if a U.S. investor purchases a corporate bond denominated in Japanese yen, and if the yen subsequently falls relative to the dollar, then the investor will lose money even if the company does not default on its bonds.

SELF-TEST

What is a bond?

What are the four main types of bonds?

Why are U.S. Treasury bonds not riskless?

To what types of risk are investors of foreign bonds exposed?

[1]The U.S. Treasury actually issues three types of securities: bills, notes, and bonds. A bond makes an equal payment every 6 months until it matures, at which time it makes an additional lump-sum payment. If the maturity at the time of issue is less than 10 years, the security is called a note rather than a bond. A T-bill has a maturity of 52 weeks or less at the time of issue, and it makes no payments at all until it matures. Thus, T-bills are sold initially at a discount to their face, or maturity, value.

GLOBAL ECONOMIC CRISIS

© uniquely India/Getty Images

The Global Economic Crisis

Betting With or Against the U.S. Government: The Case of Treasury Bond Credit Default Swaps

It might be hard to believe, but there is actually a market for U.S. Treasury bond insurance. In July 2011, investors worried that Congress would not extend the debt ceiling, inducing defaults in Treasury securities. At that time a credit default swap (CDS) on a 5-year T-bond was selling for 63.5 basis points (a basis point is 1/100 of a percentage point). This means that you could pay $6.35 a year to a counterparty who would promise to insure $1,000 of T-bond principal against default. Considering that the T-bond was yielding an amount equal to about $15 a year, the insurance would eat up a lot of the annual return for an investor who owned the bond. However, most of the trading in this CDS is by speculators and hedgers who don't even own the T-bond but are simply betting for or against the financial soundness of the U.S. government.

But it does make you wonder: "If the United States fails, who will be around to pay off the CDS?"

Note: For updates on the 5-year CDS, go to **www.bloomberg.com** and enter a quote for CT786896:IND.

5-2 Key Characteristics of Bonds

Although all bonds have some common characteristics, they do not always have identical contractual features, as described below.

WWW

An excellent site for information on many types of bonds is the FINRA Web page, **http://cxa.marketwatch.com/finra/bondcenter/default.aspx.** *The site has a great deal of information about corporates, municipals, Treasuries, and bond funds. It includes free bond searches, through which the user specifies the attributes desired in a bond and then the search returns the publicly traded bonds meeting the criteria.*

5-2a Par Value

The **par value** is the stated face value of the bond; for illustrative purposes, we generally assume a par value of $1,000. In practice, some bonds have par values that are multiples of $1,000 (for example, $5,000) and some have par values of less than $1,000 (Treasury bonds can be purchased in multiples of $100). The par value generally represents the amount of money the firm borrows and promises to repay on the maturity date.

5-2b Coupon Interest Rate

MicroDrive's bonds require the company to pay a fixed number of dollars of interest every year (or, more typically, every 6 months). When this **coupon payment**, as it is called, is divided by the par value, the result is the **coupon interest rate**. For example, MicroDrive's bonds have a $1,000 par value, and they pay $90 in interest each year. The bond's coupon interest is $90, so its coupon interest rate is $90/$1,000 = 9%. The coupon payment, which is fixed at the time the bond is issued, remains in force during the life of the bond.[2] Typically, at the time a bond is issued, its coupon payment is set at a level that will enable the bond to be issued at or near its par value.

[2]At one time, bonds literally had a number of small coupons attached to them, and on each interest payment date the owner would clip off the coupon for that date and either cash it at the bank or mail it to the company's paying agent, who would then mail back a check for the interest. For example, a 30-year, semiannual bond would start with 60 coupons. Today, most new bonds are *registered*—no physical coupons are involved, and interest checks automatically are mailed to the registered owners or directly deposited in their bank accounts.

In some cases, a bond's coupon payment will vary over time. For these **floating-rate bonds**, the coupon rate is set for, say, the initial 6-month period, after which it is adjusted every 6 months based on some market rate. Some corporate issues are tied to the Treasury bond rate; other issues are tied to other rates, such as LIBOR (the London Interbank Offered Rate). Many additional provisions can be included in floating-rate issues. For example, some are convertible to fixed-rate debt, whereas others have upper and lower limits ("caps" and "floors") on how high or low the rate can go.

Floating-rate debt is popular with investors who are worried about the risk of rising interest rates, because the interest paid on such bonds increases whenever market rates rise. This stabilizes the market value of the debt, and it also provides institutional buyers, such as banks, with income that is better geared to their own obligations. Banks' deposit costs rise with interest rates, so the income on floating-rate loans they have made rises at the same time as their deposit costs rise. The savings and loan industry was almost destroyed as a result of its former practice of making fixed-rate mortgage loans but borrowing on floating-rate terms. If you earn 6% fixed but pay 10% floating (which they were), you will soon go bankrupt (which they did). Moreover, floating-rate debt appeals to corporations that want to issue long-term debt without committing themselves to paying a historically high interest rate for the entire life of the loan.

resource

For more on zero coupon bonds, including U.S. Treasury STRIP bonds, see Web Extension 5A on the textbook's Web site.

Some bonds pay no coupons at all but are offered at a substantial discount below their par values and hence provide capital appreciation rather than interest income. These securities are called **zero coupon bonds** ("zeros"). Most zero coupon bonds are Treasury bonds, although a few corporations, such as Coca-Cola, have zero coupon bonds outstanding. Some bonds are issued with a coupon rate too low for the bond to be issued at par, so the bond is issued at a price less than its par value. In general, any bond originally offered at a price significantly below its par value is called an **original issue discount (OID) bond.**

Some bonds don't pay cash coupons but pay coupons consisting of additional bonds (or a percentage of an additional bond). These are called **payment-in-kind bonds**, or just **PIK bonds**. PIK bonds are usually issued by companies with cash flow problems, which makes them risky.

Some bonds have a step-up provision: If the company's bond rating is downgraded, then it must increase the bond's coupon rate. Step-ups are more popular in Europe than in the United States, but that is beginning to change. Note that a step-up is quite dangerous from the company's standpoint. The downgrade means that it is having trouble servicing its debt, and the step-up will exacerbate the problem. This combination has led to a number of bankruptcies.

5-2c Maturity Date

Bonds generally have a specified **maturity date** on which the par value must be repaid. MicroDrive bonds issued on January 5, 2013, will mature on January 5, 2028; thus, they have a 15-year maturity at the time they are issued. Most bonds have **original maturities** (the maturity at the time the bond is issued) ranging from 10 to 40 years, but any maturity is legally permissible.[3] Of course, the effective maturity of a bond declines each year after it has been issued. Thus, MicroDrive's bonds have a 15-year original maturity, but in 2014, a year later, they will have a 14-year maturity, and so on.

[3]In July 1993, Walt Disney Co., attempting to lock in a low interest rate, issued the first 100-year bonds to be sold by any borrower in modern times. Soon after, Coca-Cola became the second company to stretch the meaning of "long-term bond" by selling $150 million of 100-year bonds.

5-2d Provisions to Call or Redeem Bonds

Most corporate bonds contain a **call provision**, which gives the issuing corporation the right to call the bonds for redemption.[4] The call provision generally states that the company must pay the bondholders an amount greater than the par value if they are called. The additional sum, which is termed a **call premium**, is often set equal to 1 year's interest if the bonds are called during the first year, and the premium declines at a constant rate of INT/N each year thereafter (where INT = annual interest and N = original maturity in years). For example, the call premium on a $1,000 par value, 10-year, 10% bond would generally be $100 if it were called during the first year, $90 during the second year (calculated by reducing the $100, or 10%, premium by one-tenth), and so on. However, bonds are often not callable until several years (generally 5 to 10) after they are issued. This is known as a **deferred call**, and the bonds are said to have **call protection**.

Suppose a company sold bonds when interest rates were relatively high. Provided the issue is callable, the company could sell a new issue of low-yielding securities if and when interest rates drop. It could then use the proceeds of the new issue to retire the high-rate issue and thus reduce its interest expense. This process is called a **refunding operation**.

A call provision is valuable to the firm but potentially detrimental to investors. If interest rates go up, the company will not call the bond, and the investor will be stuck with the original coupon rate on the bond, even though interest rates in the economy have risen sharply. However, if interest rates fall, the company *will* call the bond and pay off investors, who then must reinvest the proceeds at the current market interest rate, which is lower than the rate they were getting on the original bond. In other words, the investor loses when interest rates go up but doesn't reap the gains when rates fall. To induce an investor to take this type of risk, a new issue of callable bonds must provide a higher coupon rate than an otherwise similar issue of noncallable bonds.

Bonds that are **redeemable at par** at the holder's option protect investors against a rise in interest rates. If rates rise, the price of a fixed-rate bond declines. However, if holders have the option of turning their bonds in and having them redeemed at par, then they are protected against rising rates. If interest rates have risen, holders will turn in the bonds and reinvest the proceeds at a higher rate.

Event risk is the chance that some sudden event will occur and increase the credit risk of a company, hence lowering the firm's bond rating and the value of its outstanding bonds. Investors' concern over event risk means that those firms deemed most likely to face events that could harm bondholders must pay extremely high interest rates. To reduce this interest rate, some bonds have a covenant called a **super poison put**, which enables a bondholder to turn in, or "put," a bond back to the issuer at par in the event of a takeover, merger, or major recapitalization.

Some bonds have a **make-whole call provision**. This allows a company to call the bond, but it must pay a call price that is essentially equal to the market value of a similar noncallable bond. This provides companies with an easy way to repurchase bonds as part of a financial restructuring, such as a merger.

5-2e Sinking Funds

Some bonds include a **sinking fund provision** that facilitates the orderly retirement of the bond issue. On rare occasions the firm may be required to deposit money with a trustee, which invests the funds and then uses the accumulated sum to retire the bonds when they

[4]A majority of municipal bonds also contain call provisions. Although the U.S. Treasury no longer issues callable bonds, some past Treasury issues were callable.

mature. Usually, though, the sinking fund is used to buy back a certain percentage of the issue each year. A failure to meet the sinking fund requirement throws the bond into default, which may force the company into bankruptcy.

In most cases, the firm is given the right to administer the sinking fund in either of two ways.

1. The company can call in for redemption (at par value) a certain percentage of the bonds each year; for example, it might be able to call 5% of the total original amount of the issue at a price of $1,000 per bond. The bonds are numbered serially, and those called for redemption are determined by a lottery administered by the trustee.
2. The company may buy the required number of bonds on the open market.

The firm will choose the least-cost method. If interest rates have risen, causing bond prices to fall, then it will buy bonds in the open market at a discount; if interest rates have fallen, it will call the bonds. Note that a call for sinking fund purposes is quite different from a refunding call as discussed previously. A sinking fund call typically requires no call premium, but only a small percentage of the issue is normally callable in any one year.[5]

Although sinking funds are designed to protect bondholders by ensuring that an issue is retired in an orderly fashion, you should recognize that sinking funds also can work to the detriment of bondholders. For example, suppose that the bond carries a 10% interest rate but that yields on similar bonds have fallen to 7.5%. A sinking fund call at par would require an investor to give up a bond that pays $100 of interest and then to reinvest in a bond that pays only $75 per year. This obviously harms those bondholders whose bonds are called. On balance, however, bonds that have a sinking fund are regarded as being safer than those without such a provision, so at the time they are issued sinking fund bonds have lower coupon rates than otherwise similar bonds without sinking funds.

5-2f Other Provisions and Features

Owners of **convertible bonds** have the option to convert the bonds into a fixed number of shares of common stock. Convertibles offer investors the chance to share in the upside if a company does well, so investors are willing to accept a lower coupon rate on convertibles than on an otherwise identical but nonconvertible bond.

Warrants are options that permit the holder to buy stock at a fixed price, thereby providing a gain if the price of the stock rises. Some bonds are issued with warrants. As with convertibles, bonds with warrants have lower coupon rates than straight bonds.

An **income bond** is required to pay interest only if earnings are high enough to cover the interest expense. If earnings are not sufficient, then the company is not required to pay interest and the bondholders do not have the right to force the company into bankruptcy. Therefore, from an investor's standpoint, income bonds are riskier than "regular" bonds.

Indexed bonds, also called **purchasing power bonds**, first became popular in Brazil, Israel, and a few other countries plagued by high inflation rates. The interest payments and maturity payment rise automatically when the inflation rate rises, thus protecting the bondholders against inflation. In January 1997, the U.S. Treasury began issuing indexed bonds called TIPS, short for Treasury Inflation-Protected Securities. Later in this chapter we show how TIPS can be used to estimate the risk-free rate.

[5]Some sinking funds require the issuer to pay a call premium.

5-2g Bond Markets

Corporate bonds are traded primarily in electronic/telephone markets rather than in organized exchanges. Most bonds are owned by and traded among a relatively small number of very large financial institutions, including banks, investment banks, life insurance companies, mutual funds, and pension funds. Although these institutions buy and sell very large blocks of bonds, it is relatively easy for bond dealers to arrange transactions because there are relatively few players in this market as compared with stock markets.

Information on bond trades is not widely published, but a representative group of bonds is listed and traded on the bond division of the NYSE and is reported on the bond market page of *The Wall Street Journal.* The most useful Web site (as of mid-2012) is provided by the Financial Industry Regulatory Authority (FINRA) at **http://cxa.marketwatch.com/finra/bondcenter/default.aspx.**

SELF-TEST

Define "floating-rate bonds" and "zero coupon bonds."

Why is a call provision advantageous to a bond issuer?

What are the two ways a sinking fund can be handled? Which method will be chosen by the firm if interest rates have risen? If interest rates have fallen?

Are securities that provide for a sinking fund regarded as being riskier than those without this type of provision? Explain.

What are income bonds and indexed bonds?

Why do convertible bonds and bonds with warrants have lower coupons than similarly rated bonds that do not have these features?

5-3 Bond Valuation

The value of any financial asset—a stock, a bond, a lease, or even a physical asset such as an apartment building or a piece of machinery—is simply the present value of the cash flows the asset is expected to produce. The cash flows from a specific bond depend on its contractual features. The following section shows the time line and cash flows for a bond.

5-3a Time Line, Cash Flows, and Valuation Formulas for a Bond

For a standard coupon-bearing bond, the cash flows consist of interest payments during the life of the bond plus the amount borrowed when the bond matures (usually a $1,000 par value):

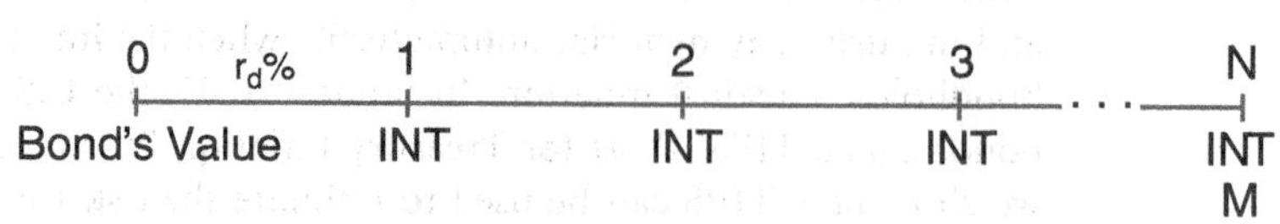

The notation in the time line is explained below.

r_d = The bond's required rate of return, which is the market rate of interest for that type of bond. This is the discount rate that is used to calculate the present value of the bond's cash flows. It is also called the "yield" or "going rate of interest." Note that r_d is *not* the coupon interest rate. It is equal to the coupon rate only if (as in this case) the bond is selling at par. Generally, most coupon bonds are issued at par, which implies that the coupon rate is set at r_d. Thereafter, interest rates, as measured by r_d, will fluctuate, but the coupon rate is fixed, so r_d will equal the coupon rate only by chance. We use the term "i" or "I" to designate the interest rate for many calculations because those terms are used on financial calculators, but "r," with the subscript "d" to designate the rate on a debt security, is normally used in finance.

N = Number of years until the bond matures. Note that N declines each year after the bond was issued, so a bond that had a maturity of 15 years when it was issued (original maturity = 15) will have N = 14 after 1 year, N = 13 after 2 years, and so on. Note also that for the sake of simplicity we assume the bond pays interest once a year, or annually, so N is measured in years. We consider bonds with semiannual payment bonds later in the chapter.

INT = Dollars of interest paid each year = (Coupon rate)(Par value). For a bond with a 9% coupon and a $1,000 par value, the annual interest is 0.09($1,000) = $90. In calculator terminology, INT = PMT = 90. If the bond had been a semiannual payment bond, the payment would have been $45 every 6 months.

M = Par, or maturity, value of the bond. This amount must be paid off at maturity, and it is often equal to $1,000.

The following general equation, written in several forms, can be used to find the value of any bond, V_B:

$$\begin{aligned} V_B &= \frac{INT}{(1+r_d)^1} + \frac{INT}{(1+r_d)^2} + \cdots + \frac{INT}{(1+r_d)^N} + \frac{M}{(1+r_d)^N} \\ &= \sum_{t=1}^{N} \frac{INT}{(1+r_d)^t} + \frac{M}{(1+r_d)^N} \\ &= INT\left[\frac{1}{r_d} - \frac{1}{r_d(1+r_d)^N}\right] + \frac{M}{(1+r_d)^N} \end{aligned} \tag{5-1}$$

Observe that the cash flows consist of an annuity of N years plus a lump-sum payment at the end of Year N. Equation 5-1 can be solved by using (1) a formula, (2) a financial calculator, or (3) a spreadsheet.

5-3b Solving for the Bond Price

Recall that MicroDrive issued a 15-year bond with an annual coupon rate of 9% and a par value of $1,000. To find the value of MicroDrive's bond by using a formula, insert values for MicroDrive's bond into Equation 5-1:

$$V_B = \sum_{t=1}^{15} \frac{\$90}{(1+0.09)^t} + \frac{\$1{,}000}{(1+0.09)^{15}}$$
$$= \$100\left[\frac{1}{0.09} - \frac{1}{0.09(1+0.09)^{15}}\right] + \frac{\$1{,}000}{(1+0.09)^{15}} \tag{5-1a}$$
$$= \$725.46 + \$274.54 = \$1{,}000$$

You could use the first line of Equation 5-1a to discount each cash flow back to the present and then sum these PVs to find the bond's value of $1,000; see Figure 5-1. This procedure is not very efficient, especially if the bond has many years to maturity.

Alternatively, you could use the formula in the second line of Equation 5-1a with a simple or scientific calculator. As shown in the third line of Equation 5-1a, the total bond value of $1,000 is the sum of the coupons' present values ($725.46) and the par value's present value ($274.54). This is easier than the step-by-step approach, but it is still somewhat cumbersome.

resource
*See **Ch05 Tool Kit.xls** on the textbook's Web site.*

A financial calculator is ideally suited for finding bond values. Here is the setup for MicroDrive's bond:

	N	I/YR	PV	PMT	FV
Inputs	15	9		90	1000
Output			-1000		

Input N = 15, I/YR = r_d = 9, INT = PMT = 90, and M = FV = 1000; then press the PV key to find the value of the bond, $1,000. Because the PV is an outflow to the investor, it is shown with a negative sign. The calculator is programmed to solve Equation 5-1: It finds the PV of an annuity of $100 per year for 15 years, discounted at 10%, then it finds the PV of the $1,000 maturity payment, and then it adds these two PVs to find the value of the bond. Notice that even though the bond has a total cash flow of $1,090 at Year 15, you should *not* enter FV = 1090! When you entered N = 15 and PMT = 90, you told the calculator that there is a $90 payment at Year 15. Thus, setting FV = 1000 accounts for any *extra* payment at Year 15, above and beyond the $90 payment.

resource
*See **Ch05 Tool Kit.xls** on the textbook's Web site.*

With *Excel*, it is easiest to use the PV function: **=PV(I,N,PMT,FV,0)**. For MicroDrive's bond, the function is **=PV(0.09,15,90,1000,0)** with a result of −$1,000. Like the financial calculator solution, the bond value is negative because PMT and FV are positive.

Excel also provides specialized functions for bond prices based on actual dates. For example, in *Excel* you could find the MicroDrive bond value as of the date it was issued by using the function wizard to enter this formula:

= PRICE(DATE(2013,1,5),DATE(2028,1,5),9%,9%,100,1,1)

The first two arguments in the function are *Excel*'s DATE function. The DATE function takes the year, month, and day as inputs and converts them into a date. The first argument is the date on which you want to find the price, and the second argument is the maturity date. The third argument in the PRICE function is the bond's coupon rate, followed by the required return on the bond, r_d. The fifth argument, 100, is the redemption value of the bond at maturity per $100 of face value; entering "100" means that the bond pays 100% of its face value when it matures. The sixth argument is the number of

FIGURE 5-1

Finding the Value of MicroDrive's Bond (V_B)

	A	B	C	D	E	F	G
19	INPUTS:						
20	Years to maturity = N =		15				
21	Coupon payment = INT =		$90				
22	Par value = M =		$1,000				
23	Required return = r_d =		9%				
24							
25	1. Step-by-Step: Divide each cash flow by $(1 + r_d)^t$						
26	Year (t)	Coupon Payment	PV of Coupon Payment	Par Value	PV of Par Value		
27	1	$90	$82.57				
28	2	$90	$75.75				
29	3	$90	$69.50				
30	4	$90	$63.76				
31	5	$90	$58.49				
32	6	$90	$53.66				
33	7	$90	$49.23				
34	8	$90	$45.17				
35	9	$90	$41.44				
36	10	$90	$38.02				
37	11	$90	$34.88				
38	12	$90	$32.00				
39	13	$90	$29.36				
40	14	$90	$26.93				
41	15	$90	$24.71	$1,000	$274.54		
42		Total =	$725.46				
43							
44	V_B = PV of all coupon payments + PV of par value =				$1,000.00		
45							
46		Inputs:	15	0		90	1,000
47	2. Financial Calculator:		N	I/YR	PV	PMT	FV
48		Output:			−$1,000.00		
49							
50	3. *Excel*:		PV function:	PV_N =	=PV(9%,15,90,1000)		
51			Fixed inputs:	PV_N =	=PV(9%,15,90,1000) =		−$1,000.00
52			Cell references:	PV_N =	=PV(C23,C20,C21,C22) =		−$1,000.00

payments per year. The last argument, 1, tells the program to base the price on the actual number of days in each month and year. This function produces a result based upon a face value of $100. In other words, if the bond pays $100 of face value at maturity, then the PRICE function result is the price of the bond. Because MicroDrive's bond pays $1,000 of face value at maturity, we must multiply the PRICE function's result by 10. In this example, the PRICE function returns a result of $100. When we multiply it by 10, we get the actual price of $1,000. This function is essential if a bond is being evaluated between coupon payment dates. See ***Ch05 Tool Kit.xls*** on the textbook's Web site for an example.[6]

5-3c Interest Rate Changes and Bond Prices

In this example, MicroDrive's bond is selling at a price equal to its par value. Whenever the going market rate of interest, r_d, is equal to the coupon rate, a *fixed-rate* bond will sell at its par value. Normally, the coupon rate is set at the going rate when a bond is issued, causing it to sell at par initially.

The coupon rate remains fixed after the bond is issued, but interest rates in the market move up and down. Looking at Equation 5-1, we see that an *increase* in the market interest rate (r_d) will cause the price of an outstanding bond to *fall*, whereas a *decrease* in rates will cause the bond's price to *rise*. For example, if the market interest rate on MicroDrive's bond increased by 5 percentage points to 14% immediately after it was issued, we would recalculate the price with the new market interest rate as follows:

	N	I/YR	PV	PMT	FV
Inputs	15	14		90	1000
Output			−692.89		

The price would fall to $692.89. Notice that the bond would then sell at a price below its par value. Whenever the going rate of interest *rises above* the coupon rate, a fixed-rate bond's price will *fall below* its par value, and it is called a **discount bond.**

On the other hand, bond prices rise when market interest rates fall. For example, if the market interest rate on MicroDrive's bond decreased by 5 percentage points to 4%, then we would once again recalculate its price:

	N	I/YR	PV	PMT	FV
Inputs	15	4		90	1000
Output			−1555.92		

In this case, the price rises to $1,555.92. In general, whenever the going interest rate *falls below* the coupon rate, a fixed-rate bond's price will *rise above* its par value, and it is called a **premium bond.**

[6]The bond prices quoted by brokers are calculated as described. However, if you bought a bond between interest payment dates, you would have to pay the basic price plus accrued interest. Thus, if you purchased a MicroDrive bond 6 months after it was issued, your broker would send you an invoice stating that you must pay $1,000 as the basic price of the bond plus $45 interest, representing one-half the annual interest of $90. The seller of the bond would receive $1,045. If you bought the bond the day before its interest payment date, you would pay $1,000 + (364/365)($90) = $1,089.75. You would receive an interest payment of $90 at the end of the next day.

SELF-TEST

Why do the prices of fixed-rate bonds fall if expectations for inflation rise?

What is a discount bond? A premium bond?

A bond that matures in 6 years has a par value of $1,000, an annual coupon payment of $80, and a market interest rate of 9%. What is its price? **($955.14)**

A bond that matures in 18 years has a par value of $1,000, an annual coupon of 10%, and a market interest rate of 7%. What is its price? **($1,301.77)**

5-4 Changes in Bond Values Over Time

At the time a coupon bond is issued, the coupon is generally set at a level that will cause the market price of the bond to equal its par value. If a lower coupon were set, investors would not be willing to pay $1,000 for the bond, and if a higher coupon were set, investors would clamor for the bond and bid its price up over $1,000. Investment bankers can judge quite precisely the coupon rate that will cause a bond to sell at its $1,000 par value.

A bond that has just been issued is known as a **new issue**. (Investment bankers classify a bond as a new issue for about a month after it has first been issued. New issues are usually actively traded and are called "on-the-run" bonds.) Once the bond has been on the market for a while, it is classified as an **outstanding bond**, also called a **seasoned issue**. Newly issued bonds generally sell very close to par, but the prices of seasoned bonds vary widely from par. Except for floating-rate bonds, coupon payments are constant, so when economic conditions change, a 9% coupon bond with a $90 coupon that sold at par when it was issued will sell for more or less than $1,000 thereafter.

MicroDrive's bonds with a 9% coupon rate were originally issued at par. If r_d remained constant at 9%, what would the value of the bond be 1 year after it was issued? Now the term to maturity is only 14 years—that is, N = 14. With a financial calculator, just override N = 15 with N = 14, press the PV key, and you find a value of $1,000. If we continued, setting N = 13, N = 12, and so forth, we would see that the value of the bond will remain at $1,000 as long as the going interest rate remains equal to the coupon rate, 9%.

Now suppose interest rates in the economy fell after the MicroDrive bonds were issued and, as a result, r_d *fell below the coupon rate,* decreasing from 9% to 4%. Both the coupon interest payments and the maturity value remain constant, but now 4% would have to be used for r_d in Equation 5-1. The value of the bond at the end of the first year would be $1,494.93:

$$V_B = \sum_{t=1}^{14} \frac{\$90}{(1+0.04)^t} + \frac{\$1,000}{(1+0.04)^{14}}$$

$$= \$100\left[\frac{1}{0.04} - \frac{1}{0.04(1+0.04)^{14}}\right] + \frac{\$1,000}{(1+0.04)^{14}}$$

$$= \$1,528.16$$

With a financial calculator, just change r_d = I/YR from 9 to 4, and then press the PV key to get the answer, $1,528.16. Thus, if r_d fell *below* the coupon rate, the bond would sell *above* par, or at a **premium**.

The arithmetic of the bond value increase should be clear, but what is the logic behind it? Because r_d has fallen to 4%, with $1,000 to invest you could buy new bonds like MicroDrive's (every day some 10 to 12 companies sell new bonds), except that these new bonds would pay $40 of interest each year rather than $90. Naturally, you would prefer $90 to $40, so you would be willing to pay more than $1,000 for a MicroDrive bond to obtain its higher coupons. All investors would react similarly; as a result, the MicroDrive bonds would be bid up in price to $1,528.16, at which point they would provide the same 4% rate of return to a potential investor as the new bonds.

Assuming that interest rates remain constant at 4% for the next 14 years, what would happen to the value of a MicroDrive bond? It would fall gradually from $1,528.16 to $1,000 at maturity, when MicroDrive will redeem each bond for $1,000. This point can be illustrated by calculating the value of the bond 1 year later, when it has 13 years remaining to maturity. With a financial calculator, simply input the values for N, I/YR, PMT, and FV, now using N = 13, and press the PV key to find the value of the bond, $1,499.28. Thus, the value of the bond will have fallen from $1,528.16 to $1,499.28, or by $28.88. If you were to calculate the value of the bond at other future dates, the price would continue to fall as the maturity date approached.

Note that if you purchased the bond at a price of $1,528.16 and then sold it 1 year later with r_d still at 4%, you would have a capital loss of 28.88, or a total dollar return of $90.00 – $28.88 = $61.12. Your percentage rate of return would consist of the rate of return due to the interest payment (called the **current yield**) and the rate of return due to the price change (called the **capital gains yield**). This total rate of return is often called the bond yield, and it is calculated as follows:

$$\begin{aligned} \text{Interest, or current, yield} &= \$90/\$1{,}528.16 = 0.0589 = 5.89\% \\ \text{Capital gains yield} &= -\$28.88/\$1{,}528.16 = -0.0189 = \underline{-1.89\%} \\ \text{Total rate of return, or yield} &= \$61.12/\$1{,}528.16 = 0.0400 = \underline{\underline{4.00\%}} \end{aligned}$$

Had interest rates risen from 9% to 14% during the first year after issue (rather than falling from 9% to 4%), then you would enter N = 14, I/YR = 14, PMT = 90, and FV = 1000, and then press the PV key to find the value of the bond, $699.90. In this case, the bond would sell below its par value, or at a discount. The total expected future return on the bond would again consist of an expected return due to interest and an expected return due to capital gains or capital losses. In this situation, the capital gains yield would be *positive.* The total return would be 14%. To see this, calculate the price of the bond with 13 years left to maturity, assuming that interest rates remain at 14%. With a calculator, enter N = 13, I/YR = 15, PMT = 90, and FV = 1000; then press PV to obtain the bond's value, $707.88.

Note that the capital gain for the year is the difference between the bond's value at Year 2 (with 13 years remaining) and the bond's value at Year 1 (with 14 years remaining), or $707.88 – $699.90 = $7.98. The interest yield, capital gains yield, and total yield are calculated as follows:

$$\begin{aligned} \text{Interest, or current, yield} &= \$90/\$699.90 = 0.1286 = 12.86\% \\ \text{Capital gains yield} &= \$7.98/\$699.90 = 0.0114 = \underline{1.14\%} \\ \text{Total rate of return, or yield} &= \$97.98/\$699.90 = 0.1400 = \underline{\underline{14.00\%}} \end{aligned}$$

Figure 5-2 graphs the value of the bond over time, assuming that interest rates in the economy (1) remain constant at 9%, (2) fall to 4% and then remain constant at that level, or (3) rise to 14% and remain constant at that level. Of course, if interest rates do *not* remain constant, then the price of the bond will fluctuate. However, regardless of what future interest rates do, the bond's price will approach $1,000 as it nears the maturity date (barring bankruptcy, which might cause the bond's value to fall dramatically).

FIGURE 5-2

Time Path of the Value of a 9% Coupon, $1,000 Par Value Bond When Interest Rates Are 4%, 9%, and 14%

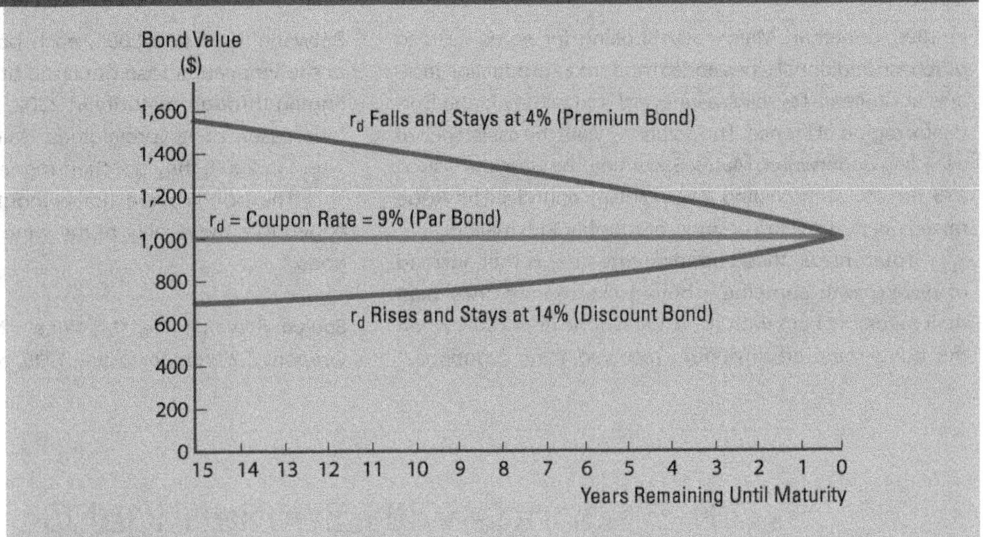

Note: The curves for 4% and 14% have a slight bow.

© Cengage Learning 2014

resource

See ***Ch05 Tool Kit.xls*** *for all calculations.*

Figure 5-2 illustrates the following key points.

1. Whenever the going rate of interest, r_d, is equal to the coupon rate, a *fixed-rate* bond will sell at its par value. Normally, the coupon rate is set equal to the going rate when a bond is issued, causing it to sell at par initially.
2. Interest rates do change over time, but the coupon rate remains fixed after the bond has been issued. Whenever the going rate of interest *rises above* the coupon rate, a fixed-rate bond's price will *fall below* its par value. Such a bond is called a discount bond.
3. Whenever the going rate of interest *falls below* the coupon rate, a fixed-rate bond's price will *rise above* its par value. Such a bond is called a premium bond.
4. Thus, an *increase* in interest rates will cause the prices of outstanding bonds to *fall,* whereas a *decrease* in rates will cause bond prices to *rise.*
5. The market value of a bond will always approach its par value as its maturity date approaches, provided the firm does not go bankrupt.

These points are very important, for they show that bondholders may suffer capital losses or make capital gains depending on whether interest rates rise or fall after the bond is purchased.

SELF-TEST

What is meant by the terms "new issue" and "seasoned issue"?

Last year, a firm issued 30-year, 8% annual coupon bonds at a par value of $1,000. (1) Suppose that 1 year later the going rate drops to 6%. What is the new price of the bonds, assuming that they now have 29 years to maturity? **($1,271.81)** (2) Suppose instead that 1 year after issue the going interest rate increases to 10% (rather than dropping to 6%). What is the price? **($812.61)**

Drinking Your Coupons

© Rob Webb/Getty Images

In 1996, Jonathan Maltus was looking for some cash to purchase additional vines and to modernize production facilities at Chateau Teyssier, a vineyard and winery in the Bordeaux region of France. The solution? With the assistance of a leading underwriter, Matrix Securities, the vineyard issued 375 bonds, each costing 2,650 British pounds. The issue raised nearly 1 million pounds, or roughly \$1.5 million.

What makes these bonds interesting is that, instead of paying with something boring like money, they paid their investors back with wine. Each June until 2002, when the bond matured, investors received their "coupons." Between 1997 and 2001, each bond provided six cases of the vineyard's rosé or claret. Starting in 1998 and continuing through maturity in 2002, investors also received four cases of its prestigious Saint Emilion Grand Cru. Then, in 2002, they got their money back.

The bonds were not without risk. Maltus acknowledged that the quality of the wine "is at the mercy of the gods."

Source: Steven Irvine, "My Wine Is My Bond, and I Drink My Coupons," *Euromoney,* July 1996, p. 7.

5-5 Bonds with Semiannual Coupons

Although some bonds pay interest annually, the vast majority actually pay interest semiannually. To evaluate semiannual payment bonds, we must modify the valuation model as follows.

1. Divide the annual coupon interest payment by 2 to determine the dollars of interest paid every 6 months.
2. Multiply the years to maturity, N, by 2 to determine the number of semiannual periods.
3. Divide the nominal (quoted) interest rate, r_d, by 2 to determine the periodic (semiannual) interest rate.

By making these changes, we obtain the following equation for finding the value of a bond that pays interest semiannually:

$$V_B = \sum_{t=1}^{2N} \frac{INT/2}{(1 + r_d/2)^t} + \frac{M}{(1 + r_d/2)^{2N}} \tag{5-2}$$

To illustrate, assume now that MicroDrive's bonds pay \$45 interest every 6 months rather than \$90 at the end of each year. Each semiannual interest payment is only half as large, but there are twice as many of them. The nominal, or quoted, coupon rate is "9%, semiannual payments."[7]

[7]In this situation, the coupon rate of "9% paid semiannually" is the rate that bond dealers, corporate treasurers, and investors generally would discuss. Of course, if this bond were issued at par, then its *effective annual rate* would be higher than 9%:

$$EAR = EFF\% = \left(1 + \frac{r_{NOM}}{M}\right)^M - 1 = \left(1 + \frac{0.09}{2}\right)^2 - 1 = (1.045)^2 - 1 = 9.20\%$$

Because 9.20% with annual payments is quite different from 9% with semiannual payments, we have assumed a change in effective rates in this section from the situation described in Section 5-3, where we assumed 9% with annual payments.

When the going (nominal) rate of interest is 4% with semiannual compounding, the value of this 15-year bond is found as follows:

Inputs	30	2		45	1000
	N	I/YR	PV	PMT	FV
Output			−1559.91		

Enter N = 30, r_d = I/YR = 2, PMT = 45, FV = 1000, and then press the PV key to obtain the bond's value, $1,559.91. The value with semiannual interest payments is slightly larger than $1,552.92, the value when interest is paid annually. This higher value occurs because interest payments are received somewhat sooner under semiannual compounding.

SELF-TEST

Describe how the annual bond valuation formula is changed to evaluate semiannual coupon bonds. Write out the revised formula.

A bond has a 25-year maturity, an 8% annual coupon paid semiannually, and a face value of $1,000. The going nominal annual interest rate (r_d) is 6%. What is the bond's price? **($1,257.30)**

5-6 Bond Yields

Unlike the coupon interest rate, which is fixed, the bond's *yield* varies from day to day depending on current market conditions. Moreover, the yield can be calculated in three different ways, and three "answers" can be obtained. These different yields are described in the following sections.

5-6a Yield to Maturity

Suppose 1 year after it was issued, you could buy MicroDrive's 14-year, 9% annual coupon, $1,000 par value bond at a price of $1,528.16. What rate of interest would you earn on your investment if you bought the bond and held it to maturity? This rate is called the bond's **yield to maturity (YTM)**, and it is the interest rate generally discussed by investors when they talk about rates of return. The yield to maturity is usually the same as the market rate of interest, r_d. To find the YTM for a bond with annual interest payments, you must solve Equation 5-1 for r_d:[8]

$$\text{Bond price} = \sum_{t=1}^{N} \frac{\text{INT}}{(1+\text{YTM})^t} + \frac{\text{M}}{(1+\text{YTM})^N} \tag{5-3}$$

For MicroDrive's yield, you must solve this equation:

$$\$1{,}528.16 = \frac{\$90}{(1+r_d)^1} + \cdots + \frac{\$90}{(1+r_d)^{14}} + \frac{\$1{,}000}{(1+r_d)^{14}}$$

[8]If the bond has semiannual payments, you must solve Equation 5-2 for r_d.

You could substitute values for r_d until you found a value that "works" and forces the sum of the PVs on the right side of the equal sign to equal $1,528.16, but this would be tedious and time-consuming.[9] As you might guess, it is much easier with a financial calculator. Here is the setup:

	N	I/YR	PV	PMT	FV
Inputs	14		−1528.16	90	1000
Output		4			

Simply enter N = 14, PV = −1,528.16, PMT = 90, and FV = 1000, and then press the I/YR key for the answer of 4%.

resource
*See **Ch05 Tool Kit.xls** on the textbook's Web site.*

You could also find the YTM with a spreadsheet. In *Excel,* you would use the RATE function for this bond, inputting N = 14, PMT = 90, PV = −1528.16, FV = 1000, 0 for Type, and leave Guess blank: **=RATE(14,90,−1528.16,1000,0)**. The result is 4%. The RATE function works only if the current date is immediately after either the issue date or a coupon payment date. To find bond yields on other dates, use *Excel*'s YIELD function. See the ***Ch05 Tool Kit.xls*** file for an example.

The yield to maturity can be viewed as the bond's *promised rate of return,* which is the return that investors will receive if all the promised payments are made. However, the yield to maturity equals the *expected rate of return* only if (1) the probability of default is zero and (2) the bond cannot be called. If there is some default risk or if the bond may be called, then there is some probability that the promised payments to maturity will not be received, in which case the calculated yield to maturity will differ from the expected return.

The YTM for a bond that sells at par consists entirely of an interest yield, but if the bond sells at a price other than its par value, then the YTM will consist of the interest yield plus a positive or negative capital gains yield. Note also that a bond's yield to maturity changes whenever interest rates in the economy change, and this is almost daily. If you purchase a bond and hold it until it matures, you will receive the YTM that existed on the purchase date, but the bond's calculated YTM will change frequently between the purchase date and the maturity date.[10]

5-6b Yield to Call

If you purchased a bond that was callable and the company called it, you would not have the option of holding the bond until it matured. Therefore, the yield to maturity would not be earned. For example, if MicroDrive's 9% coupon bonds were callable and if interest rates fell from 9% to 4%, then the company could call in the 9% bonds, replace them with 4% bonds, and save $90 − $40 = $50 interest per bond per year. This would be good for the company but not for the bondholders.

[9] Alternatively, you can substitute values of r_d into the third form of Equation 5-1 until you find a value that works.

[10] We often are asked by students if the purchaser of a bond will receive the YTM if interest rates subsequently change. The answer is definitely "yes" provided the question means "Is the realized rate of return on the investment in the bond equal to the YTM?" This is because the realized rate of return on an investment is by definition the rate that sets the present value of the realized cash flows equal to the price. If instead the question means "Is the realized rate of return on the investment in the bond and the subsequent reinvestment of the coupons equal to the YTM?" then the answer is definitely "no." Thus, the question really is one about strategy and timing. The bond, in combination with a reinvestment strategy, is really two investments, and clearly the realized rate on this combined strategy depends on the reinvestment rate (see ***Web Extension 5C*** for more on investing for a target future value). For the rest of the book, we assume that an investment in a bond is only an investment in the bond, and not a combination of the bond and a reinvestment strategy; this means the investor earns the expected YTM if the bond is held to maturity.

If current interest rates are well below an outstanding bond's coupon rate, then a callable bond is likely to be called, and investors will estimate its expected rate of return as the **yield to call (YTC)** rather than as the yield to maturity. To calculate the YTC, solve this equation for r_d:

$$\text{Price of callable bond} = \sum_{t=1}^{N} \frac{\text{INT}}{(1 + r_d)^t} + \frac{\text{Call price}}{(1 + r_d)^N} \tag{5-4}$$

Here N is the number of years until the company can call the bond, r_d is the YTC, and "Call price" is the price the company must pay in order to call the bond (it is often set equal to the par value plus 1 year's interest).

To illustrate, suppose MicroDrive's bonds had a provision that permitted the company, if it desired, to call the bonds 10 years after the issue date at a price of $1,100. Suppose further that 1 year after issuance the going interest rate had declined, causing the price of the bonds to rise to $1,528.16. Here is the time line and the setup for finding the bond's YTC with a financial calculator:

0	YTC = ?	1	2	…	8	9
−1,528.16		90	90		90	90 1,100

	N	I/YR	PV	PMT	FV
Inputs	9		−1528.16	90	1110
Output		3.15 = YTC			

The YTC is 3.15%—this is the return you would earn if you bought the bond at a price of $1,528.16 and it was called 9 years from today. (The bond could not be called until 10 years after issuance, and 1 year has gone by, so there are 9 years left until the first call date.)

Do you think MicroDrive *will* call the bonds when they become callable? MicroDrive's actions depend on the going interest rate when the bonds become callable. If the going rate remains at r_d = 4%, then MicroDrive could save 9% − 4% = 5%, or $50 per bond per year, by calling them and replacing the 9% bonds with a new 4% issue. There would be costs to the company to refund the issue, but the interest savings would probably be worth the cost, so MicroDrive would probably refund the bonds. Therefore, you would probably earn YTC = 3.15% rather than YTM = 4% if you bought the bonds under the indicated conditions.

In the balance of this chapter, we assume that bonds are not callable unless otherwise noted. However, some of the end-of-chapter problems deal with yield to call.

5-6c Current Yield

If you examine brokerage house reports on bonds, you will often see reference to a bond's **current yield**. The current yield is the annual interest payment divided by the bond's current price. For example, if MicroDrive's bonds with a 9% coupon were currently selling at $985, then the bond's current yield would be $90/$985 = 0.0914 = 9.14%.

Unlike the yield to maturity, the current yield does not represent the rate of return that investors should expect on the bond. The current yield provides information regarding the amount of cash income that a bond will generate in a given year, but it does not provide an accurate measure of the bond's total expected return, the yield to maturity. In fact, here is the relation between current yield, capital gains yield (which can be negative for a capital loss), and the yield to maturity:

$$\text{Current yield} + \text{Capital gains yield} = \text{Yield to maturity} \qquad (5\text{-}5)$$

5-6d The Cost of Debt and Intrinsic Value

The "Intrinsic Value Box" at the beginning of this chapter highlights the cost of debt, which affects the weighted average cost of capital (WACC), which in turn affects the company's intrinsic value. The pre-tax cost of debt from the company's perspective is the required return from the debtholder's perspective. Therefore, the pre-tax cost of debt is the yield to maturity (or the yield to call if a call is likely). But why do different bonds have different yields to maturity? The following sections answer this question.

SELF-TEST

Explain the difference between the yield to maturity and the yield to call.

How does a bond's current yield differ from its total return?

Could the current yield exceed the total return?

A bond currently sells for $850. It has an 8-year maturity, an annual coupon of $80, and a par value of $1,000. What is its yield to maturity? **(10.90%)** *What is its current yield?* **(9.41%)**

A bond currently sells for $1,250. It pays a $110 annual coupon and has a 20-year maturity, but it can be called in 5 years at $1,110. What are its YTM and its YTC? **(8.38%, 6.85%)** *Is the bond likely to be called if interest rates don't change?*

5-7 The Pre-Tax Cost of Debt: Determinants of Market Interest Rates

Until now we have given you r_d, the going market rate. But as we showed in Chapter 1, different debt securities often have very different market rates. What explains these differences? In general, the quoted (or nominal) interest rate on a debt security, r_d, is composed of a real risk-free rate of interest, r^*, plus several premiums that reflect inflation, the risk of the security, and the security's marketability (or liquidity). A conceptual framework is shown below:

$$\begin{aligned}\text{Quoted market interest rate} = r_d &= r^* + IP + DRP + LP + MRP \\ &= r_{RF} + DRP + LP + MRP\end{aligned} \qquad (5\text{-}6)$$

Here are definitions of the variables in Equation 5-6:

r_d = Quoted, or nominal, rate of interest on a given security.[11] There are many different securities and hence many different quoted interest rates.

r^* = Real risk-free rate of interest. Pronounced "r-star," r^* is the rate on a riskless security if zero inflation were expected.

IP = Inflation premium, which is equal to the average expected inflation rate over the life of the security. The expected future inflation rate is not necessarily equal to the current inflation rate, so IP is not necessarily equal to current inflation.

r_{RF} = r^* + IP, and it is the quoted risk-free rate of interest on a security such as a U.S. Treasury bill, which is very liquid and also free of most risks. Note that r_{RF} includes the premium for expected inflation because $r_{RF} = r^* + IP$.

DRP = Default risk premium. This premium reflects the possibility that the issuer will not pay interest or principal at the stated time and in the stated amount. The DRP is zero for U.S. Treasury securities, but it rises as the riskiness of issuers increases.

LP = Liquidity, or marketability, premium. This is a premium charged by lenders to reflect the fact that some securities cannot be converted to cash on short notice at a "reasonable" price. The LP is very low for Treasury securities and for securities issued by large, strong firms, but it is relatively high on securities issued by very small firms.

MRP = Maturity risk premium. Changes in market interest rates can cause large changes in the prices of long-term bonds, even Treasury bonds. Lenders charge a maturity risk premium to reflect this risk.

WWW

See **www.bloomberg.com** *and select MARKETS. Then select RATES AND BONDS for a partial listing of indexed Treasury bonds and their interest rates. See* **online.wsj.com** *for a complete set of Treasury quotes. See* **www.treasurydirect.gov/indiv/products/products.htm** *for a complete listing of all Treasury securities.*

We discuss the components whose sum makes up the quoted, or nominal, rate on a given security in the following sections.

SELF-TEST

Write out an equation for the nominal interest rate on any debt security.

5-8 The Real Risk-Free Rate of Interest, r*

The **real risk-free rate of interest, r***, is defined as the interest rate that would exist on a riskless security if no inflation were expected, and it may be thought of as the rate of interest on *short-term* U.S. Treasury securities in an inflation-free world. The real risk-free

[11]The term *nominal* as used here means the *stated* rate as opposed to the *real* rate, which is adjusted to remove inflation effects. Suppose you bought a 10-year Treasury bond with a quoted, or nominal, rate of about 4.6%. If inflation averages 2.5% over the next 10 years, then the real rate would be about 4.6% – 2.5% = 2.1%. To be technically correct, we should find the real rate by solving for r^* in the following equation: $(1 + r^*)(1 + 0.025) = (1 + 0.046)$. Solving the equation, we find $r^* = 2.05\%$. Because this is very close to the 2.1% just calculated, we will continue to approximate the real rate in this chapter by subtracting inflation from the nominal rate.

rate is not static—it changes over time depending on economic conditions, especially (1) the rate of return corporations and other borrowers expect to earn on productive assets, and (2) people's time preferences for current versus future consumption.[12]

In addition to its regular bond offerings, in 1997 the U.S. Treasury began issuing **indexed bonds,** with payments linked to inflation. These bonds are called **TIPS,** short for **Treasury Inflation-Protected Securities.** (For details on how TIPS are adjusted to protect against inflation, see ***Web Extension 5B*** on the textbook's Web site.) Because the payments (including the principal) are tied to inflation, the yield on a TIPS with 1 year until maturity is a good estimate of the real risk-free rate. In theory, we would like an even shorter maturity to estimate the real risk-free rate, but short-term TIPS are thinly traded and the reported yields are not as reliable.

Historically, the real interest rate has averaged around 1.5% to 2.5%. In March 2012, the TIPS with about 1 year remaining until maturity had a *−2.00%* yield. Although unusual, negative real rates are possible. In spring 2008, the combination of stagnant economic growth, a high level of investor uncertainty, fears of inflation, and the Federal Reserve's reduction in nominal short-term interest rates caused the real rate to fall below zero, as measured by negative yields on several short-term TIPS. The yields on short-term TIPS have remained low since then. Negative real rates are possible, but negative nominal rates are impossible (or at least extraordinarily rare) because investors would just hold cash instead of investing in a negative-yield bond.

SELF-TEST

What security provides a good estimate of the real risk-free rate?

5-9 The Inflation Premium (IP)

Inflation has a major effect on interest rates because it erodes the purchasing power of the dollar and lowers the real rate of return on investments. To illustrate, suppose you invest $3,000 in a default-free zero coupon bond that matures in 1 year and pays a 5% interest rate. At the end of the year, you will receive $3,150—your original $3,000 plus $150 of interest. Now suppose that the inflation rate during the year is 10% and that it affects all items equally. If gas had cost $3 per gallon at the beginning of the year, it would cost $3.30 at the end of the year. Therefore, your $3,000 would have bought $3,000/$3 = 1,000 gallons at the beginning of the year but only $3,150/$3.30 = 955 gallons at the end. In *real terms,* you would be worse off—you would receive $150 of interest, but it would not be sufficient to offset inflation. You would thus be better off buying 1,000 gallons of gas (or some other storable asset) than buying the default-free bond.

Investors are well aware of inflation's effects on interest rates, so when they lend money, they build in an **inflation premium (IP)** equal to the average expected inflation rate over the life of the security. For a short-term, default-free U.S. Treasury bill, the

[12]The real rate of interest as discussed here is different from the *current* real rate as often discussed in the press. The current real rate is often estimated as the current interest rate minus the current (or most recent) inflation rate, whereas the real rate, as used here (and in the fields of finance and economics generally) without the word "current," is the current interest rate minus the *expected future* inflation rate over the life of the security. For example, suppose the current quoted rate for a 1-year Treasury bill is 5%, inflation during the previous year was 2%, and inflation expected for the coming year is 4%. Then the *current* real rate would be approximately 5% − 2% = 3%, but the *expected* real rate would be approximately 5% − 4% = 1%.

actual interest rate charged, $r_{T\text{-bill}}$, would be the real risk-free rate, r*, plus the inflation premium (IP):

$$r_{T\text{-bill}} = r_{RF} = r^* + IP$$

Therefore, if the real short-term risk-free rate of interest were r* = 0.6% and if inflation were expected to be 1.0% (and hence IP = 1.0%) during the next year, then the quoted rate of interest on 1-year T-bills would be 0.6% + 1.0% = 1.6%.

It is important to note that the inflation rate built into interest rates is *the inflation rate expected in the future,* not the rate experienced in the past. Thus, the latest reported figures might show an annual inflation rate of 2%, but that is for the *past* year. If people on average expect a 6% inflation rate in the future, then 6% would be built into the current interest rate.

Note also that the inflation rate reflected in the quoted interest rate on any security is the *average rate of inflation expected over the security's life.* Thus, the inflation rate built into a 1-year bond is the expected inflation rate for the next year, but the inflation rate built into a 30-year bond is the average rate of inflation expected over the next 30 years. If I_t is the expected inflation during year t, then the inflation premium for an N-year bond's yield (IP_N) can be approximated as

$$IP_N = \frac{I_1 + I_2 + \cdots + I_N}{N} \tag{5-7}$$

For example, if investors expect inflation to average 3% during Year 1 and 5% during Year 2, then the inflation premium built into a 2-year bond's yield can be approximated by[13]

$$IP_2 = \frac{I_1 + I_2}{2} = \frac{3\% + 5\%}{2} = 4\%$$

In the previous section, we saw that the yield on an inflation-indexed Treasury bond (TIPS) is a good estimate of the real interest rate. We can also use TIPS to estimate inflation premiums. For example, in early 2012 the yield on a 5-year nonindexed T-bond was 1.21% and the yield on a 5-year TIPS was – 1.05%. Thus, the 5-year inflation premium was 1.21% – (–1.05%) = 2.26%, implying that investors expected inflation to average 2.26% over the next 5 years.[14] Similarly, the rate on a 20-year nonindexed T-bond was 2.97% and the rate on a 20-year indexed T-bond was 0.58%. Thus, the 20-year inflation premium was approximately 2.97% – 0.58% = 2.39%, implying that investors expected inflation to average 2.39% over the long term.[15] These calculations are summarized below:

---

[13]To be mathematically correct, we should take the *geometric average:* $(1 + IP_2)^2 = (1 + I_1)(1 + I_2)$. In this example, we have $(1 + IP_2)^2 = (1 + 0.03)(1 + 0.05)$. Solving for IP_2 yields 3.9952, which is close to our approximation of 4%.

[14]As we noted in the previous footnote, the mathematically correct approach is to use a *geometric average* and solve the following equation: (1 + IP)(1 + –0.0105) = 1 + .0121. Solving for IP gives IP = 2.28%, which is very close to our approximation.

Note, though, that the difference in yield between a T-bond and a TIPS of the same maturity reflects both the expected inflation *and* any risk premium for bearing inflation risk. So the difference in yields is really an upper limit on the expected inflation.

[15]There are several other sources for the estimated inflation premium. The Congressional Budget Office regularly updates the estimates of inflation that it uses in its forecasted budgets; see **www.cbo.gov**; select Economic Projections. A second source is the University of Michigan's Institute for Social Research, which regularly polls consumers regarding their expectations for price increases during the next year; see **www.sca.isr.umich.edu** for the survey.

We prefer using inflation premiums derived from indexed and nonindexed Treasury securities, as described in the text, because these are based on how investors actually spend their money, not on theoretical models or opinions.

Yields	Maturity		
	1 Year	5 Years	20 Years
Nonindexed U.S. Treasury Bond	0.23%	1.21%	2.97%
TIPS	−2.00%	−1.05%	0.58%
Inflation premium	2.23%	2.26%	2.39%

Expectations for future inflation are closely, but not perfectly, correlated with rates experienced in the recent past. Therefore, if the inflation rate reported for last month increases, people often raise their expectations for future inflation, and this change in expectations will cause an increase in interest rates.

Note that Germany, Japan, and Switzerland have, over the past several years, had lower inflation rates than the United States, so their interest rates have generally been lower than ours. South Africa, Brazil, and most South American countries have experienced higher inflation, which is reflected in their interest rates.

SELF-TEST

Explain how a TIPS and a nonindexed Treasury security can be used to estimate the inflation premium.

The yield on a 15-year TIPS is 3% and the yield on a 15-year Treasury bond is 5%. What is the inflation premium for a 15-year security? **(2%)**

5-10 The Nominal, or Quoted, Risk-Free Rate of Interest, r_{RF}

The **nominal, or quoted, risk-free rate,** r_{RF}, is the real risk-free rate plus a premium for expected inflation: $r_{RF} = r^* + IP$. To be strictly correct, the risk-free rate should mean the interest rate on a totally risk-free security—one that has no risk of default, no maturity risk, no liquidity risk, no risk of loss if inflation increases, and no risk of any other type. There is no such security, so there is no observable truly risk-free rate. When the term "risk-free rate" is used without either the modifier "real" or the modifier "nominal," people generally mean the quoted (nominal) rate, and we will follow that convention in this book. Therefore, when we use the term "risk-free rate, r_{RF}," we mean the nominal risk-free rate, which includes an inflation premium equal to the average expected inflation rate over the life of the security. In general, we use the T-bill rate to approximate the short-term risk-free rate and use the T-bond rate to approximate the long-term risk-free rate (even though it also includes a maturity premium). So, whenever you see the term "risk-free rate," assume that we are referring either to the quoted U.S. T-bill rate or to the quoted T-bond rate.

Because $r_{RF} = r^* + IP$, we can express the quoted rate as

$$\text{Nominal, or quoted, rate} = r_d = r_{RF} + DRP + LP + MRP \quad (5\text{-}8)$$

SELF-TEST

What security is a good approximation of the nominal risk-free rate?

5-11 The Default Risk Premium (DRP)

If the issuer defaults on a payment, investors receive less than the promised return on the bond. The quoted interest rate includes a default risk premium (DRP)—the greater the default risk, the higher the bond's yield to maturity.[16] The default risk on Treasury securities is virtually zero, but default risk can be substantial for corporate and municipal bonds. In this section, we consider some issues related to default risk.

5-11a Bond Contract Provisions That Influence Default Risk

Default risk is affected by both the financial strength of the issuer and the terms of the bond contract, especially whether collateral has been pledged to secure the bond. Several types of contract provisions are discussed next.

Bond Indentures

An **indenture** is a legal document that spells out the rights of both bondholders and the issuing corporation. A **trustee** is an official (usually a bank) who represents the bondholders and makes sure the terms of the indenture are carried out. The indenture may be several hundred pages in length, and it will include **restrictive covenants** that cover such points as the conditions under which the issuer can pay off the bonds prior to maturity, the levels at which certain ratios must be maintained if the company is to issue additional debt, and restrictions against the payment of dividends unless earnings meet certain specifications.

The Securities and Exchange Commission (1) approves indentures and (2) makes sure that all indenture provisions are met before allowing a company to sell new securities to the public. A firm will have different indentures for each of the major types of bonds it issues, but a single indenture covers all bonds of the same type. For example, one indenture will cover a firm's first mortgage bonds, another its debentures, and a third its convertible bonds.

Mortgage Bonds

A corporation pledges certain assets as security for a **mortgage bond**. The company might also choose to issue *second-mortgage bonds* secured by the same assets that were secured by a previously issued mortgage bond. In the event of liquidation, the holders of these second mortgage bonds would have a claim against the property, but only after the first mortgage bondholders had been paid off in full. Thus, second mortgages are sometimes called *junior mortgages* because they are junior in priority to the claims of *senior mortgages*, or *first-mortgage bonds*. All mortgage bonds are subject to an indenture that usually limits the amount of new bonds that can be issued.

Debentures and Subordinated Debentures

A **debenture** is an unsecured bond, and as such it provides no lien against specific property as security for the obligation. Debenture holders are, therefore, general creditors whose claims are protected by property not otherwise pledged.

[16]Suppose two bonds have the same promised cash flows, coupon rate, maturity, liquidity, and inflation exposure, but one bond has more default risk than the other. Investors will naturally pay less for the bond with the greater chance of default. As a result, bonds with higher default risk will have higher interest rates.

GLOBAL ECONOMIC CRISIS

© uniquely india/Getty Images

The Global Economic Crisis

Insuring with Credit Default Swaps: Let the Buyer Beware!

A credit default swap (CDS) is like an insurance policy. The purchaser of the CDS agrees to make annual payments to a counterparty that agrees to pay if a particular bond defaults. During the 2000s, investment banks often would purchase CDS for the mortgage-backed securities (MBS) they were creating in order to make the securities more attractive to investors. But how good was this type of insurance? As it turned out, not very. For example, Lehman Brothers might have bought a CDS from AIG in order to sell a Lehman-created MBS to an investor. But when the MBS began defaulting, neither Lehman nor AIG was capable of making full restitution to the investor.

The term *subordinate* means "below" or "inferior to"; thus, in the event of bankruptcy, subordinated debt has claims on assets only after senior debt has been paid off. **Subordinated debentures** may be subordinated either to designated notes payable (usually bank loans) or to all other debt. In the event of liquidation or reorganization, holders of subordinated debentures cannot be paid until all senior debt, as named in the debentures' indentures, has been paid.

Development Bonds

Some companies may be in a position to benefit from the sale of either **development bonds** or **pollution control bonds**. State and local governments may set up both *industrial development agencies* and *pollution control agencies*. These agencies are allowed, under certain circumstances, to sell **tax-exempt bonds** and then make the proceeds available to corporations for specific uses deemed (by Congress) to be in the public interest. For example, a Detroit pollution control agency might sell bonds to provide Ford with funds for purchasing pollution control equipment. Because the income from the bonds would be tax exempt, the bonds would have relatively low interest rates. Note, however, that these bonds are guaranteed by the corporation that will use the funds, not by a governmental unit, so their rating reflects the credit strength of the corporation using the funds.

Municipal Bond Insurance

Municipalities can have their bonds insured, which means that an insurance company guarantees to pay the coupon and principal payments should the issuer default. This reduces risk to investors, who will thus accept a lower coupon rate for an insured bond than for a comparable but uninsured one. Even though the municipality must pay a fee to have its bonds insured, its savings due to the lower coupon rate often make insurance cost-effective. Keep in mind that the insurers are private companies, and the value added by the insurance depends on the creditworthiness of the insurer. The larger insurers are strong companies, and their own ratings are AAA.

5-11b Bond Ratings

Since the early 1900s, bonds have been assigned quality ratings that reflect their probability of going into default. The three major rating agencies are Moody's Investors Service (Moody's), Standard & Poor's Corporation (S&P), and Fitch Ratings. As shown in Columns (3) and (4) of Table 5-1, triple-A and double-A bonds are extremely safe, rarely

TABLE 5-1
Bond Ratings, Default Risk, and Yields

Rating Agency[a]		Percent Defaulting Within:[b]		Median Ratios[c]		Percent Upgraded or Downgraded in 2011[b]		
S&P and Fitch (1)	Moody's (2)	1 year (3)	5 years (4)	Return on capital (5)	Total debt/ Total capital (6)	Down (7)	Up (8)	Yield[d] (9)
Investment-grade bonds								
AAA	Aaa	0.00%	0.00%	27.6%	12.4%	0.00%	NA	4.11%
AA	Aa	0.03	0.12	27.0	28.3	29.24	0.00	3.38
A	A	0.09	0.74	17.5	37.5	7.79	0.00	3.37
BBB	Baa	0.23	2.54	13.4	42.5	3.29	2.95	6.24
Junk bonds								
BB	Ba	1.17	6.91	11.3	53.7	4.82	8.13	6.28
B	B	2.14	9.28	8.7	75.9	3.48	7.59	7.02
CCC	Caa	24.47	35.23	3.2	113.5	16.67	20.00	9.98

Notes: [a]The ratings agencies also use "modifiers" for bonds rated below triple-A. S&P and Fitch use a plus and minus system; thus, A+ designates the strongest A-rated bonds and A– the weakest. Moody's uses a 1, 2, or 3 designation, with 1 denoting the strongest and 3 the weakest; thus, within the double-A category, Aa1 is the best, Aa2 is average, and Aa3 is the weakest.

[b]Default data are from Fitch Ratings Global Corporate Finance 2011 Transition and Default Study, March 16, 2012: see **www.fitchratings.com/creditdesk/reports/report_frame.cfm?rpt_id=669829.**

[c]Median ratios are from Standard & Poor's 2006 Corporate Ratings Criteria, April 23, 2007: see **www2.standardandpoors.com/spf/pdf/fixedincome/Corporate_Ratings_2006.pdf.**

[d]Composite yields for 10-year AAA, AA, A, and BBB bonds can be found at **www.bondsonline.com/Todays_Market/Composite_Bond_Yields_table.php.** Representative yields for 10-year BB, B, and CCC bonds can be found using the bond screener at **http://cxa.marketwatch.com/finra/bondcenter/AdvancedScreener.aspx.** Thin markets cause the AAA rate to be unusually high.

defaulting even within 5 years of being assigned a rating. Single-A and triple-B bonds are also strong enough to be called **investment-grade bonds**, and they are the lowest-rated bonds that many banks and other institutional investors are permitted by law to hold. Double-B and lower bonds are speculative bonds and are often called **junk bonds**. These bonds have a significant probability of defaulting.

5-11c Bond Rating Criteria, Upgrades, and Downgrades

Bond ratings are based on both quantitative and qualitative factors, as we describe below.

1. **Financial Ratios.** Many ratios potentially are important, but the return on invested capital, debt ratio, and interest coverage ratio are particularly valuable for predicting financial distress. For example, Columns (1), (5), and (6) in Table 5-1 show a strong relationship between ratings and the return on capital and the debt ratio.
2. **Bond Contract Terms.** Important provisions for determining the bond's rating include whether the bond is secured by a mortgage on specific assets, whether the bond is subordinated to other debt, any sinking fund provisions, guarantees by some other party with a high credit ranking, and *restrictive covenants* such as requirements that the

firm keep its debt ratio below a given level or that it keep its times interest earned ratio above a given level.

3. **Qualitative Factors.** Included here would be such factors as sensitivity of the firm's earnings to the strength of the economy, how it is affected by inflation, whether it is having or is likely to have labor problems, the extent of its international operations (including the stability of the countries in which it operates), potential environmental problems, potential antitrust problems, and so on. Today (2012), a critical factor is exposure to sub-prime loans, including the difficulty of determining the extent of this exposure owing to the complexity of the assets backed by such loans.

Rating agencies review outstanding bonds on a periodic basis and re-rate if necessary. Columns (7) and (8) in Table 5-1 show the percentages of companies in each rating category that were downgraded or upgraded in 2011 by Fitch Ratings. The year 2011 was a difficult one, as more bonds were downgraded than upgraded.

Over the long run, ratings agencies have done a reasonably good job of measuring the average credit risk of bonds and of changing ratings whenever there is a significant change in credit quality. However, it is important to understand that ratings do not adjust immediately to changes in credit quality, and in some cases there can be a considerable lag between a change in credit quality and a change in rating. For example, Enron's bonds still carried an investment-grade rating on a Friday in December 2001, but the company declared bankruptcy two days later, on Sunday. Many other abrupt downgrades occurred in 2007 and 2008, leading to calls by Congress and the SEC for changes in rating agencies and the way they rate bonds. Clearly, improvements can be made, but there will always be occasions when completely unexpected information about a company is released, leading to a sudden change in its rating.

5-11d Bond Ratings and the Default Risk Premium

Why are bond ratings so important? First, most bonds are purchased by institutional investors rather than individuals, and many institutions are restricted to investment-grade securities. Thus, if a firm's bonds fall below BBB, it will have a difficult time selling new bonds because many potential purchasers will not be allowed to buy them. Second, many bond covenants stipulate that the coupon rate on the bond automatically increases if the rating falls below a specified level. Third, because a bond's rating is an indicator of its default risk, the rating has a direct, measurable influence on the bond's yield. Column (9) of Table 5-1 shows that an AA bond has a yield of 3.38% and that yields increase as the rating falls. In fact, an investor would earn 9.98% on a CCC bond if it didn't default.

A **bond spread** is the difference between a bond's yield and the yield on some other security of the same maturity. Unless specified differently, the term "spread" generally means the difference between a bond's yield and the yield on a Treasury bond of similar maturity.

Figure 5-3 shows the spreads between an index of AAA bonds and a 10-year Treasury bond; it also shows spreads for an index of BBB bonds relative to the T-bond. Figure 5-3 illustrates three important points. First, the BAA spread always is greater than the AAA spread. This is because a BAA bond is riskier than an AAA bond, so BAA investors require extra compensation for their extra risk. The same is true for other ratings: Lower-rated bonds have higher yields.

Second, the spreads are not constant over time. For example, look at the AAA spread. It was exceptionally low during the boom years of 2005–2007 but rose dramatically as the economy declined in 2008 and 2009.

Third, the difference between the BAA spread and the AAA spread isn't constant over time. The two spreads were quite close to one another in early 2000 but were very far

GLOBAL ECONOMIC CRISIS

© uniquely india/Getty Images

The Global Economic Crisis

U.S. Treasury Bonds Downgraded!

The worsening recession that began at the end of 2007 led Congress to pass a huge economic stimulus package in early 2009. The combination of the stimulus package and the government's bailouts of financial institutions caused the U.S. government to increase its borrowing substantially. The current (March 2012) level of public debt is $10.4 trillion, about 68% of gross domestic product (GDP). The Congressional Budget Office long-term projections show this percentage growing to 70% to 90%, depending on the assumptions. Any way you look at it, this is a lot of money, even by Washington standards!

With so much debt outstanding and enormous annual deficits continuing, in mid-2011 Congress was faced with the need to increase the amount of debt the federal government is allowed to issue. Although Congress had increased the debt ceiling 74 times previously, and 10 times since 2001, partisan and heated debate seriously delayed approval of the measure and brought the federal government to the brink of default on its obligations by August. At the last minute, Congress approved a debt ceiling increase, narrowly avoiding a partial government shutdown. However, the deficit reduction package that accompanied the legislation was small, doing little to address the structural revenue and spending imbalance the federal government faces going forward.

On August 5, 2011, the combination of a dysfunctional political process apparently incapable of reliably performing basic financial housekeeping chores, and the lack of a clear plan to address future deficits, raised enough questions about the U.S. government's financial stability to induce Standard & Poor's (S&P), the credit rating agency, to downgrade U.S. public debt from AAA to AA+, effectively removing it from its list of risk-free investments. Financial markets quickly responded to this dark assessment with the Dow Jones Industrial Average plunging some 13% over the next week. Moody's and Fitch, the other two major rating agencies, however, kept their ratings of U.S. public debt at their highest levels. With 2 out of 3 agencies rating U.S. debt at the highest level, is the yield on U.S. debt still a proxy for the riskless rate? Only time will tell.

apart in early 2009. In other words, BAA investors didn't require much extra return over that of an AAA bond to induce them to take on that extra risk most years, but in 2009 they required a very large risk premium.

Not only do spreads vary with the rating of the security, they also usually increase as maturity increases. This should make sense. If a bond matures soon, investors are able to forecast the company's performance fairly well. But if a bond has a long time until it matures, investors have a difficult time forecasting the likelihood that the company will fall into financial distress. This extra uncertainty creates additional risk, so investors demand a higher required return.

SELF-TEST

Differentiate between mortgage bonds and debentures.

Name the major rating agencies, and list some factors that affect bond ratings.

What is a bond spread?

How do bond ratings affect the default risk premium?

A 10-year T-bond has a yield of 6%. A 10-year corporate bond with a rating of AA has a yield of 7.5%. If the corporate bond has excellent liquidity, what is an estimate of the corporate bond's default risk premium? **(1.5%)**

FIGURE 5-3
Bond Spreads

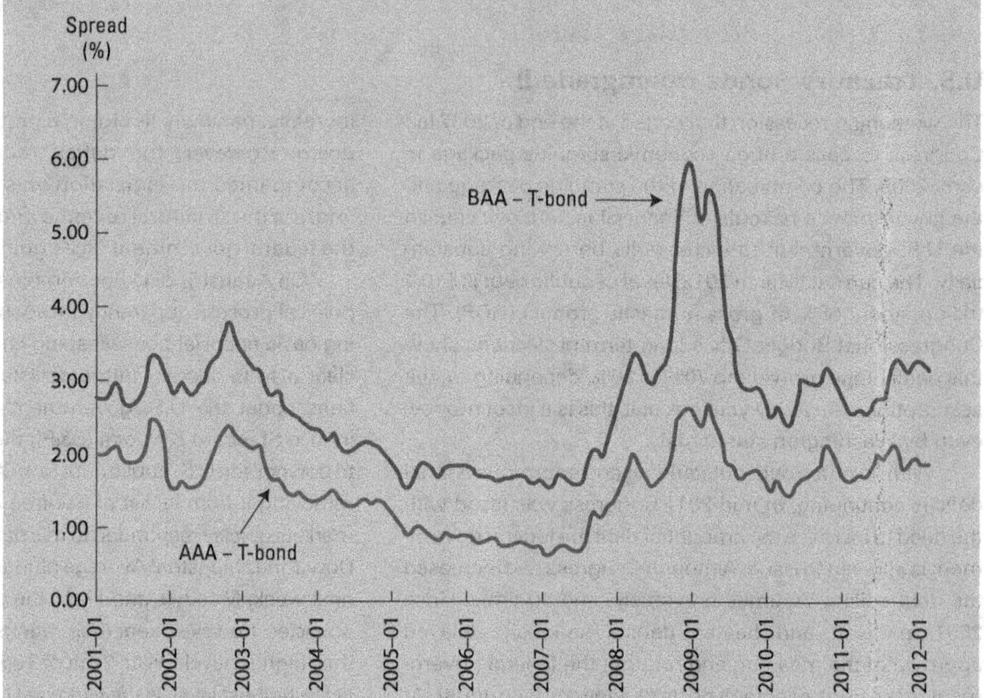

Note: All data are from the Federal Reserve Bank of St. Louis's Economic Database, FRED: **research.stlouisfed.org/fred2.** The spreads are defined as the yield on the risky bond (AAA or BAA) minus the yield on a 10-year Treasury bond.

5-12 The Liquidity Premium (LP)

A "liquid" asset can be converted to cash quickly and at a "fair market value." Financial assets are generally more liquid than real assets. Because liquidity is important, investors include **liquidity premiums (LPs)** when market rates of securities are established. Although liquidity premiums are difficult to measure accurately, a differential of at least 2 percentage points (and perhaps up to 4 or 5 percentage points) exists between the least liquid and the most liquid financial assets of similar default risk and maturity. Corporate bonds issued by small companies are traded less frequently than those issued by large companies, so small-company bonds tend to have a higher liquidity premium.

For example, liquidity in the market for mortgage-backed securities evaporated in 2008 and early 2009. The few transactions that occurred were priced such that the yields on these MBS were extremely high, which was partially due to a much higher liquidity premium caused by the extremely low liquidity of MBS.

SELF-TEST

Which bond usually will have a higher liquidity premium: one issued by a large company or one issued by a small company?

The Few, the Proud, the... AAA-Rated Companies!

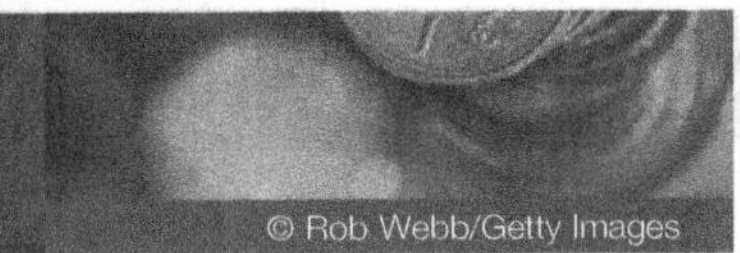

© Rob Webb/Getty Images

AAA-rated companies are members of an elite group. Over the last 20 years, this cream of the crop has included such powerhouses as 3M, Abbott Labs, BellSouth, ExxonMobil, GE, Kellogg, Microsoft, and UPS. Only large companies with stable cash flows make it into this group, and for years they guarded their AAA ratings vigilantly. In recent years, however, the nonfinancial AAA-rated corporation has become a vanishing breed. In March 2012, the major ratings agencies (Fitch, S&P, and Moody's) only agreed on the highest rating for three nonfinancial companies without government backing: ExxonMobil, XTO Energy (a subsidiary of ExxonMobil), and Johnson & Johnson. When the list is expanded to more than just nonfinancials, it is interesting to note that many of the powerhouses are not-for-profits. For example, Saddleback Valley Community Church, a megachurch located in Southern California, has a top rating, as do MIT and Princeton University.

Why do so few companies have AAA ratings? One reason may be that the recent financial crisis and recession have hurt the creditworthiness of even large, stable companies. A more likely explanation, however, is that in recent years large, stable companies have increased their debt levels to take greater advantage of the tax savings that they afford. With higher debt levels, these companies are no longer eligible for the highest rating. In essence, they have sacrificed their AAA rating for lower taxes. Does this sound like a good tradeoff to you? We will discuss how companies choose the level of debt in Chapter 15.

Source: **www.finra.org/Investors/InvestmentChoices/Bonds**

5-13 The Maturity Risk Premium (MRP)

All bonds, even Treasury bonds, are exposed to two additional sources of risk: interest rate risk and reinvestment risk. The net effect of these two sources of risk upon a bond's yield is called the **maturity risk premium, MRP**. The following sections explain how interest rate risk and reinvestment risk affect a bond's yield.

5-13a Interest Rate Risk

Interest rates go up and down over time, and an increase in interest rates leads to a decline in the value of outstanding bonds. This risk of a decline in bond values due to rising interest rates is called **interest rate risk**. To illustrate, suppose you bought some 9% MicroDrive bonds at a price of $1,000, and then interest rates rose in the following year to 14%. As we saw earlier, the price of the bonds would fall to $692.89, so you would have a loss of $307.11 per bond.[17] Interest rates can and do rise, and rising rates cause a loss of value for bondholders. Thus, bond investors are exposed to risk from changing interest rates.

This point can be demonstrated by showing how the value of a 1-year bond with a 10% annual coupon fluctuates with changes in r_d and then comparing these changes with those on a 25-year bond. The 1-year bond's value for $r_d = 5\%$ is shown below:

	N	I/YR	PV	PMT	FV
Inputs	1	5		100	1000
Output (Bond Value):			−1047.62		

[17]You would have an *accounting* (and tax) loss only if you sold the bond; if you held it to maturity, you would not have such a loss. However, even if you did not sell, you would still have suffered a *real economic loss in an opportunity cost sense* because you would have lost the opportunity to invest at 14% and would be stuck with a 9% bond in a 14% market. In an economic sense, "paper losses" are just as bad as realized accounting losses.

GLOBAL ECONOMIC CRISIS

© uniquely india/Getty Images

The Global Economic Crisis

Fear and Rationality

The graph below shows two measures of fear. One is the "Hi-Yield" spread between the yields on junk bonds and Treasury bonds. The second is the **TED spread**, which is the difference between the 3-month LIBOR rate and the 3-month T-bill rate. Both are measures of risk aversion. The Hi-Yield spread measures the amount of extra compensation investors need to induce them to take on risky junk bonds. The TED spread measures the extra compensation that banks require to induce them to lend to one another. Observe that the yields were very low from mid-2003 through the end of 2007. During these boom years, investors and bankers had a voracious appetite for risk and simply didn't require much extra return for additional risk. But as the economy began to deteriorate in 2008, investors and bankers reversed course and became extremely risk averse, with spreads skyrocketing. Interestingly, the pre-financial crisis appetite for risk has returned seems to have returned, with spreads again very low. It is hard to reconcile such drastic changes in risk aversion with careful, deliberate, and rational behavior!

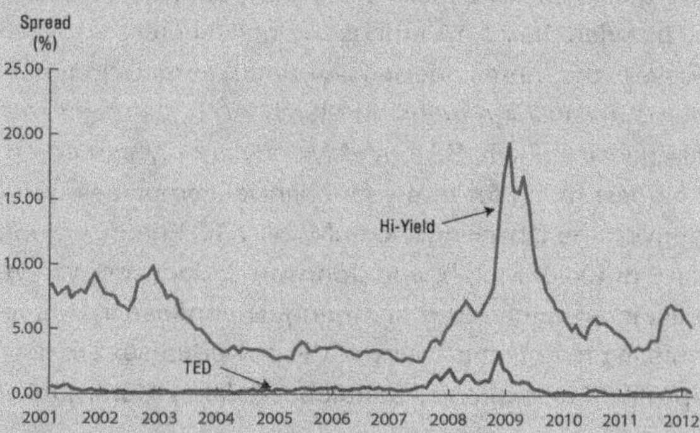

Source: The Hi-Yield spread is the average monthly value of the BofA Merrill Lynch US High Yield Master II Effective Yield minus the 10-year T-bond yield. TED is the difference between the 3-month LIBOR rate and the 3-month T-bill rate. All data are from the Federal Reserve Bank of St. Louis's Economic Database, FRED: **http://research.stlouisfed.org/fred2**.

Using either a calculator or a spreadsheet, you could calculate the bond values for a 1-year and a 25-year bond at several current market interest rates; these results are plotted in Figure 5-4. Note how much more sensitive the price of the 25-year bond is to changes in interest rates. At a 10% interest rate, both the 25-year and the 1-year bonds are valued at $1,000. When rates rise to 15%, the 25-year bond falls to $676.79 but the 1-year bond falls only to $956.52.

resource

See Ch05 Tool Kit.xls.

For bonds with similar coupons, this differential sensitivity to changes in interest rates always holds true: The longer the maturity of the bond, the more its price changes in response to a given change in interest rates. Thus, even if the risk of default on two bonds is exactly the same, the one with the longer maturity is exposed to more risk from a rise in interest rates.

The explanation for this difference in interest rate risk is simple. Suppose you bought a 25-year bond that yielded 10%, or $100 a year. Now suppose interest rates on bonds of comparable risk rose to 15%. You would be stuck with only $100 of interest for the next 25 years. On the other hand, had you bought a 1-year bond, you would have a low return for only 1 year. At the end of the year, you would get your $1,000 back, and you could then reinvest it and receive a 15% return ($150) for the next year. Thus, interest rate risk reflects the length of time one is committed to a given investment.

In addition to maturity, interest rate sensitivity reflects the size of coupon payments. Intuitively, this is because more of a high-coupon bond's value is received sooner than

FIGURE 5-4

Value of Long- and Short-Term 10% Annual Coupon Bonds at Different Market Interest Rates

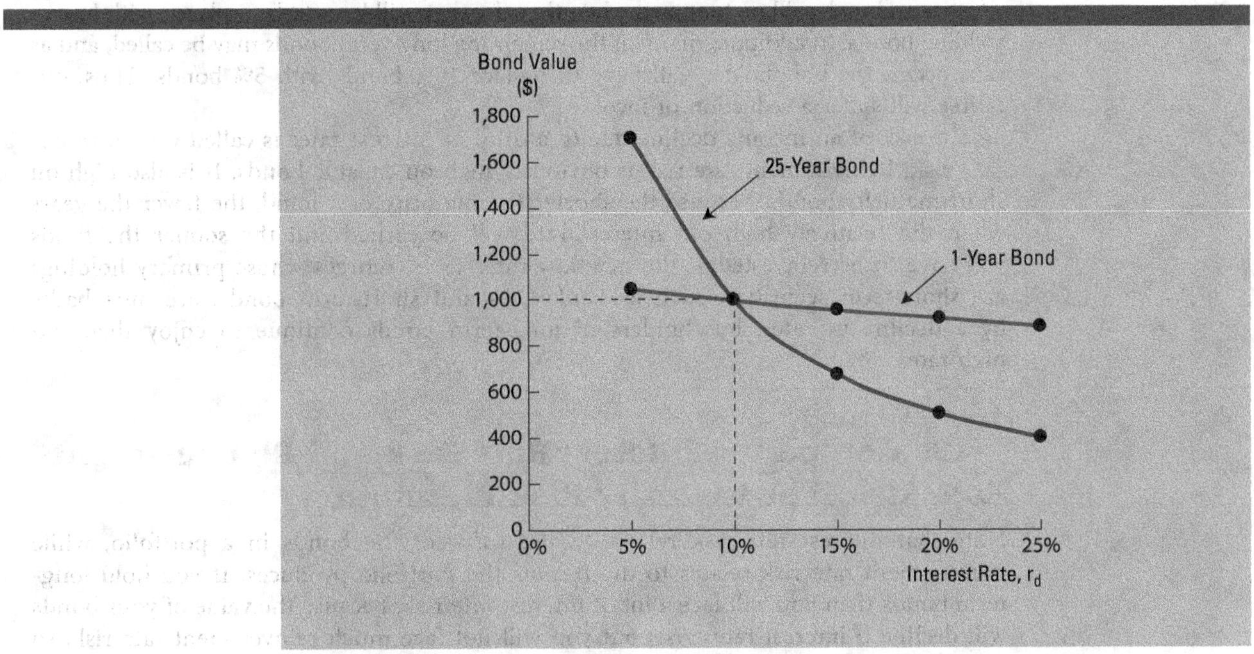

© Cengage Learning 2014

that of a low-coupon bond of the same maturity. This intuitive concept is measured by "duration," which finds the average number of years that the bond's PV of cash flows (coupons and principal payments) remains outstanding; see ***Web Extension 5C*** and ***Ch05 Tool Kit.xls*** for the exact calculation. A zero coupon bond, which has no payments until maturity, has a duration equal to its maturity. Coupon bonds have durations that are shorter than maturity, and the higher the coupon rate, the shorter the duration.

resource

For more on bond risk, including duration analysis, see Web Extension 5C on the textbook's Web site.

Duration measures a bond's sensitivity to interest rates in the following sense: Given a change in interest rates, the percentage change in a bond's price is proportional to its duration:[18]

$$\%\text{ change in } V_B = (\%\text{ change in } 1 + r_d)(-\text{Duration})$$

Excel's DURATION function provides an easy way to calculate a bond's duration. See ***Web Extension 5C*** and ***Ch05 Tool Kit.xls*** for more discussion of duration and its use in measuring and managing interest rate risk.

5-13b Reinvestment Rate Risk

As we saw in the preceding section, an *increase* in interest rates will hurt bondholders because it will lead to a decline in the value of a bond portfolio. But can a *decrease* in interest rates also hurt bondholders? The answer is "yes," because if interest rates fall then a bondholder may suffer a reduction in his or her income. For example, consider a retiree

[18]This is true for the case in which the term structure (which we discuss in Section 5-14) is flat and can only shift up and down. However, other duration measures can be developed for other term structure assumptions.

who has a portfolio of bonds and lives off the income they produce. The bonds, on average, have a coupon rate of 10%. Now suppose that interest rates decline to 5%. The short-term bonds will mature, and when they do, they will have to be replaced with lower-yielding bonds. In addition, many of the remaining long-term bonds may be called, and as calls occur, the bondholder will have to replace 10% bonds with 5% bonds. Thus, our retiree will suffer a reduction of income.

The risk of an income decline due to a drop in interest rates is called **reinvestment rate risk**. Reinvestment rate risk is obviously high on callable bonds. It is also high on short-maturity bonds, because the shorter the maturity of a bond, the fewer the years when the relatively high old interest rate will be earned and the sooner the funds will have to be reinvested at the new low rate. Thus, retirees whose primary holdings are short-term securities, such as bank CDs and short-term bonds, are hurt badly by a decline in rates, but holders of long-term bonds continue to enjoy their old high rates.

5-13c Comparing Interest Rate Risk and Reinvestment Rate Risk: The Maturity Risk Premium

Note that interest rate risk relates to the *value* of the bonds in a portfolio, while reinvestment rate risk relates to the *income* the portfolio produces. If you hold long-term bonds then you will face a lot of interest rate risk, because the value of your bonds will decline if interest rates rise; but you will not face much reinvestment rate risk, so your income will be stable. On the other hand, if you hold short-term bonds, you will not be exposed to much interest rate risk because the value of your portfolio will be stable, but you will be exposed to considerable reinvestment rate risk because your income will fluctuate with changes in interest rates. We see, then, that no fixed-rate bond can be considered totally riskless—even most Treasury bonds are exposed to both interest rate risk and reinvestment rate risk.[19]

Bond prices reflect the trading activities of the marginal investors, defined as those who trade often enough and with large enough sums to determine bond prices. Although one particular investor might be more averse to reinvestment risk than to interest rate risk, the data suggest that the marginal investor is more averse to interest rate risk than to reinvestment risk. To induce the marginal investor to take on interest rate risk, long-term bonds must have a higher expected rate of return than short-term bonds. Holding all else equal, this additional return is the maturity risk premium (MRP).

SELF-TEST

Differentiate between interest rate risk and reinvestment rate risk.

To which type of risk are holders of long-term bonds more exposed? Short-term bondholders?

Assume that the real risk-free rate is r = 3% and that the average expected inflation rate is 2.5% for the foreseeable future. The DRP and LP for a bond are each 1%, and the applicable MRP is 2%. What is the bond's yield?* **(9.5%)**

[19]Although indexed Treasury bonds are almost riskless, they pay a relatively low real rate. Note also that risks have not disappeared—they have simply been transferred from bondholders to taxpayers.

5-14 The Term Structure of Interest Rates

The **term structure of interest rates** describes the relationship between long-term and short-term rates. The term structure is important both to corporate treasurers deciding whether to borrow by issuing long-term or short-term debt and to investors who are deciding whether to buy long-term or short-term bonds.

Interest rates for bonds with different maturities can be found in a variety of publications, including *The Wall Street Journal* and the *Federal Reserve Bulletin*, as well as on a number of Web sites, including Bloomberg, Yahoo!, CNN Financial, and the Federal Reserve Board. Using interest rate data from these sources, we can determine the term structure at any given point in time. For example, Figure 5-5 presents interest rates for different maturities on three different dates. The set of data for a given date, when plotted on a graph such as Figure 5-5, is called the **yield curve** for that date.

As the figure shows, the yield curve changes both in position and in slope over time. In March 1980, all rates were quite high because high inflation was expected. However, the rate of inflation was expected to decline, so the inflation premium (IP) was larger for short-term bonds than for long-term bonds. This caused short-term yields to be higher than long-term yields, resulting in a *downward-sloping* yield curve. By February 2000, inflation had indeed declined and thus all rates were lower. The yield curve had become **humped**—medium-term rates were higher than either short- or long-term rates. In March 2012, all rates were below the 2000 levels. Because short-term rates had dropped below long-term rates, the yield curve was *upward sloping.*

Historically, long-term rates are generally higher than short-term rates owing to the maturity risk premium, so the yield curve usually slopes upward. For this reason, people often call an upward-sloping yield curve a **"normal" yield curve** and a yield curve that

FIGURE 5-5
U.S. Treasury Bond Interest Rates on Different Dates

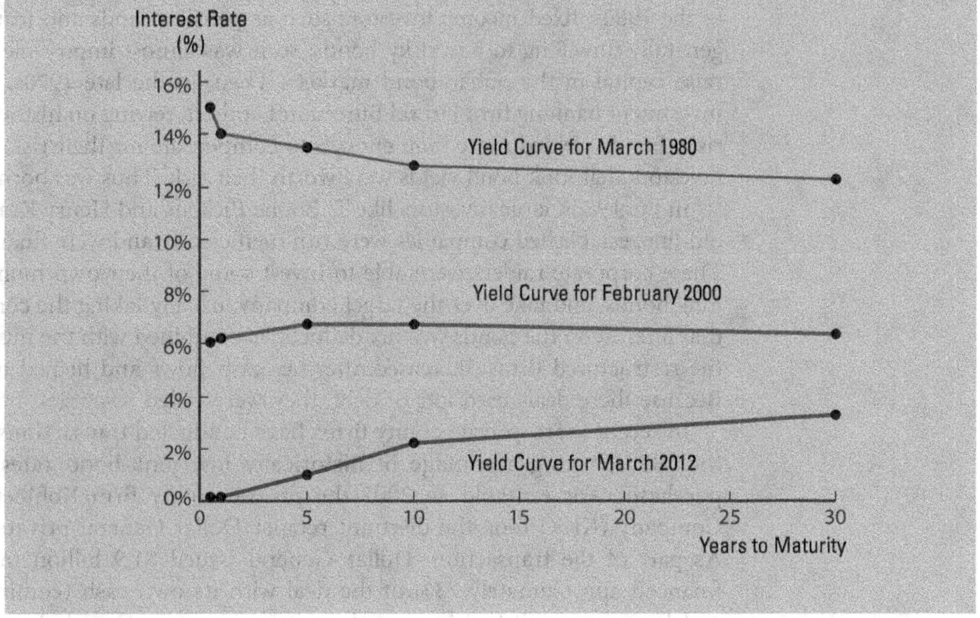

© Cengage Learning 2014

slopes downward an **inverted**, or **"abnormal," curve**. Thus, in Figure 5-5 the yield curve for March 1980 was inverted, whereas the yield curve in March 2012 was normal. As stated above, the February 2000 curve was humped.

resource

For a discussion of the expectations theory, see Web Extension 5D on the textbook's Web site.

A few academics and practitioners contend that large bond traders who buy and sell securities of different maturities each day dominate the market. According to this view, a bond trader is just as willing to buy a 30-year bond to pick up a short-term profit as to buy a 3-month security. Strict proponents of this view argue that the shape of the yield curve is therefore determined only by market expectations about future interest rates, a position that is called the **pure expectations theory**, or sometimes just the **expectations theory**. If this were true, then the maturity risk premium (MRP) would be zero and long-term interest rates would simply be a weighted average of current and expected future short-term interest rates. See ***Web Extension 5D*** for a more detailed discussion of the expectations theory.

SELF-TEST

What is a yield curve, and what information would you need to draw this curve?

Distinguish among the shapes of a "normal" yield curve, an "abnormal" curve, and a "humped" curve.

If the interest rates on 1-, 5-, 20-, and 30-year bonds are (respectively) 4%, 5%, 6%, and 7%, then how would you describe the yield curve? How would you describe it if the rates were reversed?

5-15 Financing with Junk Bonds

Recall that bonds rated less than BBB are noninvestment-grade debt, also called junk bonds or high-yield debt. There are two ways that a bond can become a junk bond. First, the bond might have been investment-grade debt when it was issued but its rating declined because the issuing corporation had fallen on hard times. Such bonds are called "fallen angels," and there are many such bonds as we write this in 2012.

Some bonds are junk bonds at the time they are issued, but this was not always true. Prior to the 1980s, fixed-income investors such as pension funds and insurance companies were generally unwilling to buy risky bonds, so it was almost impossible for risky companies to raise capital in the public bond markets. Then, in the late 1970s, Michael Milken of the investment banking firm Drexel Burnham Lambert, relying on historical studies that showed risky bonds yielded more than enough to compensate for their risk, convinced institutional investors that junk bond yields were worth their risk. Thus was born the junk bond market.

In the 1980s, large investors like T. Boone Pickens and Henry Kravis thought that certain old-line, established companies were run inefficiently and were financed too conservatively. These corporate raiders were able to invest some of their own money, borrow the rest via junk bonds, and take over the target company, usually taking the company private. The fact that interest on the bonds was tax deductible, combined with the much higher debt ratios of the restructured firms, increased after-tax cash flows and helped make the deals feasible. Because these deals used lots of debt, they were called **leveraged buyouts (LBOs)**.

In recent years, private equity firms have conducted transactions similar to the LBOs of the 1980s, taking advantage of historically low junk-bond rates to help finance their purchases. For example, in 2007 the private equity firm Kohlberg Kravis Roberts and Company (KKR) took the discount retailer Dollar General private in a $6.9 billion deal. As part of the transaction, Dollar General issued $1.9 billion in junk bonds. So KKR financed approximately 73% of the deal with its own cash (coming from its own equity and from money it had borrowed on its own account) and about 27% of the deal with money that Dollar General raised, for a net investment of about $5 billion. In late 2009, KKR took Dollar General public again at $21 per share with a resulting market value of equity of $7.1 billion and a very tidy gain!

SELF-TEST

What are junk bonds?

5-16 Bankruptcy and Reorganization

A business is *insolvent* when it does not have enough cash to meet its interest and principal payments. When this occurs, either the creditors or the company may file for bankruptcy in the United States Bankruptcy Court. After hearing from the creditors and the company's managers, a federal bankruptcy court judge decides whether to dissolve the firm through *liquidation* or to permit it to *reorganize* and thus stay alive. Chapter 7 of the federal bankruptcy statutes addresses liquidation and Chapter 11 addresses reorganization.

The decision to force a firm to liquidate versus permit it to reorganize depends on whether the value of the reorganized firm is likely to be greater than the value of the firm's assets if they are sold off piecemeal. In a reorganization, the firm's creditors negotiate with management on the terms of a potential reorganization. The reorganization plan may call for a *restructuring* of the firm's debt, in which case the interest rate may be reduced, the term to maturity may be lengthened, or some of the debt may be exchanged for equity. The point of the restructuring is to reduce the financial charges to a level that the firm's cash flows can support. Of course, the common stockholders also have to give up something: They often see their position diluted as a result of additional shares being given to debtholders in exchange for accepting a reduced amount of debt principal and interest. In fact, the original common stockholders often end up with nothing. The court may appoint a trustee to oversee the reorganization, but usually the existing management is allowed to retain control.

Liquidation occurs if the company is deemed to be too far gone to be saved—if it is worth more dead than alive. If the bankruptcy court orders liquidation, then assets are sold off and the cash obtained is distributed as specified in Chapter 7 of the Bankruptcy Act. Here is the priority of claims: (1) past-due property taxes; (2) secured creditors who are entitled to the proceeds from the sale of collateral; (3) the trustee's costs of administering and operating the bankrupt firm; (4) expenses incurred after bankruptcy was filed; (5) wages due workers, up to a limit of $2,000 per worker; (6) claims for unpaid contributions to employee benefit plans (with wages and claims not to exceed $2,000 per worker); (7) unsecured claims for customer deposits up to $900 per customer; (8) federal, state, and local taxes due; (9) unfunded pension plan liabilities (although some limitations exist); (10) general unsecured creditors; (11) preferred stockholders (up to the par value of their stock); and (12) common stockholders (although usually nothing is left for them).

The key points for you to know are: (1) the federal bankruptcy statutes govern both reorganization and liquidation, (2) bankruptcies occur frequently, and (3) a priority of the specified claims must be followed when distributing the assets of a liquidated firm.

SELF-TEST

Differentiate between a Chapter 7 liquidation and a Chapter 11 reorganization.

List the priority of claims for the distribution of a liquidated firm's assets.

SUMMARY

This chapter described the different types of bonds that governments and corporations issue, explained how bond prices are established, and discussed how investors estimate the rates of return they can expect to earn. The rate of return required by debtholders is the company's pre-tax cost of debt, and this rate depends on the risk that investors face when they buy bonds.

- A **bond** is a long-term promissory note issued by a business or governmental unit. The issuer receives money in exchange for promising to make interest payments and to repay the principal on a specified future date.
- Some special types of long-term financing include **zero coupon bonds**, which pay no annual interest but are issued at a discount; see ***Web Extension 5A*** for more on zero coupon bonds. Other types are **floating-rate debt**, whose interest payments fluctuate with changes in the general level of interest rates; and **junk bonds**, which are high-risk, high-yield instruments issued by firms that use a great deal of financial leverage.
- A **call provision** gives the issuing corporation the right to redeem the bonds prior to maturity under specified terms, usually at a price greater than the maturity value (the difference is a **call premium**). A firm will typically call a bond if interest rates fall substantially below the coupon rate.
- A **sinking fund** is a provision that requires the corporation to retire a portion of the bond issue each year. The purpose of the sinking fund is to provide for the orderly retirement of the issue. A sinking fund typically requires no call premium.
- The **value of a bond** is found as the present value of an **annuity** (the interest payments) plus the present value of a lump sum (the **principal**). The bond is evaluated at the appropriate periodic interest rate over the number of periods for which interest payments are made.
- The equation used to find the value of an annual coupon bond is

$$V_B = \sum_{t=1}^{N} \frac{INT}{(1 + r_d)^t} + \frac{M}{(1 + r_d)^N}$$

- An adjustment to the formula must be made if the bond pays interest **semiannually**: divide INT and r_d by 2, and multiply N by 2.
- The expected rate of return on a bond held to maturity is defined as the bond's **yield to maturity (YTM)**:

$$\text{Bond price} = \sum_{t=1}^{N} \frac{INT}{(1 + YTM)^t} + \frac{M}{(1 + YTM)^N}$$

- The expected rate of return on a callable bond held to its call date is defined as the **yield to call (YTC)**.
- The **nominal (or quoted) interest rate** on a debt security, r_d, is composed of the real risk-free rate, r*, plus premiums that reflect inflation (IP), default risk (DRP), liquidity (LP), and maturity risk (MRP):

$$r_d = r^* + IP + DRP + LP + MRP$$

- The **risk-free rate of interest** r_{RF}, is defined as the real risk-free rate, r*, plus an inflation premium, IP: $r_{RF} = r^* + IP$.
- **Treasury Inflation-Protected Securities (TIPS)** are U.S. Treasury bonds that have no inflation risk. See ***Web Extension 5B*** for more discussion of TIPS.

- The longer the maturity of a bond, the more its price will change in response to a given change in interest rates; this is called **interest rate risk**. However, bonds with short maturities expose investors to high **reinvestment rate risk**, which is the risk that income from a bond portfolio will decline because cash flows received from bonds will be rolled over at lower interest rates.
- **Duration** is a measure of interest rate risk. See ***Web Extension 5C*** for a discussion of duration.
- Corporate and municipal bonds have **default risk**. If an issuer defaults, investors receive less than the promised return on the bond. Therefore, investors should evaluate a bond's default risk before making a purchase.
- Bonds are assigned **ratings** that reflect the probability of their going into default. The highest rating is AAA, and they go down to D. The higher a bond's rating, the lower its risk and therefore its interest rate.
- The relationship between the yields on securities and the securities' maturities is known as the **term structure of interest rates**, and the **yield curve** is a graph of this relationship.
- The shape of the yield curve depends on two key factors: (1) *expectations about future inflation* and (2) *perceptions about the relative risk of securities with different maturities*.
- The yield curve is normally **upward sloping**—this is called a **normal yield curve**. However, the curve can slope downward (an **inverted yield curve**) if the inflation rate is expected to decline. The yield curve also can be **humped**, which means that interest rates on medium-term maturities are higher than rates on both short- and long-term maturities.
- The **expectations theory** states that yields on long-term bonds reflect expected future interest rates. ***Web Extension 5D*** discusses this theory.

QUESTIONS

(5-1) Define each of the following terms:

a. Bond; Treasury bond; corporate bond; municipal bond; foreign bond
b. Par value; maturity date; coupon payment; coupon interest rate
c. Floating-rate bond; zero coupon bond; original issue discount bond (OID)
d. Call provision; redeemable bond; sinking fund
e. Convertible bond; warrant; income bond; indexed, or purchasing power, bond
f. Premium bond; discount bond
g. Current yield (on a bond); yield to maturity (YTM); yield to call (YTC)
h. Indentures; mortgage bond; debenture; subordinated debenture
i. Development bond; municipal bond insurance; junk bond; investment-grade bond
j. Real risk-free rate of interest, r^*; nominal risk-free rate of interest, r_{RF}
k. Inflation premium (IP); default risk premium (DRP); liquidity; liquidity premium (LP)
l. Interest rate risk; maturity risk premium (MRP); reinvestment rate risk
m. Term structure of interest rates; yield curve
n. "Normal" yield curve; inverted ("abnormal") yield curve

(5-2) "Short-term interest rates are more volatile than long-term interest rates, so short-term bond prices are more sensitive to interest rate changes than are long-term bond prices." Is this statement true or false? Explain.

(5-3) The rate of return on a bond held to its maturity date is called the bond's yield to maturity. If interest rates in the economy rise after a bond has been issued, what will happen to the bond's price and to its YTM? Does the length of time to maturity affect the extent to which a given change in interest rates will affect the bond's price? Why or why not?

(5-4) If you buy a *callable* bond and interest rates decline, will the value of your bond rise by as much as it would have risen if the bond had not been callable? Explain.

(5-5) A sinking fund can be set up in one of two ways. Discuss the advantages and disadvantages of each procedure from the viewpoint of both the firm and its bondholders.

SELF-TEST PROBLEM Solution Appears in Appendix A

(ST-1) Bond Valuation

The Pennington Corporation issued a new series of bonds on January 1, 1990. The bonds were sold at par ($1,000), had a 12% coupon, and matured in 30 years on December 31, 2019. Coupon payments are made semiannually (on June 30 and December 31).

a. What was the YTM on the date the bonds were issued?
b. What was the price of the bonds on January 1, 1995 (5 years later), assuming that interest rates had fallen to 10%?
c. Find the current yield, capital gains yield, and total yield on January 1, 1995, given the price as determined in part b.
d. On July 1, 2013 (6.5 years before maturity), Pennington's bonds sold for $916.42. What are the YTM, the current yield, and the capital gains yield for that date?
e. Now assume that you plan to purchase an outstanding Pennington bond on March 1, 2013, when the going rate of interest given its risk is 15.5%. How large a check must you write to complete the transaction? (*Hint:* Don't forget the accrued interest.)

PROBLEMS Answers Appear in Appendix B

Easy Problems 1–6

(5-1) Bond Valuation with Annual Payments

Jackson Corporation's bonds have 12 years remaining to maturity. Interest is paid annually, the bonds have a $1,000 par value, and the coupon interest rate is 8%. The bonds have a yield to maturity of 9%. What is the current market price of these bonds?

(5-2) Yield to Maturity for Annual Payments

Wilson Wonders's bonds have 12 years remaining to maturity. Interest is paid annually, the bonds have a $1,000 par value, and the coupon interest rate is 10%. The bonds sell at a price of $850. What is their yield to maturity?

(5-3) Current Yield for Annual Payments

Heath Foods's bonds have 7 years remaining to maturity. The bonds have a face value of $1,000 and a yield to maturity of 8%. They pay interest annually and have a 9% coupon rate. What is their current yield?

(5-4) Determinant of Interest Rates

The real risk-free rate of interest is 4%. Inflation is expected to be 2% this year and 4% during the next 2 years. Assume that the maturity risk premium is zero. What is the yield on 2-year Treasury securities? What is the yield on 3-year Treasury securities?

(5-5) Default Risk Premium

A Treasury bond that matures in 10 years has a yield of 6%. A 10-year corporate bond has a yield of 9%. Assume that the liquidity premium on the corporate bond is 0.5%. What is the default risk premium on the corporate bond?

(5-6) Maturity Risk Premium

The real risk-free rate is 3%, and inflation is expected to be 3% for the next 2 years. A 2-year Treasury security yields 6.3%. What is the maturity risk premium for the 2-year security?

Intermediate Problems 7–20

(5-7) Bond Valuation with Semiannual Payments

Renfro Rentals has issued bonds that have a 10% coupon rate, payable semiannually. The bonds mature in 8 years, have a face value of $1,000, and a yield to maturity of 8.5%. What is the price of the bonds?

(5-8) Yield to Maturity and Call with Semiannual Payments

Thatcher Corporation's bonds will mature in 10 years. The bonds have a face value of $1,000 and an 8% coupon rate, paid semiannually. The price of the bonds is $1,100. The bonds are callable in 5 years at a call price of $1,050. What is their yield to maturity? What is their yield to call?

(5-9) Bond Valuation and Interest Rate Risk

The Garraty Company has two bond issues outstanding. Both bonds pay $100 annual interest plus $1,000 at maturity. Bond L has a maturity of 15 years, and Bond S has a maturity of 1 year.

a. What will be the value of each of these bonds when the going rate of interest is (1) 5%, (2) 8%, and (3) 12%? Assume that there is only one more interest payment to be made on Bond S.
b. Why does the longer-term (15-year) bond fluctuate more when interest rates change than does the shorter-term bond (1 year)?

(5-10) Yield to Maturity and Required Returns

The Brownstone Corporation's bonds have 5 years remaining to maturity. Interest is paid annually, the bonds have a $1,000 par value, and the coupon interest rate is 9%.

a. What is the yield to maturity at a current market price of (1) $829 or (2) $1,104?
b. Would you pay $829 for one of these bonds if you thought that the appropriate rate of interest was 12%—that is, if r_d = 12%? Explain your answer.

(5-11) Yield to Call and Realized Rates of Return

Seven years ago, Goodwynn & Wolf Incorporated sold a 20-year bond issue with a 14% annual coupon rate and a 9% call premium. Today, G&W called the bonds. The bonds originally were sold at their face value of $1,000. Compute the realized rate of return for investors who purchased the bonds when they were issued and who surrender them today in exchange for the call price.

(5-12) Bond Yields and Rates of Return

A 10-year, 12% semiannual coupon bond with a par value of $1,000 may be called in 4 years at a call price of $1,060. The bond sells for $1,100. (Assume that the bond has just been issued.)

a. What is the bond's yield to maturity?
b. What is the bond's current yield?
c. What is the bond's capital gain or loss yield?
d. What is the bond's yield to call?

(5-13) Yield to Maturity and Current Yield

You just purchased a bond that matures in 5 years. The bond has a face value of $1,000 and has an 8% annual coupon. The bond has a current yield of 8.21%. What is the bond's yield to maturity?

(5-14) Current Yield with Semiannual Payments

A bond that matures in 7 years sells for $1,020. The bond has a face value of $1,000 and a yield to maturity of 10.5883%. The bond pays coupons semiannually. What is the bond's current yield?

(5-15)
Yield to Call, Yield to Maturity, and Market Rates

Absalom Motors's 14% coupon rate, semiannual payment, $1,000 par value bonds that mature in 30 years are callable 5 years from now at a price of $1,050. The bonds sell at a price of $1,353.54, and the yield curve is flat. Assuming that interest rates in the economy are expected to remain at their current level, what is the best estimate of the nominal interest rate on new bonds?

(5-16)
Interest Rate Sensitivity

A bond trader purchased each of the following bonds at a yield to maturity of 8%. Immediately after she purchased the bonds, interest rates fell to 7%. What is the percentage change in the price of each bond after the decline in interest rates? Fill in the following table:

	Price @ 8%	Price @ 7%	Percentage Change
10-year, 10% annual coupon	______	______	______
10-year zero	______	______	______
5-year zero	______	______	______
30-year zero	______	______	______
$100 perpetuity	______	______	______

(5-17)
Bond Value as Maturity Approaches

An investor has two bonds in his portfolio. Each bond matures in 4 years, has a face value of $1,000, and has a yield to maturity equal to 9.6%. One bond, Bond C, pays an annual coupon of 10%; the other bond, Bond Z, is a zero coupon bond. Assuming that the yield to maturity of each bond remains at 9.6% over the next 4 years, what will be the price of each of the bonds at the following time periods? Fill in the following table:

t	Price of Bond C	Price of Bond Z
0	______	______
1	______	______
2	______	______
3	______	______
4	______	______

(5-18)
Determinants of Interest Rates

The real risk-free rate is 2%. Inflation is expected to be 3% this year, 4% next year, and then 3.5% thereafter. The maturity risk premium is estimated to be $0.0005 \times (t - 1)$, where t = number of years to maturity. What is the nominal interest rate on a 7-year Treasury security?

(5-19)
Maturity Risk Premiums

Assume that the real risk-free rate, r*, is 3% and that inflation is expected to be 8% in Year 1, 5% in Year 2, and 4% thereafter. Assume also that all Treasury securities are highly liquid and free of default risk. If 2-year and 5-year Treasury notes both yield 10%, what is the difference in the maturity risk premiums (MRPs) on the two notes; that is, what is MRP_5 minus MRP_2?

(5-20)
Inflation Risk Premiums

Because of a recession, the inflation rate expected for the coming year is only 3%. However, the inflation rate in Year 2 and thereafter is expected to be constant at some level above 3%. Assume that the real risk-free rate is r* = 2% for all maturities and that there are no maturity premiums. If 3-year Treasury notes yield 2 percentage points more than 1-year notes, what inflation rate is expected after Year 1?

Challenging Problems 21–23

(5-21) Bond Valuation and Changes in Maturity and Required Returns

Suppose Hillard Manufacturing sold an issue of bonds with a 10-year maturity, a $1,000 par value, a 10% coupon rate, and semiannual interest payments.

a. Two years after the bonds were issued, the going rate of interest on bonds such as these fell to 6%. At what price would the bonds sell?

b. Suppose that 2 years after the initial offering, the going interest rate had risen to 12%. At what price would the bonds sell?

c. Suppose that 2 years after the issue date (as in part a) interest rates fell to 6%. Suppose further that the interest rate remained at 6% for the next 8 years. What would happen to the price of the bonds over time?

(5-22) Yield to Maturity and Yield to Call

Arnot International's bonds have a current market price of $1,200. The bonds have an 11% annual coupon payment, a $1,000 face value, and 10 years left until maturity. The bonds may be called in 5 years at 109% of face value (call price = $1,090).

a. What is the yield to maturity?

b. What is the yield to call if they are called in 5 years?

c. Which yield might investors expect to earn on these bonds, and why?

d. The bond's indenture indicates that the call provision gives the firm the right to call them at the end of each year beginning in Year 5. In Year 5, they may be called at 109% of face value, but in each of the next 4 years the call percentage will decline by 1 percentage point. Thus, in Year 6 they may be called at 108% of face value, in Year 7 they may be called at 107% of face value, and so on. If the yield curve is horizontal and interest rates remain at their current level, when is the latest that investors might expect the firm to call the bonds?

(5-23) Determinants of Interest Rates

Suppose you and most other investors expect the inflation rate to be 7% next year, to fall to 5% during the following year, and then to remain at a rate of 3% thereafter. Assume that the real risk-free rate, r*, will remain at 2% and that maturity risk premiums on Treasury securities rise from zero on very short-term securities (those that mature in a few days) to a level of 0.2 percentage points for 1-year securities. Furthermore, maturity risk premiums increase 0.2 percentage points for each year to maturity, up to a limit of 1.0 percentage point on 5-year or longer-term T-notes and T-bonds.

a. Calculate the interest rate on 1-, 2-, 3-, 4-, 5-, 10-, and 20-year Treasury securities, and plot the yield curve.

b. Now suppose ExxonMobil's bonds, rated AAA, have the same maturities as the Treasury bonds. As an approximation, plot an ExxonMobil yield curve on the same graph with the Treasury bond yield curve. (*Hint:* Think about the default risk premium on ExxonMobil's long-term versus short-term bonds.)

c. Now plot the approximate yield curve of Long Island Lighting Company, a risky nuclear utility.

SPREADSHEET PROBLEMS

(5-24) Build a Model: Bond Valuation

Start with the partial model in the file ***Ch05 P24 Build a Model.xls*** on the textbook's Web site. A 20-year, 8% semiannual coupon bond with a par value of $1,000 may be called in 5 years at a call price of $1,040. The bond sells for $1,100. (Assume that the bond has just been issued.)

resource

a. What is the bond's yield to maturity?
b. What is the bond's current yield?
c. What is the bond's capital gain or loss yield?
d. What is the bond's yield to call?
e. How would the price of the bond be affected by a change in the going market interest rate? (*Hint:* Conduct a sensitivity analysis of price to changes in the going market interest rate for the bond. Assume that the bond will be called if and only if the going rate of interest *falls below* the coupon rate. This is an oversimplification, but assume it for purposes of this problem.)
f. Now assume the date is October 25, 2014. Assume further that a 12%, 10-year bond was issued on July 1, 2014, pays interest semiannually (on January 1 and July 1), and sells for $1,100. Use your spreadsheet to find the bond's yield.

MINI CASE

Sam Strother and Shawna Tibbs are vice presidents of Mutual of Seattle Insurance Company and co-directors of the company's pension fund management division. An important new client, the North-Western Municipal Alliance, has requested that Mutual of Seattle present an investment seminar to the mayors of the represented cities, and Strother and Tibbs, who will make the actual presentation, have asked you to help them by answering the following questions.

a. What are the key features of a bond?
b. What are call provisions and sinking fund provisions? Do these provisions make bonds more or less risky?
c. How does one determine the value of any asset whose value is based on expected future cash flows?
d. How is the value of a bond determined? What is the value of a 10-year, $1,000 par value bond with a 10% annual coupon if its required rate of return is 10%?
e. (1) What would be the value of the bond described in part d if, just after it had been issued, the expected inflation rate rose by 3 percentage points, causing investors to require a 13% return? Would we now have a discount or a premium bond?
   (2) What would happen to the bond's value if inflation fell and r_d declined to 7%? Would we now have a premium or a discount bond?
   (3) What would happen to the value of the 10-year bond over time if the required rate of return remained at 13%? If it remained at 7%? (*Hint:* With a financial calculator, enter PMT, I/YR, FV, and N, and then change N to see what happens to the PV as the bond approaches maturity.)
f. (1) What is the yield to maturity on a 10-year, 9% annual coupon, $1,000 par value bond that sells for $887.00? That sells for $1,134.20? What does the fact that a bond sells at a discount or at a premium tell you about the relationship between r_d and the bond's coupon rate?
   (2) What are the total return, the current yield, and the capital gains yield for the discount bond? (Assume the bond is held to maturity and the company does not default on the bond.)
g. How does the equation for valuing a bond change if semiannual payments are made? Find the value of a 10-year, semiannual payment, 10% coupon bond if the nominal r_d = 13%.

h. Suppose a 10-year, 10% semiannual coupon bond with a par value of $1,000 is currently selling for $1,135.90, producing a nominal yield to maturity of 8%. However, the bond can be called after 5 years for a price of $1,050.
   (1) What is the bond's *nominal* yield to call (YTC)?
   (2) If you bought this bond, do you think you would be more likely to earn the YTM or the YTC? Why?
i. Write a general expression for the yield on any debt security (r_d) and define these terms: real risk-free rate of interest (r*), inflation premium (IP), default risk premium (DRP), liquidity premium (LP), and maturity risk premium (MRP).
j. Define the nominal risk-free rate (r_{RF}). What security can be used as an estimate of r_{RF}?
k. Describe a way to estimate the inflation premium (IP) for a t-year bond.
l. What is a *bond spread* and how is it related to the default risk premium? How are bond ratings related to default risk? What factors affect a company's bond rating?
m. What is *interest rate* (or *price*) *risk?* Which bond has more interest rate risk: an annual payment 1-year bond or a 10-year bond? Why?
n. What is *reinvestment rate risk?* Which has more reinvestment rate risk: a 1-year bond or a 10-year bond?
o. How are interest rate risk and reinvestment rate risk related to the maturity risk premium?
p. What is the term structure of interest rates? What is a yield curve?
q. Briefly describe bankruptcy law. If a firm were to default on its bonds, would the company be liquidated immediately? Would the bondholders be assured of receiving all of their promised payments?

SELECTED ADDITIONAL CASES

The following cases from CengageCompose cover many of the concepts discussed in this chapter and are available at **compose.cengage.com**.

Klein-Brigham Series:

Case 3, "Peachtree Securities, Inc. (B)"; Case 72, "Swan Davis"; and Case 78, "Beatrice Peabody."

Brigham-Buzzard Series:

Case 3, "Powerline Network Corporation (Bonds and Preferred Stock)."

© Adalberto Rios Szalay/Sexto Sol/Getty Images

CHAPTER 7

Valuation of Stocks and Corporations

Stock brokerage companies, mutual fund companies, financial services institutions, pension funds, and financial advisory firms are among the many companies that employ security analysts to estimate the value and risk of stocks.

"Sell side" analysts work for investment banks and brokerages. They write reports that are distributed to investors, generally through brokers. "Buy side" analysts work for mutual funds, hedge funds, pension funds, and other institutional investors. Those institutions obtain information from the buy-side analysts, but they also do their own research and ignore the buy side if they disagree.

The analysts on both sides generally focus on specific industries, and many of them were hired as analysts after working for a time in the industry they cover. Physics PhDs are often electronics analysts, biologists analyze biotech stocks, and so on. The analysts pore over financial statements and *Excel* models, but they also go on the road and talk with company officials, companies' customers, and their suppliers. The analysts' primary objective is to predict corporate earnings, dividends, and free cash flow—and thus stock prices.

Stock prices are volatile, so it is difficult to estimate a stock's value. However, some analysts are better than others, and the material in this chapter can help you be better than average.

How much is a company worth? What can managers do to make a company more valuable? Why are stock prices so volatile? This chapter addresses those questions through the application of two widely used valuation models: the dividend growth model and the free cash flow valuation model. But before plunging into stock valuation, we begin with a closer look at what it means to be a stockholder.

Corporate Valuation and Stock Prices

© Rob Webb/Getty Images

Free cash flows (FCF) are the cash flows that are available for distribution to all of a company's investors; the weighted average cost of capital is the overall return required by all of a company's investors. So the present value of a company's free cash flows, discounted by the company's weighted average cost of capital, is the total value of the company to all its investors. It is called the value of operations because operating activities generate the FCF.

We can use this approach to estimate the stock price, but we can do this more directly in some circumstances. Recall that one use of FCF is to pay dividends, which are distributed to stockholders. Chapter 6 showed how to estimate stockholders' required return. Therefore, discounting the cash flows to stockholders (the dividends) at the rate required by stockholders determines the stock's value.

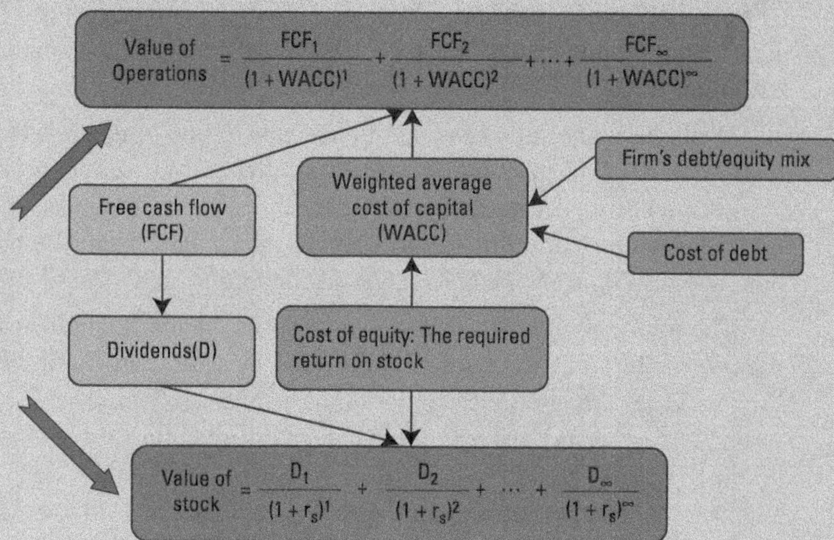

© Cengage Learning 2014

resource

The textbook's Web site contains an Excel *file that will guide you through the chapter's calculations. The file for this chapter is* ***Ch07 Tool Kit.xls,*** *and we encourage you to open the file and follow along as you read the chapter.*

7-1 Legal Rights and Privileges of Common Stockholders

Common stockholders are the *owners* of a corporation, and as such they have certain rights and privileges as discussed in this section.

7-1a Control of the Firm

A firm's common stockholders have the right to elect its directors, who, in turn, elect the officers who manage the business. In a small firm, the largest stockholder typically serves as president and chairperson of the board. In a large, publicly owned firm, the managers typically have some stock, but their personal holdings are generally insufficient to give them voting control. Thus, the managers of most publicly owned firms can be removed by the stockholders if the management team is not effective.

Corporations must hold periodic elections to select directors, usually once a year, with the vote taken at the annual meeting. At some companies, all directors are elected each year for a 1-year term. At other companies, the terms are staggered. For example, one-third of the directors are elected each year for a 3-year term.

Each share of stock has one vote, so the owner of 1,000 shares has 1,000 votes for each director.[1] Stockholders can appear at the annual meeting and vote in person, but typically they transfer their right to vote to another party by means of a **proxy**. Management always solicits stockholders' proxies and usually gets them. However, if earnings are poor and stockholders are dissatisfied, an outside group may solicit the proxies in an effort to overthrow management and take control of the business. This is known as a **proxy fight**. Proxy fights are discussed in detail in Chapter 13.

7-1b The Preemptive Right

Common stockholders often have the right, called the **preemptive right**, to purchase any additional shares sold by the firm. In some states, the preemptive right is automatically included in every corporate charter; in others, it is used only if it is specifically inserted into the charter.

WWW

Note that **http://finance.yahoo.com** *provides an easy way to find stocks meeting specified criteria. Under the Investing tab, select Stocks and then Stock Screener. To find the largest companies in terms of market value, for example, choose More Preset Screens, then select Largest Market Cap. You can also create custom screens to find stocks meeting other criteria.*

The preemptive right enables current stockholders to maintain control, and it also prevents a transfer of wealth from current stockholders to new stockholders. If not for this safeguard, the management of a corporation could issue additional shares at a low price and purchase these shares itself. Management could thereby seize control of the corporation and steal value from the current stockholders. For example, suppose 1,000 shares of common stock, each with a price of \$100, were outstanding, making the total market value of the firm \$100,000. If an additional 1,000 shares were sold at \$50 a share, or for \$50,000, this would raise the total market value to \$150,000. When total market value is divided by new total shares outstanding, a value of \$75 a share is obtained. The old stockholders thus lose \$25 per share, and the new stockholders have an instant profit of \$25 per share. Thus, selling common stock at a price below the market value would dilute its price and transfer wealth from the present stockholders to those who were allowed to purchase the new shares. The preemptive right prevents such occurrences.

SELF-TEST

What is a proxy fight?
What are the two primary reasons for using preemptive rights?

7-2 Types of Common Stock

Although most firms have only one type of common stock, in some instances companies use **classified stock** to meet special needs. Generally, when special classifications are used, one type is designated *Class A*, another *Class B*, and so on. Small, new companies seeking funds from outside sources frequently use different types of common stock. For example, when Genetic Concepts went public, its Class A stock was sold to the public and paid a dividend, but this stock had no voting rights for 5 years. Its Class B stock, which the firm's organizers retained, had full voting rights for 5 years, but the legal terms stated that the company could not pay dividends on the Class B stock until it had established its earning

[1]In the situation described, a 1,000-share stockholder could cast 1,000 votes for each of three directors if there were three contested seats on the board. An alternative procedure that may be prescribed in the corporate charter calls for *cumulative voting*. Here the 1,000-share stockholder would get 3,000 votes if there were three vacancies, and he or she could cast all of them for one director. Cumulative voting helps minority stockholders (i.e., those who do not own a majority of the shares) get representation on the board.

power and built up retained earnings to a designated level. The use of classified stock thus enabled the public to take a position in a conservatively financed growth company without sacrificing income, while the founders retained absolute control during the crucial early stages of the firm's development. At the same time, outside investors were protected against excessive withdrawals of funds by the original owners. As is often the case in such situations, the Class B stock was called **founders' shares.**[2]

As these examples illustrate, the right to vote is often a distinguishing characteristic between different classes of stock. Suppose two classes of stock differ in only one respect: One class has voting rights but the other does not. As you would expect, the stock with voting rights would be more valuable. In the United States, which has a legal system with fairly strong protection for minority stockholders (that is, noncontrolling stockholders), voting stock typically sells at a price 4% to 6% above that of otherwise similar nonvoting stock. Thus, if a stock with no voting rights sold for $50, then one with voting rights would probably sell for $52 to $53. In countries with legal systems that provide less protection for minority stockholders, the right to vote is far more valuable. For example voting stock in Israel sells for 45% more on average than nonvoting stock, and voting stock in Italy has an 82% higher value than nonvoting stock.

Some companies have multiple lines of business, with each line having different growth prospects. Because cash flows for all business lines are mingled on financial statements, some companies worry that investors are not able to value the high-growth business lines correctly. To separate the cash flows and to allow separate valuations, occasionally a company will have classes of stock with dividends tied to a particular part of a company. This is called **tracking stock,** or **target stock.** For example, in 2006 Liberty Media Corporation, a conglomerate that owned such entertainment assets as the Starz movie channel and investments in Time Warner, issued two different tracking stocks to track its two different business lines. One of these, Liberty Interactive tracking stock, was designed to track the performance of its QVC home shopping network and other high-growth Internet-based interactive assets. The other, Liberty Capital Group, comprised slower-growth holdings like the Starz Entertainment Group. The idea was that investors would assign a higher value to the high growth portion of the company if it traded separately.

However, many analysts are skeptical as to whether tracking stock increases a company's total market value. Companies still report consolidated financial statements for the entire company and have considerable leeway in allocating costs, deploying capital, and reporting the financial results for the various divisions, even those with tracking stock. Thus, a tracking stock is far from identical to the stock of an independent, stand-alone company.

SELF-TEST

What are some reasons why a company might use classified stock?

7-3 Stock Market Reporting

Fifty years ago, investors who wanted real-time information would sit in brokerage firms' offices watching a "ticker tape" go by that displayed prices of stocks as they were traded. Those who did not need current information could find the previous day's prices from the business section of a daily newspaper like *The Wall Street Journal.* Today, though, one can get quotes

[2]Note that the terms "Class A," "Class B," and so on have no standard meanings. Most firms have no classified shares, but a firm that does could designate its Class B shares as founders' shares and its Class A shares as those sold to the public; another firm might reverse these designations.

FIGURE 7-1

Stock Quote and Other Key Data for GE, February 24, 2012

General Electric Company Common (GE) – NYSE

19.24 ↓0.07 (0.36%) Feb 24, 4:00PM EST | After Hours: 19.21 ↓0.03 (0.16%) Feb 24, 7:56PM EST

Prev Close:	19.31	Day's Range:	19.14 - 19.37
Open:	19.36	52wk Range:	14.02 - 21.17
Bid	19.01 x 1000	Volume:	23,927,033
Ask:	19.24 x 100	Avg Vol (3m):	58,203,500
1y Target Est:	21.71	Market Cap:	203.29B
Beta:	1.86	P/E (ttm):	15.55
Next Earnings Date:	N/A	EPS (ttm):	1.24
		Div & Yield:	0.68 (3.50%)

Source: **http://finance.yahoo.com.**

throughout the day from many different Internet sources, including Yahoo!.[3] Figure 7-1 shows the quote for General Electric, which is traded on the NYSE under the symbol GE, on February 24, 2012. GE ended the regular trading day (4 p.m. EST) at $19.24, down $0.07, which was a 0.36% decrease from the previous day. However, in after-hours trading the stock fell by an additional 3 cents. The data also show that GE opened the day at $19.36 and traded in a range from $19.14 to $19.37. If this quote had been obtained during trading hours, it would also have provided current information about the quotes at which the stock could be bought (the Ask quote) or sold (the Bid quote). During past 52 weeks, the price hit a high of $21.17 and a low of $14.02. A total of 23.93 million GE shares traded that day, which was below the average trading volume of 58.20 million shares during the past 3 months.

The screen with the stock quote information also gives the total market value of GE's common stock (the Market Cap), the dividend, the dividend yield, the most recent "ttm" ("trailing twelve months") EPS and P/E ratios, and a graph showing the stock's performance during the day. (However, the graph can be changed to show the stock's performance over a number of time periods up to and including 5 years.) In addition to this information, the Web page has links to financial statements, research reports, historical ratios, analysts' forecasts of EPS and EPS growth rates, and a wealth of other data.

SELF-TEST

What information is provided on the Internet in addition to the stock's latest price?

7-4 Valuing Common Stocks

Common stocks are expected to provide a stream of future cash flows, and a stock's value is found the same way as the values of other financial assets—namely, as the present value of its expected future cash flow stream. In later sections we will show how to estimate a

[3]Most free sources actually provide quotes that are delayed by 20 minutes, but if you subscribe to a paid site like *The Wall Street Journal*'s online service, or if you have a brokerage account, you can generally get real-time quotes online.

stock's value as part of a company's total value, but we begin here by directly valuing a stock's cash flows to shareholders.

7-4a Definitions of Terms Used in Stock Valuation Models

It's obvious why an investor needs a stock valuation model, but why does a manager also need a valuation model? For the reasons given in Chapter 1, a manager should seek to maximize the intrinsic value of her firm's stock. To do this, a manager needs to know how her actions are likely to affect the stock's value. In other words, managers need a stock valuation model just as much as investors do.

We begin by defining key terms:

D_t = Dividend the stockholder *expects* to receive at the end of Year t. D_0 is the most recent dividend, which has already been paid; D_1 is the first dividend expected, which will be paid at the end of this year; D_2 is the dividend expected at the end of Year 2; and so forth. D_1 represents the first cash flow that a new purchaser of the stock will receive, because D_0 has just been paid. D_0 is known with certainty, but all future dividends are expected values.[4]

P_0 = Actual **market price** of the stock today.

$\hat{P}_1$ = Expected price of the stock at the end of each Year t (pronounced "P hat t"). $\hat{P}_0$ is estimated value of the stock today as seen by the particular investor doing the analysis; $\hat{P}_1$ is the price expected at the end of 1 year; and so on.

D_1/P_0 = Expected **dividend yield** during the coming year. For example, if a stock to pay a dividend of $D_1 = \$1$ during the next 12 months and if its current price is $P_0 = \$10$, then the expected dividend yield is $\$1/\$10 = 0.10 = 10\%$.

$\frac{\hat{P}_1 - P_0}{P_0}$ = Expected **capital gains yield** during the coming year. If the stock sells for \$10 today and if it is expected to rise to \$10.50 at the end of one year, then the expected capital gain is $\hat{P}_1 - P_0 = \$10.50 - \$10.00 = \$0.50$, and the expected capital gains yield is $\$0.50/\$10 = 0.05 = 5\%$.

g = Expected **growth rate** in dividends as predicted by a marginal investor.

r_s = The **required rate of return** on the stock. As shown in Chapter 6, the primary determinants of r_s include the risk-free rate and adjustments for the stock's risk.

$\hat{r}_s$ = **Expected rate of return** that an investor who buys the stock expects to receive in the future. $\hat{r}_s$ (pronounced "r hat s") could be above or below r_s, but one would buy the stock only if $\hat{r}_s \geq r_s$. Note that the expected return($\hat{r}_s$) is equal to the expected dividend yield (D_1/P_0) plus

[4]Stocks generally pay dividends quarterly, so theoretically we should evaluate them on a quarterly basis. However, in stock valuation, most analysts work on an annual basis because the data generally are not precise enough to warrant refinement to a quarterly model. For additional information on the quarterly model, see Robert Brooks and Billy Helms, "An N-Stage, Fractional Period, Quarterly Dividend Discount Model," *Financial Review*, November 1990, pp. 651–657.

the expected capital gains yield ($[\hat{P}_1 - P_0]/P_0$). In our example, $\hat{r}_s = 10\% + 5\% = 15\%$.

$\bar{r}_s$ = **Actual**, or **realized**, ***after-the-fact* rate of return**, pronounced "r bar s." For a risky security, the actual return can differ considerably from the expected return.

7-4b Expected Dividends as the Basis for Stock Values

Like all financial assets, the value of a stock is estimated by finding the present value of a stream of expected future cash flows. What are the cash flows that corporations are expected to provide to their stockholders? First, think of yourself as an investor who buys a stock with the intention of holding it (in your family) forever. In this case, all that you (and your heirs) will receive is a stream of dividends, and the value of the stock today is calculated as the present value of an infinite stream of dividends:

$$\text{Value of stock} = \hat{P}_0 = \text{PV of expected future dividends}$$
$$= \frac{D_1}{(1+r_s)^1} + \frac{D_2}{(1+r_s)^2} + \cdots + \frac{D_\infty}{(1+r_s)^\infty} \quad (7\text{-}1)$$
$$= \sum_{t=1}^{\infty} \frac{D_t}{(1+r_s)^t}$$

What about the more typical case, where you expect to hold the stock for a finite period and then sell it—what is the value of $\hat{P}_0$ in this case? Unless the company is likely to be liquidated or sold and thus to disappear, *the value of the stock is again determined by Equation 7-1.* To see this, recognize that for any individual investor, the expected cash flows consist of expected dividends plus the expected sale price of the stock. However, the sale price a current investor receives will depend on the dividends some future investor expects. Therefore, for all present and future investors in total, expected cash flows must be based on expected future dividends. Put another way, unless a firm is liquidated or sold to another concern, the cash flows it provides to its stockholders will consist only of a stream of dividends. Therefore, the value of a share of its stock must be the present value of that expected dividend stream.

The general validity of Equation 7-1 can also be confirmed by solving the following problem. Suppose I buy a stock and expect to hold it for 1 year. I will receive dividends during the year plus the value $\hat{P}_1$ when I sell at the end of the year. But what will determine the value of $\hat{P}_1$? The answer is that it will be determined as the present value of the dividends expected during Year 2 plus the stock price at the end of that year, which, in turn, will be determined as the present value of another set of future dividends and an even more distant stock price. This process can be continued ad infinitum, and the ultimate result is Equation 7-1.[5]

[5]It is ironic that investors periodically lose sight of the long-run nature of stocks as investments and forget that, in order to sell a stock at a profit, one must find a buyer who will pay the higher price. If you analyze a stock's value in accordance with Equation 7-1, conclude that the stock's market price exceeds a reasonable value, and then buy the stock anyway, you would be following the "bigger fool" theory of investment—you think that you may be a fool to buy the stock at its excessive price, but you think that when you get ready to sell it, you can find someone who is an even bigger fool. Many investors might have been following the bigger fool theory during the big stock run-ups prior to the bursting bubbles in 2000 and 2007.

SELF-TEST

What are the two components of most stocks' expected total return?

How does one calculate the capital gains yield and the dividend yield of a stock?

If $D_1 = \$3.00$, $P_0 = \$50$, and $\hat{P}_1 = \$52$, what are the stock's expected dividend yield, expected capital gains yield, and expected total return for the coming year? **(6%, 4%, 10%)**

7-5 Valuing a Constant Growth Stock

Equation 7-1 is a generalized stock valuation model in that the time pattern of D_t can be anything: D_t can be rising, falling, fluctuating randomly, or even zero for several years, yet Equation 7-1 will still hold. With a computer spreadsheet we can easily use this equation to find a stock's value for any pattern of dividends, up to the limit of the computer's memory. However, if future dividends are expected to grow at a constant rate, we can use the constant growth model.

7-5a The Constant Growth Model

In the long run, dividends can't grow faster than earnings. A dollar used to pay dividends can't be used for reinvestment in the firm or to pay down debt, so everything else equal, higher dividends must be associated either with declining earnings growth due to a lack of reinvestment or with increasing debt levels. Growth in dividends can be supported by increasing debt for a while, but to avoid unacceptably high levels of debt, long-term dividend growth must be limited to long-term earnings growth.

Long-term earnings per share (EPS) growth depends on economy-wide factors (such as recessions and inflation), industry-wide factors (such as technological innovations), and firm-specific factors (management skill, brand identity, patent protection, etc.). For a firm to grow faster than the economy, either the industry must become a bigger part of the economy or the firm must take market share from its competitors. But as markets mature, competition and market saturation will tend to limit EPS growth to a constant long-term rate, approximately equal to the sum of population growth and inflation.

Some companies are in growing industries and won't hit their long-term constant growth rate for many years, but some mature firms in saturated industries are already at their constant long-term growth rate. We will address valuation of faster-growing firms later in the chapter, but for a mature company whose dividends are growing at a constant rate, Equation 7-1 can be rewritten as follows:

resource

The last term in Equation 7-2 is derived in Web Extension 7A on the textbook's Web site.

$$\begin{aligned}\hat{P}_0 &= \frac{D_0(1+g)^1}{(1+r_s)^1} + \frac{D_0(1+g)^2}{(1+r_s)^2} + \cdots + \frac{D_0(1+g)^\infty}{(1+r_s)^\infty} \\ &= D_0 \sum_{t=1}^{\infty} \frac{(1+g)^t}{(1+r_s)^t} \\ &= \frac{D_0(1+g)}{r_s - g} = \frac{D_1}{r_s - g}\end{aligned} \tag{7-2}$$

The last term of Equation 7-2 is called the **constant growth model**, or the **Gordon model**, after Myron J. Gordon, who did much to develop and popularize it.

A necessary condition for the validity of Equation 7-2 is that r_s be greater than g. Look back at the second form of Equation 7-2. If g is larger than r_s, then $(1 + g)^t/(1 + r_s)^t$ must always be greater than 1. In this case, the second line of Equation 7-2 is the sum of an infinite number of terms, with each term being larger than 1. Therefore, if g were constant and greater than r_s, the resulting stock price would be infinite! Because no company is worth an infinite amount, it is impossible to have a constant growth rate that is greater than r_s forever. Unfortunately, a student will occasionally plug a value for g that is greater than r_s into the last form of Equation 7-2 and report a negative stock price. Always keep in mind that the last form of Equation 7-2 is valid only when g is less than r_s. *If g is greater than r_s then the constant growth model cannot be used, and the answer you would get from using Equation 7-2 would be wrong and misleading.*

7-5b Illustration of a Constant Growth Stock

Assume that R&R Enterprises just paid a dividend of \$1.15 (that is, D_0 = \$1.15). Its stock has a required rate of return, r_s, of 13.4%, and investors expect the dividend to grow at a constant 8% rate in the future. The estimated dividend 1 year hence would be D_1 = \$1.15 (1.08) = \$1.24; D_2 would be \$1.34; and the estimated dividend 5 years hence would be \$1.69:

$$D_t = D_0(1 + g)^t = \$1.15(1.08)^5 = \$1.69$$

We could use this procedure to estimate each future dividend and then use Equation 7-1 to determine the current stock value, $\hat{P}_0$. In other words, we could find each expected future dividend, calculate its present value, and then sum all the present values to find the estimated value of the stock.

Such a process would be time-consuming, but we can take a shortcut—just insert the illustrative data into Equation 7-2 to find the stock's estimated value:

$$\hat{P}_0 = \frac{\$1.15(1.08)}{0.134 - 0.08} = \frac{\$1.242}{0.054} = \$23.00$$

The concept underlying the valuation process for a constant growth stock is graphed in Figure 7-2. Dividends are growing at the rate g = 8%, but because $r_s > g$, the present value of each future dividend is declining. For example, the dividend in Year 1 is $D_1 = D_0(1 + g)^1$ = \$1.15(1.08) = \$1.242. However, the present value of this dividend, discounted at 13.4%, is $PV(D_1) = \$1.242/(1.134)^1$ = \$1.095. The dividend expected in Year 2 grows to \$1.242(1.08) = \$1.341, but the present value of this dividend falls to \$1.043. Continuing, D_3 = \$1.449 and $PV(D_3)$ = \$0.993, and so on. Thus, the expected dividends are growing, but the present value of each successive dividend is declining, because the dividend growth rate (8%) is less than the rate used for discounting the dividends to the present (13.4%).

If we summed the present values of each future dividend, this summation would be the value of the stock, $\hat{P}_0$. When g is a constant, this summation is equal to $D_1/(r_s - g)$, as shown in Equation 7-2. Therefore, if we extend the lower step-function curve in Figure 7-2 on out to infinity and add up the present values of each future dividend, the summation would be identical to the value given by Equation 7-2, \$23.00.

Although Equation 7-2 assumes there are *infinite* time periods, most of the value is based on dividends during a *finite* time period. In our example, 70% of the value is attributed to the first 25 years, 91% to the first 50 years, and 99.4% to the first 100 years. This means that companies don't have to survive forever to justify using the Gordon growth model.

FIGURE 7-2

Present Value of Dividends of a Constant Growth Stock Where D_0 = \$1.15, g = 8%, and r_s = 13.4%

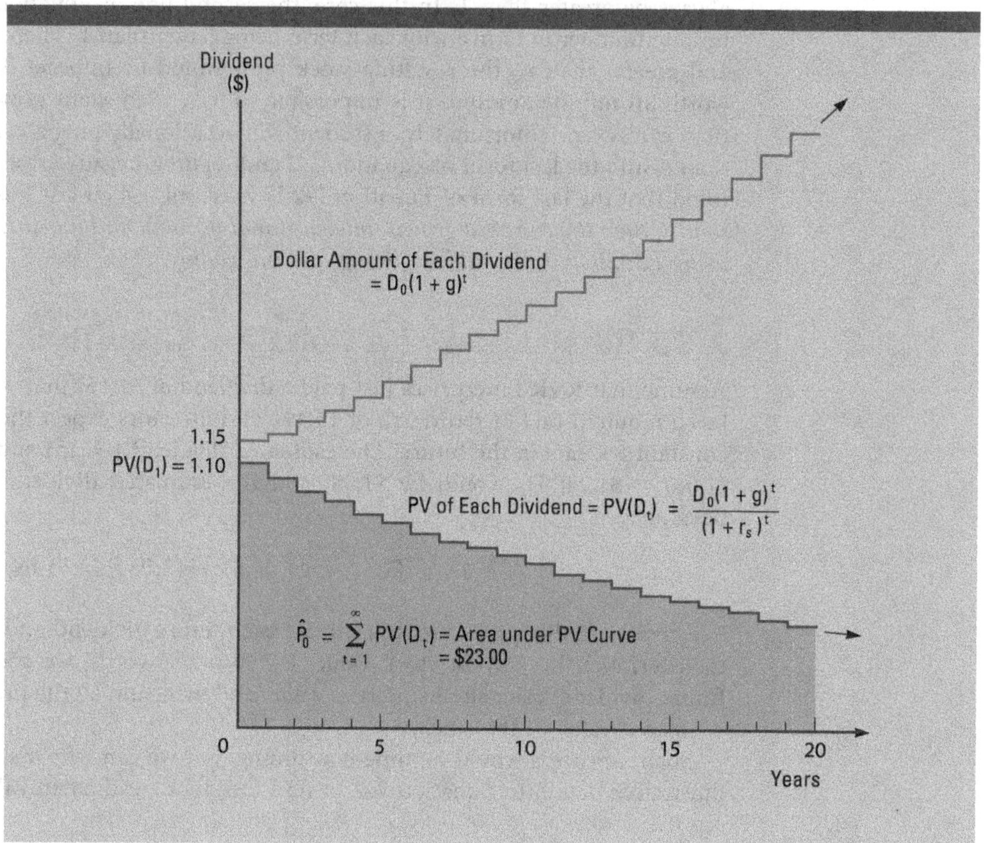

© Cengage Learning 2014

WWW

The popular Motley Fool Web site ***www.fool.com*** *provides a good description of benefits and drawbacks of a few of the more commonly used valuation procedures. Select Investing Commentary tab, choose Basics, then "How to Value Stocks."*

7-5c Do Stock Prices Reflect Long-Term or Short-Term Events?

Managers often complain that the stock market is shortsighted and that investors care only about conditions over the next few years. Let's use the constant growth model to test this assertion. R&R's most recent dividend was \$1.15, and it is expected to grow at a rate of 8% per year. Because we know the growth rate, we can forecast the dividends for each of the next 5 years and then find their present values:

$$\begin{aligned}
PV &= \frac{D_0(1+g)^1}{(1+r_s)^1} + \frac{D_0(1+g)^2}{(1+r_s)^2} + \frac{D_0(1+g)^3}{(1+r_s)^3} + \frac{D_0(1+g)^4}{(1+r_s)^4} + \frac{D_0(1+g)^5}{(1+r_s)^5} \\
&= \frac{\$1.15(1.08)^1}{(1.134)^1} + \frac{\$1.15(1.08)^2}{(1.134)^2} + \frac{\$1.15(1.08)^3}{(1.134)^3} + \frac{\$1.15(1.08)^4}{(1.134)^4} + \frac{\$1.15(1.08)^5}{(1.134)^5} \\
&= \frac{\$1.242}{(1.134)^1} + \frac{\$1.341}{(1.134)^2} + \frac{\$1.449}{(1.134)^3} + \frac{\$1.565}{(1.134)^4} + \frac{\$1.690}{(1.134)^5} \\
&= 1.095 + 1.043 + 0.993 + 0.946 + 0.901 \\
&\approx \$5.00
\end{aligned}$$

Recall that R&R's stock price is $23.00. Therefore, only $5.00, or $5/$23 = 0.22 = 22%, of the $23.00 stock price is attributable to short-term cash flows. This means that R&R's managers will affect the stock price more by working to increase long-term cash flows than by focusing on short-term flows. This situation holds for most companies. Indeed, a number of professors and consulting firms have used actual company data to show that more than 80% of a typical company's stock price is due to cash flows expected farther than 5 years in the future.

This brings up an interesting question. If most of a stock's value is due to long-term cash flows, then why do managers and analysts pay so much attention to quarterly earnings? Part of the answer lies in the information conveyed by short-term earnings. For example, when actual quarterly earnings are lower than expected not because of fundamental problems but only because a company has increased its research and development (R&D) expenditures, studies have shown that the stock price probably won't decline and may actually increase. This makes sense, because R&D should increase future cash flows. On the other hand, if quarterly earnings are lower than expected because customers don't like the company's new products, then this new information will have negative implications for future values of g, the long-term growth rate. As we show later in this chapter, even small changes in g can lead to large changes in stock prices. Therefore, short-term quarterly earnings themselves might not contribute a large portion to a stock's price, but the information they convey about future prospects can be extremely important.

Another reason many managers focus on short-term earnings is that some firms pay managerial bonuses on the basis of current earnings rather than stock prices (which reflect future earnings). For these managers, the concern with quarterly earnings is not due to their effect on stock prices—it's due to their effect on bonuses. Many apparent puzzles in finance can be explained either by managerial compensation systems or by peculiar features of the Tax Code. So, if you can't explain a firm's behavior in terms of economic logic, look to compensation procedures or taxes as possible explanations.

7-5d Stock Price Volatility

Recall from Chapter 6 that a typical company's stock returns are very volatile. Indeed, many stocks declined by 80% or more during 2012, and some enjoyed gains of over 100%. At the risk of understatement, the stock market is volatile! To see why stock prices are volatile, we estimate R&R's stock value after making small changes to the inputs of the constant growth model, as shown in Table 7-1. The estimated price is $23 for the original

TABLE 7-1

Estimated Stock Value of R&R Enterprise for Different Inputs of Growth and Required Return (D_0 = $1.15)

	Required Return: r_s				
Growth Rate: g	**11.4%**	**12.4%**	**13.4%**	**14.4%**	**15.4%**
6%	$22.57	$19.05	$16.47	$14.51	$12.97
7%	$27.97	$22.79	$19.23	$16.63	$14.65
8%	$36.53	$28.23	$23.00	$19.41	$16.78
9%	$52.23	$36.87	$28.49	$23.21	$19.59
10%	$90.36	$52.71	$37.21	$28.75	$23.43

© Cengage Learning 2014

inputs, shown in the boxed cell. Notice that even small changes in the required return or estimated growth rate cause large changes in the estimated stock value.

What might cause investors to change their expectations about the growth rate or risk of future dividends? It could be new information about the company, such as preliminary results for an R&D program, initial sales of a new product, or the discovery of harmful side effects from the use of an existing product. Or new information that will affect many companies could arrive, such as the collapse of the credit markets in 2008. Given the existence of computers and telecommunications networks, new information hits the market on an almost continuous basis, and it causes frequent and sometimes large changes in stock prices. In other words, *ready availability of information causes stock prices to be volatile.*

If a stock's price is stable, this probably means that little new information is arriving. But if you think it's risky to invest in a volatile stock, imagine how risky it would be to invest in a company that rarely releases new information about its sales or operations. It may be bad to see your stock's price jump around, but it would be a lot worse to see a stable quoted price most of the time and then to see huge moves on the rare days when new information is released.[6] Fortunately, in our economy timely information is readily available, and evidence suggests that stocks—especially those of large companies—adjust rapidly to new information.

7-5e Expected Rate of Return on a Constant Growth Stock

When using Equation 7-2, we first estimated D_1 and r_s, the *required* rate of return on the stock; then we solved for the stock's intrinsic value, which we compared to its actual market price. We can also reverse the process, observing the actual stock price, substituting it into Equation 7-2, and solving for the rate of return. In doing so, we are finding the *expected* rate of return (recall from Chapter 6 that if the market is in equilibrium, the expected return will equal the *required* rate of return, $\hat{r}_s = r_s$):

$$\begin{aligned}\hat{r}_s = \text{Expected rate of return} &= \text{Expected dividend yield} + \text{Expected capital gains yield} \\ &= \text{Expected dividend yield} + \text{Expected growth rate} \\ &= \frac{D_1}{P_0} + g\end{aligned} \tag{7-3}$$

Thus, if you buy a stock for a price P_0 = \$23, and if you expect the stock to pay a dividend D_1 = \$1.242 in a year and to grow at a constant rate g = 8% in the future, then your expected rate of return will be 13.4%:

$$\hat{r}_s = \frac{\$1.242}{\$23} + 8\% = 5.4\% + 8\% = 13.4\%$$

In this form, we see that $\hat{r}_s$ is the *expected total return* and that it consists of an *expected dividend yield*, D_1/P_0 = 5.4%, plus an *expected growth rate* (which is also the *expected capital gains yield*) of g = 8%.

[6]Note, however, that if information came out infrequently, stock prices would probably be stable for a time and then experience large price swings when news did come out. This would be a bit like not having a lot of little earthquakes (frequent new information) that relieve stress along the fault and instead building up stress for a number of years before a massive earthquake.

Suppose that the current price, P_0, is equal to \$23 and that the Year-1 expected dividend, D_1, is equal to \$1.242. What is the expected price at the end of the first year, immediately after D_1 has been paid? First, we can estimate the expected Year-2 dividend as $D_2 = D_1(1 + g) = \$1.242(1.08) = \$1.3414$. Then we can apply a version of Equation 7-2 that is shifted ahead by 1 year, using D_2 instead of D_1 and solving for $\hat{P}_1$ instead of $\hat{P}_0$:

$$\hat{P}_1 = \frac{D_2}{r_s - g} = \frac{\$1.3414}{0.134 - 0.08} = \$24.84$$

Even easier, notice that $\hat{P}_1$ must be 8% larger than \$23, the price found 1 year earlier for P_0:

$$\$23(1.08) = \$24.84$$

Either way, we expect a capital gain of \$24.84 – \$23.00 = \$1.84 during the year, which is a capital gains yield of 8%:

$$\text{Capital gains yield} = \frac{\text{Capital gain}}{\text{Beginning price}} = \frac{\$1.84}{\$23.00} = 0.08 = 8\%$$

We could extend the analysis, and in each future year the expected capital gains yield would always equal g, the expected dividend growth rate.

The dividend yield during the year could be estimated as follows:

$$\text{Dividend yield} = \frac{D_2}{\hat{P}_1} = \frac{\$1.3414}{\$24.84} = 0.054 = 5.4\%$$

The dividend yield for the following year could also be calculated, and again it would be 5.4%. Thus, *for a constant growth stock*, the following conditions must hold:

1. The dividend is expected to grow forever at a constant rate, g.
2. The stock price will also grow at this same rate.
3. The expected dividend yield is constant.
4. The expected capital gains yield is also constant and is equal to g, the dividend (and stock price) growth rate.
5. The expected total rate of return, $\hat{r}_s$, is equal to the expected dividend yield plus the expected growth rate: $\hat{r}_s$= dividend yield + g.

SELF-TEST

Write out and explain the valuation formula for a constant growth stock.

Are stock prices affected more by long-term or short-term performance? Explain.

Why doesn't a volatile stock price necessarily imply irrational pricing?

What conditions must hold in order for a stock to be evaluated using the constant growth model?

A stock is expected to pay a dividend of \$2 at the end of the year. The required rate of return is r_s = 12%. What would the stock's price be if the constant growth rate in dividends were 4%? **(\$25.00)** *What would the price be if g = 0%?* **(\$16.67)**

If D_0 = \$4.00, r_s = 9%, and g = 5% for a constant growth stock, what are the stock's expected dividend yield and capital gains yield for the coming year? **(4%, 5%)**

7-6 Valuing Nonconstant Growth Stocks

For many companies, it is not appropriate to assume that dividends will grow at a constant rate. Firms typically go through *life cycles*. During their early years, their growth is much faster than that of the economy as a whole; then they match the economy's growth; and finally their growth is slower than that of the economy. Automobile manufacturers in the 1920s, software companies such as Microsoft in the 1990s, and technology firms such as Cisco in the 2000s are examples of firms in the early part of the cycle; these firms are called **supernormal**, or **nonconstant, growth** firms.

Suppose R&R, the company from the previous section, was not yet in its constant growth phase but was expected to grow at a 30% rate for the first year, 20% for the second year, 10% for the third year, after which the growth rate is expected to fall to 8% and remain there. Chapters 12 and 14 explain how to forecast dividends, but for now just accept the forecasts for R&R. Figure 7-3 illustrates this pattern of nonconstant growth and also compares it with normal growth, zero growth, and negative growth.[7]

The value of R&R is the present value of its expected future dividends as determined by Equation 7-1. When D_t is growing at a constant rate, we simplify Equation 7-1 to $\hat{P}_0 = D_1/(r_s - g)$. In the nonconstant case, however, the expected growth rate is not a constant during the first 3 years, so we cannot apply the constant growth formula during these years.

Because Equation 7-2 requires a constant growth rate, we obviously cannot use it at Year 0 to value stocks that subsequently have nonconstant growth. However, assuming a company currently experiencing nonconstant growth will eventually slow down and become a constant growth stock, we can use Equation 7-2 to help find the stock's value.

FIGURE 7-3

Illustrative Dividend Growth at Different Rates

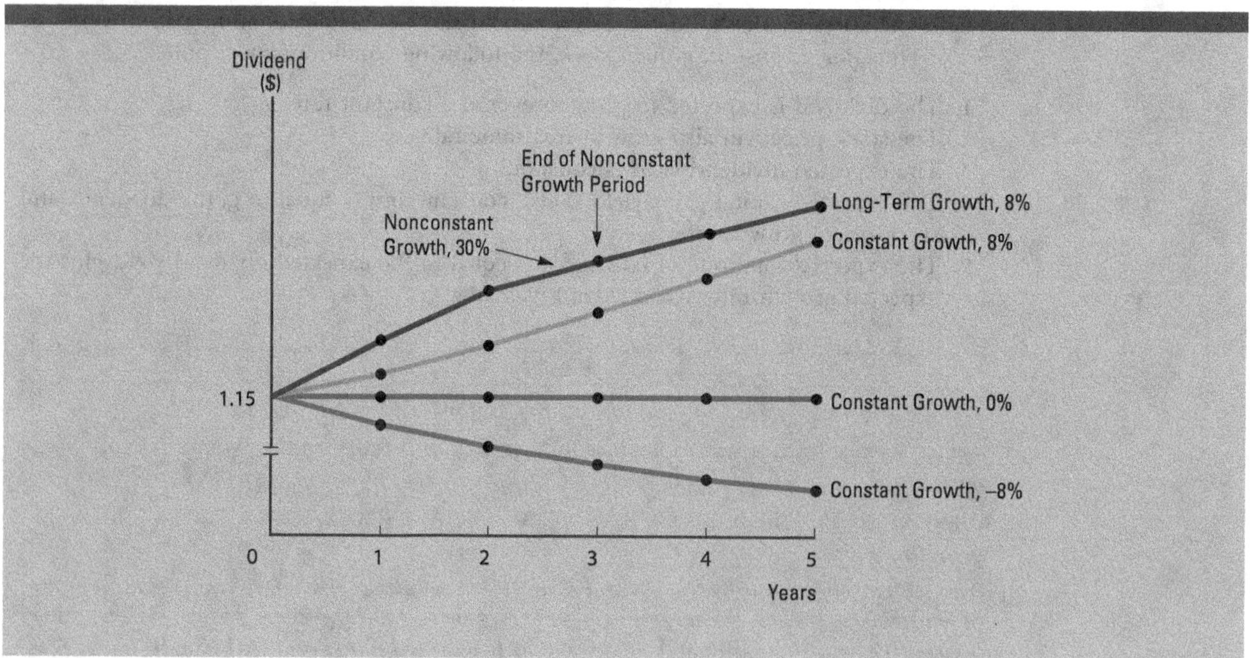

© Cengage Learning 2014

[7]A negative growth rate indicates a declining company. A mining company whose profits are falling because of a declining ore body is an example. Someone buying such a company would expect its earnings, and consequently its dividends and stock price, to decline each year, and this would lead to capital losses rather than capital gains. Obviously, a declining company's stock price will be relatively low, and its dividend yield must be high enough to offset the expected capital loss and still produce a competitive total return. Students sometimes argue that they would never be willing to buy a stock whose price was expected to decline. However, if the annual dividends are large enough to *more than offset* the falling stock price, the stock could still provide a fair return.

First, we assume that the dividend will grow at nonconstant rates (generally at relatively high rates) for N periods, after which it will grow at a constant rate, g_L. Often N is called the **horizon date** or the **terminal date.**

Recall that a stock's current estimated value, $\hat{P}_0$, is the present value of all dividends after Time 0, discounted back to Time 0. Similarly, the estimated value of a stock at Time N is the present value of all dividends beyond Time N, discounted back to Time N. When dividends beyond Time N are expected to grow at a constant long-term rate of g_L, we can use a variation of the constant growth formula, Equation 7-2, to estimate the stock's intrinsic value at Time N. The estimated value at Time N is often called the **horizon value** or the **terminal value.** For stocks, $\hat{P}_N$, denotes the horizon value of the expected stock price at Time N:

$$\text{Horizon value for stock} = \hat{P}_N = \frac{D_{N+1}}{r_s - g_L} = \frac{D_N(1+g_L)}{r_s - g_L} \tag{7-4}$$

A stock's estimated value today, $\hat{P}_0$, is the present value of the dividends during the nonconstant growth period plus the present value of the dividends after the horizon date:

$$\hat{P}_0 = \underbrace{\frac{D_1}{(1+r_s)^1} + \frac{D_2}{(1+r_s)^2} + \cdots + \frac{D_N}{(1+r_s)^N}}_{} + \underbrace{\frac{D_{N+1}}{(1+r_s)^{N+1}} + \cdots + \frac{D_\infty}{(1+r_s)^\infty}}_{}$$

= PV of dividends during the nonconstant growth period $t = 1$ to N + PV of dividends during the constant growth period $t = N + 1$ to ∞

The horizon value is the value of all dividends beyond Time N discounted back to Time N. Discounting the horizon value from Time N to Time 0 provides an estimate of the present value of all dividends beyond the nonconstant growth period. Thus, the stock's current estimated value is the present value of all dividends during the nonconstant growth period plus the present value of the horizon value:

$$\begin{aligned} \hat{P}_0 &= \left[\frac{D_1}{(1+r_s)^1} + \frac{D_2}{(1+r_s)^2} + \cdots + \frac{D_N}{(1+r_s)^N}\right] + \frac{\hat{P}_N}{(1+r_s)^N} \\ &= \left[\frac{D_1}{(1+r_s)^1} + \frac{D_2}{(1+r_s)^2} + \cdots + \frac{D_N}{(1+r_s)^N}\right] + \frac{[(D_{N+1})/(r_s - g_L)]}{(1+r_s)^N} \end{aligned} \tag{7-5}$$

To implement Equation 7-5, we go through the following three steps.

1. Estimate the expected dividends for each year during the period of nonconstant growth.
2. Find the expected price of the stock at the end of the nonconstant growth period, at which point it has become a constant growth stock.
3. Find the present values of the expected dividends during the nonconstant growth period and the present value of the expected stock price at the end of the nonconstant growth period. Their sum is the estimated value of the stock, $\hat{P}_0$.

Figure 7-4 illustrates the process for valuing a nonconstant growth stock. Notice that the dividends are projected using the appropriate growth rate for each year. The estimated horizon value, $\hat{P}_3$, is the value of all dividends from Year 4 through infinity, discounted back to Year 3 by application of the constant growth model at Year 3. The horizon value is actually the value a split-second after D_3 has been paid. Therefore, the estimated value at Time 0 is the present value of the first three dividends plus the present value of $\hat{P}_3$, for an estimated current value of $31.13. A detailed explanation is set forth in the steps below the diagram.

SELF-TEST

Explain how to find the value of a nonconstant growth stock.

Explain what is meant by the terms "horizon (terminal) date" and "horizon (terminal) value."

Suppose D_0 = $5.00 and r_s = 10%. The expected growth rate from Year 0 to Year 1 (g_1) = 20%, the expected growth rate from Year 1 to Year 2 (g_2) = 10%, and the constant growth rate beyond Year 2 is g_L = 5%. What are the expected dividends for Year 1 and Year 2? **($6.00 and $6.60)** *What is the expected horizon value price at Year 2 ($\hat{P}_3$)?* **($138.60)** *What is $\hat{P}_0$?* **($125.45)**

7-7 The Free Cash Flow Valuation Model

As stated earlier, managers should estimate and evaluate the impact of alternative strategies on their firms' values, which means that managers need a valuation model. The dividend growth model provides many meaningful insights, such as (1) the relative importance of long-term cash flows versus short-term cash flows and (2) the reason stock prices are so volatile. However, the dividend growth model is unsuitable in many situations.

For example, suppose a start-up company is formed to develop and market a new product. Its managers will focus on product development, marketing, and raising capital. They will probably be thinking about an eventual IPO, or perhaps the sale of the company to a larger firm; for example, Google, Cisco, Microsoft, Intel, IBM, or another of the industry leaders buy hundreds of successful new companies each year. For the managers of such a start-up, the decision to initiate dividend payments in the foreseeable future will be totally off the radar screen. Thus, the dividend growth model is not useful for valuing most start-up companies.

Also, many established firms pay no dividends. Investors may expect them to pay dividends sometime in the future—but when, and how much? As long as internal opportunities and acquisitions are so attractive, the initiation of dividends will be postponed, and this makes the dividend growth model of little use. Even Apple, one of the world's most successful companies, paid no dividends from 1995 until 2012, when it initiated quarterly dividend payments.

Finally, the dividend growth model is generally of limited use for internal management purposes, even for a dividend-paying company. If the firm consisted of just one big asset and if that asset produced all of the cash flows used to pay dividends, then alternative strategies could be judged through the use of the dividend growth model. However, most firms have several different divisions with many assets, so the corporation's value depends on the cash flows from many different assets and on the actions of many managers. These managers need a way to measure the effects of

FIGURE 7-4

Process for Finding the Value of a Nonconstant Growth Stock

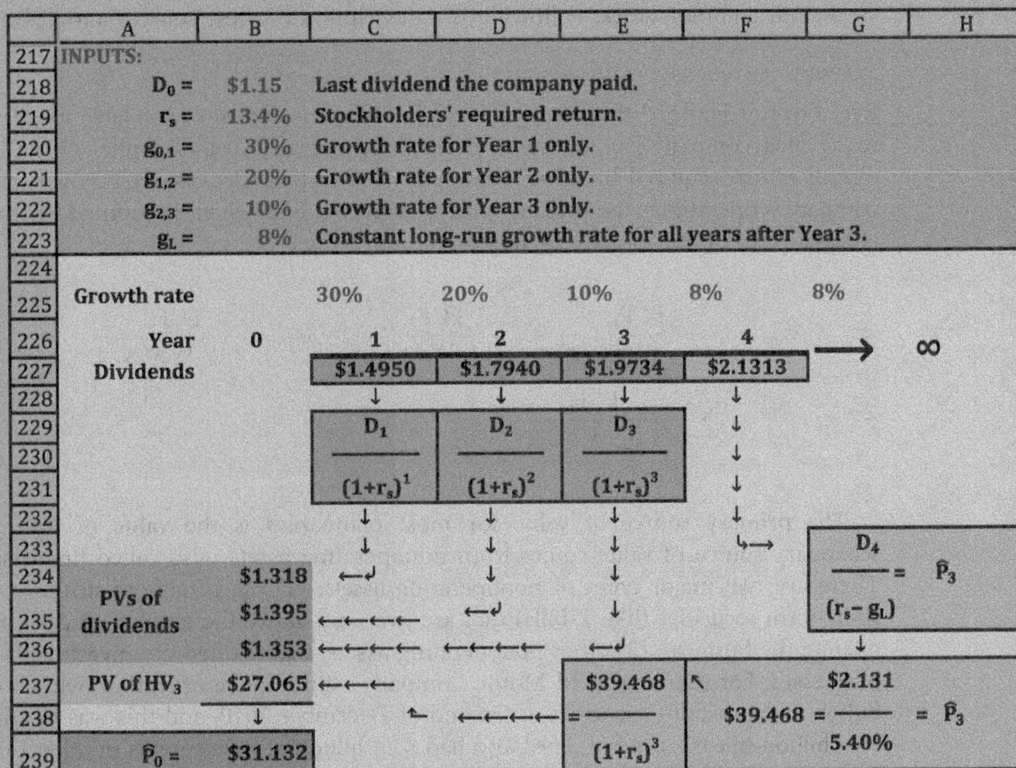

Notes:

Step 1. Calculate the dividends expected at the end of each year during the nonconstant growth period. Calculate the first dividend, $D_1 = D_0(1 + g_{0,1}) = \$1.15(1.30) = \$1.4950$. Here $g_{0,1}$ is the growth rate (30%) during the first year of the nonconstant growth period. Show the \$1.4950 on the time line as the cash flow at Year 1. Then calculate $D_2 = D_1(1 + g_{1,2}) = \$1.4950(1.20) = \$1.7940$ and then $D_3 = D_2(1 + g_{2,3}) = \$1.7940(1.10) = \$1.9734$. (The figure shows the values rounded to four decimal places, but all calculations used nonrounded values.) Show these values on the time line as the cash flows at Year 2 and Year 3. Note that D_0 is used only to calculate D_1.

Step 2. At Year 3, the stock becomes a constant growth stock. Therefore, we can use the constant growth formula to find $\hat{P}_3$, which is the PV of the dividends from Year 4 to infinity as evaluated at Year 3. First we determine $D_4 = \$1.9734(1.08) = \$2.1313$ for use in the formula, and then we calculate $\hat{P}_3$ as follows:

$$\hat{P}_3 = \frac{D_4}{r_s - g_L} = \frac{\$2.1313}{0.134 - 0.08} = \$39.4680$$

We show this \$39.468 on the time line as a second cash flow at Year 3. The \$39.468 is a Year-3 cash flow in the sense that the owner of the stock could sell it for \$39.468 at Year 3 and also in the sense that \$39.468 is the value at Year 3 of the dividend cash flows from Year 4 to infinity.

Step 3. Now that the cash flows have been placed on the time line, we can discount each cash flow at the required rate of return, $r_s = 13.4\%$. This produces the PVs shown to the left below the time line, and the sum of the PVs is the value of the nonconstant growth stock, \$31.13.

In the figure we show the setup for an *Excel* solution. With a financial calculator, you could use the cash flow (CFLO) register of your calculator. Enter 0 for CF_0 because you get no cash flow at Time 0, $CF_1 = 1.495$, $CF_2 = 1.7940$, and $CF_3 = 1.9734 + 39.468 = 41.4414$. Then enter I/YR = 13.4 and press the NPV key to find the value of the stock, \$31.1315.

their decisions on corporate value, but the discounted dividend model isn't very useful because individual divisions don't pay dividends.

resource

*See **Ch07 Tool Kit.xls** on the textbook's Web site.*

Fortunately, the free cash flow valuation model does not depend on dividends, and it can be applied to divisions and subunits as well as to the entire firm.

7-7a Sources of Value and Claims on Value

Companies have two primary sources of value, the value of operations and the value of nonoperating assets. There are three major types of claims on this value: debt, preferred stock, and common stock. Following is a description of these sources and claims.

Sources of Value

Recall from Chapter 2 that free cash flow (FCF) is the cash flow available for distribution to *all* of a company's investors. The weighted average cost of capital (WACC) is the overall return required by *all* of a company's investors. Because FCF is generated by a company's operations, the present value of expected FCF when discounted by the WACC is equal to the value of a company's operations, V_{op}:

$$V_{op} = \frac{FCF_1}{(1+WACC)^1} + \frac{FCF_2}{(1+WACC)^2} + \cdots + \frac{FCF_\infty}{(1+WACC)^\infty} = \sum_{t=1}^{\infty} \frac{FCF_t}{(1+WACC)^t} \quad (7\text{-}6)$$

The primary source of value for most companies is the value of operations. A secondary source of value comes from nonoperating assets (also called financial assets). There are two major types of nonoperating assets: (1) marketable securities, which are short-term securities (like T-bills) that are over and above the amount of cash needed to operate the business; (2) other nonoperating assets, which often are investments in other businesses. For example, Ford Motor Company's automotive operation held about \$14.2 billion in marketable securities at the end of December 2010, and this was in addition to \$6.3 billion in cash. Second, Ford also had \$2.4 billion of investments in other businesses, which were reported on the asset side of the balance sheet as "Equity in Net Assets of Affiliated Companies." In total, Ford had \$14.2 + \$2.4 = \$16.6 billion of nonoperating assets, amounting to 26% of its \$64.6 billion of total automotive assets. For most companies, the percentage is much lower. For example, as of the end of October 2010, Walmart's percentage of nonoperating assets was less than 1%, which is more typical.

We see, then, that for most companies operating assets are far more important than nonoperating assets. Moreover, companies can influence the values of their operating assets, whereas the values of nonoperating assets are largely beyond their direct control.

Claims on Value

For a company that is a going concern, debtholders have the first claim on value in the sense that interest and scheduled principal payments must be paid before any preferred or common dividends can be paid. Preferred stockholders have the next claim because preferred dividends must be paid before common dividends. Common shareholders come last in this pecking order and have a residual claim on the company's value.

7-7b Estimating the Value of Operations

The free cash flow (FCF) model is analogous to the dividend growth model, except the FCF valuation model (1) discounts free cash flows instead of dividends and (2) the discount rate is the weighted average cost of capital (WACC) instead of the required return on stock. Free cash flow is generated by operations, FCF is the cash flow available for all investors, and the WACC is the overall required return of all investors; therefore, the result of the FCF model is the total value of operations, not just the value of the stock.

We will illustrate the FCF valuation model using MagnaVision Inc., which produces optical systems for use in medical photography. Growth has been rapid in the past, but the market is becoming saturated, so the sales growth rate is projected to decline from 21% in 2013 to a sustainable rate of 5% in 2016 and beyond. Profit margins are expected to improve as the production process becomes more efficient and because MagnaVision will no longer be incurring marketing costs associated with the introduction of a major product. All items on the financial statements are projected to grow at a 5% rate after 2016.

Chapter 2 explained how to calculate FCF if you have historical financial statements; however, you need *forecasted* financial statements to apply the FCF valuation model. To better focus on the free cash flow valuation model in this example, we provide MagnaVision's projected free cash flows in Figure 7-5 and defer forecasting until Chapter 12.[8] We also provide MagnaVision's weighted average cost of capital, 10.84%; we will explain how to estimate the cost of capital in Chapter 9. All calculations in Figure 7-5 are explained in the following paragraphs.

resource

*See **Ch07 Tool Kit.xls** on the textbook's Web site.*

Notice that MagnaVision has negative free cash flows in the first two projected years. Negative free cash flow in early years is typical for young, high-growth companies. Even though net operating profit after taxes (NOPAT) may be positive, free cash flow often is negative due to investments in operating assets during the high-growth years. As growth slows, free cash flow will become positive and eventually grow at a constant rate.

FIGURE 7-5

MagnaVision's Value of Operations (Millions of Dollars)

	A	B	C	D	E	F	G	H
263	INPUTS:							
264	g_L =	5.00%						
265	WACC =	10.84%	Projections					
266	Year	2012	2013	2014	2015	2016		
267	FCF		−$18.00	−$23.00	$46.40	$49.00	→	
268			↓	↓	↓	↓		↓
269			FCF_{2013}	FCF_{2014}	FCF_{2015}	FCF_{2016}		↓
270								↓
271			$(1+WACC)^1$	$(1+WACC)^2$	$(1+WACC)^3$	$(1+WACC)^4$		$HV = V_{op(12/31/16)}$
272			↓	↓	↓	↓		↓
273			↓	↓	↓	↓		$FCF_{2016}(1+g_L)$
274		−$16.240	←	↓	↓	↓		
275	PVs of FCFs	−$18.721	←	←	↓	↓		$(WACC-g_L)$
276		$34.074	←	←	←	↓		↓
277		$32.465	←	←	←	←		↓
278	PV of HV	$583.696				$880.993	←	$51.450
279		↓				=		=
280	V_{op} =	$615.27				$(1+WACC)^4$		5.84%

[8]We have provided MagnaVision's projected statements and calculations of projected FCF in a worksheet in ***Ch07 Tool Kit.xls***.

To estimate MagnaVision's value of operations, we use an approach similar to the nonconstant dividend growth model for stocks and proceed as follows.

1. Recognize that growth after Year N will be constant, so we can use a constant growth formula to find the firm's value at Year N. The value at Year N is the sum of the PVs of FCF for year N + 1 and all subsequent years, discounted back to Year N.
2. Find the PV of the free cash flows for each of the N nonconstant growth years. Also, find the PV of the firm's value at Year N.
3. Now sum all the PVs, those of the annual free cash flows during the nonconstant period plus the PV of the Year-N value, to find the firm's value of operations.

A variant of the constant growth dividend model is shown in Equation 7-7, in which FCF replaces dividends and the WACC replaces r_s. This equation can be used to find the value of MagnaVision's operations at time N, when its free cash flows stabilize and begin to grow at a constant rate. This is the value of all FCFs beyond time N, discounted back to time N (which is 2016 for MagnaVision):

$$V_{op\,(at\ time\ N)} = \sum_{t=N+1}^{\infty} \frac{FCF_t}{(1+WACC)^{t-N}} = \frac{FCF_{N+1}}{WACC - g_L} = \frac{FCF_N(1+g_L)}{WACC - g_L} \tag{7-7}$$

Based on a 10.84% cost of capital, \$49 million of free cash flow in 2016, and a 5% growth rate, the value of MagnaVision's operations as of December 31, 2016, is estimated to be \$880.99 million:

$$V_{op(12/31/16)} = \frac{FCF_{12/31/16}(1+g_L)}{WACC - g_L} = \frac{\$49(1+0.05)}{0.1084-0.05} = \frac{\$51.45}{0.1084-0.05} = \$880.99 \tag{7-7a}$$

This \$880.99 million figure is called the company's horizon value because it is the value at the end of the forecast period. It is also sometimes called a continuing value or terminal value. It is the amount that MagnaVision could expect to receive if it sold its operating assets on December 31, 2016.

Figure 7-5 shows the free cash flow for each year during the nonconstant growth period along with the horizon value of operations in 2016. To find the value of operations as of "today," December 31, 2012, we find the PV of the horizon value and each annual free cash flow in Figure 7-5, discounting at the 10.84% cost of capital:

$$\begin{aligned} V_{op(12/31/12)} &= \frac{-\$18.00}{(1+0.1084)^1} + \frac{-\$23.00}{(1+0.1084)^2} + \frac{\$46.40}{(1+0.1084)^3} \\ &\quad + \frac{\$49.00}{(1+0.1084)^4} + \frac{\$880.99}{(1+0.1084)^4} \\ &= \$615.27 \end{aligned}$$

The sum of the PVs is approximately \$615 million, and it represents an estimate of the price MagnaVision could expect to receive if it sold its operating assets "today," December 31, 2012.

7-7c Estimating the Price per Share

In addition to the value of operations, we need to know the value of MagnaVision's nonoperating assets, claims on value (such as debt and preferred stock), and the number of shares. Those values are shown in the INPUTS section of Figure 7-6. The other calculations in Figure 7-6 are explained as follows.

Think of a company's value as though it were a pie whose size is determined by the value of operations and the value of any financial (nonoperating) assets. The first piece of pie belongs to debtholders, the second to preferred stockholders, and the remaining piece (if there is one) to common shareholders. In other words, common shareholders have a residual claim.

resource

*See **Ch07 Tool Kit.xls** on the textbook's Web site.*

On December 31, 2012, MagnaVision reported owning $63 million of marketable securities. We don't need to calculate a present value for marketable securities because short-term financial assets as reported on the balance sheet are at (or close to) their market value. Therefore, MagnaVision's total value on December 31, 2012, is $615.27 + $63 = $678.27 million.

The value of common equity is the remaining value after other claims. Figure 7-6 shows that MagnaVision has $247 million in debt and $62 million in preferred stock.[9] Therefore, the value left for common stockholders is $678.27 − $247 − $62 = $369.27 million.[10]

Figure 7-7 illustrates the sources of and claims on MagnaVision's value.

FIGURE 7-6

Estimating the Value of MagnaVision's Stock Price (Millions, Except for Per Share Data)

	A	B	C	D	E
289	INPUTS:				
290				Value of operations =	$615.27
291				Value of nonoperating assets =	$63.00
292				All debt =	$247.00
293				Preferred stock =	$62.00
294				Number of shares of common stock =	100.00
295	Estimating Price Per Share				
296				Value of operations	$615.27
297				+ Value of nonoperating assets	63.00
298				Total estimated value of firm	$678.27
299				− Debt	247.00
300				− Preferred stock	62.00
301				Estimated value of equity	$369.27
302				÷ Number of shares	100.00
303				Estimated stock price per share =	$3.69

[9]Accounts payable and accruals were part of the calculation of FCF, so their impact on value is already incorporated into the valuation of the company's operations. It would be double-counting to subtract them now from the value of operations.

[10]When estimating the intrinsic market value of equity, it would be better to subtract the market values of debt and preferred stock rather than their book values. However, in most cases (including this one), the book values of fixed-income securities are close to their market values. When this is true, one can simply use book values.

FIGURE 7-7

MagnaVision's Sources of Value and Claims on Value (Millions of Dollars)

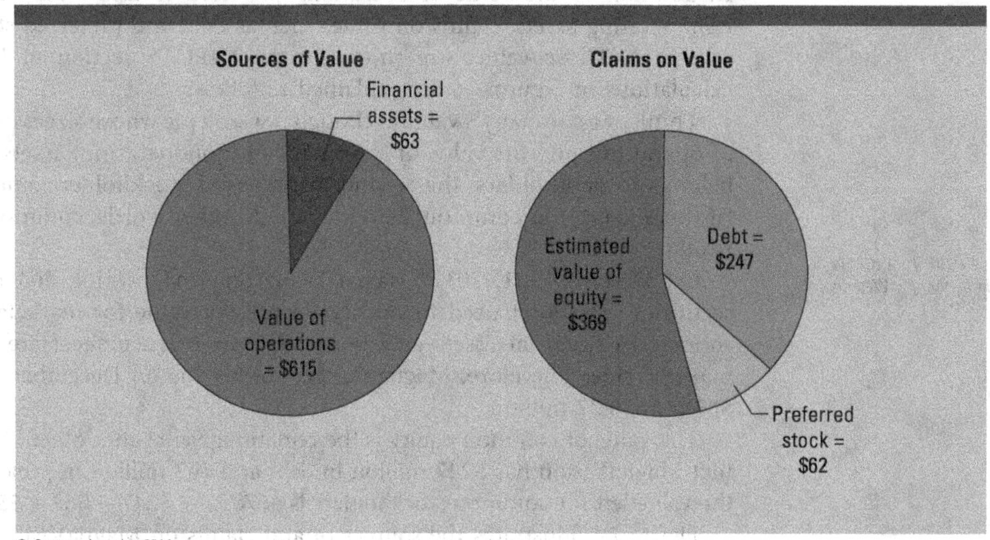

© Cengage Learning 2014

As shown in Figure 7-6, MagnaVision has 100 million shares outstanding. Its estimated equity value is $369.27 million. Therefore, the estimated value of a single share is $369.27/100 = $3.69.

7-7d Comparing the Free Cash Flow Valuation and Dividend Growth Models

In Chapter 12 we show that the free cash flow valuation model and the dividend growth model give the same estimated stock price if you are very careful to be consistent with the implicit assumptions underlying the projections of free cash flows and dividends.[11] Which model should you use, as they both give the same answer? If you were a financial analyst estimating the value of a mature company whose dividends are expected to grow steadily in the future, it would probably be more efficient to use the dividend growth model. In this case you would need to estimate only the growth rate in dividends, not the entire set of forecasted financial statements.

However, if a company is paying a dividend but is still in the high-growth stage of its life cycle, you would need to project the future financial statements before you could make a reasonable estimate of future dividends. After you have estimated future financial statements, it would be a toss-up as to whether the corporate valuation model or the dividend growth model would be easier to apply. If you were trying to estimate the value of a company that has never paid a dividend, a private company (including companies nearing an IPO), or a division of a company, then there would be no choice: You would have to estimate future financial statements and use the corporate valuation model.

[11]For a more detailed explanation of corporate valuation and forecasting financial statements, see P. Daves, M. Ehrhardt, and R. Shrieves, *Corporate Valuation: A Guide for Managers and Investors* (Mason, OH: Thomson/South-Western, 2004).

SELF-TEST

Why is the free cash flow valuation model applicable in more circumstances than the dividend growth model?

Write out the equation for the value of operations.

What is the horizon value? *Why is it also called the* terminal value *or* continuing value?

Explain how to estimate the price per share using the corporate free cash flow valuation model.

A company expects FCF of –$10 million at Year 1 and FCF of $20 million at Year 2; after Year 2, FCF is expected to grow at a 5% rate. If the WACC is 10%, then what is the horizon value of operations, $V_{op(Year\ 2)}$? **($420 million)** *What is the current value of operations,* $V_{op(Year\ 0)}$? **($354.55 million)**

A company has a current value of operations of $800 million, and it holds $100 million in short-term investments. If the company has $400 million in debt and has 10 million shares outstanding, what is the estimated price per share? **($50.00)**

7-8 Market Multiple Analysis

Some analysts use **market multiple analysis** to estimate a company's value. The analyst chooses a metric for the firm—say, its EPS—and then multiplies the company's EPS by a market-determined multiple such as the average P/E ratio for a sample of similar companies. This would give an estimate of the stock's intrinsic value. Market multiples can also be applied to total net income, to sales, to book value, or to number of subscribers for businesses such as cable TV or cellular telephone systems. Whereas the discounted dividend method applies valuation concepts by focusing on expected cash flows, market multiple analysis is more judgmental.

To illustrate the concept, suppose Tapley Products is a privately held firm whose forecasted earnings per share are $7.70, and suppose the average price/earnings (P/E) ratio for a set of similar publicly traded companies is 12. To estimate the intrinsic value of Tapley's stock we would simply multiply its $7.70 EPS by the multiple 12, obtaining the value $7.70(12) = $92.40.

Another commonly used metric is *earnings before interest, taxes, depreciation, and amortization (EBITDA)*. The EBITDA *multiple* is the total value of a company (the market value of its equity plus that of its debt) divided by EBITDA. This multiple is based on total value, since EBITDA is used to compensate the firm's stockholders and bondholders. Therefore, it is called an **entity multiple**. The EBITDA market multiple is the average EBITDA multiple for a group of similar publicly traded companies. This procedure gives an estimate of the company's total value, and to find the estimated intrinsic value of the stock we would subtract the value of the debt from total value and then divide by the shares of stock outstanding.

As suggested previously, in some businesses, such as cable TV and cellular telephone, a critical factor is the number of customers the company has. For example, when a telephone company acquires a cellular operator, it might pay a price that is based on the number of customers. Managed care companies such as HMOs have applied similar logic in acquisitions, basing valuations primarily on the number of people insured. Some Internet companies have been valued by the number of "eyeballs," which is the number of hits on the site.

SELF-TEST

What is market multiple analysis?
What is an entity multiple?

7-9 Preferred Stock

Preferred stock is a *hybrid*—it's similar to bonds in some respects and to common stock in others. Like bonds, preferred stock has a par value, and a fixed amount of dividends must be paid on it before dividends can be paid on the common stock. However, if the preferred dividend is not earned, the directors can omit (or "pass") it without throwing the company into bankruptcy. So, although preferred stock has a fixed payment like bonds, a failure to make this payment will not lead to bankruptcy.

The dividends on preferred stock are fixed, and if they are scheduled to go on forever, the issue is a perpetuity whose value is found as follows:

$$V_{ps} = \frac{D_{ps}}{r_{ps}} \tag{7-8}$$

V_{ps} is the value of the preferred stock, D_{ps} is the preferred dividend, and r_{ps} is the required rate of return. Notice that Equation 7-8 is just a special case of the constant dividend growth model for which growth is zero.

MicroDrive has preferred stock outstanding that pays a dividend of \$8 per year. If the required rate of return on this preferred stock is 8%, then its value is \$100:

$$V_{ps} = \frac{\$8.00}{0.8} = \$100.00$$

If we know the current price of a preferred stock and its dividend, we can transpose terms and solve for the expected rate of return as follows:

$$\hat{r}_{ps} = \frac{D_{ps}}{V_{ps}} \tag{7-9}$$

Some preferred stock has a stated maturity, say, 50 years. If a firm's preferred stock matures in 50 years, pays a \$8 annual dividend, has a par value of \$100, and has a required return of 6%, then we can find its price using a financial calculator: Enter N = 50, I/YR = 6, PMT = 8, and FV = 100. Then press PV to find the price, V_{ps} = \$131.52. If you know the price of a share of preferred stock, you can solve for I/YR to find the expected rate of return, $\hat{r}_{ps}$.

Most preferred stock pays dividends quarterly. This is true for MicroDrive, so we could find the effective rate of return on its preferred stock as follows:

$$\text{EFF\%} = \text{EAR} = \left(1+\frac{r_{NOM}}{M}\right)^M - 1 = \left(1+\frac{0.08}{4}\right)^4 - 1 = 8.24\%$$

If an investor wanted to compare the returns on MicroDrive's bonds and its preferred stock, it would be best to convert the nominal rates on each security to effective rates and then compare these "equivalent annual rates."

SELF-TEST

Explain the following statement: "Preferred stock is a hybrid security."

Is the equation used to value preferred stock more like the one used to evaluate perpetual bonds or the one used for common stock? Explain.

A preferred stock has an annual dividend of $5. The required return is 8%. What is the V_{ps}? **($62.50)**

SUMMARY

Corporate decisions should be analyzed in terms of how alternative courses of action are likely to affect a firm's value. However, it is necessary to know how stock prices are established before attempting to measure how a given decision will affect a firm's value. This chapter showed how stock values are determined and also how investors go about estimating the rates of return they expect to earn. The key concepts covered are listed below.

- A **proxy** is a document that gives one person the power to act for another, typically the power to vote shares of common stock. A **proxy fight** occurs when an outside group solicits stockholders' proxies in an effort to overthrow the current management.
- Stockholders often have the right to purchase any additional shares sold by the firm. This right, called the **preemptive right**, protects the present stockholders' control and prevents dilution of their value.
- Although most firms have only one type of common stock, in some instances **classified stock** is used to meet the special needs of the company. One type is **founders' shares.** This is stock owned by the firm's founders that carries sole voting rights but restricted dividends for a specified number of years.
- The equation used to find **estimated value of a constant growth stock** is

$$\hat{P}_0 = \frac{D_1}{r_s - g}$$

  Web Extension 7A provides a derivation of this formula.
- The **expected total rate of return** from a stock consists of an **expected dividend yield** plus an **expected capital gains yield.** For a constant growth firm, both the dividend yield and the capital gains yield are expected to remain constant in the future.
- The equation for $\hat{r}_s$, the **expected rate of return on a constant growth stock,** is

$$\hat{r}_s = \frac{D_1}{P_0} + g$$

- A **zero growth stock** is one whose future dividends are not expected to grow at all. A **nonconstant growth stock** is one whose earnings and dividends are expected to grow much faster than the economy as a whole over some specified time period and then to grow at a sustainable long-term rate.

- To estimate the **present value of a nonconstant growth stock**, (1) forecast the dividends expected during the nonconstant growth period, (2) estimate the projected price of the stock at the end of the nonconstant growth period, (3) discount the dividends and the projected price back to the present, and (4) sum these PVs to find the current estimated value of the stock, $\hat{P}_0$.
- The **horizon (terminal) date** is the date when individual dividend forecasts are no longer made because the dividend growth rate is assumed to be constant thereafter.
- The **horizon value** for a stock is the present value of all dividends *after* the horizon date discounted back to horizon date:

$$\hat{P}_N = \frac{D_{N+1}}{r_s - g}$$

- **Preferred stock** is a hybrid security having some characteristics of debt and some of equity.
- The **value of a share of perpetual preferred stock** is found as the dividend divided by the required rate of return:

$$V_{ps} = \frac{D_{ps}}{r_{ps}}$$

- **Preferred stock** that has a finite maturity is evaluated with a formula that is identical in form to the bond value formula.
- The **value of operations** is the present value of all the future free cash flows expected from operations when discounted at the weighted average cost of capital:

$$V_{op\,(at\ time\ 0)} = \sum_{t=1}^{\infty} \frac{FCF_t}{(1 + WACC)^t}$$

- **Nonoperating assets** include **financial assets** such as investments in marketable securities and noncontrolling interests in the stock of other companies.
- The **value of nonoperating assets** is usually close to the figure reported on the balance sheet.
- The **horizon value** of operations is the value of operations at the end of the explicit forecast period. It is also called the **terminal value** or **continuing value**, and it is equal to the present value of all free cash flows beyond the forecast period, discounted back to the end of the forecast period at the weighted average cost of capital:

$$\text{Continuing value} = V_{op(at\ time\ N)} = \frac{FCF_{N+1}}{WACC - g} = \frac{FCF_N(1+g)}{WACC - g}$$

- The **free cash flow model** can be used to calculate the total value of a company by finding the value of operations plus the value of nonoperating assets.
- The estimate **value of equity** is the total value of the company minus the value of the debt and preferred stock. The intrinsic **price per share** is the total value of the equity divided by the number of shares.

QUESTIONS

(7-1) Define each of the following terms:

a. Proxy; proxy fight; preemptive right; classified stock; founders' shares

b. Estimated value ($\hat{P}_0$); market price (P_0)

c. Required rate of return, r_s; expected rate of return, $\hat{r}_s$; actual, or realized, rate of return, $\bar{r}_s$
d. Capital gains yield; dividend yield; expected total return
e. Constant growth; nonconstant growth; zero growth stock
f. Preferred stock
g. Nonoperating assets
h. Value of operations; horizon value; free cash flow valuation model

(7-2) Two investors are evaluating General Electric's stock for possible purchase. They agree on the expected value of D_1 and also on the expected future dividend growth rate. Further, they agree on the risk of the stock. However, one investor normally holds stocks for 2 years and the other normally holds stocks for 10 years. On the basis of the type of analysis done in this chapter, they should both be willing to pay the same price for General Electric's stock. True or false? Explain.

(7-3) A bond that pays interest forever and has no maturity date is a perpetual bond, also called a perpetuity or a consol. In what respect is a perpetual bond similar to (1) a no-growth common stock and (2) a share of preferred stock?

(7-4) Explain how to use the corporate valuation model to find the price per share of common equity.

SELF-TEST PROBLEMS Solutions Appear in Appendix A

(ST-1) Constant Growth Stock Valuation

Ewald Company's current stock price is \$36, and its last dividend was \$2.40. In view of Ewald's strong financial position and its consequent low risk, its required rate of return is only 12%. If dividends are expected to grow at a constant rate g in the future, and if r_s is expected to remain at 12%, then what is Ewald's expected stock price 5 years from now?

(ST-2) Nonconstant Growth Stock Valuation

Snyder Computer Chips Inc. is experiencing a period of rapid growth. Earnings and dividends are expected to grow at a rate of 15% during the next 2 years, at 13% in the third year, and at a constant rate of 6% thereafter. Snyder's last dividend was \$1.15, and the required rate of return on the stock is 12%.

a. Calculate the value of the stock today.
b. Calculate $\hat{P}_1$ and $\hat{P}_2$.
c. Calculate the dividend yield and capital gains yield for Years 1, 2, and 3.

(ST-3) Free Cash Flow Valuation Model

Watkins Inc. has never paid a dividend, and when the firm might begin paying dividends is not known. Its current free cash flow is \$100,000, and this FCF is expected to grow at a constant 7% rate. The weighted average cost of capital is WACC = 11%. Watkins currently holds \$325,000 of nonoperating marketable securities. Its long-term debt is \$1,000,000, but it has never issued preferred stock. Watkins has 50,000 shares of stock outstanding.

a. Calculate Watkins's value of operations.
b. Calculate the company's total value.
c. Calculate the estimated value of common equity.
d. Calculate the estimated per share stock price.

PROBLEMS Answers Appear in Appendix B

Easy Problems 1–7

(7-1) DPS Calculation Thress Industries just paid a dividend of $1.50 a share (i.e., D_0 = $1.50). The dividend is expected to grow 5% a year for the next 3 years and then 10% a year thereafter. What is the expected dividend per share for each of the next 5 years?

(7-2) Constant Growth Valuation Boehm Incorporated is expected to pay a $1.50 per share dividend at the end of this year (i.e., D_1 = $1.50). The dividend is expected to grow at a constant rate of 6% a year. The required rate of return on the stock, r_s, is 13%. What is the estimated value per share of Boehm's stock?

(7-3) Constant Growth Valuation Woidtke Manufacturing's stock currently sells for $22 a share. The stock just paid a dividend of $1.20 a share (i.e., D_0 = $1.20), and the dividend is expected to grow forever at a constant rate of 10% a year. What stock price is expected 1 year from now? What is the estimated required rate of return on Woidtke's stock (assume the market is in equilibrium with the required return equal to the expected return)?

(7-4) Preferred Stock Valuation Nick's Enchiladas Incorporated has preferred stock outstanding that pays a dividend of $5 at the end of each year. The preferred sells for $50 a share. What is the stock's required rate of return (assume the market is in equilibrium with the required return equal to the expected return)?

(7-5) Nonconstant Growth Valuation A company currently pays a dividend of $2 per share ($D_0$ = $2). It is estimated that the company's dividend will grow at a rate of 20% per year for the next 2 years, and then at a constant rate of 7% thereafter. The company's stock has a beta of 1.2, the risk-free rate is 7.5%, and the market risk premium is 4%. What is your estimate of the stock's current price?

(7-6) Value of Operations of Constant Growth Firm EMC Corporation has never paid a dividend. Its current free cash flow of $400,000 is expected to grow at a constant rate of 5%. The weighted average cost of capital is WACC = 12%. Calculate EMC's estimated value of operations.

(7-7) Horizon Value Current and projected free cash flows for Radell Global Operations are shown below. Growth is expected to be constant after 2015, and the weighted average cost of capital is 11%. What is the horizon (continuing) value at 2016 if growth from 2015 remains constant?

	Actual		Projected	
	2013	2014	2015	2016
Free cash flow (millions of dollars)	$606.82	$667.50	$707.55	$750.00

Intermediate Problems 8–17

(7-8) Constant Growth Rate, g A stock is trading at $80 per share. The stock is expected to have a year-end dividend of $4 per share ($D_1$ = $4), and it is expected to grow at some constant rate g throughout time. The stock's required rate of return is 14% (assume the market is in equilibrium with the required return equal to the expected return). What is your forecast of g?

(7-9) Constant Growth Valuation Crisp Cookware's common stock is expected to pay a dividend of $3 a share at the end of this year (D_1 = $3.00); its beta is 0.8; the risk-free rate is 5.2%; and the market risk premium is 6%. The dividend is expected to grow at some constant rate g, and the stock currently sells for $40 a share. Assuming the market is in equilibrium, what does the market believe will be the stock's price at the end of 3 years (i.e., what is $\hat{P}_3$)?

(7-10) Preferred Stock Rate of Return What is the required rate of return on a preferred stock with a \$50 par value, a stated annual dividend of 7% of par, and a current market price of (a) \$30, (b) \$40, (c) \$50, and (d) \$70 (assume the market is in equilibrium with the required return equal to the expected return)?

(7-11) Declining Growth Stock Valuation Brushy Mountain Mining Company's coal reserves are being depleted, so its sales are falling. Also, environmental costs increase each year, so its costs are rising. As a result, the company's earnings and dividends are declining at the constant rate of 4% per year. If D_0 = \$6 and r_s = 14%, what is the estimated value of Brushy Mountain's stock?

(7-12) Nonconstant Growth Stock Valuation Assume that the average firm in your company's industry is expected to grow at a constant rate of 6% and that its dividend yield is 7%. Your company is about as risky as the average firm in the industry, but it has just successfully completed some R&D work that leads you to expect that its earnings and dividends will grow at a rate of 50% [$D_1 = D_0(1 + g) = D_0(1.50)$] this year and 25% the following year, after which growth should return to the 6% industry average. If the last dividend paid (D_0) was \$1, what is the estimated value per share of your firm's stock?

(7-13) Nonconstant Growth Stock Valuation Simpkins Corporation does not pay any dividends because it is expanding rapidly and needs to retain all of its earnings. However, investors expect Simpkins to begin paying dividends, with the first dividend of \$0.50 coming 3 years from today. The dividend should grow rapidly—at a rate of 80% per year—during Years 4 and 5. After Year 5, the company should grow at a constant rate of 7% per year. If the required return on the stock is 16%, what is the value of the stock today (assume the market is in equilibrium with the required return equal to the expected return)?

(7-14) Preferred Stock Valuation Several years ago, Rolen Riders issued preferred stock with a stated annual dividend of 10% of its \$100 par value. Preferred stock of this type currently yields 8%. Assume dividends are paid annually.

a. What is the estimated value of Rolen's preferred stock?

b. Suppose interest rate levels have risen to the point where the preferred stock now yields 12%. What would be the new estimated value of Rolen's preferred stock?

(7-15) Return on Common Stock You buy a share of The Ludwig Corporation stock for \$21.40. You expect it to pay dividends of \$1.07, \$1.1449, and \$1.2250 in Years 1, 2, and 3, respectively, and you expect to sell it at a price of \$26.22 at the end of 3 years.

a. Calculate the growth rate in dividends.

b. Calculate the expected dividend yield.

c. Assuming that the calculated growth rate is expected to continue, you can add the dividend yield to the expected growth rate to obtain the expected total rate of return. What is this stock's expected total rate of return (assume the market is in equilibrium with the required return equal to the expected return)?

(7-16) Constant Growth Stock Valuation Investors require a 13% rate of return on Brooks Sisters's stock (r_s = 13%).

a. What would the estimated value of Brooks's stock be if the previous dividend were D_0 = \$3.00 and if investors expect dividends to grow at a constant annual rate of (1) −5%, (2) 0%, (3) 5%, and (4) 10%?

b. Using data from part a, what is the constant growth model's estimated value for Brooks Sisters's stock if the required rate of return is 13% and the expected growth rate is (1) 13% or (2) 15%? Are these reasonable results? Explain.

c. Is it reasonable to expect that a constant growth stock would have $g > r_s$?

(7-17) Value of Operations Kendra Enterprises has never paid a dividend. Free cash flow is projected to be \$80,000 and \$100,000 for the next 2 years, respectively; after the second year, FCF is expected to grow at a constant rate of 8%. The company's weighted average cost of capital is 12%.

a. What is the terminal, or horizon, value of operations? (*Hint:* Find the value of all free cash flows beyond Year 2 discounted back to Year 2.)
b. Calculate the value of Kendra's operations.

(7-18) Free Cash Flow Valuation

Dozier Corporation is a fast-growing supplier of office products. Analysts project the following free cash flows (FCFs) during the next 3 years, after which FCF is expected to grow at a constant 7% rate. Dozier's weighted average cost of capital is WACC = 13%.

	Year		
	1	2	3
Free cash flow ($ millions)	−$20	$30	$40

a. What is Dozier's terminal, or horizon, value? (*Hint:* Find the value of all free cash flows beyond Year 3 discounted back to Year 3.)
b. What is the current value of operations for Dozier?
c. Suppose Dozier has $10 million in marketable securities, $100 million in debt, and 10 million shares of stock. What is the intrinsic price per share?

Challenging Problems 19–21

(7-19) Constant Growth Stock Valuation

You are analyzing Jillian's Jewlery (JJ) stock for a possible purchase. JJ just paid a dividend of $1.50 *yesterday*. You expect the dividend to grow at the rate of 6% per year for the next 3 years; if you buy the stock, you plan to hold it for 3 years and then sell it.

a. What dividends do you expect for JJ stock over the next 3 years? In other words, calculate D_1, D_2, and D_3. Note that D_0 = $1.50.
b. JJ's stock has a required return of 13% and so this is the rate you'll use to discount dividends. Find the present value of the dividend stream; that is, calculate the PV of D_1, D_2, and D_3, and then sum these PVs.
c. JJ stock should trade for $27.05 3 years from now (i.e., you expect $\hat{P}_3$ = $27.05). Discounted at a 13% rate, what is the present value of this expected future stock price? In other words, calculate the PV of $27.05.
d. If you plan to buy the stock, hold it for 3 years, and then sell it for $27.05, what is the most you should pay for it?
e. Use the constant growth model to calculate the present value of this stock. Assume that g = 6% and is constant.
f. Is the value of this stock dependent on how long you plan to hold it? In other words, if your planned holding period were 2 years or 5 years rather than 3 years, would this affect the value of the stock today, $\hat{P}_0$? Explain your answer.

(7-20) Nonconstant Growth Stock Valuation

Reizenstein Technologies (RT) has just developed a solar panel capable of generating 200% more electricity than any solar panel currently on the market. As a result, RT is expected to experience a 15% annual growth rate for the next 5 years. By the end of 5 years, other firms will have developed comparable technology, and RT's growth rate will slow to 5% per year indefinitely. Stockholders require a return of 12% on RT's stock. The most recent annual dividend (D_0), which was paid yesterday, was $1.75 per share.

a. Calculate RT's expected dividends for t = 1, t = 2, t = 3, t = 4, and t = 5.
b. Calculate the estimated intrinsic value of the stock today, $\hat{P}_0$. Proceed by finding the present value of the dividends expected at t = 1, t = 2, t = 3, t = 4, and t = 5 plus the present value of the stock price that should exist at t = 5, $\hat{P}_5$. The $\hat{P}_5$ stock price can

be found by using the constant growth equation. Note that to find $\hat{P}_5$ you use the dividend expected at t = 6, which is 5% greater than the t = 5 dividend.

c. Calculate the expected dividend yield ($D_1/\hat{P}_0$), the capital gains yield expected during the first year, and the expected total return (dividend yield plus capital gains yield) during the first year. (Assume that $\hat{P}_0 = P_0$, and recognize that the capital gains yield is equal to the total return minus the dividend yield.) Also calculate these same three yields for t = 5 (e.g., $D_6/\hat{P}_5$).

(7-21) Nonconstant Growth Stock Valuation

Conroy Consulting Corporation (CCC) has been growing at a rate of 30% per year in recent years. This same nonconstant growth rate is expected to last for another 2 years ($g_{0,1} = g_{1,2} = 30\%$).

a. If $D_0 = \$2.50$, $r_s = 12\%$, and $g_L = 7\%$, then what is CCC's stock worth today? What are its expected dividend yield and capital gains yield at this time?

b. Now assume that CCC's period of nonconstant growth is to last another 5 years rather than 2 years ($g_{0,1} = g_{1,2} = g_{2,3} = g_{3,4} = g_{4,5} = 30\%$). How would this affect its price, dividend yield, and capital gains yield? Answer in words only.

c. What will CCC's dividend yield and capital gains yield be once its period of nonconstant growth ends? (*Hint:* These values will be the same regardless of whether you examine the case of 2 or 5 years of nonconstant growth, and the calculations are very easy.)

d. Of what interest to investors is the relationship over time between dividend yield and capital gains yield?

SPREADSHEET PROBLEMS

(7-22) Build a Model: Nonconstant Growth and Corporate Valuation

Start with the partial model in the file ***Ch07 P22 Build a Model.xls*** on the textbook's Web site. Hamilton Landscaping's dividend growth rate is expected to be 30% in the next year, drop to 15% from Year 1 to Year 2, and drop to a constant 5% for Year 2 and all subsequent years. Hamilton has just paid a dividend of \$2.50, and its stock has a required return of 11%.

resource

a. What is Hamilton's estimated stock price today?

b. If you bought the stock at Year 0, what are your expected dividend yield and capital gains for the upcoming year?

c. What are your expected dividend yield and capital gains for the second year (from Year 1 to Year 2)? Why aren't these the same as for the first year?

(7-23) Build a Model: Free Cash Flow Valuation Model

Start with the partial model in the file ***Ch07 P23 Build a Model.xls*** on the textbook's Web site. Selected data for the Derby Corporation are shown below. Use the data to answer the following questions.

resource

a. Calculate the estimated horizon value (i.e., the value of operations at the end of the forecast period immediately after the Year-4 free cash flow).

b. Calculate the present value of the horizon value, the present value of the free cash flows, and the estimated Year-0 value of operations.

c. Calculate the estimated Year-0 price per share of common equity.

INPUTS (In Millions)	Year				
	Current	Projected			
	0	1	2	3	4
Free cash flow		−$20.0	$20.0	$80.0	$84.0
Marketable securities	$40				
Notes payable	$100				
Long-term bonds	$300				
Preferred stock	$50				
WACC	9.00%				
Number of shares of stock	40				

THOMSON ONE Business School Edition Problem

THOMSON REUTERS

Use the Thomson ONE—Business School Edition online database to work this chapter's questions.

Estimating ExxonMobil's Intrinsic Stock Value with Thomson ONE—Business School Edition

In this chapter we described the various factors that influence stock prices and the approaches analysts use to estimate a stock's intrinsic value. By comparing these intrinsic value estimates to the current price, an investor can assess whether it makes sense to buy or sell a particular stock. Stocks trading at a price far below their estimated intrinsic values may be good candidates for purchase, whereas stocks trading at prices far in excess of their intrinsic value may be good stocks to avoid or sell.

Although estimating a stock's intrinsic value is a complex exercise that requires reliable data and good judgment, we can use the data available in Thomson ONE to arrive at a quick "back of the envelope" calculation of intrinsic value.

Thomson ONE—BSE Discussion Questions

1. For the purposes of this exercise, let's take a closer look at the stock of ExxonMobil Corporation (XOM). Looking at the Company Overview, we can immediately see the company's current stock price and its performance relative to the overall market in recent months. What is ExxonMobil's current stock price? How has the stock performed relative to the market over the past few months?
2. Click on the "News" tab to see the recent news stories for the company. Have there been any recent events affecting the company's stock price, or have things been relatively quiet?
3. To provide a starting point for gauging a company's relative valuation, analysts often look at a company's price-to-earnings (P/E) ratio. Returning to the Company Overview page, you can see XOM's current P/E ratio. To put this number in perspective, it is useful to compare this ratio with other companies in the same industry and to take a look at how this ratio has changed over time. If you want to see how XOM's P/E ratio stacks up to its peers, click on the tab labeled Comparables, then select Key Financial Ratios.

Toward the bottom of the table you should see information on the P/E ratio in the section titled Market Value Ratios. Toward the top, you should see an item that says Click Here To Select New Peer Set—do this if you want to compare XOM to a different set of firms.

For the most part, is XOM's P/E ratio above or below that of its peers? Off the top of your head, can these factors explain why XOM's P/E ratio differs from its peers?

4. To see how XOM's P/E ratio has varied over time, return to the Company Overview page. Next click Financials—Growth Ratios and then select Worldscope—Income Statement Ratios. Is XOM's current P/E ratio well above or well below its historical average? If so, do you have any explanation for why the current P/E deviates from its historical trend? On the basis of this information, does XOM's current P/E suggest that the stock is undervalued or overvalued? Explain.
5. In the text, we discussed using the dividend growth model to estimate a stock's intrinsic value. To keep things as simple as possible, let's assume at first that XOM's dividend is expected to grow at some constant rate over time. Then its intrinsic value would equal D_1 / (r_s − g), where D_1 is the expected annual dividend 1 year from now, r_s is the stock's required rate of return, and g is the dividend's constant growth rate. To estimate the dividend growth rate, it's helpful first to look at XOM's dividend history. Staying on the current Web page (Worldscope—Income Statement Ratios), you should immediately find the company's annual dividend for the past several years. On the basis of this information, what has been the average annual dividend growth rate? Another way to obtain estimates of dividend growth rates is to look at analysts' forecasts for future dividends, which can be found on the Estimates tab, which should bring up the Thomson Estimated Tearsheet. Scrolling down the page, you should see an area marked Consensus Estimates; select Thomson Forecast Reports and a tab under Available Measures. Here you click on the down arrow key and select Dividends Per Share (DPS). What is the median year-end dividend forecast? You can use this as an estimate of D_1 in your measure of intrinsic value. You can also use this forecast along with the historical data to arrive at a measure of the forecasted dividend growth rate, g.
6. The required return on equity, r_s, is the final input needed to estimate intrinsic value. For our purposes you can either assume a number (say, 8% or 9%) or use the CAPM to calculate an estimated cost of equity using the data available in Thomson ONE. (For more details, see the Thomson ONE exercise for Chapter 6.) Having decided on your best estimates for D_1, r_s, and g, you can then calculate XOM's intrinsic value. How does this estimate compare with the current stock price? Does your preliminary analysis suggest that XOM is undervalued or overvalued? Explain.
7. Often it is useful to perform a sensitivity analysis, in which you show how your estimate of intrinsic value varies according to different estimates of D_1, r_s, and g. To do so, recalculate your intrinsic value estimate for a range of different estimates for each of these key inputs. One convenient way to do this is to set up a simple data table in *Excel*. Refer to the *Excel* tutorial accessed through the textbook's Web site for instructions on data tables. On the basis of this analysis, what inputs justify the current stock price?
8. On the basis of the dividend history you uncovered in question 5 and your assessment of XOM's future dividend payout policies, do you think it is reasonable to assume that the constant growth model is a good proxy for intrinsic value? If not, how would you use the available data in Thomson ONE to estimate intrinsic value using the nonconstant growth model?

9. Finally, you can also use the information in Thomson ONE to value the entire corporation. This approach requires that you estimate XOM's annual free cash flows. Once you estimate the value of the entire corporation, you subtract the value of debt and preferred stock to arrive at an estimate of the company's equity value. Divide this number by the number of shares of common stock outstanding, which yields an alternative estimate of the stock's intrinsic value. This approach may take some more time and involve more judgment concerning forecasts of future free cash flows, but you can use the financial statements and growth forecasts in Thomson ONE as useful starting points. Go to Worldscope's Cash Flow Ratios Report (which you find by clicking on Financials, Fundamental Ratios, and Worldscope Ratios) to find an estimate of "free cash flow per share." Although this number is useful, Worldscope's definition of free cash flow subtracts out dividends per share; therefore, to make it comparable to the measure used in this text, you must add back dividends. To see Worldscope's definition of free cash flow (or any term), click on Search For Companies from the left toolbar and then select the Advanced Search tab. In the middle of your screen, on the right-hand side, you will see a dialog box with terms. Use the down arrow to scroll through the terms, highlighting the term for which you would like to see a definition. Then, click on the Definition button immediately below the dialog box.

MINI CASE

Your employer, a mid-sized human resources management company, is considering expansion into related fields, including the acquisition of Temp Force Company, an employment agency that supplies word processor operators and computer programmers to businesses with temporary heavy workloads. Your employer is also considering the purchase of a Biggerstaff & Biggerstaff (B&B), a privately held company owned by two brothers, each with 5 million shares of stock. B&B currently has free cash flow of $24 million, which is expected to grow at a constant rate of 5%. B&B's financial statements report marketable securities of $100 million, debt of $200 million, and preferred stock of $50 million. B&B's WACC is 11%. Answer the following questions.

a. Describe briefly the legal rights and privileges of common stockholders.
b. (1) Write out a formula that can be used to value any stock, regardless of its dividend pattern.
   (2) What is a constant growth stock? How are constant growth stocks valued?
   (3) What happens if a company has a constant g that exceeds its r_s? Will many stocks have expected $g > r_s$ in the short run (i.e., for the next few years)? In the long run (i.e., forever)?
c. Assume that Temp Force has a beta coefficient of 1.2, that the risk-free rate (the yield on T-bonds) is 7.0%, and that the market risk premium is 5%. What is the required rate of return on the firm's stock?
d. Assume that Temp Force is a constant growth company whose last dividend (D_0, which was paid yesterday) was $2.00 and whose dividend is expected to grow indefinitely at a 6% rate.
   (1) What is the firm's current estimated intrinsic stock price?
   (2) What is the stock's expected value 1 year from now?
   (3) What are the expected dividend yield, the expected capital gains yield, and the expected total return during the first year?

e. Suppose Temp Force's stock price is selling for $30.29. Is the stock price based more on long-term or short-term expectations? Answer this by finding the percentage of Temp Force's current stock price that is based on dividends expected during Years 1, 2, and 3.
f. Why are stock prices volatile? Using Temp Force as an example, what is the impact on the estimated stock price if g falls to 5% or rises to 7%? If r_s changes to 12%% or to 14%?
g. Now assume that the stock is currently selling at $30.29. What is its expected rate of return?
h. Now assume that Temp Force's dividend is expected to experience nonconstant growth of 30% from Year 0 to Year 1, 25% from Year 1 to Year 2, and 15% from Year 2 to Year 3. After Year 3, dividends will grow at a constant rate of 6%. What is the stock's intrinsic value under these conditions? What are the expected dividend yield and capital gains yield during the first year? What are the expected dividend yield and capital gains yield during the fourth year (from Year 3 to Year 4)?
i. What is free cash flow (FCF)? What is the weighted average cost of capital? What is the free cash flow valuation model?
j. Use a pie chart to illustrate the sources that comprise a hypothetical company's total value. Using another pie chart, show the claims on a company's value. How is equity a residual claim?
k. Use B&B's data and the free cash flow valuation model to answer the following questions.
   (1) What is its estimated value of operations?
   (2) What is its estimated total corporate value?
   (3) What is its estimated intrinsic value of equity?
   (4) What is its estimated intrinsic stock price per share?
l. You have just learned that B&B has undertaken a major expansion that will change its expected free cash flows to −$10 million in 1 year, $20 million in 2 years, and $35 million in 3 years. After 3 years, free cash flow will grow at a rate of 5%. No new debt or preferred stock was added; the investment was financed by equity from the owners. Assume the WACC is unchanged at 11% and that there are still 10 million shares of stock outstanding.
   (1) What is the company's horizon value (i.e., its value of operations at Year 3)? What is its current value of operations (i.e., at Time 0)?
   (2) What is its estimated intrinsic value of equity on a price-per-share basis?
m. Compare and contrast the free cash flow valuation model and the dividend growth model.
n. What is market multiple analysis?
o. What is preferred stock? Suppose a share of preferred stock pays a dividend of $2.10 and investors require a return of 7%. What is the estimated value of the preferred stock?

SELECTED ADDITIONAL CASES

The following cases from CengageCompose cover many of the concepts discussed in this chapter and are available at **compose.cengage.com**.

Klein-Brigham Series:
Case 3, "Peachtree Securities, Inc. (B)"; Case 71, "Swan Davis"; Case 78, "Beatrice Peabody"; and Case 101, "TECO Energy."
Brigham-Buzzard Series:
Case 4, "Powerline Network Corporation (Stocks)."

© lulu/fotolia.com

PART 4

Projects and Their Valuation

CHAPTER 9
The Cost of Capital 357

CHAPTER 10
The Basics of Capital Budgeting: Evaluating Cash Flows 397

CHAPTER 11
Cash Flow Estimation and Risk Analysis 437

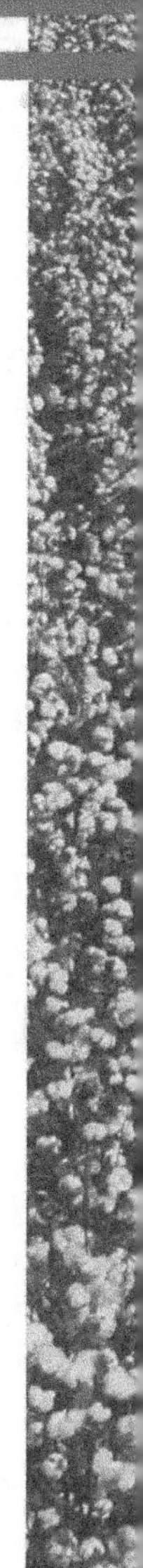

© Adalberto Rios Szalay/Sexto Sol/Getty Images

CHAPTER 9

The Cost of Capital

When companies consider investing in new projects, the cost of capital plays a major role. Sunny Delight Beverage Co. is making big investments to upgrade its juice factories, but would this happen if low interest rates had not driven down the cost of capital? According to CEO Billy Cyr, "When the cost of capital goes up, it is harder to justify an equipment purchase." The opposite is true when the cost of capital goes down.

Among its businesses, Phoenix Stamping Group LLC produces components for equipment used in agriculture and transportation. After modernizing two factories, Phoenix President Brandyn Chapman said, "The cost of capital certainly helps that decision."

For these and many other companies, the historically low cost of capital is making possible major investments in machinery, equipment, and technology. Many of these investments are designed to increase productivity, which will lead to lower prices for consumers and higher cash flows for shareholders. On the other hand, productivity gains mean not as many employees are needed to run the business.

Think about these issues as you read this chapter.

Source: **Adapted from Timothy Aeppel, "Man vs. Machine, a Jobless Recovery—Companies Are Spending to Upgrade Factories but Hiring Lags; Robots Pump Out Sunny Delight,"** ***The Wall Street Journal,*** **January 17, 2012, B1.**

Corporate Valuation and the Cost of Capital

© Rob Webb/Getty Images

In Chapter 1, we told you that managers should strive to make their firms more valuable and that the value of a firm is determined by the size, timing, and risk of its free cash flows (FCF). Indeed, a firm's intrinsic value is estimated as the present value of its FCFs, discounted at the weighted average cost of capital (WACC). In previous chapters, we examined the major sources of financing (stocks, bonds, and preferred stock) and the costs of those instruments. In this chapter, we put those pieces together and estimate the WACC that is used to determine intrinsic value.

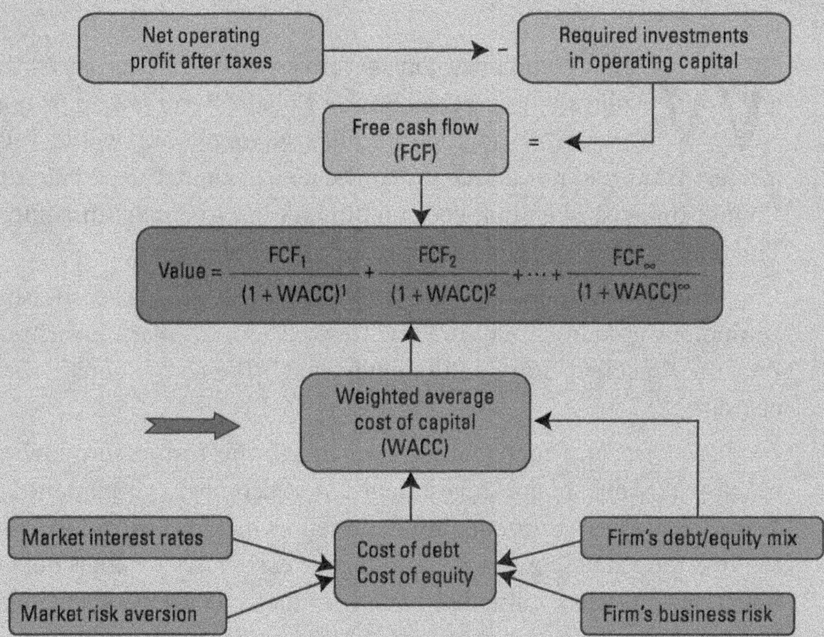

© Cengage Learning 2014

resource

The textbook's Web site contains an Excel file that will guide you through the chapter's calculations. The file for this chapter is ***Ch09 Tool Kit.xls****, and we encourage you to open the file and follow along as you read the chapter.*

Businesses require capital to develop new products, build factories and distribution centers, install information technology, expand internationally, and acquire other companies. For each of these actions, a company must estimate the total investment required and then decide whether the expected rate of return exceeds the cost of the capital. The cost of capital is also a factor in compensation plans, with bonuses dependent on whether the company's return on invested capital exceeds the cost of that capital. This cost is also a key factor in choosing the firm's mixture of debt and equity and in decisions to lease rather than buy assets. As these examples illustrate, the cost of capital is a critical element in many business decisions.[1]

[1]The cost of capital is also an important factor in the regulation of electric, gas, and water companies. These utilities are natural monopolies in the sense that one firm can supply service at a lower cost than could two or more firms. Because it has a monopoly, an unregulated electric or water company could exploit its customers. Therefore, regulators (1) determine the cost of the capital investors have provided the utility and then (2) set rates designed to permit the company to earn its cost of capital, no more and no less.

9-1 The Weighted Average Cost of Capital

The value of a company's operations is the present value of the expected free cash flows (FCF) discounted at the weighted average cost of capital (WACC):

$$V_{op} = \sum_{t=1}^{\infty} \frac{FCF_t}{(1 + WACC)^t} \quad (9\text{-}1)$$

We defined free cash flows (FCF) in Chapter 2, explained how to find present values in Chapter 4, and used the valuation equation in Chapter 7. Now we define the **weighted average cost of capital (WACC)**:

$$WACC = w_d r_d (1 - T) + w_{std} r_{std} (1 - T) + w_{ps} r_{ps} + w_s r_s \quad (9\text{-}2)$$

Some of these variables should be familiar to you from previous chapters, but some are new. All are defined as follows:

r_d = Coupon rate on new long-term debt being issued by the firm. Recall from Chapter 5 that r_d is the required return on a bond; for previously issued bonds, r_d, is equal to the bond's yield to maturity.

T = The firm's effective marginal tax rate.

r_{std} = Interest rate on short-term debt, such as notes payable.

r_{ps} = Required return on preferred stock, as defined in Chapter 7.

r_s = Required return on common stock, as defined in Chapter 7.

w = w_d, w_{std}, w_{ps}, and w_s, = weights of long-term debt, short-term debt, preferred stock, and common stock in the firm's target capital structure. The weights are the percentages of the different sources of capital the firm plans to use on a regular basis, with the percentages based on the market values of those sources of capital in the target capital structure.

In the following sections we explain how to estimate the WACC of a specific company, MicroDrive, Inc., but let's begin with a few general concepts. First, companies are financed by several sources of investor-supplied capital, which are called **capital components**. We have included short-term debt and preferred stock because some companies use them as sources of funding, but most companies only use two major sources of investor-supplied capital, long-term debt, and common stock.

Second, investors providing the capital components require rates of return (r_d, r_{std}, r_{ps}, and r_s) commensurate with the risks of the components in order to induce them to make the investments. Previous chapters defined those required returns from an investor's view, but those returns are costs from a company's viewpoint. This is why we call the WACC a *cost* of capital.

Third, recall that FCF is the cash flow available for distribution to all investors. Therefore, the free cash flows must provide an overall rate of return sufficient to compensate investors for their exposure to risk. Intuitively, it makes sense that this overall return should be a weighted average of the capital components' required returns. This intuition is confirmed by applying algebra to the definitions of required returns, free cash flow, and the value of operations: The discount rate used in Equation 9-1 is equal to the WACC as defined in Equation 9-2. In other words, the correct rate for estimating the present value of a company's (or project's) cash flows is the *weighted* average cost of capital.

SELF-TEST

Identify a firm's major capital structure components and give the symbols for their respective costs and weights.

What is a component cost?

9-2 Choosing Weights for the Weighted Average Cost of Capital

Figure 9-1 selected data for MicroDrive, Inc., including: (1) liabilities and equity (L&E) from the balance sheets; (2) percentages of total L&E comprised by each liability or equity account; (3) book values (as reported on the balance sheets) and percentages of financing from investor-supplied capital; (4) current market values and percentages of financing from investor-supplied capital; and (5) target capital structure weights.

Notice that we exclude accounts payable and accruals from capital structure weights. Capital is provided by *investors*—interest-bearing debt, preferred stock, and common equity. Accounts payable and accruals arise from operating decisions, not from financing decisions. Recall that the impact of payables and accruals is incorporated into a firm's free cash flows and a project's cash flows rather than into the cost of capital. Therefore, we consider only investor-supplied capital when discussing capital structure weights.

Figure 9-1 reports percentages of financing based on book values, market values, and target weights. Book values are a record of the cumulative amounts of capital supplied by investors over the life of the company. For equity, stockholders have supplied capital directly when MicroDrive issued stock, but they have also supplied capital indirectly when MicroDrive retained earnings instead of paying bigger dividends. The WACC is used to find the present value of *future* cash flows, so it would be inconsistent to use weights based on the *past* history of the company.

Stock prices are volatile, so current market values of total common equity often change dramatically from day to day. Companies certainly don't try to maintain the weights in their capital structures daily by issuing stock, repurchasing stock, issuing debt, or repaying debt in response to changes in their stock price. Therefore, the capital structure weights based on the current market values might not be a good estimate of the capital structure that the company will have on average during the future.

The target capital structure is defined as the average capital structure weights (based on market values) that a company will have during the future. MicroDrive has chosen a target capital structure composed of 2% short-term debt, 28% long-term debt, 3% preferred stock, and 67% common equity. MicroDrive presently has more debt in its actual capital structure (using either book values or market values), but it intends to move towards its target capital structure in the near future. We explain how firms choose their capital structures in Chapter 15, but for now just accept the given target weights for MicroDrive.

The following sections explain how to estimate the required returns for the capital structure components.

FIGURE 9-1

MicroDrive, Inc.: Selected Capital Structure Data (Millions of Dollars, December 31, 2013)

	A	B	C	D	E	F	G	H	I	J
30					Investor-Supplied Capital					
31					Book		Market		Target	
32				Percent	Book	Percent	Market	Percent	Capital	
33	*Liabilities and Equity*			of Total	Value	of Total	Value	of Total	Structure	
34	Accounts payable		$ 200	5.6%						
35	Notes payable		280	7.9%	$ 280	9.2%	$ 280	9.9%	w_{std} =	2%
36	Accruals		300	8.5%						
37	Total C.L.		$ 780	22.0%						
38	Long-term debt		1,200	33.8%	1,200	39.3%	1,200	42.4%	w_d =	28%
39	Total liabilities		$1,980	55.8%						
40	Preferred stock		100	2.8%	100	3.3%	100	3.5%	w_{ps} =	3%
41	Common stock		500	14.1%						
42	Retained earnings		970	27.3%						
43	Total common equity		$1,470	41.4%	$1,470	48.2%	$1,250	44.2%	w_s =	67%
44	Total L&E		$3,550	100.0%	$3,050	100.0%	$2,830	100.0%		100%
45										
46	Other Data (Millions, except per share data):									
47	Number of common shares outstanding =				50					
48	Price per share of common stock =				$25.00					
49	Number of preferred shares outstanding =				1					
50	Price per share of preferred stock =				$100.00					

Notes:

1. The market value of the notes payable is equal to the book value. Some of the long-term bonds sell at a discount and some sell at a premium, but their aggregate market value is approximately equal to their aggregate book value.
2. The common stock price is $25 per share. There are 50 million shares outstanding, for a total market value of equity of $25(50) = $1,250 million.
3. The preferred stock price is $100 per share. There are 1 million shares outstanding, for a total market value of preferred stock of $100(1) = $100 million.

SELF-TEST

What is a target capital structure?

9-3 After-Tax Cost of Debt: $r_d(1 - T)$ and $r_{std}(1 - T)$

The first step in estimating the cost of debt is to determine the rate of return lenders require.

9-3a The Before-Tax Cost of Short-Term Debt: r_{std}

Short-term debt should be included in the capital structure only if it is a permanent source of financing in the sense that the company plans to continually repay and refinance the short-term debt. This is the case for MicroDrive, whose bankers charge 10% on notes payable. Therefore, MicroDrive's short-term lenders have a required return of r_{std} = 10%, which is MicroDrive's before-tax cost of short-term debt.

Some large companies use commercial paper as a source of short-term financing. We discuss this in Chapter 16.

9-3b The Before-Tax Cost of Long-Term Debt: r_d

For long-term debt, estimating r_d is conceptually straightforward, but some problems arise in practice. Companies use both fixed- and floating-rate debt, both straight and convertible debt, both long- and short-term debt, as well as debt with and without sinking funds. Each type of debt may have a somewhat different cost.

It is unlikely that the financial manager will know at the beginning of a planning period the exact types and amounts of debt that will be used during the period. The type or types used will depend on the specific assets to be financed and on capital market conditions as they develop over time. Even so, the financial manager does know what types of debt are typical for his firm. For example, MicroDrive typically issues 15-year bonds to raise long-term debt used to help finance its capital budgeting projects. Because the WACC is used primarily in capital budgeting, MicroDrive's treasurer uses the cost of 15-year bonds in her WACC estimate.

Assume that it is January 2014 and that MicroDrive's treasurer is estimating the WACC for the coming year. How should she calculate the component cost of debt? Most financial managers begin by discussing current and prospective interest rates with their investment bankers. Assume MicroDrive's bankers believe that a new, 15-year, noncallable, straight bond issue would require a 9% coupon rate with semiannual payments. It can be offered to the public at its $1,000 par value. Therefore, their estimate of r_d is 9%.[2]

Note that 9% is the cost of **new**, or **marginal, debt**, and it will probably not be the same as the average rate on MicroDrive's previously issued debt, which is called the **historical**, or **embedded, rate**. The embedded cost is important for some decisions but not for others. For example, the average cost of all the capital raised in the past and still outstanding is used by regulators when they determine the rate of return that a public utility should be allowed to earn. However, in financial management the WACC is used primarily to make investment decisions, and these decisions hinge on projects' expected future returns versus the cost of the new, or marginal, capital that will be used to finance those projects. *Thus, for our purposes, the relevant cost is the marginal cost of new debt to be raised during the planning period.*

MicroDrive has issued debt in the past and the bonds are publicly traded. The financial staff can use the market price of the bonds to find the yield to maturity (or yield to call, if the bonds sell at a premium and are likely to be called). This yield is the rate of return that current bondholders expect to receive, and it is also a good estimate of r_d, the rate of return that new bondholders will require.

MicroDrive's outstanding bonds were recently issued and have a 9% coupon, paid semiannually. The bonds mature in 15 years and have a par value of $1,000. These bonds are trading at $1,000. We can find the yield to maturity by using a financial calculator with these inputs: N = 30, PV = −1000, PMT = 45, and FV = 1000. Solving for the rate, we find I/YR = 4.5%. This is a semiannual periodic rate, so the nominal annual rate is 9.0%. This is consistent with the investment bankers' estimated rate, so 9% is a reasonable estimate for r_d.

[2]Because it is a semiannual bond, the effective annual rate is $(1 + 0.09/2)^2 - 1 = 9.2\%$, but MicroDrive and most other companies use nominal rates for all component costs.

MicroDrive's outstanding bonds are trading at par, so the yield is equal to the coupon rate. But consider a hypothetical example for which the market price isn't par but instead is \$923.14. We can find the yield to maturity by using a financial calculator with these inputs: N = 30, PV = −923.14, PMT = 45, and FV = 1000. Solving for the rate, we find I/YR = 5%, which implies a hypothetical nominal annual rate of 10%. As this hypothetical example illustrates, it is not necessary for the bond to trade at par in order to estimate the cost of debt.

Even if MicroDrive had no publicly traded debt, its staff could still look at the yields on publicly traded debt of similar firms for a reasonable estimate of r_d.

Be alert to situations in which there is a significant probability that the company will default on its debt. In such a case, the yield to maturity (whether calculated from market prices of an outstanding bond or taken as the coupon rate on a newly issued bond) overstates the investor's expected return and hence the company's expected cost. For example, let's reconsider MicroDrive's 15-year semiannual bonds that can be issued at par if the coupon rate is 9%. As shown previously, the nominal annual yield to maturity is 9%. But suppose investors believe there is a significant chance that MicroDrive will default. To keep the example simple, suppose investors believe that the bonds will default in 14 years and that the recovery rate on the par value will be 70%. Here are the new inputs: N = 2(14) = 28, PV = −1000, PMT = 45, and FV = 0.70(1000) = 700. Solving for the rate, we find I/YR = 3.9%, implying an annual expected return of 7.8%. This is an extremely simple example, but it illustrates that the expected return on a bond is less than the yield to maturity as it is normally calculated. For bonds with a relatively low expected default rate, we recommend using the yield to maturity. But for bonds with high expected default rates, it would be necessary to do a scenario analysis (such as the one in Section 6.2) to estimate the bond's expected return.

9-3c The After-Tax Cost of Debt: $r_d(1 - T)$ and $r_{std}(1 - T)$

The required return to debtholders, r_d, is not equal to the company's cost of debt because interest payments are deductible, which means the government in effect pays part of the total cost. As a result, the weighted average cost of capital is calculated using the **after-tax cost of debt**, $r_d(1 - T)$, which is the interest rate on debt, r_d, less the tax savings that result because interest is deductible. Here T is the firm's marginal tax rate.[3]

$$\begin{aligned}\text{After-tax component cost of debt} &= \text{Interest rate} - \text{Tax savings}\\ &= r_d - r_dT\\ &= r_d(1-T)\end{aligned} \tag{9-3}$$

If we assume that MicroDrive's marginal federal-plus-state tax rate is 40%, then its after-tax cost of debt is 5.4%:[4]

[3]The federal tax rate for most corporations is 35%. However, most corporations are also subject to state income taxes, so the marginal tax rate on most corporate income is about 40%. For illustrative purposes, we assume that the effective federal-plus-state tax rate on marginal income is 40%. The effective tax rate is *zero* for a firm with such large current or past losses that it does not pay taxes. In this situation, the after-tax cost of debt is equal to the pre-tax interest rate.

[4]Strictly speaking, the after-tax cost of debt should reflect the *expected* cost of debt. Although MicroDrive's bonds have a promised return of 9%, there is some chance of default and so its bondholders' expected return (and consequently MicroDrive's cost) is a bit less than 9%. However, for a relatively strong company such as MicroDrive, this difference is quite small.

How Effective Is the Effective Corporate Tax Rate?

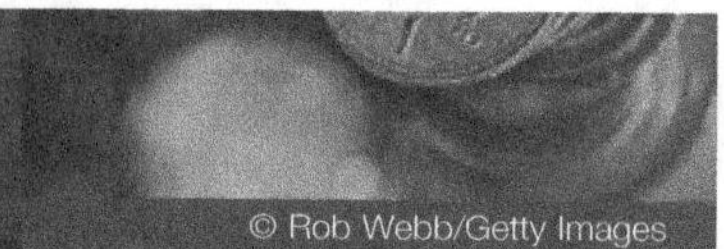

© Rob Webb/Getty Images

The statutory U.S. federal corporate tax rate is 35%. With Japan cutting its tax rate in 2012, U.S. corporations face the highest combined federal and state taxes in the world. Or do they? The following chart shows the actual federal corporate tax receipts as a percentage of domestic economic profits. Notice that the effective tax rate averaged around 25% for about 15 years after the tax reforms of 1986, but that it has gyrated wildly since 2000, dropping to an all-time low of 12.1% in 2011, probably due to temporary changes in the tax code made to stimulate the economy in response to the recession. International comparisons are difficult due to data availability and complexity (and due to the analysts' political leanings), but the average effective tax rate on corporations in developed countries usually is around 25%.

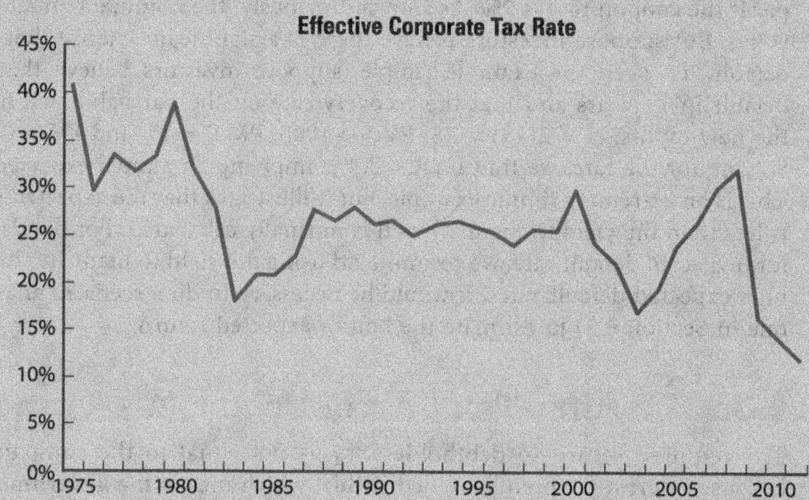

Source: Adapted from the Congressional Budget Office report on January 19, 2012, *The Budget and Economic Outlook: Fiscal Years 2012 to 2022*. To see the report, go to **www.cbo.gov/publication/42905**. To get the data in an *Excel* workbook, select Data Underlying Figures.

$$\begin{aligned} r_d(1-T) &= 9\%(1.0-0.4) \\ &= 9\%(0.6) \\ &= 5.4\% \end{aligned}$$

For MicroDrive's short-term debt, the after-tax cost is 6%: $r_{std}(1-T) = 10\%(1.0-0.4) = 6\%$.

9-3d Flotation Costs and the Cost of Debt

Most debt offerings have very low flotation costs, especially for privately placed debt. Because flotation costs are usually low, most analysts ignore them when estimating the after-tax cost of debt. However, the following example illustrates the procedure for incorporating flotation costs as well as their impact on the after-tax cost of debt.

Suppose MicroDrive can issue 30-year debt with an annual coupon rate of 9%, with coupons paid semiannually. The flotation costs, F, are equal to 1% of the value of the issue. Instead of finding the pre-tax yield based upon pre-tax cash flows and then adjusting it to reflect taxes, as we did before, we can find the after-tax, flotation-adjusted cost by using this formula:

$$M(1-F) = \sum_{t=1}^{N} \frac{INT(1-T)}{[1+r_d(1-T)]^t} + \frac{M}{[1+r_d(1-T)]^N} \quad (9\text{-}4)$$

Here M is the bond's maturity (or par) value, F is the **percentage flotation cost** (i.e., the percentage of proceeds paid to the investment bankers), N is the number of payments, T is the firm's tax rate, INT is the dollars of interest per period, and $r_d(1 - T)$ is the after-tax cost of debt adjusted for flotation costs. With a financial calculator, enter N = 60, PV = −1000(1 − 0.01) = −990, PMT = 45(1 − 0.40) = 27, and FV = 1000. Solving for I/YR, we find I/YR = $r_d(1 - T)$ = 2.73%, which is the semiannual after-tax component cost of debt. The nominal after-tax cost of debt is 5.46%. Note that this is quite close to the original 5.40% after-tax cost, so in this instance adjusting for flotation costs doesn't make much difference.[5]

However, the flotation adjustment would be higher if F were larger or if the bond's life were shorter. For example, if F were 10% rather than 1%, then the nominal annual flotation-adjusted $r_d(1 - T)$ would be 6.13%. With N at 1 year rather than 30 years and F still equal to 1%, the nominal annual $r_d(1 - T)$ = 6.45%. Finally, if F = 10% and N = 1, then the nominal annual $r_d(1 - T)$ = 16.67%. In all of these cases, the effect of flotation costs would be too large to ignore.

As an alternative to adjusting the cost of debt for flotation costs, in some situations it makes sense to instead adjust the project's cash flows. For example, **project financing** is a special situation in which a large project, such as an oil refinery, is financed with debt plus other securities that have a specific claim on the project's cash flows. This is different from the usual debt offering, in which the debt has a claim on all of the corporation's cash flows. Because project financing is funded by securities with claims tied to a particular project, the flotation costs can be included with the project's other cash flows when evaluating the project's value. However, project financing is relatively rare, so when we incorporate the impact of flotation costs, we usually do so by adjusting the component cost of the new debt.

SELF-TEST

Why is the after-tax cost of debt, rather than its before-tax cost, used to calculate the weighted average cost of capital?

Is the relevant cost of debt when calculating the WACC the interest rate on already outstanding debt or the rate on new debt? Why?

A company has outstanding long-term bonds with a face value of $1,000, a 10% coupon rate, 25 years remaining until maturity, and a current market value of $1,214.82. If it pays interest semiannually, then what is the nominal annual pre-tax cost of debt? ***(8%)*** If the company's tax rate is 40%, what is the after-tax cost of debt? **(4.8%)**

[5]Equation 9-4 produces the correct after-tax cost of debt only for bonds issued at par. For bonds with a price other than par, the after-tax cash flows must be adjusted to take into account the actual taxation of the discount or premium. See ***Web Extension 5A*** on the textbook's Web site for a discussion of the taxation of original issue discount bonds. Also, we ignored the tax shield due to amortization of flotation costs because it has very little effect on the cost of debt; see ***Ch09 Tool Kit.xls*** for an example that incorporates the amortization tax shield.

9-4 Cost of Preferred Stock, r_{ps}

Many firms (including MicroDrive) use, or plan to use, preferred stock as part of their financing mix. Preferred dividends are not tax deductible, so the company bears their full cost. Therefore, *no tax adjustment is used when calculating the cost of preferred stock.* Some preferred stocks are issued without a stated maturity date, but today most have a sinking fund that effectively limits their life. Finally, although it is not mandatory that preferred dividends be paid, firms generally have every intention of doing so, because otherwise (1) they cannot pay dividends on their common stock, (2) they will find it difficult to raise additional funds in the capital markets, and (3) in some cases preferred stockholders can take control of the firm.

The **component cost of preferred stock,** r_{ps}, is the cost used in the WACC calculation. For preferred stock with a stated maturity date, we use the same approach as in the previous section for the cost of debt, keeping in mind that a firm has no tax savings with preferred stock. For preferred stock without a stated maturity date, r_{ps} is

$$\text{Component cost of preferred stock} = r_{ps} = \frac{D_{ps}}{P_{ps}(1-F)} \quad (9\text{-}5)$$

Here D_{ps} is the preferred dividend, P_{ps} is the preferred stock price, and F is the flotation cost as a percentage of proceeds.

To illustrate the calculation, assume MicroDrive has preferred stock that pays an $8 dividend per share and sells for $100 per share. If MicroDrive issued new shares of preferred, then it would incur an underwriting (or flotation) cost of 2.5%, or $2.50 per share, so it would net $97.50 per share. Therefore, MicroDrive's cost of preferred stock is 8.2%:

$$r_{ps} = \$8/\$97.50 = 8.2\%$$

If we had not incorporated flotation costs, we would have incorrectly estimated $r_{ps} = \$8/\$100 = 8.0\%$, which is too big a difference to ignore. Therefore, analysts usually include flotation costs when estimating the firm's cost of preferred stock.

Although preferred stock is riskier than debt, MicroDrive's preferred stock has a lower return to investors than does its debt: 8% versus 9%. However, recall that most preferred stock is held by other companies, which are allowed to exclude 70% of preferred stocks' dividends from taxation. Thus, the after-tax return to these investors is higher for preferred stock than for debt, which is consistent with preferred stock being riskier than debt.

SELF-TEST

Does the component cost of preferred stock include or exclude flotation costs? Explain.

Why is no tax adjustment made to the cost of preferred stock?

A company's preferred stock currently trades for $50 per share and pays a $3 annual dividend. Flotation costs are equal to 3% of the gross proceeds. If the company issues preferred stock, what is the cost of that stock? **(6.19%)**

9-5 Cost of Common Stock: The Market Risk Premium, RP_M

Before addressing the required return for an individual stock, let's start with the big picture, which is the required return for the entire stock market. In other words, how much return do investors require to induce them to invest in stocks? It often is more convenient to focus on the extra return that investors require to induce them to invest in risky equities over and beyond the return on a Treasury bond. As Chapter 6 explained, this extra return is called the market risk premium, RP_M. Sometimes this is called the **equity risk premium**, or just the **equity premium**.

Unfortunately, the required return on the market, and hence the equity premium, is not directly observable. Three approaches may be used to estimate the market risk premium: (1) calculate historical premiums and use them to estimate the current premium; (2) survey experts; and (3) use the current value of the market to estimate forward-looking premiums. Following are descriptions of each approach.

9-5a Historical Risk Premium

Historical risk premium data for U.S. securities, updated annually, are available from many sources, including Ibbotson Associates.[6] Using data from 1926 through the most recent year, Ibbotson calculates the actual realized rate of return each year for the stock market and for long-term government bonds. Ibbotson defines the annual equity risk premium as the difference between the historical realized returns on stocks and the historical yields to maturity on long-term T-bonds.[7] Ibbotson recently reported a 6.6% arithmetic average historical risk premium.[8] How should these data be used?

First, stock returns are quite volatile, which leads to low statistical confidence in estimated averages. For example, the estimated historical average premium is 6.6%, but based on the market return's standard deviation of around 20%, the 95% confidence interval ranges about plus or minus 3% from 6.6%. In other words, the historical average is helpful in deciding whether the risk premium is on the order of 6% or 20%, but it isn't very helpful in deciding whether the premium should be 4% or 6%.

Second, the historical average is extremely sensitive to the period over which it is calculated. For example, we provide annual data for the period 1968–2011 in the file ***Ch09 Tool Kit.xls.*** For this period, the estimated historic risk premium is just 3.9%.

Third, changes in the risk premium can occur if investors' tolerance for risk changes. This causes problems in interpreting historical returns because a change in the required risk premium causes an *opposite change in the observed* premium. For example, an increase in the required premium means that investors have become more risk averse and require a higher return on stocks. But applying a higher discount rate to a stock's future cash flows causes a decline in stock price. Thus, an *increase* in the required premium causes a simultaneous *decrease* in the observed premium. Part of the market's precipitous decline in 2008 and 2009 surely was due to investors' increased risk aversion.

---

[6]See *Ibbotson Stocks, Bonds, Bills, and Inflation: 2012 Valuation Yearbook* (Chicago: Morningstar, Inc., 2012) for the most recent estimates.

[7]The risk premium should be defined using the yield on T-bonds. As a proxy for yield, Ibbotson uses the return on 20-year T-bonds that is due to coupons. This underestimates yield for discount bonds and overstates yield for premium bonds, but the error probably averages out to zero in most years.

[8]The arithmetic average often is used as an estimate of next year's risk premium; this is most appropriate if investor risk aversion had actually been constant during the sample period. On the other hand, the geometric average would be most appropriate to estimate the longer-term risk premium, say, for the next 20 years. The geometric average for this time period is 4.7%, which is less than the arithmetic average.

9-5b Surveys of Experts

What do the experts think about the market risk premium? Two professors at Duke University, John Graham and Campbell Harvey (working in conjunction with *CFO* magazine), have surveyed CFOs quarterly beginning in 2000.[9] One survey question asks CFOs what they expect the S&P 500 return to be over the next 10 years; the CFOs are also given the yield on a 10-year T-bond. Their average response in the March 2012 survey implied an average expected risk premium of about 4.35%.

Professor Fernando Fernandez of the IESE Business School regularly surveys professors, analysts, and companies.[10] For 2011, based on the average U.S. responses, professors recommend a premium of 5.7%, analysts recommend 5.0%, and companies recommend 5.5%.

In summary, in 2011–2012, experts predicted a premium within the range of about 4.35% to 5.7%.

9-5c Forward-Looking Risk Premiums

An alternative to the historical risk premium is the forward-looking, or ex ante, risk premium. As shown in Chapter 7, if we assume that the market dividend will grow at a constant rate and that the firms that make up the market pay out as dividends all the funds available for distribution (i.e., the firms make no stock repurchases or purchases of short-term investments), then the expected market rate of return, $\hat{r}_M$ is:

$$\hat{r}_M = \frac{D_1}{P_0} + g \tag{9-6}$$

If we also assume that the market is in equilibrium, then required return on the market, r_M, is equal to the expected return, $\hat{r}_M$, found by using Equation 9-6. Thus, the required return on the market can be estimated as the sum of the market's expected dividend yield plus the expected constant growth rate in dividends.

resource

*For current estimates, see instructions in **Ch09 Tool Kit.xls**.*

Simplified Illustration of Estimating a Forward-Looking Risk Premium

Following is an illustration for how to use Equation 9-6 to estimate the required return on the market. First, you need an estimate of the expected dividend. In April 2012, Standard & Poor's Web site reported a projected dividend yield of 2.16% for the S&P 500, based on declared dividends. Second, you need an estimate of the constant dividend growth rate, g. One approach is to use the historical average growth rate in dividends for the S&P 500, which is about 4.4% (for 1926–2011). Using these estimates produces an estimate of the required market return:

$$\begin{aligned} r_M = \hat{r}_M &= \frac{D_1}{P_0} + g \\ &= 2.16\% + 4.4\% \\ &= 6.56\% \end{aligned}$$

---

[9]See John Graham and Campbell Harvey, "The Equity Risk Premium in 2012," Working Paper, Duke University, 2012. For periodic updates, see Professor Graham's Web site, **http://faculty.fuqua.duke.edu/~jgraham/resume.html**, and look for the section on Permanent Working Papers.

[10]See Pablo Fernández, "Market Risk Premium Used in 56 Countries in 2011: A Survey with 6,014 Answers," at SSRN: **ssrn.com/abstract=1822192**.

At the time we estimated r_M, the 10-year T-bond yield was 2.19%. Using the previously estimated r_M of 6.56%, the estimated forward-looking market risk premium is:

$$RP_M = r_M - r_{RF}$$
$$= 6.56\% - 2.19\%$$
$$= 4.37\%$$

Complications When Estimating a Forward-Looking Risk Premium

We made numerous simplifying assumptions in the previous example regarding three complications that arise in practice. First, the growth rate in dividends probably will not be constant in the near future but might instead take many years before leveling out. Second, the historical average growth rate in dividends might not be a good estimate of the expected long-term dividend growth rate. Long-term growth in dividends is probably related to long-term sales and profits, which in turn depend on inflation (which affects reported dollar value of sales), population growth (which affects the unit volume of sales), and productivity (which affects profits). Third, the model is based on dividends per share, but it ignores the impact of stock repurchases on the number of outstanding shares (which then changes the growth rate of dividends per share).

Fortunately, there are ways to address these technical issues, including the use of a multistage growth model. The interested reader should see ***Web Extension 9A*** and the corresponding worksheet, ***Web 9A,*** in ***Ch9 Tool Kit.xls.***

9-5d Our View on the Market Risk Premium

After reading the previous sections, you might well be confused about the best way to estimate the market risk premium. Here's our opinion: The risk premium is driven primarily by investors' attitudes toward risk, and there are good reasons to believe that investors' risk aversion changes over time. The introduction of pension plans, Social Security, health insurance, and disability insurance over the last 50 years means that people today can take more chances with their investments, which should make them less risk averse. Moreover, many households have dual earners, allowing households to take more chances. Therefore, we think the risk premium is lower now than it was 50 years ago.

In our consulting, we currently (spring 2012) use a risk premium of about 5% to 6%, but we would have a hard time arguing with someone who used a risk premium anywhere in the range of 3% to 7%. We believe that investors' aversion to risk is relatively stable much of the time, but it is not absolutely constant from year to year and is certainly not constant during periods of great stress, such as during the 2008–2009 financial crisis. When stock prices are relatively high, investors feel less risk averse, so we use a risk premium at the low end of our range. Conversely, when prices are depressed, we use a premium at the high end of the range. The bottom line is that there is no way to prove that a particular risk premium is either right or wrong, though we'd be suspicious of an estimated market premium that is less than 3% or greater than 7%.

SELF-TEST

Explain both the historical and the forward-looking approaches to estimating the market risk premium.

9-6 Using the CAPM to Estimate the Cost of Common Stock, r_s

Before estimating the return required by MicroDrive's shareholders, r_s, it is worth considering the two ways that a company can raise common equity: (1) Sell newly issued shares to the public. (2) Reinvest (retain) earnings by not paying out all net income as dividends.

Does new equity capital raised by reinvesting earnings have a cost? The answer is a resounding "yes!" If earnings are reinvested, then stockholders will incur an **opportunity cost**—the earnings could have been paid out as dividends or used to repurchase stock, and in either case stockholders would have received funds that they could reinvest in other securities. *Thus, the firm should earn on its reinvested earnings at least as much as its stockholders could earn on alternative investments of equivalent risk.*

What rate of return could stockholders expect to earn on equivalent-risk investments? The answer is r_s, because they could presumably earn that return by simply buying the stock of the firm in question or that of a similar firm. *Therefore, r_s is the cost of common equity raised internally as reinvested earnings.* If a company can't earn at least r_s on reinvested earnings, then it should pass those earnings on to its stockholders as dividends and let them invest the money themselves in assets that do yield r_s.

9-6a The Capital Asset Pricing Model

To estimate the cost of common stock using the Capital Asset Pricing Model as discussed in Chapter 6, we proceed as follows.

1. Estimate the risk-free rate, r_{RF}.
2. Estimate the current market risk premium, RP_M, which is the required market return in excess of the risk-free rate.
3. Estimate the stock's beta coefficient, b_i, which measures the stock's relative risk. The subscript i signifies Stock i's beta.
4. Use these three values to estimate the stock's required rate of return:

$$r_s = r_{RF} + (RP_M)b_i \quad (9\text{-}7)$$

Equation 9-7 shows that the CAPM estimate of r_s begins with the risk-free rate, r_{RF}. We then add a risk premium that is equal to the risk premium on the market, RP_M, scaled up or down to reflect the particular stock's risk as measured by its beta coefficient. The following sections explain how to implement this four-step process.

9-6b Estimating the Risk-Free Rate, r_{RF}

The starting point for the CAPM cost-of-equity estimate is r_{RF}, the risk-free rate. There is no such thing as a truly riskless asset in the U.S. economy. Treasury securities are essentially free of default risk; however, nonindexed long-term T-bonds will suffer capital losses if interest rates rise, indexed long-term bonds will decline if the real rate rises, and a portfolio of short-term T-bills will provide a volatile earnings stream because the rate earned on T-bills varies over time.

WWW

To find the rate on a T-bond, go to **www.federalreserve.gov**. *Select "Economic Research & Data" and then select "Statistical Releases andHistorical Data." Click on "Daily" for "H.15: Selected Interest Rates."*

Because we cannot, in practice, find a truly riskless rate upon which to base the CAPM, what rate should we use? Keep in mind that our objective is to estimate the cost of capital, which will be used to discount a company's free cash flows or a project's cash flows. Free cash flows occur over the life of the company and many projects last for many years.

Because the cost of capital will be used to discount relatively long-term cash flows, it seems appropriate to use a relatively long-term risk-free rate, such as the yield on a 10-year Treasury bond. Indeed, a survey of highly regarded companies shows that about two-thirds of them use the rate on 10-year Treasury bonds.[11]

T-bond rates can be found in *The Wall Street Journal*, the *Federal Reserve Bulletin*, or on the Internet. Although most analysts use the yield on a 10-year T-bond as a proxy for the risk-free rate, yields on 20- or 30-year T-bonds are also reasonable proxies.

9-6c Estimating the Market Risk Premium, RP_M

We described three approaches for estimating the market risk premium, RP_M, in Section 9.5: (1) use historical averages, (2) survey experts, and (3) estimate forward-looking expected market returns. All three approaches provide estimates in the same ballpark, around 3% to 7%. The final choice really boils down to judgment informed by the current state of the market and the estimates provided by the three approaches. We will use a market risk premium of 6% in this example.

9-6d Estimating Beta, b_i

W W W

To find an estimate of beta, go to ***www.valueline.com*** *and then enter the ticker symbol for a stock quote. Or go to Thomson ONE—Business School Edition. Beta is shown in the Key Fundamentals section.*

Recall from Chapter 6 a stock's beta, b_i, can be estimated as:

$$b_i = \left(\frac{\sigma_i}{\sigma_M}\right)\rho_{iM} \tag{9-8}$$

where ρ_{iM} is the correlation between Stock i's return and the market return, σ_i is the standard deviation of Stock i's return, and σ_M is the standard deviation of the market's return. This definition is also equal to the estimated slope coefficient in a regression, with the company's stock returns on the y-axis and market returns on the x-axis.

It is easy to gather historical returns from the Web and then estimate your own beta, as we show in the Chapter 6 ***Tool Kit***. Also, many Web sources provide estimates of beta. The good news is that there is no shortage of beta estimates; the bad news is that many estimates differ from one another. We will discuss this in the next section.

9-6e An Illustration of the CAPM Approach: MicroDrive's Cost of Equity, r_s

Following is an application of the CAPM approach to MicroDrive. As estimated in Chapter 6, MicroDrive's beta, b_i, is 1.43. We assume that the market risk premium, RP_M, is about 6%. For this example, assume that the risk-free rate, r_{RF}, is 5%. Using Equation 9-7, we estimate MicroDrive's required return as about 13.6%:

$$\begin{aligned} r_s &= 5\% + (6\%)(1.43) \\ &= 5\% + 8.58\% \\ &= 13.58\% \approx 13.6\% \end{aligned}$$

[11]See Robert E. Bruner, Kenneth M. Eades, Robert S. Harris, and Robert C. Higgins, "Best Practices in Estimating the Cost of Capital: Survey and Synthesis," *Financial Practice and Education*, Spring/Summer 1998, pp. 13–28.

This estimate of 13.6% is a required return from an investor's point of view, but it is a cost of equity from a company's perspective.

Always keep in mind that the estimated cost of equity is indeed an estimate, for several reasons. First, the yield on any long-term T-bond would be an appropriate estimate of the risk-free rate, and different yields would lead to different estimates of r_s. Second, no one truly knows the correct market risk premium. We can narrow the estimated RP_M down to a fairly small range, but different estimates in this range would lead to different estimates of r_s. Third, estimates of beta are inexact. In addition to a large range of the confidence interval around an estimated beta, using slightly different time periods to estimate beta can lead to rather large differences in the estimated beta.

Still, in our judgment, it is possible to develop "reasonable" estimates of the required inputs, and we believe that the CAPM can be used to obtain reasonable estimates of the cost of equity. Indeed, despite the difficulties we have noted, surveys indicate that the CAPM is by far the most widely used method. Although most firms use more than one method, almost 74% of respondents in one survey (and 85% in another) used the CAPM.[12] This is in sharp contrast to a 1982 survey, which found that only 30% of respondents used the CAPM.[13]

SELF-TEST

What are the two primary sources of equity capital?

Explain why there is a cost to using reinvested earnings; that is, why aren't reinvested earnings a free source of capital?

Which is generally considered the more appropriate estimate of the risk-free rate: the yield on a short-term T-bill or the yield on a 10-year T-bond?

A company's beta is 1.4, the yield on a 10-year T-bond is 4%, and the market risk premium is 4.5%. What is r_s? **(10.3%)**

9-7 Dividend-Yield-Plus-Growth-Rate, or Discounted Cash Flow (DCF), Approach

In Chapter 7, we saw that if an investor expects dividends to grow at a constant rate and if the company makes all payouts in the form of dividends (the company does not repurchase stock), then the price of a stock can be found as follows:

$$\hat{P}_0 = \frac{D_1}{r_s - g} \tag{9-9}$$

[12]See John R. Graham and Campbell Harvey, "The Theory and Practice of Corporate Finance: Evidence from the Field," *Journal of Financial Economics,* 2001, pp. 187–243, and the paper cited in footnote 10. It is interesting that a growing number of firms (about 34%) also are using CAPM-type models with more than one factor. Of these firms, over 40% include factors for interest rate risk, foreign exchange risk, and business cycle risk (proxied by gross domestic product). More than 20% of these firms include a factor for inflation, size, and exposure to particular commodity prices. Less than 20% of these firms make adjustments due to distress factors, book-to-market ratios, or momentum factors.

[13]See Lawrence J. Gitman and Vincent Mercurio, "Cost of Capital Techniques Used by Major U.S. Firms: Survey Analysis of *Fortune's* 1000," *Financial Management,*1982, pp. 21–29.

Here $\hat{P}_0$ is the intrinsic value of the stock for the investor, D_1 is the dividend expected to be paid at the end of Year 1, g is the expected growth rate in dividends, and r_s is the required rate of return. For the marginal investor, the required return is equal to the expected return. If this investor is the marginal investor then $\hat{P}_0 = P_0$, the market price of the stock, and we can solve for r_s to obtain the required rate of return on common equity:

$$\hat{r}_s = r_s = \frac{D_1}{P_0} + \text{Expected g} \quad (9\text{-}10)$$

Thus, investors expect to receive a dividend yield, D_1/P_0, plus a capital gain, g, for a total expected return of $\hat{r}_s$. In equilibrium this expected return is also equal to the required return, r_s. This method of estimating the cost of equity is called the **discounted cash flow,** or **DCF, method.** Henceforth, we will assume that markets are at equilibrium (which means that $r_s = \hat{r}_s$), and this permits us to use the terms r_s and $\hat{r}_s$ interchangeably.

9-7a Estimating Inputs for the DCF Approach

Three inputs are required to use the DCF approach: the current stock price, the current dividend, and the marginal investor's expected dividend growth rate. The stock price and the dividend are easy to obtain, but the expected growth rate is difficult to estimate, as we will see in the following sections.

Historical Growth Rates

If earnings and dividend growth rates have been relatively stable in the past, and if investors expect these trends to continue, then the past realized growth rate may be used as an estimate of the expected future growth rate. Unfortunately, such situations occur only at a handful of very mature, slow-growing companies, which precludes the usefulness of historical growth rates as predictors of future growth rates for most companies.

Retention Growth Model

Most firms pay out some of their net income as dividends and reinvest, or retain, the rest. The more they retain, and the higher the earned rate of return on those retained earnings, the larger their growth rate. This is the idea behind the retention growth model.

The **payout ratio** is the percent of net income that the firm pays out in dividends, and the **retention ratio** is the complement of the payout ratio: Retention ratio = (1 − Payout ratio). To illustrate, consider Aldabra Corporation, a mature company. Aldabra's payout ratio has averaged 63% over the past 15 years, so its retention rate has averaged 1.0 − 0.63 = 0.37 = 37%. Also, Aldabra's return on equity (ROE) has averaged 14.5% over the past 15 years. We know that, other things held constant, the earnings growth rate depends on the amount of income the firm retains and the rate of return it earns on those retained earnings, and the **retention growth equation** can be expressed as follows:

$$g = \text{ROE}(\text{Retention ratio}) \quad (9\text{-}11)$$

Using Aldabra's 14.5% average ROE and its 37% retention rate, we can use Equation 9-11 to find the estimated g:

$$g = 14.5\%(0.37) = 5.365 \approx 5.4\%$$

Although easy to implement, this approach requires four major assumptions: (1) the payout rate, and thus the retention rate, remain constant; (2) the ROE on new investments remains constant and equal to the ROE on existing assets; (3) the firm is not expected to repurchase or issue new common stock, or, if it does, this new stock will be sold at a price equal to its book value; and (4) future projects are expected to have the same degree of risk as the firm's existing assets. Unfortunately, these assumptions apply in very few situations, limiting the usefulness of the retention growth model.

Analysts' Forecasts

A third technique calls for using security analysts' forecasts. As we discussed earlier, analysts publish earnings' growth rate estimates for most of the larger publicly owned companies. For example, *Value Line* provides such dividend forecasts on about 1,700 companies. Several sources compile analysts' earnings forecasts on a regular basis, and these earnings growth rates can be used as proxies for dividend growth rates.

However, analysts usually forecast nonconstant growth, which limits the usefulness of the constant growth model. Instead, a multistage model must be used. See ***Web Extension 9A*** on the textbook's Web site for an explanation of multistage approach; all calculations are in the worksheet ***Web 9A*** in the file ***Ch9 Tool Kit.xls.***

9-7b An Illustration of the DCF Approach

To illustrate the DCF approach, suppose Aldabra's stock sells for \$32, its next expected dividend is \$1.82, and its expected constant growth rate is 5.4%. Aldabra is not expected to repurchase any stock. Aldabra's stock is thought to be in equilibrium, so its expected and required rates of return are equal. Based on these assumptions, its estimated DCF cost of common equity is 11.1%:

$$\begin{aligned} \hat{r}_s = r_s &= \frac{\$1.82}{\$32.00} + 5.4\% \\ &= 5.7\% + 5.4\% \\ &= 11.1\% \end{aligned}$$

As previously noted, it is difficult to apply the DCF approach because dividends do not grow at a constant rate for most companies. Surveys show that 16% of responding firms use the DCF approach, down from 31% in 1982.[14]

SELF-TEST

What inputs are required for the DCF method?

What are three ways to estimate the expected dividend growth rate?

A company's estimated growth rate in dividends is 6%, its current stock price is \$40, and its expected annual dividend is \$2. Using the DCF approach, what is the firm's r_s? **(11%)**

---

[14]See the sources cited in footnotes 12 and 13.

9-8 The Weighted Average Cost of Capital (WACC)

As we mentioned earlier in this chapter (and as we discuss in more detail in Chapter 15), each firm has an optimal capital structure, which is defined as the mix of debt, preferred stock, and common equity that maximizes its stock price. Therefore, a value-maximizing firm must attempt to find its *target (or optimal) capital structure* and then raise new capital in a manner that will keep the actual capital structure on target over time. In this chapter, we assume that the firm has identified its optimal capital structure, that it uses this optimum as the target, and that it finances so as to remain constantly on target. How the target is established is examined in Chapter 15. The target proportions of debt, preferred stock, and common equity, along with the component costs of capital, are used to calculate the WACC, as shown previously in Equation 9-2:

$$\text{WACC} = w_d r_d (1 - T) + w_{std} r_{std} (1 - T) + w_{ps} r_{ps} + w_s r_s \tag{9-2}$$

Here w_d, w_{std}, w_{ps}, and w_s are the target weights for long-term debt, short-term debt, preferred stock, and common equity, respectively.

To illustrate, we first note that MicroDrive has a target capital structure calling for 28% long-term debt, 2% short-term debt, 3% preferred stock, and 67% common equity. Before-tax cost of long-term debt, r_d, is 9%; before-tax cost of short-term debt, r_{std}, is 10%; cost of preferred stock, r_{ps}, is 8.16%; cost of common equity, r_s, is 13.58%; and marginal tax rate is 40%. We can now calculate MicroDrive's weighted average cost of capital as follows:

$$\begin{aligned}\text{WACC} &= 0.28(9.0\%)(1 - 0.4) + 0.02(10.0\%)(1 - 0.4) + 0.03(8.16\%) + 0.67(13.58\%)\\ &= 11\%\end{aligned}$$

Three points should be noted. First, the WACC is the cost the company would incur to raise each new, or *marginal*, dollar of capital—it is not the average cost of dollars raised in the past. Second, the percentages of each capital component, called *weights*, should be based on management's target capital structure, not on the particular sources of financing in any single year. Third, the target weights should be based on market values and not on book values. The following sections explain these points.

9-8a Marginal Rates versus Historical Rates

The required rates of return for a company's investors, whether they are new or old, are always marginal rates. For example, a stockholder might have invested in a company last year when the risk-free interest rate was 6% and the required return on equity was 12%. If the risk-free rate subsequently falls and is now 4%, then the investor's required return on equity is now 10% (holding all else constant). This is the same required rate of return that a new equity holder would have, whether the new investor bought stock in the secondary market or through a new equity offering. In other words, whether the shareholders are already equity holders or are brand-new equity holders, they all have the same required rate of return, which is the current required rate of return on equity. The same reasoning applies for the firm's bondholders. All bondholders, whether old or new, have a required rate of return equal to today's yield on the firm's debt, which is based on current market conditions.

Because investors' required rates of return are based on *current* market conditions, not on market conditions when they purchased their securities, it follows that the cost of capital depends on current conditions and not on past market conditions.

9-8b Target Weights versus Annual Financing Choices

We have heard managers (and students!) say, "Our debt has a 5% after-tax cost versus a 10% WACC and a 14% cost of equity. Therefore, because we will finance only with debt this year, we should evaluate this year's projects at a 5% cost." There are two flaws in this line of reasoning.

First, suppose the firm exhausts its capacity to issue low-cost debt this year to take on projects with after-tax returns as low as 5.1% (which is slightly higher than the after-tax cost of debt). Then next year, when the firm must finance with common equity, it will have to turn down projects with returns as high as 13.9% (which is slightly lower than the cost of equity). To avoid this problem, a firm that plans to remain in business indefinitely should evaluate all projects using the 10% WACC.

Second, both existing and new investors have claims on *all* future cash flows. For example, if a company raises debt and also invests in a new project that same year, the new debtholders don't have a specific claim on that specific project's cash flows (assuming it is not non-recourse project financing). In fact, new debtholders receive a claim on the cash flows being generated by existing as well as new projects, while old debtholders (and equity holders) have claims on both new and existing projects. Thus, the decision to take on a new project should depend on the project's ability to satisfy all of the company's investors, not just the new debtholders, even if only debt is being raised that year.

9-8c Weights for Component Costs: Book Values versus Market Values versus Targets

Our primary reason for calculating the WACC is to use it in capital budgeting or corporate valuation. In particular, we need to compare the expected returns on projects and stocks with investors' required returns to determine whether investors are compensated fairly for the risk they bear. The total amount of required compensation depends both on the *rate of required return* and the *amount* investors have at stake.

Regarding the rate of return required by investors, the previous sections showed that investors require a rate of return equal to the current rate they could get on alternative investments of equivalent risk. In other words, the required rate is the opportunity cost.

Regarding the amount that investors have at stake, we again apply the "opportunity" concept. Investors have the opportunity to sell their investment at the market value, so this is the amount that investors have at stake. Notice that the amount at stake is not equal to the book values as reported on the financial statements. Book values are a record of historical investments, not the current market value of the investment. Because the WACC is used to discount future cash flows, the weights should be based on the market value weights expected on average in the future, not necessarily the current weights based on current market values.

In summary, the weights should not be based on book values but instead should be based on the market-value weights in the target capital structure. Obviously, the target capital structure must be realistic—companies can't take on so much debt that they will almost certainly go bankrupt. Also, a company must try to adjust its market value weights toward the target weights; otherwise the average weights over time might differ significantly from those in the target capital structure. We discuss capital structures, including how fast companies adjust their weights, in Chapter 15.

Global Variations in the Cost of Capital

© Rob Webb/Getty Images

For U.S. firms to be competitive with foreign companies, they must have a cost of capital no greater than that faced by their international competitors. In the past, many experts argued that U.S. firms were at a disadvantage. In particular, Japanese firms enjoyed a very low cost of capital, which lowered their total costs and thus made it hard for U.S. firms to compete with them. Recent events, however, have considerably narrowed cost-of-capital differences between U.S. and Japanese firms. In particular, the U.S. stock market has outperformed the Japanese market in recent years, which has made it easier and cheaper for U.S. firms to raise equity capital.

As capital markets become increasingly integrated, cross-country differences in the cost of capital are declining. Today, most large corporations raise capital throughout the world; hence, we are moving toward one global capital market instead of distinct capital markets in each country. Government policies and market conditions can affect the cost of capital within a given country, but this primarily affects smaller firms that do not have access to global capital markets, and even these differences are becoming less important as time passes. What matters most is the risk of the individual firm, not the market in which it raises capital.

SELF-TEST

How is the weighted average cost of capital calculated? Write out the equation.

Should the weights used to calculate the WACC be based on book values, market values, or something else? Explain.

A firm has the following data: target capital structure of 25% debt, 10% preferred stock, and 65% common equity; tax rate = 40%; r_d = 7%; r_{ps} = 7.5%; and r_s = 11.5%. Assume the firm will not issue new stock. What is this firm's WACC? **(9.28%)**

9-9 Adjusting the Cost of Equity for Flotation Costs

Few firms with moderate or slow growth issue new shares of common stock through public offerings.[15] In fact, less than 2% of all new corporate funds come from the external public equity market, for two very good reasons, negative signaling and direct costs. We discuss signaling in Chapter 15, but we address direct costs here.

The direct costs of new issuance are called **flotation costs**. Table 9-1 shows the average flotation costs for debt and equity U.S. corporations issued in the 1990s. Notice that flotation costs, as a *percentage* of capital raised, fall as the *amount* of capital raised increases. The common stock flotation costs are for non-IPO issues. For IPOs, flotation costs are higher—about 17% higher if less than $10 million is raised and higher still as issue size increases. The data in Table 9-1 include both utility and nonutility companies; if utilities had been excluded, the reported flotation costs would have been higher. Table 9-1 shows that flotation costs are significantly higher for equity than for debt. One reason for higher equity flotation costs is that corporate debt is sold mainly in large blocks to institutional investors, whereas common

[15]A few companies issue new shares through new-stock dividend reinvestment plans, which we discuss in Chapter 14. Many companies sell stock to their employees, and companies occasionally issue stock to finance huge projects or mergers. Also, some utilities regularly issue common stock.

TABLE 9-1

Average Flotation Costs for Debt and Equity

Amount of Capital Raised (Millions of Dollars)	Average Flotation Cost for Common Stock (% of Total Capital Raised)	Average Flotation Cost for New Debt (% of Total Capital Raised)
2–9.99	13.28%	4.39%
10–19.99	8.72	2.76
20–39.99	6.93	2.42
40–59.99	5.87	2.32
60–79.99	5.18	2.34
80–99.99	4.73	2.16
100–199.99	4.22	2.31
200–499.99	3.47	2.19
500 and up	3.15	1.64

Source: "The Costs of Raising Capital," Inmoo Lee, Scott Lochhead, Jay Ritter, and Quanshui Zhao. Copyright © 1996 by *The Journal of Financial Research.* Reproduced with permission of John Wiley & Sons, Ltd.

stock is sold in smaller amounts to many different investors; this imposes higher costs on the investment banks, which pass these costs on to the issuing company. Also, stock values are harder to estimate than debt values, which make selling stock more difficult, again leading to higher costs for the investment banks.

For companies that do issue new common stock, the **cost of new common equity, r_e,** or external equity, is higher than the cost of equity raised internally by reinvesting earnings, r_s, because of the flotation costs involved in issuing new common stock. What rate of return must be earned on new investments to make issuing stock worthwhile? Put another way, what is the cost of new common stock?

r_e = component cost of *external equity*, or common equity raised by issuing new stock. As we will see, r_e is equal to r_s plus a factor that reflects the cost of issuing new stock.

The answer, for a constant growth firm, is found by applying this formula:

$$r_e = \hat{r}_e = \frac{D_1}{P_0(1-F)} + g \quad (9\text{-}12)$$

In Equation 9-12, F is the percentage flotation cost incurred in selling the new stock, so $P_0(1 - F)$ is the net price per share received by the company.

Here is an example. In Section 9.7b, we estimated Aldabra's cost of common equity using the DCF approach as 11.1%, assuming Aldabra didn't issue new equity. Now assume that Aldabra must issue new equity with a flotation cost of 12.5%. The cost of new outside equity is calculated as follows:

$$r_e = \frac{\$1.82}{\$32(1-0.125)} + 5.4\%$$

$$= 6.5\% + 5.4\% = 11.9\%$$

Because of flotation costs, Aldabra must earn 11.9% on the new equity capital in order to provide shareholders the 11.1% they require.

As we noted previously, most analysts use the CAPM to estimate the cost of equity. How would the analyst incorporate flotation costs into a CAPM cost estimate? If application of the DCF methodology gives a cost of internally generated equity of 11.1% but a cost of 11.9% when flotation costs are involved, then the flotation costs add 0.8 percentage points to the cost of equity. To incorporate flotation costs into the CAPM estimate, we would simply add 0.8% to the CAPM estimate.

As an alternative to adjusting the cost of equity for flotation costs, many companies simply include the flotation costs as a negative cash flow when they perform project analysis. See Chapter 11 for a description of cash flow estimation for projects.

SELF-TEST

What are flotation costs?

Why are flotation costs higher for stock than for debt?

A firm has common stock with D_1 = \$3.00; P_0 = \$30; g = 5%; and F = 4%. If the firm must issue new stock, what is its cost of external equity, r_e? **(15.42%)**

9-10 Privately Owned Firms and Small Businesses

So far our discussion of the cost of capital has been focused on publicly owned corporations. Privately owned firms and small businesses have different situations calling for slightly different approaches.

9-10a Estimating the Cost of Stock by the Comparison Approach

When we estimated the rate of return required by public stockholders, we use stock returns to estimate beta as an input for the CAPM approach and stock prices as input data for the DCF method. But how can one measure the cost of equity for a firm whose stock is not traded? Most analysts begin by identifying one or more publicly traded firms that are in the same industry and that are approximately the same size as the privately owned firm.[16] The analyst then estimates the betas for these publicly traded firms and uses their average beta as an estimate of the beta of the privately owned firm.

9-10b Own-Bond-Yield-Plus-Judgmental-Risk-Premium Approach

From Chapter 5, we know that a company's cost of debt is above the risk-free rate due to the default risk premium. We also know that a company's cost of stock should be greater than its cost of debt because equity is riskier than debt. Therefore, some

[16]In Chapter 15, we show how to adjust if these comparison firms have differences in capital structures.

analysts use a subjective, ad hoc procedure to estimate a firm's cost of common equity: They simply add a judgmental risk premium of 3% to 5% to the cost of debt. In this approach,

$$r_s = r_d + \text{Judgmental risk premium} \qquad (9\text{-}13)$$

For example, consider a privately held company with a 10% cost of debt. Using 4% as the judgmental risk premium (because it is the mid-point of the 3%–5% range), the estimated cost of equity is 14%:

$$r_s = 10\% + 4\% = 14\%$$

9-10c Adjusting for Lack of Liquidity

The stock of a privately held firm is less liquid than that of a publicly held firm. As we explained in Chapter 5, investors require a liquidity premium on thinly traded bonds. Therefore, many analysts make an ad hoc adjustment to reflect this lack of liquidity by adding 1 to 3 percentage points to the firm's cost of equity. This rule of thumb is not theoretically satisfying because we don't know exactly how large the liquidity premium should be, but it is logical and is also a common practice.

9-10d Estimating Consistent Weights in the Capital Structure

Suppose a privately held firm is concerned that its current capital structure weights are appropriate. The first step for a publicly traded company would be to estimate the capital structure weights based on current market values. However, a privately held firm can't directly observe its market value, so it can't directly observe its market value weights.

To resolve this problem, many analysts begin by making a trial guess as to the value of the firm's equity. The analysts then use this estimated value of equity to estimate the cost of capital, next use the cost of capital to estimate the value of the firm, and finally complete the circle by using the estimated value of the firm to estimate the value of its equity. If this newly estimated equity value is different from their trial guess, analysts repeat the process but start the iteration with the newly estimated equity value as the trial value of equity. After several iterations, the trial value of equity and the resulting estimated equity value usually converge. Although somewhat tedious, this process provides consistent estimates of the weights, the cost of capital, and the value of the firm.

SELF-TEST

Identify problems that occur when estimating the cost of capital for a privately held firm. What are some solutions to these problems?

Explain the reasoning behind the bond-yield-plus-judgmental-risk-premium approach.

A company's bond yield is 7%. If the appropriate own-bond-yield risk premium is 3.5%, then what is r_s? **(10.5%)**

9-11 Managerial Issues and the Cost of Capital

We describe several managerial issues in this section, starting with how managerial decisions affect the cost of capital.

9-11a How Managerial Decisions Affect the Cost of Capital

The cost of capital is affected by some factors that are under a firm's control and some that are not.

Four Factors the Firm Cannot Control

Four factors are beyond managerial control: (1) interest rates, (2) credit crises, (3) the market risk premium, and (4) tax rates.

Interest Rates. Interest rates in the economy affect the costs of both debt and equity, but they are beyond a manager's control. Even the Fed can't control interest rates indefinitely. For example, interest rates are heavily influenced by inflation, and when inflation hit historic highs in the early 1980s, interest rates followed. Rates trended mostly down for 25 years through the recession accompanying the 2008 financial crisis. Strong actions by the federal government in the spring of 2009 brought rates even lower, which contributed to the official ending of the recession in June 2009. These actions encouraged investment, and there is little doubt that they will eventually lead to stronger growth. However, many observers fear that the government's actions will also reignite long-run inflation, which would lead to higher interest rates.

Credit Crisis. Although rare, sometimes credit markets are so disrupted that it is virtually impossible for a firm to raise capital at reasonable rates. This happened in 2008 and 2009, before the U.S. Treasury and the Federal Reserve intervened to open up the capital markets. During such times, firms tend to cut back on growth plans; if they must raise capital, its cost can be extraordinarily high.

Market Risk Premium. Investors' aversion to risk determines the market risk premium. Individual firms have no control over the RP_M, which affects the cost of equity and thus the WACC.

Tax Rates. Tax rates, which are influenced by the president and set by Congress, have an important effect on the cost of capital. They are used when we calculate the after-tax cost of debt for use in the WACC. In addition, the lower tax rate on dividends and capital gains than on interest income favors financing with stock rather than bonds, as we discuss in detail in Chapter 15.

Three Factors the Firm Can Control

A firm can affect its cost of capital through (1) its capital structure policy, (2) its dividend policy, and (3) its investment (capital budgeting) policy.

Capital Structure Policy. In this chapter, we assume the firm has a given target capital structure, and we use weights based on that target to calculate its WACC. However, a firm can change its capital structure, and such a change can affect the cost of capital. For example, the after-tax cost of debt is lower than the cost of equity, so if the firm decides to use more debt and less common equity, then this increase in debt will tend to lower the WACC. However, an increased use of debt will increase the risk of debt and the equity, offsetting to some extent the effect due to a greater weighting of debt. In Chapter 15 we discuss this in more depth, and we demonstrate that the optimal capital structure is the one that minimizes the WACC, which maximizes the intrinsic value of the stock.

Dividend Policy. As we will see in Chapter 14, the percentage of earnings paid out in dividends may affect a stock's required rate of return, r_s. Also, if the payout ratio is so high that the firm must issue new stock to fund its capital budget, then the resulting flotation costs will also affect the WACC.

Investment Policy. When we estimate the cost of capital, we use as the starting point the required rates of return on the firm's outstanding stocks and bonds, which reflect the risks inherent in the existing assets. Therefore, we are implicitly assuming that new capital will be invested in assets with the same degree of risk as existing assets. This assumption is generally correct, because most firms invest in assets similar to those they currently use. However, the equal risk assumption is incorrect if a firm dramatically changes its investment policy. For example, if a company invests in an entirely new line of business, then its marginal cost of capital should reflect the risk of that new business. For example, we can see with hindsight that GE's huge investments in the TV and movie businesses, as well as its investment in mortgages, increased its risk and thus its cost of capital.

The following section explains how to adjust the cost of capital to reflect the risk of individual divisions and projects.

9-11b Adjusting the Cost of Capital for Risk: Divisions and Projects

As we have calculated it, the weighted average cost of capital reflects the average risk and overall capital structure of the entire firm. No adjustments are needed when using the WACC as the discount rate when estimating the value of a company by discounting its cash flows. However, adjustments for risk are often needed when evaluating a division or project. For example, what if a firm has divisions in several business lines that differ in risk? Or what if a company is considering a project that is much riskier than its typical project? It is not logical to use the overall cost of capital to discount divisional or project-specific cash flows that don't have the same risk as the company's average cash flows. The following sections explain how to adjust the cost of capital for divisions and for specific projects.

Divisional Costs of Capital

Consider Starlight Sandwich Shops, a company with two divisions—a bakery operation and a chain of cafes. The bakery division is low-risk and has a 10% WACC. The cafe division is riskier and has a 14% WACC. Each division is approximately the same size, so Starlight's overall cost of capital is 12%. The bakery manager has a project with an 11% expected rate of return, and the cafe division manager has a project with a 13% expected return. Should these projects be accepted or rejected? Starlight will create value if it accepts the bakery's project, because its rate of return is greater than its cost of capital (11% > 10%), but the cafe project's rate of return is less than its cost of capital (13% < 14%), so it should reject that project. However, if management simply compared the two projects' returns with Starlight's 12% overall cost of capital, then the bakery's value-adding project would be rejected while the cafe's value-destroying project would be accepted.

Many firms use the CAPM to estimate the cost of capital for specific divisions. To begin, recall that the Security Market Line (SML) equation expresses the risk–return relationship as follows:

$$r_s = r_{RF} + (RP_M)b_i$$

As an example, consider the case of Huron Steel Company, an integrated steel producer operating in the Great Lakes region. For simplicity, assume that Huron has only one division and uses only equity capital, so its cost of equity is also its corporate cost of capital, or WACC. Huron's beta = b = 1.1, r_{RF} = 5%, and RP_M = 6%. Thus, Huron's cost of equity (and WACC) is 11.6%:

$$r_s = 5\% + (6\%)1.1 = 11.6\%$$

This suggests that investors should be willing to give Huron money to invest in new, average-risk projects if the company expects to earn 11.6% or more on this money. By "average risk" we mean projects having risk similar to the firm's existing division.

Now suppose Huron creates a new transportation division consisting of a fleet of barges to haul iron ore, and suppose barge operations typically have betas of 1.5 rather than 1.1. The barge division, with b = 1.5, has a 14.0% cost of capital:

$$r_{Barge} = 5\% + (6\%)1.5 = 14.0\%$$

On the other hand, if Huron adds a low-risk division, such as a new distribution center with a beta of only 0.5, then that division's cost of capital would be 8%:

$$r_{Center} = 5\% + (6\%)0.5 = 8.0\%$$

A firm itself may be regarded as a "portfolio of assets," and because the beta of a portfolio is a weighted average of the betas of its individual assets, adding the barge and distribution center divisions will change Huron's overall beta. The exact value of the new corporate beta would depend on the size of the investments in the new divisions relative to Huron's original steel operations. If 70% of Huron's total value ends up in the steel division, 20% in the barge division, and 10% in the distribution center, then its new corporate beta would be calculated as follows:

$$\text{New beta} = 0.7(1.1) + 0.2(1.5) + 0.1(0.5) = 1.12$$

Thus, investors in Huron's stock would require a return of

$$r_{Huron} = 5\% + (6\%)1.12 = 11.72\%$$

Even though investors require an overall return of 11.72%, they should expect a rate of return on projects in each division at least as high as the division's required return based on the SML. In particular, they should expect a return of at least 11.6% from the steel division, 14.0% from the barge division, and 8.0% from the distribution center.

Our example suggests a level of precision that is much higher than firms can obtain in the real world. Still, managers should be aware of this example'slogic, and they should strive to measure the required inputs as accurately as possible.

Techniques for Measuring Divisional Betas

In Chapter 6 we discussed the estimation of betas for stocks and indicated how difficult it is to measure beta precisely. Estimating divisional betas is much more difficult, primarily because divisions do not have their own publicly traded stock. Therefore, we must estimate the beta that the division would have if it were an independent, publicly traded company. Two approaches can be used to estimate divisional betas: the pure play method and the accounting beta method.

The Pure Play Method. In the **pure play method**, the company tries to find the betas of several publicly held specialized companies in the same line of business as the division being evaluated, and it then averages those betas to determine the cost of capital for its own division. For example, suppose Huron found three companies devoted exclusively to operating barges, and suppose that Huron's management believes its barge division would be subject to the same risks as those firms. Then Huron could use the average beta of those firms as an estimate of its barge division's beta.[17]

The Accounting Beta Method. As noted above, it may be impossible to find specialized publicly traded firms suitable for the pure play approach. If that is the case, we may be able to use the **accounting beta method**. Betas are normally found by regressing the returns of a particular company's *stock* against returns on a *stock market index*. However, we could run a regression of the division's *accounting return on assets* against the *average return on assets* for a large sample of companies, such as those included in the S&P 500. Betas determined in this way (that is, by using accounting data rather than stock market data) are called **accounting betas**.

Estimating the Cost of Capital for Individual Projects

In Chapter 11 we examine ways to estimate the risk inherent in individual projects, but at this point it is useful to consider how project risk is reflected in measures of the firm's cost of capital. First, although it is intuitively clear that riskier projects have a higher cost of capital, it is difficult to measure projects' relative risks. Also, note that three separate and distinct types of risk can be identified.

1. **Stand-alone risk**, which is the variability of the project's expected returns.
2. **Corporate**, or **within-firm**, **risk**, which is the variability the project contributes to the corporation's returns, giving consideration to the fact that the project represents only one asset of the firm's portfolio of assets and so some of its risk will be diversified away.
3. **Market**, or **beta**, **risk**, which is the risk of the project as seen by a well-diversified stockholder who owns many different stocks. A project's market risk is measured by its effect on the firm's overall beta coefficient.

Taking on a project with a high degree of either stand-alone or corporate risk will not necessarily increase the corporate beta. However, if the project has highly uncertain returns and if those returns are highly correlated with returns on the firm's other assets and with most other assets in the economy, then the project will have a high degree of all types of risk.

Of the three measures, market risk is theoretically the most relevant because of its direct effect on stock prices. Unfortunately, the market risk for a project is also the most difficult to estimate. In practice, most decision makers consider all three risk measures in a subjective manner.

[17]If the pure play firms employ different capital structures than that of Huron, then this must be addressed by adjusting the beta coefficients. See Chapter 15 for a discussion of this aspect of the pure play method. For a technique that can be used when pure play firms are not available, see Yatin Bhagwat and Michael Ehrhardt, "A Full Information Approach for Estimating Divisional Betas," *Financial Management*, Summer 1991, pp. 60–69.

The first step is to determine the divisional cost of capital before grouping divisional projects into subjective risk categories. Then, using the divisional WACC as a starting point, **risk-adjusted costs of capital** are developed for each category. For example, a firm might establish three risk classes—high, average, and low—and then assign average-risk projects the divisional cost of capital, higher-risk projects an above-average cost, and lower-risk projects a below-average cost. Thus, if a division's WACC were 10%, its managers might use 10% to evaluate average-risk projects in the division, 12% for high-risk projects, and 8% for low-risk projects. Although this approach is better than ignoring project risk, these adjustments are necessarily subjective and somewhat arbitrary. Unfortunately, given the data, there is no completely satisfactory way to specify exactly how much higher or lower we should go in setting risk-adjusted costs of capital.

9-12 Four Mistakes to Avoid

We often see managers and students make the following mistakes when estimating the cost of capital. Although we have discussed these errors previously at separate places in the chapter, they are worth repeating here.

1. *Never base the cost of debt on the coupon rate on a firm's existing debt.* The cost of debt must be based on the interest rate the firm would pay if it issued new debt today.
2. *When estimating the market risk premium for the CAPM method, never use the historical average return on stocks in conjunction with the current return on T-bonds.* The historical average return on bonds should be subtracted from the past average return on stocks to calculate the *historical market risk premium.* On the other hand, it is appropriate to subtract today's yield on T-bonds from an estimate of the expected future return on stocks to obtain the *forward-looking market risk premium.* A case can be made for using either the historical or the current risk premium, but it would be wrong to take the *historical* rate of return on stocks, subtract from it the *current* rate on T-bonds, and then use the difference as the market risk premium.
3. *Never use the current book value capital structure to obtain the weights when estimating the WACC.* Your first choice should be to use the firm's target capital structure for the weights. However, if you are an outside analyst and do not know the target weights, it would probably be best to estimate weights based on the current market values of the capital components. If the company's debt is not publicly traded, then it is reasonable to use the book value of debt to estimate the weights because book and market values of debt, especially short-term debt, are usually close to one another. However, stocks' market values in recent years have generally been at least 2–3 times their book values, so using book values for equity could lead to serious errors. The bottom line: If you don't know the target weights then use the market value, not the book value, of equity when calculating the WACC.
4. *Always remember that capital components are funds that come from investors.* If it's not from an investor, then it's not a capital component. Sometimes the argument is made that accounts payable and accruals should be included in the calculation of the WACC. However, these funds are not provided by investors, but instead, they arise from operating relationships with suppliers and employees. As such, the impact of accounts payable and accruals is incorporated into the calculations of free cash flows and project cash flows. Therefore, accounts payable and accruals should not be included as capital components when we calculate the WACC.

SELF-TEST

Name some factors that are generally beyond the firm's control but still affect its cost of capital.

What three policies under the firm's control affect its cost of capital?

Explain how a change in interest rates in the economy would be expected to affect each component of the weighted average cost of capital.

Based on the CAPM, how would one adjust the corporation's overall cost of capital to establish the required return for most projects in a low-risk division and in a high-risk division?

Describe the pure play and the accounting beta methods for estimating divisional betas.

What are the three types of risk to which projects are exposed? Which type of risk is theoretically the most relevant? Why?

Describe a procedure firms can use to establish costs of capital for projects with differing degrees of risk.

What four mistakes are commonly made when estimating the WACC?

SUMMARY

This chapter discussed how the cost of capital is developed for use in capital budgeting. The key points covered are listed below.

- The cost of capital used in capital budgeting is a **weighted average** of the types of capital the firm uses—typically long-term debt, short-term debt, preferred stock, and common equity.
- The **component cost of debt** is the **after-tax cost of new debt.** It is found by multiplying the interest rate paid on new debt by 1 − T, where T is the firm's marginal tax rate: $r_d(1 - T)$.
- Most debt is raised directly from lenders without the use of investment bankers; hence no flotation costs are incurred. However, a **debt flotation cost adjustment** should be made if large flotation costs are incurred. We reduce the bond's issue price by the flotation expenses, reduce the bond's cash flows to reflect taxes, and then solve for the after-tax yield to maturity.
- The **component cost of preferred stock** is calculated as the preferred dividend divided by the net price the firm receives after deducting flotation costs: $r_{ps} = D_{ps}/[P_{ps}(1-F)]$. Flotation costs on preferred stock are usually fairly high, so we typically include the impact of flotation costs when estimating r_{ps}. Also note that if the preferred stock is convertible into common stock, then the true cost of the preferred stock will exceed the flotation-adjusted yield of the preferred dividend.
- The **cost of common equity,** r_s, also called the **cost of common stock,** is the rate of return required by the firm's stockholders.
- To use the **CAPM approach,** we (1) estimate the firm's beta, (2) multiply this beta by the market risk premium to obtain the firm's risk premium, and then (3) add the firm's risk premium to the risk-free rate to obtain its cost of common stock: $r_s = r_{PF} + (RP_M)b_i$.

- The best proxy for the **risk-free rate** is the yield on long-term T-bonds, with 10 years the maturity used most frequently.
- To use the **dividend-yield-plus-growth-rate approach**, which is also called the **discounted cash flow (DCF) approach**, add the firm's expected dividend growth rate to its expected dividend yield: $r_s = \hat{r} = D_1/P_0 + g$. ***Web Extension 9A*** shows how to estimate the DCF cost of equity (and the market risk premium) if dividends are not growing at a constant rate.
- The growth rate for use in the DCF model can be based on security analysts' **published forecasts**, on **historical growth rates** of earnings and dividends, or on the **retention growth model**, g = (1 − Payout)(Return on equity).
- The **own-bond-yield-plus-judgmental-risk-premium approach** calls for adding a subjective risk premium of 3 to 5 percentage points to the interest rate on the firm's own long-term debt: r_s = Bond yield + Judgmental risk premium.
- When calculating the **cost of new common stock**, r_e, the DCF approach can be used to estimate the flotation cost. For a constant growth stock, the flotation-adjusted cost can be expressed as $r_s = \hat{r}_e = D_1/[P_0(1 - F)] + g$. Note that flotation costs cause r_e to be greater than r_s. We can find the difference between r_e and r_s and then add this differential to the CAPM estimate of r_s to find the CAPM estimate of r_e.
- Each firm has a **target capital structure**, which is defined as the mix of debt, preferred stock, and common equity that minimizes its **weighted average cost of capital (WACC)**:

$$\text{WACC} = w_d r_d(1 - T) + w_{std} r_{std}(1 - T) + w_{ps} r_{ps} + w_s r_s$$

- Various factors affect a firm's cost of capital. Some are determined by the financial environment, but the firm can influence others through its financing, investment, and dividend policies.
- Many firms estimate **divisional costs of capital** that reflect each division's risk and capital structure.
- The **pure play** and **accounting beta methods** can be used to estimate betas for large projects or for divisions.
- A project's **stand-alone risk** is the risk the project would have if it were the firm's only asset and if stockholders held only that one stock. Stand-alone risk is measured by the variability of the asset's expected returns.
- **Corporate**, or **within-firm**, **risk** reflects the effect of a project on the firm's risk, and it is measured by the project's effect on the firm's earnings variability.
- **Market**, or **beta**, **risk** reflects the effects of a project on stockholders' risk, assuming they hold diversified portfolios. Market risk is measured by the project's effect on the firm's beta coefficient.
- Most decision makers consider all three risk measures in a subjective manner and then classify projects into risk categories. Using the firm's WACC as a starting point, risk-adjusted costs of capital are developed for each category. The **risk-adjusted cost of capital** is the cost of capital appropriate for a given project, given its risk. The greater a project's risk, the higher its cost of capital.

The cost of capital as developed in this chapter is used in the next two chapters to evaluate potential capital budgeting projects, and it is used later in the text to determine the value of a corporation.

QUESTIONS

(9-1) Define each of the following terms:

a. Weighted average cost of capital, WACC; after-tax cost of debt, $r_d(1 - T)$; after-tax cost of short-term debt, $r_{std}(1 - T)$
b. Cost of preferred stock, r_{ps}; cost of common equity (or cost of common stock), r_s
c. Target capital structure
d. Flotation cost, F; cost of new external common equity, r_e

(9-2) How can the WACC be both an average cost and a marginal cost?

(9-3) How would each of the factors in the following table affect a firm's cost of debt, $r_d(1 - T)$; its cost of equity, r_s; and its weighted average cost of capital, WACC? Indicate by a plus (+), a minus (−), or a zero (0) if the factor would increase, reduce, or have an indeterminate effect on the item in question. Assume that all other factors are held constant. Be prepared to justify your answer, but recognize that several of the parts probably have no single correct answer; these questions are designed to stimulate thought and discussion.

	Effect on:		
	$r_d(1 - T)$	r_s	WACC
a. The corporate tax rate is lowered.	_______	_______	_______
b. The Federal Reserve tightens credit.	_______	_______	_______
c. The firm uses more debt.	_______	_______	_______
d. The firm doubles the amount of capital it raises during the year.	_______	_______	_______
e. The firm expands into a risky new area.	_______	_______	_______
f. Investors become more risk averse.	_______	_______	_______

(9-4) Distinguish between beta (i.e., market) risk, within-firm (i.e., corporate) risk, and stand-alone risk for a potential project. Of the three measures, which is theoretically the most relevant, and why?

(9-5) Suppose a firm estimates its overall cost of capital for the coming year to be 10%. What might be reasonable costs of capital for average-risk, high-risk, and low-risk projects?

SELF-TEST PROBLEM Solution Appears in Appendix A

(ST-1) WACC Longstreet Communications Inc. (LCI) has the following capital structure, which it considers to be optimal: debt = 25% (LCI has only long-term debt), preferred stock = 15%, and common stock = 60%. LCI's tax rate is 40%, and investors expect earnings and dividends to grow at a constant rate of 6% in the future. LCI paid a dividend of \$3.70 per share last year (D_0), and its stock currently sells at a price of \$60 per share. Ten-year Treasury bonds yield 6%, the market risk premium is 5%, and LCI's beta is 1.3. The following terms would apply to new security offerings.

Preferred: New preferred stock could be sold to the public at a price of \$100 per share, with a dividend of \$9. Flotation costs of \$5 per share would be incurred.
Debt: Debt could be sold at an interest rate of 9%.
Common: New common equity will be raised only by retaining earnings.

a. Find the component costs of debt, preferred stock, and common stock.
b. What is the WACC?

PROBLEMS Answers Appear in Appendix B

Easy Problems 1–8

(9-1) **After-Tax Cost of Debt** Calculate the after-tax cost of debt under each of the following conditions:

a. r_d of 13%, tax rate of 0%
b. r_d of 13%, tax rate of 20%
c. r_d of 13%, tax rate of 35%

(9-2) **After-Tax Cost of Debt** LL Incorporated's currently outstanding 11% coupon bonds have a yield to maturity of 8%. LL believes it could issue new bonds at par that would provide a similar yield to maturity. If its marginal tax rate is 35%, what is LL's after-tax cost of debt?

(9-3) **Cost of Preferred Stock** Duggins Veterinary Supplies can issue perpetual preferred stock at a price of $50 a share with an annual dividend of $4.50 a share. Ignoring flotation costs, what is the company's cost of preferred stock, r_{ps}?

(9-4) **Cost of Preferred Stock with Flotation Costs** Burnwood Tech plans to issue some $60 par preferred stock with a 6% dividend. A similar stock is selling on the market for $70. Burnwood must pay flotation costs of 5% of the issue price. What is the cost of the preferred stock?

(9-5) **Cost of Equity: DCF** Summerdahl Resort's common stock is currently trading at $36 a share. The stock is expected to pay a dividend of $3.00 a share at the end of the year (D_1 = $3.00), and the dividend is expected to grow at a constant rate of 5% a year. What is its cost of common equity?

(9-6) **Cost of Equity: CAPM** Booher Book Stores has a beta of 0.8. The yield on a 3-month T-bill is 4%, and the yield on a 10-year T-bond is 6%. The market risk premium is 5.5%, and the return on an average stock in the market last year was 15%. What is the estimated cost of common equity using the CAPM?

(9-7) **WACC** Shi Importers's balance sheet shows $300 million in debt, $50 million in preferred stock, and $250 million in total common equity. Shi's tax rate is 40%, $r_d = 6\%$, $r_{ps} = 5.8\%$, and $r_s = 12\%$. If Shi has a target capital structure of 30% debt, 5% preferred stock, and 65% common stock, what is its WACC?

(9-8) **WACC** David Ortiz Motors has a target capital structure of 40% debt and 60% equity. The yield to maturity on the company's outstanding bonds is 9%, and the company's tax rate is 40%. Ortiz's CFO has calculated the company's WACC as 9.96%. What is the company's cost of equity capital?

Intermediate Problems 9–14

(9-9) **Bond Yield and After-Tax Cost of Debt** A company's 6% coupon rate, semiannual payment, $1,000 par value bond that matures in 30 years sells at a price of $515.16. The company's federal-plus-state tax rate is 40%. What is the firm's after-tax component cost of debt for purposes of calculating the WACC? (*Hint:* Base your answer on the *nominal* rate.)

(9-10) **Cost of Equity** The earnings, dividends, and stock price of Shelby Inc. are expected to grow at 7% per year in the future. Shelby's common stock sells for $23 per share, its last dividend was $2.00, and the company will pay a dividend of $2.14 at the end of the current year.

a. Using the discounted cash flow approach, what is its cost of equity?
b. If the firm's beta is 1.6, the risk-free rate is 9%, and the expected return on the market is 13%, then what would be the firm's cost of equity based on the CAPM approach?

c. If the firm's bonds earn a return of 12%, then what would be your estimate of r_s using the own-bond-yield-plus-judgmental-risk-premium approach? (*Hint:* Use the midpoint of the risk premium range.)

d. On the basis of the results of parts a through c, what would be your estimate of Shelby's cost of equity?

(9-11) Cost of Equity Radon Homes's current EPS is \$6.50. It was \$4.42 5years ago. The company pays out 40% of its earnings as dividends, and the stock sells for \$36.

a. Calculate the historical growth rate in earnings. (*Hint:* This is a 5-year growth period.)

b. Calculate the *next* expected dividend per share, D_1. (*Hint:* $D_0 = 0.4(\$6.50) = \$2.60$.) Assume that the past growth rate will continue.

c. What is Radon's cost of equity, r_s?

(9-12) Calculation of g and EPS Spencer Supplies's stock is currently selling for \$60 a share. The firm is expected to earn \$5.40 per share this year and to pay a year-end dividend of \$3.60.

a. If investors require a 9% return, what rate of growth must be expected for Spencer?

b. If Spencer reinvests earnings in projects with average returns equal to the stock's expected rate of return, then what will be next year's EPS? (*Hint:* g = ROE × Retention ratio.)

(9-13) The Cost of Equity and Flotation Costs Messman Manufacturing will issue common stock to the public for \$30. The expected dividend and the growth in dividends are \$3.00 per share and 5%, respectively. If the flotation cost is 10% of the issue's gross proceeds, what is the cost of external equity, r_e?

(9-14) The Cost of Debt and Flotation Costs Suppose a company will issue new 20-year debt with a par value of \$1,000 and a coupon rate of 9%, paid annually. The tax rate is 40%. If the flotation cost is 2% of the issue proceeds, then what is the after-tax cost of debt? Disregard the tax shield from the amortization of flotation costs.

Challenging Problems 15–17

(9-15) WACC Estimation On January 1, the total market value of the Tysseland Company was \$60 million. During the year, the company plans to raise and invest \$30 million in new projects. The firm's present market value capital structure, shown below, is considered to be optimal. There is no short-term debt.

Debt	\$30,000,000
Common equity	30,000,000
Total capital	\$60,000,000

New bonds will have an 8% coupon rate, and they will be sold at par. Common stock is currently selling at \$30 a share. The stockholders' required rate of return is estimated to be 12%, consisting of a dividend yield of 4% and an expected constant growth rate of 8%. (The next expected dividend is \$1.20, so the dividend yield is \$1.20/\$30 = 4%.) The marginal tax rate is 40%.

a. In order to maintain the present capital structure, how much of the new investment must be financed by common equity?

b. Assuming there is sufficient cash flow for Tysseland to maintain its target capital structure without issuing additional shares of equity, what is its WACC?

c. Suppose now that there is not enough internal cash flow and the firm must issue new shares of stock. Qualitatively speaking, what will happen to the WACC?No numbers are required to answer this question.

(9-16) Market Value Capital Structure

Suppose the Schoof Company has this *book value* balance sheet:

Current assets	$ 30,000,000	Current liabilities	$ 20,000,000
		Notes payable	$ 10,000,000
Fixed assets	70,000,000	Long-term debt	30,000,000
		Common stock (1 million shares)	1,000,000
		Retained earnings	39,000,000
Total assets	$100,000,000	Total liabilities and equity	$100,000,000

The notes payable are to banks, and the interest rate on this debt is 10%, the same as the rate on new bank loans. These bank loans are not used for seasonal financing but instead are part of the company's permanent capital structure. The long-term debt consists of 30,000 bonds, each with a par value of $1,000, an annual coupon interest rate of 6%, and a 20-year maturity. The going rate of interest on new long-term debt, r_d, is 10%, and this is the present yield to maturity on the bonds. The common stock sells at a price of $60 per share. Calculate the firm's *market value* capital structure.

(9-17) WACC Estimation

The table below gives the balance sheet for Travellers Inn Inc. (TII), a company that was formed by merging a number of regional motel chains.

Travellers Inn: December 31, 2013 (Millions of Dollars)

Cash	$ 10	Accounts payable	$ 10
Accounts receivable	20	Accruals	10
Inventories	20	Short-term debt	5
Current assets	$ 50	Current liabilities	$ 25
Net fixed assets	50	Long-term debt	30
		Preferred stock	5
		Common equity	
		Common stock	$ 10
		Retained earnings	30
		Total common equity	$ 40
Total assets	$100	Total liabilities and equity	$100

The following facts also apply to TII.

(1) Short-term debt consists of bank loans that currently cost 10%, with interest payable quarterly. These loans are used to finance receivables and inventories on a seasonal basis, so bank loans are zero in the off-season.

(2) The long-term debt consists of 20-year, semiannual payment mortgage bonds with a coupon rate of 8%. Currently, these bonds provide a yield to investors of r_d = 12%. If new bonds were sold, they would have a 12% yield to maturity.

(3) TII's perpetual preferred stock has a $100 par value, pays a quarterly dividend of $2, and has a yield to investors of 11%. New perpetual preferred stock would have

to provide the same yield to investors, and the company would incur a 5% flotation cost to sell it.

(4) The company has 4 million shares of common stock outstanding. P_0 = \$20, but the stock has recently traded in the price range from \$17 to \$23. D_0 = \$1 and EPS_0 = \$2. ROE based on average equity was 24% in 2012, but management expects to increase this return on equity to 30%; however, security analysts and investors generally are not aware of management's optimism in this regard.

(5) Betas, as reported by security analysts, range from 1.3 to 1.7; the T-bond rate is 10%; and RP_M is estimated by various brokerage houses to range from 4.5% to 5.5%. Some brokerage house analysts report forecasted growth dividend growth rates in the range of10% to 15% over the foreseeable future.

(6) TII's financial vice president recently polled some pension fund investment managers who hold TII's securities regarding what minimum rate of return on TII's common would make them willing to buy the common rather than TII bonds, given that the bonds yielded 12%. The responses suggested a risk premium over TII bonds of 4 to 6 percentage points.

(7) TII is in the 40% federal-plus-state tax bracket.

(8) TII's principal investment banker predicts a decline in interest rates, with r_d falling to 10% and the T-bond rate to 8%, although the bank acknowledges that an increase in the expected inflation rate could lead to an increase rather than a decrease in interest rates.

Assume that you were recently hired by TII as a financial analyst and that your boss, the treasurer, has asked you to estimate the company's WACC under the assumption that no new equity will be issued. Your cost of capital should be appropriate for use in evaluating projects that are in the same risk class as the assets TII now operates.

SPREADSHEET PROBLEM

(9-18)
Build a Model: WACC

resource

Start with the partial model in the file ***Ch09 P18 Build a Model.xls*** on the textbook's Web site. The stock of Gao Computing sells for \$50, and last year's dividend was \$2.10. A flotation cost of 10% would be required to issue new common stock. Gao's preferred stock pays a dividend of \$3.30 per share, and new preferred stock could be sold at a price to net the company \$30 per share. Security analysts are projecting that the common dividend will grow at a rate of 7% a year. The firm can issue additional long-term debt at an interest rate (or a before-tax cost) of 10%, and its marginal tax rate is 35%. The market risk premium is 6%, the risk-free rate is 6.5%, and Gao's beta is 0.83. In its cost-of-capital calculations, Gao uses a target capital structure with 45% debt, 5% preferred stock, and 50% common equity.

a. Calculate the cost of each capital component—in other words, the after-tax cost of debt, the cost of preferred stock (including flotation costs), and the cost of equity (ignoring flotation costs). Use both the DCF method and the CAPM method to find the cost of equity.
b. Calculate the cost of new stock using the DCF model.
c. What is the cost of new common stock based on the CAPM? (*Hint:* Find the difference between r_e and r_s as determined by the DCF method and then add that difference to the CAPM value for r_s.)
d. Assuming that Gao will not issue new equity and will continue to use the same target capital structure, what is the company's WACC?
e. Suppose Gao is evaluating three projects with the following characteristics.

(1) Each project has a cost of $1 million. They will all be financed using the target mix of long-term debt, preferred stock, and common equity. The cost of the common equity for each project should be based on the beta estimated for the project. All equity will come from reinvested earnings.
(2) Equity invested in Project A would have a beta of 0.5 and an expected return of 9.0%.
(3) Equity invested in Project B would have a beta of 1.0 and an expected return of 10.0%.
(4) Equity invested in Project C would have a beta of 2.0 and an expected return of 11.0%.

f. Analyze the company's situation, and explain why each project should be accepted or rejected.

THOMSON ONE Business School Edition Problem

THOMSON REUTERS

Use the Thomson ONE—Business School Edition online database to work this chapter's questions.

Calculating 3M's Cost of Capital

In this chapter we described how to estimate a company's WACC, which is the weighted average of its costs of debt, preferred stock, and common equity. Most of the data we need to do this can be found in Thomson ONE. Here, we walk through the steps used to calculate Minnesota Mining & Manufacturing's (MMM) WACC.

Thomson ONE—BSE Discussion Questions

1. As a first step, we need to estimate what percentage of MMM's capital comes from long-term debt, preferred stock, and common equity. If we click on FINANCIALS, we can see immediately from the balance sheet the amount of MMM's long-term debt and common equity (as of mid-2012, MMM had no preferred stock). Alternatively, you can click on FUNDAMENTAL RATIOS in the next row of tabs below and then select WORLDSCOPE'S BALANCE SHEET RATIOS. Here, you will also find a recent measure of long-term debt as a percentage of total capital.

   Recall that the weights used in the WACC are based on the company's target capital structure. If we assume the company wants to maintain the same mix of capital that it currently has on its balance sheet, then what weights should you use to estimate the WACC for MMM? (In Chapter 15, we will see that we might arrive at different estimates for these weights if we assume that MMM bases its target capital structure on the market values,rather than the book values, of debt and equity.)
2. Once again, we can use the CAPM to estimate MMM's cost of equity. Thomson ONE provides various estimates of beta; select the measure that you believe is best and combine this with your estimates of the risk-free rate and the market risk premium to obtain an estimate of its cost of equity. (See the Thomson ONE exercise in Chapter 6 more details.) What is your estimate for the cost of equity? Why might it not make much sense to use the DCF approach to estimate MMM's cost of equity?
3. Next, we need to calculate MMM's cost of debt. Unfortunately, Thomson ONE doesn't provide a direct measure of the cost of debt. However, we can use different approaches to

estimate it. One approach is to take the company's long-term interest expense and divide it by the amount of long-term debt. This approach works only if the historical cost of debt equals the yield to maturity in today's market (that is, only if MMM's outstanding bonds are trading at close to par). This approach may produce misleading estimates in the years during which MMM issues a significant amount of new debt.

For example, if a company issues a lot of debt at the end of the year, then the full amount of debt will appear on the year-end balance sheet. However, we still may not see a sharp increase in interest expense on the annual income statement because the debt was outstanding for only a small portion of the entire year. When this situation occurs, the estimated cost of debt will likely understate the true cost of debt.

Another approach is to try to find this number in the notes to the company's annual report by accessing the company's home page and its Investor Relations section. Remember that you need the after-tax cost of debt to calculate a firm's WACC, so you will need MMM's average tax rate (which has been about 37% in recent years). What is your estimate of MMM's after-tax cost of debt?

4. Putting all this information together, what is your estimate of MMM's WACC? How confident are you in this estimate? Explain your answer.

MINI CASE

During the last few years, Harry Davis Industries has been too constrained by the high cost of capital to make many capital investments. Recently, though, capital costs have been declining, and the company has decided to look seriously at a major expansion program proposed by the marketing department. Assume that you are an assistant to Leigh Jones, the financial vice president. Your first task is to estimate Harry Davis's cost of capital. Jones has provided you with the following data, which she believes may be relevant to your task:

(1) The firm's tax rate is 40%.

(2) The current price of Harry Davis's 12% coupon, semiannual payment, noncallable bonds with 15 years remaining to maturity is $1,153.72. Harry Davis does not use short-term interest-bearing debt on a permanent basis. New bonds would be privately placed with no flotation cost.

(3) The current price of the firm's 10%, $100 par value, quarterly dividend, perpetual preferred stock is $116.95. Harry Davis would incur flotation costs equal to 5% of the proceeds on a new issue.

(4) Harry Davis's common stock is currently selling at $50 per share. Its last dividend (D_0) was $3.12, and dividends are expected to grow at a constant rate of 5.8% in the foreseeable future. Harry Davis's beta is 1.2, the yield on T-bonds is 5.6%, and the market risk premium is estimated to be 6%. For the own-bond-yield-plus-judgmental-risk-premium approach, the firm uses a 3.2% risk premium.

(5) Harry Davis's target capital structure is 30% long-term debt, 10% preferred stock, and 60% common equity.

To help you structure the task, Leigh Jones has asked you to answer the following questions.

a. (1) What sources of capital should be included when you estimate Harry Davis's weighted average cost of capital?

(2) Should the component costs be figured on a before-tax or an after-tax basis?
(3) Should the costs be historical (embedded) costs or new (marginal) costs?

b. What is the market interest rate on Harry Davis's debt, and what is the component cost of this debt for WACC purposes?

c. (1) What is the firm's cost of preferred stock?
(2 Harry Davis's preferred stock is riskier to investors than its debt, yet the preferred stock's yield to investors is lower than the yield to maturity on the debt. Does this suggest that you have made a mistake? (*Hint:* Think about taxes.)

d. (1) What are the two primary ways companies raise common equity?
(2) Why is there a cost associated with reinvested earnings?
(3) Harry Davis doesn't plan to issue new shares of common stock. Using the CAPM approach, what is Harry Davis's estimated cost of equity?

e. (1) What is the estimated cost of equity using the discounted cash flow (DCF) approach?
(2) Suppose the firm has historically earned 15% on equity (ROE) and has paid out 62% of earnings, and suppose investors expect similar values to obtain in the future. How could you use this information to estimate the future dividend growth rate, and what growth rate would you get? Is this consistent with the 5.8% growth rate given earlier?
(3) Could the DCF method be applied if the growth rate were not constant? How?

f. What is the cost of equity based on the own-bond-yield-plus-judgmental-risk-premium method?

g. What is your final estimate for the cost of equity, r_s?

h. What is Harry Davis's weighted average cost of capital (WACC)?

i. What factors influence a company's WACC?

j. Should the company use its overall WACC as the hurdle rate for each of its divisions?

k. What procedures can be used to estimate the risk-adjusted cost of capital for a particular division? What approaches are used to measure a division's beta?

l. Harry Davis is interested in establishing a new division that will focus primarily on developing new Internet-based projects. In trying to determine the cost of capital for this new division, you discover that specialized firms involved in similar projects have, on average, the following characteristics: (1) their capital structure is 10% debt and 90% common equity; (2) their cost of debt is typically 12%; and (3) they have a beta of 1.7. Given this information, what would your estimate be for the new division's cost of capital?

m. What are three types of project risk? How can each type of risk be considered when thinking about the new division's cost of capital?

n. Explain in words why new common stock that is raised externally has a higher percentage cost than equity that is raised internally by retaining earnings.

o. (1) Harry Davis estimates that if it issues new common stock, the flotation cost will be 15%. Harry Davis incorporates the flotation costs into the DCF approach. What is the estimated cost of newly issued common stock, taking into account the flotation cost?
(2) Suppose Harry Davis issues 30-year debt with a par value of $1,000 and a coupon rate of 10%, paid annually. If flotation costs are 2%, what is the after-tax cost of debt for the new bond issue?

p. What four common mistakes in estimating the WACC should Harry Davis avoid?

SELECTED ADDITIONAL CASES

The following cases from CengageCompose cover many of the concepts discussed in this chapter and are available at **compose.cengage.com.**

Klein-Brigham Series:
Case 42, "West Coast Semiconductor"; Case 54, "Ace Repair"; Case 55, "Premier Paint & Body"; Case 6, "Randolph Corporation"; Case 75, "The Western Company"; and Case 81, "Pressed Paper Products."

Brigham-Buzzard Series:
Case 5, "Powerline Network Corporation (Determining the Cost of Capital)."

© Adalberto Rios Szalay/Sexto Sol/Getty Images

CHAPTER 10

The Basics of Capital Budgeting: Evaluating Cash Flows

Nothing runs like a Deere, according to Deere & Co., the manufacturer of the iconic green tractors and agricultural equipment. Commonly known as John Deere, the company is indeed running fast with a multibillion dollar expansion. Some of the additional capacity will be overseas, as Deere announced plans to build seven new factories in the BRIC countries (Brazil, Russia, India, and China). Deere is making major upgrades to several of its domestic production facilities, including its Waterloo, Iowa, tractor factory.

Deere is projecting increased demand for its equipment based on global population growth and increased purchasing power from a larger worldwide middle class. Deere is not basing its plans on intuition. In the 2011 annual report, CEO Samuel R. Allen states that Deere focuses on "operating consistency and a disciplined approach to asset and cost management."

As you read this chapter, think about how capital budgeting methods are a vital part of asset selection and expansion decisions.

Sources: See the 2011 Deere & Company Annual Report, p. 3. Also see Bob Tita, "Deere Bets Big on Expanding Global Demand," *The Wall Street Journal*, May 17, 2012, p. B8.

Corporate Valuation and Capital Budgeting

© Rob Webb/Getty Images

You can calculate the cash flows (CF) for a project in much the same way as you do for a firm. When the project's cash flows are discounted at the appropriate risk-adjusted weighted average cost of capital ("r" for simplicity), the result is the project's value. When valuing an entire firm you discount its free cash flows at the overall weighted average cost of capital, but when valuing a project you discount its cash flows at the project's own risk-adjusted cost of capital. The firm's free cash flows are the total of all the net cash flows from its past projects. Thus, if a project is accepted and put into operation, it will provide cash flows that add to the firm's free cash flows and thus to the firm's value.

Subtracting the initial cost of the project from the discounted future expected cash flows gives the project's net present value (NPV). A project that has a positive NPV adds value to the firm. In fact, the firm's Market Value Added (MVA) is the sum of all its projects' NPVs. The key point, though, is that the process of evaluating projects, or capital budgeting, is critical to a firm's success.

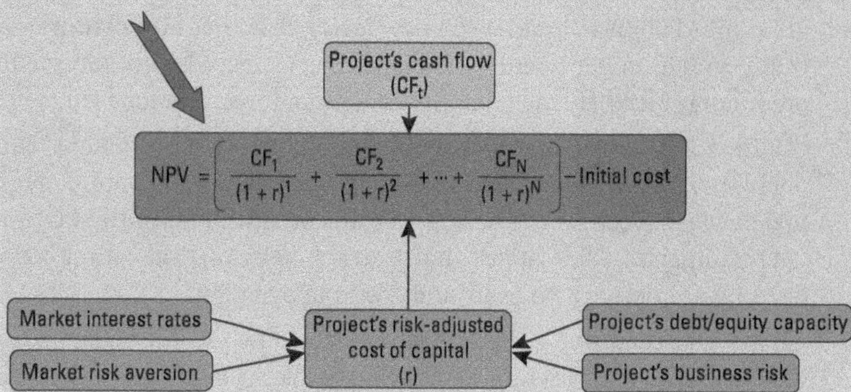

© Cengage Learning 2014

resource

*The textbook's Web site contains an Excel file that will guide you through the chapter's calculations. The file for this chapter is **Ch10 Tool Kit.xls**, and we encourage you to open the file and follow along as you read the chapter.*

In Chapters 10 and 11, we discuss *capital budgeting.* Here *capital* refers to long-term assets used in production, and a *budget* is a plan that outlines projected expenditures during a future period. Thus, the *capital budget* is a summary of planned investments of assets that will last for more than a year, and **capital budgeting** is the whole process of analyzing projects and deciding which ones to accept and thus include in the capital budget. Chapter 10 explains the measures companies use to evaluate projects, including the measures' strengths and weaknesses. Chapter 10 also describes several other issues that arise in the capital budgeting process. Chapter 11 explains how to estimate cash flows and evaluate project risk.

10-1 An Overview of Capital Budgeting

A firm's ability to remain competitive and to survive depends on a constant flow of ideas for new products, improvements in existing products, and ways to operate more efficiently. Therefore, it is vital for a company to evaluate proposed projects accurately.

However, analyzing project proposals requires skill, effort, and time. For certain types of projects, an extremely detailed analysis may be warranted, whereas simpler procedures are adequate for other projects. Accordingly, firms generally categorize projects and analyze those in each category somewhat differently:

1. *Replacement needed to continue profitable operations.* An example would be replacing an essential pump on a profitable offshore oil platform. The platform manager could make this investment without an elaborate review process.
2. *Replacement to reduce costs.* An example would be the replacement of serviceable but obsolete equipment in order to lower costs. A fairly detailed analysis would be needed, with more detail required for larger expenditures.
3. *Expansion of existing products or markets.* These decisions require a forecast of growth in demand, so a more detailed analysis is required. Go/no-go decisions are generally made at a higher level in the organization than are replacement decisions.
4. *Expansion into new products or markets.* These investments involve strategic decisions that could change the fundamental nature of the business. A detailed analysis is required, and top officers make the final decision, possibly with board approval.
5. *Contraction decisions.* Especially during bad recessions, companies often find themselves with more capacity than they are likely to need. Rather than continue to operate plants at, say, 50% of capacity and incur losses as a result of excessive fixed costs, management decides to downsize. That generally requires payments to laid-off workers and additional costs for shutting down selected operations. These decisions are made at the board level.
6. *Safety and/or environmental projects.* Expenditures necessary to comply with environmental orders, labor agreements, or insurance policy terms fall into this category. How these projects are handled depends on their size, with small ones being treated much like the Category 1 projects and large ones requiring expenditures that might even cause the firm to abandon the line of business.
7. *Other.* This catch-all includes items such as office buildings, parking lots, and executive aircraft. How they are handled varies among companies.
8. *Mergers.* Buying a whole firm (or division) is different from buying a machine or building a new plant. Still, basic capital budgeting procedures are used when making merger decisions.

Relatively simple calculations, and only a few supporting documents, are required for most replacement decisions, especially maintenance investments in profitable plants. More detailed analyses are required as we move on to more complex expansion decisions, especially for investments in new products or areas. Also, within each category projects are grouped by their dollar costs: Larger investments require increasingly detailed analysis and approval at higher levels. Thus, a plant manager might be authorized to approve maintenance expenditures up to $10,000 using a simple payback analysis, but the full board of directors might have to approve decisions that involve either amounts greater than $1 million or expansions into new products or markets.

If a firm has capable and imaginative executives and employees, and if its incentive system is working properly, then many ideas for capital investment will be forthcoming. Some ideas will be good and should be funded, but others should be killed. Therefore, the following measures have been established for screening projects and deciding which to accept or reject:[1]

[1]One other rarely used measure, the Accounting Rate of Return, is covered in the chapter's *Excel Tool Kit* model and ***Web Extension 10A***.

1. Net Present Value (NPV)
2. Internal Rate of Return (IRR)
3. Modified Internal Rate of Return (MIRR)
4. Profitability Index (PI)
5. Regular Payback
6. Discounted Payback

As we shall see, the NPV is the best single measure, primarily because it directly relates to the firm's central goal of maximizing intrinsic value. However, all of the measures provide some useful information, and all are used in practice.

SELF-TEST

Identify the major project classification categories, and explain how and why they are used.

List six procedures for screening projects and deciding which to accept or reject.

10-2 The First Step in Project Analysis

In the sections that follow, we will evaluate two projects that Guyton Products Company (GPC) is considering. GPC is a high-tech "lab-bench-to-market" development company that takes cutting-edge research advances and translates them into consumer products. GPC has recently licensed a nano-fabrication coating technology from a university that promises to significantly increase the efficiency with which solar energy can be harvested and stored as heat. GPC is considering using this technology in two different product lines. In the first, code-named "Project S" for "solid," the technology would be used to coat rock and concrete structures to be used as passive heat sinks and sources for energy-efficient residential and commercial buildings. In the second, code-named "Project L" for "liquid," it would be used to coat the collectors in a high-efficiency solar water heater. GPC must decide whether to undertake either of these two projects.

The first step in project analysis is to estimate the project's expected cash flows. We will explain cash flow estimation for Project L in Chapter 11, including the impact of depreciation, taxes, and salvage values. However, we want to focus now on the six evaluation measures, so we will specify the cash flows used in the following examples.[2]

Recall from Chapter 9 that a company's weighted average cost of capital (WACC) reflects the average risk of all the company's projects and that the appropriate cost of capital for a particular project may differ from the company's WACC. Chapter 11 explains how to estimate a project's risk-adjusted cost of capital, but for now assume that Projects L and S are equally risky and both have a 10% cost of capital.

Figure 10-1 shows the inputs for GPC's Projects S and L, including the projects' cost of capital and the time line of expected cash flows (with the initial cost shown at Year 0). Although Projects S and L are GPC's "solid" and "liquid" coating projects, you may also find it helpful to think of S and L as standing for *Short* and *Long*. Project S is a short-term project in the sense that its biggest cash inflows occur relatively soon; Project L has more total cash inflows, but its largest cash flows occur in the later years.

[2]We will see in Chapter 11 that project cash flows are, in fact, free cash flows as calculated in Chapter 3 and used in Chapter 7 to estimate corporate value.

FIGURE 10-1

Cash Flows and Selected Evaluation Measures for Projects S and L (Millions of Dollars)

	A	B	C	D	E	F
19	**Panel A: Inputs for Project Cash Flows and Cost of Capital, r**					
20						
21	INPUTS:					
22	r = 10%					
23			Initial Cost and Expected Cash Flows			
24	Year	0	1	2	3	4
25	Project S	−$10,000	$5,300	$4,300	$1,874	$1,500
26	Project L	−$10,000	$1,900	$2,700	$2,345	$7,800
27						
28	**Panel B: Summary of Selected Evaluation Measures**					
29			Project S	Project L		
30	Net present value, NPV		$804.38	$1,048.02		
31	Internal rate of return, IRR		14.69%	13.79%		
32	Modified IRR, MIRR		12.15%	10.19%		
33	Profitability index, PI		1.08	1.10		
34	Payback		2.21	3.39		
35	Discounted payback		3.21	3.80		

resource

See Ch10 Tool Kit.xls on the textbook's Web site.

The second step in project analysis is to calculate the evaluation measures, which are shown in Panel B of Figure 10-1. The following sections explain how each measure is calculated.

SELF-TEST

What is the first step in project analysis?

10-3 Net Present Value (NPV)

The **net present value (NPV)** is defined as the present value of a project's expected cash flows (including its initial cost) discounted at the appropriate risk-adjusted rate. The NPV measures how much wealth the project contributes to shareholders. When deciding which projects to accept, NPV is generally regarded as the best single criterion.

10-3a Calculating NPV

We can calculate NPV with the following steps.

1. Calculate the present value of each cash flow discounted at the project's risk-adjusted cost of capital, which is r = 10% in our example.
2. The sum of the discounted cash flows is defined as the project's NPV.

The equation for the NPV, set up with input data for Project S, is

$$\text{NPV} = \text{CF}_0 + \frac{\text{CF}_1}{(1+r)^1} + \frac{\text{CF}_2}{(1+r)^2} + \cdots + \frac{\text{CF}_N}{(1+r)^N}$$
$$= \sum_{t=0}^{N} \frac{\text{CF}_t}{(1+r)^t} \quad \text{(10-1)}$$

Applying Equation 10-1 to Project S, we have

$$\begin{aligned}\text{NPV}_S &= -\$10{,}000 + \frac{\$5{,}300}{(1.10)^1} + \frac{\$4{,}300}{(1.10)^2} + \frac{\$1{,}874}{(1.10)^3} + \frac{\$1{,}500}{(1.10)^4} \\ &= -\$10{,}000 + \$4{,}818.18 + \$3{,}553.72 + \$1{,}407.96 + \$1{,}024.52 \\ &= \$804.38 \text{ million}\end{aligned}$$

Here CF_t is the expected net cash flow at Time t, r is the project's risk-adjusted cost of capital (or WACC), and N is its life. Projects generally require an initial investment—for example, developing the product, buying the equipment needed to make it, building a factory, and stocking inventory. The initial investment is a negative cash flow. For Projects S and L, only CF_0 is negative; large projects often have outflows for several years before cash inflows begin.

Figure 10-2 shows the cash flow time line for Project S as taken from Figure 10-1. The initial cash flow is –\$10,000, which is not discounted because it occurs at t = 0. The PV of each cash inflow and the sum of the PVs are shown in Column B. You could find the PVs of the cash flows with a calculator or with *Excel*, and the result would be the numbers in Column B. When we sum the PVs of the inflows and subtract the cost, the result is \$804.38, which is NPV_S. The NPV for Project L, \$1,048.02, can be found similarly, but there is a much easier way. The bottom section of Figure 10-2 shows how to use *Excel's* NPV function to calculate Project L's NPV. Notice that the NPV function uses the range of cash flows beginning with the Year 1 cash flow, not the Year 0 cash flow. Therefore, you must add the Year 0 cash flow to the result of the NPV function to calculate the net present value.

FIGURE 10-2

Finding the NPV for Projects S and L (Millions of Dollars)

	A	B	C	D	E	F
46	INPUTS:					
47	r =	10%				
48			Initial Cost and Expected Cash Flows			
49	Year	0	1	2	3	4
50	Project S	-\$10,000	\$5,300	\$4,300	\$1,874	\$1,500
51		4,818.18	←←↵	↓	↓	↓
52		3,553.72	←←←←←←	←←↵	↓	↓
53		1,407.96	←←←←←←	←←←←←	←←↵	↓
54		1,024.52	←←←←←←	←←←←←	←←←←←	←←↵
55	NPV_S =	\$804.38	Long way:			
56			Sum the PVs of the CFs to find NPV			
57			Initial Cost and Expected Cash Flows			
58	Year	0	1	2	3	4
59	Project L	-\$10,000	\$1,900	\$2,700	\$2,345	\$7,800
60	NPV_L =	\$1,048.02	Short way: Use *Excel's* NPV function			
61			=NPV(B47,C59:F59)+B59			

resource
See *Ch10 Tool Kit.xls* on the textbook's Web site.

It is also possible to calculate the NPV with a financial calculator. As we discussed in Chapter 4, all calculators have a "cash flow register" that can be used to evaluate uneven cash flows such as those for Projects S and L. Equation 10-1 is programmed into these calculators, and all you need to do is enter the cash flows (with the correct signs) along with r = I/YR = 10. Once you have entered the data, press the NPV key to get the answer, 804.38, on the screen.[3]

10-3b Applying NPV as an Evaluation Measure

Before using these NPVs in the decision process, we need to know whether Projects S and L are **independent** or **mutually exclusive**. The cash flows for independent projects are not affected by other projects. For example, if Walmart were considering a new store in Boise and another in Atlanta, those projects would be independent. If both had positive NPVs, Walmart should accept both.

Mutually exclusive projects, on the other hand, are two different ways of accomplishing the same result, so if one project is accepted then the other must be rejected. A conveyor-belt system to move goods in a warehouse and a fleet of forklifts for the same purpose would be mutually exclusive—accepting one implies rejecting the other.

What should the decision be if Projects S and L are independent? In this case, both should be accepted because both have positive NPVs and thus add value to the firm. However, if they are mutually exclusive, then Project L should be chosen because it has the higher NPV and thus adds more value than S. We can summarize these criteria with the following rules:

1. *Independent projects:* If NPV exceeds zero, accept the project. Because S and L both have positive NPVs, accept them both if they are independent.
2. *Mutually exclusive projects:* Accept the project with the highest positive NPV. If no project has a positive NPV, then reject them all. If S and L are mutually exclusive, the NPV criterion would select L.

Projects must be either independent or mutually exclusive, so one or the other of these rules applies to every project.

SELF-TEST

Why is NPV the primary capital budgeting decision criterion?

What is the difference between "independent" and "mutually exclusive" projects?

Projects SS and LL have the following cash flows:

	End-of-Year Cash Flows			
	0	**1**	**2**	**3**
SS	−700	500	300	100
LL	−700	100	300	600

If the cost of capital is 10%, then what are the projects' NPVs? **(NPV_{SS} = \$77.61; NPV_{LL} = \$89.63)**

What project or set of projects would be in your capital budget if SS and LL were (a) independent or (b) mutually exclusive? **(Both; LL)**

10-4 Internal Rate of Return (IRR)

In Chapter 5 we discussed the yield to maturity on a bond, and we explained that if you hold a bond to maturity then you will earn the yield to maturity on your investment. The YTM is found as the discount rate that forces the present value of the cash inflows to

[3]The keystrokes for finding the NPV are shown for several calculators in the calculator tutorials we provide on the textbook's Web site.

equal the price of the bond. This same concept is used in capital budgeting when we calculate a project's **internal rate of return**, or **IRR**. A project's IRR is the discount rate that forces the PV of the expected future cash flows to equal the initial cash flow. This is equivalent to forcing the NPV to equal zero.

Why is the discount rate that causes a project's NPV to equal zero helpful as an evaluation measure? The reason is that the IRR is an estimate of the project's rate of return. If this return exceeds the cost of the funds used to finance the project, then the difference benefits the firm's stockholders. On the other hand, if the IRR is less than the cost of capital, stockholders must make up the shortfall.

10-4a Calculating the IRR

To calculate the IRR, begin with Equation 10-1 for the NPV, replace r in the denominator with the term "IRR," and choose a value of r so that the NPV is equal to zero. This transforms Equation 10-1 into Equation 10-2, the one used to find the IRR. The rate that forces NPV to equal zero is the IRR.[4]

$$NPV = CF_0 + \frac{CF_1}{(1+IRR)^1} + \frac{CF_2}{(1+IRR)^2} + \cdots + \frac{CF_N}{(1+IRR)^N} = 0$$
$$= \sum_{t=0}^{N} \frac{CF_t}{(1+IRR)^t} = 0 \qquad \text{(10-2)}$$

For Project S, we have

$$NPV_s = 0 = -\$10{,}000 + \frac{\$5{,}300}{(1+IRR)^1} + \frac{\$4{,}300}{(1+IRR)^2} + \frac{\$1{,}874}{(1+IRR)^3} + \frac{\$1{,}500}{(1+IRR)^4}$$

Figure 10-3 illustrates the process for finding the IRR of Project S.

Three procedures can be used to find the IRR:

resource
See *Ch10 Tool Kit.xls* on the textbook's Web site.

1. *Trial-and-error.* We could use a trial-and-error procedure: Try a discount rate, see if the equation solves to zero, and if it doesn't, try a different rate. Continue until you find the rate that forces the NPV to zero, and that rate will be the IRR. This procedure is rarely done by hand calculations, however. IRR usually is calculated using either a financial calculator or *Excel* (or some other computer program) as described below.
2. *Calculator solution.* Enter the cash flows into the calculator's cash flow register just as you did to find the NPV, and then press the calculator key labeled "IRR." Instantly, you get the internal rate of return. Here are the values for Projects S and L:

$$IRR_S = 14.686\%$$
$$IRR_L = 13.786\%$$

3. *Excel solution.* It is even easier to find IRRs using *Excel*, as Figure 10-3 shows for Project L. Notice that with *Excel's* IRR function, the range in the function includes the initial cash flow at Year 0. This is in contrast to the NPV function's range, which starts with the Year 1 cash flow. Be alert to this difference when you use these functions, because it is easy to mis-specify the range of inputs.

[4]For a large, complex project like an FPL power plant, costs are incurred for several years before cash inflows begin. That simply means that we have a number of negative cash flows before the positive cash flows begin.

FIGURE 10-3
Finding the IRR

	A	B	C	D	E	F
73	INPUTS:					
74			Initial Cost and Expected Cash Flows			
75	Year	0	1	2	3	4
76	Project S	-$10,000	$5,300	$4,300	$1,874	$1,500
77		4,621.33	←←↲	↓	↓	↓
78		3,269.26	←←←←←←	←←↲	↓	↓
79		1,242.34	←←←←←←	←←←←←	←←↲	↓
80		867.07	←←←←←←	←←←←←	←←←←←	←←↲
81–83	NPV$_S$ =	$0.00	Long way: Try a value for r, sum the PVs of the CFs to find NPV. If NPV is not zero, try another value for r. Or use Goal Seek to find the value of r that makes the NPV = 0.			
84	IRR = r =	14.69%	Value of r that makes NPV = 0.			
85						
86			Initial Cost and Expected Cash Flows			
87	Year	0	1	2	3	4
88	Project L	-$10,000	$1,900	$2,700	$2,345	$7,800
89–90	IRR$_L$ =	13.79%	Short way: Use *Excel*'s IRR function =IRR(B88:F88)			

10-4b A Potential Problem with the IRR: Multiple Internal Rates of Return[5]

If a project has a *normal* cash flow pattern, which is one or more cash outflows followed only by cash inflows (or the reverse, one or more cash inflows followed only by outflows), then the project can have only one positive real IRR. Here are some examples of normal cash flow patterns:

Normal: $- + + +$ or $- - + + +$ or $+ + - -$

Notice that the sign of the cash flows only changes once for any of these examples, either from negative to positive or positive to negative.

However, some projects have cash flows with signs that change more than once. For example, consider a strip coal mine where the company first spends money to buy the property and prepare the site for mining. The mining company has positive inflows for several years, and then spends more money to return the land to its original condition. For this project, the cash flow sign goes from negative to positive and then changes again from positive to negative. This is a *nonnormal* cash flow pattern; here are some examples:

Nonnormal: $- + + + + -$ or $- + + + - + + +$

If a project's cash flows have a nonnormal pattern (i.e., the cash flows have more than one sign change), it is possible for the project to have more than one positive real IRR—that is, **multiple IRRs.**[6]

---

[5]This section is relatively technical, and some instructors may choose to omit it without loss of continuity.

[6]Equation 10-2 is a polynomial of degree n, so it has n different roots, or solutions. All except one of the roots are imaginary numbers when investments have normal cash flows (one or more cash outflows followed by cash inflows), so in the normal case only one value of IRR appears. However, the possibility of multiple real roots, and hence of multiple IRRs, arises when negative net cash flows occur after the project has been placed in operation.

To illustrate multiple IRRs, suppose a firm is considering a potential strip mine (Project M) that has a cost of \$1.6 million and will produce a cash flow of \$10 million at the end of Year 1; however, the firm must spend \$10 million to restore the land to its original condition at the end of Year 2. Therefore, the project's expected net cash flows are as follows (in millions):

	Year 0	End of Year 1	End of Year 2
Cash flows	−\$1.6	+\$10	−\$10

We can substitute these values into Equation 10-2 and then solve for the IRR:

$$\text{NPV} = \frac{-\$1.6 \text{ million}}{(1 + \text{IRR})^0} + \frac{\$10 \text{ million}}{(1 + \text{IRR})^1} + \frac{-\$10 \text{ million}}{(1 + \text{IRR})^2} = 0$$

resource
*See **Ch10 Tool Kit.xls** on the textbook's Web site for all calculations.*

For Project M's cash flows, the NPV equals 0 when IRR = 25%, but it also equals 0 when IRR = 400%.[7] Therefore, Project M has one IRR of 25% and another of 400%. Are either of these IRRs helpful in deciding whether to proceed with Project M? No! To see this, look at Figure 10-4, which shows Project M's NPV for different costs of capital. Notice that Project M has a negative NPV for costs of capital less than 25%. Therefore, Project M should be rejected for reasonable costs of capital.

When you evaluate a project, always look at the projected cash flows and count the number of times that the sign changes. If the sign changes more than once, don't even calculate the IRR, because it is at best useless and at worst misleading.

FIGURE 10-4

Graph for Multiple IRRs: Project M (Millions of Dollars

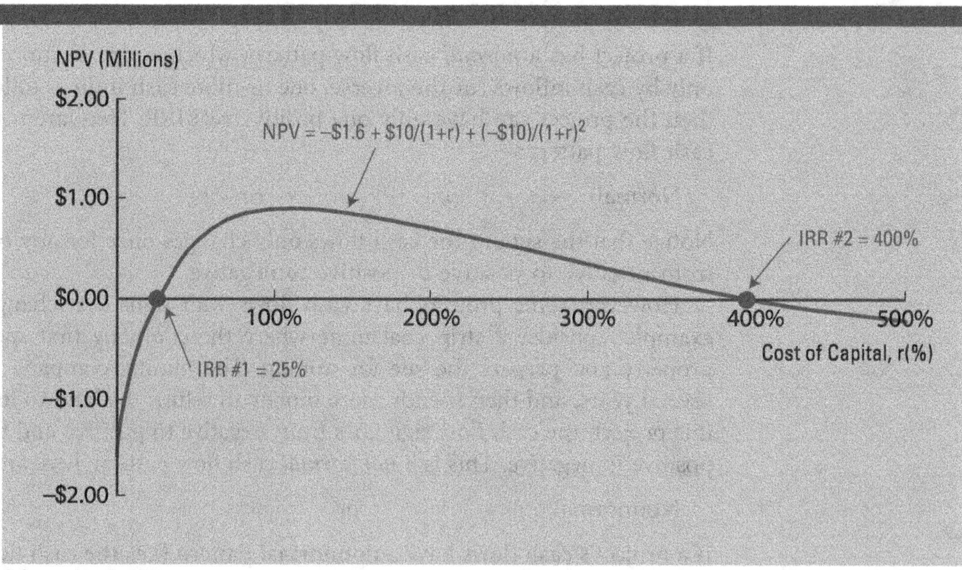

© Cengage Learning 2014

[7]If you attempt to find Project M's IRR with an HP calculator, you will get an error message, whereas TI calculators give only the IRR closest to zero. When you encounter either situation, you can find the approximate IRRs by first calculating NPVs using several different values for r = I/YR, constructing a graph with NPV on the vertical axis and cost of capital on the horizontal axis, and then visually determining approximately where NPV = 0. The intersection with the x-axis gives a rough idea of the IRRs' values. With some calculators and with *Excel*, you can find both IRRs by entering guesses, as we explain in our calculator and *Excel* tutorials.

10-4c Potential Problems When Using the IRR to Evaluate Mutually Exclusive Projects

Potential problems can arise when using the IRR to choose among mutually exclusive projects. Projects S and L are independent, but suppose for illustrative purposes that they are mutually exclusive. Their NPVs and IRRs are shown below:

	NPV	IRR
Project S	$804.38	14.69%
Project L	$1,048.02	13.79%

If using NPV as a decision criterion, Project L is preferred. But Project S is preferred if using IRR as a decision criterion. How do we resolve this conflict?

Resolving a Conflict between the IRR and NPV for Mutually Exclusive Projects: Pick the Project with the Highest NPV

Consider these two hypothetical games we offer our students in class. In Game 1, we offer to give a student $2 at the end of class if the student will give us $1 at the beginning. Assuming we can be trusted, Game 1 has a 100% rate of return. In Game 2, we offer to give a student $25 at the end of class in exchange for $20 at the beginning of class. The games are mutually exclusive and may not be repeated—a student can choose only one game and can play it only once. Which game would you choose? If you are like our students, you would choose Game 2 because your wealth goes up by $5, which is better than the $1 increase in wealth offered by Game 1. So even though Game 1 has a higher rate of return, people prefer more wealth to less wealth.

The same is true for the shareholders. If projects are mutually exclusive, managers should choose the project that provides the greatest increase in wealth (as measured by the NPV) even though it may not have the highest rate of return (as measured by the IRR). Therefore, if Projects S and L were mutually exclusive, managers would choose Project L because it has a higher NPV and generates more wealth for shareholders.

The Causes of Possible Conflicts between the IRR and NPV for Mutually Exclusive Projects: Timing and Scale Differences

Figure 10-5 illustrates the situation with a **net present value profile** for each project. This profile has a project's NPV plotted on the y-axis for different costs of capital. Notice the IRR for each project, which is the point at which the project has a zero NPV (it is also the place where the curve crosses the x-axis). As the figure shows, Project S has the largest IRR (the curve for Project S crosses the x-axis to the right of Project L's curve). Notice the NPV for each project when the cost of capital is 10%. Project L's NPV is above that of Project S.

The two NPV profile lines cross at a cost of capital of 12.247%, which is called the **crossover rate**. Find the crossover rate by calculating the IRR of the differences in the projects' cash flows, as demonstrated below:

	Year				
	0	1	2	3	4
Project S:	−$10,000	$5,300	$4,300	$1,874	$1,500
Project L:	−10,000	1,900	2,700	2,345	7,800
$\Delta = CF_S - CF_L$:	$0	$3,400	$1,600	−$471	−$6,300

IRR Δ = 12.274%

FIGURE 10-5
NPV Profiles for Projects S and L

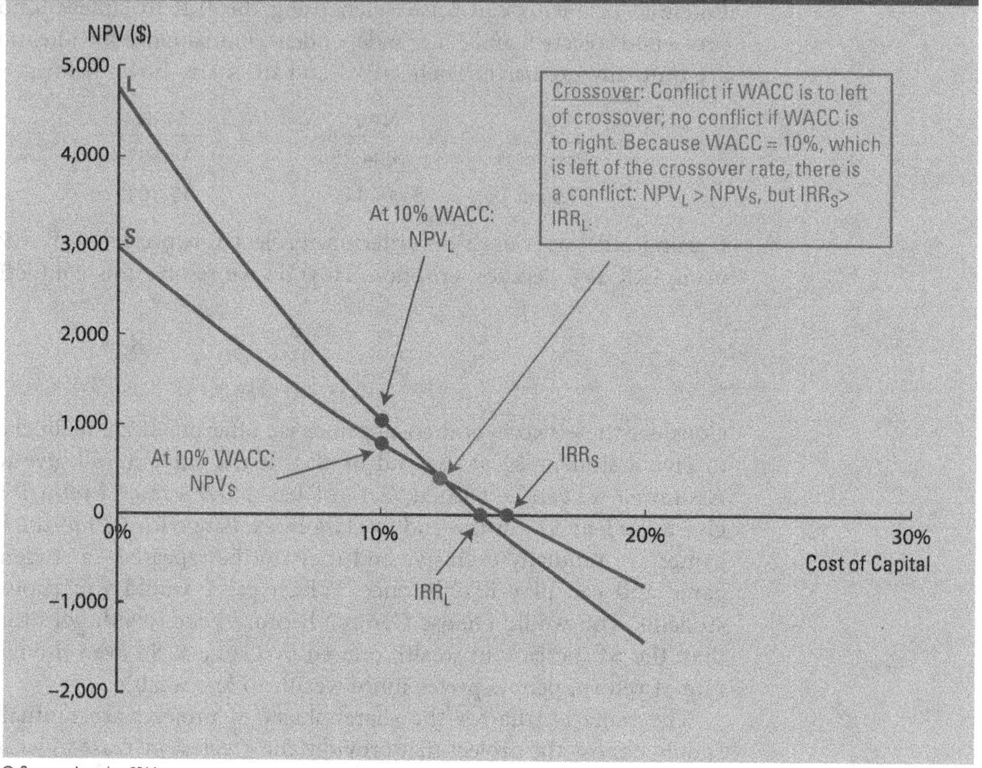

© Cengage Learning 2014

If the cost of capital is *less* than the crossover rate, Project L has the higher NPV. But if the cost of capital is *greater* than the crossover rate, Project S has the higher NPV.

Many projects don't have different rankings—if a project has a larger NPV, it usually has a higher IRR. But for projects whose rankings conflict, you must determine the source of the conflict. Note that in order for a conflict to exist, both projects must have positive NPVs and there must be a crossover rate. For a crossover rate to exist, the difference in cash flows between the two projects must have a normal pattern, as described in the previous section: The cash flows must have one and only one sign change. Therefore, a crossover rate only can exist for projects with positive NPVs if the cash flows have timing differences, size (or scale) differences, or some combination.[8] For example, consider the cash flows of Project Sooner and Project Later. Both have a 10% cost of capital; their cash flows are shown below:

	Year				
	0	1	2	NPV	IRR
Project Sooner:	−$1,000	$1,020	$120	$26	12.7%
Project Later:	−$1,000	$120	$1,120	$35	12.0%
$\Delta = CF_S - CF_L$:	$0	$900	−$1,000		11.1%

[8]Also, if mutually exclusive projects have different lives (as opposed to different cash flow patterns over a common life), further complications arise; thus, for meaningful comparisons, some mutually exclusive projects must be evaluated over a common life. This point is discussed later in the chapter.

Both projects have the same scale (each requires an initial investment of $1,000), so the difference in their initial cost is zero. However, Project Sooner has most of its future cash flows in Year 1 and Project Later has most of its future cash flows in Year 2. This causes their difference in Year 1 to be positive and their difference in Year 2 to be negative. In other words, there is one and only one sign change, so a crossover rate exists. As this illustrates, projects with the same scale must have timing differences in future cash flows for there to be one and only one sign change.

What about a situation in which projects don't have timing differences but do have a scale difference? Projects Smaller and Larger each have a 10% cost of capital, and their cash flows are shown below:

	Year				
	0	1	2	NPV	IRR
Smaller	–$90	$12	$112	$13	18.4%
Larger	–$1,000	$120	$1,120	$35	12.0%
$\Delta = CF_S - CF_L$	$910	–$108	–$1,008		11.3%

There are no timing differences in the future cash flows; in fact, Project Smaller's future cash flows are 10% of Project Larger's. However, there is a scale difference because Project Smaller's initial cost is much less than that of Project Larger. The scale difference causes the difference in the initial cash flow to be positive. However, the differences in the future cash flows are negative. This causes one and only one sign change, so a crossover rate exists.

10-4d Applying IRR as an Evaluation Measure

When using the IRR, it is important to distinguish between independent projects and mutually exclusive projects.

If you are evaluating an independent project with normal cash flows, then the NPV and IRR criteria always lead to the same accept/reject decision: If NPV says accept then IRR also says accept, and vice versa. To see why this is so, look at Figure 10-5 and notice (1) that the IRR says accept Project S if the cost of capital is less than (or to the left of) the IRR and (2) that if the cost of capital is less than the IRR, then the NPV must be positive. Thus, at any cost of capital less than 14.686%, Project S will be recommended by both the NPV and IRR criteria, but both methods reject the project if the cost of capital is greater than 14.686%. A similar statement can be made for Project L, or any other normal project, and we would always reach the same conclusion: For normal, independent projects, if the IRR says to accept it, then so will the NPV.

Now assume that Projects S and L are mutually exclusive rather than independent. Therefore, we can choose either S or L, or we can reject both, but we can't accept both. Now look at Figure 10-5 and note these points.

- $IRR_S > IRR_L$, so the IRR decision rule would say to accept Project S over Project L.
- As long as the cost of capital is *greater than* the crossover rate of 12.274%, both methods agree that Project S is better: $NPV_S > NPV_L$ and $IRR_S > IRR_L$. Therefore, if r is *greater* than the crossover rate, no conflict occurs.
- However, if the cost of capital is *less than* the crossover rate, a conflict arises: NPV ranks L higher, but IRR ranks S higher. In this situation, select the project with the highest NPV even if it has a lower IRR.

SELF-TEST

In what sense is a project's IRR similar to the YTM on a bond?

The cash flows for Projects SS and LL are as follows:

	End-of-Year Cash Flows			
	0	1	2	3
SS	−700	500	300	100
LL	−700	100	300	600

Assume that the firm's WACC = r = 10%. What are the two projects' IRRs? **(IRR_{SS} = 18.0%; IRR_{LL} = 15.6%)**

Which project would the IRR method select if the firm has a 10% cost of capital and the projects are (a) independent or (b) mutually exclusive? **(Both; SS)**

What condition regarding cash flows would cause more than one IRR to exist?

Project MM has the following cash flows:

End-of-Year Cash Flows			
0	1	2	3
−$1,000	$2,000	$2,000	−$3,350

Calculate MM's NPV at discount rates of 0%, 10%, 12.2258%, 25%, 122.147%, and 150%. **(−$350; −$46; $0; $165; $0; −$94)**

What are MM's IRRs? **(12.23% and 122.15%)**

If the cost of capital were 10%, should the project be accepted or rejected? **(Rejected because NPV < 0)**

Describe in words how an NPV profile is constructed. How do you determine the intercepts for the x-axis and the y-axis?

What is the crossover rate, and how does it interact with the cost of capital to determine whether or not a conflict exists between NPV and IRR?

What two characteristics can lead to conflicts between the NPV and the IRR when evaluating mutually exclusive projects??

10-5 Modified Internal Rate of Return (MIRR)

Recall from Chapter 5 that an investor who purchases a bond and holds it to maturity (assuming no default) will receive the bond's yield to maturity (YTM) even if interest rates change. This happens because the realized rate of return on an investment is by definition the rate that sets the present value of the realized cash flows equal to the purchase price. However, the realized rate of return on the investment in the bond and the subsequent reinvestment of the coupons will not necessarily equal the YTM if interest rates change. Similar reasoning can be applied to a project—the project's expected return is equal to its IRR, but the expected return on the project and any reinvested cash flows is not necessarily equal to the IRR.

If a manager wishes to evaluate a project based on the return expected from the project and its reinvested cash flows, then the IRR overstates this return because it is more likely that the project's future cash flows can be reinvested at the cost of capital and not at the project's IRR. The **Modified IRR (MIRR)** is similar to the regular IRR, except it is based on the assumption that cash flows are reinvested at the WACC (or some other explicit

FIGURE 10-6

Finding the MIRR for Projects S and L

	A	B	C	D	E	F	G
293	INPUTS:						
294	r = 10%						
295			Initial Cost and Expected Cash Flows				
296	Year	0	1	2	3	4	
297	Project S	-$10,000	$5,300	$4,300	$1,874	$1,500	
298		↓	↓	↓	↳→→	$2,061	
299		↓	↓	↳→ →	→→→→→	$5,203	
300	Present Value of	↓	↳→ →	→→→→→	→→→→→	$7,054	
301	Negative CF (PV) =	-$10,000	Terminal Value of Positive CF (TV) =			$15,819	
302							
303	Calculator: N = 4, PV = −10000, PMT = 0, FV = 15819. Press I/YR to get:					$MIRR_S$ =	12.15%
304	*Excel* Rate function–Easier:		=RATE(F296,0,B301,F301)			$MIRR_S$ =	12.15%
305	*Excel* MIRR function–Easiest:		=MIRR(B297:F297,B294,B294)			$MIRR_S$ =	12.15%
306							
307	Year	0	1	2	3	4	
308	Project L	-$10,000	$1,900	$2,700	$2,345	$7,800	
309							
310	For Project L, using the MIRR function:			=MIRR(B308:F308,B294,B294)		$MIRR_L$ =	12.78%

Notes:

1. The terminal value (TV) is the future value of all positive cash flows. The present value (PV) is the present value of all negative cash flows.
2. Find the discount rate that forces the TV positive cash flows to equal the PV of negative cash flows. That discount rate is defined as the MIRR.

$$\text{PV of negative cash flows} = (\text{TV of positive cash flows})/(1 + \text{MIRR})^N$$

$$\$10{,}000 = \$15{,}819/(1 + \text{MIRR})^4$$

We can find the MIRR with a calculator or *Excel.*

rate if that is a more reasonable assumption). Refer to Figure 10-6 as you read the following steps that explain the MIRR's calculation.

1. Project S has just one outflow, a negative $10,000 at t = 0. Because it occurs at Time 0, it is not discounted, and its PV is −$10,000. If the project had additional outflows, we would find the PV at t = 0 for each one and then sum them for use in the MIRR calculation.
2. Next, we find the future value of each *inflow*, compounded at the WACC out to the "terminal year," which is the year the last inflow is received. We assume that cash flows are reinvested at the WACC. For Project S, the first cash flow, $5,300, is compounded at WACC = 10% for 3 years, and it grows to $7,054. The second inflow, $4,300, grows to $5,203, and the third inflow, $1,874, grows to $2,061. The last inflow, $1,500, is received at the end, so it is not compounded at all. The sum of the future values, $15,819, is called the "terminal value," or TV.
3. We now have the PV at t = 0 of all negative cash flows, −$10,000, and the TV at Year 4 of all positive cash flows, $15,819. There is some discount rate that will cause the PV of the terminal value to equal the cost. *That interest rate is defined as the Modified Internal Rate of Return (MIRR).* In a calculator, enter N = 4, PV = −10000, PMT = 0, and FV = 15819. Then pressing the I/YR key yields the MIRR, 12.15%.

4. The MIRR can be found in a number of ways. Figure 10-6 illustrates how the MIRR is calculated: We compound each cash inflow, sum them to determine the TV, and then find the rate that causes the PV of the TV to equal the cost. That rate in this example is 12.15%. However, *Excel* and some of the better calculators have a built-in MIRR function that streamlines the process. We explain how to use the MIRR function in our calculator tutorials, and we explain how to find MIRR with *Excel* in this chapter's *Excel Tool Kit.*[9]

The MIRR has two significant advantages over the regular IRR. First, the MIRR assumes that cash flows are reinvested at the cost of capital (or some other explicit rate). Because reinvestment at the IRR is generally not correct, the MIRR is usually a better indicator of the rate of return on the project and its reinvested cash flows. Second, the MIRR eliminates the multiple IRR problem—there can never be more than one MIRR, and it can be compared with the cost of capital when deciding to accept or reject projects.

Our conclusion is that the MIRR is better than the regular IRR; however, this question remains: Is MIRR as good as the NPV? Here is our take on the situation.

- For *independent* projects, the NPV, IRR, and MIRR always reach the same accept–reject conclusion, so the three criteria are equally good when evaluating independent projects.
- However, if projects are *mutually exclusive* and if they differ in size, conflicts can arise. In such cases the NPV is best because it selects the project that maximizes value.[10]
- Our overall conclusions are that (1) the MIRR is superior to the regular IRR as an indicator of a project's "true" rate of return, but (2) NPV is better than either IRR or MIRR when choosing among competing projects. If managers want to know the expected rates of return on projects, it would be better to give them MIRRs than IRRs because MIRRs are more likely to be the rates that are actually earned if the projects' cash flows are reinvested in future projects.

---

[9]If we let COF_t and CIF_t denote cash outflows and inflows, respectively, then Equations 10-2a and 10-2b summarize the steps just described:

$$\sum_{t=0}^{N} \frac{COF_t}{(1+r)^t} = \frac{\sum_{t=0}^{N} CIF_t(1+r)^{N-t}}{(1+MIRR)^N} \tag{10-2a}$$

$$\text{PV costs} = \frac{TV}{(1+MIRR)^N} \tag{10-2b}$$

Also, note that there are alternative definitions for the MIRR. One difference relates to whether negative cash flows after the positive cash flows begin should be compounded and treated as part of the TV or discounted and treated as a cost. A related issue is whether negative and positive flows in a given year should be netted or treated separately. For more discussion, see David M. Shull, "Interpreting Rates of Return: A Modified Rate of Return Approach," *Financial Practice and Education,* Fall 1993, pp. 67–71.

[10]For projects of equal size but different lives, the MIRR will always lead to the same decision as the NPV if the MIRRs are both calculated using as the terminal year the life of the longer project. (Fill in zeros for the shorter project's missing cash flows.)

SELF-TEST

What's the primary difference between the MIRR and the regular IRR?

Projects A and B have the following cash flows:

	0	1	2
A	−$1,000	$1,150	$100
B	−$1,000	$100	$1,300

The cost of capital is 10%. What are the projects' IRRs, MIRRs, and NPVs? **(IRR_A = 23.1%, IRR_B = 19.1%; $MIRR_A$ = 16.8%, $MIRR_B$ = 18.7%; NPV_A = $128.10, NPV_B = $165.29)**

Which project would each method select? **(IRR: A; MIRR: B; NPV: B)**

10-6 Profitability Index (PI)

A fourth method used to evaluate projects is the **profitability index (PI)**:

$$PI = \frac{\text{PV of future cash flows}}{\text{Initial cost}} = \frac{\sum_{t=1}^{N} \frac{CF_t}{(1+r)^t}}{CF_0} \quad (10\text{-}3)$$

Here CF_t represents the expected future cash flows and CF_0 represents the initial cost. The PI shows the *relative* profitability of any project, or the present value per dollar of initial cost. As we can see from Figure 10-7, the PI for Project S, based on a 10% cost of capital, is $10,804.38/$10,000 = 1.0804; the PI for Project L is 1.1048. Thus, Project S is expected to produce $1.0804 of present value for each $1 of investment whereas L should produce $1.1048 for each dollar invested.

A project is acceptable if its PI is greater than 1.0, and the higher the PI, the higher the project's ranking. Therefore, both S and L would be accepted by the PI criterion if they were independent, and L would be ranked ahead of S if they were mutually exclusive.

Mathematically, the NPV, IRR, MIRR, and PI methods will always lead to the same accept/reject decisions for *normal, independent* projects: If a project's NPV is positive, its IRR and MIRR will always exceed r and its PI will always be greater than 1.0. However, these methods can give conflicting rankings for *mutually exclusive* projects if the projects differ in size or in the timing of cash flows. If the PI ranking conflicts with the NPV, then the NPV ranking should be used.

FIGURE 10-7

Profitability Index (PI)

	A	B	C	D	E
332	**Project S:**		**PI_S = PV of future cash flows**	**÷**	**Initial cost**
333			**PI_S = $10,804.38**	**÷**	**$10,000**
334			**PI_S = 1.0804**		
335					
336	**Project L:**		**PI_L = PV of future cash flows**	**÷**	**Initial cost**
337			**PI_L = $11,048.02**	**÷**	**$10,000**
338			**PI_L = 1.1048**		

SELF-TEST

Explain how the PI is calculated. What does it measure?

A project has the following expected cash flows: $CF_0 = -\$500$, $CF_1 = \$200$, $CF_2 = \$200$, and $CF_3 = \$400$. If the project's cost of capital is 9%, what is the PI? **(1.32)**

10-7 Payback Period

NPV and IRR are the most commonly used methods today, but historically the first selection criterion was the **payback period**, defined as the number of years required to recover the funds invested in a project from its operating cash flows. Equation 10-4 is used for the calculation, and the process is diagrammed in Figure 10-8. We start with the project's cost, a negative number, and then add the cash inflow for each year until the cumulative cash flow turns positive. The payback year is the year *prior to* full recovery, plus a fraction equal to the shortfall at the end of the prior year divided by the cash flow during the year when full recovery occurs:[11]

$$\text{Payback} = \begin{matrix}\text{Number of}\\ \text{years prior to}\\ \text{full recovery}\end{matrix} + \frac{\begin{matrix}\text{Unrecovered cost}\\ \text{at start of year}\end{matrix}}{\begin{matrix}\text{Cash flow during}\\ \text{full recovery year}\end{matrix}} \tag{10-4}$$

FIGURE 10-8

Payback Period

	A	B	C	D	E	F	G
365	Project S	Year	0	1	2	3	4
366		Cash flow	-$10,000	$5,300	$4,300	$1,874	$1,500
367		Cumulative cash flow	-$10,000	-$4,700	-$400	$1,474	$2,974
368	Intermediate calculation for payback		—	—	—	2.21	3.98
369						↑	
370					Intermediate calculation:		
371	Manual calculation of Payback S = 2 + $400/$1,874 =			2.21	=IF(F367>0,E365+ABS(E367/F366),"—")		
372	*Excel* calculation of Payback S =			2.21		2.21	
373							
374	Project L	Year	0	1	2	3	4
375		Cash flow	-$10,000	$1,900	$2,700	$2,345	$7,800
376		Cumulative cash flow	-$10,000	-$8,100	-$5,400	-$3,055	$4,745
377							
378	Manual calculation of Payback L = 3 + $3,055/$7,800 =			3.39	Payback switches from negative to positive cash flow.		
379	Alternative *Excel* calculation of Payback L =						
380	=PERCENTRANK(C376:G376,0,6)*G374			3.39			

[11] Equation 10-4 assumes that cash flows come in uniformly during the full recovery year.

resource
*See **Ch10 Tool Kit.xls** on the textbook's Web site.*

The cash flows for Projects S and L, together with their paybacks, are shown in Figure 10-8.[12] The shorter the payback, the better the project. Therefore, if the firm requires a payback of 3 years or less, then S would be accepted but L would be rejected. If the projects were mutually exclusive, S would be ranked over L because of its shorter payback.

The regular payback has three flaws: (1) Dollars received in different years are all given the same weight—that is, the time value of money is ignored. (2) Cash flows beyond the payback year are given no consideration whatsoever, regardless of how large they might be. (3) Unlike the NPV or the IRR, which tell us how much wealth a project adds or how much a project's rate of return exceeds the cost of capital, the payback merely tells us how long it takes to recover our investment. There is no necessary relationship between a given payback period and investor wealth, so we don't know how to specify an acceptable payback. The firm might use 2 years, 3 years, or any other number as the minimum acceptable payback, but the choice is arbitrary.

To counter the first criticism, financial analysts developed the **discounted payback**, where cash flows are discounted at the WACC and then those discounted cash flows are used to find the payback. In Figure 10-9, we calculate the discounted paybacks for S and L, assuming both have a 10% cost of capital. Each inflow is divided by $(1 + r)^t = (1.10)^t$, where t is the year in which the cash flow occurs and r is the project's cost of capital, and then those PVs are used to find the payback. Project S's discounted payback is 3.21 years and L's is 3.80 years.

resource
*See **Ch10 Tool Kit.xls** on the textbook's Web site.*

Note that the payback is a "break-even" calculation in the sense that if cash flows come in at the expected rate, then the project will at least break even. However, because the regular payback doesn't consider the cost of capital, it doesn't specify the true break-even year. The discounted payback does consider capital costs, but it disregards cash flows

FIGURE 10-9
Discounted Payback

	A	B	C	D	E	F	G
393	Project WACC =	10%					
394	Project S	Year	0	1	2	3	4
395		Cash flow	-$10,000	$5,300	$4,300	$1,874	$1,500
396		Discounted cash flow	-$10,000	$4,818	$3,554	$1,408	$1,025
397		Cumulative discounted CF	-$10,000	-$5,182	-$1,628	-$220	$804
398							
399	Discounted Payback S = 3 + $220.14/$1,024.52 =			3.21		Switches from negative to	
400	*Excel* calculation of Discounted Payback S =					positive cash flow.	
401	=PERCENTRANK(C397:G397,0,6)*G394			3.21			
402							
403	Project L	Year	0	1	2	3	4
404		Cash flow	-$10,000	$1,900	$2,700	$2,345	$7,800
405		Discounted cash flow	-$10,000	$1,727	$2,231	$1,762	$5,328
406		Cumulative discounted CF	-$10,000	-$8,273	-$6,041	-$4,279	$1,048
407							
408	Discounted Payback L = 3 + $4,279.49/$5,327.50 =			3.80		Switches from negative to	
409	*Excel* calculation of Discounted Payback L =					positive cash flow.	
410	=PERCENTRANK(C406:G406,0,6)*G403			3.80			

[12]There is not an *Excel* function for payback. But if the cash flows are normal, then the PERCENTRANK function can be used to find payback, as illustrated in Figures 10-8 and 10-9.

poor decisions. Finally, there is no way to determine how short the payback periods must be to justify accepting a project.

Although the payback methods have faults as ranking criteria, they do provide information about *liquidity* and *risk*. The shorter the payback, other things held constant, the greater the project's liquidity. This factor is often important for smaller firms that don't have ready access to the capital markets. Also, cash flows expected in the distant future are generally riskier than near-term cash flows, so the payback period is also a risk indicator.

SELF-TEST

What two pieces of information does the payback method provide that are absent from the other capital budgeting decision methods?

What three flaws does the regular payback method have? Does the discounted payback method correct all of those flaws? Explain.

Project P has a cost of $1,000 and cash flows of $300 per year for 3 years plus another $1,000 in Year 4. The project's cost of capital is 15%. What are P's regular and discounted paybacks? **(3.10, 3.55)** *If the company requires a payback of 3 years or less, would the project be accepted? Would this be a good accept/reject decision, considering the NPV and/or the IRR?* **(NPV = $256.72, IRR = 24.78%)***?*

10-8 How to Use the Different Capital Budgeting Methods

We have discussed six capital budgeting decision criteria: NPV, IRR, MIRR, PI, payback, and discounted payback. We compared these methods and highlighted their strengths and weaknesses. In the process, we may have created the impression that "sophisticated" firms should use only one method, the NPV. However, virtually all capital budgeting decisions are analyzed by computer, so it is easy to use all six methods. In making the accept–reject decision, most firms usually calculate and consider all six because each method provides a somewhat different piece of information about the decision.

10-8a A Comparison of the Methods

NPV is the single best criterion because it provides a direct measure of the value a project adds to shareholder wealth. IRR and MIRR measure profitability expressed as a percentage rate of return, which decision makers like to consider. The PI also measures profitability but in relation to the amount of the investment. Further, IRR, MIRR, and PI all contain information concerning a project's "safety margin." To illustrate, consider a firm, whose WACC is 10%, which must choose between these two mutually exclusive projects: SS (for small) has a cost of $10,000 and is expected to return $16,500 at the end of 1 year; LL (for large) has a cost of $100,000 and is expected to return $115,550 at the end of 1 year. SS has a huge IRR, 65%, while LL's IRR is a more modest 15.6%. The NPV paints a somewhat different picture: At the 10% cost of capital, SS's NPV is $5,000 while LL's is $5,045. By the NPV rule we would choose LL. However, SS's IRR indicates that it has a much larger margin for error: Even if its cash flow were 39% below the $16,500 forecast, the firm would still recover its $10,000 investment. On the other hand, if LL's inflows fell by only 13.5% from its forecasted $115,550, the firm would not recover its investment. Further, if neither project generated any cash flows at all, the firm would lose only $10,000 on SS but would lose $100,000 by accepting LL.

The modified IRR has all the virtues of the IRR, but it avoids the problem of multiple rates of return that can occur with the IRR. The MIRR also measures the expected return of the project and its reinvested cash flows, which provides additional insight into the project. So if decision makers want to know projects' rates of return, the MIRR is a better indicator than the regular IRR.

The PI tells a similar story to the IRR. Here PI_{LL} is only 1.05 while PI_{SS} is 1.50. As with the IRR, this indicates that Project SS's cash inflow could fall by a lot before it loses money, whereas a small decline in LL's cash flows would result in a loss.

Payback and discounted payback provide indications of a project's *liquidity* and *risk.* A long payback means that investment dollars will be locked up for a long time; hence the project is relatively illiquid. In addition, a long payback means that cash flows must be forecast far into the future, and that probably makes the project riskier than one with a shorter payback. A good analogy for this is bond valuation. An investor should never compare the yields to maturity on two bonds without also considering their terms to maturity, because a bond's risk is influenced significantly by its maturity. The same holds true for capital projects.

In summary, the different measures provide different types of useful information. It is easy to calculate all of them: Simply put the cost of capital and the cash flows into an *Excel* model like the one provided in this chapter's ***Tool Kit*** and the model will instantly calculate all six criteria. Therefore, most sophisticated companies consider all six measures when making capital budgeting decisions. For most decisions, the greatest weight should be given to the NPV, but it would be foolish to ignore the information provided by the other criteria.

10-8b The Decision Process: What Is the Source of a Project's NPV?

Just as it would be foolish to ignore these capital budgeting methods, it would also be foolish to make decisions based *solely* on them. One cannot know at Time 0 the exact cost of future capital or the exact future cash flows. These inputs are simply estimates, and if they turn out to be incorrect then so will be the calculated NPVs and IRRs. Thus, *quantitative methods provide valuable information, but they should not be used as the sole criteria for accept–reject decisions* in the capital budgeting process. Rather, managers should use quantitative methods in the decision-making process but should also consider the likelihood that actual results will differ from the forecasts. Qualitative factors, such as the chances of a tax increase, or a war, or a major product liability suit, should also be considered. In summary, *quantitative methods such as NPV and IRR should be considered as an aid to informed decisions but not as a substitute for sound managerial judgment.*

In this same vein, managers should ask sharp questions about any project that has a large NPV, a high IRR, or a high PI. In a perfectly competitive economy, there would be no positive-NPV projects—all companies would have the same opportunities, and competition would quickly eliminate any positive NPV. The existence of positive-NPV projects must be predicated on some imperfection in the marketplace, and the longer the life of the project, the longer that imperfection must last. Therefore, managers should be able to identify the imperfection and explain why it will persist before accepting that a project will really have a positive NPV. Valid explanations might include patents or proprietary technology, which is how pharmaceutical and software firms create positive-NPV projects. Pfizer's Lipitor (a cholesterol-reducing medicine) and Microsoft's Windows 7 operating system are examples. Companies can also create positive NPV by being the first entrant into a new market or by creating new products that meet some previously unidentified consumer needs. Post-it notes invented by 3M are an example. Similarly, Dell developed procedures for direct sales of microcomputers and, in the process, created projects with enormous NPV. Also, companies such as Southwest Airlines have trained and motivated their workers better than their competitors, and this has led to positive-NPV projects. In all of these cases, the companies developed some source of competitive advantage, and that advantage resulted in positive-NPV projects.

This discussion suggests three things: (1) If you can't identify the reason a project has a positive projected NPV, then its actual NPV will probably not be positive. (2) Positive-NPV projects don't just happen—they result from hard work to develop some competitive advantage. At the risk of oversimplification, the primary job of a manager is to find and develop areas of competitive advantage. (3) Some competitive advantages last longer than others, with their durability depending on competitors' ability to replicate them. Patents, the control of scarce resources, or large size in an industry where strong economies of scale exist can keep competitors at bay. However, it is relatively easy to replicate product features that cannot be patented. The bottom line is that managers should strive to develop nonreplicable sources of competitive advantage. If such an advantage cannot be demonstrated, then you should question projects with high NPV—especially if they have long lives.

10-8c Decision Criteria Used in Practice

Table 10-1 reports survey evidence and shows that a large majority of companies use NPV and IRR. As we suggested in the previous section, other methods are also used.

The table also reports the factors CEOs consider important in allocating capital within the firm. The ranking of projects by NPV is the factor that most CEOs consider important. Interestingly, CEOs also consider the manager who is proposing the project, both in terms of the manager's past success and the manager's confidence in the project. Confidence is often expressed through the range of possible outcomes for the project, with smaller ranges conveying more confidence. Chapter 11 explains how to estimate such confidence intervals.

TABLE 10-1
Capital Budgeting in Practice

Quantitative Measures Used by Companies	Percent Using	Factors Considered Important by CEOs when Allocating Capital within the Company	Percent Agreeing
NPV	75%	Project's ranking based on NPV	78.6%
IRR	76	Proposing manager's track record	71.3
Payback	57	Proposing manager's confidence in project	68.8
Discounted payback	29	Timing of project's cash flows	65.3
		Project's ability to protect market share	51.9
		Proposing division's track record	51.2

Sources: The percentages of companies using particular quantitative measures are from John R. Graham and Campbell R. Harvey, "The Theory and Practice of Corporate Finance: Evidence from the Field," *Journal of Financial Economics,* 2001, pp. 187–244. The percentages of CEOs agreeing with the capital allocation factors are from John R. Graham, Campbell R. Harvey, and Manju Puri, "Capital Allocation and Delegation of Decision Making Authority within Firms," NBER Working Paper 1730, 2011, **www.nber.org/papers/w17370.**

SELF-TEST

Describe the advantages and disadvantages of the six capital budgeting methods.

Should capital budgeting decisions be made solely on the basis of a project's NPV, with no regard to the other criteria? Explain your answer.

What are some possible reasons that a project might have a high NPV?

10-9 Other Issues in Capital Budgeting

Three other issues in capital budgeting are discussed in this section: (1) how to deal with mutually exclusive projects whose lives differ; (2) the potential advantage of terminating a project before the end of its physical life; and (3) the optimal capital budget when the cost of capital rises as the size of the capital budget increases.

10-9a Mutually Exclusive Projects with Unequal Lives

When choosing between two mutually exclusive alternatives with significantly different lives, an adjustment is necessary. For example, suppose a company is planning to modernize its production facilities and is considering either a conveyor system (Project C) or a fleet of forklift trucks (Project F) for moving materials. The first two sections of Figure 10-10 show the expected net cash flows, NPVs, and IRRs for these two mutually exclusive alternatives. We see that Project C, when discounted at the firm's 12% cost of capital, has the higher NPV and thus appears to be the better project.

resource
See Ch10 Tool Kit.xls on the textbook's Web site.

Although the NPVs shown in Figure 10-10 suggest that Project C should be selected, this analysis is incomplete, and the decision to choose Project C is actually incorrect. If we choose Project F, we will have an opportunity to make a similar investment in 3 years, and

FIGURE 10-10
Analysis of Projects C and F (r = 12%)

	A	B	C	D	E	F	G	H
438	WACC = r =	12.0%						
439								
440	Data on Project C, Conveyor System:							
441	Year	0	1	2	3	4	5	6
442	Cash flows for C	−$40,000	$8,000	$14,000	$13,000	$12,000	$11,000	$10,000
443		NPV_C =	$6,491		IRR_C =	17.5%		
444								
445	Data on Project F, Forklifts:							
446	Year	0	1	2	3			
447	Cash flows for F	−$20,000	$7,000	$13,000	$12,000			
448		NPV_F =	$5,155		IRR_F =	25.2%		
449								
450	Common Life Approach with F Repeated (Project FF):							
451	Year	0	1	2	3	4	5	6
452	CF_t for 1st F	−$20,000	$7,000	$13,000	$12,000			
453	CF_t for 2nd F				−$20,000	$7,000	$13,000	$12,000
454	All CFs for FF	−$20,000	$7,000	$13,000	−$8,000	$7,000	$13,000	$12,000
455		NPV_{FF} =	$8,824		IRR_{FF} =	25.2%		

if cost and revenue conditions continue at the levels shown in Figure 10-10, then this second investment will also be profitable. However, if we choose Project C, we cannot make this second investment. Two approaches can be used to compare Projects C and F, as shown in Figure 10-10 and discussed next.

Replacement Chains

The key to the *replacement chain,* or *common life, approach* is to analyze both projects over an equal life. In our example, Project C has a 6-year life, so we assume that Project F will be repeated after 3 years and then analyze it over the same 6-year period. We can then calculate the NPV of C and compare it to the extended-life NPV of Project F. The NPV for Project C, as shown in Figure 10-10, is already based on the 6-year common life. For Project F, however, we must add in a second project to extend the overall life to 6 years. The time line for this extended project, denoted as "All CFs for FF," is shown in Figure 10-10. Here we assume (1) that Project F's cost and annual cash inflows will not change if the project is repeated in 3 years and (2) that the cost of capital will remain at 12%.

The NPV of this extended Project F is $8,824, and its IRR is 25.2%. (The IRR of two Project Fs is the same as the IRR for one Project F.) However, the $8,824 extended NPV of Project F is greater than Project C's $6,491 NPV, so Project F should be selected.

Alternatively, we could recognize that Project F has an NPV of $5,155 at Time 0 and a second NPV of that same amount at Time 3, find the PV of the second NPV at Time 0, and then sum the two to find Project F's extended-life NPV of $8,824.

Equivalent Annual Annuities (EAA)

Electrical engineers designing power plants and distribution lines were the first to encounter the unequal life problem. They could install transformers and other equipment that had relatively low initial costs but short lives, or they could use equipment that had higher initial costs but longer lives. The services would be required into the indefinite future, so this was the issue: Which choice would result in a higher NPV in the long run? The engineers converted the annual cash flows under the alternative investments into a constant cash flow stream whose NPV was equal to, or equivalent to, the NPV of the initial stream. This was called the **equivalent annual annuity (EAA) method.** To apply the EAA method to Projects C and F, for each project find the constant payment streams that the projects' NPVs ($6,491 for C and $5,155 for F) would provide over their respective lives. Using a financial calculator for Project C, we enter N = 6, I/YR = 12, PV = −6491, and FV = 0. Then, when we press the PMT key, we find EAA_C = $1,579. For Project F, we enter N = 3, I/YR = 12, PV = −5155, and FV = 0; solving for PMT, we find EAA_F = $2,146. Project F would thus produce a higher cash flow stream over the 6 years, so it is the better project.

Conclusions about Unequal Lives

When should we worry about analysis of unequal lives? The unequal life issue (1) does not arise for independent projects but (2) can arise if mutually exclusive projects with significantly different lives are being compared. However, even for mutually exclusive projects, it is not always appropriate to extend the analysis to a common life. This should be done if and only if there is a high probability that the projects will actually be repeated at the end of their initial lives.

We should note several potentially serious weaknesses in this type of analysis. (1) If inflation occurs, then replacement equipment will have a higher price. Moreover, both sales prices and operating costs would probably change. Thus, the static conditions built into the analysis would be invalid. (2) Replacements that occur down the road would probably employ new technology, which in turn might change the cash flows. (3) It is difficult enough to estimate the lives of most projects, and even more so to estimate the lives of a series of projects. In view of these problems, no experienced financial analyst would be too concerned about comparing mutually exclusive projects with lives of, say, 8 years and 10 years. Given all the uncertainties in the estimation process, we would assume that such projects would, for all practical purposes, have the same life. Still, it is important to recognize that a problem exists if mutually exclusive projects have substantially different lives.

When we encounter situations with significant differences in project lives, we first use a computer spreadsheet to build expected inflation and/or possible efficiency gains directly into the cash flow estimates and then use the replacement chain approach. We prefer the replacement chain approach for two reasons. First, it is easier to explain to those who are responsible for approving capital budgets. Second, it is easier to build inflation and other modifications into a spreadsheet and then go on to make the replacement chain calculations.

10-9b Economic Life versus Physical Life

Projects are normally evaluated under the assumption that the firm will operate them over their full physical lives. However, this may not be the best plan—it may be better to terminate a project before the end of its potential life. For example, the cost of maintenance for trucks and machinery can become quite high if they are used for too many years, so it might be better to replace them before the end of their potential lives.

Figure 10-11 provides data for an asset with a physical life of 3 years. However, the project can be terminated at the end of any year and the asset sold at the indicated salvage values. All of the cash flows are after taxes, and the firm's cost of capital is 10%. The undiscounted cash flows are shown in Columns C and D in the upper part of the figure, and the present values of these flows are shown in Columns E and F. We find the project's NPV under different assumptions about how long it will be operated. If the project is operated for its full 3-year life, it will have a negative NPV. The NPV will be positive if it is operated for 2 years and then the asset is sold for a relatively high salvage value; the NPV will be negative if the asset is disposed after only 1 year of operation. Therefore, the project's optimal life is 2 years.

resource
*See **Ch10 Tool Kit.xls** on the textbook's Web site.*

This type of analysis is used to determine a project's **economic life**, which is the life that maximizes the NPV and thus shareholder wealth. For our project, the economic life is 2 years versus the 3-year **physical**, or **engineering, life**. Note that this analysis was based on the expected cash flows and the expected salvage values, and it should always be conducted as a part of the capital budgeting evaluation if salvage values are relatively high.

10-9c The Optimal Capital Budget

The **optimal capital budget** is defined as the set of projects that maximizes the value of the firm. Finance theory states that all independent projects with positive NPVs should be accepted, as should the mutually exclusive projects with the highest NPVs. Therefore, the optimal capital budget consists of that set of projects. However, two complications arise in practice: (1) The cost of capital might increase as the size of the capital budget increases, making it hard to know the proper discount rate to use when evaluating projects; and (2) sometimes firms set an upper limit on the size of their capital budgets, which is also known as *capital rationing.*

FIGURE 10-11
Economic Life versus Physical Life

	A	B	C	D	E	F	G
495	WACC = 10%				PVs of the Cash Flows		
496			Operating	Salvage	Operating	Salvage	
497		Year	Cash Flow	Value	Cash Flow	Value	
498		0	-$4,800				
499		1	2,000	$3,000	$1,818.18	$2,727.27	
500		2	2,000	1,650	1,652.89	1,363.64	
501		3	1,750	0	1,314.80	0.00	
502					PV of		PV of
503	NPV at Different Operating Lives:		Initial Cost	+	Operating	+	Salvage
504					Cash Flows		Value
505	Operate for 3 Years:						
506	NPV_3:	-$14.12	-$4,800	+	$4,785.88	+	$0.00
507	Operate for 2 Years:						
508	NPV_2:	$34.71	-$4,800	+	$3,471.07	+	$1,363.64
509	Operate for 1 Year:						
510	NPV_1:	-$254.55	-$4,800	+	$1,818.18	+	$2,727.27

Note: The project is profitable if and only if it is operated for just 2 years.

An Increasing Cost of Capital

The cost of capital may increase as the capital budget increases—this is called an *increasing marginal cost of capital.* As we discussed in Chapter 9, flotation costs associated with issuing new equity can be quite high. This means that the cost of capital will increase once a company has invested all of its internally generated cash and must sell new common stock. In addition, once a firm has used up its normal credit lines and must seek additional debt capital, it may encounter an increase in its cost of debt. This means that a project might have a positive NPV if it is part of a $10 million capital budget, but the same project might have a negative NPV if it is part of a $20 million capital budget because the cost of capital might increase.

Fortunately, these problems rarely occur for most firms, especially those that are stable and well established. When a rising cost of capital is encountered, we would proceed as indicated below. You can look at Figure 10-12 as you read through our points.

- Find the IRR (or MIRR) on all potential projects, arrange them in rank order (along with their initial costs), and then plot them on a graph with the IRR on the vertical axis and the cumulative costs on the horizontal axis. The firm's data are shown in Figure 10-12, and the IRRs are plotted in the graph. The line is called the Investment Opportunity Schedule (IOS), and it shows the marginal return on capital.
- Next, determine how much capital can be raised before it is necessary to issue new common stock or go to higher-cost sources of debt, and identify the amounts of higher-cost capital. Use this information to calculate the WACC that corresponds to the different amounts of capital raised. In this example, the firm can raise $300 before the WACC rises, but the WACC increases as additional capital is raised. The

FIGURE 10-12

IOS and MCC Schedules

	A	B	C	D	E	F
517	Investment Opportunity Schedule (IOS)			Marginal Cost of Capital (MCC)		
518			Highest to	Cumulative		Lowest to
519	Projects	Cost	Lowest IRR	Cost		Highest WACC
520	A	$100	14.0%	$100		9.0%
521	B	$100	13.0%	$200		9.0%
522	C	$100	11.5%	$300		9.0%
523	D	$100	10.0%	$400		10.0%
524	E	$50	9.5%	$450		11.0%
525	F	$50	9.0%	$500		12.0%
526	G	$100	8.5%	$600		15.0%

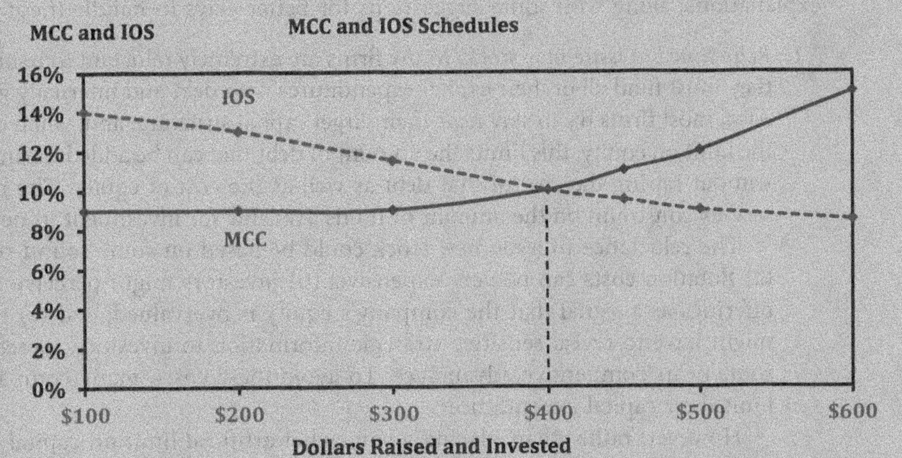

Note: Use WACC = 10% as the base rate for finding base risk-adjusted project WACCs.

resource

*See **Ch10 Tool Kit.xls** on the textbook's Web site.*

increasing WACC represents the marginal cost of capital, and its graph is called the Marginal Cost of Capital (MCC) schedule.

- The intersection of the IOS and MCC schedules indicates the amount of capital the firm should raise and invest, and it is analogous to the familiar marginal cost versus marginal revenue schedule discussed in introductory economics courses. In our example, the firm should have a capital budget of $400; if it uses a WACC of 10% then it will accept projects A, B, C, and D, which have a cumulative cost of $400. The 10% WACC should be used for average-risk projects, but it should be scaled up or down for more or less risky projects as discussed in Chapter 9.

Our example illustrates the case of a firm that cannot raise all the money it needs at a constant WACC. Firms should not try to be too precise with this process—the data are not good enough for precision—but they should be aware of the concept and get at least a rough idea of how raising additional capital will affect the WACC.

Capital Rationing

Armbrister Pyrotechnics, a manufacturer of fireworks and lasers for light shows, has identified 40 potential independent projects, of which 15 have a positive NPV based on the firm's 12% cost of capital. The total investment required to implement these 15 projects would be $75 million and so, according to finance theory, the optimal capital budget is $75 million. Thus, Armbrister should accept the 15 projects with positive NPVs and invest $75 million. However, Armbrister's management has imposed a limit of $50 million for capital expenditures during the upcoming year. Because of this restriction, the company must forgo a number of value-adding projects. This is an example of **capital rationing**, defined as a situation in which a firm limits its capital expenditures to an amount less than would be required to fund the optimal capital budget. Despite being at odds with finance theory, this practice is quite common.

Why would any company forgo value-adding projects? Here are some potential explanations, along with some suggestions for better ways to handle these situations.

1. *Reluctance to issue new stock.* Many firms are extremely reluctant to issue new stock, so they must fund all of their capital expenditures with debt and internally generated cash. Also, most firms try to stay near their target capital structure, and, when combined with the limit on equity, this limits the amount of debt that can be added during any one year without raising the cost of that debt as well as the cost of equity. The result can be a serious constraint on the amount of funds available for investment in new projects.

   The reluctance to issue new stock could be based on some sound reasons: (a) flotation costs can be very expensive; (b) investors might perceive new stock offerings as a signal that the company's equity is overvalued; and (c) the company might have to reveal sensitive strategic information to investors, thereby reducing some of its competitive advantages. To avoid these costs, many companies simply limit their capital expenditures.

   However, rather than placing a somewhat artificial limit on capital expenditures, companies might be better off explicitly incorporating the costs of raising external capital into their costs of capital along the lines shown in Figure 10-12. If there still are positive-NPV projects even with the higher cost of capital, then the company should go ahead and raise external equity and accept the projects.
2. *Constraints on nonmonetary resources.* Sometimes a firm simply doesn't have the necessary managerial, marketing, or engineering talent to immediately accept all positive-NPV projects. In other words, the potential projects may be independent from a demand standpoint but not from an internal standpoint, because accepting them all would raise the firm's costs. To avoid potential problems due to spreading existing talent too thin, many firms simply limit the capital budget to a size that can be accommodated by their current personnel.

   A better solution might be to employ a technique called **linear programming**. Each potential project has an expected NPV, and each potential project requires a certain level of support by different types of employees. A linear program can identify the set of projects that maximizes NPV *subject to the constraint* that the total amount of support required for these projects does not exceed the available resources.
3. *Controlling estimation bias.* Many managers become overly optimistic when estimating the cash flows for a project. Some firms try to control this estimation bias by requiring managers to use an unrealistically high cost of capital. Others try to control the bias by limiting the size of the capital budget. Neither solution is generally effective, because managers quickly learn the rules of the game and then increase their own estimates of project cash flows, which might have been biased upward to begin with.

A better solution is to implement a post-audit program and to link the accuracy of forecasts to the compensation of the managers who initiated the projects.

SELF-TEST

Briefly describe the replacement chain (common life) approach and differentiate it from the Equivalent Annual Annuity (EAA) approach.

Differentiate between a project's physical *life and its* economic *life.*

What factors can lead to an increasing marginal cost of capital? How might this affect capital budgeting?

What is capital rationing?

What are three explanations for capital rationing? How might firms otherwise handle these situations?

SUMMARY

This chapter has described six techniques used in capital budgeting analysis: NPV, IRR, MIRR, PI, payback, and discounted payback. Each approach provides a different piece of information, so in this age of computers, managers often look at all of them when evaluating projects. However, NPV is the best single measure, and almost all firms now use NPV. The key concepts covered in this chapter are listed below.

- **Capital budgeting** is the process of analyzing potential projects. Capital budgeting decisions are probably the most important ones that managers must make.
- The **net present value (NPV) method** discounts all cash flows at the project's cost of capital and then sums those cash flows. The project should be accepted if the NPV is positive because such a project increases shareholders' value.
- The **internal rate of return (IRR)** is defined as the discount rate that forces a project's NPV to equal zero. The project should be accepted if the IRR is greater than the cost of capital.
- The NPV and IRR methods make the same accept–reject decisions for **independent projects**, but if projects are **mutually exclusive** then ranking conflicts can arise. In such cases, the NPV method should generally be relied upon.
- It is possible for a project to have more than one IRR if the project's cash flows change signs more than once.
- Unlike the IRR, a project never has more than one **modified IRR (MIRR)**. MIRR requires finding the **terminal value** (TV) of the cash inflows, compounding them at the firm's cost of capital, and then determining the discount rate that forces the present value of the TV to equal the present value of the outflows.
- The **profitability index (PI)** is calculated by dividing the present value of cash inflows by the initial cost, so it measures relative profitability—that is, the amount of the present value per dollar of investment.
- The regular **payback period** is defined as the number of years required to recover a project's cost. The regular payback method has three flaws: It ignores cash flows beyond the payback period, it does not consider the time value of money, and it doesn't give a precise acceptance rule. The payback method does, however, provide an indication of a project's risk and liquidity, because it shows how long the invested capital will be tied up.
- The **discounted payback** is similar to the regular payback except that it discounts cash flows at the project's cost of capital. It considers the time value of money, but it still ignores cash flows beyond the payback period.

- The chapter's ***Tool Kit Excel*** model and ***Web Extension 10A*** describe another, but seldom-used, evaluation method—the **accounting rate of return.**
- If mutually exclusive projects have **unequal lives,** it may be necessary to adjust the analysis to put the projects on an equal-life basis. This can be done using the **replacement chain (common life) approach** or the **equivalent annual annuity (EAA) approach.**
- A project's true value may be greater than the NPV based on its **physical life** if it can be **terminated** at the end of its **economic life.**
- Flotation costs and increased risk associated with unusually large expansion programs can cause the **marginal cost of capital** to increase as the size of the capital budget increases.
- **Capital rationing** occurs when management places a constraint on the size of the firm's capital budget during a particular period.

QUESTIONS

(10-1) Define each of the following terms:

a. Capital budgeting; regular payback period; discounted payback period
b. Independent projects; mutually exclusive projects
c. DCF techniques; net present value (NPV) method; internal rate of return (IRR) method; profitability index (PI)
d. Modified internal rate of return (MIRR) method
e. NPV profile; crossover rate
f. Nonnormal cash flow projects; normal cash flow projects; multiple IRRs
g. Reinvestment rate assumption
h. Replacement chain; economic life; capital rationing; equivalent annual annuity (EAA)

(10-2) What types of projects require the least detailed and the most detailed analysis in the capital budgeting process?

(10-3) Explain why the NPV of a relatively long-term project, defined as one for which a high percentage of its cash flows are expected in the distant future, is more sensitive to changes in the cost of capital than is the NPV of a short-term project.

(10-4) When two mutually exclusive projects are being compared, explain why the short-term project might be ranked higher under the NPV criterion if the cost of capital is high whereas the long-term project might be deemed better if the cost of capital is low. Would changes in the cost of capital ever cause a change in the IRR ranking of two such projects? Why or why not?

(10-5) Suppose a firm is considering two mutually exclusive projects. One has a life of 6 years and the other a life of 10 years. Would the failure to employ some type of replacement chain analysis bias an NPV analysis against one of the projects? Explain.

SELF-TEST PROBLEM Solution Appears in Appendix A

(ST-1) Project Analysis

You are a financial analyst for the Hittle Company. The director of capital budgeting has asked you to analyze two proposed capital investments, Projects X and Y. Each project has a cost of $10,000, and the cost of capital for each is 12%. The projects' expected net cash flows are as follows:

Year	Expected Net Cash Flows Project X	Project Y
0	−$10,000	−$10,000
1	6,500	3,500
2	3,000	3,500
3	3,000	3,500
4	1,000	3,500

a. Calculate each project's payback period, net present value (NPV), internal rate of return (IRR), modified internal rate of return (MIRR), and profitability index (PI).

b. Which project or projects should be accepted if they are independent?

c. Which project should be accepted if they are mutually exclusive?

d. How might a change in the cost of capital produce a conflict between the NPV and IRR rankings of these two projects? Would this conflict exist if r were 5%? (*Hint:* Plot the NPV profiles.)

e. Why does the conflict exist?

PROBLEMS Answers Appear in Appendix B

Easy Problems 1–7

(10-1) NPV A project has an initial cost of $40,000, expected net cash inflows of $9,000 per year for 7 years, and a cost of capital of 11%. What is the project's NPV? (*Hint:* Begin by constructing a time line.)

(10-2) IRR Refer to Problem 10-1. What is the project's IRR?

(10-3) MIRR Refer to Problem 10-1. What is the project's MIRR?

(10-4) Profitability Index Refer to Problem 10-1. What is the project's PI?

(10-5) Payback Refer to Problem 10-1. What is the project's payback period?

(10-6) Discounted Payback Refer to Problem 10-1. What is the project's discounted payback period?

(10-7) NPV Your division is considering two investment projects, each of which requires an up-front expenditure of $15 million. You estimate that the investments will produce the following net cash flows:

Year	Project A	Project B
1	$ 5,000,000	$20,000,000
2	10,000,000	10,000,000
3	20,000,000	6,000,000

a. What are the two projects' net present values, assuming the cost of capital is 5%? 10%? 15%?

b. What are the two projects' IRRs at these same costs of capital?

Intermediate Problems 8–18

(10-8) NPVs, IRRs, and MIRRs for Independent Projects

Edelman Engineering is considering including two pieces of equipment, a truck and an overhead pulley system, in this year's capital budget. The projects are independent. The cash outlay for the truck is $17,100 and that for the pulley system is $22,430. The firm's cost of capital is 14%. After-tax cash flows, including depreciation, are as follows:

Year	Truck	Pulley
1	$5,100	$7,500
2	5,100	7,500
3	5,100	7,500
4	5,100	7,500
5	5,100	7,500

Calculate the IRR, the NPV, and the MIRR for each project, and indicate the correct accept–reject decision for each.

(10-9) NPVs and IRRs for Mutually Exclusive Projects

Davis Industries must choose between a gas-powered and an electric-powered forklift truck for moving materials in its factory. Because both forklifts perform the same function, the firm will choose only one. (They are mutually exclusive investments.) The electric-powered truck will cost more, but it will be less expensive to operate; it will cost $22,000, whereas the gas-powered truck will cost $17,500. The cost of capital that applies to both investments is 12%. The life for both types of truck is estimated to be 6 years, during which time the net cash flows for the electric-powered truck will be $6,290 per year and those for the gas-powered truck will be $5,000 per year. Annual net cash flows include depreciation expenses. Calculate the NPV and IRR for each type of truck, and decide which to recommend.

(10-10) Capital Budgeting Methods

Project S has a cost of $10,000 and is expected to produce benefits (cash flows) of $3,000 per year for 5 years. Project L costs $25,000 and is expected to produce cash flows of $7,400 per year for 5 years. Calculate the two projects' NPVs, IRRs, MIRRs, and PIs, assuming a cost of capital of 12%. Which project would be selected, assuming they are mutually exclusive, using each ranking method? Which should actually be selected?

(10-11) MIRR and NPV

Your company is considering two mutually exclusive projects, X and Y, whose costs and cash flows are shown below:

Year	X	Y
0	–$5,000	–$5,000
1	1,000	4,500
2	1,500	1,500
3	2,000	1,000
4	4,000	500

The projects are equally risky, and their cost of capital is 12%. You must make a recommendation, and you must base it on the modified IRR (MIRR). Which project has the higher MIRR?

(10-12) NPV and IRR Analysis

After discovering a new gold vein in the Colorado mountains, CTC Mining Corporation must decide whether to go ahead and develop the deposit. The most cost-effective method of mining gold is sulfuric acid extraction, a process that could result in environmental damage.

Before proceeding with the extraction, CTC must spend $900,000 for new mining equipment and pay $165,000 for its installation. The gold mined will net the firm an estimated $350,000 each year for the 5-year life of the vein. CTC's cost of capital is 14%. For the purposes of this problem, assume that the cash inflows occur at the end of the year.

a. What are the project's NPV and IRR?
b. Should this project be undertaken if environmental impacts were not a consideration?
c. How should environmental effects be considered when evaluating this, or any other, project? How might these concepts affect the decision in part b?

(10-13) NPV and IRR Analysis

Cummings Products is considering two mutually exclusive investments whose expected net cash flows are as follows:

	EXPECTED NET CASH FLOWS	
Year	**Project A**	**Project B**
0	−$400	−$650
1	−528	210
2	−219	210
3	−150	210
4	1,100	210
5	820	210
6	990	210
7	−325	210

a. Construct NPV profiles for Projects A and B.
b. What is each project's IRR?
c. If each project's cost of capital were 10%, which project, if either, should be selected? If the cost of capital were 17%, what would be the proper choice?
d. What is each project's MIRR at the cost of capital of 10%? At 17%? (*Hint:* Consider Period 7 as the end of Project B's life.)
e. What is the crossover rate, and what is its significance?

(10-14) Timing Differences

The Ewert Exploration Company is considering two mutually exclusive plans for extracting oil on property for which it has mineral rights. Both plans call for the expenditure of $10 million to drill development wells. Under Plan A, all the oil will be extracted in 1 year, producing a cash flow at t = 1 of $12 million; under Plan B, cash flows will be $1.75 million per year for 20 years.

a. What are the annual incremental cash flows that will be available to Ewert Exploration if it undertakes Plan B rather than Plan A? (*Hint:* Subtract Plan A's flows from B's.)
b. If the company accepts Plan A and then invests the extra cash generated at the end of Year 1, what rate of return (reinvestment rate) would cause the cash flows from reinvestment to equal the cash flows from Plan B?
c. Suppose a firm's cost of capital is 10%. Is it logical to assume that the firm would take on all available independent projects (of average risk) with returns greater than 10%? Further, if all available projects with returns greater than 10% have been taken, would this mean that cash flows from past investments would have an opportunity cost of only 10%, because all the firm could do with these cash flows would be to replace money that has a cost of 10%? Finally, does this imply that the cost of capital is the correct rate to assume for the reinvestment of a project's cash flows?
d. Construct NPV profiles for Plans A and B, identify each project's IRR, and indicate the crossover rate.

(10-15) Scale Differences The Pinkerton Publishing Company is considering two mutually exclusive expansion plans. Plan A calls for the expenditure of $50 million on a large-scale, integrated plant that will provide an expected cash flow stream of $8 million per year for 20 years. Plan B calls for the expenditure of $15 million to build a somewhat less efficient, more labor-intensive plant that has an expected cash flow stream of $3.4 million per year for 20 years. The firm's cost of capital is 10%.

a. Calculate each project's NPV and IRR.
b. Set up a Project Δ by showing the cash flows that will exist if the firm goes with the large plant rather than the smaller plant. What are the NPV and the IRR for this Project Δ?
c. Graph the NPV profiles for Plan A, Plan B, and Project Δ.

(10-16) Unequal Lives Shao Airlines is considering the purchase of two alternative planes. Plane A has an expected life of 5 years, will cost $100 million, and will produce net cash flows of $30 million per year. Plane B has a life of 10 years, will cost $132 million, and will produce net cash flows of $25 million per year. Shao plans to serve the route for only 10 years. Inflation in operating costs, airplane costs, and fares is expected to be zero, and the company's cost of capital is 12%. By how much would the value of the company increase if it accepted the better project (plane)? What is the equivalent annual annuity for each plane?

(10-17) Unequal Lives The Perez Company has the opportunity to invest in one of two mutually exclusive machines that will produce a product it will need for the foreseeable future. Machine A costs $10 million but realizes after-tax inflows of $4 million per year for 4 years. After 4 years, the machine must be replaced. Machine B costs $15 million and realizes after-tax inflows of $3.5 million per year for 8 years, after which it must be replaced. Assume that machine prices are not expected to rise because inflation will be offset by cheaper components used in the machines. The cost of capital is 10%. By how much would the value of the company increase if it accepted the better machine? What is the equivalent annual annuity for each machine?

(10-18) Unequal Lives Filkins Fabric Company is considering the replacement of its old, fully depreciated knitting machine. Two new models are available: Machine 190-3, which has a cost of $190,000, a 3-year expected life, and after-tax cash flows (labor savings and depreciation) of $87,000 per year; and Machine 360-6, which has a cost of $360,000, a 6-year life, and after-tax cash flows of $98,300 per year. Knitting machine prices are not expected to rise, because inflation will be offset by cheaper components (microprocessors) used in the machines. Assume that Filkins's cost of capital is 14%. Should the firm replace its old knitting machine? If so, which new machine should it use? By how much would the value of the company increase if it accepted the better machine? What is the equivalent annual annuity for each machine?

Challenging Problems 19–22

(10-19) Multiple Rates of Return The Ulmer Uranium Company is deciding whether or not to open a strip mine whose net cost is $4.4 million. Net cash inflows are expected to be $27.7 million, all coming at the end of Year 1. The land must be returned to its natural state at a cost of $25 million, payable at the end of Year 2.

a. Plot the project's NPV profile.
b. Should the project be accepted if r = 8%? If r = 14%? Explain your reasoning.
c. Can you think of some other capital budgeting situations in which negative cash flows during or at the end of the project's life might lead to multiple IRRs?
d. What is the project's MIRR at r = 8%? At r = 14%? Does the MIRR method lead to the same accept–reject decision as the NPV method?

(10-20) Present Value of Costs

The Aubey Coffee Company is evaluating the within-plant distribution system for its new roasting, grinding, and packing plant. The two alternatives are (1) a conveyor system with a high initial cost but low annual operating costs, and (2) several forklift trucks, which cost less but have considerably higher operating costs. The decision to construct the plant has already been made, and the choice here will have no effect on the overall revenues of the project. The cost of capital for the plant is 8%, and the projects' expected net costs are listed in the following table:

	Expected Net Cost	
Year	Conveyor	Forklift
0	−$500,000	−$200,000
1	−120,000	−160,000
2	−120,000	−160,000
3	−120,000	−160,000
4	−120,000	−160,000
5	−20,000	−160,000

a. What is the IRR of each alternative?
b. What is the present value of the costs of each alternative? Which method should be chosen?

(10-21) Payback, NPV, and MIRR

Your division is considering two investment projects, each of which requires an up-front expenditure of $25 million. You estimate that the cost of capital is 10% and that the investments will produce the following after-tax cash flows (in millions of dollars):

Year	Project A	Project B
1	5	20
2	10	10
3	15	8
4	20	6

a. What is the regular payback period for each of the projects?
b. What is the discounted payback period for each of the projects?
c. If the two projects are independent and the cost of capital is 10%, which project or projects should the firm undertake?
d. If the two projects are mutually exclusive and the cost of capital is 5%, which project should the firm undertake?
e. If the two projects are mutually exclusive and the cost of capital is 15%, which project should the firm undertake?
f. What is the crossover rate?
g. If the cost of capital is 10%, what is the modified IRR (MIRR) of each project?

(10-22) Economic Life

The Scampini Supplies Company recently purchased a new delivery truck. The new truck cost $22,500, and it is expected to generate net after-tax operating cash flows, including depreciation, of $6,250 per year. The truck has a 5-year expected life. The expected salvage values after tax adjustments for the truck are given below. The company's cost of capital is 10%.

Year	Annual Operating Cash Flow	Salvage Value
0	-$22,500	$22,500
1	6,250	17,500
2	6,250	14,000
3	6,250	11,000
4	6,250	5,000
5	6,250	0

a. Should the firm operate the truck until the end of its 5-year physical life? If not, then what is its optimal economic life?
b. Would the introduction of salvage values, in addition to operating cash flows, ever *reduce* the expected NPV and/or IRR of a project?

SPREADSHEET PROBLEM

(10-23)
Build a Model:
Capital Budgeting
Tools

resource

Start with the partial model in the file ***Ch10 P23 Build a Model.xls*** on the textbook's Web site. Gardial Fisheries is considering two mutually exclusive investments. The projects' expected net cash flows are as follows:

	Expected Net Cash Flows	
Year	Project A	Project B
0	-$375	-$575
1	-300	190
2	-200	190
3	-100	190
4	600	190
5	600	190
6	926	190
7	-200	0

a. If each project's cost of capital is 12%, which project should be selected? If the cost of capital is 18%, what project is the proper choice?
b. Construct NPV profiles for Projects A and B.
c. What is each project's IRR?
d. What is the crossover rate, and what is its significance?
e. What is each project's MIRR at a cost of capital of 12%? At r = 18%? (*Hint:* Consider Period 7 as the end of Project B's life.)
f. What is the regular payback period for these two projects?
g. At a cost of capital of 12%, what is the discounted payback period for these two projects?
h. What is the profitability index for each project if the cost of capital is 12%?

MINI CASE

You have just graduated from the MBA program of a large university, and one of your favorite courses was "Today's Entrepreneurs." In fact, you enjoyed it so much you have decided you want to "be your own boss." While you were in the master's program, your grandfather died and left you $1 million to do with as you please. You are not an inventor, and you do not have a trade skill that you can market; however, you have decided that you would like to purchase at least one established franchise in the fast-foods area, maybe two (if profitable). The problem is that you have never been one to stay with any project for too long, so you figure that your time frame is 3 years. After 3 years you will go on to something else.

You have narrowed your selection down to two choices: (1) Franchise L, Lisa's Soups, Salads, & Stuff, and (2) Franchise S, Sam's Fabulous Fried Chicken. The net cash flows shown below include the price you would receive for selling the franchise in Year 3 and the forecast of how each franchise will do over the 3-year period. Franchise L's cash flows will start off slowly but will increase rather quickly as people become more health-conscious, while Franchise S's cash flows will start off high but will trail off as other chicken competitors enter the marketplace and as people become more health-conscious and avoid fried foods. Franchise L serves breakfast and lunch whereas Franchise S serves only dinner, so it is possible for you to invest in both franchises. You see these franchises as perfect complements to one another: You could attract both the lunch and dinner crowds and the health-conscious and not-so-health-conscious crowds without the franchises directly competing against one another.

Here are the net cash flows (in thousands of dollars):

	Expected Net Cash Flows	
Year	**Franchise L**	**Franchise S**
0	–$100	–$100
1	10	70
2	60	50
3	80	20

Depreciation, salvage values, net working capital requirements, and tax effects are all included in these cash flows.

You also have made subjective risk assessments of each franchise and concluded that both franchises have risk characteristics that require a return of 10%. You must now determine whether one or both of the franchises should be accepted.

a. What is capital budgeting?
b. What is the difference between independent and mutually exclusive projects?
c. (1) Define the term *net present value (NPV)*. What is each franchise's NPV?
   (2) What is the rationale behind the NPV method? According to NPV, which franchise or franchises should be accepted if they are independent? Mutually exclusive?
   (3) Would the NPVs change if the cost of capital changed?
d. (1) Define the term *internal rate of return (IRR)*. What is each franchise's IRR?
   (2) How is the IRR on a project related to the YTM on a bond?
   (3) What is the logic behind the IRR method? According to IRR, which franchises should be accepted if they are independent? Mutually exclusive?
   (4) Would the franchises' IRRs change if the cost of capital changed?
e. (1) Draw NPV profiles for Franchises L and S. At what discount rate do the profiles cross?
   (2) Look at your NPV profile graph without referring to the actual NPVs and IRRs. Which franchise or franchises should be accepted if they are independent? Mutually exclusive? Explain. Are your answers correct at any cost of capital less than 23.6%?

f. What is the underlying cause of ranking conflicts between NPV and IRR?

g. Define the term *modified IRR (MIRR)*. Find the MIRRs for Franchises L and S.

h. What does the profitability index (PI) measure? What are the PIs of Franchises S and L?

i. (1) What is the payback period? Find the paybacks for Franchises L and S.
   (2) What is the rationale for the payback method? According to the payback criterion, which franchise or franchises should be accepted if the firm's maximum acceptable payback is 2 years and if Franchises L and S are independent? If they are mutually exclusive?
   (3) What is the difference between the regular and discounted payback periods?
   (4) What is the main disadvantage of discounted payback? Is the payback method of any real usefulness in capital budgeting decisions?

j. As a separate project (Project P), you are considering sponsorship of a pavilion at the upcoming World's Fair. The pavilion would cost $800,000, and it is expected to result in $5 million of incremental cash inflows during its single year of operation. However, it would then take another year, and $5 million of costs, to demolish the site and return it to its original condition. Thus, Project P's expected net cash flows look like this (in millions of dollars):

Year	Net Cash Flows
0	–$0.8
1	5.0
2	–5.0

The project is estimated to be of average risk, so its cost of capital is 10%.
   (1) What are normal and nonnormal cash flows?
   (2) What is Project P's NPV? What is its IRR? Its MIRR?
   (3) Draw Project P's NPV profile. Does Project P have normal or nonnormal cash flows? Should this project be accepted?

k. In an unrelated analysis, you have the opportunity to choose between the following two mutually exclusive projects, Project T (which lasts for two years) and Project F (which lasts for four years):

	Expected Net Cash Flows	
Year	Project T	Project F
0	–$100,000	–$100,000
1	60,000	33,500
2	60,000	33,500
3	—	33,500
4	—	33,500

The projects provide a necessary service, so whichever one is selected is expected to be repeated into the foreseeable future. Both projects have a 10% cost of capital.
   (1) What is each project's initial NPV without replication?
   (2) What is each project's equivalent annual annuity?
   (3) Apply the replacement chain approach to determine the projects' extended NPVs. Which project should be chosen?
   (4) Assume that the cost to replicate Project T in 2 years will increase to $105,000 due to inflation. How should the analysis be handled now, and which project should be chosen?

l. You are also considering another project that has a physical life of 3 years; that is, the machinery will be totally worn out after 3 years. However, if the project were terminated prior to the end of 3 years, the machinery would have a positive salvage value. Here are the project's estimated cash flows:

Year	Initial Investment and Operating Cash Flows	End-of-Year Net Salvage Value
0	–$5,000	$5,000
1	2,100	3,100
2	2,000	2,000
3	1,750	0

Using the 10% cost of capital, what is the project's NPV if it is operated for the full 3 years? Would the NPV change if the company planned to terminate the project at the end of Year 2? At the end of Year 1? What is the project's optimal (economic) life?

SELECTED ADDITIONAL CASES

The following cases from CengageCompose cover many of the concepts discussed in this chapter and are available at ***compose.cengage.com***.

Klein-Brigham Series:
Case 11, "Chicago Valve Company."
Brigham-Buzzard Series:

Case 6, "Powerline Network Corporation (Basics of Capital Budgeting)."

© Adalberto Rios Szalay/Sexto Sol/Getty Images

CHAPTER 11

Cash Flow Estimation and Risk Analysis

Procter & Gamble, Unilever, and the Thales Group are among the many companies that understand the importance of cash flow estimation and risk analysis. For example, P&G conducts risk analysis on a wide variety of capital budgeting projects, from routine cost savings proposals at domestic facilities to cross-border facility location choices. P&G's Associate Director for Investment Analysis, Bob Hunt, says that risk analysis, especially the use of decision trees, "has been very useful in helping us break complex projects down into individual decision options, helping us understand the uncertainties, and ultimately helping us make superior decisions."

Unilever created its Decision Making Under Uncertainty (DMUU) approach to avoid overlooking risk during its project selection process. Unilever applies DMUU to conduct risk analysis for many types of projects, but especially when it must choose among multiple proposals.

Project evaluation is always difficult, but it is even more so when rapidly evolving technology is involved. For firms bidding for government and business contracts, the bidding process itself ramps up the already difficult task of project evaluation. The Thales Group competes in this market by providing communication systems for the defense and aerospace industries. Not only does Thales use risk analysis to better identify the expected levels and risks of project cash flows, but it also uses risk analysis to better understand and manage the risks associated with submitting bids for projects.

Keep these companies in mind as you read the chapter.

Source: **Palisade Corporation is a leading developer of software for risk evaluation and decision analysis. For examples of companies using risk analysis, see the case analyses at www.palisade.com/cases.**

Project Valuation, Cash Flows, and Risk Analysis

© Rob Webb/Getty Images

When we estimate a project's cash flows (CF) and then discount them at the project's risk-adjusted cost of capital, r, the result is the project's NPV, which tells us how much the project increases the firm's value. This chapter focuses on how to estimate the size and risk of a project's cash flows.

Note too that project cash flows, once a project has been accepted and placed in operation, are added to the firm's free cash flows from other sources. Therefore, projects' cash flows essentially determine the firm's free cash flows as discussed in Chapter 2 and thus form the basis for the firm's market value and stock price.

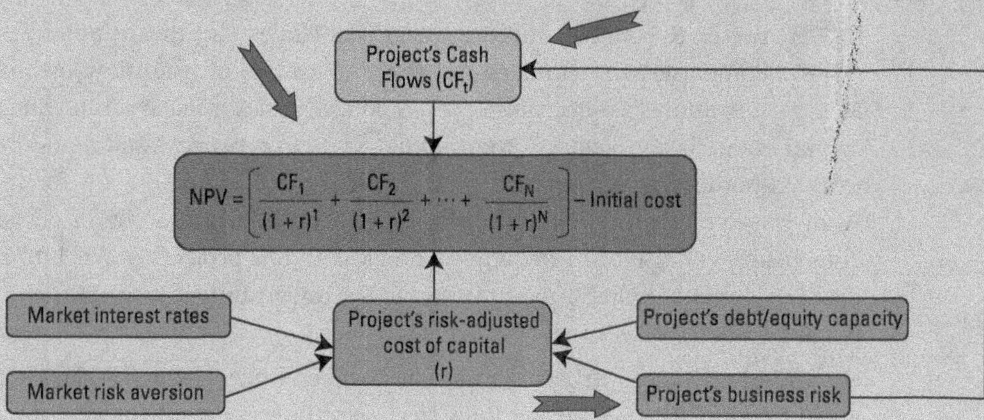

© Cengage Learning 2014

resource

*The textbook's Web site contains an Excel file that will guide you through the chapter's calculations. The file for this chapter is **Ch11 Tool Kit.xls**, and we encourage you to open the file and follow along as you read the chapter.*

Chapter 10 assumed that a project's cash flows had already been estimated. Now we cover cash flow estimation and identify the issues a manager faces in producing relevant and realistic cash flow estimates. In addition, cash flow estimates are just that: estimates! It is crucial for a manager to incorporate uncertainty into project analysis if a company is to make informed decisions regarding project selection. We begin with a discussion of procedures for estimating relevant and realistic cash flows.

11-1 Identifying Relevant Cash Flows

The most important—and difficult—step in capital budgeting is estimating a proposal's relevant **project cash flows**, which are the differences between the cash flows the firm will have if it implements the project versus the cash flows it will have if it rejects the project. These are called **incremental cash flows**:

$$\text{Incremental cash flows} = \begin{matrix}\text{Company's cash flows} \\ \textit{with} \text{ the project}\end{matrix} - \begin{matrix}\text{Company's cash flows} \\ \textit{without} \text{ the project}\end{matrix}$$

Estimating incremental cash flows might sound easy, but there are many potential pitfalls. In this section, we identify the key concepts that will help you avoid these pitfalls and then apply the concepts to an actual project to illustrate their application to cash flow estimation.

11-1a Cash Flow versus Accounting Income

We saw in Chapter 2 that free cash flow differs from accounting income: Free cash flow is cash flow that is available for distribution to investors, making free cash flow the basis of a firm's value. It is common in the practice of finance to speak of a firm's free cash flow and a project's cash flow (or net cash flow), but these are based on the same concepts. In fact, a project's cash flow is identical to the project's free cash flow, and a firm's total net cash flow from all projects is equal to the firm's free cash flow. We will follow the typical convention and refer to a project's free cash flow simply as project cash flow, but keep in mind that the two concepts are identical.[1]

Because net income is not equal to the cash flow available for distribution to investors, in the last chapter we discounted *net cash flows,* not accounting income, to find projects' NPVs. *For capital budgeting purposes it is the project's net cash flow, not its accounting income, which is relevant.* Therefore, when analyzing a proposed capital budgeting project, disregard the project's net income and focus exclusively on its net cash flow. Be especially alert to the following differences between cash flow and accounting income.

The Cash Flow Effect of Asset Purchases and Depreciation

Most projects require assets, and asset purchases represent *negative* cash flows. Even though the acquisition of assets results in a cash outflow, accountants do not show the purchase of fixed assets as a deduction from accounting income. Instead, they deduct a depreciation expense each year throughout the life of the asset. Depreciation shelters income from taxation, and this has an impact on cash flow, but depreciation itself is not a cash flow. Therefore, depreciation must be added back when estimating a project's operating cash flow.

Depreciation is the most common noncash charge, but there are many other noncash charges that might appear on a company's financial statements. Just as with depreciation, all other noncash charges should be added back when calculating a project's net cash flow.

Changes in Net Operating Working Capital

Normally, additional inventories are required to support a new operation, and expanded sales tie up additional funds in accounts receivable. However, payables and accruals increase as a result of the expansion, and this reduces the cash needed to finance inventories and receivables. The difference between the required increase in operating current assets and the increase in operating current liabilities is the change in net operating working capital. If this change is positive, as it generally is for expansion projects, then additional financing—beyond the cost of the fixed assets—will be needed.

Toward the end of a project's life, inventories will be used but not replaced, and receivables will be collected without corresponding replacements. As these changes occur the firm will receive cash inflows; as a result, the investment in net operating working capital will be returned by the end of the project's life.

[1]When the financial press refers to a firm's "net cash flow," it is almost always equal to the definition we provide in Chapter 2 (which simply adds back depreciation and any other noncash charges to net income). However, as we explained in Chapter 2, the net cash flow from operations (from the statement of cash flows) and the firm's free cash flow are much more useful measures of cash flow. When financial analysts within a company use the term "a project's net cash flow," they almost always calculate it as we do in this chapter, which is in essence the project's free cash flow. Thus, free cash flow means the same thing whether you calculate it for a firm or for a project. On the other hand, when the financial press talks about a firm's net cash flow or when an internal analyst talks about a project's net cash flow, those "net cash flows" are not the same.

INTEREST CHARGES ARE *NOT* INCLUDED IN PROJECT CASH FLOWS

Interest is a cash expense, so at first blush it would seem that interest on any debt used to finance a project should be deducted when we estimate the project's net cash flows. However, this is not correct. Recall from Chapter 10 that we discount a project's cash flows by its risk-adjusted cost of capital, which is a weighted average (WACC) of the costs of debt, preferred stock, and common equity, adjusted for the project's risk and debt capacity. This project cost of capital is the rate of return necessary to satisfy *all* of the firm's investors, including stockholders and debtholders. A common mistake made by many students and financial managers is to subtract interest payments when estimating a project's cash flows. This is a mistake because the cost of debt is already embedded in the cost of capital, so subtracting interest payments from the project's cash flows would amount to double-counting interest costs. Therefore, *you should not subtract interest expenses when finding a project's cash flows.*

11-1b Timing of Cash Flows: Yearly versus Other Periods

In theory, in capital budgeting analyses we should discount cash flows based on the exact moment when they occur. Therefore, one could argue that daily cash flows would be better than annual flows. However, it would be costly to estimate daily cash flows and laborious to analyze them. In general the analysis would be no better than one using annual flows because we simply can't make accurate forecasts of daily cash flows more than a couple of months into the future. Therefore, it is generally appropriate to assume that all cash flows occur at the end of the various years. For projects with highly predictable cash flows, such as constructing a building and then leasing it on a long-term basis (with monthly payments) to a financially sound tenant, we would analyze the project using monthly periods.

11-1c Expansion Projects and Replacement Projects

Two types of projects can be distinguished: (1) *expansion projects,* in which the firm makes an investment in, for example, a new Home Depot store in Seattle; and (2) *replacement projects,* in which the firm replaces existing assets, generally to reduce costs. In expansion projects, the cash expenditures on buildings, equipment, and required working capital are obviously incremental, as are the sales revenues and operating costs associated with the project. The incremental costs associated with replacement projects are not so obvious. For example, Home Depot might replace some of its delivery trucks to reduce fuel and maintenance expenses. Replacement analysis is complicated by the fact that most of the relevant cash flows are the cash flow differences between the existing project and the replacement project. For example, the fuel bill for a more efficient new truck might be $10,000 per year versus $15,000 for the old truck, and the $5,000 fuel savings would be an incremental cash flow associated with the replacement decision. We analyze an expansion and replacement decision later in the chapter.

11-1d Sunk Costs

A **sunk cost** is an outlay related to the project that was incurred in the past and that cannot be recovered in the future regardless of whether or not the project is accepted. Therefore, sunk costs are *not incremental costs* and thus are not relevant in a capital budgeting analysis.

To illustrate, suppose Home Depot spent $2 million to investigate sites for a potential new store in a given area. That $2 million is a sunk cost—the money is gone, and it won't come back regardless of whether or not a new store is built. Therefore, the $2 million should not be included in a capital budgeting decision. Improper treatment of sunk costs can lead to bad decisions. For example, suppose Home Depot completed the analysis for a new store and found that it must spend an additional (or incremental) $17 million to build and supply the store, on top of the $2 million already spent on the site study. Suppose the present value of future cash flows is $18 million. Should the project be accepted? If the sunk costs are mistakenly included, the NPV is −$2 million + (−$17 million) + $18 million = −$1 million and the project would be rejected. However, *that would be a bad decision.* The real issue is whether the *incremental* $17 million would result in enough *incremental* cash flow to produce a positive NPV. If the $2 million sunk cost were disregarded, as it should be, then the NPV on an incremental basis would be a *positive* $1 million.

11-1e Opportunity Costs Associated with Assets the Firm Already Owns

Another conceptual issue relates to **opportunity costs** related to assets the firm already owns. Continuing our example, suppose Home Depot (HD) owns land with a current market value of $2 million that can be used for the new store if it decides to build the store. If HD goes forward with the project, only another $15 million will be required, not the full $17 million, because it will not need to buy the required land. Does this mean that HD should use the $15 million incremental cost as the cost of the new store? The answer is definitely "no." If the new store is *not* built, then HD could sell the land and receive a cash flow of $2 million. This $2 million is an *opportunity cost*—it is cash that HD would not receive if the land is used for the new store. Therefore, the $2 million must be charged to the new project, and failing to do so would cause the new project's calculated NPV to be too high.

11-1f Externalities

Another conceptual issue relates to **externalities**, which are the effects of a project on other parts of the firm or on the environment. As explained in what follows, there are three types of externalities: negative within-firm externalities, positive within-firm externalities, and environmental externalities.

Negative Within-Firm Externalities

If a retailer like Home Depot opens a new store that is close to its existing stores, then the new store might attract customers who would otherwise buy from the existing stores, reducing the old stores' cash flows. Therefore, the new store's incremental cash flow must be reduced by the amount of the cash flow lost by its other units. This type of externality is called **cannibalization**, because the new business eats into the company's existing business. Many businesses are subject to cannibalization. For example, each new iPod model cannibalizes existing models. Those lost cash flows should be considered, and that means charging them as a cost when analyzing new products.

Dealing properly with negative externalities requires careful thinking. If Apple decided not to come out with a new model of iPod because of cannibalization, another company might come out with a similar new model, causing Apple to lose sales on existing models.

Apple must examine the total situation, and this is definitely more than a simple, mechanical analysis. Experience and knowledge of the industry is required to make good decisions in most cases.

One of the best examples of a company getting into trouble as a result of not dealing correctly with cannibalization was IBM's response to the development of the first personal computers in the 1970s. IBM's mainframes dominated the computer industry, and they generated huge profits. IBM used its technology to enter the PC market, and initially it was the leading PC company. However, its top managers decided to deemphasize the PC division because they were afraid it would hurt the more profitable mainframe business. That decision opened the door for Apple, Dell, Hewlett Packard, Sony, and Chinese competitors to take PC business away from IBM. As a result, IBM went from being the most profitable firm in the world to one whose very survival was threatened. IBM's experience highlights that it is just as important to understand the industry and the long-run consequences of a given decision as it is to understand the theory of finance. Good judgment is an essential element for good financial decisions.

Positive Within-Firm Externalities

As we noted earlier, cannibalization occurs when a new product competes with an old one. However, a new project can also be *complementary* to an old one, in which case cash flows in the old operation will be *increased* when the new one is introduced. For example, Apple's iPod was a profitable product, but when Apple considered an investment in its music store it realized that the store would boost sales of iPods. So, even if an analysis of the proposed music store indicated a negative NPV, the analysis would not be complete unless the incremental cash flows that would occur in the iPod division were credited to the music store. Consideration of positive externalities often changes a project's NPV from negative to positive.

Environmental Externalities

The most common type of negative externality is a project's impact on the environment. Government rules and regulations constrain what companies can do, but firms have some flexibility in dealing with environmental issues. For example, suppose a manufacturer is studying a proposed new plant. The company could meet current environmental regulations at a cost of $1 million, but the plant would still emit fumes that would cause some bad will in its neighborhood. Those ill feelings would not show up in the cash flow analysis, but they should be considered. Perhaps a relatively small additional expenditure would reduce the emissions substantially, make the plant look good relative to other plants in the area, and provide goodwill that in the future would help the firm's sales and its negotiations with governmental agencies.

Of course, all firms' profits ultimately depend on the Earth remaining healthy, so companies have some incentive to do things that protect the environment even though those actions are not currently required. However, if one firm decides to take actions that are good for the environment but quite costly, then it must either raise its prices or suffer a decline in earnings. If its competitors decide to get by with less costly but environmentally unfriendly processes, they can price their products lower and make more money. Of course, the more environmentally friendly companies can advertise their environmental efforts, and this might—or might not—offset their higher costs. All this illustrates why government regulations are often necessary. Finance, politics, and the environment are all interconnected.

SELF-TEST

Why should companies use a project's net cash flows rather than accounting income when determining a project's NPV?

Explain the following terms: incremental cash flow, sunk cost, opportunity cost, externality, cannibalization, and complementary project.

Provide an example of a "good" externality—that is, one that increases a project's true NPV over what it would be if just its own cash flows were considered.

11-2 Analysis of an Expansion Project

In Chapter 10, we worked with the cash flows associated with one of Guyton Products Company's expansion projects. Recall that Project L is the application of a radically new liquid nano-coating technology to a new type of solar water heater module, which will be manufactured under a 4-year license from a university. In this section we show how these cash flows are estimated (we only show estimates for Project L in the chapter, but we also show estimates GPC's other project from Chapter 10, Project S, in ***Ch11 Tool Kit.xls***). It's not clear how well the water heater will work, how strong demand for it will be, how long it will be before the product becomes obsolete, or whether the license can be renewed after the initial 4 years. Still, the water heater has the potential for being profitable, though it could also fail miserably. GPC is a relatively large company and this is one of many projects, so a failure would not bankrupt the firm but would hurt profits and the stock's price.

11-2a Base Case Inputs and Key Results

resource

*See **Ch11 Tool Kit.xls** on the textbook's Web site.*

We used *Excel* to do the analysis. We could have used a calculator and paper, but *Excel* is *much* easier when dealing with capital budgeting problems. You don't need to know *Excel* to understand our discussion, but if you plan to work in finance—or, really, in any business field—you must know how to use *Excel*, so we recommend that you open the *Excel* ***Tool Kit*** for this chapter and scroll through it as the textbook explains the analysis.

Figure 11-1 shows the Part 1 of the *Excel* model used in this analysis; see the first worksheet in ***Ch11 Tool Kit.xls*** named ***1-Base-Case.*** The base-case inputs are in the blue section. For example, the cost of required equipment to manufacture the water heaters is $7,750 and is shown in the blue input section. (All dollar values in Figure 11-1 and in our discussion here are reported in thousands, so the equipment actually costs $7,750,000.) The actual number-crunching takes place in Part 2 of the model, shown in Figure 11-2. Part 2 takes the inputs from the blue section of Figure 11-1 and generates the project's cash flows. Part 2 of the model also performs calculations of the project performance measures discussed in Chapter 10 and then reports those results in the orange section of Figure 11-1. This structure allows you (or your manager) to change and input and instantly see the impact on the reported performance measures.

We have saved these base-case inputs in ***Ch11 Tool Kit.xls*** with *Excel's* Scenario Manager. If you change some inputs but want to return to the original base-case inputs, you can select Data, What-If Analysis, Scenario Manager, pick the scenario named "Base-Case for Project L," and click Show. This will replace any changes with the original inputs. Scenario Manager is a very useful tool and we will have more to say about it later in this chapter.

FIGURE 11-1

Analysis of an Expansion Project: Inputs and Key Results (Thousands of Dollars)

	A	B	C	D	E	F	G	H	I
54	Part 1. Inputs and Key Results								
55									
56	Inputs				Base-Case		Key Results		
57	Equipment cost				$7,750		NPV		$1,048
58	Salvage value, equipment, Year 4				$639		IRR		13.79%
59	Opportunity cost				$0		MIRR		12.78%
60	Externalities (cannibalization)				$0		PI		1.10
61	Units sold, Year 1				10,000		Payback		3.39
62	Annual change in units sold, after Year 1				15%		Discounted payback		3.80
63	Sales price per unit, Year 1				$1.50				
64	Annual change in sales price, after Year 1				4%				
65	Variable cost per unit (VC), Year 1				$1.07				
66	Annual change in VC, after Year 1				3%				
67	Nonvariable cost (Non-VC), Year 1				$2,120				
68	Annual change in Non-VC, after Year 1				3%				
69	Project WACC				10%				
70	Tax rate				40%				
71	Working capital as % of next year's sales				15%				

11-2b Cash Flow Projections: Intermediate Calculations

resource

See Ch11 Tool Kit.xls on the textbook's Web site.

Figure 11-2 shows Part 2 of the model. When setting up *Excel* models, we prefer to have more rows but shorter formulas. So instead of having very complicated formulas in the section for cash flow forecasts, we put intermediate calculations in a separate section. The blue section of Figure 11-2 shows these intermediate calculations for the GPC project, as we explain in the following sections.

Annual Unit Sales, Unit Prices, Unit Costs, and Inflation

Rows 85–88 show annual unit sales, unit sale prices, unit variable costs, and nonvariable costs. These values are all projected to grow at the rates assumed in Part 1 of the model in Figure 11-1. If you ignore growth in prices and costs when estimating cash flows, you are likely to *underestimate* a project's value because the project's weighted average cost of capital (WACC) includes the impact of inflation. In other words, the estimated cash flows will be too low relative to the WACC, so the estimated net present value (NPV) also will be too low relative to the true NPV. To see that the WACC includes inflation, recall from Chapter 5 that the cost of debt includes an inflation premium. Also, the capital asset pricing model from Chapter 6 defines the cost of equity as the sum of the risk-free rate and a risk premium. Like the cost of debt, the risk-free rate also has an inflation premium. Therefore, if the WACC includes the impact of inflation, the estimated cash flows must also include inflation. It is theoretically possible to ignore inflation when estimating the cash flows but adjust the WACC so that it, too, doesn't incorporate inflation, but we have never seen this accomplished correctly in practice. Therefore, you should always include growth rates in prices and costs when estimating cash flows.

FIGURE 11-2

Analysis of an Expansion Project: Cash Flows and Performance Measures (Thousands of Dollars)

	A–B	C–D	E	F	G	H	I
83	**Part 2. Cash Flows and Performance Measures**						
84	Intermediate Calculations		0	1	2	3	4
85	Unit sales			10,000	11,500	13,225	15,209
86	Sales price per unit			$1.50	$1.56	$1.62	$1.69
87	Variable cost per unit (excl. depr.)			$1.07	$1.10	$1.14	$1.17
88	Nonvariable costs (excl. depr.)			$2,120	$2,184	$2,249	$2,317
89	Sales revenues = Units × Price/unit			$15,000	$17,940	$21,456	$25,662
90	$NOWC_t$ = 15%($Revenues_{t+1}$)		$2,250	$2,691	$3,218	$3,849	$0
91	Basis for depreciation		$7,750				
92	Annual depreciation rate (MACRS)			33.33%	44.45%	14.81%	7.41%
93	Annual depreciation expense			$2,583	$3,445	$1,148	$574
94	Remaining undepreciated value			$5,167	$1,722	$574	$0
95	Cash Flow Forecast				Cash Flows at End of Year		
96			0	1	2	3	4
97	Sales revenues = Units × Price/unit			$15,000	$17,940	$21,456	$25,662
98	Variable costs = Units × Cost/unit			$10,700	$12,674	$15,013	$17,782
99	Nonvariable costs (excluding depr.)			$2,120	$2,184	$2,249	$2,317
100	Depreciation			$2,583	$3,445	$1,148	$574
101	Earnings before int. and taxes (EBIT)			−$403	−$363	$3,047	$4,988
102	Taxes on operating profit (40% rate)			−$161	−$145	$1,219	$1,995
103	Net operating profit after taxes			−$242	−$218	$1,828	$2,993
104	Add back depreciation			$2,583	$3,445	$1,148	$574
105	Equipment purchases		−$7,750				
106	Profit from salvage value						$639
107	Cash flow due to tax on salv. val.						−$256
108	Cash flow due to change in WC		−$2,250	−$441	−$527	−$631	$3,849
109	Opportunity cost, after taxes		$0	$0	$0	$0	$0
110	After-tax externalities			$0	$0	$0	$0
111	Project net cash flows: Time Line		−$10,000	$1,900	$2,700	$2,345	$7,800
112	Project Evaluation Measures						
113	NPV	$1,048	=NPV(E69,F111:I111)+E111				
114	IRR	13.79%	=IRR(E111:I111)				
115	MIRR	12.78%	=MIRR(E111:I111,E69,E69)				
116	Profitability index	1.10	=NPV(E69,F111:I111)/(-E111)				
117	Payback	3.39	=PERCENTRANK(E120:I120,0,6)*I119				
118	Disc. payback	3.80	=PERCENTRANK(E122:I122,0,6)*I119				
119	Calculations for Payback	Year:	0	1	2	3	4
120	Cumulative cash flows for payback		−$10,000	−$8,100	−$5,400	−$3,055	$4,745
121	Disc. cash flows for disc. payback		−$10,000	$1,727	$2,231	$1,762	$5,328
122	Cumulative discounted cash flows		−$10,000	−$8,273	−$6,041	−$4,279	$1,048

Net Operating Working Capital (NOWC)

Virtually all projects require working capital, and this one is no exception. For example, raw materials must be purchased and replenished each year as they are used. In Part 1 (Figure 11-1) we assume that GPC must have an amount of net operating working capital on hand equal to 15% of the upcoming year's sales. For example, in Year 0, GPC must have 15%($15,000) = $2,250 in working capital on hand. As sales grow, so does the required working capital. Rows 89–90 show the annual sales revenues (the product of units sold and sales price) and the required working capital.

Depreciation Expense

Rows 91–94 report intermediate calculations related to depreciation, beginning with the depreciation basis, which is the cost of acquiring and installing a project. The basis for GPC's project is $7,750.[2] The depreciation expense for a year is the product of the basis and that year's depreciation rate. Depreciation rates depend on the type of property and its useful life. Even though GPC's project will operate for 4 years, it is classified as 3-year property for tax purposes. The depreciation rates in Row 92 are for 3-year property using the modified cost accelerated cost recovery system (MACRS); see Appendix 11A and the chapter's ***Tool Kit*** for more discussion of depreciation.[3] The remaining undepreciated value is equal to the original basis less the accumulated depreciation; this is called the book value of the asset and is used later in the model when calculating the tax on the salvage value.

resource

*See **Ch11 Tool Kit.xls** on the textbook's Web site.*

11-2c Cash Flow Projections: Estimating Net Operating Profit after Taxes (NOPAT)

The yellow section in the middle of Figure 11-2 shows the steps in calculating the project's net operating profit after taxes (NOPAT). Projected sales revenues are on Row 97. Annual variable unit costs are multiplied by the number of units sold to determine total variable costs, as shown on Row 98. Nonvariable costs are shown on Row 99, and depreciation expense is shown on Row 100. Subtracting variable costs, nonvariable costs, and depreciation from sales revenues results in operating profit, as shown on Row 101.

When discussing a company's income statement, operating profit often is called earnings before interest and taxes (EBIT). Remember, though, that we do not subtract interest when estimating a project's cash flows, because the project's WACC is the overall rate of return required by all the company's investors and not just shareholders. Therefore, the cash flows must also be the cash flows available to all investors and not just shareholders, so we do not subtract interest expense. We calculate taxes in Row 102 and subtract them to get the project's net operating profit after taxes (NOPAT) on Row 103. The project has negative earnings before interest and taxes in Years 1 and 2. When multiplied by the 40% tax rate, Row 102 shows negative taxes for Years 1 and 2. This negative tax is subtracted from EBIT and actually makes the after-tax operating profit larger than the pre-tax profit! For example, the Year 1 pre-tax profit is −$403 and the reported tax is −$161, leading to an after-tax profit of −$403 − (−$161) = −$242. In other words, it is as though the IRS is sending GPC a check for $161. How can this be correct?

Recall the basic concept underlying the relevant cash flows for project analysis—what are the company's cash flows with the project versus the company's cash flows without the project? Applying this concept, if GPC expects to have taxable income from other projects in excess of $403 in Year 1, then the project will shelter that income from $161 in taxes. Therefore, the project will generate $161 in cash flow for GPC in Year 1 due to the tax savings.[4]

---

[2]Regardless of whether accelerated or straight-line depreciation is used, the basis is not adjusted by the expected salvage value when calculating the depreciation expense that is used to determine taxable income. This is in contrast to the calculation of depreciation for purposes of financial reporting.

[3]MACRS assumes that property is placed in service in the middle of a year, so only one-half a year's depreciation is allowed in the first year. A final one-half year's depreciation is allowed in the fourth year.

[4]Even if GPC doesn't expect to have other taxable income in Year 1 but does have taxable income from the past two years, GPC can carryback the loss in Year 1 and receive a tax refund. If GPC doesn't have past taxable income, then we would report zero taxes for the project in Year 1 and carryforward the loss until GPC or the project does have taxable income.

11-2d Cash Flow Projections: Adjustments to NOPAT

Row 103 reports the project's NOPAT, but we must adjust NOPAT to determine the project's actual cash flows. In particular, we must account for depreciation, asset purchases and dispositions, changes in working capital, opportunity costs, externalities, and sunk costs.

Adjustments to Determine Cash Flows: Depreciation

The first step is to add back depreciation, which is a noncash expense. You might be wondering why we subtract depreciation on Row 100 only to add it back on Row 104, and the answer is due to depreciation's impact on taxes. If we had ignored the Year 1 depreciation of $2,583 when calculating NOPAT, the pre-tax income (EBIT) for Year 1 would have been $15,000 – $10,700 – $2,120 = $2,180 instead of –$403. Taxes would have been 40%($2,180) = $872 instead of –$161. This is a difference of $872 – (–$161) = $1,033. Cash flows should reflect the actual taxes, but we must add back the noncash depreciation expense to reflect the actual cash flow.[5]

Adjustments to Determine Cash Flows: Asset Purchases and Dispositions

GPC purchased the asset at the beginning of the project for $7,750, which is a negative cash flow shown on Row 105. Had GPC purchased additional assets in other years, we would report those purchases, too.

GPC expects to salvage the investment at Year 4 for $639. In our example, GPC's project was fully depreciated by the end of the project, so the $639 salvage value is a taxable profit. At a 40% tax rate, GPC will owe 40%($639) = $256 in taxes, as shown on Row 107.

Suppose instead that GPC terminates operations before the equipment is fully depreciated. The after-tax salvage value depends on the price at which GPC can sell the equipment *and* on the book value of the equipment (i.e., the original basis less all previous depreciation charges). Suppose GPC terminates at Year 2, at which time the book value is $1,722, as shown on Row 94. We consider two cases, gains and losses. In the first case, the salvage value is $2,200 and so there is a reported gain of $2,200 – $1,722 = $478. This gain is taxed as ordinary income, so the tax is 40%($478) = $191. The after-tax cash flow is equal to the sales price less the tax: $2,200 – $191 = $2,009.

Now suppose the salvage value at Year 2 is only $500. In this case, there is a reported loss: $500 – $1,722 = –$1,222. This is treated as an ordinary expense, so its tax is 40% (–$1,222) = –$489. This "negative" tax acts as a credit if GPC has other taxable income, so the net after-tax cash flow is $500 – (–$489) = $989.

Adjustments to Determine Cash Flows: Working Capital

Row 90 shows the total amount of net operating working capital needed each year. Row 108 shows the incremental investment in working capital required each year. For example, at the start of the project, Cell E108 shows a cash flow of –$2,250 will be needed at the beginning of the project to support Year 1 sales. Row 90 shows working capital must increase from $2,250 to $2,691 to support Year 2 sales. Thus, GPC must invest $2,691 – $2,250 = $441 in working capital in Year 1, and this is shown as a negative number (because it is an investment) in Cell F108. Similar calculations are made for Years 2 and 3. At the end of Year 4, all of the

[5]Notice that the tax savings due to depreciation also may be calculated as the product of the tax rate and the depreciation expense: 40%($2,583) = $1,033.20. The numbers shown in the textbook are rounded, but the numbers used in the *Excel* model are not.

investments in working capital will be recovered. Inventories will be sold and not replaced, and all receivables will be collected by the end of Year 4. Total net working capital recovered at t = 4 is the sum of the initial investment at t = 0, $2,250, plus the additional investments during Years 1 through 3; the total is $3,849.

Adjustments to Determine Cash Flows: Sunk Costs, Opportunity Costs, and Externalities

GPC's project doesn't have any sunk costs, opportunity costs, or externalities, but the following sections show how we would adjust the cash flows if GPC did have some of these issues.

Sunk Costs. Suppose that last year GPC spent $1,500 on a marketing and feasibility study for the project. Should $1,500 be included in the project's cost? The answer is no. That money already has been spent and accepting or rejecting the project will not change that fact.

Opportunity Costs. Now suppose the $7,750 equipment cost was based on the assumption that the project would use space in a building that GPC now owns but that the space could be leased to another company for $200 per year, after taxes, if the project is rejected. The $200 would be an *opportunity cost,* and it should be reflected in the cash flow calculations.

Externalities. As noted earlier, the solar water heater project does not lead to any cannibalization effects. Suppose, however, that it would reduce the net after-tax cash flows of another GPC division by $50 per year and that no other firm could take on this project if GPC turns it down. In this case, we would use the cannibalization line at Row 110, deducting $50 each year. As a result, the project would have a lower NPV. On the other hand, if the project would cause additional inflows to some other GPC division because it was complementary to that other division's products (i.e., if a positive externality exists), then those after-tax inflows should be attributed to the water heater project and thus shown as a positive inflow on Row 110.

11-2e Evaluating Project Cash Flows

We sum Rows 103 to 110 to get the project's annual net cash flows, set up as a time line on Row 111. These cash flows are then used to calculate NPV, IRR, MIRR, PI, payback, and discounted payback, performance measures that are shown in the orange portion at the bottom of Figure 11-2.

Preliminary Evaluation of the Base-Case Scenario

Based on this analysis, the preliminary evaluation indicates that the project is acceptable. The NPV is $1,048, which is fairly large when compared to the initial investment of $10,000. Its IRR and MIRR are both greater than the 10% WACC, and the PI is larger than 1.0. The payback and discounted payback are almost as long as the project's life, which is somewhat concerning, and is something that needs to be explored by conducting a risk analysis of the project.

Scenario Manager

Excel's Scenario Manager is a very powerful and useful tool. We illustrate its use here as we examine two topics, the impact of forgetting to include inflation and the impact of accelerated depreciation versus straight-line depreciation. To use Scenario Manager in the worksheet named ***1-Base-Case*** in ***Ch11 Tool Kit.xls,*** Select Data, What-If Analysis, and Scenario Manager. There are five scenarios: (1) Base-Case for Project L but Forget Inflation, (2) Base-Case for Project L, (3) Project S, (4) MACRS Depreciation, and (5) Straight-Line Depreciation. The first three scenarios change the inputs in Rows 56–71. The last two scenarios change the depreciation rates in Row 92. This structure allows you to choose a set of inputs and then choose a depreciation method. Sometimes we include all the changing cells in each scenario, and sometimes we separate the scenarios into different groups as we did in this example.

The advantage of having all changing cells in each scenario is that you only have to select a single scenario to show all the desired inputs in the model. The disadvantage is that each scenario can get complicated by having many changing cells.

The advantage of having groups of scenarios is that you can focus on particular aspects of the analysis, such as the choice of depreciation methods. The disadvantage is that you must know which other scenarios are active in order to properly interpret your results.

For some models it makes sense to have only one group of scenarios in which each scenario has the same changing cells; for other models it makes sense to have different groups of scenarios.

The Impact of Inflation. It is easy to overlook inflation, but it is important to include it. For example, had we forgotten to include inflation in the GPC example, the estimated NPV would have dropped from $1,048 to $225. You can see this by changing all the price and cost growth rates to zero and then looking at the NPV. An easy way to do this is with the Scenario Manager—just choose the scenario named "Base-Case for Project L but Forget Inflation." Forgetting to include inflation in a capital budgeting analysis typically causes the estimated NPV to be lower than the true NPV, which could cause a company to reject a project that it should have accepted. You can return to the original inputs by going back into Scenario Manager, selecting "Base-Case for Project L," and clicking on "Show."

Accelerated Depreciation versus Straight-Line Depreciation. Congress permits firms to depreciate assets using either the straight-line method or an accelerated method. The results we have discussed thus far were based on accelerated depreciation. To see the impact of using straight-line depreciation, go to the Scenario Manager and select "Straight-Line Depreciation." Be sure that you have also selected "Base-Case for Project L." After selecting and showing these two scenarios, you will have a set of inputs for the base-case and straight-line deprecation rates.

The results indicate that the project's NPV is $921 when using straight-line depreciation, which is lower than the $1,048 NPV when using accelerated depreciation. In general, *profitable firms are better off using accelerated depreciation* because more depreciation is taken in the early years under the accelerated method, so taxes are lower in those years and higher in later years. Total depreciation, total cash flows, and total taxes are the same under both depreciation methods, but receiving the cash earlier under the accelerated method results in a higher NPV, IRR, and MIRR.

Suppose Congress wants to encourage companies to increase their capital expenditures and thereby boost economic growth and employment. What changes in depreciation regulations would have the desired effect? The answer is "Make accelerated depreciation even more accelerated." For example, if GPC could write off equipment at rates of 67%, 22%, 7%, and 4% rather than 33.33%, 44.45%, 14.81%, and 7.41%, then its early tax payments would be even lower, early cash flows would be even higher, and the project's NPV would exceed the value shown in Figure 11-2.[6]

Be sure to return the scenarios to "Base-Case for Project L" and "MACRS Depreciation."

[6]This is exactly what Congress did in 2008 and 2009, in response to the global economic crisis, by establishing a temporary "bonus" depreciation to stimulate investment. The depreciation in the first year is the regular accelerated depreciation plus a bonus of 50% of the original basis. This bonus was increased to 100% of the original basis for 2011, effectively allowing companies to fully expense certain capital expenditures in 2011. The bonus drops back to 50% for 2012. The provisions are set to expire at the end of 2012.

Project S. Recall from Chapter 10 that GPC was also considering Project S, which used solid coatings. You can use the Scenario Manager to show this project by selecting the scenario "Project S," which will show the cash flows used in Chapter 10. Be sure to return the scenarios in the worksheet ***1-Base-Case*** to "Base-Case for Project L" and "MACRS Depreciation."

SELF-TEST

In what way is the setup for finding a project's cash flows similar to the projected income statements for a new, single-product firm? In what way would the two statements be different?

Would a project's NPV for a typical firm be higher or lower if the firm used accelerated rather than straight-line depreciation? Explain.

How could the analysis in Figure 11-2 be modified to consider cannibalization, opportunity costs, and sunk costs?

Why does net working capital appear with both negative and positive values in Figure 11-2?

11-3 Risk Analysis in Capital Budgeting[7]

Projects differ in risk, and risk should be reflected in capital budgeting decisions. There are three separate and distinct types of risk.

1. **Stand-alone risk** is a project's risk assuming (a) that it is the firm's only asset and (b) that each of the firm's stockholders holds only that one stock in his portfolio. Stand-alone risk is based on uncertainty about the project's expected cash flows. It is important to remember that *stand-alone risk ignores diversification by both the firm and its stockholders.*
2. **Within-firm risk** (also called **corporate risk**) is a project's risk to the corporation itself. Within-firm risk recognizes that the project is only one asset in the firm's portfolio of projects; hence some of its risk is eliminated by diversification within the firm. However, *within-firm risk ignores diversification by the firm's stockholders.* Within-firm risk is measured by the project's impact on uncertainty about the firm's future total cash flows.
3. **Market risk** (also called **beta risk**) is the risk of the project as seen by a well-diversified stockholder who recognizes that (a) the project is only one of the firm's projects and (b) the firm's stock is but one of her stocks. The project's market risk is measured by its effect on the firm's beta coefficient.

Taking on a project with a lot of stand-alone and/or corporate risk will not necessarily affect the firm's beta. However, if the project has high stand-alone risk and if its cash flows are highly correlated with cash flows on the firm's other assets and with cash flows of most other firms in the economy, then the project will have a high degree of all three types of risk. Market risk is, *theoretically*, the most relevant because it is the one that, according to the CAPM, is reflected in stock prices. Unfortunately, market risk is also the most difficult to measure, primarily because new projects don't have "market prices" that can be related to stock market returns.

[7]Some professors may choose to cover some of the risk sections and skip others. We offer a range of choices, and we tried to make the exposition clear enough that interested and self-motivated students can read these sections on their own if they are not assigned.

resource

See Web Extension 11A on the textbook's Web site for a more detailed discussion on alternative methods for incorporating project risk into the capital budgeting decision process.

Most decision makers conduct a *quantitative* analysis of stand-alone risk and then consider the other two types of risk in a *qualitative* manner. They classify projects into several categories; then, using the firm's overall WACC as a starting point, they assign a **risk-adjusted cost of capital** to each category. For example, a firm might establish three risk classes and then assign the corporate WACC to average-risk projects, add a 5% risk premium for higher-risk projects, and subtract 2% for low-risk projects. Under this setup, if the company's overall WACC were 10%, then 10% would be used to evaluate average-risk projects, 15% for high-risk projects, and 8% for low-risk projects. Although this approach is probably better than not making any risk adjustments, these adjustments are highly subjective and difficult to justify. Unfortunately, there's no perfect way to specify how high or low the risk adjustments should be.[8]

SELF-TEST

What are the three types of project risk?

Which type is theoretically the most relevant? Why?

Describe a type of classification scheme that firms often use to obtain risk-adjusted costs of capital.

11-4 Measuring Stand-Alone Risk

A project's stand-alone risk reflects uncertainty about its cash flows. The required dollars of investment, unit sales, sales prices, and operating costs as shown in Figure 11-1 for GPC's project are all subject to uncertainty. First-year sales are projected at 10,000 units to be sold at a price of $1.50 per unit (recall that all dollar values are reported in thousands). However, unit sales will almost certainly be somewhat higher or lower than 10,000, and the price will probably turn out to be different from the projected $1.50 per unit. Similarly, the other variables would probably differ from their indicated values. Indeed, *all the inputs are expected values, not known values, and actual values can and do vary from expected values.* That's what risk is all about!

Three techniques are used in practice to assess stand-alone risk: (1) sensitivity analysis, (2) scenario analysis, and (3) Monte Carlo simulation. We discuss them in the sections that follow.

SELF-TEST

What does a project's stand-alone risk reflect?

What three techniques are used to assess stand-alone risk?

11-5 Sensitivity Analysis

Intuitively, we know that a change in a key input variable such as units sold or the sales price will cause the NPV to change. **Sensitivity analysis** *measures the percentage change in NPV that results from a given percentage change in an input variable when other inputs are held at their expected values.* This is by far the most commonly used type of risk analysis. It begins with a base-case scenario in which the project's NPV is found using the base-case

[8]Note that the CAPM approach can be used for projects provided there are specialized publicly traded firms in the same business as that of the project under consideration. See the discussion in Chapter 10 regarding techniques for measuring divisional betas.

value for each input variable. GPC's base-case inputs were given in Figure 11-1, but it's easy to imagine changes in the inputs, and any changes would result in a different NPV.

11-5a Sensitivity Graph

When GPC's senior managers review a capital budgeting analysis, they are interested in the base-case NPV, but they always go on to ask a series of "what if" questions: "What if unit sales fall to 9,000?" "What if market conditions force us to price the product at $1.40, not $1.50?" "What if variable costs are higher than we have forecasted?" Sensitivity analysis is designed to provide answers to such questions. Each variable is increased or decreased by a specified percentage from its expected value, holding other variables constant at their base-case levels. Then the NPV is calculated using the changed input. Finally, the resulting set of NPVs is plotted to show how sensitive NPV is to changes in the different variables.

Figure 11-3 shows GPC's project's sensitivity graph for six key variables. The data below the graph give the NPVs based on different values of the inputs, and those NPVs were then plotted to make the graph. Figure 11-3 shows that, as unit sales and the sales price are increased, the project's NPV increases; in contrast, increases in variable costs, nonvariable costs, equipment

FIGURE 11-3

Sensitivity Graph for Solar Water Heater Project (Thousands of Dollars)

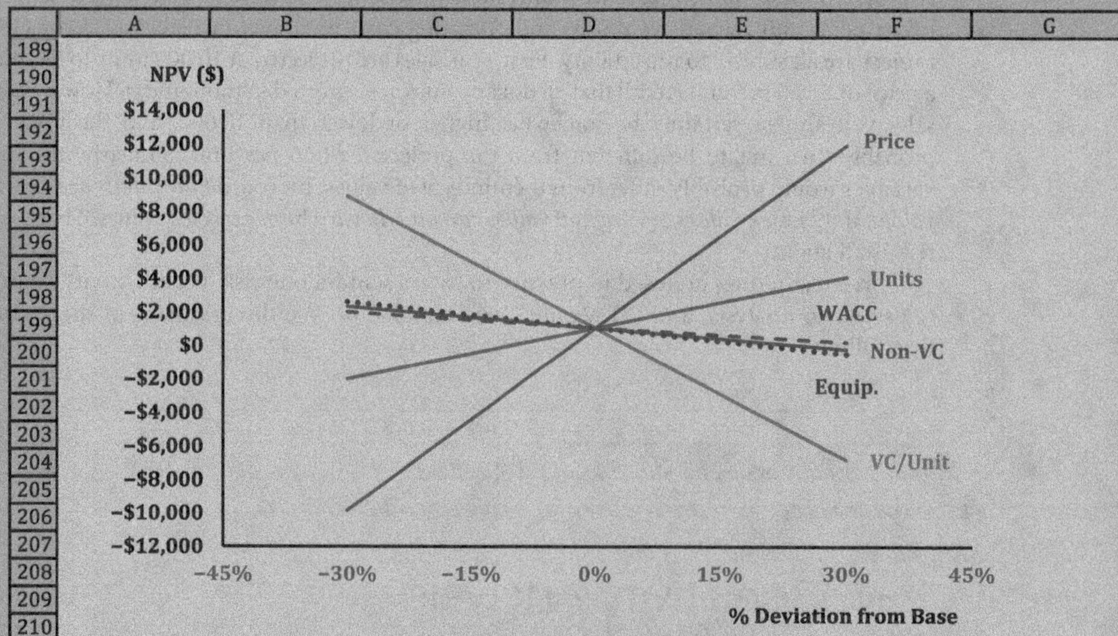

Deviation from Base	Equip.	Price	Units	VC/Unit	Non-VC	WACC
	Data for Sensitivity Graph					
	NPV with Variables at Different Deviations from Base					
-30%	$2,599	-$9,852	-$1,999	$8,901	$2,309	$1,999
0%	$1,048	$1,048	$1,048	$1,048	$1,048	$1,048
30%	-$503	$11,949	$4,096	-$6,805	-$213	$205
Range	$3,102	$21,801	$6,095	$15,706	$2,521	$1,794

costs, and WACC lower the project's NPV. The slopes of the lines in the graph and the ranges in the table below the graph indicate how sensitive NPV is to each input: *The larger the range, the steeper the variable's slope, and the more sensitive the NPV is to this variable.* We see that NPV is extremely sensitive to changes in the sales price; fairly sensitive to changes in variable costs, units sold, and fixed costs; and not especially sensitive to changes in the equipment's cost and the WACC. Management should, of course, try especially hard to obtain accurate estimates of the variables that have the greatest impact on the NPV. See ***2-Sens*** in ***Ch11 Tool Kit.xls*** for all calculations.

resource
*See **Ch11 Tool Kit.xls** on the textbook's Web site.*

If we were comparing two projects, then the one with the steeper sensitivity lines would be riskier (other things held constant), because relatively small changes in the input variables would produce large changes in the NPV. Thus, sensitivity analysis provides useful insights into a project's risk.[9] Note, however, that even though NPV may be highly sensitive to certain variables, if those variables are not likely to change much from their expected values, then the project may not be very risky in spite of its high sensitivity. Also, if several of the inputs change at the same time, the combined effect on NPV can be much greater than sensitivity analysis suggests.

11-5b Tornado Diagrams

Tornado diagrams are another way to present results from sensitivity analysis. The first steps are to calculate the range of possible NPVs for each of the input variables being changed and then rank these ranges. In our example, the range for sales price per unit is the largest and the range for WACC is the smallest. The ranges for each variable are then plotted, with the largest range on top and the smallest range on the bottom. It is also helpful to plot a vertical line showing the base-case NPV. We present a tornado diagram in Figure 11-4. Notice that the diagram is like a tornado in the sense that it is widest at the top and smallest at the bottom; hence its name. The tornado diagram makes it immediately obvious which inputs have the greatest impact on NPV: sales price and variable costs in this case.

11-5c NPV Break-Even Analysis

resource
*See **Ch11 Tool Kit.xls** on the textbook's Web site.*

A special application of sensitivity analysis is called **NPV break-even analysis**. In a break-even analysis, we find the level of an input that produces an NPV of exactly zero. We used *Excel*'s Goal Seek feature to do this. See ***Ch11 Tool Kit.xls*** on the textbook's Web site for an explanation of how to use this *Excel* feature.

Table 11-1 shows the values of the inputs discussed previously that produce a zero NPV. For example, the number of units sold in Year 1 can drop to 9,868 before the project's NPV falls to zero. Break-even analysis is helpful in determining how bad things can get before the project has a negative NPV.

11-5d Extensions of Sensitivity Analysis

resource
*See **Ch11 Tool Kit.xls** on the textbook's Web site.*

In our examples, we showed how one output, NPV, varied with a change in a single input. Sensitivity analysis can easily be extended to show how multiple outputs, such as NPV and IRR, vary with a change in an input. See ***Ch11 Tool Kit.xls*** on the textbook's Web site for an example showing how to use *Excel*'s Data Table feature to present multiple outputs.

---

[9]Sensitivity analysis is tedious with a regular calculator but easy with a spreadsheet. We used the chapter's *Excel **Tool Kit*** to calculate the NPVs and then to draw the graph in Figure 11-3. To conduct such an analysis by hand would be quite time-consuming, and if the basic data were changed even slightly—say, the cost of the equipment was increased slightly—then all of the calculations would have to be redone. With a spreadsheet, we can simply type over the old input with the new one, and the analysis and the graph change instantaneously.

FIGURE 11-4

Tornado Diagram for Solar Water Heater Project: Range of Outcomes for Input Deviations from Base Case (Thousands of Dollars)

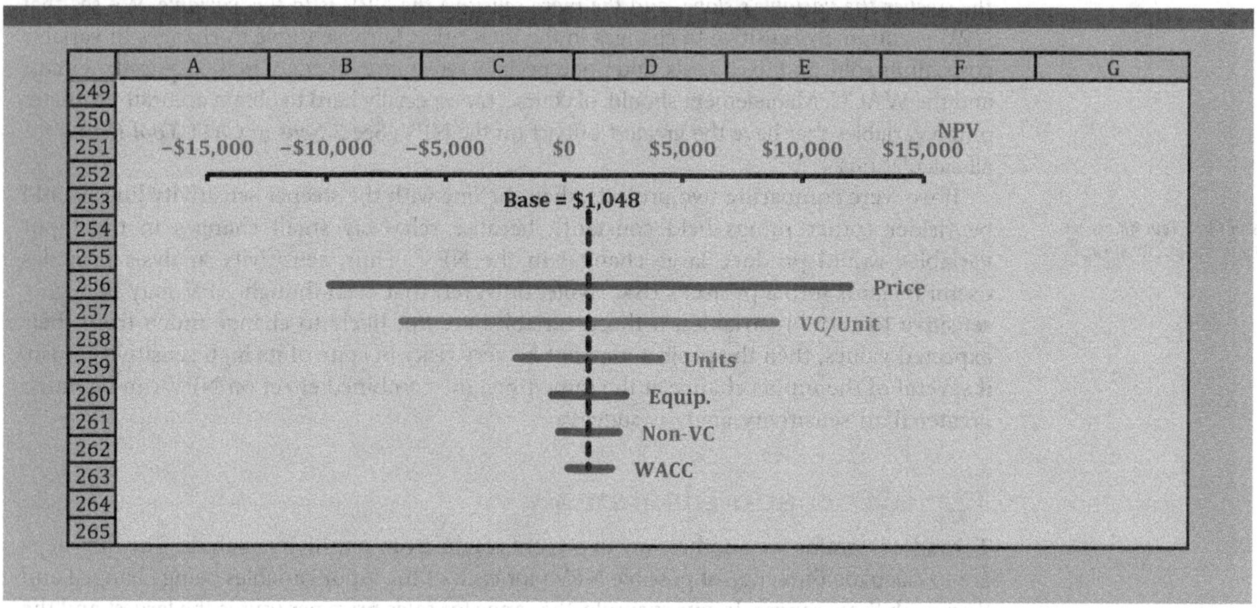

TABLE 11-1

NPV Break-Even Analysis (Thousands of Dollars)

Input	Input Value That Produces Zero NPV, Holding All Else Constant
Sales price per unit, Year 1	$1.457
Variable cost per unit (VC), Year 1	$1.113
Annual change in units sold after Year 1	7.40%
Units sold, Year 1	8,968
Nonvariable cost (Non-VC), Year 1	$2,649
Project WACC	13.79%

© Cengage Learning 2014

It is also possible to use a Data Table to show how a single output, such as NPV, varies for changes in two inputs, such as the number of units sold and the sales price per unit. See ***Ch11 Tool Kit.xls*** on the textbook's Web site for an example. However, when we examine the impact of a change in more than one input, we usually use scenario analysis, which is described in the following section.

SELF-TEST

What is sensitivity analysis?

Briefly explain the usefulness of a sensitivity graph.

Discuss the following statement: "A project may not be very risky in spite of its high sensitivity to certain variables."

11-6 Scenario Analysis

In the sensitivity analysis just described, we changed one variable at a time. However, it is useful to know what would happen to the project's NPV if several of the inputs turn out to be better or worse than expected, and this is what we do in a **scenario analysis.** Also, scenario analysis allows us to assign probabilities to the base (or most likely) case, the best case, and the worst case; then we can find the *expected value and standard deviation* of the project's NPV to get a better idea of the project's risk.

In a scenario analysis, we begin with the base-case scenario, which uses the most likely value for each input variable. We then ask marketing, engineering, and other operating managers to specify a worst-case scenario (low unit sales, low sales price, high variable costs, and so on) and a best-case scenario. Often, the best and worst cases are defined as having a 25% probability of occurring, with a 50% probability for the base-case conditions. Obviously, conditions could take on many more than three values, but such a scenario setup is useful to help get some idea of the project's riskiness.

After much discussion with the marketing staff, engineers, accountants, and other experts in the company, a set of worst-case and best-case values were determined for several key inputs. Figure 11-5, taken from worksheet *3a-Scen* of the chapter *Tool Kit* model, shows the probability and inputs assumed for the base-case, worst-case, and best-case scenarios, along with selected key results.

resource

See Ch11 Tool Kit.xls on the textbook's Web site.

FIGURE 11-5

Inputs and Key Results for Each Scenario (Thousands of Dollars)

	A B C D	E	F	G
34			Scenarios:	
35	Scenario Name	Base	Worst	Best
36	Probability of Scenario	50%	25%	25%
37	Inputs:			
38	Equipment cost	$7,750	$8,250	$7,250
39	Salvage value of equip. in Year 4	$639	$639	$639
40	Opportunity cost	$0	$0	$0
41	Externalities (cannibalization)	$0	$0	$0
42	Units sold, Year 1	10,000	8,500	11,500
43	% Δ in units sold, after Year 1	15%	5%	25%
44	Sales price per unit, Year 1	$1.50	$1.25	$1.75
45	% Δ in sales price, after Year 1	4%	4%	4%
46	Var. cost per unit (VC), Year 1	$1.07	$1.17	$0.97
47	% Δ in VC, after Year 1	3%	3%	3%
48	Nonvar. cost (Non-VC), Year 1	$2,120	$2,330	$1,910
49	% Δ in Non-VC, after Year 1	3%	3%	3%
50	Project WACC	10%	10%	10%
51	Tax rate	40%	50%	30%
52	NOWC as % of next year's sales	15%	15%	15%
53	Key Results:			
54	NPV	$1,048	−$7,543	$19,468
55	IRR	13.79%	−29.40%	62.41%
56	MIRR	12.78%	−22.23%	43.49%
57	Profitability index	1.10	0.23	2.90
58	Payback	3.39	Not found	1.83
59	Discounted payback	3.80	Not found	2.07

resource
*See **Ch11 Tool Kit.xls** on the textbook's Web site.*

The project's cash flows and performance measures under each scenario are calculated; see ***3a-Scen*** in the ***Tool Kit*** for the calculations. The net cash flows for each scenario are shown in Figure 11-6, along with a probability distribution of the possible outcomes for NPV. If the project is highly successful, then a low initial investment, high sales price, high unit sales, and low production costs would combine to result in a very high NPV, $19,468. However, if things turn out badly, then the NPV would be a *negative* $7,543. This wide range of possibilities, and especially the large potential negative value, suggests that this is a risky project. If bad conditions materialize, the project will not bankrupt the company—this is just one project for a large company. Still, losing $7,543 (actually $7,543,000, as the units are thousands of dollars) would certainly hurt the company's value and the reputation of the project's manager.

If we multiply each scenario's probability by the NPV for that scenario and then sum the products, we will have the project's expected NPV of $3,505, as shown in Figure 11-6. Note that the *expected* NPV differs from the *base-case* NPV, which is the most likely outcome because it has a 50% probability. This is not an error—mathematically they are not equal.[10] We also calculate the standard deviation of the expected NPV; it is $9,861. Dividing the standard deviation by the expected NPV yields the **coefficient of variation**, 2.81, which is a measure of stand-alone risk. The coefficient of variation measures the amount of risk per dollar of NPV, so the coefficient of variation can be helpful when comparing the risk of projects with different NPVs. GPC's average project has a coefficient of variation of about 1.2, so the 2.81 indicates that this project is riskier than most of GPC's other typical projects.

GPC's corporate WACC is 9%, so that rate should be used to find the NPV of an average-risk project. However, the water heater project is riskier than average, so a higher discount rate should be used to find its NPV. There is no way to determine the precisely correct discount rate—this is a judgment call. Management decided to evaluate the project using a 10% rate.[11]

Note that the base-case results are the same in our sensitivity and scenario analyses, but in the scenario analysis the worst case is much worse than in the sensitivity analysis and the best case is much better. This is because in scenario analysis all of the variables are set at their best or worst levels, whereas in sensitivity analysis only one variable is adjusted and all the others are left at their base-case levels.

The project has a positive NPV, but its coefficient of variation (CV) is 2.81, which is more than double the 1.2 CV of an average project. With the higher risk, it is not clear if the project should be accepted or not. At this point, GPC's CEO will ask the CFO to investigate the risk further by performing a simulation analysis, as described in the next section.

---

[10]This result occurs for two reasons. First, although in this scenario analysis, the base-case input values happen to equal the average of the best- and worst-case values, this is by no means necessary. Best- and worst-case values need not be the same distance from the base case. Second, even though the base-case values are midway between the best- and worst-case values, in our model two uncertain variables, sales volume and sales price, are multiplied together to obtain dollar sales, and this process causes the NPV distribution to be skewed to the right. A large number multiplied by another large number produces a very big number, and this in turn causes the average value (or expected value) to increase.

[11]One could argue that the best-case scenario should be evaluated with a relatively low WACC, the worst-case scenario with a relatively high WACC, and the base case with the average corporate WACC. However, one could also argue that, at the time of the initial decision, we don't know what case will occur and hence a single rate should be used. Observe that, in the worst-case scenario, all of the cash flows are negative. If we used a high WACC because of this branch's risk, this would lower the PV of these negative cash flows, making the worst case much better than if we used the average WACC. Determining the "right" WACC to use in the analysis is not an easy task!

FIGURE 11-6

Scenario Analysis: Expected NPV and Its Risk (Thousands of Dollars)

	A	B	C	D	E	F	G	H	I
94			Predicted Cash Flows for Alternative Scenarios						
95		Prob:	0	1	2	3	4	WACC	NPV
96	Best →	25%	-$10,269	$4,761	$6,673	$8,237	$20,065	10.00%	$19,468
97									
98	(1) → Base →	50%	-$10,000	$1,900	$2,700	$2,345	$7,800	10.00%	$1,048
99									
100	Worst →	25%	-$9,844	$403	$897	-$281	$2,055	10.00%	-$7,543
101								Expected NPV =	$3,505
102								Standard Deviation (SD) =	$9,861
103								Coefficient of Variation (CV) = Std. Dev./Expected NPV =	2.81

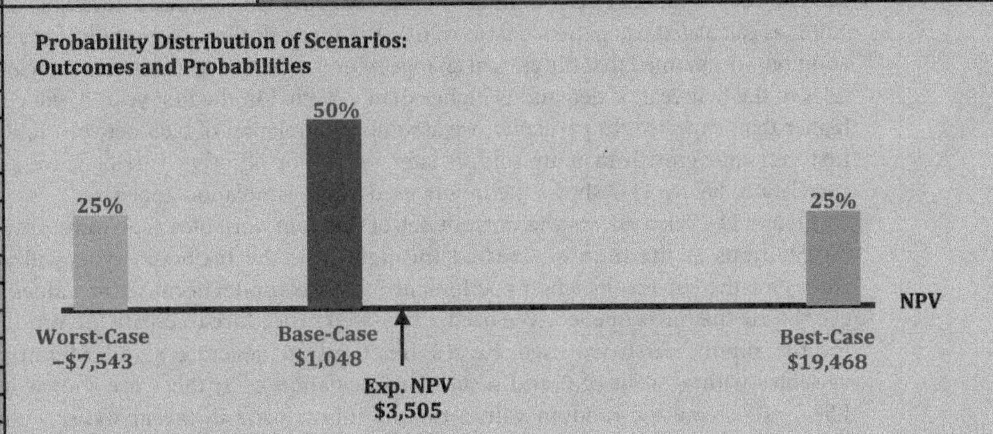

SELF-TEST

What is scenario analysis?

Differentiate between sensitivity analysis and scenario analysis. What advantage does scenario analysis have over sensitivity analysis?

11-7 Monte Carlo Simulation[12]

Monte Carlo simulation ties together sensitivities, probability distributions, and correlations among the input variables. It grew out of work in the Manhattan Project to build the first atomic bomb and was so named because it utilized the mathematics of casino gambling. Although Monte Carlo simulation is considerably more complex than scenario analysis, simulation software packages make the process manageable. Many of these packages can be used as add-ins to *Excel* and other spreadsheet programs.

In a simulation analysis, a probability distribution is assigned to each input variable—sales in units, the sales price, the variable cost per unit, and so on. The computer begins by picking a random value for each variable from its probability distribution. Those values are then entered into the model, the project's NPV is calculated, and the NPV is stored in the

---

[12]This section is relatively technical, and some instructors may choose to skip it with no loss in continuity.

computer's memory. This is called a trial. After completing the first trial, a second set of input values is selected from the input variables' probability distributions, and a second NPV is calculated. This process is repeated many times. The NPVs from the trials can be charted on a histogram, which shows an estimate of the project's outcomes. The average of the trials' NPVs is interpreted as a measure of the project's expected NPV, with the standard deviation (or the coefficient of variation) of the trials' NPV as a measure of the project's risk.

Using this procedure, we conducted a simulation analysis of GPC's solar water heater project. To compare apples and apples, we focused on the same six variables that were allowed to change in the previously conducted scenario analysis. We assumed that each variable can be represented by its own continuous normal distribution with means and standard deviations that are consistent with the base-case scenario. For example, we assumed that the units sold in Year 1 come from a normal distribution with a mean equal to the base-case value of 10,000. We used the probabilities and outcomes of the three scenarios from Section 11-6 to estimate the standard deviation (all calculations are in the ***Tool Kit***). The standard deviation of units sold is 1,061, as calculated using the scenario values. We made similar assumptions for all variables. In addition, we assumed that the annual change in unit sales will be positively correlated with unit sales in the first year: If demand is higher than expected in the first year, it will continue to be higher than expected. In particular, we assume a correlation of 0.65 between units sold in the first year and growth in units sold in later years. For all other variables, we assumed zero correlation. Figure 11-7 shows the inputs used in the simulation analysis.

Figure 11-7 also shows the current set of random variables that were drawn from the distributions at the time we created the figure for the textbook—you will see different values for the key results when you look at the *Excel* model because the values are updated every time the file is opened. We used a two-step procedure to create the random variables for the inputs. First, we used *Excel*'s functions to generate standard normal random variables with a mean of 0 and a standard deviation of 1; these are shown in Cells E38:E51.[13] To create the random values for the inputs used in the analysis, we multiplied a random standard normal variable by the standard deviation and added the expected value. For example, *Excel* drew the value −0.07 for first-year unit sales (Cell E42) from a standard normal distribution. We calculated the value for first-year unit sales to use in the current trial as 10,000 + 1,061(−0.07) = 9,927, which is shown in Cell F42.[14]

We used the inputs in Cells F38:F52 to generate cash flows and to calculate performance measures for the project (the calculations are in the ***Tool Kit***). For the trial reported in Figure 11-7, the NPV is $15,121. We used a Data Table in the ***Tool Kit*** to generate additional trials. For each trial, the Data Table saved the value of the input variables and the value of the trial's NPV. Figure 11-8 presents selected results from the simulation for 10,000 trials. (The worksheet ***4a-Sim100*** in the ***Tool Kit*** shows only 100 trials; the worksheet ***4b-Sim10000*** has the ability to perform 10,000 simulations, but we have turned off the Data Table in that worksheet because simulating 10,000 trials reduces *Excel*'s speed when performing other calculations in the file.)

After running a simulation, the first thing we do is verify that the results are consistent with our assumptions. The resulting sample mean and standard deviation of units sold in the first year are 9,982 and 1,057, which are virtually identical to our assumptions in Figure 11-7. The same is true for all the other inputs, so we can be reasonably confident that the simulation is doing what we are asking. Figure 11-8 also reports summary statistics for the project's NPV. The mean is $1,120, which suggests that the project should be accepted. However, the range of outcomes is quite large, from a loss of $16,785 to a gain of

resource

*See **Ch11 Tool Kit.xls** on the textbook's Web site.*

[13]See the ***Tool Kit*** for detailed explanations on using *Excel* to generate random variables.

[14]There may be slight rounding differences because *Excel* doesn't round in intermediate steps. We used a slightly more complicated procedure to generate a random variable for the annual change in sales to ensure that it had 0.65 correlation with the first-year units sold. See the ***Tool Kit*** for details.

FIGURE 11-7

Inputs and Key Results for the Current Simulation Trial (Thousands of Dollars)

	A	B	C	D	E	F
33			Inputs for Simulation		Random Variables Used in	
34			Probability Distributions		Current Simulation Trial	
35			Expected	Standard	Standard	
36			Value of	Deviation of	Normal	Value Used in
37			Input	Input	Random	Current Trial
38	Equipment cost		$7,750	$354	−0.165	$7,692
39	Salvage value of equip. in Year 4		—	—	—	$639
40	Opportunity cost		—	—	—	$0
41	Externalities (cannibalization)		—	—	—	$0
42	Units sold, Year 1		$10,000	$1,061	−0.069	$9,927
43	% Δ in units sold, after Year 1		15.00%	7.07%	0.734	20.19%
44	Sales price per unit, Year 1		$1.50	$0.18	1.931	$1.84
45	% Δ in sales price, after Year 1		—	—	—	4.00%
46	Var. cost per unit (VC), Year 1		$1.07	$0.07	−1.087	$0.99
47	% Δ in VC, after Year 1		—	—	—	3.00%
48	Nonvar. cost (Non-VC), Year 1		$2,120	$148	0.514	$2,196
49	% Δ in Non-VC, after Year 1		—	—	—	3.00%
50	Project WACC		—	—	—	10.00%
51	Tax rate		40.00%	7.07%	−1.511	29.32%
52	NOWC as % of next year's sales		—	—	—	15.00%
53	Assumed correlation between units sold in Year 1 and annual change in					
54	units sold in later years:			ρ = 65.00%		
55	Key Results Based on Current Trial					
56		NPV	$15,121			
57		IRR	53.23%			
58		MIRR	37.61%			
59		PI	2.45			
60		Payback	1.98			
61		Discounted payback	$2.25			

$26,406, so the project is clearly risky. The standard deviation of $5,132 indicates that losses could easily occur, which is consistent with this wide range of possible outcomes.[15] Figure 11-8 also reports a median NPV of $737, which means that half the time the project will have an NPV of less than $737. In fact, there is only 56.4% probability that the project will have a positive NPV.

A picture is worth a thousand words, and Figure 11-8 shows the probability distribution of the outcomes. Note that the distribution of outcomes is slightly skewed to the right. As the

[15]Note that the standard deviation of NPV in the simulation is much smaller than the standard deviation in the scenario analysis. In the scenario analysis, we assumed that all of the poor outcomes would occur together in the worst-case scenario and that all of the positive outcomes would occur together in the best-case scenario. In other words, we implicitly assumed that all of the risky variables were perfectly positively correlated. In the simulation, we assumed that the variables were independent (except for the correlation between unit sales and growth). The independence of variables in the simulation reduces the range of outcomes. For example, in the simulation, sometimes the sales price is high but the sales growth is low. In the scenario analysis, a high sales price is always coupled with high growth. Because the scenario analysis assumption of perfect correlation is unlikely, simulation may provide a better estimate of project risk. However, if the standard deviations and correlations used as inputs in the simulation are inaccurately estimated, then the simulation output will likewise be inaccurate.

FIGURE 11-8

Summary of Simulation Results (Thousands of Dollars)

	A	B	C	D	E	F	G	H	I
156	Number of Trials	10,000	Input Variables						
157–160	Summary Statistics for Simulated Input Variables		Equip. cost	Units sold, Year 1	% Δ in units sold, after Year 1	Sales price per unit, Year 1	Variable cost per unit (VC), Year 1	Nonvar. cost (Non-VC), Year 1	Tax rate
161		Average	$7,750	9,982	15.0%	$1.50	$1.07	$2,122	39.9%
162		Standard deviation	$354	1,057	7.1%	$0.18	$0.07	$150	7.1%
163		Maximum	$9,072	14,005	45.0%	$2.15	$1.32	$2,682	68.7%
164		Minimum	$6,397	6,172	−13.97%	$0.81	$0.78	$1,549	13.5%
165		Correlation with unit sales			65.4%				

	Summary Statistics for Simulated Results	NPV
168	Average	$1,120
169	Standard deviation	$5,132
170	Maximum	$26,406
171	Minimum	−$16,785
172	Median	$737
173	Probability of NPV > 0	56.4%
174	Coefficient of variation	4.58

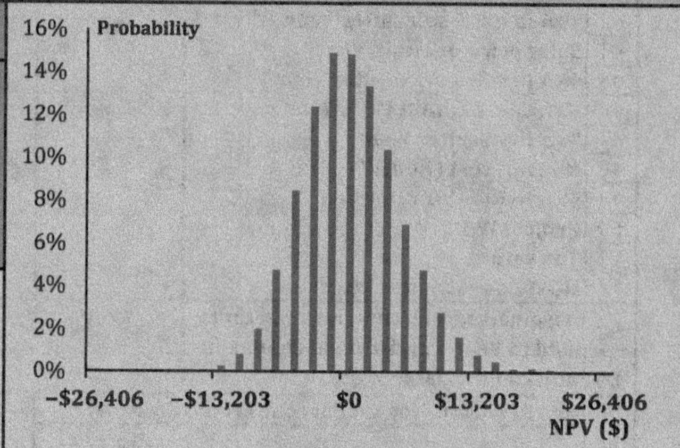

resource

See Ch11 Tool Kit.xls on the textbook's Web site.

figure shows, the potential downside losses are not as large as the potential upside gains. Our conclusion is that this is a very risky project, as indicated by the coefficient of variation, but it does have a positive expected NPV and the potential to be a "home run."

If the company decides to go ahead with the project, senior management should also identify possible contingency plans for responding to changes in market conditions. Senior managers always should consider qualitative factors in addition to the quantitative project analysis.

SELF-TEST

What is Monte Carlo simulation?

11-8 Project Risk Conclusions

We have discussed the three types of risk normally considered in capital budgeting: stand-alone risk, within-firm (or corporate) risk, and market risk. However, two important questions remain: (1) Should firms care about stand-alone and corporate risk, given that finance theory says that market (beta) risk is the only relevant risk? (2) What do we do when the stand-alone, within-firm, and market risk assessments lead to different conclusions?

There are no easy answers to these questions. Strict adherents of the CAPM would argue that well-diversified investors are concerned only with market risk, that managers should be concerned only with maximizing stock price, and thus that market (beta) risk ought to be given virtually all the weight in capital budgeting decisions. However, we know that not all investors are well diversified, that the CAPM does not operate exactly as the theory says it should, and that measurement problems keep managers from having complete confidence in the CAPM inputs. In addition, the CAPM ignores bankruptcy costs, even though such costs can be substantial, and the probability of bankruptcy depends on a firm's corporate risk, not on its beta risk. Therefore, even well-diversified investors should want a firm's management to give at least some consideration to a project's corporate risk, and that means giving some consideration to stand-alone project risk.

Although it would be nice to reconcile these problems and to measure risk on some absolute scale, the best we can do in practice is to estimate risk in a somewhat nebulous, relative sense. For example, we can generally say with a fair degree of confidence that a particular project has more, less, or about the same stand-alone risk as the firm's average project. Then, because stand-alone and corporate risks generally are correlated, the project's stand-alone risk generally is a reasonably good measure of its corporate risk. Finally, assuming that market risk and corporate risk are correlated, as is true for most companies, a project with a relatively high or low corporate risk will also have a relatively high or low market risk. We wish we could be more specific, but one simply must use a lot of judgment when assessing projects' risks.

SELF-TEST

In theory, should a firm be equally concerned with stand-alone, corporate, and market risk? Would your answer be the same if we substituted "In practice" for "In theory"? Explain your answers.

If a project's stand-alone, corporate, and market risk are known to be highly correlated, would this make the task of evaluating the project's risk easier or harder? Explain.

11-9 Replacement Analysis

In the previous sections we assumed that the solar water heater project was an entirely new project, so all of its cash flows were incremental—they would occur if and only if the project were accepted. However, for replacement projects we must find the cash flow *differentials* between the new and old projects, and these differentials are the *incremental cash flows* that we must analyze.

We evaluate a replacement decision in Figure 11-9, which is set up much like Figures 11-1 and 11-2 but with data on both a new, highly efficient machine and data on the old machine. In Part I we show the key inputs in the analysis, including depreciation on the new and old machines. In Part II we find the cash flows the firm will have if it continues to use the old machine, and in Part III we find the cash flows if the firm replaces the old machine. Then, in Part IV, we subtract the old flows from the new to arrive at the *incremental cash flows,* and we evaluate those flows in Part V to find the NPV, IRR, and MIRR. Replacing the old machine appears to be a good decision.[16]

resource

*See **Ch11 Tool Kit.xls** on the textbook's Web site.*

In some instances, replacements add capacity as well as lower operating costs. In this case, sales revenues in Part III would be increased, and if that leads to a need for more working capital, then this would be shown as a Time 0 expenditure along with a recovery at the end of the project's life. These changes would, of course, be reflected in the incremental cash flows on Row 52.

[16]The same sort of risk analysis discussed in previous sections can be applied to replacement decisions.

FIGURE 11-9
Replacement Analysis

	A B C	D	E	F	G	H	I
15				Applies to:			
16	**Part I. Inputs:**		Both Machines	Old Machine	New Machine		
17	Cost of new machine				$2,000		
18	After-tax salvage value old machine			$400			
19	Sales revenues (fixed)		$2,500				
20	Annual operating costs except depr.			$1,200	$280		
21	Tax rate		40%				
22	WACC		10%				
23	Depreciation	1	2	3	4	Totals:	
24	Depr. rates (new machine)	33.33%	44.45%	14.81%	7.41%	100%	
25	Depreciation on new machine	$667	$889	$296	$148	$2,000	
26	Depreciation on old machine	$334	$333	$0	$0	$667	
27	Δ: Change in depreciation	$333	$556	$296	$148	$1,333	
28	**Part II. Net Cash Flows before Replacement: Old Machine**						
29			0	1	2	3	4
30	Sales revenues			$2,500	$2,500	$2,500	$2,500
31	Operating costs except depreciation			1,200	1,200	1,200	1,200
32	Depreciation			334	333	0	0
33	Total operating costs			$1,534	$1,533	$1,200	$1,200
34	Operating income			$966	$967	$1,300	$1,300
35	Taxes 40%			386	387	520	520
36	After-tax operating income			$580	$580	$780	$780
37	Add back depreciation			334	333	0	0
38	Net cash flows before replacement		$0	$914	$913	$780	$780
39	**Part III. Net Cash Flows after Replacement: New Machine**						
40			0	1	2	3	4
41	New machine cost:		-$2,000				
42	After-tax salvage value, old machine		$400				
43	Sales revenues			$2,500	$2,500	$2,500	$2,500
44	Operating costs except depreciation			$280	$280	$280	$280
45	Depreciation			$667	$889	$296	$148
46	Total operating costs			$947	$1,169	$576	$428
47	Operating income			$1,553	$1,331	$1,924	$2,072
48	Taxes 40%			$621	$532	$770	$829
49	After-tax operating income			$932	$799	$1,154	$1,243
50	Add back depreciation			$667	$889	$296	$148
51	Net cash flows after replacement		-$1,600	$1,599	$1,688	$1,450	$1,391
52	**Part IV. Incremental CF: Row 51 – Row 38**		-$1,600	$685	$774	$670	$611
53	**Part V. Evaluation**	NPV =	$584.02	IRR =	26.33%	MIRR =	18.90%

SELF-TEST

How are incremental cash flows found in a replacement analysis?

If you were analyzing a replacement project and suddenly learned that the old equipment could be sold for $1,000 rather than $400, would this new information make the replacement look better or worse? Explain.

In Figure 11-9 we assumed that output would remain stable if the old machine were replaced. Suppose output would double. How would this change be dealt with in the framework of Figure 11-9?

11-10 Real Options

According to traditional capital budgeting theory, a project's NPV is the present value of its expected future cash flows discounted at a rate that reflects the riskiness of those cash flows. Note, however, that this says nothing about actions taken *after* the project has been accepted and placed in operation that might lead to an increase in the cash flows. In other words, traditional capital budgeting theory assumes that a project is like a roulette wheel. A gambler can choose whether to spin the wheel, but once the wheel has been spun, nothing can be done to influence the outcome. Once the game begins, the outcome depends purely on chance, and no skill is involved.

Contrast roulette with a game such as poker. Chance plays a role in poker, and it continues to play a role after the initial deal because players receive additional cards throughout the game. However, poker players are able to respond to their opponents' actions, so skilled players usually win.

Capital budgeting decisions have more in common with poker than roulette because (1) chance plays a continuing role throughout the life of the project, but (2) managers can respond to changing market conditions and to competitors' actions. Opportunities to respond to changing circumstances are called **managerial options** (because they give managers a chance to influence the outcome of a project), **strategic options** (because they are often associated with large, strategic projects rather than routine maintenance projects), and **embedded options** (because they are a part of the project). Finally, they are called **real options** to differentiate them from financial options because they involve real, rather than financial, assets. The following sections describe projects with several types of real options.

11-10a Investment Timing Options

Conventional NPV analysis implicitly assumes that projects either will be accepted or rejected, which implies they will be undertaken now or never. In practice, however, companies sometimes have a third choice—delay the decision until later, when more information is available. Such **investment timing options** can dramatically affect a project's estimated profitability and risk, as we saw in our example of GPC's solar water heater project.

Keep in mind, though, that the *option to delay* is valuable only if it more than offsets any harm that might result from delaying. For example, while one company delays, some other company might establish a loyal customer base that makes it difficult for the first company to enter the market later. The option to delay is usually most valuable to firms with proprietary technology, patents, licenses, or other barriers to entry, because these factors lessen the threat of competition. The option to delay is valuable when market demand is uncertain, but it is also valuable during periods of volatile interest rates, because the ability to wait can allow firms to delay raising capital for a project until interest rates are lower.

11-10b Growth Options

A **growth option** allows a company to increase its capacity if market conditions are better than expected. There are several types of growth options. One lets a company *increase the capacity of an existing product line*. A "peaking unit" power plant illustrates this type of growth option. Such units have high variable costs and are used to produce additional power only if demand, thus prices, are high.

The second type of growth option allows a company to *expand into new geographic markets*. Many companies are investing in China, Eastern Europe, and Russia even though standard NPV analysis produces negative NPVs. However, if these developing markets really take off, the option to open more facilities could be quite valuable.

The third type of growth option is the opportunity to *add new products,* including complementary products and successive "generations" of the original product. Auto companies are losing money on their first electric autos, but the manufacturing skills and consumer recognition those cars will provide should help turn subsequent generations of electric autos into moneymakers.

11-10c Abandonment Options

Consider the value of an **abandonment option**. Standard DCF analysis assumes that a project's assets will be used over a specified economic life. But even though some projects must be operated over their full economic life—in spite of deteriorating market conditions and hence lower than expected cash flows—other projects can be abandoned. Smart managers negotiate the right to abandon if a project turns out to be unsuccessful as a condition for undertaking the project.

Note, too, that some projects can be structured so that they provide the option to *reduce capacity* or *temporarily suspend operations.* Such options are common in the natural resources industry, including mining, oil, and timber, and they should be reflected in the analysis when NPVs are being estimated.

11-10d Flexibility Options

Many projects offer **flexibility options** that permit the firm to alter operations depending on how conditions change during the life of the project. Typically, either inputs or outputs (or both) can be changed. BMW's Spartanburg, South Carolina, auto assembly plant provides a good example of output flexibility. BMW needed the plant to produce sports coupes. If it built the plant configured to produce only these vehicles, the construction cost would be minimized. However, the company thought that later on it might want to switch production to some other vehicle type, and that would be difficult if the plant were designed just for coupes. Therefore, BMW decided to spend additional funds to construct a more flexible plant: one that could produce different types of vehicles should demand patterns shift. Sure enough, things did change. Demand for coupes dropped a bit and demand for sport-utility vehicles soared. But BMW was ready, and the Spartanburg plant began to produce hot-selling SUVs. The plant's cash flows were much higher than they would have been without the flexibility option that BMW "bought" by paying more to build a more flexible plant.

Electric power plants provide an example of input flexibility. Utilities can build plants that generate electricity by burning coal, oil, or natural gas. The prices of those fuels change over time in response to events in the Middle East, changing environmental policies, and weather conditions. Some years ago, virtually all power plants were designed to burn just one type of fuel, because this resulted in the lowest construction costs. However, as fuel cost volatility increased, power companies began to build higher-cost but more flexible plants, especially ones that could switch from oil to gas and back again depending on relative fuel prices.

11-10e Valuing Real Options

A full treatment of real option valuation is beyond the scope of this chapter, but there are some things we can say. First, if a project has an embedded real option, then management should at least recognize and articulate its existence. Second, we know that a financial option is more valuable if it has a long time until maturity or if the underlying asset is very risky. If either of these characteristics applies to a project's real option, then management should know that its value is probably relatively high. Third, management might be able to model the real option along the lines of a decision tree, as we illustrate in the following section.

SELF-TEST

Explain the relevance of the following statement: "Capital budgeting decisions have more in common with poker than roulette."

What are managerial options? Strategic options?

Identify some different types of real options and differentiate among them.

11-11 Phased Decisions and Decision Trees

Up to this point we have focused primarily on techniques for estimating a project's risk. Although this is an integral part of capital budgeting, managers are just as interested in *reducing* risk as in *measuring* it. One way to reduce risk is to structure projects so that expenditures can be made in stages over time rather than all at once. This gives managers the opportunity to reevaluate decisions using new information and then to either invest additional funds or terminate the project. This type of analysis involves the use of *decision trees.*

11-11a The Basic Decision Tree

resource

*See **Ch11 Tool Kit.xls** on the textbook's Web site.*

GPC's analysis of the solar water heater project thus far has assumed that the project cannot be abandoned once it goes into operation, even if the worst-case situation arises. However, GPC is considering the possibility of terminating (abandoning) the project at Year 2 if the demand is low. The net after-tax cash flow from salvage, legal fees, liquidation of working capital, and all other termination costs and revenues is $5,000. Using these assumptions, the GPC ran a new scenario analysis; the results are shown in Figure 11-10, which is a simple decision tree.

FIGURE 11-10

Simple Decision Tree: Abandoning Project in Worst-Case Scenario

	A	B	C	D	E	F	G	H	I
123			Predicted Cash Flows for Alternative Scenarios						
124		Prob:	0	1	2	3	4	WACC	NPV
125	Best →	25%	−$10,269	$4,761	$6,673	$8,237	$20,065	10%	$19,468
126									
127	(1) →Base→	50%	−$10,000	$1,900	$2,700	$2,345	$7,800	10%	$1,048
128									
129			−$9,844	$403	$897	−$281	$2,055		
130	Worst →	25%							
131			−$9,844	$403	(2) $5,000	$0	$0	10%	−$5,345
132	If abandon, can liquidate for $5,000 at t = 2.								
133							Expected NPV =		$4,055
134							Standard Deviation (SD) =		$9,273
135							Coefficient of Variation (CV) = Std. Dev./Expected NPV =		2.29

Here we assume that, if the worst case materializes, then this will be recognized after the low Year-1 cash flow and GPC will abandon the project. Rather than continue realizing low cash flows in Years 2, 3, and 4, the company will shut down the operation and liquidate the project for $5,000 at t = 2. Now the expected NPV rises from $3,505 to $4,055 and the CV declines from 2.81 to 2.29. So, securing the right to abandon the project if things don't work out raised the project's expected return and lowered its risk. This will give you an approximate value, but keep in mind that you may not have a good estimate of the appropriate discount rate because the real option changes the risk, and hence the required return, of the project.[17]

11-11b Staged Decision Tree

After the management team thought about the decision-tree approach, other ideas for improving the project emerged. The marketing manager stated that he could undertake a study that would give the firm a better idea of demand for the product. If the marketing study found favorable responses to the product, the design engineer stated that she could build a prototype solar water heater to gauge consumer reactions to the actual product. After assessing consumer reactions, the company could either go ahead with the project or abandon it. This type of evaluation process is called a **staged decision tree** and is shown in Figure 11-11.

Decision trees such as the one in Figure 11-11 often are used to analyze multistage, or sequential, decisions. Each circle represents a decision point, also known as a **decision node**. The dollar value to the left of each decision node represents the net cash flow at that point, and the cash flows shown under t = 3, 4, 5, and 6 represent the cash inflows if the project is pushed on to completion. Each diagonal line leads to a **branch** of the decision tree, and each

FIGURE 11-11

Decision Tree with Multiple Decision Points

	A	B	C	D	E	F	G	H	I	J	K
144	Firm can abandon the project at t = 2									WACC =	10%
145				Time Periods, Cash Flows, Probabilities, and Decision Points						WACC =	10%
146	0	1		2		3	4	5	6	WACC =	10%
147	1st Invest	Prob.	2nd Invest	Prob.	3rd Invest	Inflow	Inflow	Inflow	Inflow	NPV	Joint Prob
148											
149				45%	−$10,269 (3)	$4,761	$6,673	$8,237	$20,065	$15,534	36%
150											
151		80%	−$500 (2)	40%	−$10,000 (3)	$1,900	$2,700	$2,345	$7,800	$312	32%
152											
153	−$100 (1)			15%	Stop (3)	$0	$0	$0	$0	−$555	12%
154											
155		20%	Stop (2)		$0	$0	$0	$0	$0	−$100	20%
156											100%
157									Expected NPV =	$5,606	
158									Standard Deviation (SD) =	$7,451	
159									Coefficient of Variation (CV) = Std. Dev./Expected NPV =	1.33	

[17]For more on real option valuation, see M. Amram and N. Kulatilaka, *Real Options: Managing Strategic Investment in an Uncertain World* (Boston: Harvard Business School Press, 1999); and H. Smit and L. Trigeorgis, *Strategic Investments: Real Options and Games* (Princeton, NJ: Princeton University Press, 2004).

branch has an estimated probability. For example, if the firm decides to "go" with the project at Decision Point 1, then it will spend $100,000 on the marketing study. Management estimates that there is a 0.8 probability that the study will produce *positive* results, leading to the decision to make an additional investment and thus move on to Decision Point 2, and a 0.2 probability that the marketing study will produce *negative* results, indicating that the project should be canceled after Stage 1. If the project is canceled, the cost to the company will be the $100,000 spent on the initial marketing study.

If the marketing study yields positive results, then the firm will spend $500,000 on the prototype water heater module at Decision Point 2. Management estimates (even before making the initial $100,000 investment) that there is a 45% probability of the pilot project yielding good results, a 40% probability of average results, and a 15% probability of bad results. If the prototype works well, then the firm will spend several millions more at Decision Point 3 to build a production plant, buy the necessary inventory, and commence operations. The operating cash flows over the project's 4-year life will be good, average, or bad, and these cash flows are shown under Years 3 through 6.

The column of joint probabilities in Figure 11-11 gives the probability of occurrence of each branch—and hence of each NPV. Each joint probability is obtained by multiplying together all the probabilities on that particular branch. For example, the probability that the company will, if Stage 1 is undertaken, move through Stages 2 and 3, and that a strong demand will produce the indicated cash flows, is (0.8)(0.45) = 0.36 = 36.0%. There is a 32% probability of average results, a 12% probability of building the plant and then getting bad results, and a 20% probability of getting bad initial results and stopping after the marketing study. The NPV of the top (most favorable) branch as shown in Column J is $15,534, calculated as follows:

$$\begin{aligned} \text{NPV} &= -\$100 - \frac{\$500}{(1.10)^1} - \frac{\$10{,}269}{(1.10)^2} + \frac{\$4{,}761}{(1.10)^3} + \frac{\$6{,}673}{(1.10)^4} + \frac{\$8{,}237}{(1.10)^5} + \frac{\$20{,}065}{(1.10)^6} \\ &= \$15{,}534 \end{aligned}$$

The NPVs for the other branches are calculated similarly.[18]

The last column in Figure 11-11 gives the product of the NPV for each branch times the joint probability of that branch's occurring, and the sum of these products is the project's expected NPV. Based on the expectations used to create Figure 11-11 and a cost of capital of 10%, the project's expected NPV is $5,606, or $5.606 million.[19] In addition, the CV declines from 2.81 to 1.33, and the maximum anticipated loss is a manageable –$555,000. At this point, the solar water heater project looked good, and GPC's management decided to accept it.

As this example shows, decision-tree analysis requires managers to articulate explicitly the types of risk a project faces and to develop responses to potential scenarios. Note also that our example could be extended to cover many other types of decisions and could even be incorporated into a simulation analysis. All in all, decision-tree analysis is a valuable tool for analyzing project risks.[20]

---

[18]The calculations in *Excel* use nonrounded annual cash flows, so there may be small differences when calculating by hand with rounded annual cash flows.

[19]As we mentioned concerning the abandonment option, the presence of the real options in Figure 11-11 might cause the discount rate to change.

[20]In this example we glossed over an important issue: the appropriate cost of capital for the project. Adding decision nodes to a project clearly changes its risk, so we would expect the cost of capital for a project with few decision nodes to have a different risk than one with many nodes. If this is so then the projects should have different costs of capital. In fact, we might expect the cost of capital to change over time as the project moves to different stages, because the stages themselves differ in risk.

SELF-TEST

What is a decision tree? A branch? A node?

If a firm can structure a project such that expenditures can be made in stages rather than all at the beginning, how would this affect the project's risk and expected NPV? Explain.

SUMMARY

In this chapter, we developed a framework for analyzing a project's cash flows and its risk. The key concepts covered are listed below.

- The most important (and most difficult) step in analyzing a capital budgeting project is **estimating the incremental after-tax cash flows** the project will produce.
- A project's **net cash flow** is different from its accounting income. Project net cash flow reflects (1) cash outlays for fixed assets, (2) sales revenues, (3) operating costs, (4) the tax shield provided by depreciation, and (5) cash flows due to changes in net working capital. A project's net cash flow does *not* include interest payments, because they are accounted for by the discounting process. If we deducted interest and then discounted cash flows at the WACC, this would double-count interest charges.
- In determining incremental cash flows, **opportunity costs** (the cash flows forgone by using an asset) must be included, but **sunk costs** (cash outlays that have been made and that cannot be recouped) are not included. Any **externalities** (effects of a project on other parts of the firm) should also be reflected in the analysis. Externalities can be *positive* or *negative* and may be *environmental.*
- **Cannibalization** is an important type of externality that occurs when a new project leads to a reduction in sales of an existing product.
- **Tax laws** affect cash flow analysis in two ways: (1) taxes reduce operating cash flows, and (2) tax laws determine the depreciation expense that can be taken in each year.
- **Price level changes (inflation** or **deflation)** must be considered in project analysis. The best procedure is to build expected price changes into the cash flow estimates. Recognize that output prices and costs for a product can decline over time even though the economy is experiencing inflation.
- The chapter illustrates both **expansion projects,** in which the investment generates new sales, and **replacement projects,** where the primary purpose of the investment is to operate more efficiently and thus reduce costs.
- We discuss three types of risk: **Stand-alone risk, corporate** (or **within-firm) risk,** and **market** (or **beta) risk.** Stand-alone risk does not consider diversification at all; corporate risk considers risk among the firm's own assets; and market risk considers risk at the stockholder level, where stockholders' own diversification is considered.
- **Risk** is important because it affects the discount rate used in capital budgeting; in other words, a project's WACC depends on its risk.
- Assuming the CAPM holds true, **market risk** is the most important risk because (according to the CAPM) it is the risk that affects stock prices. However, usually *it is difficult to measure a project's market risk.*

- **Corporate risk** is important because it influences the firm's ability to use low-cost debt, to maintain smooth operations over time, and to avoid crises that might consume management's energy and disrupt its employees, customers, suppliers, and community. Also, a project's corporate risk is generally easier to measure than its market risk, and, because corporate and market risks are generally thought to be correlated, corporate risk can often serve as a proxy for market risk.
- **Stand-alone risk** is easier to measure than either market or corporate risk. Also, most of a firm's projects' cash flows are correlated with one another, and the firm's total cash flows are correlated with those of most other firms. These correlations mean that a project's stand-alone risk generally can be used as a proxy for hard-to-measure market and corporate risk. As a result, most risk analysis in capital budgeting focuses on stand-alone risk.
- **Sensitivity analysis** is a technique that shows how much a project's NPV will change in response to a given change in an input variable, such as sales, when all other factors are held constant.
- **Scenario analysis** is a risk analysis technique in which the best- and worst-case NPVs are compared with the project's base-case NPV.
- **Monte Carlo simulation** is a risk analysis technique that uses a computer to simulate future events and thereby estimate a project's profitability and riskiness.
- The **risk-adjusted discount rate**, or **project cost of capital**, is the rate used to evaluate a particular project. It is based on the corporate WACC, a value that is increased for projects that are riskier than the firm's average project and decreased for less risky projects.
- A **decision tree** shows how different decisions during a project's life can affect its value.
- A **staged decision tree** divides the analysis into different phases. At each phase a decision is made either to proceed or to stop the project. These decisions are represented on the decision trees by circles and are called **decision nodes**.
- Opportunities to respond to changing circumstances are called **real options** or **managerial options** because they give managers the option to influence the returns on a project. They are also called **strategic options** if they are associated with large, strategic projects rather than routine maintenance projects. Finally, they are also called "real" options because they involve "real" (or "physical") rather than "financial" assets. Many projects include a variety of these **embedded options** that can dramatically affect the true NPV.
- An **investment timing option** involves the possibility of delaying major expenditures until more information on likely outcomes is known. The opportunity to delay can dramatically change a project's estimated value.
- A **growth option** occurs if an investment creates the opportunity to make other potentially profitable investments that would not otherwise be possible. These include (1) options to expand the original project's output, (2) options to enter a new geographical market, and (3) options to introduce complementary products or successive generations of products.
- An **abandonment option** is the ability to discontinue a project if the operating cash flow turns out to be lower than expected. It reduces the risk of a project and increases its value. Instead of total abandonment, some options allow a company to reduce capacity or temporarily suspend operations.
- A **flexibility option** is the option to modify operations depending on how conditions develop during a project's life, especially the type of output produced or the inputs used.

QUESTIONS

(11-1) Define each of the following terms:

a. Project cash flow; accounting income
b. Incremental cash flow; sunk cost; opportunity cost; externality; cannibalization; expansion project; replacement project
c. Net operating working capital changes; salvage value
d. Stand-alone risk; corporate (within-firm) risk; market (beta) risk
e. Sensitivity analysis; scenario analysis; Monte Carlo simulation analysis
f. Risk-adjusted discount rate; project cost of capital
g. Decision tree; staged decision tree; decision node; branch
h. Real options; managerial options; strategic options; embedded options
i. Investment timing option; growth option; abandonment option; flexibility option

(11-2) Operating cash flows, rather than accounting profits, are used in project analysis. What is the basis for this emphasis on cash flows as opposed to net income?

(11-3) Why is it true, in general, that a failure to adjust expected cash flows for expected inflation biases the calculated NPV downward?

(11-4) Explain why sunk costs should not be included in a capital budgeting analysis but opportunity costs and externalities should be included.

(11-5) Explain how net operating working capital is recovered at the end of a project's life and why it is included in a capital budgeting analysis.

(11-6) How do simulation analysis and scenario analysis differ in the way they treat very bad and very good outcomes? What does this imply about using each technique to evaluate project riskiness?

(11-7) Why are interest charges not deducted when a project's cash flows are calculated for use in a capital budgeting analysis?

(11-8) Most firms generate cash inflows every day, not just once at the end of the year. In capital budgeting, should we recognize this fact by estimating daily project cash flows and then using them in the analysis? If we do not, will this bias our results? If it does, would the NPV be biased up or down? Explain.

(11-9) What are some differences in the analysis for a replacement project versus that for a new expansion project?

(11-10) Distinguish among beta (or market) risk, within-firm (or corporate) risk, and stand-alone risk for a project being considered for inclusion in a firm's capital budget.

(11-11) In theory, market risk should be the only "relevant" risk. However, companies focus as much on stand-alone risk as on market risk. What are the reasons for the focus on stand-alone risk?

SELF-TEST PROBLEMS Solutions Appear in Appendix A

(ST-1) New-Project Analysis

You have been asked by the president of the Farr Construction Company to evaluate the proposed acquisition of a new earth mover. The mover's basic price is $50,000, and it would cost another $10,000 to modify it for special use. Assume that the mover falls into the MACRS 3-year class (see Appendix 11A), that it would be sold after 3 years for $20,000, and that it would require an increase in net working capital (spare parts inventory) of $2,000 at the start of the project. This working capital will be recovered at

Year 3. The earth mover would have no effect on revenues, but it is expected to save the firm $20,000 per year in before-tax operating costs, mainly labor. The firm's marginal federal-plus-state tax rate is 40%.

a. What are the Year-0 cash flows?
b. What are the operating cash flows in Years 1, 2, and 3?
c. What are the additional (nonoperating) cash flows in Year 3?
d. If the project's cost of capital is 10%, should the earth mover be purchased?

(ST-2) Corporate Risk Analysis

The staff of Porter Manufacturing has estimated the following net after-tax cash flows and probabilities for a new manufacturing process:

	Net After-Tax Cash Flows		
Year	P = 0.2	P = 0.6	P = 0.2
0	−$100,000	−$100,000	−$100,000
1	20,000	30,000	40,000
2	20,000	30,000	40,000
3	20,000	30,000	40,000
4	20,000	30,000	40,000
5	20,000	30,000	40,000
5*	0	20,000	30,000

Line 0 gives the cost of the process, Lines 1 through 5 give operating cash flows, and Line 5* contains the estimated salvage values. Porter's cost of capital for an average-risk project is 10%.

a. Assume that the project has average risk. Find the project's expected NPV. (*Hint:* Use expected values for the net cash flow in each year.)
b. Find the best-case and worst-case NPVs. What is the probability of occurrence of the worst case if the cash flows are perfectly dependent (perfectly positively correlated) over time? If they are independent over time?
c. Assume that all the cash flows are perfectly positively correlated. That is, assume there are only three possible cash flow streams over time—the worst case, the most likely (or base) case, and the best case—with respective probabilities of 0.2, 0.6, and 0.2. These cases are represented by each of the columns in the table. Find the expected NPV, its standard deviation, and its coefficient of variation.

PROBLEMS Answers Appear in Appendix B

Easy Problems 1–4

(11-1) Investment Outlay

Talbot Industries is considering launching a new product. The new manufacturing equipment will cost $17 million, and production and sales will require an initial $5 million investment in net operating working capital. The company's tax rate is 40%.

a. What is the initial investment outlay?
b. The company spent and expensed $150,000 on research related to the new product last year. Would this change your answer? Explain.
c. Rather than build a new manufacturing facility, the company plans to install the equipment in a building it owns but is not now using. The building could be sold for $1.5 million after taxes and real estate commissions. How would this affect your answer?

(11-2) Operating Cash Flow The financial staff of Cairn Communications has identified the following information for the first year of the roll-out of its new proposed service:

Projected sales	$18 million
Operating costs (not including depreciation)	$ 9 million
Depreciation	$ 4 million
Interest expense	$ 3 million

The company faces a 40% tax rate. What is the project's operating cash flow for the first year (t = 1)?

(11-3) Net Salvage Value Allen Air Lines must liquidate some equipment that is being replaced. The equipment originally cost $12 million, of which 75% has been depreciated. The used equipment can be sold today for $4 million, and its tax rate is 40%. What is the equipment's after-tax net salvage value?

(11-4) Replacement Analysis Although the Chen Company's milling machine is old, it is still in relatively good working order and would last for another 10 years. It is inefficient compared to modern standards, though, and so the company is considering replacing it. The new milling machine, at a cost of $110,000 delivered and installed, would also last for 10 years and would produce after-tax cash flows (labor savings and depreciation tax savings) of $19,000 per year. It would have zero salvage value at the end of its life. The firm's WACC is 10%, and its marginal tax rate is 35%. Should Chen buy the new machine?

Intermediate Problems 5–11

(11-5) Depreciation Methods Wendy's boss wants to use straight-line depreciation for the new expansion project because he said it will give higher net income in earlier years and give him a larger bonus. The project will last 4 years and requires $1,700,000 of equipment. The company could use either straight line or the 3-year MACRS accelerated method. Under straight-line depreciation, the cost of the equipment would be depreciated evenly over its 4-year life (ignore the half-year convention for the straight-line method). The applicable MACRS depreciation rates are 33.33%, 44.45%, 14.81%, and 7.41%, as discussed in Appendix 11A. The company's WACC is 10%, and its tax rate is 40%.

a. What would the depreciation expense be each year under each method?
b. Which depreciation method would produce the higher NPV, and how much higher would it be?
c. Why might Wendy's boss prefer straight-line depreciation?

(11-6) New-Project Analysis The Campbell Company is considering adding a robotic paint sprayer to its production line. The sprayer's base price is $1,080,000, and it would cost another $22,500 to install it. The machine falls into the MACRS 3-year class, and it would be sold after 3 years for $605,000. The MACRS rates for the first three years are 0.3333, 0.4445, and 0.1481. The machine would require an increase in net working capital (inventory) of $15,500. The sprayer would not change revenues, but it is expected to save the firm $380,000 per year in before-tax operating costs, mainly labor. Campbell's marginal tax rate is 35%.

a. What is the Year 0 net cash flow?
b. What are the net operating cash flows in Years 1, 2, and 3?
c. What is the additional Year-3 cash flow (i.e., the after-tax salvage and the return of working capital)?
d. If the project's cost of capital is 12%, should the machine be purchased?

(11-7) **New-Project Analysis** The president of the company you work for has asked you to evaluate the proposed acquisition of a new chromatograph for the firm's R&D department. The equipment's basic price is $70,000, and it would cost another $15,000 to modify it for special use by your firm. The chromatograph, which falls into the MACRS 3-year class, would be sold after 3 years for $30,000. The MACRS rates for the first three years are 0.3333, 0.4445, and 0.1481. Use of the equipment would require an increase in net working capital (spare parts inventory) of $4,000. The machine would have no effect on revenues, but it is expected to save the firm $25,000 per year in before-tax operating costs, mainly labor. The firm's marginal federal-plus-state tax rate is 40%.

a. What is the Year-0 net cash flow?
b. What are the net operating cash flows in Years 1, 2, and 3?
c. What is the additional (nonoperating) cash flow in Year 3?
d. If the project's cost of capital is 10%, should the chromatograph be purchased?

(11-8) **Inflation Adjustments** The Rodriguez Company is considering an average-risk investment in a mineral water spring project that has a cost of $150,000. The project will produce 1,000 cases of mineral water per year indefinitely. The current sales price is $138 per case, and the current cost per case is $105. The firm is taxed at a rate of 34%. Both prices and costs are expected to rise at a rate of 6% per year. The firm uses only equity, and it has a cost of capital of 15%. Assume that cash flows consist only of after-tax profits, because the spring has an indefinite life and will not be depreciated.

a. Should the firm accept the project? (*Hint:* The project is a growing perpetuity, so you must use the constant growth formula to find its NPV.)
b. Suppose that total costs consisted of a fixed cost of $10,000 per year plus variable costs of $95 per unit and only the variable costs were expected to increase with inflation. Would this make the project better or worse? Continue to assume that the sales price will rise with inflation.

(11-9) **Replacement Analysis** The Gilbert Instrument Corporation is considering replacing the wood steamer it currently uses to shape guitar sides. The steamer has 6 years of remaining life. If kept, the steamer will have depreciation expenses of $650 for five years and $325 for the sixth year. Its current book value is $3,575, and it can be sold on an Internet auction site for $4,150 at this time. If the old steamer is not replaced, it can be sold for $800 at the end of its useful life.

Gilbert is considering purchasing the *Side Steamer 3000*, a higher-end steamer, which costs $12,000 and has an estimated useful life of 6 years with an estimated salvage value of $1,500. This steamer falls into the MACRS 5-year class, so the applicable depreciation rates are 20.00%, 32.00%, 19.20%, 11.52%, 11.52%, and 5.76%. The new steamer is faster and allows for an output expansion, so sales would rise by $2,000 per year; the new machine's much greater efficiency would reduce operating expenses by $1,900 per year. To support the greater sales, the new machine would require that inventories increase by $2,900, but accounts payable would simultaneously increase by $700. Gilbert's marginal federal-plus-state tax rate is 40%, and its WACC is 15%. Should it replace the old steamer?

(11-10) **Replacement Analysis** St. Johns River Shipyard's welding machine is 15 years old, fully depreciated, obsolete, and has no salvage value. However, even though it is obsolete, it is perfectly functional as originally designed and can be used for quite a while longer. A new welder will cost $182,500 and have an estimated life of 8 years with no salvage value. The new welder will be much more efficient, however, and this enhanced efficiency will increase earnings before depreciation from $27,000 to $74,000 per year. The new machine will be depreciated over its 5-year MACRS recovery period, so the applicable depreciation rates are 20.00%, 32.00%, 19.20%, 11.52%, 11.52%, and 5.76%. The applicable corporate tax rate is 40%, and the firm's WACC is 12%. Should the old welder be replaced by the new one?

Challenging Problems 11–17

(11-11) Scenario Analysis

Shao Industries is considering a proposed project for its capital budget. The company estimates the project's NPV is $12 million. This estimate assumes that the economy and market conditions will be average over the next few years. The company's CFO, however, forecasts there is only a 50% chance that the economy will be average. Recognizing this uncertainty, she has also performed the following scenario analysis:

Economic Scenario	Probability of Outcome	NPV
Recession	0.05	–$70 million
Below average	0.20	–25 million
Average	0.50	12 million
Above average	0.20	20 million
Boom	0.05	30 million

What is the project's expected NPV, its standard deviation, and its coefficient of variation?

(11-12) New-Project Analysis

Madison Manufacturing is considering a new machine that costs $350,000 and would reduce pre-tax manufacturing costs by $110,000 annually. Madison would use the 3-year MACRS method to depreciate the machine, and management thinks the machine would have a value of $33,000 at the end of its 5-year operating life. The applicable depreciation rates are 33.33%, 44.45%, 14.81%, and 7.42%, as discussed in Appendix 11A. Working capital would increase by $35,000 initially, but it would be recovered at the end of the project's 5-year life. Madison's marginal tax rate is 40%, and a 10% WACC is appropriate for the project.

a. Calculate the project's NPV, IRR, MIRR, and payback.
b. Assume management is unsure about the $110,000 cost savings—this figure could deviate by as much as plus or minus 20%. What would the NPV be under each of these extremes?
c. Suppose the CFO wants you to do a scenario analysis with different values for the cost savings, the machine's salvage value, and the working capital (WC) requirement. She asks you to use the following probabilities and values in the scenario analysis:

Scenario	Probability	Cost Savings	Salvage Value	WC
Worst case	0.35	$ 88,000	$28,000	$40,000
Base case	0.35	110,000	33,000	35,000
Best case	0.30	132,000	38,000	30,000

Calculate the project's expected NPV, its standard deviation, and its coefficient of variation. Would you recommend that the project be accepted?

(11-13) Replacement Analysis

The Everly Equipment Company's flange-lipping machine was purchased 5 years ago for $55,000. It had an expected life of 10 years when it was bought and its remaining depreciation is $5,500 per year for each year of its remaining life. As the older flange-lippers are robust and useful machines, it can be sold for $20,000 at the end of its useful life.

A new high-efficiency, digital-controlled flange-lipper can be purchased for $120,000, including installation costs. During its 5-year life, it will reduce cash operating expenses by $30,000 per year, although it will not affect sales. At the end of its useful life, the high-efficiency machine is estimated to be worthless. MACRS depreciation will be used, and the machine will be depreciated over its 3-year class life rather than its 5-year economic life, so the applicable depreciation rates are 33.33%, 44.45%, 14.81%, and 7.41%.

The old machine can be sold today for $35,000. The firm's tax rate is 35%, and the appropriate WACC is 16%.

a. If the new flange-lipper is purchased, what is the amount of the initial cash flow at Year 0?
b. What are the incremental net cash flows that will occur at the end of Years 1 through 5?
c. What is the NPV of this project? Should Everly replace the flange-lipper?

(11-14)
Replacement Analysis

DeYoung Entertainment Enterprises is considering replacing the latex molding machine it uses to fabricate rubber chickens with a newer, more efficient model. The old machine has a book value of $450,000 and a remaining useful life of 5 years. The current machine would be worn out and worthless in 5 years, but DeYoung can sell it now to a Halloween mask manufacturer for $135,000. The old machine is being depreciated by $90,000 per year for each year of its remaining life.

The new machine has a purchase price of $775,000, an estimated useful life and MACRS class life of 5 years, and an estimated salvage value of $105,000. The applicable depreciation rates are 20.00%, 32.00%, 19.20%, 11.52%, 11.52%, and 5.76%. Being highly efficient, it is expected to economize on electric power usage, labor, and repair costs, and, most importantly, to reduce the number of defective chickens. In total, an annual savings of $185,000 will be realized if the new machine is installed. The company's marginal tax rate is 35%, and it has a 12% WACC.

a. What is the initial net cash flow if the new machine is purchased and the old one is replaced?
b. Calculate the annual depreciation allowances for both machines, and compute the change in the annual depreciation expense if the replacement is made.
c. What are the incremental net cash flows in Years 1 through 5?
d. Should the firm purchase the new machine? Support your answer.
e. In general, how would each of the following factors affect the investment decision, and how should each be treated?
   (1) The expected life of the existing machine decreases.
   (2) The WACC is not constant but is increasing as DeYoung adds more projects into its capital budget for the year.

(11-15)
Risky Cash Flows

The Bartram-Pulley Company (BPC) must decide between two mutually exclusive investment projects. Each project costs $6,750 and has an expected life of 3 years. Annual net cash flows from each project begin 1 year after the initial investment is made and have the following probability distributions:

Project A		Project B	
Probability	**Net Cash Flows**	**Probability**	**Net Cash Flows**
0.2	$6,000	0.2	$ 0
0.6	6,750	0.6	6,750
0.2	7,500	0.2	18,000

BPC has decided to evaluate the riskier project at a 12% rate and the less risky project at a 10% rate.

a. What is the expected value of the annual net cash flows from each project? What is the coefficient of variation (CV)? (*Hint:* σ_B = $5,798 and $CV_B = 0.76$.)
b. What is the risk-adjusted NPV of each project?

c. If it were known that Project B is negatively correlated with other cash flows of the firm whereas Project A is positively correlated, how would this affect the decision? If Project B's cash flows were negatively correlated with gross domestic product (GDP), would that influence your assessment of its risk?

(11-16) Simulation Singleton Supplies Corporation (SSC) manufactures medical products for hospitals, clinics, and nursing homes. SSC may introduce a new type of X-ray scanner designed to identify certain types of cancers in their early stages. There are a number of uncertainties about the proposed project, but the following data are believed to be reasonably accurate.

Probability	Developmental Costs	Random Numbers
0.3	$2,000,000	00–29
0.4	4,000,000	30–69
0.3	6,000,000	70–99

Probability	Project Life	Random Numbers
0.2	3 years	00–19
0.6	8 years	20–79
0.2	13 years	80–99

Probability	Sales in Units	Random Numbers
0.2	100	00–19
0.6	200	20–79
0.2	300	80–99

Probability	Sales Price	Random Numbers
0.1	$13,000	00–09
0.8	13,500	10–89
0.1	14,000	90–99

Probability	Cost per Unit (Excluding Developmental Costs)	Random Numbers
0.3	$5,000	00–29
0.4	6,000	30–69
0.3	7,000	70–99

SSC uses a cost of capital of 15% to analyze average-risk projects, 12% for low-risk projects, and 18% for high-risk projects. These risk adjustments primarily reflect the uncertainty about each project's NPV and IRR as measured by their coefficients of variation. The firm is in the 40% federal-plus-state income tax bracket.

a. What is the expected IRR for the X-ray scanner project? Base your answer on the expected values of the variables. Also, assume the after-tax "profits" figure that you develop is equal to annual cash flows. All facilities are leased, so depreciation may be disregarded. Can you determine the value of σ_{IRR} short of actual simulation or complex statistical analysis?

b. Assume that SSC uses a 15% cost of capital for this project. What is the project's NPV? Could you estimate σ_{NPV} without either simulation or a complex statistical analysis?

c. Show the process by which a computer would perform a simulation analysis for this project. Use the random numbers 44, 17, 16, 58, 1; 79, 83, 86; and 19, 62, 6 to illustrate the process with the first computer run. Calculate the first-run NPV and IRR. Assume the cash flows for each year are independent of cash flows for other years. Also, assume the computer operates as follows: (1) A developmental cost and a project life are estimated for the first run using the first two random numbers. (2) Next, sales volume, sales price, and cost per unit are estimated using the next three random numbers and used to derive a cash flow for the first year. (3) Then, the next three random numbers are used to estimate sales volume, sales price, and cost per unit for the second year, hence the cash flow for the second year. (4) Cash flows for other years are developed similarly, on out to the first run's estimated life. (5) With the developmental cost and the cash flow stream established, NPV and IRR for the first run are derived and stored in the computer's memory. (6) The process is repeated to generate perhaps 500 other NPVs and IRRs. (7) Frequency distributions for NPV and IRR are plotted by the computer, and the distributions' means and standard deviations are calculated.

(11-17)
Decision Tree

The Yoran Yacht Company (YYC), a prominent sailboat builder in Newport, may design a new 30-foot sailboat based on the "winged" keels first introduced on the 12-meter yachts that raced for the America's Cup.

First, YYC would have to invest $10,000 at t = 0 for the design and model tank testing of the new boat. YYC's managers believe there is a 60% probability that this phase will be successful and the project will continue. If Stage 1 is not successful, the project will be abandoned with zero salvage value.

The next stage, if undertaken, would consist of making the molds and producing two prototype boats. This would cost $500,000 at t = 1. If the boats test well, YYC would go into production. If they do not, the molds and prototypes could be sold for $100,000. The managers estimate the probability is 80% that the boats will pass testing and that Stage 3 will be undertaken.

Stage 3 consists of converting an unused production line to produce the new design. This would cost $1 million at t = 2. If the economy is strong at this point, the net value of sales would be $3 million; if the economy is weak, the net value would be $1.5 million. Both net values occur at t = 3, and each state of the economy has a probability of 0.5. YYC's corporate cost of capital is 12%.

a. Assume this project has average risk. Construct a decision tree and determine the project's expected NPV.
b. Find the project's standard deviation of NPV and coefficient of variation of NPV. If YYC's average project had a CV of between 1.0 and 2.0, would this project be of high, low, or average stand-alone risk?

SPREADSHEET PROBLEM

(11-18)
Build a Model: Issues in Capital Budgeting

resource

Start with the partial model in the file ***Ch11 P18 Build a Model.xls*** on the textbook's Web site. Webmaster.com has developed a powerful new server that would be used for corporations' Internet activities. It would cost $10 million at Year 0 to buy the equipment necessary to manufacture the server. The project would require net working capital at the beginning of a year in an amount equal to 10% of the year's projected sales: $NOWC_0 = 10\%(Sales_1)$. The servers would sell for $24,000 per unit, and Webmasters believes that variable costs would amount to $17,500 per unit. After Year 1, the sales price and variable costs will increase at the inflation rate of 3%. The company's nonvariable costs would be $1 million at Year 1 and would increase with inflation.

The server project would have a life of 4 years. If the project is undertaken, it must be continued for the entire 4 years. Also, the project's returns are expected to be highly correlated with returns on the firm's other assets. The firm believes it could sell 1,000 units per year.

The equipment would be depreciated over a 5-year period, using MACRS rates. The estimated market value of the equipment at the end of the project's 4-year life is $500,000. Webmaster's federal-plus-state tax rate is 40%. Its cost of capital is 10% for average-risk projects, defined as projects with an NPV coefficient of variation between 0.8 and 1.2. Low-risk projects are evaluated with a WACC of 8% and high-risk projects at 13%.

a. Develop a spreadsheet model, and use it to find the project's NPV, IRR, and payback.
b. Conduct a sensitivity analysis to determine the sensitivity of NPV to changes in the sales price, variable costs per unit, and number of units sold. Set these variables' values at 10% and 20% above and below their base-case values. Include a graph in your analysis.
c. Conduct a scenario analysis. Assume that there is a 25% probability that best-case conditions, with each of the variables discussed in part b being 20% better than its base-case value, will occur. There is a 25% probability of worst-case conditions, with the variables 20% worse than base, and a 50% probability of base-case conditions.
d. If the project appears to be more or less risky than an average project, find its risk-adjusted NPV, IRR, and payback.
e. On the basis of information in the problem, would you recommend the project should be accepted?

MINI CASE

Shrieves Casting Company is considering adding a new line to its product mix, and the capital budgeting analysis is being conducted by Sidney Johnson, a recently graduated MBA. The production line would be set up in unused space in Shrieves's main plant. The machinery's invoice price would be approximately $200,000, another $10,000 in shipping charges would be required, and it would cost an additional $30,000 to install the equipment. The machinery has an economic life of 4 years, and Shrieves has obtained a special tax ruling that places the equipment in the MACRS 3-year class. The machinery is expected to have a salvage value of $25,000 after 4 years of use.

The new line would generate incremental sales of 1,250 units per year for 4 years at an incremental cost of $100 per unit in the first year, excluding depreciation. Each unit can be sold for $200 in the first year. The sales price and cost are both expected to increase by 3% per year due to inflation. Further, to handle the new line, the firm's net working capital would have to increase by an amount equal to 12% of sales revenues. The firm's tax rate is 40%, and its overall weighted average cost of capital is 10%.

a. Define "incremental cash flow."
   (1) Should you subtract interest expense or dividends when calculating project cash flow?
   (2) Suppose the firm spent $100,000 last year to rehabilitate the production line site. Should this be included in the analysis? Explain.
   (3) Now assume the plant space could be leased out to another firm at $25,000 per year. Should this be included in the analysis? If so, how?
   (4) Finally, assume that the new product line is expected to decrease sales of the firm's other lines by $50,000 per year. Should this be considered in the analysis? If so, how?

b. Disregard the assumptions in part a. What is Shrieves's depreciable basis? What are the annual depreciation expenses?
c. Calculate the annual sales revenues and costs (other than depreciation). Why is it important to include inflation when estimating cash flows?
d. Construct annual incremental operating cash flow statements.
e. Estimate the required net working capital for each year and the cash flow due to investments in net working capital.
f. Calculate the after-tax salvage cash flow.
g. Calculate the net cash flows for each year. Based on these cash flows, what are the project's NPV, IRR, MIRR, PI, payback, and discounted payback? Do these indicators suggest that the project should be undertaken?
h. What does the term "risk" mean in the context of capital budgeting; to what extent can risk be quantified; and, when risk is quantified, is the quantification based primarily on statistical analysis of historical data or on subjective, judgmental estimates?
i. (1) What are the three types of risk that are relevant in capital budgeting?
(2) How is each of these risk types measured, and how do they relate to one another?
(3) How is each type of risk used in the capital budgeting process?
j. (1) What is sensitivity analysis?
(2) Perform a sensitivity analysis on the unit sales, salvage value, and cost of capital for the project. Assume each of these variables can vary from its base-case, or expected, value by ±10%, ±20%, and ±30%. Include a sensitivity diagram, and discuss the results.
(3) What is the primary weakness of sensitivity analysis? What is its primary usefulness?
k. Assume that Sidney Johnson is confident in her estimates of all the variables that affect the project's cash flows except unit sales and sales price. If product acceptance is poor, unit sales would be only 900 units a year and the unit price would only be $160; a strong consumer response would produce sales of 1,600 units and a unit price of $240. Johnson believes there is a 25% chance of poor acceptance, a 25% chance of excellent acceptance, and a 50% chance of average acceptance (the base case).
(1) What is scenario analysis?
(2) What is the worst-case NPV? The best-case NPV?
(3) Use the worst-, base-, and best-case NPVs and probabilities of occurrence to find the project's expected NPV, as well as the NPV's standard deviation and coefficient of variation.
l. Are there problems with scenario analysis? Define simulation analysis, and discuss its principal advantages and disadvantages.
m. (1) Assume Shrieves's average project has a coefficient of variation in the range of 0.2 to 0.4. Would the new line be classified as high risk, average risk, or low risk? What type of risk is being measured here?
(2) Shrieves typically adds or subtracts 3 percentage points to the overall cost of capital to adjust for risk. Should the new line be accepted?
(3) Are there any subjective risk factors that should be considered before the final decision is made?
n. What is a real option? What are some types of real options?

SELECTED ADDITIONAL CASES

The following cases from CengageCompose cover many of the concepts discussed in this chapter and are available at **compose.cengage.com**.

Klein-Brigham Series:

Case 12, "Indian River Citrus Company (A)"; Case 44, "Cranfield, Inc. (A)"; and Case 14, "Robert Montoya, Inc." focus on cash flow estimation. Case 13, "Indian River Citrus (B)"; Case 45, "Cranfield, Inc. (B)"; Case 58, "Tasty Foods (B)"; Case 60, "Heavenly Foods"; and Case 15, "Robert Montoya, Inc. (B)," illustrate project risk analysis. Cases 75, 76, and 77, "The Western Company (A and B)," are comprehensive cases.

Brigham-Buzzard Series:

Case 7, "Powerline Network Corporation (Risk and Real Options in Capital Budgeting)."

© lulu/fotolia.com

Appendix 11A

Tax Depreciation

Companies often calculate depreciation one way when figuring taxes and another way when reporting income to investors: Many use the **straight-line method** for stockholder reporting (or "book" purposes), but they use the fastest rate permitted by law for tax purposes. Under the straight-line method used for stockholder reporting, one normally takes the cost of the asset, subtracts its estimated salvage value, and divides the net amount by the asset's useful economic life. For example, consider an asset with a 5-year life that costs \$100,000 and has a \$12,500 salvage value; its annual straight-line depreciation charge is (\$100,000 − \$12,500)/5 = \$17,500. Note, however, as we stated earlier, salvage value is a factor in financial reporting but it is *not* considered for tax depreciation purposes.

For tax purposes, Congress changes the permissible tax depreciation methods from time to time. Prior to 1954, the straight-line method was required for tax purposes, but in 1954 **accelerated methods** (double-declining balance and sum-of-years'-digits) were permitted. Then, in 1981, the old accelerated methods were replaced by a simpler procedure known as the Accelerated Cost Recovery System (ACRS). The ACRS system was changed again in 1986 as a part of the Tax Reform Act, and it is now known as the **Modified Accelerated Cost Recovery System (MACRS)**; a 1993 tax law made further changes in this area.

Note that U.S. tax laws are complicated, and in this text we can provide only an overview of MACRS that will give you a basic understanding of the impact of depreciation on capital budgeting decisions. Further, the tax laws change so often that the numbers we present may be outdated before the book is published. Thus, when dealing with tax depreciation in real-world situations, always consult current Internal Revenue Service (IRS) publications or individuals with expertise in tax matters.

For tax purposes, the entire cost of an asset is expensed over its depreciable life. Historically, an asset's depreciable life was set equal to its estimated useful economic life; it was intended that an asset would be fully depreciated at approximately the same time that it reached the end of its useful economic life. However, MACRS totally abandoned that practice and set simple guidelines that created several classes of assets, each with a more-or-less arbitrarily prescribed life called a *recovery period* or *class life.* The MACRS class lives bear only a rough relationship to assets' expected useful economic lives. A major effect of the MACRS system has been to shorten the depreciable lives of assets, thus giving businesses larger tax deductions early in the assets' lives and thereby increasing the present value of the cash flows. Table 11A-1 describes the types of property that fit into the different class life groups, and Table 11A-2 sets forth the MACRS recovery allowance percentages (depreciation rates) for selected classes of investment property.

Consider Table 11A-1, which gives the MACRS class lives and the types of assets that fall into each category. Property in the 27.5- and 39-year categories (real estate) must be depreciated by the straight-line method, but 3-, 5-, 7-, and 10-year property (personal

TABLE 11A-1

Major Classes and Asset Lives for MACRS

Class	Type of Property
3-year	Certain special manufacturing tools
5-year	Automobiles, light-duty trucks, computers, and certain special manufacturing equipment
7-year	Most industrial equipment, office furniture, and fixtures
10-year	Certain longer-lived types of equipment
27.5-year	Residential rental real property such as apartment buildings
39-year	All nonresidential real property, including commercial and industrial buildings

© Cengage Learning 2014

property) can be depreciated either by the accelerated method set forth in Table 11A-2 or by the straight-line method.[1]

As we saw earlier in the chapter, higher depreciation expenses result in lower taxes in the early years and hence lead to a higher present value of cash flows. Therefore, because firms have the choice of using straight-line rates or the accelerated rates shown in Table 11A-2, most elect to use the accelerated rates.

The yearly recovery allowance, or depreciation expense, is determined by multiplying each asset's *depreciable basis* by the applicable recovery percentage shown in Table 11A-2. You might be wondering why 4 years of deprecation rates are shown for property in the 3-year class. Under MACRS, the assumption is generally made that property is placed in service in the middle of the first year. Thus, for 3-year-class property, the recovery period begins in the middle of the year the asset is placed in service and ends 3 years later. The effect of the *half-year convention* is to extend the recovery period out one more year, so 3-year-class property is depreciated over 4 calendar years, 5-year property is depreciated over 6 calendar years, and so on. This convention is incorporated into Table 11A-2's recovery allowance percentages.[2]

SELF TEST

What do the acronyms ACRS and MACRS stand for? Briefly describe the tax depreciation system under MACRS.

[1]The Tax Code currently (for 2012) permits companies to *expense*, which is equivalent to depreciating over 1 year, up to $125,000 of equipment; see IRS Publication 946 for details. This is a benefit primarily for small companies. Thus, if a small company bought one asset worth up to $125,000, it could write the asset off in the year it was acquired. This is called "Section 179 expensing." We shall disregard this provision throughout the book. Also, Congress enacted the Job Creation and Worker Assistance Act of 2002 following the terrorist attacks on the World Trade Center and Pentagon. This act, among other things, temporarily changed how depreciation is charged for property acquired after September 10, 2001, and before September 11, 2004, and put in service before January 1, 2005. We shall disregard this provision throughout the book as well.

[2]The half-year convention also applies if the straight-line alternative is used, with half of one year's depreciation taken in the first year, a full year's depreciation taken in each of the remaining years of the asset's class life, and the remaining half-year's depreciation taken in the year following the end of the class life. You should recognize that virtually all companies have computerized depreciation systems. Each asset's depreciation pattern is programmed into the system at the time of its acquisition, and the computer aggregates the depreciation allowances for all assets when the accountants close the books and prepare financial statements and tax returns.

TABLE 11A-2

Recovery Allowance Percentage for Personal Property

	Class of Investment			
Ownership Year	**3-Year**	**5-Year**	**7-Year**	**10-Year**
1	33.33%	20.00%	14.29%	10.00%
2	44.45	32.00	24.49	18.00
3	14.81	19.20	17.49	14.40
4	7.41	11.52	12.49	11.52
5		11.52	8.93	9.22
6		5.76	8.92	7.37
7			8.93	6.55
8			4.46	6.55
9				6.56
10				6.55
11				3.28
	100%	100%	100%	100%

Notes:

1. We developed these recovery allowance percentages based on the 200% declining balance method prescribed by MACRS, with a switch to straight-line depreciation at some point in the asset's life. For example, consider the 5-year recovery allowance percentages. The straight-line percentage would be 20% per year, so the 200% declining balance multiplier is 2.0(20%) = 40% = 0.4. However, because the half-year convention applies, the MACRS percentage for Year 1 is 20%. For Year 2, there is 80% of the depreciable basis remaining to be depreciated, so the recovery allowance percentage is 0.40(80%) = 32%. In Year 3, 20% + 32% = 52% of the depreciation has been taken, leaving 48%, so the percentage is 0.4(48%) = 19.2%. In Year 4, the percentage is 0.4(28.8%) = 11.52%. After 4 years, straight-line depreciation exceeds the declining balance depreciation, so a switch is made to straight-line (which is permitted under the law). However, the half-year convention must also be applied at the end of the class life, and the remaining 17.28% of depreciation must be taken (amortized) over 1.5 years. Thus, the percentage in Year 5 is 17.28%/1.5 = 11.52%, and in Year 6 it is 17.28% − 11.52% = 5.76%. Although the tax tables carry the allowance percentages out to two decimal places, we have rounded to the nearest whole number for ease of illustration. See the worksheet *7. App. A* in the file ***Ch11 Tool Kit.xls*** on the textbook's Web site for the exact recovery percentages specified by the IRS.
2. Residential rental property (apartments) is depreciated over a 27.5-year life, whereas commercial and industrial structures are depreciated over 39 years. In both cases, straight-line depreciation must be used. The depreciation allowance for the first year is based, pro rata, on the month the asset was placed in service, with the remainder of the first year's depreciation being taken in the 28th or 40th year. A half-month convention is assumed; that is, an asset placed in service in February would receive 10.5 months of depreciation in the first year.

© Cengage Learning 2014

resource

*See **Ch11 Tool Kit.xls** on the textbook's Web site for all calculations.*

© lulu/fotolia.com

Web Extension 11A

Certainty Equivalents and Risk-Adjusted Discount Rates

Two alternative methods have been developed for incorporating project risk into the capital budgeting decision process. One is the **certainty equivalent method,** in which the expected cash flows are adjusted to reflect project risk: Risky cash flows are scaled down because the riskier the flows, the lower their certainty equivalent values. The second is the **risk-adjusted discount rate method,** where differential project risk is dealt with by changing the discount rate: Average-risk projects are discounted at the firm's corporate cost of capital, above-average-risk projects are discounted at a higher cost of capital, and below-average-risk projects are discounted at a rate below the corporate cost of capital. Most companies use the risk-adjusted discount rate method, so we focused on it in earlier chapters. However, the certainty equivalent approach does have some advantages, so financial managers should be familiar with it as well.

It is not always possible to find existing models for financial options that correspond to all real options. In such a situation, the analyst must use financial engineering techniques. One technique, **risk-neutral valuation,** is analogous to the certainty equivalent method, except it is applied using simulation.

11A-1 The Certainty Equivalent Method

The certainty equivalent (CE) method follows directly from the concept of utility theory. Under the CE approach, the decision maker must first evaluate a cash flow's risk and then specify how much money, to be received with certainty, will make him indifferent between the riskless and the risky cash flows. To illustrate, suppose a rich eccentric offered you the following two choices:

1. Flip a fair coin. If heads comes up you receive \$1 million, but if tails comes up you get nothing. The expected value of the gamble is (0.5)(\$1,000,000) + (0.5)(\$0) = \$500,000, but the actual outcome will be either \$0 or \$1 million, so this choice is risky.
2. Do not flip the coin and simply pocket \$300,000 cash.

If you find yourself indifferent between the two alternatives, then \$300,000 is your certainty equivalent for this particular risky \$500,000 expected cash flow. The certain (or riskless) \$300,000 thus provides you with the same *utility* as the risky \$500,000 expected return.

Now ask yourself this question: In the preceding example, exactly how much cash-in-hand would it actually take to make you indifferent between a certain sum and the risky \$500,000 expected return? If you are like most people, your certainty equivalent would be significantly less than \$500,000, indicating that you are risk averse. In general, people are risk averse, and the lower the certainty equivalent, the greater the decision maker's risk aversion.

© 2014 Cengage Learning. All Rights Reserved. May not be scanned, copied or duplicated, or posted to a publicly accessible website, in whole or in part.

FIGURE 11A-1

Project A: Certainty Equivalent Analysis

Year	Expected Net Cash Flow	Degree of Risk	Certainty Equivalent Cash Flow
0	($2,000)	Zero	($2,000)
1	1,000	Average	700
2	1,000	Average	700
3	1,000	Average	700
4	1,000	Average	700

© Cengage Learning 2014

The certainty equivalent concept can be applied to capital budgeting decisions, at least in theory, in the following way.

1. Estimate the certainty equivalent cash flow in each Year t, CE_t, based on the expected cash flow and its riskiness.
2. Given these certainty equivalents, discount by the risk-free rate to obtain the project's NPV.[1]

To illustrate, suppose Project A, whose expected net cash flows are shown in Figure 11A-1, is to be evaluated using the certainty equivalent method. Assume that the initial net cost, $2,000, is fixed by contract and hence known with certainty. Further, assume that the capital budgeting analyst estimates that the cash inflows in Years 1 through 4 all have average risk, and that the appropriate certainty equivalent is $700. The project's NPV, found using a risk-free discount rate of 5%, is $482.17:

$$NPV_A = -\$2{,}000 + \frac{\$700}{(1.05)^1} + \frac{\$700}{(1.05)^2} + \frac{\$700}{(1.05)^3} + \frac{\$700}{(1.05)^4} = \$482.17$$

Because the risk-adjusted NPV is positive, the project should be accepted.

The certainty equivalent method is simple and neat. Moreover, it can easily accommodate differential risk among cash flows. For example, if the Year-4 expected net cash flow of $1,000 included a very risky estimated salvage value, then we could simply reduce the certainty equivalent from $700 to, say, $500 and then recalculate the project's NPV. Unfortunately, there is no practical way to estimate certainty equivalents. Each individual would have her own estimate, and these could vary significantly. Note that certainty equivalents should reflect shareholders' risk preferences rather than those of management. For these reasons, the certainty equivalent method is seldom used in corporate decision making. However, it is conceptually a powerful tool, and later in this extension it will be used to help us recognize some assumptions that are embodied in constant risk-adjusted discount rates.

[1]Note that, unlike the WACC, the risk-free rate normally does not reflect the tax advantage of debt. Thus, either the certainty equivalent estimates or the risk-free rate should be constructed so that they capture this benefit.

© 2014 Cengage Learning. All Rights Reserved. May not be scanned, copied or duplicated, or posted to a publicly accessible website, in whole or in part.

11A-2 The Risk-Adjusted Discount Rate Method

With the risk-adjusted discount rate method, we use the expected cash flow values, CF_t, and the risk adjustment is made to the denominator of the NPV equation (the discount rate) rather than to the numerator. To illustrate, again consider Project A, whose expected cash flows were given in Figure 11A-1. Suppose the firm evaluating Project A had a corporate cost of capital of 15%. Thus, all average-risk projects would be evaluated using a discount rate of 15%. Now assume that a risk analysis of Project A indicated that the project had above-average risk, so a project cost of capital of 22% was subjectively assigned to the project. In this situation, the risk-adjusted discount rate method produces an NPV of $493.64:

$$NPV_A = -\$2{,}000 + \frac{\$1{,}000}{(1.22)^1} + \frac{\$1{,}000}{(1.22)^2} + \frac{\$1{,}000}{(1.22)^3} + \frac{\$1{,}000}{(1.22)^4} = \$493.64$$

In theory, if managers were able to estimate precisely both a project's certainty equivalent cash flows and its risk-adjusted discount rate (or rates), the two methods would produce the identical NPV. However, the risk-adjusted discount rate method is easier to use in practice because the discount rate for average-risk projects (the firm's corporate cost of capital) can be estimated from observable market data, whereas no market data are available to help managers estimate certainty equivalent cash flows.

11A-3 Certainty Equivalents versus Risk-Adjusted Discount Rates

As already noted, investment risk can be handled by making adjustments either to the numerator of the present value equation (the certainty equivalent, or CE, method) or to its denominator (the risk-adjusted discount rate, or RADR, method). The RADR method dominates in practice because people find it easier to estimate suitable discount rates based on current market data than to derive certainty equivalent cash flows. Some financial theorists have suggested that the certainty equivalent approach is theoretically superior, but other theorists have shown that if risk increases with time then the risk-adjusted discount rate is a valid procedure to use.[2]

Risk-adjusted rates lump together the pure time value of money as represented by the risk-free rate and a risk premium: $RADR = r_{RF} + r_{RP}$. In contrast, the CE approach keeps risk and the time value of money separate. This separation gives a theoretical advantage to certainty equivalents, because lumping together the time value of money and the risk premium compounds the risk premium over time. By compounding the risk premium over time, the RADR method automatically assigns more risk to cash flows that occur in the distant future—and the farther into the future, the greater the implied risk. Because the CE method assigns risk to each cash flow individually, it does not impose any assumptions regarding the relationship between risk and time.

[2]See Alexander A. Robichek and Stewart C. Myers, "Conceptual Problems in the Use of Risk-Adjusted Discount Rates," *Journal of Finance,* December 1966, pp. 727–730; and Houng-Yhi Chen, "Valuation under Uncertainty," *Journal of Financial and Quantitative Analysis,* September 1967, pp. 313–326.

© 2014 Cengage Learning. All Rights Reserved. May not be scanned, copied or duplicated, or posted to a publicly accessible website, in whole or in part.

11A-4 Implications

A firm using the RADR approach for its capital budgeting decisions will have a corporate cost of capital that reflects its overall market-determined riskiness. This rate should be used for "average" projects—that is, for projects that have the same risk as the firm's existing assets. Lower rates should be used for less risky projects, and higher rates should be used for riskier projects. To facilitate the decision process, corporate headquarters generally prescribes rates for different classes of investments (for example, replacement, expansion of existing lines, and expansion into new lines). Then, investments of a given class within a given division are analyzed in terms of the prescribed rate. For example, replacement decisions in the retailing division of an oil company might all be evaluated with a 10% discount rate, while exploratory drilling projects might be evaluated at a 20% rate.

However, a constant RADR implies that risk increases with time, and it therefore imposes a relatively severe burden on long-term projects. This means that short-payoff projects will tend to be selected over those with longer payoffs when, for example, there are alternative ways of performing a given task. This is often appropriate, but there are projects for which distant returns are *not* more risky than near-term returns. For example, the estimated returns on a water pipeline serving a developing community may be highly uncertain in the short run, because the rate of growth of the community is uncertain. However, the water company may be quite sure that, in time, the community will be fully developed and will utilize the full capacity of the pipeline. Similar situations could exist in many public projects—water projects, highway programs, schools, and so forth—and when industrial firms are building plants or when retailers are building stores to serve growing geographic markets.

To the extent that the implicit assumption of rising risk over time reflects the facts, then a constant discount rate may be appropriate. Indeed, in the vast majority of business situations, risk undoubtedly is an increasing function of time and so a constant risk-adjusted discount rate is generally reasonable. However, one should be aware of the relationships described in this section and avoid the pitfall of unwittingly penalizing long-term projects when they are not, in fact, more risky than short-term projects.

11A-5 Risky Cash Outflows: An Application of the CE and RADR Methods

Projects often have negative cash flows during their lives, and when this occurs, special problems may arise. To illustrate, suppose Duke Power Company has concluded that it needs a new generating plant, and it is choosing between a nuclear plant and a coal-fired plant. Both plants will produce the same amount of electricity and hence will generate identical revenues. However, the coal plant will have a smaller investment requirement but higher operating costs, so it will have smaller annual cash flows. Also, the nuclear plant will have to be closed down at the end of its 30-year life. The company knows that the costs of tearing down the plant and removing the radioactive material will be high, but the exact cost is highly uncertain at the present time.

Figure 11A-2 shows the projected cash flows from the two plants. The coal plant has a cost of $2 billion and is expected to produce net cash flows of $250 million per year for 30 years. The nuclear plant has a cost of $4 billion and is expected to produce cash flows of $474 million per year for 30 years, after which the company expects it will have to spend $2 billion in order to decommission the radioactive plant. All of the cash flows except the decommissioning costs

© 2014 Cengage Learning. All Rights Reserved. May not be scanned, copied or duplicated, or posted to a publicly accessible website, in whole or in part.

FIGURE 11A-2

Expected Cash Flows, Coal versus Nuclear Power Plant (Millions of Dollars)

Panel A: Operating Cash Flows		
	CASH FLOWS FROM:	
Year	Coal Plant	Nuclear Plant
0	($2,000)	($4,000)
1	250	474
2	250	474
.	.	.
.	.	.
.	.	.
28	250	474
29	250	474
30	250	474
NPV of operating cash flows @ 10%	$ 357	$ 468

Panel B: Present Value of Nuclear Plant's Shutdown Costs	
Year	Nuclear Plant's Shutdown Costs
31	($2,000)
If Cost of Capital = 10%	
PV of shutdown costs	($ 104)
Total NPV of operations and shutdown	$ 364
If Cost of Capital = 15%	
PV of shutdown costs	($ 26)
Total NPV of operations and shutdown	$ 442
If Cost of Capital = 5.38%	
PV of shutdown costs	($ 394)
Total NPV of operations and shutdown	$ 74

have the same risk as Duke Power's other cash flows; hence they are to be discounted at the company's WACC of 10%. However, the decommissioning costs are much more uncertain, so they should be discounted at a rate that reflects their higher risks.

Panel A of Figure 11A-2 shows the operating cash flows' NPVs. The NPV of the coal plant, discounting at the 10% WACC, is $357 million. At the 10% WACC, the nuclear plant's operating cash flows have a higher NPV, $468 million, but this value does not reflect the nuclear plant's decommissioning costs. We might discount the shutdown costs at WACC = 10%. Panel B shows that this gives a –$104 PV of shutdown costs, which gives a total NPV of the nuclear plant of $468 – $104 = $364 million. This is higher than the NPV of the coal plant but doesn't reflect the higher risk of the shutdown costs. Our first inclination is to discount the decommissioning costs at a higher rate to reflect their greater risk. Using a discount rate of 15% for the decommissioning costs, we get a PV of shutdown costs of –$26 million and a total NPV of $468 – $26 = $442 million. But note

© 2014 Cengage Learning. All Rights Reserved. May not be scanned, copied or duplicated, or posted to a publicly accessible website, in whole or in part.

that something is amiss. We applied a higher risk-adjusted discount rate to penalize the nuclear plant for its higher risk, but this *improved* its relative position!

This is where the certainty equivalent method can help. Discussions with the company's managers revealed that they would be more willing to suffer a certain −$2.4 billion cash flow than the uncertain −$2 billion for decommissioning the nuclear power plant in 31 years. Because the −$2.4 billion is a certainty equivalent, we can find the PV of the shutdown costs by discounting the −$2.4 billion at the risk-free rate of 6%: $PV = -\$2.4/(1 + 0.06)^{31} = -\$394$ million. This produces a total NPV for the nuclear plant of $468 − $394 = $74 million, which is much less than the NPV of the coal plant. Alternatively, we could have discounted the risky −$2 billion shutdown cost at a lower discount rate of 5.38%. Panel B of Figure 13A-2 shows that this produces a PV of −$394 million, the same as the certainty equivalent method. The appropriate RADR for this cash outflow is not only less than the cost of capital, it is even less than the risk-free rate!

The key to understanding why a lower RADR might be used for a risky outflow is to ask why the managers were willing to commit to a certain payment of $2.4 billion rather than the risky payment of $2 billion. In terms of total corporate risk, the managers must have feared that the shutdown costs would be especially negative when the other cash flows of the firm were low. In other words, they were worried that the shutdown costs would be worse at a time when the company could ill afford them. Therefore, they were willing to pay more than the expected $2 billion to avoid that risk. Putting this in the framework of corporate risk, the managers believed the shutdown cash flows were positively correlated with the firm's other cash flows. For example, if the firm's other cash flows were low, the shutdown cash flows would be even worse than −$2 billion; if the firm's other cash flows were high, the shutdown costs would be better than −$2 billion. The proof is too complicated for a financial management course, but it can be shown that if a negative expected cash flow has positive correlation with the firm's other cash flows, then the discount rate for the negative cash flow has a negative beta.[3] In the CAPM, a negative beta leads to a discount rate that is less than the risk-free rate, which explains the very low discount rate in Panel B of Figure 11A-2.

The managers in the example subjectively estimated the certainty equivalent for the shutdown costs. However, it is possible to add some discipline to their judgment. If the managers can estimate the standard deviation of the expected cash flow and its correlation with the firm's other cash flows, then it is possible to calculate the certainty equivalent and the appropriate discount rate. See the paper cited in footnote 3 for details.

In summary, some projects have cash flows with risk different from the firm's normal operating cash flows, so the firm's cost of capital is not the appropriate rate for the different cash flow. The appropriate rate might be either higher or lower than the firm's cost of capital, depending on the nature of the risk. If the cash flow has a negative expected value and is positively correlated with the firm's other cash flows, then the appropriate discount rate has a negative beta, and the project's cost of capital is less than the risk-free rate. This is the case with our power plant example. On the other hand, if the negative expected cash flow is negatively correlated with the firm's other projects, then the discount rate has a positive beta and the project's cost of capital is greater than the risk-free rate—and possibly greater than the firm's overall cost of capital.

The same analysis can be applied to a project with *positive* expected cash flow that differs in risk from the firm's normal operating cash flows; the only difference in this case is that the sign on the resulting beta is reversed. If the positive expected cash flow is positively correlated with the firm's other cash flows, then the beta used to obtain the

[3]See Phillip R. Daves and Michael C. Ehrhardt, "Capital Budgeting: The Valuation of Unusual, Irregular, or Extraordinary Cash Flows," *Financial Practice and Education*, Fall/Winter 2000, pp. 106–114.

© 2014 Cengage Learning. All Rights Reserved. May not be scanned, copied or duplicated, or posted to a publicly accessible website, in whole or in part.

discount rate is positive. If the positive expected cash flow is negatively correlated with the firm's other cash flows, then the beta used to obtain the discount rate is negative.

Finally, some negative cash flows are so large that they might put the firm in jeopardy of bankruptcy. In this case, it is better to use real option techniques. A bankruptcy usually includes some very large direct costs, such as legal fees and the sale of assets at low prices. Therefore, accepting a project with a large risky negative cash flow is like writing a put option on the bankruptcy costs. If the negative cash flow doesn't turn out to be too negative, then the firm doesn't go bankrupt and doesn't have to pay the bankruptcy costs. However, if the negative cash flow does turn out to be very negative, then the firm must pay the direct bankruptcy costs. We can then use real option techniques to estimate the cost of this real option.

© 2014 Cengage Learning. All Rights Reserved. May not be scanned, copied or duplicated, or posted to a publicly accessible website, in whole or in part.

© lulu/fotolia.com

PART 5

Corporate Valuation and Governance

CHAPTER 12
Corporate Valuation and Financial Planning 487

© Adalberto Rios Szalay/Sexto Sol/Getty Images

CHAPTER 12 Corporate Valuation and Financial Planning

A survey of CFOs disclosed a paradox regarding financial planning. On one hand, almost all CFOs stated that financial planning is both important and highly useful for allocating resources. On the other hand, 45% also said that budgeting is "contentious, political, and time-consuming," and 53% went on to say that the budgeting process can encourage undesirable behavior among managers as they negotiate budgets to meet their own rather than the company's objectives. They also said that instead of basing growth and incentive compensation targets on an analysis of what markets and competitors are likely to do in the future, firms often set their targets at last year's levels plus a percentage increase, which is dangerous in a dynamic economy.

To resolve these issues, many companies use *demand-pull* budgeting, which links the budget to a sales forecast and updates the sales forecast to reflect changing economic conditions. This approach is often augmented with a *rolling forecast,* in which companies make 1-year and 5-year forecasts but then modify the 1-year forecast each month as new operating results become available.

Another survey shows that high-performance companies also focus on the links between forecasting, planning, and business strategy rather than on just cost management and cost accounting. According to John McMahan of the Hackett Group, such changes are leading to greater forecasting accuracy, higher employee morale, and better corporate performance. These issues are often thought of as "management" rather than "finance," but this is a false distinction. Much of finance is numbers-oriented, but as any CFO will tell you, his or her primary job is to help the firm as a whole achieve good results. The procedures discussed in this chapter can help firms improve their operations and results.

Sources: J. McCafferty, "Planning for the Best," *CFO,* February 2007, p. 24; and Don Durfee, "Alternative Budgeting," *CFO,* June 2006, p. 28.

Corporate Valuation and Financial Planning

© Rob Webb/Getty Images

The value of a firm is determined by the size, timing, and risk of its expected future free cash flows (FCF). Managers use projected financial statements to estimate the impact that different operating plans have on intrinsic value. Managers also use projected statements to identify deficits that must be financed in order to implement the operating plans. This chapter explains how to project financial statements that incorporate operating assumptions and financial policies.

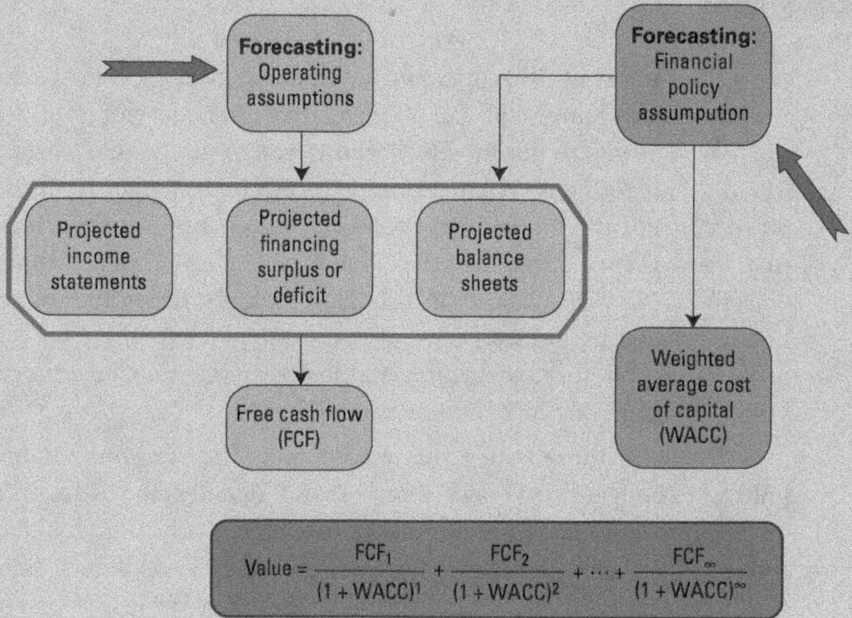

© Cengage Learning 2014

resource
*The textbook's Web site contains an Excel file that will guide you through the chapter's calculations. The file for this chapter is **Ch12 Tool Kit.xls**, and we encourage you to open the file and follow along as you read the chapter.*

Our primary objective in this book is to explain how financial managers can make their companies more valuable. However, value creation is impossible unless the company has well-designed operating and financial plans. As Yogi Berra once said, "You've got to be careful if you don't know where you're going, because you might not get there."

A vital step in financial planning is to forecast financial statements, which are called **projected financial statements** or **pro forma financial statements**. Managers use projected financial statements in four ways: (1) By looking at projected statements, they can assess whether the firm's anticipated performance is in line with the firm's own general targets and with investors' expectations. (2) Pro forma statements can be used to estimate the effect of proposed operating changes, enabling managers to conduct "what if" analyses. (3) Managers use pro forma statements to anticipate the firm's future financing needs. (4) Managers forecast free cash flows under different operating plans, forecast their capital requirements, and then choose the plan that maximizes shareholder value. Security analysts make the same types of projections, forecasting future earnings, cash flows, and stock prices.

12-1 Overview of Financial Planning

The two most important components of financial planning are the operating plan and the financial plan.

12-1a The Operating Plan

As its name suggests, an operating plan provides detailed implementation guidance for a firm's operations, including the firm's choice of market segments, product lines, sales and marketing strategies, production processes, and logistics. An operating plan can be developed for any time horizon, but most companies use a 5-year horizon, with the plan being quite detailed for the first year but less and less specific for each succeeding year. The plan explains who is responsible for each particular function and when specific tasks are to be accomplished.

An important part of the operating plan is the forecast of sales, production costs, inventories, and other operating items. In fact, this part of the operating plan actually is a forecast of the company's expected free cash flow. (Recall from Chapter 2 that free cash flow is defined as net operating profit after taxes (NOPAT) minus the investment in total operating capital.)

Free cash flow is the primary source of a company's value. Using what-if analysis, managers can analyze different operating plans to estimate their impact on value. In addition, managers can apply sensitivity analysis, scenario analysis, and simulation to estimate the risk of different operating plans, which is an important part of risk management.

12-1b The Financial Plan

By definition, a company's operating assets can grow only by the purchase of additional assets. Therefore, a growing company must continually obtain cash to purchase new assets. Some of this cash might be generated internally by its operations, but some might have to come externally from shareholders or debtholders. This is the essence of financial planning—forecasting the additional sources of financing required to fund the operating plan.

There is a strong connection between financial planning and free cash flow. A company's operations generate the free cash flow, but the financial plan determines how the company will use the free cash flow. Recall from Chapter 2 that free cash flow can be used in five ways: (1) pay dividends, (2) repurchase stock, (3) pay the net after-tax interest on debt, (4) repay debt, or (5) purchase financial assets such as marketable securities. A company's financial plan must use free cash flow differently if FCF is negative than if FCF is positive.

If free cash flow is positive, the financial plan must identify how much FCF to allocate among its investors (shareholders or debtholders) and how much to put aside for future needs by purchasing marketable securities. If free cash flow is negative, either because the company is growing rapidly (which requires large investments in operating capital) or because the company has low NOPAT, then the total uses of free cash flow must also be negative. For example, instead of repurchasing stock, the company might have to issue stock; instead of repaying debt, the company might have to issue debt.

Therefore, the financial plan must incorporate (1) the company's dividend policy, which determines the targeted size and method of cash distributions to shareholders, and (2) the capital structure, which determines the targeted mix of debt and equity used to finance the firm, which in turn determines the relative mix of distributions to shareholders and payments to debtholders.

SELF-TEST

Briefly describe the key elements of an operating plan.

Identify the five uses of free cash flow and how these uses are related to a financial plan.

12-2 Financial Planning at MicroDrive, Inc.

As we described in Chapters 2 and 3, MicroDrive's operating performance and stock price have declined in recent years. As a result, MicroDrive's board recently installed a new management team: A new CEO, CFO, marketing manager, sales manager, inventory manager, and credit manager—only the production manager was retained. The new team met for a 3-day retreat with the goal of developing a plan to improve the company's performance.

One of the first steps was to develop forecasts based on the status quo to give the management team a better idea of where the company is now and where it will be if they don't make changes. The new CFO began by developing an *Excel* model to forecast the operating plan and the financial plan. Refer to ***Ch12 Tool Kit.xls*** as we explain MicroDrive's financial planning.

The CFO's first step was to examine the current and recent historical data. Figure 12-1 shows MicroDrive's most recent financial statements and selected additional data; see Chapters 2 and 3 for a full discussion of the process used to assess MicroDrive's current position and trends.

FIGURE 12-1

MicroDrive's Most Recent Financial Statements (Millions, Except for Per Share Data)

	A	B	C	D	E	F	G
15	INCOME STATEMENTS			BALANCE SHEETS			
16		2012	2013	*Assets*		2012	2013
17	Net sales	$ 4,760	$ 5,000	Cash		$ 60	$ 50
18	COGS (excl. depr.)	3,560	3,800	ST Investments		40	-
19	Depreciation	170	200	Accounts receivable		380	500
20	Other operating expenses	480	500	Inventories		820	1,000
21	EBIT	$ 550	$ 500	Total CA		$ 1,300	$ 1,550
22	Interest expense	100	120	Net PP&E		1,700	2,000
23	Pretax earnings	$ 450	$ 380	Total assets		$ 3,000	$ 3,550
24	Taxes (40%)	180	152				
25	NI before pref. div.	$ 270	$ 228	*Liabilities and equity*			
26	Preferred div.	8	8	Accounts payable		$ 190	$ 200
27	Net income	$ 262	$ 220	Accruals		280	300
28				Notes payable		130	280
29	*Other Data*			Total CL		$ 600	$ 780
30	Common dividends	$48	$50	Long-term bonds		1,000	1,200
31	Addition to RE	$214	$170	Total liabilities		$ 1,600	$ 1,980
32	Tax rate	40%	40%	Preferred stock		100	100
33	Shares of common stock	50	50	Common stock		500	500
34	Earnings per share	$5.24	$4.40	Retained earnings		800	970
35	Dividends per share	$0.96	$1.00	Total common equity		$ 1,300	$ 1,470
36	Price per share	$40.00	$27.00	Total liabs. & equity		$ 3,000	$ 3,550
37							

FIGURE 12-2

MicroDrive's Forecast: Inputs for the Status Quo Scenario

	A	B	C	D	E	F	G	H	I
60	Status Quo	Industry	MicroDrive		MicroDrive				
61	**Inputs**	Actual	Actual		Forecast				
62	*1. Operating Ratios*	2013	2012	2013	2014	2015	2016	2017	2018
63	Sales growth rate	5%	15%	5%	10%	8%	7%	5%	5%
64	COGS (excl. depr.) / Sales	76%	75%	76%	76%	76%	76%	76%	76%
65	Depreciation / Net PP&E	9%	10%	10%	10%	10%	10%	10%	10%
66	Other op. exp. / Sales	10%	10%	10%	10%	10%	10%	10%	10%
67	Cash / Sales	1%	1%	1%	1%	1%	1%	1%	1%
68	Acc. rec. / Sales	8%	8%	10%	10%	10%	10%	10%	10%
69	Inventory / Sales	15%	17%	20%	20%	20%	20%	20%	20%
70	Net PP&E / Sales	33%	36%	40%	40%	40%	40%	40%	40%
71	Acc. pay. / Sales	4%	4%	4%	4%	4%	4%	4%	4%
72	Accruals / Sales	7%	6%	6%	6%	6%	6%	6%	6%
73	Tax rate	40%	40%	40%	40%	40%	40%	40%	40%
74	*2. Capital Structure*	Actual Market Weights			Target Market Weights				
75	% Long-term debt	22%	31%	41%	28%	28%	28%	28%	28%
76	% Short-term debt	3%	4%	10%	2%	2%	2%	2%	2%
77	% Preferred stock	0%	3%	3%	3%	3%	3%	3%	3%
78	% Common stock	75%	62%	46%	67%	67%	67%	67%	67%
79	*3. Costs of Capital*				Forecast				
80	Rate on LT debt				9.0%	9%	9%	9%	9%
81	Rate on ST debt				10.0%	10%	10%	10%	10%
82	Rate on preferred stock (ignoring flotation costs)				8.0%	8%	8%	8%	8%
83	Cost of equity				13.58%	14%	14%	14%	14%
84	*4. Target Dividend Policy*		Actual						
85	Growth rate of dividends		11%	4.2%	5%	5%	5%	5%	5%

The CFO's second step was to choose a forecasting framework. Many companies, including MicroDrive, forecast their entire financial statements as part of the planning process. This approach is called **forecasted financial statements (FFS) method** of financial planning.

Figure 12-2 shows the inputs MicroDrive uses to forecast different scenarios for its operating plan and financial plan. The inputs are for the Status Quo scenario, which assumes most of MicroDrive's operating activities and financial policies remain unchanged. The figure shows actual values for industry peers (the silver section), actual values for MicroDrive's past two years, and forecasted values for MicroDrive's 5-year forecast. The blue section shows inputs for the first year and inputs for any subsequent years that differ from the previous year. Section 1 shows the ratios required to project the items required for an operating plan, Section 2 shows the inputs related to the capital structure, Section 3 shows the costs of the capital components, and Section 4 shows the target dividend policy. We will describe each of these sections as they are applied to the forecast, beginning with the forecast of operations.

12-3 Forecasting Operations

The first row in Section 1 of Figure 12-2 shows the forecast of the sales growth rate. After discussions with teams from marketing, sales, product development, and production, MicroDrive's CFO chose a growth rate of 10% for the next year. Keep in mind that this is just a preliminary estimate and that it is easy to make changes in the *Excel* model (after doing the hard work to build the model!). Notice that MicroDrive is forecasting sales growth to decline and level off by the end of the forecast. Recall from Chapter 7 that the growth rate for a company's sales and free cash flows must level off at some future date in order to apply the constant growth model at the forecast horizon. Had MicroDrive's managers projected nonconstant growth for more than five years, Figure 12-2 would need to be extended until growth does level out.

Other than sales growth, MicroDrive's managers assumed that the operating ratios for 2014 would remain constant for the entire forecast period. However, it would be quite easy for them to input changes in the future ratios, with one caveat. The operating ratios must level off by the end of the forecast period, or else the free cash flows *will not* be growing at a constant rate by the end of the forecast period even if sales *are* growing at a constant rate.

The following sections explain how MicroDrive uses the ratios in Figure 12-2 to forecast its operations. For convenience, the operating ratio inputs are repeated in Panel A of Figure 12-3; Panel B reports the resulting operating forecast.

12-3a Sales Revenues

Section B1 of Figure 12-3 shows the forecast of net sales based on the previous year's sales and the forecasted growth rate in sales. For example, the forecast of net sales for 2014 is (1 + 0.10)($5,000) = $5,500.

12-3b Operating Assets

Section B2 of Figure 12-3 shows the forecast of operating assets. As noted earlier, MicroDrive's assets must increase if sales are to increase, and some types of assets grow proportionately to sales, including cash.

MicroDrive writes and deposits checks every day. Because its managers don't know exactly when all of the checks will clear, they can't predict exactly what the balance in their checking accounts will be on any given day. Therefore, they must maintain a balance of cash and cash equivalents (such as very short-term marketable securities) to avoid overdrawing their accounts. We discuss the issue of cash management in Chapter 16, but MicroDrive's CFO assumed that the cash required to support MicroDrive's operations is proportional to its sales. For example, the forecasted cash in 2014 is 1%(2014 sales) = 1%($5,500) = $55. The CFO applied the same process to project cash in subsequent years.

Unless a company changes its credit policy or has a change in its customer base, accounts receivable should be proportional to sales. The CFO assumed that the credit policy and customers' paying patterns would remain constant and so projected accounts receivable as 10%($5,500) = $550.

As sales increase, firms generally must carry more inventories. The CFO assumed here that inventory would be proportional to sales. (Chapter 16 will discuss inventory management in detail). The projected inventory is 20%($5,500) = $1,100.

It might be reasonable to assume that cash, accounts receivable, and inventories will be proportional to sales, but will the amount of net property, plant, and equipment go up and down as sales go up and down? The correct answer could be either yes or no. When companies acquire PP&E, they often install more capacity than they currently need due to economies of scale in building capacity. Moreover, even if a plant is operating at its maximum-rated capacity, most companies can produce additional units by reducing

FIGURE 12-3

MicroDrive's Forecast of Operations for the Status Quo Scenario (Millions of Dollars, Except for Per Share Data)

	A	B	C	D	E	F	G	H	I
116	Status Quo	Industry	MicroDrive		MicroDrive				
117	**Panel A: Inputs**	Actual	Actual		Forecast				
118	*A1. Operating Ratios*	2013	2012	2013	2014	2015	2016	2017	2018
119	Sales growth rate	5%	*15%*	*5%*	10%	8%	7%	5%	5%
120	COGS (excl. depr.) / Sales	76%	*75%*	*76%*	76%	76%	76%	76%	76%
121	Depreciation / Net PP&E	9%	*10%*	*10%*	10%	10%	10%	10%	10%
122	Other op. exp. / Sales	10%	*10%*	*10%*	10%	10%	10%	10%	10%
123	Cash / Sales	1%	*1%*	*1%*	1%	1%	1%	1%	1%
124	Acc. rec. / Sales	8%	*8%*	*10%*	10%	10%	10%	10%	10%
125	Inventory / Sales	15%	*17%*	*20%*	20%	20%	20%	20%	20%
126	Net PP&E / Sales	33%	*36%*	*40%*	40%	40%	40%	40%	40%
127	Acc. pay. / Sales	4%	*4%*	*4%*	4%	4%	4%	4%	4%
128	Accruals / Sales	7%	*6%*	*6%*	6%	6%	6%	6%	6%
129	Tax rate	40%	*40%*	*40%*	40%	40%	40%	40%	40%
130	**Panel B: Results**			Actual	Forecast				
131	*B1. Sales Revenues*			*2013*	2014	2015	2016	2017	2018
132	Net sales			*$5,000*	$5,500	$5,940	$6,356	$6,674	$7,007
133	*B2. Operating Assets and Operating Liabilities*								
134	Cash			*$50*	$55	$59	$64	$67	$70
135	Accounts receivable			*$500*	$550	$594	$636	$667	$701
136	Inventories			*$1,000*	$1,100	$1,188	$1,271	$1,335	$1,401
137	Net PP&E			*$2,000*	$2,200	$2,376	$2,542	$2,669	$2,803
138	Accounts payable			*$200*	$220	$238	$254	$267	$280
139	Accruals			*$300*	$330	$356	$381	$400	$420
140	*B3. Operating Income*								
141	COGS (excl. depr.)			*$3,800*	$4,180	$4,514	$4,830	$5,072	$5,326
142	Depreciation			*$200*	$220	$238	$254	$267	$280
143	Other operating expenses			*$500*	$550	$594	$636	$667	$701
144	EBIT			*$500*	$550	$594	$636	$667	$701
145	Net operating profit after taxes			*$300*	$330	$356	$381	$400	$420
146	*B4. Free Cash Flows*								
147	Net operating working capital			*$1,050*	$1,155	$1,247	$1,335	$1,401	$1,472
148	Total operating capital			*$3,050*	$3,355	$3,623	$3,877	$4,071	$4,274
149	FCF = NOPAT − Δ op capital			*−$260*	$25	$88	$128	$207	$217
150	*B5. Estimated Intrinsic Value*								
151	Target WACC				11.0%	11.0%	11.0%	11.0%	11.0%
152	Return on invested capital			*9.8%*	9.8%	9.8%	9.8%	9.8%	9.8%
153	Growth in FCF					252%	45.1%	61.7%	5.0%
154									
155	**Horizon Value:**							Value of operations	$2,719
156								+ ST investments	$0
157	$HV_{2018} = \frac{FCF_{2018}(1+g_L)}{(WACC - g_L)}$ =		$3,814					Estimated total intrinsic value	$2,719
158								− All debt	$1,480
159	**Value of Operations:**							− Preferred stock	$100
160	Present value of HV		$2,267					Estimated intrinsic value of equity	$1,139
161	+ Present value of FCF		$453					÷ Number of shares	$50
162	Value of operations =		$2,719					Estimated intrinsic stock price =	$22.78

downtime for scheduled maintenance, by running machinery at a higher than optimal speed, or by adding a second or third shift. Therefore, at least in the short run, sales and net PP&E may not have a close relationship.

However, some companies do have a close relationship between sales and net PP&E, even in the short term. For example, new stores in many retail chains achieve the same sales during their first year as the chain's existing stores. The only way such retailers can grow (beyond inflation) is by adding new stores. Such companies therefore have a strong proportional relationship between fixed assets and sales.

Finally, in the long term there is a close relationship between sales and net PP&E for virtually all companies: Few companies can continue to increase sales unless they also add capacity. Therefore, it is reasonable to assume that the long-term ratio of net PP&E to sales will be constant.

For the first years in a forecast, managers generally build in the actual planned expenditures on plant and equipment. If those estimates are not available, it is generally best to assume a constant ratio of net PP&E to sales.

MicroDrive is a relatively large company and makes capital expenditures every year, so the CFO forecast net PP&E as a percent of sales. The projected net PP&E is 40%($5,500) = $2,200.

12-3c Operating Liabilities

Section B2 of Figure 12-3 shows the forecast of operating liabilities. Some types of liabilities grow proportionately to sales; these are called **spontaneous liabilities**, as we explain next.

As sales increase, so will purchases of raw materials, and those additional purchases will spontaneously lead to a higher level of accounts payable. MicroDrive's forecast of accounts payable in 2014 is 4%($5,500) = $220.

Higher sales require more labor, and higher sales normally result in higher taxable income and thus taxes. Therefore, accrued wages and taxes both increase as sales increase. The projection of accruals is 6%($5,500) = $330.

12-3d Operating Income

For most companies, the cost of goods sold (COGS) is highly correlated with sales, and MicroDrive is no exception. MicroDrive's forecast of COGS for 2014 is 76%($5,500) = $4,180.

Because depreciation depends on an asset's depreciable basis, as described in Chapter 11, it is more reasonable to forecast depreciation as a percent of net plant and equipment rather than of sales. MicroDrive's projection of depreciation in 2014 is 10%(2014 Net PP&E) = 10%($2,200) = $220.

MicroDrive's other operating expenses include items such as salaries of executives, insurance fees, and marketing costs. These items tend to be related to a company's size, which is related to sales. MicroDrive's projection is 10%($5,500) = $550.

Subtracting the COGS, depreciation, and other operating expenses from net sales gives the earnings before interest and taxes (EBIT). Recall from Chapter 2 that the net operating profit after taxes (NOPAT) is defined as EBIT(1 − T), where T is the tax rate.

12-3e Free Cash Flow (FCF)

Section B4 calculates free cash flow (FCF) using the process described in Chapter 2. The first row in Section B4 begins with a calculation of net operating capital (NOWC), which is defined as operating current assets minus operating current liabilities. Operating current assets is the sum of cash, accounts receivable, and inventories; operating current liabilities is the sum or accounts payable and accruals. The second row shows the forecast of total operating capital, which is NOWC plus net PP&E. All of the items required for these calculations were previously forecast in Section B2.

Recall from Chapter 2 that free cash flow is equal to NOPAT minus the investment in total operating capital; the forecast of NOPAT is in Section B3 and the forecast of total net operating capital is in the second row of Section B4.

12-3f Estimated Intrinsic Value

Section B5 begins with the estimated target WACC, calculated using the inputs from Sections 2 and 3 of Figure 12-2. These values are the same ones used in Chapter 9 to estimate MicroDrive's weighted average cost of capital, with the exception of the cost of preferred stock. To simplify the forecast of preferred dividends when projecting the income statement, MicroDrive's CFO decided to ignore flotation costs because they have a negligible impact on the WACC.

The weighted average cost of capital is calculated based on the target capital structure. MicroDrive's CFO decided to use the target capital structure for all scenarios, but to modify the projections later if the board decides to change the capital structure.

The second row in Section B5 of Figure 12-3 reports return on invested capital (ROIC) for easy comparison to the WACC. The third row shows the growth rate in FCF. Notice that the growth rate is very high in the early years of the forecast but then levels out at the sustainable growth rate of sales, 5%. Had it not done so, the forecast period would need to be extended until the growth in FCF became constant.

Using the estimated FCF, WACC, and long-term constant growth rate in FCF, Section B5 shows the calculation of the value of operations using the constant growth horizon value formula from Chapter 7. To find the value of operations, it is necessary to find the present value of the horizon value and the present value of the forecasted free cash flows, and then sum them, as shown at the lower-left corner of the figure.

The panel on the lower right of Section B5 estimates the intrinsic stock price using the approach in Chapter 7. For the Status Quo forecast, the estimated intrinsic value is $22.78. This estimate is about 16% lower than the price of $27 observed on December 31, 2013. What can account for this difference? First, keep in mind that MicroDrive's standard deviation of stock returns is about 49%, as estimated in Chapter 6. This high standard deviation makes the 16% difference between the estimated and actual stock price look pretty small. It could well be that the estimated intrinsic value would have been exactly equal to the actual stock price on a day during the week before or after December 31, 2013. Second, it could be that investors (who determine the price through their buying and selling activities) expect MicroDrive's performance in the future to be better than the Status Quo scenario.

We will have more to say about the operating forecast after completing the forecast of financial statements.

12-3g Enhancements to the Basic Model

Although the assumption that operating assets and operating liabilities grow proportionally to sales is a very good approximation for most companies, there are a few circumstances that might require more complicated modeling techniques. We describe four possible refinements in Section 12-7: economies of scale, nonlinear relationships, lumpy purchases of assets, and excess capacity adjustments. However, always keep in mind that additional complexity in a model might not be worth the incremental improvement in accuracy.

SELF-TEST

Which items comprise operating current assets? Why is it reasonable to assume that they grow proportionally to sales?

What are some reasons that net PP&E might grow proportionally to sales, and what are some reasons that it might not?

What are spontaneous liabilities?

12-4 Projecting MicroDrive's Financial Statements

A key output of a financial plan is the set of projected financial statements. The basic approach in projecting statements is a simple, three-step process: (1) forecast the operating items, (2) forecast the amounts of debt, equity, and dividends that are determined by the company's preliminary short-term financial policy, and (3) ensure that the company has sufficient but not excess financing to fund the operating plan.

Despite the simple process, projecting financial statements can be similar to peeling onions—but not because it smells bad and brings tears to your eyes! Just as there are many different onions (white, purple, large, small, sweet, sour, etc.), there are many different variations on the basic approach. And just as onions have many layers, a financial plan can have many layers of complexity. It would be impossible for us to cover all the different methods and details used when projecting financial statements, so we are going to focus on the straightforward method MicroDrive's CFO used, which is applicable to most companies.

Here are the three steps in this method:

1. MicroDrive will project all the operating items that are part of the operating plan.
2. For the initial forecast, MicroDrive's CFO applied the following preliminary short-term financial policy: (1) MicroDrive will not issue any long-term bonds, preferred stock, or common stock in the upcoming year; (2) MicroDrive will not pay off or increase notes payable; and (3) MicroDrive will increase regular dividends at the sustainable long-term growth rate discussed previously in the sales forecast.
3. If the short-term financial policies described in the second step do not provide sufficient additional financing to fund the additional operating assets needed by the operating plan described in the first step, MicroDrive will draw on a special line of credit. If the financial policies provide surplus financing, MicroDrive will pay a special dividend.

12-4a Forecast the Accounts from the Operating Plan

Figure 12-4 shows MicroDrive's projected financial statements for the Status Quo scenario for the upcoming year. MicroDrive's CFO forecast the operating plan in Section 12-3, so it is an easy matter to replicate the process and forecast the corresponding operating items on the financial statement accounts. Column C shows the most recent year, Column D shows the inputs from Figure 12-2, Columns E and F describe how the inputs are applied, and Column G shows the forecast for the upcoming year. Notice that the forecasts for the operating items in Figure 12-4 are identical to those in Figure 12-3.

FIGURE 12-4

MicroDrive's Projected Financial Statements (Millions of Dollars, Except for Per Share Data)

	A	B	C	D	E	F	G
201	Status Quo						
202	*1. Balance Sheets*		Most Recent				Forecast
203			2013	Input	Basis for 2014 Forecast		2014
204	*Assets*						
205	Cash		$50.0	1.00%	× 2014 Sales		$55.00
206	Accounts receivable		500.0	10.00%	× 2014 Sales		$550.00
207	Inventories		1,000.0	20.00%	× 2014 Sales		$1,100.00
208	Total current assets		$1,550.0				$1,705.00
209	Net PP&E		2,000.0	40.00%	× 2014 Sales		$2,200.00
210	Total assets (TA)		$3,550.0				$3,905.00
211	*Liabilities and equity*						
212	Accounts payable		$200.0	4.00%	× 2014 Sales		$220.00
213	Accruals		300.0	6.00%	× 2014 Sales		$330.00
214	Notes payable		280.0	Carry over from previous year			$280.00
215	Line of credit		0.0	Draw on LOC if financing deficit			$117.10
216	Total CL		$780.0				$947.10
217	Long-term bonds		1,200.0	Carry over from previous year			$1,200.00
218	Total liabilities		$1,980.0				$2,147.10
219	Preferred stock		$100.0	Carry over from previous year			$100.00
220	Common stock		500.0	Carry over from previous year			$500.00
221	Retained earnings		970.0		Old RE + Add. to RE		$1,158
222	Total common equity		$1,470.0				$1,658
223	Total liabs. & equity		$3,550.0				$3,905
224				Check: TA − Total Liab. & Eq. =			$0.00
225	*2. Income Statement*		Most Recent				Forecast
226			2013	Input	Basis for 2014 Forecast		2014
227	Net sales		$5,000.0	110%	× 2013 Sales		$5,500.00
228	COGS (excl. depr.)		3,800.0	76.00%	× 2014 Sales		$4,180.00
229	Depreciation		200.0	10.00%	× 2014 Net PP&E		$220.00
230	Other operating expenses		$500.0	10.00%	× 2014 Sales		$550.00
231	EBIT		$500.0				$550.00
232	Less: Interest on notes		20.0	10.00%	× Avg notes		$28.00
233	Interest on bonds		100.0	9.00%	× Avg bonds		$108.00
234	Interest on LOC		0.0	11.50%	× Beginning LOC		$0.00
235	Pretax earnings		$380.0				$414.00
236	Taxes (40%)		152.0	40.00%	× Pretax earnings		$165.60
237	NI before pref. div.		$228.0				$248.40
238	Preferred div.		8.0	8.00%	× Avg pref. stock		$8.00
239	Net income		$220.0				$240.40
240	Regular common dividends		$50.0	105%	× 2013 Dividend		$52.50
241	Special dividends		$0.0		Pay if financing surplus		$0.00
242	Addition to RE		$170.0		Net income − Dividends		$187.90
243							
244	*3. Elimination of the Financial Deficit or Surplus*						
245	Increase in spontaneous liabilities (accounts payable and accruals)						$50.00
246	+ Increase in notes payable, long-term bonds, preferred stock and common stock						$0.00
247	+ Net income minus regular common dividends						$187.90
248	Increase in financing						$237.90
249	− Increase in total assets						$355.00
250	Amount of deficit or surplus financing:						−$117.10
251	If deficit in financing (negative), draw on line of credit					Line of credit	$117.10
252	If surplus in financing (positive), pay special dividend					Special dividend	$0.00

12-4b Forecast Items Determined by the Preliminary Short-Term Financial Policy

MicroDrive has a target capital structure and target dividend growth, shown in Figure 12-2, Sections 2–4. Like most companies, MicroDrive is willing to deviate from those targets in the short term. For the purpose of this initial forecast, MicroDrive has a preliminary short-term financial policy that sets the projected values for notes payable, long-term debt, preferred stock, and common stock equal to their previous values. In other words, the preliminary short-term financial policy does not call for any change in these items. Keep in mind that financial planning is an iterative process—specify a plan, look at the results, modify if needed, and repeat the process until the plan is acceptable and achievable.

The pale silver rows with blue print in Figure 12-4 show the items determined by the preliminary short-term financial policy. Section 1 shows the projected balance sheets, with the projected values for notes payable, long-term debt, preferred stock, and common stock unchanged from their previous values. The basic approach for projecting financial statements would remain unchanged if the preliminary short-term financial policy had called for changes in these items, such as issuing new debt or equity. In fact, MicroDrive's CFO plans on presenting long-term recommendations to the board regarding the possibility of issuing additional common stock, preferred stock, or long-term bonds after the preliminary forecast has been analyzed.

Section 2 shows the projected income statement. The interest expense on notes payable is projected as the interest rate on notes payable multiplied by the average value of the notes payable outstanding during the year. For example, MicroDrive had $280 at the end of 2013 and projected $280 at the end of 2014, so the average balance during the year is $280 = ($280 + $280)/2. If MicroDrive's plans had called for borrowing an addition $40 in notes payable during the year (resulting in an end-of-year balance of $320), the average balance would have been $300 = ($280+ $320)/2. The same process is applied to long-term bonds and preferred stock.

Basing interest expense on the average amount of debt outstanding during the year implies that the debt is added (or repaid) smoothly during the year. However, if debt is not added until the last day of the year, that year's interest expense should be based on just the debt at the beginning of the year (i.e., the debt at the end of the previous year), because virtually no interest would have accrued on the new debt. On the other hand, if the new debt is added on the first day of the year, interest would accrue all year, so the interest expense should be based on the amount of debt shown at the end of the year.

MicroDrive's preliminary short-term financial policy calls for dividend growth of 5%.

The only items on the projected statements that have not been forecast by the operating plan or the preliminary short-term financial plan are the line of credit (LOC), interest on the LOC, and the item for special dividends. These are shown in dark red ink in the pale gray rows, and we explain them in the following section.

12-4c Identify and Eliminate the Financing Deficit or Surplus in the Projected Balance Sheets

At this point in the projection, it would be extremely unlikely for the balance sheets to balance because the increase in assets required by the operating plan probably is not equal to the increase in liabilities and financing caused by the operating plan and the preliminary short-term financial policy. There will be a financing deficit if the additional financing is less than the additional assets, and a financing surplus if the additional assets are greater than the additional financing. If there is a financing deficit, MicroDrive will not be able to afford its operating plan; if there is a financing surplus, MicroDrive must use it in some manner. Therefore, a realistic projection requires balance sheets that balance.

The first step in making the sheets balance is to identify the amount of financing surplus or deficit resulting from the operating plan and the preliminary short-term financial policy. The second step is to eliminate the deficit or surplus.

Preliminary additional financing comes from three sources: (1) spontaneous liabilities, (2) external financing (such as issuing new long-term bonds or common equity), and (3) internal financing (which is the amount of earnings that are reinvested rather than paid out as dividends). Following is an explanation of how to calculate the additional financing for MicroDrive.

Section 3 in Figure 12-4 begins by adding up the additional financing in the forecast relative to the previous year. For example, MicroDrive's spontaneous liabilities (accounts payable and accruals) went from a total of $500 to $550, an increase of $50. Due to MicroDrive's preliminary short-term financial policy, there were no changes in the external financing provided by notes payable, long-term bonds, preferred stock, or common stock. MicroDrive's preliminary policy calls for no changes in external financing, but it would be easy to modify this assumption. In fact, the CFO did make changes in external financing in a final plan that we discuss later. The preliminary amount of internal financing is the difference between net income and regular common dividends—this is the amount of earnings that are being reinvested. MicroDrive projects a total increase in financing of $237.9, as shown in Section 3 of Figure 12-4.

Is this enough financing, too much, or just right? To answer this question, start by calculating MicroDrive's projected increase in total assets: $355 = $3,905 – $3,550. The difference between MicroDrive's increase in financing and its increase in projected assets is $237.9 – $355 = –$117.1. This amount is negative because the increase in MicroDrive's projected assets is greater than the increase in MicroDrive's projected financing. Therefore, MicroDrive has a preliminary financing deficit—MicroDrive needs more financing to support its operating plan. Had this value been positive, MicroDrive would have had a financing surplus. How should a company handle a financing deficit or surplus?

There are an infinite number of answers to that question, which is why financial modeling can be complicated. MicroDrive's CFO chose a simple but effective answer—if there is a deficit, draw on a line of credit even though it has a high interest rate (the rate on the LOC is 1.5 percentage points higher than the rate on notes payable); if there is a surplus, pay a special dividend. Keep in mind that this is a preliminary plan and that MicroDrive might choose a different source of financing in its final plan.

The last two rows in Section 3 of Figure 12-4 apply this logic. The cell for the LOC in the balance sheet in Section 1 (Cell C215) is linked to the cell in Section 3 (G251). The next step is to estimate the interest expense on the LOC. MicroDrive's CFO made a simplifying assumption for the preliminary projection: The LOC will be drawn upon on the last day of the year. Therefore, the LOC will not accrue interest, so the interest expense on the LOC is equal to the interest rate multiplied by the balance of the LOC at the beginning of the year rather than the end of the year.

The CFO realizes that the projected interest expense will understate the true interest expense if MicroDrive draws on the LOC earlier in the year. However, the CFO wanted to keep the model simple for the preliminary presentations at the retreat. The CFO actually made more realistic (but more complex) assumptions in another model, which we describe later in the chapter.

Now that the hard work of projecting the financial statements is done, it is time for MicroDrive's managers to discuss the projections and formulate their plans.

SELF-TEST

How are operating items projected on financial statements?

How are preliminary levels of debt, preferred stock, common stock, and dividends projected?

What is the financing surplus or deficit? How is it calculated?

12-5 Analysis and Revision of the Preliminary Plan

After explaining the process used to forecast the statements in Figure 12-4, MicroDrive's CFO constructed a 5-year forecast based on the methods and assumptions of the 1-year forecast. Important inputs and key results are shown in Figure 12-5; the full forecast is shown in ***Ch12 Tool Kit.xls.***

FIGURE 12-5

The Status Quo Scenario: Summary of Important Inputs and Key Results (Millions of Dollars, Except for Per Share Data)

	A	B	C	D	E	F	G	H
355	Status Quo	Industry			MicroDrive			
356	**Panel A: Inputs**	Actual	Actual		Forecast			
357	***A1. Operating Ratios***	2013	2013	2014	2015	2016	2017	2018
358	Sales growth rate	5%	*5%*	10%	8%	7%	5%	5%
359	COGS (excl. depr.) / Sales	76%	*76%*	76%	76%	76%	76%	76%
360	Inventory / Sales	15%	*20%*	20%	20%	20%	20%	20%
361	Net PP&E / Sales	33%	*40%*	40%	40%	40%	40%	40%
362	**Panel B: Key Results**	Industry			MicroDrive			
363		Actual	Actual		Forecast			
364	***B1. Operations***	2013	2013	2014	2015	2016	2017	2018
365	Free cash flow	NA	-$260	$25	$88	$128	$207	$217
366	Return on invested capital	15.0%	9.8%	9.8%	9.8%	9.8%	9.8%	9.8%
367	NOPAT/Sales	6.9%	6.0%	6.0%	6.0%	6.0%	6.0%	6.0%
368	Total op. capital / Sales	46.0%	61.0%	61.0%	61.0%	61.0%	61.0%	61.0%
369	Inventory turnover	5.0	4.0	4.0	4.0	4.0	4.0	4.0
370	Days sales outstanding	30.0	36.5	36.5	36.5	36.5	36.5	36.5
371	Fixed asset turnover	3.0	2.5	2.5	2.5	2.5	2.5	2.5
372	***B2. Financing***							
373	Total liabilities / TA	45.0%	55.8%	55.0%	53.5%	51.6%	49.0%	46.3%
374	Net income / Sales	6.2%	4.4%	4.4%	4.4%	4.4%	4.4%	4.6%
375	Return on assets (ROA)	11.0%	6.2%	6.2%	6.1%	6.2%	6.2%	6.4%
376	Return on equity (ROE)	19.0%	15.0%	14.5%	13.9%	13.4%	12.8%	12.4%
377	Times interest earned	10.0	4.2	4.0	4.0	4.1	4.2	4.5
378	Line of credit	NA	$0	$117	$182	$214	$173	$121
379	Payout ratio	35.0%	22.7%	21.8%	21.3%	20.7%	20.5%	20.0%
380	Regular dividends/share	NA	$1.00	$1.05	$1.10	$1.16	$1.22	$1.28
381	Special dividends/share	NA	$0.00	$0.00	$0.00	$0.00	$0.00	$0.00
382	Earnings per share	NA	$4.40	$4.81	$5.17	$5.58	$5.92	$6.38
383	***B3. Estimated intrinsic value***							
384	12/31/2013	Estimated value of operations =			$2,719			
385	12/31/2013	Estimated intrinsic stock price =			$22.78			

12-5a Analysis of the Preliminary Plan

Section B1 of Figure 12-5 shows key results from the operating plan for the Status Quo scenario. The good news is that FCF becomes positive, but the bad news is that the return on invested capital is much lower than the industry average and is lower than MicroDrive's cost of capital. Rows 367 and 368 show that MicroDrive has a lower NOPAT/Sales ratio than its peers and a higher Capital/Sales ratio. In other words, MicroDrive is less profitable and less efficient. Rows 369–371 show that MicroDrive carries too much inventory, collects more slowly from its customers, and utilizes its factories inefficiently.

The financial plan reflects the poor operating performance. The projected ratio of total liabilities to sales shows that MicroDrive will have more leverage than its peers and will need to borrow from the expensive line of credit. However, even higher leverage is not enough to boost MicroDrive's return on equity to the industry average.

The poor performance also is reflected in MicroDrive's estimated intrinsic stock value of $22.78, which is less than the current market price of $27. The management team concluded that unless they make changes soon, the market price will fall.

12-5b The Final Plan

The marketing and sales directors made the first suggestion. They felt they could boost sales growth to 12% in the next year and maintain sales growth of 6% in the post-forecast years. However, when the CFO input higher sales growth rates and left all other inputs unchanged, the intrinsic value *fell* by a small amount! (You should try this yourself in the model ***Ch12 Tool Kit.xls*** by selecting Data, What-If Analysis, Scenario Manager, and the scenario named Status Quo Except Higher Sales Growth.) The CFO explained that MicroDrive's return on invested capital was slightly lower than its cost of capital, so each additional dollar of sales is like adding a project that has small negative NPV.[1] Unless MicroDrive improves its ROIC, growth will not add value.

After much discussion, the management team concluded that, because of licensing fees and other costs, it was not feasible for the MicroDrive to reduce its COGS/Sales ratio in the next year. However, the director of R&D explained that the new products in the pipeline will have higher profit margins. If MicroDrive can fund some extra field tests, the new products can reach the market in a year and drive the ratio of COGS/Sales down to 75%.

The production, sales, and purchasing managers are jointly responsible for inventory in MicroDrive's supply chain. With some additional funding for technology to improve channels of information among suppliers and customers, MicroDrive can reduce inventory levels without hurting product availability. They estimated that the improved technology would push the Inventory/Sales ratio down to 17%.

The production and human resource managers stated that productivity could be increased with new training programs so that employees can better utilize the new production equipment that had been added the previous year. They estimated that the increased productivity would cause the ratio of PP&E/Sales to fall to 36% in the next two years.

Managers from accounting and finance estimated that the total cost for these improvement programs would be about $200 million.

[1]If the expected ROIC is less than the WACC, growth doesn't add value. The expected ROIC is defined as the projected NOPAT divided by the current level of total operating capital: Expected ROIC = $NOPAT_{t+1}$ / $Capital_t$.

The CFO entered these new inputs (except the cost to implement the new plans) into the model and named it the Final scenario. The results are shown in Figure 12-6. The value of operations increased from $3,814 million to $5,260 million. This is an increase of over $1.4 billion, well above the $200 million cost to implement the plans. Although the Final plan from the management retreat does not include the costs to implement the improvement plans, the CFO included these costs upon returning to headquarters.

Figure 12-6 shows that the ROIC improves to 12.7% by the second year, well above the WACC of 11%. Free cash flow becomes much larger, causing the estimated intrinsic stock price to increase to $51.20. With respect to financing, MicroDrive will not have to draw on its line of credit. In fact, the company will have extra cash available to distribute as a special dividend if the board chooses to do so.

The marketing and sales directors asked about the impact of growth in sales if the ROIC improves to 12.7%. The CFO input the higher growth rate and the model showed that increasing sales does increase value in scenarios that have the ROIC greater than the WACC (see the scenario named Final Except Higher Sales Growth in the ***Tool Kit***).

FIGURE 12-6

The Final Scenario: Summary of Important Inputs and Key Results (Millions of Dollars, Except for Per Share Data)

	A	B	C	D	E	F	G	H
355	Final	Industry	MicroDrive					
356	**Panel A: Inputs**	Actual	Actual	Forecast				
357	***A1. Operating Ratios***	2013	2013	2014	2015	2016	2017	2018
358	Sales growth rate	5%	*5%*	10%	8%	7%	5%	5%
359	COGS (excl. depr.) / Sales	76%	*76%*	76%	75%	75%	75%	75%
360	Inventory / Sales	15%	*20%*	17%	17%	17%	17%	17%
361	Net PP&E / Sales	33%	*40%*	39%	36%	36%	36%	36%
362	**Panel B: Key Results**	Industry	MicroDrive					
363		Actual	Actual	Forecast				
364	***B1. Operations***	2013	2013	2014	2015	2016	2017	2018
365	Free cash flow	NA	−$260	$248	$334	$210	$285	$299
366	Return on invested capital	15.0%	9.8%	10.6%	12.7%	12.7%	12.7%	12.7%
367	NOPAT/Sales	6.9%	6.0%	6.1%	6.8%	6.8%	6.8%	6.8%
368	Total op. capital / Sales	46.0%	61.0%	57.0%	54.0%	54.0%	54.0%	54.0%
369	Inventory turnover	5.0	4.0	4.7	4.6	4.6	4.6	4.6
370	Days sales outstanding	30.0	36.5	36.5	36.5	36.5	36.5	36.5
371	Fixed asset turnover	3.0	2.5	2.6	2.8	2.8	2.8	2.8
372	***B2. Financing***							
373	Total liabilities / TA	45.0%	55.8%	55.1%	54.6%	52.0%	50.3%	48.6%
374	Net income / Sales	6.2%	4.4%	4.4%	5.3%	5.4%	5.5%	5.6%
375	Return on assets (ROA)	11.0%	6.2%	6.6%	8.3%	8.5%	8.6%	8.7%
376	Return on equity (ROE)	19.0%	15.0%	15.7%	19.5%	18.6%	18.1%	17.7%
377	Times interest earned	10.0	4.2	4.1	5.0	5.3	5.6	5.9
378	Line of credit	NA	$0	$0	$0	$0	$0	$0
379	Payout ratio	35.0%	22.7%	65.1%	77.1%	34.9%	53.2%	53.8%
380	Regular dividends/share	NA	$1.00	$3.17	$4.88	$2.41	$3.91	$4.19
381	Special dividends/share	NA	$0.00	$2.12	$3.78	$1.25	$2.69	$2.91
382	Earnings per share	NA	$4.40	$4.87	$6.33	$6.90	$7.34	$7.79
383	***B3. Estimated intrinsic value***							
384	12/31/2013	Estimated value of operations =			$4,140			
385	12/31/2013	Estimated intrinsic stock price =			$51.20			

12-5c The CFO's Model[2]

The CFO's final model, shown in the worksheet named ***CFO Model*** in the file ***Ch12 Tool Kit.xls,*** has several refinements to the basic model presented in the previous sections, including the incorporation of financing feedback and implementation of the target capital structure.

Financing Feedback

The basic model assumed that no interest would accrue on the line of credit because the LOC would be added at the end of the year. However, if interest is calculated on the LOC's average balance during the year, which is more realistic, here is what happens:

1. The line of credit required to make the balance sheets balance is added to the balance sheet.
2. Interest expense increases due to the LOC.
3. Net income decreases because interest expenses are higher.
4. Internally generated financing decreases because net income decreases.
5. The financing deficit increases because internally generated financing decreases.
6. An additional amount of the LOC is added to the balance sheets to make them balance.
7. Go to step 2 and repeat the loop.

This loop is called *financing feedback* because the additional financing feeds back and causes a need for more additional financing. If programmed into *Excel,* there will be a circular reference. Sometimes *Excel* can handle this (if the iteration feature is enabled), but sometimes *Excel* freezes up. Fortunately, there is a simple way to modify the required line of credit by scaling it up so that no iterations are required. If this piques your interest, take a look at the ***CFO Model*** in the ***Tool Kit.***

Implementing the Target Capital Structure

The preliminary financial policy chosen by the CFO during the managers' retreat held external financing constant—with no additional borrowing or repayment of debt (other than the line of credit) and no new issues or repurchases of preferred stock or common stock. However, this ignores the target capital structure. Fortunately, there is a simple way to implement the target capital structure in the projected statements.

If MicroDrive implements its target capital structure, then it can find the current value of operations, as shown in Figure 12-3. Furthermore, MicroDrive also can estimate its value of operations for *each year* of the forecast, starting at the horizon and working backwards. For example, MicroDrive's horizon value from the final plan is $4,140 (to see this, select the Final scenario in the ***Tool Kit*** and look at the updated Figure 12-3). The value of operations at the horizon, 2018, is equal to the horizon value—this is the value of all FCF from 2019 and beyond discounted back to 2018. The value of operations at 2017, one year before the horizon, is equal to the value of all free cash flows beyond 2017, discounted at the WACC back to 2017. But we have already found the value of all FCF beyond 2018 discounted back to 2018 (which is equal to the value of operations at 2018), and we know the FCF of 2018. Therefore, we can discount the 2018 value of operations and the 2018 free cash flow back 1 year to get the 2017 value of operations: Value at 2017 = ($4,140 + $299)/(1 + 0.11) = $3,999. We can work our way back to the current date by repeating this process, providing estimates of the yearly values of operations.

[2]This section is relatively technical, and some instructors may choose to skip it with no loss in continuity.

We know the weights in the target capital structure for each year. For example, the target weight for long-term debt, w_d, is 28%. We can multiply this target weight by the value of operations each year to obtain the amount of long-term debt that conforms to the target capital structure. For example, in 2017 MicroDrive should have long-term debt of \$1,120= 28%(\$3,999). Repeating this process for all the capital components each year provides the amounts of external funding that match the target capital structure.

The CFO's model implements a modified version of this procedure. Instead of setting the actual capital structure weights equal to the target weights in the first year of the forecast, the CFO allows the actual weights in the capital structure each year to move smoothly from the actual current values to the target values at the horizon. See the ***CFO Model*** in the ***Tool Kit*** for details.

SELF-TEST

Suppose a company's return on invested capital is less than its WACC. What happens to the value of operations if the sales growth rate increases? Explain your answer.

12-6 Additional Funds Needed (AFN) Equation Method

A complete financial plan includes projected financial statements, but the **additional funds needed (AFN) equation** method provides a simple way to get a ballpark estimate of the additional external financing that will be required. The AFN approach identifies the financing surplus or deficit in much the same way as we did in the previous sections: (1) Identify the amount of additional funding required by the additional assets due to growth in sales. (2) Identify the amount of spontaneous liabilities (which reduces the amount of external financing that is required to support the additional assets). (3) Identify the amount of funding generated internally from net income that will be available for reinvestment in the company after paying dividends. (4) Assume no new external financing (similar to the preliminary financial policy in the Status Quo scenario). The difference between the additional assets and the sum of spontaneous liabilities and reinvested net income is the amount of additional financing needed from external sources. Following are explanations and applications of these steps.

12-6a Required Increase in Assets

In a steady-state situation in which no excess capacity exists, the firm must have additional plant and equipment, more delivery trucks, higher inventories, and so forth if sales are to increase. In addition, more sales will lead to more accounts receivable, and those receivables must be financed from the time of the sale until they are collected. Therefore, both fixed and current assets must increase if sales are to increase. Of course, if assets are to increase, liabilities and equity must also increase by a like amount to make the balance sheet balance.

12-6b Spontaneous Liabilities

The first sources of expansion funding are the "spontaneous" increases that will occur in MicroDrive's accounts payable and accrued wages and taxes. The company's suppliers give it 10 days to pay for inventory purchases, and because purchases will increase with sales, accounts payable will automatically rise. For example, if sales rise by 10%, then inventory purchases will also rise by 10%, and this will cause accounts payable to rise spontaneously by the same 10%. Similarly, because the company pays workers every 2 weeks, more workers and a larger payroll will mean more accrued wages payable. Finally, higher expected income will mean more accrued income taxes, and its higher wage bill will mean more accrued withholding taxes. Normally no interest is paid on these spontaneous funds, but their amount is limited by credit terms, contracts with workers, and tax laws. Therefore, *spontaneous funds will thus be used to the extent possible, but there is little flexibility in their usage.*

12-6c Addition to Retained Earnings

The second source of funds for expansion comes from net income. Part of MicroDrive's profit will be paid out in dividends, but the remainder will be reinvested in operating assets, as shown in the Assets section of the balance sheet; a corresponding amount will be reported as an addition to retained earnings in the Liabilities and equity section of the balance sheet. There is some flexibility in the amount of funds that will be generated from new reinvested earnings because dividends can be increased or decreased, but if the firm plans to hold its dividend steady or to increase it at a target rate, as most do, then flexibility is limited.

12-6d Calculating Additional Funds Needed (AFN)

If we start with the required new assets and then subtract both spontaneous funds and additions to retained earnings, we are left with the additional funds needed, or AFN. The AFN must come from *external sources*; hence it is sometimes called EFN. The typical sources of external funds are bank loans, new long-term bonds, new preferred stock, and newly issued common stock. The mix of the external funds used should be consistent with the firm's financial policies, especially its target debt ratio.

12-6e Using MicroDrive's Data to Implement the AFN Equation Method

Equation 12-1 summarizes the logic underlying the AFN equation method. Figure 12-7 defines the notation in Equation 12-1 and applies it to identify MicroDrive's AFN. The **additional funds needed (AFN) equation** is:

$$\begin{array}{ccccccc} \text{Required increase in assets} & - & \text{Increase in spontaneous liabilities} & - & \text{Increase in retained earnings} & = & \text{Additional funds needed} \\ (A_0^*/S_0)\Delta S & - & (L_0^*/S_0)\Delta S & - & S_1 \times M \times \left(1 - \text{Payout Ratio}\right) & = & \text{AFN} \end{array} \quad (12\text{-}1)$$

We see from Part B of Figure 12-7 that for sales to increase by $500 million, MicroDrive must increase assets by $355 million. Therefore, liabilities and capital must also increase by $355 million. Of this total, $50 million will come from spontaneous liabilities, and another $187 million will come from new retained earnings. The remaining $118 million must be raised from external sources—probably some combination of short-term bank loans, long-term bonds, preferred stock, and common stock. Notice that the AFN from this model is very close to the surplus financing required in the Status Quo model for the projected financial statements because both methods assume that the operating ratios for MicroDrive will not change.

FIGURE 12-7
Additional Funds Needed (AFN) (Millions of Dollars)

	A	B	C	D	E	F	G	H	I
397	*Part A. Inputs and Definitions*								
398	S_0:		Most recent year's sales =						$5,000
399	g:		Forecasted growth rate in sales =						10.00%
400	S_1:		Next year's sales: $S_0 \times (1 + g)$ =						$5,500
401	gS_0:		Change in sales = $S_1 - S_0 = \Delta S$ =						$500
402	A_0^*:		Most recent year's operating assets =						$3,550
403	A_0^* / S_0:		Required assets per dollar of sales =						71.00%
404	L_0^*:		Most recent year's spontaneous liabilities i.e., payables + accruals =						$500
405	L_0^* / S_0:		Spontaneous liabilities per dollar of sales =						10.00%
406	Profit margin (M):		Most recent profit margin = net income/sales =						4.40%
407	Payout ratio (POR):		Most recent year's dividends / net income = % of income paid out =						22.73%
408	*Part B. Additional Funds Needed (AFN) to Support Growth*								
409									
410	AFN	= Required Increase in		−	Increase in Spon. Liab.		−	Addition to Retained	
411		=	$(A_0^*/S_0)\Delta S$	−	$(L_0^*/S_0)\Delta S$		−	$S_1 \times M \times (1 - POR)$	
412				−			−		
413		=	$(A_0^*/S_0)(gS_0)$	−	$(L_0^*/S_0)(gS_0)$		−	$(1+g)S_0 \times M \times (1 - POR)$	
414				−			−		
415		=	(0.710)($500)	−	(0.10)($500)		−	$5,500(0.044)(1 − 0.2273)	
416		=	$355	−	$50.00		−	$187.00	
417	AFN =	$118.00							

12-6f Key Factors in the AFN Equation

The AFN equation shows that external financing requirements depend on five key factors.

1. **Sales growth (g).** Rapidly growing companies require large increases in assets and a corresponding large amount of external financing, other things held constant.
2. **Capital intensity (A_0^*/S_0).** The amount of assets required per dollar of sales, A_0^*/S_0, is the **capital intensity ratio**, which has a major effect on capital requirements. Companies with relatively high assets-to-sales ratios require a relatively large number of new assets for any given increase in sales; hence they have a greater need for external financing. If a firm can find a way to lower this ratio—for instance, by adopting a just-in-time inventory system, by going to two shifts in its manufacturing plants, or by outsourcing rather than manufacturing parts—then it can achieve a given level of growth with fewer assets and thus less new external capital.
3. **Spontaneous liabilities-to-sales ratio (L_0^*/S_0).** If a company can increase its spontaneously generated liabilities, this will reduce its need for external financing. One way of raising this ratio is by paying suppliers in, say, 20 days rather than 10 days. Such a change may be possible but, as we shall see in Chapter 16, it would probably have serious adverse consequences.
4. **Profit margin (M = Net Income/Sales).** The higher the profit margin, the more net income is available to support increases in assets—and hence the less the need for external financing. A firms' profit margin is normally as high as management can get it, but sometimes a change in operations can boost the sales price or reduce costs, thus raising the margin further. If so, this will permit a faster growth rate with less external capital.

5. **Payout ratio (POR = DPS/EPS).** The less of its income a company distributes as dividends, the larger its addition to retained earnings—hence the less its need for external capital. Companies typically like to keep their dividends stable or to increase them at a steady rate—stockholders like stable, dependable dividends, so such a dividend policy will generally lower the cost of equity and thus maximize the stock price. So even though reducing the dividend is one way a company can reduce its need for external capital, companies generally resort to this method only if they are under financial duress.

12-6g The Self-Supporting Growth Rate

One interesting question is: "What is the maximum growth rate the firm could achieve if it had no access to external capital?" This rate is called the *self-supporting growth rate*, and it can be found as the value of g that, when used in the AFN equation, results in an AFN of zero. We first replace ΔS in the AFN equation with gS_0 and $S_1$with $(1+g)S_0$ so that the only unknown is g; we then solve for g to obtain the following equation for the self-supporting growth rate:

$$\text{Self-supporting } g = \frac{M(1-POR)(S_0)}{A_0* - L_0* - M(1-POR)(S_0)} \tag{12-2}$$

The definitions of the terms used in this equation are shown in Figure 12-7.

If the firm has any positive earnings and pays out less than 100% in dividends, then it will have some additions to retained earnings, and those additions could be combined with spontaneous funds to enable the company to grow at some rate without having to raise external capital. As explained in the chapter's *Excel* ***Tool Kit***, this value can be found either algebraically or with *Excel*'s Goal Seek function. For MicroDrive, the self-supporting growth rate is 5.9%; this means it could grow at that rate even if capital markets dried up completely, with everything else held constant.

resource

*See **Ch12 Tool Kit.xls** on the textbook's Web site for details.*

SELF-TEST

If all ratios are expected to remain constant, an equation can be used to forecast AFN. Write out the equation and briefly explain it.

Describe how the following factors affect external capital requirements: (1) payout ratio, (2) capital intensity, (3) profit margin.

In what sense do accounts payable and accruals provide "spontaneous funds" to a growing firm?

Is it possible for the calculated AFN to be negative? If so, what would this imply?

Refer to data in the MicroDrive example presented, but now assume that MicroDrive's growth rate in sales is forecasted to be 15% rather than 10%. If all ratios remain constant, what would the AFN be? **($205.6 million)**

12-7 Forecasting When the Ratios Change

The versions of the percent of sales forecasting model and the AFN method assumed that the forecasted items could be estimated as a percent of sales. This implies that each of the accounts for assets, spontaneous liabilities, and operating costs is proportional to sales. In graph form, this implies the type of relationship shown in Panel a of Figure 12-8,

FIGURE 12-8

Four Possible Ratio Relationships (Millions of Dollars)

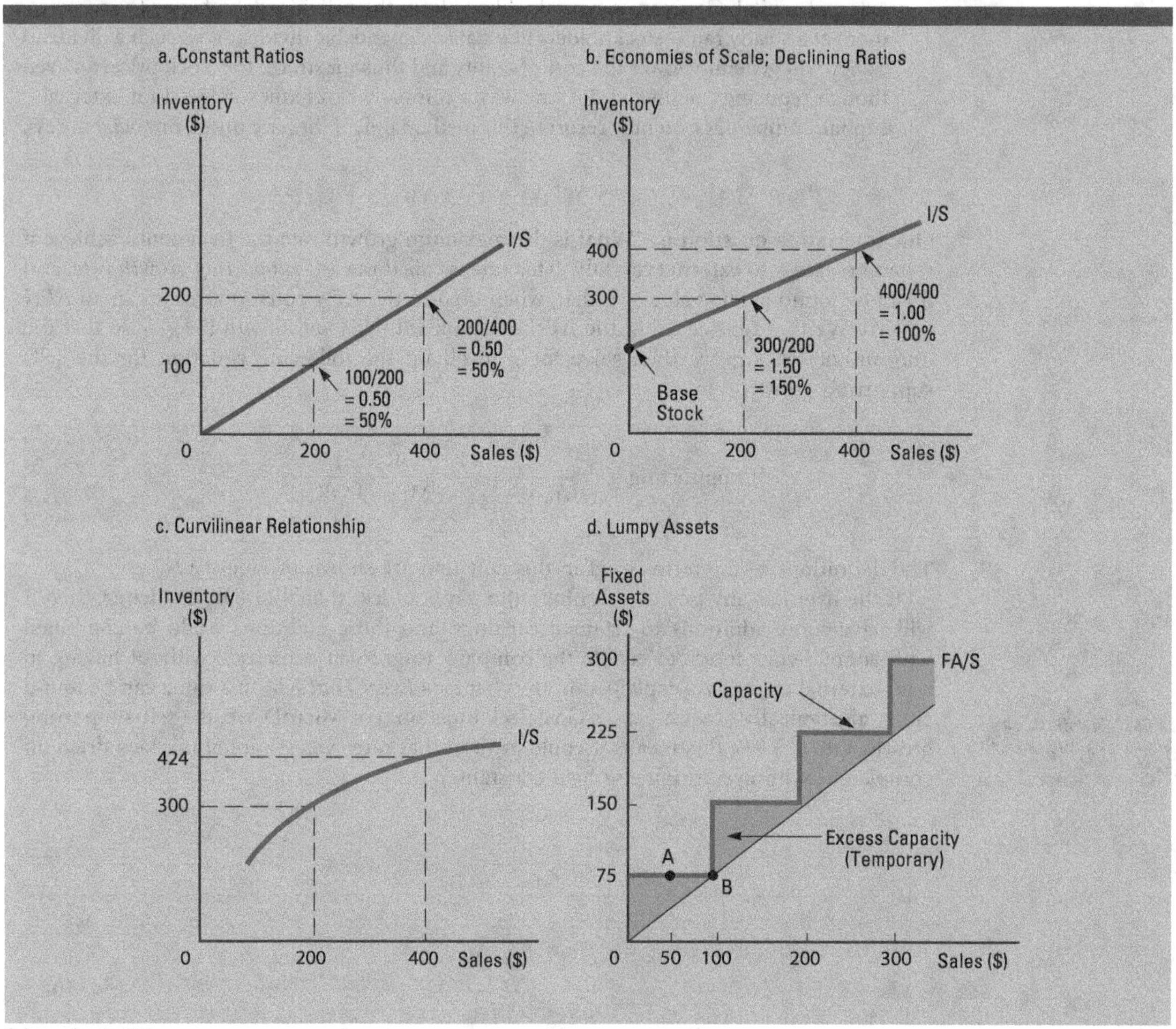

© Cengage Learning 2014

a relationship whose graph (1) is linear and (2) passes through the origin. Under those conditions, if the company's sales increase from $200 million to $400 million, or by 100%, then inventory will also increase by 100%, from $100 million to $200 million.

The assumption of constant ratios and identical growth rates is appropriate at times, but there are times when it is incorrect. We describe three such situations in the following sections.

12-7a Economies of Scale

There are economies of scale in the use of many kinds of assets, and when economies of scale occur, the ratios are likely to change over time as the size of the firm increases. For example, retailers often need to maintain base stocks of different inventory items even if current sales are quite low. As sales expand, inventories may then grow less rapidly than sales, so the ratio of inventory to sales (I/S) declines. This situation is depicted in Panel b of Figure 12-8. Here we see that the inventory/sales ratio is 1.5 (or 150%) when sales are $200 million but declines to 1.0 when sales climb to $400 million.

It is easy in *Excel* to incorporate this type of scale economy in the forecast. For example, the basic method forecasts inventory as: Inventory = m(Sales), where m is a constant. With economies of scale, forecast Inventory as: Inventory = b + m(Sales), where m and b are constants.

12-7b Nonlinear Relationships

The relationship in Panel b is linear, but nonlinear relationships often exist. Indeed, if the firm uses one popular model for establishing inventory levels (the Economic Ordering Quantity, or EOQ, model), its inventories will rise with the *square root* of sales. This situation is shown in Panel c of Figure 12-8, which shows a curved line whose slope decreases at higher sales levels. In this situation, very large increases in sales would require very little additional inventory. To incorporate this type of nonlinearity in *Excel*, for example, you could forecast inventory as a function of the square root of sales: Inventory = m($\text{Sales}^{0.5}$).

12-7c Lumpy Assets and Excess Capacity

In many industries, technological considerations dictate that if a firm is to be competitive, it must add fixed assets in large, discrete units; such assets are often referred to as **lumpy assets**. In the paper industry, for example, there are strong economies of scale in basic paper mill equipment, so when a paper company expands capacity, it must do so in large, lumpy increments. This type of situation is depicted in Panel d of Figure 12-8. Here we assume that the minimum economically efficient plant has a cost of $75 million, and that such a plant can produce enough output to reach a sales level of $100 million. If the firm is to be competitive, it simply must have at least $75 million of fixed assets.

Lumpy assets have a major effect on the ratio of fixed assets to sales (FA/S) at different sales levels and, consequently, on financial requirements. At Point A in Panel d, which represents a sales level of $50 million, the fixed assets are $75 million and so the ratio FA/S = $75/$50 = 1.5. Sales can expand by $50 million, out to $100 million, with no additions to fixed assets. At that point, represented by Point B, the ratio FA/S = $75/$100 = 0.75. However, because the firm is operating at capacity (sales of $100 million), even a small increase in sales would require a doubling of plant capacity, so a small projected sales increase would bring with it a large financial requirement.[3]

If assets are lumpy and a firm makes a major purchase, the firm will have excess capacity, which means that sales can grow before the firm must add capacity. The level of full capacity sales is

[3]Several other points should be noted about Panel d of Figure 12-7. First, if the firm is operating at a sales level of $100 million or less, then any expansion that calls for a sales increase of more than $100 million would require a *doubling* of the firm's fixed assets. A much smaller percentage increase would be involved if the firm were large enough to be operating a number of plants. Second, firms generally go to multiple shifts and take other actions to minimize the need for new fixed asset capacity as they approach Point B. However, these efforts can only go so far, and eventually a fixed asset expansion will be required. Third, firms often arrange to share excess capacity with other firms in their industry. For example, the situation in the electric utility industry is very much like that depicted in Panel d. However, electric companies often build plants jointly, or they "take turns" building plants. Then they buy power from or sell power to other utilities to avoid building new plants that would be underutilized.

$$\text{Full capacity sales} = \frac{\text{Actual sales}}{\text{Percentage of capacity at which fixed assets were operated}} \tag{12-3}$$

For example, consider MicroDrive and use the data from its financial statements in Figure 12-1, but now assume that excess capacity exists in fixed assets. Specifically, assume that fixed assets in 2013 were being utilized to only 96% of capacity. If fixed assets had been used to full capacity, then 2013 sales could have been as high as $3,125 million versus the $3,000 million in actual sales:

$$\begin{aligned}\text{Full capacity sales} &= \frac{\text{Actual sales}}{\text{Percentage of capacity at which fixed assets were operated}} \\ &= \frac{\$5{,}000 \text{ million}}{0.96} = \$5{,}208 \text{ million}\end{aligned}$$

The target fixed assets/sales ratio can be defined in terms of the full capacity sales:

$$\text{Target fixed assets/Sales} = \frac{\text{Actual fixed assets}}{\text{Full capacity sales}} \tag{12-4}$$

MicroDrive's target fixed assets/sales ratio should be 38.4% rather than 40%:

$$\begin{aligned}\text{Target fixed assets/Sales} &= \frac{\text{Actual fixed assets}}{\text{Full capacity sales}} \\ &= \frac{\$2{,}000}{\$5{,}208} = 0.384 = 38.4\%\end{aligned}$$

The required level of fixed assets depends upon this target fixed assets/sales ratio:

$$\begin{matrix}\text{Required level} \\ \text{of fixed assets}\end{matrix} = \left(\frac{\text{Target fixed assets}}{\text{Sales}}\right)\left(\begin{matrix}\text{Projected} \\ \text{sales}\end{matrix}\right) \tag{12-5}$$

Therefore, if MicroDrive's sales increase to $3,300 million, its fixed assets would have to increase to $1,056 million:

$$\begin{aligned}\begin{matrix}\text{Required level} \\ \text{of fixed assets}\end{matrix} &= \left(\frac{\text{Target fixed assets}}{\text{Sales}}\right)\left(\begin{matrix}\text{Projected} \\ \text{sales}\end{matrix}\right) \\ &= 0.384(\$5{,}500) = \$2{,}112 \text{ million}\end{aligned}$$

We previously forecasted that MicroDrive would need to increase fixed assets at the same rate as sales, or by 10%. That meant an increase of $200 million, from $2,000 million to $2,200 million under the old assumption of no excess capacity. Under the new assumption of excess capacity, the actual required increase in fixed assets is only from $2,000 million to $2,112 million, which is an increase of $112 million. Thus, the capacity-adjusted forecast is less than the earlier forecast: $200 − $112 = $88 million. With a smaller fixed asset requirement, the projected AFN would decline from an estimated $118 million to $118 − $88 = $30 million.

Note also that when excess capacity exists, sales can grow to the capacity sales as calculated above with no increase in fixed assets, but sales beyond that level would require additions of fixed assets as in our example. The same situation could occur with respect to inventories, and the required additions would be determined in exactly the same manner as for fixed assets. Theoretically, the same situation could occur with other types of assets, but as a practical matter excess capacity normally exists only with respect to fixed assets and inventories.

SELF-TEST

How do economies of scale and lumpy assets affect financial forecasting?

SUMMARY

- The **forecasted financial statements (FFS) method** of financial planning forecasts the entire set of financial statements. It usually begins with a forecast of the firm's sales and then projects many items on the financial statements as a percent of sales.
- The **additional funds needed (AFN) equation** can be used to forecast additional external financing requirements, but only for one year ahead and only if all asset-to-sales ratios are identical, all spontaneous liabilities-to-sales ratios are identical, and all cost-to-sales ratios are identical.
- A firm can determine its **AFN** by estimating the amount of new assets necessary to support the forecasted level of sales and then subtracting from this amount the spontaneous funds that will be generated from operations.
- The higher a firm's **sales growth rate** and the higher its **payout ratio**, the greater will be its need for additional financing.
- There are two major applications of forecasted financial statements. First, the forecasted free cash flows can be used to estimate the impact that changes in operating plans have on the firm's estimated intrinsic value of operations and stock price. Second, the forecasted financing surplus or deficit allows the firm to identify its future financing needs.
- Adjustments must be made if **economies of scale** exist in the use of assets, if **excess capacity** exists, or if growth must occur in large increments (**lumpy assets**).
- **Excess capacity adjustments** can be used to forecast asset requirements in situations in which assets are not expected to grow at the same rate as sales.

QUESTIONS

(12-1) Define each of the following terms:

a. Operating plan; financial plan
b. Spontaneous liabilities; profit margin; payout ratio
c. Additional funds needed (AFN); AFN equation; capital intensity ratio; self-supporting growth rate
d. Forecasted financial statement approach using percent of sales
e. Excess capacity; lumpy assets; economies of scale
f. Full capacity sales; target fixed assets/sales ratio; required level of fixed assets

(12-2) Some liability and net worth items increase spontaneously with increases in sales. Put a check (✓) by those items listed below that typically increase spontaneously:

Accounts payable	______	Mortgage bonds	______
Notes payable to banks	______	Common stock	______
Accrued wages	______	Retained earnings	______
Accrued taxes	______		

(12-3) The following equation is sometimes used to forecast financial requirements:

$$AFN = (A_0^*/S_0)(\Delta S) - (L_0^*/S_0)(\Delta S) - MS_1(1 - POR)$$

What key assumption do we make when using this equation? Under what conditions might this assumption not hold true?

(12-4) Name five key factors that affect a firm's external financing requirements.

(12-5) What is meant by the term "self-supporting growth rate"? How is this rate related to the AFN equation, and how can that equation be used to calculate the self-supporting growth rate?

(12-6) Suppose a firm makes the policy changes listed below. If a change means that external, nonspontaneous financial requirements (AFN) will increase, indicate this by a (+); indicate a decrease by a (–); and indicate no effect or an indeterminate effect by a (0). Think in terms of the *immediate* effect on funds requirements.

a. The dividend payout ratio is increased. ______

b. The firm decides to pay all suppliers on delivery, rather than after a 30-day delay, to take advantage of discounts for rapid payment. ______

c. The firm begins to offer credit to its customers, whereas previously all sales had been on a cash basis. ______

d. The firm's profit margin is eroded by increased competition, although sales hold steady. ______

e. The firm sells its manufacturing plants for cash to a contractor and simultaneously signs an outsourcing contract to purchase from that contractor goods that the firm formerly produced. ______

f. The firm negotiates a new contract with its union that lowers its labor costs without affecting its output. ______

SELF-TEST PROBLEMS Solutions Appear in Appendix A

(ST-1) Self-Supporting Growth Rate

The Barnsdale Corporation has the following ratios: $A_0^*/S_0 = 1.6$; $L_0^*/S_0 = 0.4$; profit margin = 0.10; and dividend payout ratio = 0.45, or 45%. Sales last year were \$100 million. Assuming that these ratios will remain constant, use the AFN equation to determine the firm's self-supporting growth rate—in other words, the maximum growth rate Barnsdale can achieve without having to employ nonspontaneous external funds.

(ST-2) AFN Equation

Refer to Problem ST-1, and suppose Barnsdale's financial consultants report (1) that the inventory turnover ratio (sales/inventory) is 3, compared with an industry average of 4, and (2) that Barnsdale could reduce inventories and thus raise its turnover ratio to 4 without affecting its sales, profit margin, or other asset turnover ratios. Under these conditions, use the AFN equation to determine the amount of additional funds Barnsdale would require during each of the next 2 years if sales grow at a rate of 20% per year.

(ST-3) **Excess Capacity** Van Auken Lumber's 2013 financial statements are shown below.

Van Auken Lumber: Balance Sheet as of December 31, 2013 (Thousands of Dollars)

Cash	$ 1,800	Accounts payable	$ 7,200
Receivables	10,800	Notes payable	3,472
Inventories	12,600	Line of credit	0
Total current assets	$25,200	Accruals	2,520
Net fixed assets	21,600	Total current liabilities	$13,192
		Mortgage bonds	5,000
		Common stock	2,000
		Retained earnings	26,608
Total assets	$46,800	Total liabilities and equity	$46,800

Van Auken Lumber: Income Statement for December 31, 2013 (Thousands of Dollars)

Sales	$36,000
Operating costs	30,783
Earnings before interest and taxes	$ 5,217
Interest	717
Pre-tax earnings	$ 4,500
Taxes (40%)	1,800
Net income	$ 2,700
Dividends (60%)	$ 1,620
Addition to retained earnings	$ 1,080

a. Assume that the company was operating at full capacity in 2013 with regard to all items *except* fixed assets, which in 2013 were being utilized to only 75% of capacity. By what percentage could 2014 sales increase over 2013 sales without the need for an increase in fixed assets?

b. Now suppose that 2014 sales increase by 25% over 2013 sales. Use the forecasted financial statement method to forecast a 12/31/14 balance sheet and 2014 income statement, assuming that (1) the historical ratios of operating costs/sales, cash/sales, receivables/sales, inventories/sales, accounts payable/sales, and accruals/sales remain constant; (2) Van Auken cannot sell any of its fixed assets; (3) any required financing is done at the *end* of 2014 as through a line of credit; (4) the firm earns no interest on its cash; and (5) the interest rate on all of its debt is 12%. Van Auken pays out 60% of its net income as dividends and has a tax rate of 40%. What is Van Auken's financing deficit or surplus? (*Hints:* Assume any additional financing through the line of credit will be drawn on the last day of the year. Therefore, the line of credit will not accrue interest expense during the year because any new line of credit is added at the end of the year; also, use the forecasted income statement to determine the addition to retained earnings for use in the balance sheet.)

PROBLEMS Answers Appear in Appendix B

Easy Problems 1–3

(12-1) AFN Equation Broussard Skateboard's sales are expected to increase by 15% from $8 million in 2013 to $9.2 million in 2014. Its assets totaled $5 million at the end of 2013. Broussard is already at full capacity, so its assets must grow at the same rate as projected sales. At the end of 2013, current liabilities were $1.4 million, consisting of $450,000 of accounts payable, $500,000 of notes payable, and $450,000 of accruals. The after-tax profit margin is forecasted to be 6%, and the forecasted payout ratio is 40%. Use the AFN equation to forecast Broussard's additional funds needed for the coming year.

(12-2) AFN Equation Refer to Problem 12-1. What would be the additional funds needed if the company's year-end 2013 assets had been $7 million? Assume that all other numbers, including sales, are the same as in Problem 12-1 and that the company is operating at full capacity. Why is this AFN different from the one you found in Problem 12-1? Is the company's "capital intensity" ratio the same or different?

(12-3) AFN Equation Refer to Problem 12-1. Return to the assumption that the company had $5 million in assets at the end of 2013, but now assume that the company pays no dividends. Under these assumptions, what would be the additional funds needed for the coming year? Why is this AFN different from the one you found in Problem 12-1?

Intermediate Problems 4–6

(12-4) Sales Increase Maggie's Muffins, Inc., generated $5,000,000 in sales during 2013, and its year-end total assets were $2,500,000. Also, at year-end 2013, current liabilities were $1,000,000, consisting of $300,000 of notes payable, $500,000 of accounts payable, and $200,000 of accruals. Looking ahead to 2014, the company estimates that its assets must increase at the same rate as sales, its spontaneous liabilities will increase at the same rate as sales, its profit margin will be 7%, and its payout ratio will be 80%. How large a sales increase can the company achieve without having to raise funds externally—that is, what is its self-supporting growth rate?

(12-5) Long-Term Financing Needed At year-end 2013, Wallace Landscaping's total assets were $2.17 million and its accounts payable were $560,000. Sales, which in 2013 were $3.5 million, are expected to increase by 35% in 2014. Total assets and accounts payable are proportional to sales, and that relationship will be maintained. Wallace typically uses no current liabilities other than accounts payable. Common stock amounted to $625,000 in 2013, and retained earnings were $395,000. Wallace has arranged to sell $195,000 of new common stock in 2014 to meet some of its financing needs. The remainder of its financing needs will be met by issuing new long-term debt at the end of 2014. (Because the debt is added at the end of the year, there will be no additional interest expense due to the new debt.) Its net profit margin on sales is 5%, and 45% of earnings will be paid out as dividends.

a. What were Wallace's total long-term debt and total liabilities in 2013?
b. How much new long-term debt financing will be needed in 2014? (*Hint:* AFN − New stock = New long-term debt.)

(12-6) Additional Funds Needed

The Booth Company's sales are forecasted to double from $1,000 in 2013 to $2,000 in 2014. Here is the December 31, 2013, balance sheet:

Cash	$ 100	Accounts payable	$ 50
Accounts receivable	200	Notes payable	150
Inventories	200	Accruals	50
Net fixed assets	500	Long-term debt	400
		Common stock	100
		Retained earnings	250
Total assets	$1,000	Total liabilities and equity	$1,000

Booth's fixed assets were used to only 50% of capacity during 2013, but its current assets were at their proper levels in relation to sales. All assets except fixed assets must increase at the same rate as sales, and fixed assets would also have to increase at the same rate if the current excess capacity did not exist. Booth's after-tax profit margin is forecasted to be 5% and its payout ratio to be 60%. What is Booth's additional funds needed (AFN) for the coming year?

Challenging Problems 7–9

(12-7) Forecasted Statements and Ratios

Upton Computers makes bulk purchases of small computers, stocks them in conveniently located warehouses, ships them to its chain of retail stores, and has a staff to advise customers and help them set up their new computers. Upton's balance sheet as of December 31, 2013, is shown here (millions of dollars):

Cash	$ 3.5	Accounts payable	$ 9.0
Receivables	26.0	Notes payable	18.0
Inventories	58.0	Line of credit	0
Total current assets	$ 87.5	Accruals	8.5
Net fixed assets	35.0	Total current liabilities	$ 35.5
		Mortgage loan	6.0
		Common stock	15.0
		Retained earnings	66.0
Total assets	$122.5	Total liabilities and equity	$122.5

Sales for 2013 were $350 million and net income for the year was $10.5 million, so the firm's profit margin was 3.0%. Upton paid dividends of $4.2 million to common stockholders, so its payout ratio was 40%. Its tax rate was 40%, and it operated at full capacity. Assume that all assets/sales ratios, spontaneous liabilities/sales ratios, the profit margin, and the payout ratio remain constant in 2014.

a. If sales are projected to increase by $70 million, or 20%, during 2014, use the AFN equation to determine Upton's projected external capital requirements.
b. Using the AFN equation, determine Upton's self-supporting growth rate. That is, what is the maximum growth rate the firm can achieve without having to employ nonspontaneous external funds?
c. Use the forecasted financial statement method to forecast Upton's balance sheet for December 31, 2014. Assume that all additional external capital is raised as a line of credit at the end of the year and is reflected (because the debt is added at the end of the year, there will be no additional interest expense due to the new debt).

Assume Upton's profit margin and dividend payout ratio will be the same in 2014 as they were in 2013. What is the amount of the line of credit reported on the 2014 forecasted balance sheets? (*Hint:* You don't need to forecast the income statements because you are given the projected sales, profit margin, and dividend payout ratio; these figures allow you to calculate the 2014 addition to retained earnings for the balance sheet.)

(12-8) Financing Deficit Stevens Textiles's 2013 financial statements are shown here:

Balance Sheet as of December 31, 2013 (Thousands of Dollars)

Cash	$ 1,080	Accounts payable	$ 4,320
Receivables	6,480	Accruals	2,880
Inventories	9,000	Line of credit	0
Total current assets	$16,560	Notes payable	2,100
Net fixed assets	12,600	Total current liabilities	$ 9,300
		Mortgage bonds	3,500
		Common stock	3,500
		Retained earnings	12,860
Total assets	$29,160	Total liabilities and equity	$ 29,160

Income Statement for December 31, 2013 (Thousands of Dollars)

Sales	$36,000
Operating costs	32,440
Earnings before interest and taxes	$ 3,560
Interest	460
Pre-tax earnings	$ 3,100
Taxes (40%)	1,240
Net income	$ 1,860
Dividends (45%)	$ 837
Addition to retained earnings	$ 1,023

a. Suppose 2014 sales are projected to increase by 15% over 2013 sales. Use the forecasted financial statement method to forecast a balance sheet and income statement for December 31, 2014. The interest rate on all debt is 10%, and cash earns no interest income. Assume that all additional debt in the form of a line of credit is added at the end of the year, which means that you should base the forecasted interest expense on the balance of debt at the beginning of the year. Use the forecasted income statement to determine the addition to retained earnings. Assume that the company was operating at full capacity in 2013, that it cannot sell off any of its fixed assets, and that any required financing will be borrowed as notes payable. Also, assume that assets, spontaneous liabilities, and operating costs are expected to increase by the same percentage as sales. Determine the additional funds needed.

b. What is the resulting total forecasted amount of the line of credit?

c. In your answers to Parts a and b, you should not have charged any interest on the additional debt added during 2014 because it was assumed that the new debt was added at the end of the year. But now suppose that the new debt is added throughout the year. Don't do any calculations, but how would this change the answers to parts a and b?

(12-9) Financing Deficit

Garlington Technologies Inc.'s 2013 financial statements are shown here:

Balance Sheet as of December 31, 2013

Cash	$ 180,000	Accounts payable	$ 360,000
Receivables	360,000	Notes payable	156,000
Inventories	720,000	Line of credit	0
Total current assets	$1,260,000	Accruals	180,000
Fixed assets	1,440,000	Total current liabilities	$ 696,000
		Common stock	1,800,000
		Retained earnings	204,000
Total assets	$2,700,000	Total liabilities and equity	$2,700,000

Income Statement for December 31, 2013

Sales	$3,600,000
Operating costs	3,279,720
EBIT	$ 320,280
Interest	18,280
Pre-tax earnings	$ 302,000
Taxes (40%)	120,800
Net income	$ 181,200
Dividends	$ 108,000

Suppose that in 2014 sales increase by 10% over 2013 sales and that 2014 dividends will increase to $112,000. Forecast the financial statements using the forecasted financial statement method. Assume the firm operated at full capacity in 2013. Use an interest rate of 13%, and assume that any new debt will be added at the end of the year (so forecast the interest expense based on the debt balance at the beginning of the year). Cash does not earn any interest income. Assume that the all new debt will be in the form of a line of credit.

SPREADSHEET PROBLEMS

(12-12) Build a Model: Forecasting Financial Statements

resource

Start with the partial model in the file ***Ch12 P10 Build a Model.xls*** on the textbook's Web site, which contains the 2013 financial statements of Zieber Corporation. Forecast Zieber's 2014 income statement and balance sheets. Use the following assumptions: (1) Sales grow by 6%. (2) The ratios of expenses to sales, depreciation to fixed assets, cash to sales, accounts receivable to sales, and inventories to sales will be the same in 2014 as in 2013. (3) Zieber will not issue any new stock or new long-term bonds. (4) The interest rate is 11% for long-term debt and the interest expense on long-term debt is based on the average balance during the year. (5) No interest is earned on cash. (6) Dividends grow at an 8% rate. (6) Calculate the additional funds needed (AFN). If new financing is required, assume it will be raised by drawing on a line of credit with an interest rate of 12%. Assume that any draw on the line of credit will be made on the last day of the year, so there will be no additional interest expense for the new line of credit. If surplus funds are available, pay a special dividend.

a. What are the forecasted levels of the line of credit and special dividends?
b. Now assume that the growth in sales is only 3%. What are the forecasted levels of the line of credit and special dividends?

THOMSON ONE Business School Edition Problem

THOMSON REUTERS Use the Thomson ONE—Business School Edition online database to work this chapter's questions.

Forecasting the Future Performance of Abercrombie & Fitch

Clothing retailer Abercrombie & Fitch enjoyed phenomenal success in the late 1990s. Between 1996 and 2000, its sales grew almost fourfold, from $335 million to more than $1.2 billion, and its stock price soared by more than 500%. More recently, however, its growth rate has begun to slow down, and Abercrombie has had a hard time meeting its quarterly earnings targets. These problems were compounded by the global recession in 2009 with the stock price in November 2009 falling by 90% from its high 1 year before. Abercrombie's struggles resulted from increased competition, a sluggish economy, and the challenges of staying ahead of the fashion curve.

Since 2009, the company's stock has rebounded strongly but questions remain about the firm's long-term growth prospects. Given the questions about Abercrombie's future growth rate, analysts have focused on the company's earnings reports. Thomson ONE provides a convenient and detailed summary of the company's recent earnings history along with a summary of analysts' earnings forecasts.

To access this information, we begin by entering the company's ticker symbol, ANF, on Thomson ONE's main screen and then selecting GO. This takes us to an overview of the company's recent performance. After checking out the overview, you should click on the tab labeled Estimates, near the top of your screen. Here you will find a wide range of information about the company's past and projected earnings.

Thomson ONE—BSE Discussion Questions

1. What are the mean and median forecasts for Abercrombie's earnings per share over the next fiscal year?
2. Based on analysts' forecasts, what is the firm's expected long-term growth rate in earnings?
3. Have analysts made any significant changes to their forecasted earnings for Abercrombie & Fitch in the past few months?
4. Historically, have Abercrombie's reported earnings generally met, exceeded, or fallen short of analysts' forecasted earnings?
5. How has Abercrombie's stock performed this year relative to the S&P 500?

MINI CASE

Hatfield Medical Supplies's stock price had been lagging its industry averages, so its board of directors brought in a new CEO, Jaiden Lee. Lee had brought in Ashley Novak, a finance MBA who had been working for a consulting company, to replace the old CFO, and Lee asked Ashley to develop the financial planning section of the strategic plan. In her previous job, Novak's primary task had been to help clients develop financial forecasts, and that was one reason Lee hired her.

Novak began by comparing Hatfield's financial ratios to the industry averages. If any ratio was substandard, she discussed it with the responsible manager to see what could be done to improve the situation. The following data show Hatfield's latest financial statements plus some ratios and other data that Novak plans to use in her analysis.

Hatfield Medical Supplies (Millions of Dollars Except Per Share Data)

Balance Sheet, 12/31/2013		Income Statement, Year Ending 2013	
Cash	$ 20	Sales	$2,000
Accts. rec.	280	Op. costs (excl. depr.)	1,800
Inventories	400	Depreciation	50
Total CA	$ 700	EBIT	$ 150
Net fixed assets	500	Interest	40
Total assets	$1,200	Pre-tax earnings	$ 110
		Taxes (40%)	44
Accts. pay. & accruals	$ 80	Net income	$ 66
Line of credit	$ 0		
Total CL	$ 80	Dividends	$ 20.0
Long-term debt	500	Add. to RE	$ 46.0
Total liabilities	$ 580	Common shares	10.0
Common stock	420	EPS	$ 6.60
Retained earnings	200	DPS	$ 2.00
Total common equ.	$ 620	Ending stock price	$52.80
Total liab. & equity	$1,200		

Selected Additional Data for 2013

	Hatfield	Industry		Hatfield	Industry
Op. costs/Sales	90.0%	88.0%	Total liability/Total assets	48.3%	36.7%
Depr./FA	10.0%	12.0%	Times interest earned	3.8	8.9
Cash/Sales	1.0%	1.0%	Return on assets (ROA)	5.5%	10.2%
Receivables/Sales	14.0%	11.0%	Profit margin (M)	3.30%	4.99%
Inventories/Sales	20.0%	15.0%	Sales/Assets	1.67	2.04
Fixed assets/Sales	25.0%	22.0%	Assets/Equity	1.94	1.58
Acc. pay. & accr./Sales	4.0%	4.0%	Return on equity (ROE)	10.6%	16.1%
Tax rate	40.0%	40.0%	P/E ratio	8.0	16.0
ROIC	8.0%	12.5%			
NOPAT/Sales	4.5%	5.6%			
Total op. capital/Sales	56.0%	45.0%			

a. Using Hatfield's data and its industry averages, how well run would you say Hatfield appears to be compared to other firms in its industry? What are its primary strengths and weaknesses? Be specific in your answer, and point to various ratios that support your position. Also, use the Du Pont equation (see Chapter 3) as one part of your analysis.

b. Use the AFN equation to estimate Hatfield's required new external capital for 2014 if the sales growth rate is 10%. Assume that the firm's 2013 ratios will remain the same in 2014. (*Hint:* Hatfield was operating at full capacity in 2013.)

c. Define the term capital intensity. Explain how a decline in capital intensity would affect the AFN, other things held constant. Would economies of scale combined with rapid growth affect capital intensity, other things held constant? Also, explain how changes in each of the following would affect AFN, holding other things constant: the growth rate, the amount of accounts payable, the profit margin, and the payout ratio.

d. Define the term self-supporting growth rate. What is Hatfield's self-supporting growth rate? Would the self-supporting growth rate be affected by a change in the capital intensity ratio or the other factors mentioned in the previous question? Other things held constant, would the calculated capital intensity ratio change over time if the company were growing and were also subject to economies of scale and/or lumpy assets?

e. Use the following assumptions to answer the questions below: (1) Operating ratios remain unchanged. (2) Sales will grow by 10%, 8%, 5%, and 5% for the next four years. (3) The target weighted average cost of capital (WACC) is 9%. This is the *No Change* scenario because operations remain unchanged.

   (1) For each of the next four years, forecast the following items: sales, cash, accounts receivable, inventories, net fixed assets, accounts payable & accruals, operating costs (excluding depreciation), depreciation, and earnings before interest and taxes (EBIT).

   (2) Using the previously forecasted items, calculate for each of the next four years the net operating profit after taxes (NOPAT), net operating working capital, total operating capital, free cash flow, (FCF), annual growth rate in FCF, and return on invested capital. What does the forecasted free cash flow in the first year imply about the need for external financing? Compare the forecasted ROIC with the WACC. What does this imply about how well the company is performing?

   (3) Assume that FCF will continue to grow at the growth rate for the last year in the forecast horizon (*Hint:* 5%). What is the horizon value at 2017? What is the present value of the horizon value? What is the present value of the forecasted FCF? (*Hint:* Use the free cash flows for 2014 through 2017.) What is the current value of operations? Using information from the 2013 financial statements, what is the current estimated intrinsic stock price?

f. Continue with the same assumptions for the *No Change* scenario from the previous question, but now forecast the balance sheet and income statements for 2014 (but not for the following three years) using the following preliminary financial policy. (1) Regular dividends will grow by 10%. (2) No additional long-term debt or common stock will be issued. (3) The interest rate on all debt is 8%. (4) Interest expense for long-term debt is based on the average balance during the year. (5) If the operating results and the preliminary financing plan cause a financing deficit, eliminate the deficit by drawing on a line of credit. The line of credit would be tapped on the last day of the year, so it would create no additional interest expenses for that year. (6) If there is a financing surplus, eliminate it by paying a special dividend. After forecasting the 2014 financial statements, answer the following questions.

(1) How much will Hatfield need to draw on the line of credit?

(2) What are some alternative ways than those in the preliminary financial policy that Hatfield might choose to eliminate the financing deficit?

g. Repeat the analysis performed the previous question but now assume that Hatfield is able to improve the following inputs: (1) reduce operating costs (excluding depreciation)/sales to 89.5% at a cost of $40 million, and (2) reduce inventories/sales to 16% at a cost of $10 million. This is the Improve scenario.

(1) Should Hatfield implement the plans? How much value would they add to the company?

(2) How much can Hatfield pay as a special dividend in the Improve scenario? What else might Hatfield do with the financing surplus?

SELECTED ADDITIONAL CASES

The following cases from TextChoice, *Cengage Learning's online library, cover many of the concepts discussed in this chapter and are available at* **http://www.textchoice2.com/casenet**.

Klein-Brigham Series:
Case 37, "Space-Age Materials, Inc."; Case 38, "Automated Banking Management, Inc."; Case 52, "Expert Systems"; and Case 69, "Medical Management Systems, Inc."

© Adalberto Rios Szalay/Sexto Sol/Getty Images

CHAPTER 30

Financial Management in Not-for-Profit Businesses[1]

Thus far, we have focused exclusively on the financial management of investor-owned, profit-oriented firms. However, financial management is also important in not-for-profit businesses, defined as corporations that charge a fee for their services and are expected to generate enough revenues to cover costs but that have neither outstanding stock nor stockholders. Examples of not-for-profit businesses include thousands of municipal utilities ranging from Los Angeles Power & Light and the New York Power Authority to tiny rural electric authority (REA) cooperatives; all private colleges and universities; about 85% of all U.S. hospitals, nursing homes, and other health care facilities; and even tourist attractions such as the Baltimore and Tampa aquariums.

These tens of thousands of not-for-profit firms employ millions of people and provide vital services, so it is important that they be operated efficiently. To maintain efficiency, the not-for-profits require financial management skills similar to those of investor-owned firms, but with an important difference: The not-for-profits do not have stockholders, so their goal is not to maximize shareholder wealth. As we discuss in the chapter, this difference in goals between profit and not-for-profit businesses leads to some interesting contrasts in the financial management of the two types of organizations.

[1]There is no ***Tool Kit*** for this chapter.

© 2014 Cengage Learning. All Rights Reserved. May not be scanned, copied or duplicated, or posted to a publicly accessible website, in whole or in part.

30-1 For-Profit (Investor-Owned) versus Not-for-Profit Businesses

When the average person thinks of a business, she thinks of an **investor-owned**, or **for-profit**, firm. The IBMs and General Motors of this world are investor-owned firms. Investors become owners by buying common stock either when a company first sells its shares to the public in an initial public offering (IPO) or when it issues additional shares in the primary or secondary market.

Investor-owned firms have three key characteristics: (1) The owners (stockholders) are well-defined, and they exercise control by voting for the firm's board of directors. (2) The firm's residual earnings belong to its stockholders, so management is responsible to this single, well-defined group of people for the firm's profitability. (3) The firm is subject to taxation at the federal, state, and local levels. However, if an organization meets a set of stringent requirements, it can qualify as a **tax-exempt**, or **not-for-profit, corporation.**[2] Tax-exempt status is granted to corporations that fit the definition of a charitable organization and hence qualify under Internal Revenue Service (IRS) Tax Code Section 501(c)(3). Thus, such corporations are also known as **501(c)(3) corporations.**[3]

The Tax Code defines a charitable organization as any corporation, community chest, fund, or foundation that is organized and operated exclusively for religious, charitable, scientific, public safety, literary, or educational purposes. Because the promotion of health is commonly considered a charitable activity, a corporation that provides health care services, provided it meets other requirements, can qualify for tax-exempt status. In addition to being organized for a charitable purpose, a not-for-profit corporation must be administered so that (1) it operates exclusively for the public, rather than private, interest; (2) none of the profits are used for private inurement; (3) no political activity is conducted; and (4) if liquidation occurs, the assets will continue to be used for a charitable purpose.[4]

For example, hospital corporations that qualify for tax-exempt status exhibit the following characteristics: (1) Control rests in a **board of trustees** composed mostly of community leaders who have no direct economic interest in the organization. (2) The organization maintains an open medical staff, with privileges available to all qualified physicians. (3) If the hospital leases office space to physicians, such space can be leased by any member of the medical staff. (4) The hospital operates an emergency room accessible to the general public. (5) The hospital is engaged in medical research and education. (6) The hospital undertakes various programs to improve the health of the community.

Conversely, a hospital may be disqualified from tax-exempt status if it (1) is controlled by members of the medical staff, (2) restricts staff privileges to controlling physicians,

---

[2]In the past, tax-exempt corporations were commonly called *nonprofit corporations*, but today the term *not-for-profit corporation* is more common. For more information on financial management in not-for-profit health care corporations, see Louis C. Gapenski and George H. Pink, *Understanding Health Care Financial Management*, 6th ed. (Chicago: Health Administration Press, 2011).

[3]For additional information on obtaining and maintaining tax-exempt status, see the summer 1988 issue of *Topics in Health Care Financing*, titled "Tax Management for Exempt Providers."

[4]*Private inurement* means personal benefit from the profits (net income) of the corporation. Because individuals cannot benefit from the profits that not-for-profit corporations earn, such organizations cannot pay dividends. Note, however, that prohibition of private inurement does not prevent parties to not-for-profit corporations, such as managers, from benefiting through salaries, perquisites, and the like. For example, in 1992 it was disclosed that the national chairman of the United Way received an annual salary plus perquisites that exceeded $400,000 in value. He was forced to resign in part because this level of compensation was considered too high for an employee of a not-for-profit charity. Interestingly, United Way's CEO's salary increased along with those of for-profit CEOs during the 1990s and 2000s. By 2009, the salary was about $500 thousand per year.

© 2014 Cengage Learning. All Rights Reserved. May not be scanned, copied or duplicated, or posted to a publicly accessible website, in whole or in part.

(3) leases office space to some physicians at less than fair market value, (4) limits the use of its facilities, (5) has contractual agreements that provide direct economic benefit to controlling physicians, or (6) provides only a negligible amount of charity care.

Not-for-profit corporations differ significantly from investor-owned corporations. Because not-for-profit businesses have no shareholders, no group of individuals has ownership rights to the firm's residual earnings. Similarly, no outside group exercises control of the firm; rather, control is exercised by a board of trustees that is not constrained by outside oversight. As we noted earlier, not-for-profit corporations are generally exempt from taxation, including both property and income taxes, and they have the right to issue tax-exempt debt. Finally, individual contributions to not-for-profit organizations can be deducted from taxable income by the donor, so not-for-profit businesses have access to tax-advantaged contributed capital.

Whether a firm is investor-owned or not-for-profit, there are many types of organizational structures. At the most basic level, a not-for-profit business can be a single entity with one operating unit. In this situation, all the financial management decisions are performed by a single set of managers who must raise the needed capital and decide how to allocate it within the organization. Alternatively, corporations can be set up with separate operating divisions or as holding companies, with wholly owned or partially owned subsidiary corporations, in which the different management layers have different responsibilities.

The holding company structure, which we discussed in Chapter 22, is particularly useful when a corporation is engaged in both for-profit and not-for-profit activities. For example, a typical not-for-profit hospital corporation is organized along the lines presented in Figure 30-1. This organization facilitates expansion into both tax-exempt and taxable activities well beyond patient care. However, the tax-exempt holding company must ensure that all transactions between taxable and tax-exempt subsidiaries are conducted at arm's length; if business is not transacted in this way, then the tax-exempt status of the parent holding company and its not-for-profit subsidiaries could be challenged.

The inherent differences between investor-owned and not-for-profit organizations have profound implications for many elements of financial management, including defining the goals of the firm and making financing and capital budgeting decisions. The remainder of this Web chapter will be devoted to these issues.

SELF-TEST

Define the following terms:

(1) Investor-owned firm
(2) Not-for-profit business
(3) 501(c)(3) corporation
(4) Private inurement
(5) Board of trustees

What are some major differences between investor-owned and not-for-profit businesses?

30-2 Goals of the Firm

From a financial management perspective, the primary goal of investor-owned firms is shareholder wealth maximization, which translates to stock price maximization. Because not-for-profit businesses do not have stockholders, shareholder wealth maximization

© 2014 Cengage Learning. All Rights Reserved. May not be scanned, copied or duplicated, or posted to a publicly accessible website, in whole or in part.

FIGURE 30-1

Typical Not-for-Profit Corporate Structure

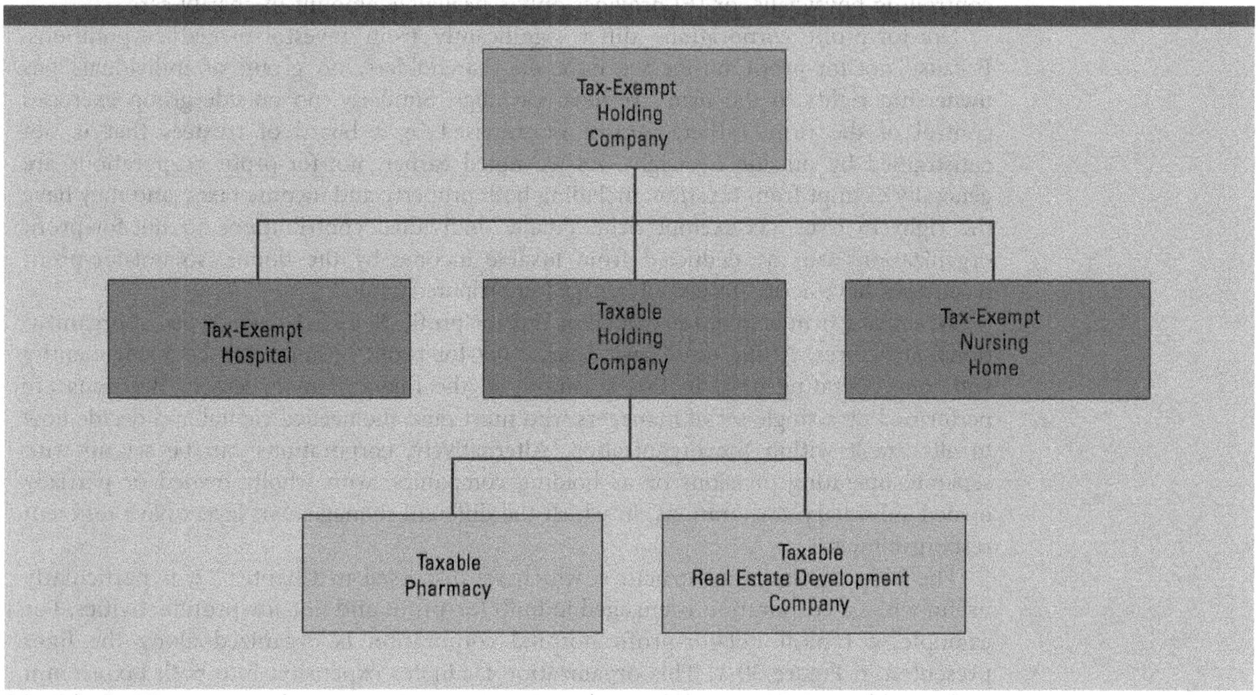

© Cengage Learning 2014

cannot be the goal of such organizations. Rather, not-for-profit businesses serve and are served by a number of **stakeholders**, which include all parties that have an interest (financial or otherwise) in the organization. For example, a not-for-profit hospital's stakeholders include its board of trustees, managers, employees, physicians, creditors, suppliers, patients, and even potential patients (that is, the entire community). Managers of investor-owned companies can focus primarily on the interests of one class of stakeholders, the stockholders, but managers of not-for-profit businesses face a different situation. They must try to please all the stakeholders because there is no single, well-defined group that exercises control.[5]

Typically, the goal of a not-for-profit business is stated in terms of some mission. For example, here is the mission statement of Ridgeway Community Hospital, a 300-bed, not-for-profit hospital:

> *Ridgeway Community Hospital, along with its medical staff, is a recognized, innovative health care leader dedicated to meeting the needs of the community. We strive to be the best comprehensive health care provider possible through our commitment to excellence.*

Although this mission statement provides Ridgeway's managers and employees with a framework for developing specific goals and objectives, it does not provide much insight about the goals of financial management. For Ridgeway to accomplish

[5]Many people argue that managers of not-for-profit firms do not have to please anyone at all, because they tend to dominate the board of trustees that is supposed to exercise oversight. However, we would argue that managers of not-for-profit firms must to some extent please all the firms' stakeholders because all are necessary to the well-being of the business. Similarly, managers of investor-owned firms should not treat any of their stakeholders unfairly, because such actions are ultimately detrimental to stockholders.

© 2014 Cengage Learning. All Rights Reserved. May not be scanned, copied or duplicated, or posted to a publicly accessible website, in whole or in part.

its mission, the hospital's managers have identified the following specific financial management goals.

1. The hospital must maintain its financial viability.
2. The hospital must generate sufficient profits to permit it to expand along with the community and to replace plant and equipment as it wears out or becomes obsolete.[6]
3. The hospital must generate sufficient profits to invest in new medical technologies and services as they become available.
4. Although the hospital has an aggressive philanthropy program in place, it does not want to be overly dependent on this program, or on government grants, to fund its operations.
5. The hospital will strive to provide services to the community as inexpensively as possible, given the above financial requirements.

In effect, Ridgeway's managers are saying that to achieve the "commitment to excellence" mentioned in its mission statement, the hospital must remain financially strong and reasonably profitable. Financially weak organizations cannot continue to accomplish their stated missions over the long run. When talking among themselves, Ridgeway's managers summarize this requirement as "No margin, no mission." Note that in many ways Ridgeway's five goals for financial management are not much different from the financial management goals of for-profit hospitals. In order to maximize shareholder wealth, the managers of for-profit hospitals must also maintain financial viability and obtain the financial resources necessary to provide new services and technologies.

SELF-TEST

What is the primary goal of investor-owned firms? Of not-for-profit businesses?

From a financial management perspective, what are the major similarities and differences between the objectives of investor-owned and not-for-profit firms?

30-3 Estimating the Cost of Capital

As we discussed in Chapter 9, a firm's weighted average (or overall) cost of capital, WACC, is a blend of the costs of the various types of capital it uses. In general, cost of capital estimation for not-for-profit businesses parallels that for investor-owned firms, but there are two major differences. First, because not-for-profit businesses pay no taxes, there are no tax effects associated with debt financing.[7] Second, investor-owned firms raise equity capital by selling new common stock and by retaining earnings rather than paying them out as dividends. Not-for-profit businesses raise the equivalent of equity capital, which is called fund capital, in three ways: (1) by earning profits, which by law must be retained within the business; (2) by receiving grants from governmental entities; and (3) by receiving contributions from individuals and companies. Fund capital is fundamentally different from equity capital, so this question arises: How do we measure the cost of fund capital?

[6]Technically, not-for-profit firms earn an "excess of revenues over expenses" rather than "profits." However, for the sake of consistent terminology, we will generally use the term **profits** or **net income** for this excess.

[7]However, most not-for-profit firms can issue tax-exempt bonds through municipal financing authorities. Thus, the cost-of-debt disadvantage of not being able to deduct interest expense from taxable income is offset for the most part by issuing lower-cost tax-exempt debt. We will discuss tax-exempt debt in detail later in the chapter.

© 2014 Cengage Learning. All Rights Reserved. May not be scanned, copied or duplicated, or posted to a publicly accessible website, in whole or in part.

Because the weighted average cost of capital is used primarily for capital budgeting decisions, it represents the opportunity cost of using capital to purchase fixed assets rather than for alternative uses. For investor-owned firms, the opportunity cost associated with equity capital is apparent—if available capital is not needed for investment in fixed assets, it can be returned to the stockholders by either paying dividends or repurchasing stock. For not-for-profit businesses, which do not have this option, the opportunity cost of fund capital is more controversial. Historically, at least four positions have been taken with regard to the cost of fund capital.[8]

1. It has been argued that fund capital has zero cost. The rationale here is (a) that contributors do not expect a monetary return on their contributions and (b) that the firm's other suppliers of fund capital, especially the customers who pay more for services than is warranted by the firm's tangible costs, do not require an explicit return on the capital retained by the firm.
2. The second position also assumes a zero cost for fund capital, but here it is recognized that, when inflation exists, fund capital must earn a return sufficient to enable the organization to replace existing assets as they wear out. For example, assume that a not-for-profit firm buys a building that costs $1,000,000. Over time, the cost of the building will be recovered by depreciation, so, at least in theory, $1,000,000 will be available to replace the building when it becomes obsolete. However, because of inflation the new building now might cost $1,500,000. If the firm has not increased its fund capital by retaining earnings, then the only way to finance the additional $500,000 will be through grants and contributions, which may not be available, or by increasing its debt and hence its debt ratio, which might not be desirable or even possible. Thus, just to maintain its existing asset base over time, a not-for-profit firm must earn a return on fund capital equal to the inflation rate; this rate must therefore be built into the firm's cost-of-capital estimate. Of course, if the asset base must increase to provide additional services, then retained earnings above those needed to keep up with inflation will be required.
3. The third position is that fund capital has some cost but that it is not very high. When a not-for-profit firm either receives contributions or retains earnings, it can always invest those funds in marketable securities rather than purchase real assets. Thus, fund capital has an opportunity cost that should be acknowledged, and this cost is roughly equal to the return available on a portfolio of short-term, low-risk securities such as T-bills.
4. Finally, others have argued that fund capital to not-for-profit businesses has about the same cost as the cost of retained earnings to similar investor-owned firms. The rationale here also rests on the opportunity cost concept, but the opportunity cost is now defined as the return available from investing the fund capital in alternative investments *of similar risk*.

Which of the four positions is correct? Think about it this way: Suppose Ridgeway Community Hospital expects to receive $500,000 in contributions in 2013 and also forecasts $1,500,000 in earnings, so it expects to have $2,000,000 of new fund capital available for investment. The $2 million could be used to purchase assets related to its core business, such as an outpatient clinic or diagnostic equipment; the money could be temporarily invested in securities with the intent of purchasing real assets sometime in the future; it could be used to retire debt; it could be used to pay management bonuses; it

[8]For one of the classic works on this topic, see Douglas A. Conrad, "Returns on Equity to Not-for-Profit Hospitals: Theory and Implementation," *Health Services Research*, April 1984, pp. 41–63. See also the follow-up articles by Pauly, by Conrad, and by Silvers and Kauer in the April 1986 issue of *Health Services Research*.

© 2014 Cengage Learning. All Rights Reserved. May not be scanned, copied or duplicated, or posted to a publicly accessible website, in whole or in part.

could be placed in a non-interest-bearing account at the bank; and so on. If it uses the capital to purchase real assets, then Ridgeway is deprived of the opportunity to use this capital for other purposes and so an opportunity cost must be assigned.

The hospital's investment in real assets should return at least as much as the return available on securities investments of similar risk.[9] What return is available on securities with similar risk to hospital assets? Generally, the best answer is the return that could be expected from investing in the stock of an investor-owned hospital company. After all, instead of using fund capital to purchase real assets, Ridgeway could always use the funds to buy the stock of an investor-owned hospital and thus generate additional funds for future use. Therefore, the cost of fund capital for a not-for-profit corporation can be proxied by estimating the beta coefficient of a similar investor-owned corporation and then using Hamada's equation as discussed in Chapter 15 to adjust for leverage and tax differences.

In general, the opportunity cost principle applies to all fund capital, and this capital has a cost that is equal to the cost of retained earnings to similar investor-owned firms. However, contributions that are designated for a specific purpose, such as a children's hospital wing, may indeed have a zero cost: Because the funds are restricted to a particular project, the firm does not have the opportunity to invest them in other alternatives.

Although the opportunity cost concept is intuitively appealing, some fundamental problems are inherent in using a publicly held for-profit hospital corporation's cost of equity as a proxy for a not-for-profit hospital's cost of fund capital. First and foremost, the market risk to equity investors is probably less than the risk embedded in fund capital because stockholders can eliminate a large portion of their investment risk by holding well-diversified portfolios. In contrast, stakeholders such as managers, patients, physicians, and employees do not have the same opportunities to diversify their hospital-related activities. Furthermore, investor-owned companies tend to have wide geographic and patient diversification, whereas not-for-profit hospitals tend to be stand-alone concerns with little risk-reducing diversification. In spite of these objections, it is reasonable to assign a cost of fund capital based on opportunity costs, and the best estimate is the cost of equity to a similar for-profit business.

SELF-TEST

What is fund capital, and how does it differ from equity capital?

How does the cost of capital estimation process differ between investor-owned and not-for-profit businesses?

30-4 Capital Structure Decisions

When making capital structure decisions within not-for-profit businesses, managers must be concerned with two issues: Is capital structure theory, particularly the "tax benefits versus financial distress costs" trade-off theory, applicable to not-for-profit businesses? And are there any characteristics of not-for-profit businesses that prevent them from following the guidance prescribed by theory?

No rigorous research has been conducted into the optimal capital structures of not-for-profit businesses, but some loose analogies can be drawn. Although not-for-profit businesses do not pay taxes and hence cannot reduce the cost of debt by the factor 1 − T,

[9]We do not mean to imply that not-for-profit firms should never invest in a project that will lose money. Not-for-profit firms do invest in negative-profit projects that benefit their stakeholders, but their managers must be aware of the financial opportunity costs inherent in such investments. We will have more to say about this issue when we discuss capital budgeting decisions.

© 2014 Cengage Learning. All Rights Reserved. May not be scanned, copied or duplicated, or posted to a publicly accessible website, in whole or in part.

many of these businesses have access to the tax-exempt debt market. As a result, not-for-profit businesses have about the same effective cost of debt as do investor-owned firms.

As discussed in the previous section, a not-for-profit firm's fund capital has an opportunity cost that is roughly equivalent to the cost of equity of an investor-owned firm of similar risk. Thus, we would expect the opportunity cost of fund capital to rise as more and more debt financing is used, just as it would for an investor-owned firm. Not-for-profit businesses are subject to the same types of financial distress and agency costs as investor-owned firms, so these costs are equally applicable. Therefore, we would expect the trade-off theory to be applicable to not-for-profit businesses, and such businesses should have optimal capital structures that are defined, at least at first blush, as a trade-off between the costs and benefits of debt financing. Note, however, that the asymmetric information theory is not applicable to not-for-profit businesses because such businesses do not issue common stock.

Although the trade-off theory may be conceptually correct for not-for-profit businesses, a problem arises when applying the theory. For-profit firms have relatively easy access to equity capital. Thus, if a for-profit firm has more capital investment opportunities than it can finance with retained earnings and debt financing, it can generally raise the needed funds by a new stock offering.[10] Furthermore, it is relatively easy for investor-owned firms to alter their capital structures. For example, if a firm is underleveraged it can simply issue more debt and use the proceeds to repurchase stock. If it has too much debt it can issue additional shares and use the proceeds to retire debt.

Not-for-profit businesses do not have access to the equity markets—their sole source of "equity" capital is through government grants, private contributions, and profits. Thus, managers of not-for-profit businesses do not have the same degree of flexibility in either capital investment or capital structure decisions as do their counterparts in for-profit firms. For this reason, it is often necessary for not-for-profit businesses (1) to delay new projects because of funding insufficiencies and (2) to use more than the theoretically optimal amount of debt because that is the only way that needed services can be financed. Although these actions may be unavoidable, managers must recognize that such strategies do increase costs. Project delays result in needed services not being provided on a timely basis, and using more debt than the optimal level pushes the firm beyond the point of the greatest net benefit of debt financing, which increases its capital costs. Therefore, if a not-for-profit firm is forced into a situation where it is using more than the optimal amount of debt financing, its managers should plan to reduce the level of debt as soon as circumstances permit.

The ability of not-for-profit businesses to obtain government grants, to attract private contributions, and to generate excess revenues plays an important role in establishing the firm's competitive position. A firm that has an adequate amount of fund capital can operate at its optimal capital structure and thus minimize capital costs. If sufficient fund capital is not available then a not-for-profit firm may be forced to rely too heavily on debt financing, resulting in higher capital costs. Also, its weakened financial condition may prevent it from acquiring capital equipment that would increase its efficiency and improve its services, thus hampering its overall operating performance.

Imagine two not-for-profit businesses that are similar in all respects except that one has more fund capital and can operate at its optimal capital structure, while the other has insufficient fund capital and thus must use more debt than its optimum. The financially strong firm has a significant competitive advantage because it can offer either more services at the same cost or matching services at a lower cost.

[10]According to the pecking order theory of capital structure, managers may not *want* to issue new stock but will do so if the investment opportunities are sufficiently attractive.

© 2014 Cengage Learning. All Rights Reserved. May not be scanned, copied or duplicated, or posted to a publicly accessible website, in whole or in part.

SELF-TEST

Is the trade-off theory of capital structure applicable to not-for-profit businesses? Explain.

What impact does the inability to issue common stock have on capital structure decisions within not-for-profit businesses?

30-5 Capital Budgeting Decisions

In this section, we discuss the effect of not-for-profit status on three elements of capital budgeting: (1) appropriate goals for project analysis, (2) cash flow estimation/decision methods, and (3) risk analysis.

30-5a The Goal of Project Analysis

The primary goal of a not-for-profit business is to provide some service to society, not to maximize shareholder wealth. In this situation, capital budgeting decisions must incorporate many factors besides the project's profitability. For example, noneconomic factors such as the well-being of the community must also be taken into account, and these factors may outweigh financial considerations.

Nevertheless, good decision making, designed to ensure the future viability of the organization, requires that the financial impact of each capital investment be fully recognized. Indeed, if a not-for-profit business takes on unprofitable projects that are not offset by profitable projects then the firm's financial condition will deteriorate. If this situation persists over time it could lead to bankruptcy and closure. Obviously, bankrupt businesses cannot meet community needs.

30-5b Cash Flow Estimation/Decision Methods

In general, the same project analysis techniques that are applicable to investor-owned firms are also applicable to not-for-profit businesses. However, two differences do exist. First, because some projects of not-for-profit businesses are expected to provide a social value in addition to a purely economic value, project analysis should consider social value along with financial, or cash flow, value. When social value is considered, the total net present value (TNPV) of a project can be expressed as follows:[11]

$$\text{TNPV} = \text{NPV} + \text{NPSV} \tag{30-1}$$

Here NPV is the standard net present value of the project's cash flow stream and NPSV is the net present social value of the project. The NPSV term clearly differentiates capital budgeting in not-for-profit businesses from that in investor-owned firms, and it represents the firm's assessment of the project's social value as opposed to its pure financial value as measured by NPV.

A project is deemed to be acceptable if its TNPV ≥ 0. Not all projects have social value, but if a project does, this value should be recognized in the decision process. Note that, for the firm's financial viability to be ensured, the sum of the NPVs of all projects initiated in

[11]For more information on the social value model, see John R. C. Wheeler and Jan P. Clement, "Capital Expenditure Decisions and the Role of the Not-For-Profit Hospital: An Application of the Social Goods Model," *Medical Care Review,* Winter 1990, pp. 467–486.

© 2014 Cengage Learning. All Rights Reserved. May not be scanned, copied or duplicated, or posted to a publicly accessible website, in whole or in part.

a planning period, plus the value of the unrestricted contributions received, must equal or exceed zero. If this restriction were not imposed then social value could eventually displace financial value, but this would not be a sustainable situation because a firm cannot continue to provide social value unless its financial integrity is maintained.

NPSV can be defined as follows:

$$\text{NPSV} = \sum_{t=1}^{n} \frac{(\text{Social value})_t}{(1 + r_s)^t} \tag{30-2}$$

Here, the social values of a project in every Year t, quantified in some manner, are discounted back to Year 0 and then summed. In essence, the suppliers of fund capital to a not-for-profit firm never receive a cash return on their investment. Instead, they receive a return on investment in the form of social dividends, such as charity care, medical research and education, and myriad other community services that for various reasons do not pay their own way. Services provided to patients at a price equal to or greater than the full cost of production are assumed not to create social value. Similarly, if governmental entities purchase care directly for beneficiaries of a program or support research, the resulting social value is attributed to the governmental entity and not to the provider of the services.

In estimating a project's NPSV (i.e., in evaluating Equation 30-2), it is necessary (1) to quantify the social value of the services provided by the project in each year and (2) to determine the discount rate to be applied to those services. First, consider how we might quantify the social value of services provided in the health care industry. When a project produces services to individuals who are willing and able to pay for those services, then the value of those services is captured by the amount the individuals actually pay. Thus, one approach to valuing the services provided to those who cannot pay, or to those who cannot pay the full amount, is to use the average net price paid by individuals who do pay. This approach has intuitive appeal, but there are four points that merit further discussion:

1. Price is a fair measure of value only if the payer has the capacity to judge the true value of the services provided. Many who are knowledgeable about the health care industry would argue that information asymmetries between the provider and the purchaser reduce the ability of the purchaser to judge true value.
2. Because most payments for health care services are made by third parties, price distortions may occur. For example, insurers might be willing to pay more for services than an individual would pay in the absence of insurance. Or the existence of monopsony power (e.g., by Medicare) might result in a net price that is less than individuals would actually be willing to pay.
3. The amount that an individual is willing to pay might be more or less than the amount a contributor or other fund supplier would be willing to pay for the same service.
4. Finally, there is a great deal of controversy over the true value of treatment in many health care situations. If we are entitled to whatever health care is available regardless of its cost and if we are not individually required to pay for the care (even though society, as a whole, is), then we may demand a level of care that is of questionable value. For example, should \$100,000 be spent to keep a comatose 87-year-old person alive for 15 more days? If the true social value of such an effort is zero, then it makes little sense to assign a \$100,000 value to the care just because that is its cost.

© 2014 Cengage Learning. All Rights Reserved. May not be scanned, copied or duplicated, or posted to a publicly accessible website, in whole or in part.

In spite of potential problems mentioned here, it still seems reasonable to assign a social value to many (but not all) health care services on the basis of the price that others are willing to pay for those services.[12]

The second element required to estimate a project's NPSV is the discount rate that is to be applied to its annual social value stream. As with the required rate of return on equity for not-for-profit businesses, there has been considerable controversy over the proper discount rate to apply to future social values. One way of looking at the issue is to recognize that fund capital can generate social value in two ways: The not-for-profit can use it to provide services itself, or it can invest the money and use the proceeds to purchase the services on the open market. For example, suppose one of the goals of a not-for-profit organization is to provide indigent medical care. First, the organization could use the funds to provide the services itself, using the money to build a hospital and provide indigent care, as well as provide care for which it receives payment. Alternatively, the not-for-profit organization could invest the funds in a portfolio of marketable securities and use the proceeds to purchase care from an existing hospital for those who cannot afford it. Because the second alternative exists, it is reasonable to argue that providers should require a return on the social value stream that approximates the return available on the equity investment in for-profit firms offering the same services.

The net present social value model formalizes the capital budgeting decision process applicable to not-for-profit businesses. Although few organizations attempt to quantify NPSV for all projects, not-for-profit businesses should at least subjectively consider the social value inherent in projects under consideration.

Another important difference between investor-owned and not-for-profit businesses involves the amount of capital available for investment. Standard capital budgeting procedures assume that firms can raise virtually unlimited amounts of capital to meet investment requirements. Presumably, as long as a firm is investing the funds in profitable (positive-NPV) projects, it should raise the debt and equity needed to fund the projects. However, not-for-profit businesses have limited access to capital—their fund capital is limited to retentions, contributions, and grants, and their debt capital is limited to the amount that can be supported by their fund capital and revenue base. Thus, not-for-profit businesses are likely to face periods in which the cost of desirable new projects will exceed the amount that can be financed, so not-for-profit businesses are often subject to capital rationing.

If capital rationing exists then, from a financial perspective, the firm should accept the set of capital projects that maximizes aggregate NPV without violating the capital constraint. This amounts to "getting the most bang for the buck," and it involves selecting projects that have the greatest positive impact on the firm's financial condition. However, in a not-for-profit setting, priority may be assigned to some low-profit or even negative-NPV projects. This is acceptable as long as these projects are offset by the selection of positive-NPV projects, which would prevent the low-profit, priority projects from eroding the firm's financial integrity.

---

[12]The issue of interpersonal values also arises: Is the value of a heart transplant the same to a 75-year-old in poor health as to a 16-year-old in otherwise good health? An even more controversial issue concerns the ability to pay. If someone can afford a Rolls Royce and wants to buy one, then she can, even though someone else may think the car is not worth the cost. To what extent is health care different from cars—or food, shelter, and clothes? Hence, to what extent should the health care industry be insulated from the kinds of economic incentives that operate in other industries? To date, our society has not come to grips with this issue, but with health care costs rising at a rate that will make them exceed the gross national product in fewer than 50 years, something must be done, and fairly soon.

© 2014 Cengage Learning. All Rights Reserved. May not be scanned, copied or duplicated, or posted to a publicly accessible website, in whole or in part.

30-5c Risk Analysis

There are three separate and distinct types of project risk: (1) stand-alone risk, which ignores portfolio effects and views the risk of a project as if it were held in isolation; (2) corporate risk, which views the risk of a project within the context of the firm's portfolio of projects; and (3) market risk, which views a project's risk from the perspective of a shareholder who holds a well-diversified portfolio of stocks. For investor-owned firms, market risk is the most relevant, although corporate risk should not be totally ignored.

For not-for-profit businesses, stand-alone risk would be relevant if a firm had only one project. In this situation, there would be no portfolio consequences, either at the firm or individual investor level, so risk could be measured by the variability of forecasted returns. However, most not-for-profit businesses offer myriad products or services, so they can be thought of as having a large number (hundreds or even thousands) of individual projects. For example, most not-for-profit health maintenance organizations (HMOs) offer health care services to a large number of diverse employee groups in numerous service areas. In this situation, the stand-alone risk of a project under consideration is not relevant because the project will not be held in isolation. Rather, the relevant risk of a new project is its corporate risk, which is the contribution of the project to the firm's overall risk as measured by the impact of the project on the variability of the firm's overall profitability.

To illustrate corporate risk in a not-for-profit setting, assume that Project P represents the expansion into a new service area by a not-for-profit HMO that has many existing projects. Table 30-1 lists the distributions of IRR for Project P and for the HMO as a whole.[13] The HMO's profitability (IRR), like that of Project P, is uncertain, and it depends on future economic events. Overall, the HMO's expected IRR is 7.0%, with a standard deviation of 2.0% and a coefficient of variation of 0.3. Thus, looking at either the standard deviation or the coefficient of variation (stand-alone risk measures), Project P is riskier than the HMO in the aggregate; that is, Project P is riskier than the HMO's average project.

TABLE 30-1

Estimated Return Distributions for Project P and the HMO

		IRR for Each Economic State	
State of Economy	**Probability of Occurrence**	**Project P**	**HMO**
Very poor	5%	2.5%	1.0%
Poor	20	5.0	6.0
Average	50	10.0	7.0
Good	20	15.0	8.0
Very good	5	17.5	13.0
Expected return		10.0%	7.0%
Standard deviation		4.0%	2.0%
Coefficient of variation		0.4	0.3
Correlation coefficient between P and HMO firm (ρ_{PF}) =		0.8	

© Cengage Learning 2014

[13]In practice, it is impossible to obtain the firm's IRR on its aggregate assets. However, a reasonable proxy is the firm's cash flow return on assets as measured by (Net income + Depreciation + Interest)/(Total assets).

© 2014 Cengage Learning. All Rights Reserved. May not be scanned, copied or duplicated, or posted to a publicly accessible website, in whole or in part.

However, the relevant risk of Project P is not its stand-alone risk but rather its contribution to the overall riskiness of the HMO, which is the project's corporate risk. Project P's corporate risk depends not only on its standard deviation but also on the correlation between the returns on Project P (the project's IRR distribution) and the returns on the HMO's average project (the firm's IRR distribution). If Project P's returns were negatively correlated with the returns on the HMO's other projects, then accepting it would reduce the riskiness of the HMO's aggregate returns, and the larger Project P's standard deviation, the greater the risk reduction. (An economic state resulting in a low return on the average project would produce a high return on Project P, and vice versa, so taking on the project would reduce the HMO's overall risk.) In this situation, Project P should be viewed as having low risk relative to the HMO's average project, in spite of its higher stand-alone risk.

In our actual case, however, Project P's returns are positively correlated with the HMO's aggregate returns ($\rho_{PF} = 0.8$), and the project has twice the standard deviation (4.0% vs. 2.0%) and a 33% larger coefficient of variation (0.4 vs. 0.3), so accepting it would increase the risk of the HMO's aggregate returns. The quantitative measure of corporate risk is a project's **corporate beta (b)**. The corporate beta is the slope of the **corporate characteristic line**, which is the regression line that results when the project's returns are plotted on the y-axis and the returns on the firm's total operations are plotted on the x-axis.

The slope (rise over run) of Project P's corporate characteristic line can be found as follows:

$$\text{Corporate } b_P = (\sigma_P/\sigma_F)\rho_{PF} \quad (30\text{-}3)$$

where

σ_P = Standard deviation of Project P's returns.

σ_F = Standard deviation of the firm's returns.

ρ_{PF} = Correlation coefficient between the returns on Project P and the firm's returns.

Thus,

$$\text{Corporate } b_P = (4.0\%/2.0\%)0.8 = 1.6$$

By definition, a company's average corporate beta is 1.0. Some individual projects would have relatively high betas and some would have relatively low betas, but the weighted average of all the individual projects' corporate betas would be 1.0. For a firm with many projects, a particular project's corporate beta indicates the relative amount of risk that the project contributes to corporate risk. For example, if a project's corporate beta is 2.0, then it contributes twice as much risk to the company as a project with a corporate beta of 1.0. A negative corporate beta, which occurs if a project's returns are negatively correlated with the firm's overall returns, indicates that the returns on the project move counter-cyclically to most of the firm's other projects. The addition of a negative-beta project to the firm's portfolio of projects would tend to reduce the firm's risk. However, negative-beta projects are hard to find because most projects are related to the firm's core line of business, so their returns are highly positively correlated. With a corporate beta of 1.6, Project P has significantly more corporate risk than the HMO's average project, and the HMO's WACC should be increased to reflect the differential risk prior to evaluating the project.

© 2014 Cengage Learning. All Rights Reserved. May not be scanned, copied or duplicated, or posted to a publicly accessible website, in whole or in part.

As with investor-owned firms, in most situations it is very difficult, if not impossible, to develop accurate quantitative assessments of projects' corporate risk. Therefore, managers are often left with only an assessment of a project's stand-alone risk plus a subjective notion about how it fits in with the firm's other operations. Generally, the project under consideration will be in the same line of business as the firm's (or division's) other projects; in this situation, stand-alone and corporate risk are highly correlated and so a project's stand-alone risk will be a good measure of its corporate risk. This suggests that managers of not-for-profit businesses can get a feel for the relevant risk of most projects by conducting scenario, simulation, and/or decision-tree analyses.

Ultimately, capital budgeting decisions in not-for-profit organizations require the blending of objective and subjective factors to reach a conclusion about a project's risk, social value, effects on debt capacity, profitability, and overall acceptability. The process is not precise, and often there is a temptation to ignore risk considerations because they are so nebulous. Nevertheless, a project's riskiness should be assessed and incorporated into the decision-making process.[14]

SELF-TEST

Why should not-for-profit businesses worry about the profitability of proposed projects?

Describe the net present social value model for making capital budgeting decisions. How might social value be measured?

Which are more likely to experience capital rationing: investor-owned businesses or not-for-profit businesses? Why?

What project risk measure is most relevant for investor-owned businesses? For not-for-profit businesses?

What is a corporate beta? How does a corporate beta differ from a market beta?

30-6 Long-Term Financing Decisions

Not-for-profit businesses have access to many of the same types of capital as investor-owned firms, but there are two major differences: (1) interest earned on debt issued by not-for-profit firms is exempt from taxes; (2) not-for-profit firms cannot issue equity (although they can solicit tax-exempt contributions) and all earnings (which are not subject to corporate income taxes) must be retained because not-for-profit firms cannot pay dividends.

30-6a Long-Term Debt Financing

With regard to debt financing, the major difference between investor-owned and not-for-profit businesses is that not-for-profit businesses can issue **tax-exempt**, or **municipal, bonds**, generally called **munis**.[15] There are several types of munis. For example, **general obligation bonds** are secured by the full faith and credit of a government unit (that is,

[14]Risk considerations are generally much more important than debt capacity considerations because a project's cost of capital is affected to a much greater degree by differential risk than by differential debt capacity.

[15]*Municipal bond* is the name given to long-term debt obligations issued by states and their political subdivisions, such as counties, cities, port authorities, toll road or hospital authorities, and so on. Short-term municipal notes are issued primarily to meet temporary cash needs, and long-term municipal bonds are typically used to finance capital projects.

© 2014 Cengage Learning. All Rights Reserved. May not be scanned, copied or duplicated, or posted to a publicly accessible website, in whole or in part.

they are backed by the full taxing authority of the issuer), whereas **special tax bonds** are secured by a specified tax, such as a tax on utility services. Of specific interest to not-for-profit businesses are **revenue bonds**, where the revenues derived from such projects as roads and bridges, airports, water and sewage systems, and not-for-profit health care facilities are pledged as security for the bonds. Most municipal bonds are sold in **serial form**, which means that a portion of the issue comes due periodically—generally every 6 months or every year—over the life of the issue. The shorter maturities are essentially equivalent to sinking fund payments on corporate bonds, and they help to ensure that the bonds are retired before the revenue-producing asset has been fully depreciated. Munis are typically issued in denominations or multiples of $5,000; most are tax exempt, but some that have been issued since 1986 are taxable to investors.

In contrast to corporate bonds, municipal issues are not required to be registered with the Securities and Exchange Commission (SEC). Information about municipal issues is found in each issue's **official statement**, which is prepared before the issue is brought to market. To assist buyers and sellers of municipal bonds in the secondary market, the SEC requires issuers of municipal bonds to provide an audited annual report on their current financial condition and to release, in a timely fashion, information that is "material" to the credit quality of their outstanding debt.

Whereas the majority of federal government and corporate bonds are held by institutions, close to 50% of all municipal bonds outstanding are held by individual investors. The primary attraction of most municipal bonds is their exemption from federal and state (in the state of issue) taxes. For example, the interest rate on an AAA-rated long-term corporate bond in July 2012 was 4.12%, while the rate on a triple-A muni was 3.49%. To an individual investor in the 40% federal-plus-state tax bracket, the muni bond's equivalent taxable yield is 3.49%/(1 − 0.40) = 3.49%/0.6 = 5.82%. It is easy to see why high-tax-bracket investors often prefer municipal bonds to corporates.[16]

To illustrate the use of municipal bonds by a not-for-profit hospital, consider the June 2012, $56 million issue by the Orange County (Florida) Health Facilities Authority. The authority is a public body created under Florida's Health Facilities Authorities Law, and it issues health facilities municipal revenue bonds and then gives the proceeds to the qualifying health care provider. For this particular bond issue, the provider was the South-Central Medical Center, a not-for-profit hospital, and the primary purpose of the issue was to raise funds to build and equip a children's hospital facility. The bonds were secured solely by the revenues of South-Central Medical Center, so the actual issuer—the Orange County Health Facilities Authority—had no responsibility regarding the interest or principal payments on the issue. The bonds were rated AAA, not on the basis of the financial strength of South-Central Medical Center but rather because the bonds were insured by the Municipal Bond Investors Assurance (MBIA) Corporation.[17] Table 30-2 shows the maturities and interest rates associated with the issue.

Note the following points regarding the South-Central Medical Center municipal bond issue:

1. The issue is a serial issue; that is, the $56,000,000 in bonds is composed of 13 series, or individual issues, with maturities ranging from about 2 years to 30 years.
2. Because the yield curve was normal, or upward sloping, at the time of issue, the interest rates increase as the series' maturities increase.

[16]For more information on tax-exempt financing by not-for-profit firms, see Bradley M. Odegard, "Tax-Exempt Financing under the Tax Reform Act of 1986," *Topics in Health Care Financing*, Summer 1988, pp. 35–45. Also see Kenneth Kaufman and Mark L. Hall, *The Capital Management of Health Care Organizations* (Ann Arbor, MI: Health Administration Press, 1990), Chapter 5.

[17]Municipal bond insurance, which is called **credit enhancement**, will be discussed in more detail later in the section.

© 2014 Cengage Learning. All Rights Reserved. May not be scanned, copied or duplicated, or posted to a publicly accessible website, in whole or in part.

TABLE 30-2
South-Central Medical Center Municipal Bond Issue: Maturities, Amounts, and Interest Rates

Maturity[a]	Amount	Interest Rate
2014	$ 705,000	3.35%
2015	740,000	3.45
2016	785,000	3.60
2017	825,000	3.75
2018	880,000	3.90
2019	925,000	4.00
2020	985,000	4.10
2021	1,050,000	4.20
2022	1,115,000	4.30
2023	1,190,000	4.40
2027	5,590,000	4.80
2032	9,435,000	4.90
2042	31,775,000	5.00
	$56,000,000	

[a]All serial issues mature on June 1 of the listed year.

© Cengage Learning 2014

3. The bonds that mature in 2027, 2032, and 2042 are called "term bonds," and they have sinking fund provisions that require the hospital to place a specified dollar amount with a trustee each year to ensure that funds are available to retire the issues as they become due. The trustee may either buy up the relevant bonds in the open market or call the bonds at par for redemption. If interest rates have fallen and the bonds sell at a premium, the trustee will call the bonds; but if rates have risen, then the trustee will make open market purchases.
4. Although it is not shown in the table, South-Central's **debt service requirements**—the total amount of principal and interest that it must pay on the issue—are relatively constant over time, at about $3.5 million per year. In effect, the debt payments are spread relatively evenly over time. The purpose of structuring the series in this way is to match the maturity of the asset with the maturities of the bonds. Think about it this way: The children's hospital has a life of about 30 years. During this time, it will be generating revenues more or less evenly, and its value will decline more or less evenly. Thus, the issuer has structured the debt series so that the debt service requirements can be met by the revenues associated with the children's hospital. At the end of 30 years, the debt will be paid off and South-Central will probably be planning for a replacement facility to be funded, at least in part, by a new bond issue.

One feature unique to municipal bonds is **credit enhancement**, or **bond insurance**, which is a relatively recent development used for upgrading an issue's rating to AAA. Credit enhancement is offered by several credit insurers; the two largest are the Municipal Bond Investors Assurance (MBIA) Corporation and AMBAC Indemnity Corporation. Currently, about 40% of all new municipal issues carry bond insurance.

© 2014 Cengage Learning. All Rights Reserved. May not be scanned, copied or duplicated, or posted to a publicly accessible website, in whole or in part.

Here is how credit enhancement works. Regardless of the inherent credit rating of the issuer, the bond insurance company guarantees that bondholders will receive the promised interest and principal payments. Thus, bond insurance protects investors against default by the issuer. Because the insurer gives its guarantee that payments will be made, the bond carries the credit rating of the insurance company, not of the issuer. For example, in our previous discussion on the bonds issued by the Orange County Health Facilities Authority on behalf of South-Central Medical Center, we noted that the bonds were rated AAA because of MBIA insurance. The hospital itself has an A rating; hence, bonds issued without credit enhancement would be rated A. The guarantee by MBIA resulted in the AAA rating.

Credit enhancement gives the issuer access to the lowest possible interest rate, but not without a cost—bond insurers typically charge an upfront fee of about 0.7 to 1.0% of the total debt service over the life of the bond. Of course, the lower the hospital's inherent credit rating, the higher the cost of bond insurance. Additionally, bond insurers typically will not insure issues that would have a rating below A if uninsured.

To illustrate credit enhancement, again consider the South-Central Medical Center bonds. The total debt service (principal and interest) on the bonds amounts to roughly \$120 million on the \$56 million issue (interest adds up quickly). Assuming an insurance cost of 1.0%, the fee for the insurance would be \$1.2 million. Is it worth it? South-Central Medical Center apparently thought so. To perform an analysis, simply discount the interest savings that result from the AAA rating (as opposed to the uninsured A rating) back to the present and then compare this present value with the insurance cost. If the present value of the savings exceeds the cost of the bond insurance, then insurance should be purchased.

30-6b Equity (Fund) Financing

Investor-owned firms have two sources of equity financing: retained earnings and proceeds from new stock offerings. Not-for-profit businesses can, and do, retain earnings, but they cannot sell stock to raise equity capital. They can, however, raise equity capital through **charitable contributions**. Individuals as well as firms are motivated to contribute to not-for-profit businesses for a variety of reasons, including concern for the well-being of others, the recognition that often accompanies large contributions, and tax deductibility.

To illustrate, consider not-for-profit hospitals, most of which received their initial, start-up equity capital from religious, educational, or governmental entities (some hospitals also receive ongoing funding from these sources). Since the 1970s, these sources have provided a much smaller proportion of hospital funding, forcing many not-for-profit hospitals to rely more on retained earnings and charitable contributions. Further, federal programs—such as the Hill-Burton Act, which provided large amounts of funds for hospital expansion following World War II—have been discontinued.

On the surface, it appears that investor-owned firms have a significant advantage in raising equity capital because new common stock can in theory be issued at any time and in any amount. Conversely, charitable contributions are much less reliable—pledges are not always collected, so funds that were counted on may not be available. Furthermore, the planning, solicitation, and collection periods can take years. Also, whereas the proceeds of new stock offerings may be used for any purpose, charitable contributions are often **restricted**, which means that they can be used only for a designated purpose. Note, however, that managers of investor-owned firms do not have complete freedom to raise capital in the equity markets—if

© 2014 Cengage Learning. All Rights Reserved. May not be scanned, copied or duplicated, or posted to a publicly accessible website, in whole or in part.

market conditions are poor and the stock is selling at a low price, then a new stock issue can be harmful to the firm's current stockholders. Also, as we discussed in Chapter 15, a new stock offering may be viewed by investors as a signal by management that the firm's stock is overvalued, so new stock issues tend to have a negative effect on the firm's stock price, which discourages their use.

SELF-TEST

Define the following terms:

(1) Municipal bonds
(2) Revenue bonds
(3) Serial bonds
(4) Official statement
(5) Debt service requirements
(6) Credit enhancement

Do municipal financing authorities that issue revenue bonds generally have any obligations regarding the payment of interest and principal? Explain.

How could a not-for-profit firm's financial manager evaluate whether or not to buy bond insurance?

30-7 Financial Analysis, Planning, and Forecasting

The general procedures for financial analysis, planning, and forecasting discussed in Chapters 12 and 13 pertain to both investor-owned and not-for-profit businesses. The primary difference is the accounting procedures used, which affects the "look" of the financial statements.

For illustrative purposes, consider the health care industry again. As in all industries, financial reporting in health care follows a set of standards (established by the accounting profession) called **generally accepted accounting principles (GAAP)**.[18] The two primary organizations that promulgate standards for the health care industry are the **Financial Accounting Standards Board (FASB)**, which deals with issues pertaining to private organizations, and the **Government Accounting Standards Board (GASB)**, which deals with issues related to governmental entities. Generally, the principles promulgated by FASB and GASB relate to issues that are relevant to most industries, while industry-specific issues are addressed by the various industry committees of the American Institute of Certified Public Accountants (AICPA). In 1972, the AICPA Health Care Institutions Committee issued the first of six editions of the *Hospital Audit Guide*, which became the bible for those preparing hospital financial statements. In 1990 the committee, which is

[18]Publicly traded companies in the United States will eventually have to adhere to a set of standards that is more consistent with the standards that companies in other countries use. These standards, called International Financial Reporting Standards (IFRS), differ from U.S. GAAP standards; see Chapter 2 for a discussion of GAAP versus IFRS. The current schedule calls for IFRS adoption by 2015 for large companies, but not-for-profits will likely migrate from U.S. GAAP to some form of IFRS standard over several years following the adoption by for-profit entities. For more information on the various organizations involved in setting accounting principles for the health care industry, see Woodrin Grossman and William Warshauer, Jr., "An Overview of the Standard Setting Process," *Topics in Health Care Financing,* Summer 1990, pp. 1–8.

© 2014 Cengage Learning. All Rights Reserved. May not be scanned, copied or duplicated, or posted to a publicly accessible website, in whole or in part.

now called the Health Care Committee, published an entirely new guide entitled *Audits of Providers of Health Care Services*, which superseded the old guides. Here are some of the more important provisions of the guide.[19]

1. The guide applies to all private organizations providing health care services to individuals. Thus, it applies to both investor-owned and private not-for-profit organizations such as hospitals, nursing homes, managed care plans, home health agencies, medical group practices, and clinics.[20]
2. The guide contains complete sets of sample financial statements, including footnote disclosures, for the major types of providers.
3. Prior to the issuance of the guide, providers reported revenues on the income statement on the basis of charges (gross revenues), whether or not the charges were expected to be collected. Then, the various deductions from charges—such as contractual allowances (discounts), bad-debt losses, and charity care—were subtracted from gross revenue. The guide prescribes that only net revenue should be shown on the income statement because charges not billed or not expected to be collected do not represent expected revenue to the provider. Bad-debt losses constitute an operating expense and continue to be shown directly on the income statement, but contractual allowances and charity care are now reported in the footnotes.[21]
4. The guide blurs the distinction between operating and nonoperating cash flows. Essentially, **operating revenues and expenses** occur because of an organization's central mission and operations. On the other hand, **nonoperating gains and losses** result from transactions that are incidental or peripheral to the organization's mission. Considerable latitude exists in what an organization defines as its central mission and operations, but most organizations classify most revenues and expenses as operating. In general, only contributions, investment income, and gains and losses on financial transactions such as bond refundings are classified as nonoperating.
5. The guide validates cash flows as the best measure of transactions. Thus, the statement of cash flows has become a standard financial statement for not-for-profit health care providers.
6. Finally, the guide contains detailed guidance on issues that are unique to the health care industry. Examples include the reporting of third-party payments from insurance companies such as Blue Cross/Blue Shield and malpractice insurance.

Tables 30-3 and 30-4 show the 2012 and 2013 income statements (also called statements of revenues and expenses) and balance sheets for a typical not-for-profit hospital. Three points about the statements are worth noting. First, the formats for the statements are similar to those of investor-owned firms. Second, the hospital had an excess of revenues over expenses (or net income) of $8,572,000 in 2013. Of course, being a not-for-profit firm, the hospital paid no taxes or dividends, so it retained all of this

[19]For a more detailed review of the audit guide, see Robert G. Colbert, "The New Health Care Audit and Accounting Guide," *Topics in Health Care Financing*, Summer 1990, pp. 14–23; and J. William Tillett and William R. Titera, "What AICPA Audit Guide Revisions Mean for Providers," *Healthcare Financial Management*, July 1990, pp. 52–62.

[20]Most governmental providers will also have to follow the guide, but GASB statements will have precedence over the guide when conflicts occur.

[21]If a provider does not expect to collect for services rendered, then the care is classified as charity care and does not constitute revenue. However, if a provider expects to collect for services rendered but fails to do so, the expected revenue becomes a bad-debt loss.

© 2014 Cengage Learning. All Rights Reserved. May not be scanned, copied or duplicated, or posted to a publicly accessible website, in whole or in part.

TABLE 30-3
Income Statement for a Typical Not-for-Profit Hospital: Years Ending December 31 (Thousands of Dollars)

	2013	2012
Net patient services revenue	$108,600	$ 97,393
Other operating revenue	6,205	9,364
Total operating revenue	$114,805	$106,757
Operating expenses		
Nursing services	$ 58,285	$ 56,752
Dietary services	5,424	4,718
General services	13,198	11,655
Administrative services	11,427	11,585
Employee health and welfare	10,250	10,705
Provision for uncollectibles	3,328	3,469
Provision for malpractice	1,320	1,204
Depreciation	4,130	4,025
Interest expense	1,542	1,521
Total operating expenses	$108,904	$105,634
Income from operations	$ 5,901	$ 1,123
Contributions and grants	$ 2,253	$ 874
Investment income	418	398
Nonoperating gain (loss)	$ 2,671	$ 1,272
Excess of revenues over expenses	$ 8,572	$ 2,395

© Cengage Learning 2014

income. Third, the claims against assets are of two types: liabilities (money the company owes) and fund capital. Fund capital is any excess of assets relative to liabilities. Thus, for 2013:

$$\begin{aligned}\text{Fund capital} &= \text{Assets} - \text{All liabilities}\\ &= \$151{,}278{,}000 - (\$13{,}332{,}000 + \$30{,}582{,}000)\\ &= \$107{,}364{,}000\end{aligned}$$

Fund capital is the not-for-profit equivalent of equity capital and serves essentially the same function. A balance sheet fund account for a not-for-profit business is built up over time primarily by retentions and contributions but is reduced by operating losses.

SELF-TEST

What organizations prescribe standards for reporting by not-for-profit businesses?

How do the financial statements of investor-owned and not-for-profit businesses differ?

© 2014 Cengage Learning. All Rights Reserved. May not be scanned, copied or duplicated, or posted to a publicly accessible website, in whole or in part.

TABLE 30-4
Balance Sheet for a Typical Not-for-Profit Hospital: Years Ending December 31 (Thousands of Dollars)

	2013	2012
Cash and securities	$ 6,263	$ 5,095
Accounts receivable	21,840	20,738
Inventories	3,177	2,982
Total current assets	$ 31,280	$ 28,815
Gross plant and equipment	$145,158	$140,865
Accumulated depreciation	25,160	21,030
Net plant and equipment	$119,998	$119,835
Total assets	$151,278	$148,650
Accounts payable	$ 4,707	$ 5,145
Accrued expenses	5,650	5,421
Notes payable	825	4,237
Current portion of long-term debt	2,150	2,000
Total current liabilities	$ 13,332	$ 16,803
Long-term debt	$ 28,750	$ 30,900
Capital lease obligations	1,832	2,155
Total long-term liabilities	$ 30,582	$ 33,055
Fund capital	$107,364	$ 98,792
Total liabilities and funds	$151,278	$148,650

© Cengage Learning 2014

SUMMARY

This Web chapter focuses on financial management within not-for-profit businesses. The key concepts covered are listed below.

- Although most finance graduates will go to work for investor-owned firms, many financial management professionals work for or closely with **not-for-profit organizations**, which range from government agencies such as school districts and colleges to charities such as the United Way and the American Heart Association.
- If an organization meets a set of stringent requirements, it can qualify for **tax-exempt status**. Such organizations, which must be incorporated, are called **not-for-profit corporations**. One type of not-for-profit organization is the **not-for-profit business**, which sells goods and/or services to the public but has not-for-profit status.
- The goal of a not-for-profit business is typically stated in terms of some **mission** rather than shareholder wealth maximization.
- Not-for-profit businesses raise the equivalent of equity capital, which is called **fund capital**, in three ways: (1) by earning profits, which by law are retained within the business, (2) by receiving grants from governmental entities, and (3) by receiving contributions from individuals and companies.
- In not-for-profit businesses, the **weighted average cost of capital** is developed in the same way as in investor-owned firms. Although there is no direct tax benefit to the

© 2014 Cengage Learning. All Rights Reserved. May not be scanned, copied or duplicated, or posted to a publicly accessible website, in whole or in part.

issuer associated with debt financing, there is a benefit to investors because interest received is often tax exempt; thus, the net cost of debt is similar for investor-owned and not-for-profit businesses.

- For cost of capital purposes, fund capital has an **opportunity cost** that is roughly equal to the cost of equity of similar investor-owned firms.
- The **trade-off theory of capital structure** generally applies to not-for-profit firms, but such firms do not have as much financial flexibility as investor-owned firms because not-for-profit firms cannot issue new common stock.
- The **social value** version of the net present value model recognizes that not-for-profit businesses should value social contributions as well as cash flows.
- In general, the relevant capital budgeting risk for not-for-profit businesses is **corporate risk** rather than market risk. Corporate risk is measured by a project's **corporate beta**.
- Many not-for-profit organizations can raise funds in the **municipal bond** market.
- **Credit enhancement** upgrades the rating of a municipal bond issue to that of the insurer. However, issuers must pay a fee to the insurer to obtain credit enhancement.
- With minor exceptions, the financial statement formats of investor-owned and not-for-profit businesses are the same.
- Short-term financial management is generally unaffected by the ownership type.

QUESTIONS

(30-1) What is the major difference in ownership structure between investor-owned and not-for-profit businesses?

(30-2) Does the asymmetric information theory of capital structure apply to not-for-profit businesses? Explain.

(30-3) Does a not-for-profit firm's marginal cost of capital schedule have a retained earnings break point? Explain. (*Hint:* See Chapter 9 for a discussion of the marginal cost of capital faced by for-profit firms.)

(30-4) Assume that a not-for-profit firm does not have access to tax-exempt (municipal) debt and thus gains no benefits from the use of debt financing.

a. What would be the firm's optimal capital structure according to the cost–benefit trade-off theory?
b. Is it likely that the firm would be able to operate at its theoretically optimal structure?

(30-5) Describe how social value can be incorporated into the NPV decision model. Would not-for-profit firms normally try to quantify net present social value, or would they merely treat it as a qualitative factor?

(30-6) Why is corporate risk the most relevant project risk measure for not-for-profit businesses?

(30-7) Suppose that all buyers and sellers in a market have easy access to the same information. In that case, would firms gain any cost advantage by purchasing bond insurance (credit enhancement)?

MINI CASE

Sandra McCloud, a finance major in her last term of college, is currently scheduling her placement interviews through the university's career resource center. Her list of companies is typical of most finance majors: several commercial banks, a few industrial firms,

© 2014 Cengage Learning. All Rights Reserved. May not be scanned, copied or duplicated, or posted to a publicly accessible website, in whole or in part.

and one brokerage house. However, she noticed that a representative of a not-for-profit hospital is scheduling interviews next week, and the position—that of financial analyst—appears to be exactly what Sandra has in mind. Sandra wants to sign up for an interview, but she is concerned that she knows nothing about not-for-profit organizations and how they differ from the investor-owned firms she has studied in her finance classes. In spite of her worries, Sandra scheduled an appointment with the hospital representative, and she now wants to learn more about not-for-profit businesses before the interview.

To begin the learning process, Sandra drew up the following set of questions. See if you can help her answer them.

a. First, consider some basic background information concerning the differences between not-for-profit organizations and investor-owned firms.
   (1) What are the key features of investor-owned firms? How do a firm's owners exercise control?
   (2) What is a not-for-profit corporation? What are the major control differences between investor-owned and not-for-profit businesses?
   (3) How do goals differ between investor-owned and not-for-profit businesses?

b. Now consider the cost of capital estimation process.
   (1) Is the weighted average cost of capital (WACC) relevant to not-for-profit businesses?
   (2) Is there any difference between the WACC formula for investor-owned firms and that for not-for-profit businesses?
   (3) What is fund capital? How is the cost of fund capital estimated?

c. Just as in investor-owned firms, not-for-profit businesses use a mix of debt and equity (fund) financing.
   (1) Is the trade-off theory of capital structure applicable to not-for-profit businesses? What about the asymmetric information theory?
   (2) What problems do not-for-profit businesses encounter when they attempt to implement the trade-off theory?

d. Consider the following questions relating to capital budgeting decisions.
   (1) Why is capital budgeting important to not-for-profit businesses?
   (2) What is social value? How can the net present value method be modified to include the social value of proposed projects?
   (3) Which of the three project risk measures—stand-alone, corporate, and market—is relevant to not-for-profit businesses?
   (4) What is a corporate beta? How does it differ from a market beta?
   (5) In general, how is project risk actually measured within not-for-profit businesses? How is project risk incorporated into the decision process?

e. Not-for-profit businesses have access to many of the same long-term financing sources as investor-owned firms.
   (1) What are municipal bonds? How do not-for-profit health care businesses access the municipal bond market?
   (2) What is credit enhancement, and what effect does it have on debt costs?
   (3) What are a not-for-profit business's sources of fund capital?
   (4) What effect does the inability to issue common stock have on a not-for-profit business's capital structure and capital budgeting decisions?

f. What unique problems do not-for-profit businesses encounter in financial analysis and planning? What about short-term financial management?

© 2014 Cengage Learning. All Rights Reserved. May not be scanned, copied or duplicated, or posted to a publicly accessible website, in whole or in part.

© lulu/fotolia.com

Appendix B

Answers to End-of-Chapter Problems

We present here some intermediate steps and final answers to selected end-of-chapter problems. Please note that your answer may differ slightly from ours because of rounding differences. Also, although we hope not, some of the problems may have more than one correct solution, depending on what assumptions are made when working the problem. Finally, many of the problems involve some verbal discussion as well as numerical calculations; this verbal material is not presented here.

2-1 5.8%.

2-2 25%.

2-3 $3,000,000.

2-4 $2,000,000.

2-5 $3,600,000.

2-6 $25,000,000.

2-7 Tax = $107,855;
NI = $222,145;
Marginal tax rate = 39%;
Average tax rate = 33.8%.

2-8 a. Tax = $3,575,000.
b. Tax = $350,000.
c. Tax = $105,000.

2-9 AT&T bond = 4.875%;
AT&T preferred stock =5.37%;
Florida bond = 5%.

2-10 NI = $450,000;
NCF = $650,000.

2-11 a. $2,400,000.
b. NI = $0;
NCF = $3,000,000.
c. NI = $1,350,000;
NCF = $2,100,000.

2-12 a. NOPAT = $756 million.
b. $NOWC_{12}$ = $3.0 billion;
$NOWC_{13}$ = $3.3 billion.
c. Op. $capital_{12}$ = $6.5 billion;
Op. $capital_{13}$ = $7.15 billion.
d. FCF = $106 million.
e. ROIC = 10.57%.
f. Answers in millions:
A-T int. = $72.
Inc. in debt = −$284.
Div. = $220.
Rep. stock = $88.
Purch. ST inv. = $10.

2-13 Refund = $120,000.
Future taxes = $0; $0;
$40,000; $60,000; $60,000.

3-1 AR = $400,000.

3-2 Debt ratio = 15%.

3-3 M/B = 10.

3-4 P/E = 16.0.

3-5 ROE = 12%.

3-6 S/TA = 2.4; TA/E = 1.67.

3-7 CL = $2,000,000;
Inv = $1,000,000.

3-8 Net profit margin = 3.33%;
L/A = 42.86%.
Debt ratio = 21.43%.

3-9 $262,500; 1.19.

3-10 TIE = 4.13.

3-11 Sales = $600,000;
COGS = $450,000;
Cash = $28,000;
AR = $60,000;

Inv. = $120,000;
FA = $192,000.
AP = $110,000;
Common stock = $140,000;

3-12 Sales = $2,580,000.

3-13 a. Current ratio = 2.01;
DSO = 77 days;
Inv TO = 5.67;
FA turnover = 5.56;
TA turnover = 1.75;
PM = 1.5%;
ROA = 2.6%;
ROE = 6.4%;
Debt ratio = 33%.
L/TA = 59%.

3-14 Quick ratio = 0.8;
CA/CL = 2.3;
Inv. TO = 4.2;
DSO = 37 days;
FA TO = 10.0;
TA TO = 2.3;
ROA = 5.9%;
ROE = 13.1%;
PM = 2.5%;
Debt ratio = 27.5%.
L/TA = 54.8%.
PE ratio = 5.0;
P/CF ratio = 2.0;
M/B ratio = 0.65.

4-1 FV_5 = $16,105.10.

4-2 PV = $1,292.10.

4-3 I/YR = 8.01%.

4-4 N = 11.01 years.

4-5 N = 11 years.

4-6 FVA_5 = $1,725.22;
$FVA_{5\ Due}$ = $1,845.99.

4-7 PV = $923.98;
FV = $1,466.24.

4-8 PMT = $444.89;
EAR = 12.6825%.

4-9 a. $530.
b. $561.80.
c. $471.70.
d. $445.00.

4-10 a. $895.42.
b. $1,552.92.
c. $279.20.
d. $160.99.

4-11 a. N = 10.24 ≈ 10 years.
b. N = 7.27 ≈ 7 years.
c. N = 4.19 ≈ 4 years.
d. N = 1.00 ≈ 1 year.

4-12 a. $6,374.97.
b. $1,105.13.
c. $2,000.00.
d. (1) $7,012.46.
(2) $1,160.38.
(3) $2,000.00.

4-13 a. $2,457.83.
b. $865.90.
c. $2,000.00.
d. (1) $2,703.61.
(2) $909.19.
(3) $2,000.00.

4-14 a. PV_A = $1,251.25.
PV_B = $1,300.32.
b. PV_A = $1,600.
PV_B = $1,600.

4-15 a. 7%.
b. 7%.
c. 9%.
d. 15%.

4-16 a. $881.17.
b. $895.42.
c. $903.06.
d. $908.35.

4-17 a. $279.20.
b. $276.84.
c. $443.72.

4-18 a. $5,272.32.
b. $5,374.07.

4-19 a. Universal, EAR = 7%;
Regional, EAR = 6.14%.

4-20 a. PMT = $6,594.94;
$Interest_1$ = $2,500;
$Interest_2$ = $2,090.51.
b. $13,189.87.
c. $8,137.27.

4-21 a. I = 14.87% ≈ 15%.

4-22 I = 7.18%.

4-23 I = 9%.

4-24 a. $33,872.11.
b. (1) $26,243.16.
(2) $0.

4-25 N = 14.77 ≈ 15 years.

4-26 6 years; $1,106.01.

4-27 (1) $1,428.57.
(2) $714.29.

4-28 $893.26.

4-29 $984.88.

4-30 57.18%.

4-31 a. $1,432.02.
b. $93.07.

4-32 I_{NOM} = 15.19%.

4-33 PMT = $36,949.61.

4-34 First PMT = $9,736.96.

5-1 $928.39.

5-2 12.48%.

5-3 8.55%.

5-4 7%; 7.33%.

5-5 2.5%.

5-6 0.3%.

5-7 $1,085.80.

5-8 YTM = 6.62%; YTC = 6.49%.

5-9 a. 5%: V_L = $1,518.98;
V_S = $1,047.62.
8%: V_L = $1,171.19;
V_S = $1,018.52.
12%: V_L = $863.78;
V_S = $982.14.

5-10 a. YTM at $829 = 13.98%;
YTM at $1,104 = 6.50%.

5-11 14.82%.

5-12 a. 10.37%.
b. 10.91%.
c. −0.54%.
d. 10.15%.

5-13 8.65%.

5-14 10.78%.

5-15 YTC = 6.47%.

5-16 a. 10-year, 10% coupon = 6.75%;
10-year zero = 9.75%;
5-year zero = 4.76%;
30-year zero = 32.19%;
$100 perpetuity = 14.29%.

5-17 C_0 = $1,012.79; Z_0 = $693.04;
C_1 = $1,010.02; Z_1 = $759.57;
C_2 = $1,006.98; Z_2 = $832.49;
C_3 = $1,003.65; Z_3 = $912.41;
C_4 = $1,000.00; Z_4 = $1,000.00.

5-18 5.8%.

5-19 1.5%.

5-20 6.0%.

5-21 a. $1,251.22.
b. $898.94.

5-22 a. 8.02%.
b. 7.59%.

5-23 a. r_1 = 9.20%; r_5 = 7.20%.

6-1 b = 1.08.

6-2 r_s = 10.40%.

6-3 r_M = 12%; r_{sB} = 16.9%.

6-4 15.96%.

6-5 $\hat{r}$ = 11.40%; σ = 26.69%.

6-6 a. $\hat{r}_M$ = 13.5%; $\hat{r}_j$ = 11.6%.
b. σ_M = 3.85%; σ_j = 6.22%.

6-7 a. b_A = 1.40.
b. r_A = 15%.

6-8 a. r_i = 14.8%.
b. (1) r_M = 13%; r_i = 15.8%.
(2) r_M = 11%; r_i = 13.8%.
c. (1) r_i = 17.6%.
(2) r_i = 13.4%.

6-9 b_N = 1.25.

6-10 b_p = 0.7625; r_p = 12.1%.

6-11 b_N = 1.1250.

6-12 4.5%.

6-13 a. $\bar{r}_A$ = 11.80%; $\bar{r}_B$ = 11.80%.
b. $\bar{r}_p$ = 11.80%
c. σ_A = 25.3%; σ_B = 24.3%;
σ_p = 16.3%.

6-14 a. $b_X = 1.3471$; $b_Y = 0.6508$.
b. $r_X = 12.7355\%$; $r_Y = 9.254\%$.
c. $r_p = 12.04\%$.

7-1 $D_1 = \$1.5750$; $D_3 = \$1.7364$; $D_5 = \$2.1011$.

7-2 $\hat{P}_0 = \$21.43$.

7-3 $\hat{P}_1 = \$24.20$; $\hat{r}_s = 16.00\%$.

7-4 $r_{ps} = 10\%$.

7-5 $50.50.

7-6 $V_{op} = \$6,000,000$.

7-7 V_{op} at 2016 = $15,000 (Million of $).

7-8 $g = 9\%$.

7-9 $\hat{P}_3 = \$43.08$.

7-10 a. 11.67%.
b. 8.75%.
c. 7.00%.
d. 5.00%.

7-11 $32.00.

7-12 $25.03.

7-13 $\hat{P}_0 = \$10.76$.

7-14 a. $125.
b. $83.33.

7-15 a. 7%.
b. 5%.
c. 12%.

7-16 a. (1) $15.83.
(2) $23.08.
(3) $39.38.
(4) $110.00.
b. (1) Undefined.

7-17 a. $HV_2 = \$2,700,000$.
b. $2,303,571.43.

7-18 a. $713.33 million.
b. $527.89 million.
c. $43.79.

7-19 a. $1.79
b. PV = $3.97.
c. $18.74.
d. $22.71.

7-20 a. $2.01, $2.31, $2.66, $3.06, $3.52.
b. $\hat{P}_0 = \$39.42$.
c. $D_1/P_0 = 5.10\%$;
$D_6/P_5 = 7.00\%$.

7-21 $\hat{P}_0 = \$78.35$.

8-1 $5; $2.

8-2 $27.00; $37.00.

8-3 $1.67.

8-4 $3.70.

8-5 $1.90.

8-6 $2.39.

8-7 $1.91.

9-1 a. 13%.
b. 10.4%.
c. 8.45%.

9-2 5.2%.

9-3 9%.

9-4 5.41%.

9-5 13.33%.

9-6 10.4%.

9-7 9.17%.

9-8 13%.

9-9 7.2%.

9-10 a. 16.3%.
b. 15.4%.
c. 16%.

9-11 a. 8%.
b. $2.81.
c. 15.81%.

9-12 a. $g = 3\%$.
b. $EPS_1 = \$5.562$.

9-13 16.1%.

9-14 $(1 - T)r_d = 5.57\%$.

9-15 a. $15,000,000.
b. 8.4%.

9-16 Short-term debt = 11.14%;
Long-term debt = 22.03%;
Common equity = 66.83%.

9-17 w_{std} = 0%; w_d = 20%;
w_{ps} = 4%; w_s = 76%;
r_d(After-tax) = 7.2%;
r_{ps} = 11.6%; $r_s \approx$ 17.5%.

10-1 NPV = $2,409.77.

10-2 IRR = 12.84%.

10-3 MIRR = 11.93%.

10-4 PI = 1.06.

10-5 4.44 years.

10-6 6.44 years.

10-7 a. 5%: NPV_A = $16,108,952;
NPV_B = $18,300,939.
10%: NPV_A = $12,836,213;
NPV_B = $15,954,170.
15%: NPV_A = $10,059,587;
NPV_B = $13,897,838.
b. IRR_A = 43.97%; IRR_B = 82.03%

10-8 NPV_T = $409; IRR_T = 15%;
$MIRR_T$ = 14.54%; Accept.
NPV_P = $3,318; IRR_P = 20%;
$MIRR_P$ = 17.19%; Accept.

10-9 NPV_E = $3,861; IRR_E = 18%;
NPV_G = $3,057; IRR_G = 18%;
Purchase electric-powered forklift because it has a higher NPV.

10-10 NPV_S = $814.33;
NPV_L = $1,675.34;
IRR_S = 15.24%;
IRR_L = 14.67%;
$MIRR_S$ = 13.77%;
$MIRR_L$ = 13.46%;
PI_S = 1.081; PI_L = 1.067.

10-11 $MIRR_X$ = 17.49%;
$MIRR_Y$ = 18.39%.

10-12 a. NPV = $136,578;
IRR = 19.22%.

10-13 b. IRR_A = 20.7%;
IRR_B = 25.8%.
c. 10%: NPV_A = $478.83;
NPV_B = $372.37.
17%: NPV_A = $133.76;
NPV_B = $173.70.
d. (1) $MIRR_A$ = 14.91%;
$MIRR_B$ = 17.35%.
(2) $MIRR_A$ = 18.76%;
$MIRR_B$ = 21.03%.
e. Crossover rate = 14.76%.

10-14 a. $0; −$10,250,000;
$1,750,000.
b. 16.07%.

10-15 a. NPV_A = $18,108,510;
NPV_B = $13,946,117;
IRR_A = 15.03%; IRR_B = 22.26%.
b. NPV_Δ = $4,162,393;
IRR_Δ = 11.71%.

10-16 Extended NPV_A = $12.76 million;
Extended NPV_B = $9.26 million.
EAA_A = $2.26 million;
EAA_B = $1.64 million.

10-17 Extended NPV_A = $4.51 million.
EAA_A = $0.85 million;
EAA_B = $0.69 million.

10-18 NPV of 360-6 = $22,256.
Extended NPV of 190-3 = $20,070.
EAA of 360-6 = $5,723.30;
EAA of 190-3 = $5,161.02.

10-19 d. 7.61%; 15.58%.

10-20 a. Undefined.
b. NPV_C = −$911,067;
NPV_F = −$838,834.

10-21 a. A = 2.67 years;
B = 1.5 years.
b. A = 3.07 years;
B = 1.825 years.
c. NPV_A = $12,739,908; IRR_A = 27.27%;
NPV_B = $11,554,880; IRR_B = 36.15%;
Choose both.
d. NPV_A = $18,243,813;
NPV_B = $14,964,829;
Choose A.
e. NPV_A = $8,207,071; NPV_B = $8,643,390;
Choose B.
f. 13.53%.
g. $MIRR_A$ = 21.93%;
$MIRR_B$ = 20.96%.

10-22 a. 3 years; NPV_3 = $1,307.
b. No.

11-1 a. \$22,000,000.
b. No.
c. Charge it against project and add \$1.5 million to initial investment outlay.

11-2 \$7,000,000.

11-3 \$3,600,000.

11-4 NPV = \$6,746.78

11-5 a. Straight Line: \$425,000 per year. MACRS: \$566,610; \$755,650; \$251,770; \$125,970.
b. MACRS, \$27,043.62 higher.

11-6 a. −\$1,118,000.
b. \$375,612; \$418,521; \$304,148.
c. \$437,343.
d. NPV = \$78,790; Purchase.

11-7 a. −\$89,000
b. \$26,332; \$30,113; \$20,035.
c. \$24,519.
d. NPV = −\$6,700; Don't purchase.

11-8 a. NPV = \$106,520.

11-9 NPV of replace = \$2,083.51.

11-10 NPV of replace = \$11,468.48.

11-11 E(NPV) = \$3 million; σ_{NPV} = \$23.622 million; CV_{NPV} = 7.874.

11-12 a. NPV = \$15,732; IRR = 11.64%; MIRR = 10.88%; Payback = 3.75 years.
b. \$65,770; −\$34,307.
c. E(NPV) = \$13,041; σ_{NPV} = \$43,289; CV = 3.32.

11-13 a. −\$87,625.
b. \$31,574; \$36,244; \$23,795; \$20,687; \$4,575.
c. -\$4,623.

11-14 a. −\$529,750.
b. New depreciation: \$155,000; \$248,000; \$148,800; \$89,280; \$89,280.
c. Net incremental cash flows: \$143,000; \$175,550; \$140,830; \$119,998; \$203,872.
d. NPV = \$30,059.

11-15 a. Expected CF_A = \$6,750; Expected CF_B = \$7,650; CV_A = 0.0703.
b. NPV_A = \$10,036; NPV_B = \$11,624.

11-16 a. E(IRR) ≈ 15.3%.
b. \$38,589.

11-17 a. \$117,779.
b. σ_{NPV} = \$445,060; CV_{NPV} = 3.78.

12-1 AFN = \$283,800.

12-2 AFN = \$583,800.

12-3 AFN = \$63,000.

12-4 ΔS = \$202,312.

12-5 a. \$590,000; \$1,150,000.
b. \$238,563.

12-6 AFN = \$360.

12-7 a. \$13.44 million.
b. 6.38%.
c. LOC = \$13.44 million.

12-8 a. Total assets = \$ 33,534 (thousands); Deficit = \$2,128 (thousands).
b. LOC = \$4,228 (thousands).

12-9 LOC = \$128,783.

14-1 Payout = 33.33%.

14-2 Payout = 20%.

14-3 Payout = 52%.

14-4 V_{op} = \$175 million; n = 8.75 million.

14-5 P_0 = \$80.

14-6 \$6,900,000.

14-7 n = 4,000; EPS = \$5.00; DPS = \$1.50; P = \$40.00.

14-8 D_0 = \$4.25.

14-9 Payout = 17.89%.

14-10 a. (1) \$2,808,000.
(2) \$3.34 Million.
(3) \$7,855,000.
(4) Regular = \$2,808,000; Extra = \$5,047,000.

14-11 a. $10,500,000.
b. DPS = $0.50; Payout = 4.55%.
c. $9,000,000.
d. No.
e. 40%.
f. $1,500,000.
g. $12,875,143.

14-12 a. $848 million.
b. $450 million.
c. $30.
d. 1 million; 14 million.
e. $420 million; $30.

15-1 20,000.

15-2 1.0.

15-3 3.6%.

15-4 $300 million.

15-5 $30.

15-6 40 million.

15-7 a. ΔProfit = $850,000; Return = 21.25% > r_s = 15%.
b. $Q_{BE,Old}$ = 40; $Q_{BE,New}$ = 45.45.

15-8 a. V = $3,348,214.
b. $16.74.
c. $1.84.
d. 10%.

15-9 30% debt:
WACC = 11.14%;
V = $101.023 million.

50% debt:
WACC = 11.25%;
V = $100 million.

70% debt:
WACC = 11.94%;
V = $94.255 million.

15-10 a. 0.870.
b. b = 1.218; r_s = 10.872%.
c. WACC = 8.683%; V = $103.188 million.

15-11 WACC at optimal debt level: 8.89%.

16-1 $3,000,000.

16-2 AR = $59,500.

16-3 r_{NOM} = 75.26%; EAR = 109.84%.

16-4 EAR = 8.49%.

16-5 $7,500,000.

16-6 a. DSO = 38 days.
b. AR = $156,164.
c. AR = $141,781.

16-7 a. 73.74%.
b. 14.90%.
c. 32.25%.
d. 21.28%.
e. 29.80%.

16-8 a. 45.15%.

16-9 Nominal cost = 14.90%; Effective cost = 15.89%.

16-10 14.91%.

16-11 a. 60 days.
b. $420,000.
c. 7.3.

16-12 a. 56.8 days.
b. (1) 2.7082.
(2) 18.96%.
c. (1) 36.6 days.
(2) 2.95.
(3) 20.68%.

16-13 a. ROE_T = 11.75%; ROE_M = 10.80%; ROE_R = 9.16%.

16-14 a. Feb. surplus = $2,000.
b. $164,400.

16-15 a. $100,000.
b. (1) $300,000.
(2) Nominal cost = 37.24%; Effective cost = 44.59%.
c. Nominal cost = 24.83%; Effective cost = 27.86%.

16-16 a. 14.35%.

16-17 a. $300,000.
b. $2,000.
c. (1) $322,500.
(2) $26,875.
(3) 13.57%.
(4) 14.44%.

17-1 12.358 yen per peso.

17-2 f_t = $0.00907.

17-3 1 euro = $0.9091 or
$1 = 1.1 euros.

17-4 0.6667 euros per dollar.

17-5 1.5152 SFr.

17-6 2.4 Swiss francs per pound.

17-7 $r_{NOM-U.S.}$ = 4.6%.

17-8 117 pesos.

17-9 +$500,000.

17-10 $24,500.

17-11 a. $1,658,925.
b. $$1,646,091.
c. $2,000,000.

17-12 b. f_t = 1.3990 dollars per Swiss franc; discount.

17-13 $322 million.

17-14 a. $89,357; 20%.
b. 1,039.90 won per U.S. dollar and 1029.95 won per U.S. dollar.
c. 78,150,661 won; 18.85%.

18-1 a. $700,000.
b. $3,700,000.
c. −$2,300,000.

18-2 964,115 shares.

18-3 10,000 shares at $20 per share.

18-4 a. $$22,016,893; $ 40.03per share.
b. Abercrombe: D/A 30.43%;
P/E 15.91; M/B 2.19; ROE 13.8%; P/FCF 21.47
Gunter: D/A 20.00%;
P/E 15.02; M/B 2.35; ROE 15.7%; P/FCF 18.50.
B&C: D/A 18.18%%;
P/E 15.40; M/B 2.22; ROE 14.4%; P/FCF 20.02.
c. Price based on: Abercrombe P/E $41.36; Gunter P/E $39.04.
Price based on: Abercrombe M/B $39.38; Gunter M/B $42.30.
Price based on: Abercrombe P/FCF $42.94; Gunter P/FCF $37.01.

18-5 $14.74; $13.708 million.

18-6 a. After-tax call cost = $2,640,000.
b. Flotation cost = $1,600,000.
c. $1,920,000; $768,000.
d. $3,472,000.
e. New tax savings = $16,000;
Lost tax savings = $19,200.
f. $360,000.
g. PV = $9,109,413.
h. $5,637,413.

18-7 a. NPV = $2,717,128.

19-1 a. (1) 50%.
(2) 60%.
(3) 50%.

19-2 Cost of owning = −$127;
Cost of leasing = −$128;
NAL = −$1.

19-3 a. Energen: Debt/TA = 50%;
Hastings: Debt/TA = 33%.
b. TA = $200.

19-4 a. NAL = $108,147.

19-5 a. PV of leasing = −667,261;
PV of owning =
−$713,300;
NAL = $46,039
b. $245,703.

20-1 $182.16.

20-2 20 shares.

20-3 a. (1) $0.
(2) $0.
(3) $5.
(4) $75.
b. 10%; $100.

20-4 Premium = 10%: $46.20;
Premium = 30%: $54.60.

20-5 a. 14.1%.
b. $12 million before tax.
c. $331.89.
d. Value as a straight bond = $699.25; Value in conversion = $521.91.
e. Value as a straight bond = $1,000.00; Value in conversion = $521.91.

20-6 a. Plan 1, 49%; Plan 2, 53%;
Plan 3, 53%.

b. Plan 1, \$0.59; Plan 2, \$0.64; Plan 3, \$0.88.
c. Plan 1, 19%; Plan 2, 19%; Plan 3, 50%.

20-7 a. Year = 7; CV_7 = \$1,210.422; CF_7 = \$1,290.422.
b. 10.20%.

21-1 \$500 million.

21-2 \$821 million.

21-3 \$620.68 million.

21-4 \$813.125 million.

21-5 a. b_U = 1.125.
b. r_{sU} = 15.625%.
c. 16.62%; 18.04%; 20.23%.
d. 20.23%.

21-6 a. $V_U = V_L$ = \$20 million.
b. r_{sU} = 10%; r_{sL} = 15%.
c. S_L = \$10 million.
d. $WACC_U$ = 10%; $WACC_L$ = 10%.

21-7 a. V_U = \$12 million; V_L = \$16 million.
b. r_{sU} = 10%; r_{sL} = 15%.
c. S_L = \$6 million.
d. $WACC_U$ = 10%; $WACC_L$ = 7.5%.

21-8 a. V_U = \$12 million; V_L = \$15.33 million; \$3.33 million.
b. $V_L = V_U$ = \$20 million; \$0.
c. V_U = \$12 million; V_L = \$16 million; \$4 million.
d. V_U = \$12 million; V_L = \$16 million; \$4 million.

21-9 a. V_U = \$12.5 million.
b. V_L = \$16 million; r_{sL} = 15.7%.
c. V_L = \$14.5 million; r_{sL} = 14.9%.

21-10 a. $V_U = V_L$ = \$14,545,455.
b. At D = \$6 million: r_{sL} = 14.51%; WACC = 11.0%.
c. V_U = \$8,727,273; V_L = \$11,127,273.
d. At D = \$6 million: r_{sL} = 14.51%; WACC = 8.63%.
e. D = V = \$14,545,455.

21-11 a. V = \$3.29 million.
b. D = \$1.71 million; Yield = 8.1%.
c. V = \$3.23 million; D = \$1.77 million; Yield = 6.3%.

21-12 a. \$713.33 million.
b. \$563.29 million.
c. \$71.33 million.
d. \$57.86 million.
e. \$621.15 million.

22-1 P_0 = \$25.26.

22-2 P_0 = \$41.54.

22-3 \$25.26 to \$41.54.

22-4 Value of equity = \$46.30 million.

22-5 a. $V_{op\ Unlevered}$ = \$32.02 million; $V_{Tax\ shields}$ = \$11.50 million.
b. V_{op} = \$43.52 million; max = \$33.52 million.

22-6 a. 10.96%.
b. (All in millions) FCF_1 = \$23.12, TS_1 = \$14.00; FCF_3 = \$12.26, TS_3 = \$16.45; FCF_5 = \$23.83, TS_5 = \$18.90.
c. HV_{TS} = \$510.68 million; HV_U = \$643.89 million.
d. Value of equity = \$508.57 million.

23-1 Net payment = LIBOR + 0.2%.

23-2 r_d = 7.01%.

23-3 r_d = 5.96%; Futures = \$89,748.42.

23-4 Net to Carter = 9.95% fixed; Net to Brence = LIBOR + 3.05% floating.

23-5 a. Sell 105 contracts.
b. Bond = −\$1,414,552.69; Futures = \$1,951,497.45; Net = +\$536,944.76.

24-1 AP = \$375,000;
NP = \$750,000;
SD = \$750,000; Stockholders = \$343,750.

24-2 a. Total assets: \$327 million.
b. Income: \$7 million.
c. Before, \$15.6 million;
After, \$13.0 million.
d. Before, 35.7%;
After, 64.2%.

24-3 a. \$0.
b. First mortgage holders, \$300,000; Second mortgage holders, \$100,000 plus \$12,700 as a general claimant.
c. Trustee's expenses, \$50,000;
Wages due, \$30,000;
Taxes due, \$40,000.
d. *Before subordination*
Accounts payable = \$6,350;
Notes payable = \$22,860;
Second mortgage = \$12,700 + \$100,000;
Debentures = \$25,400;
Sub. debentures = \$12,700.
After subordination
Notes payable = \$35,560;
Sub. debentures = \$0.

24-4 a. \$0 for stockholders.
b. AP = 24%; NP = 100%; WP = 100%;
TP = 100%; Mortgage = 85%; Subordinated debentures = 9%; Trustee = 100%.

25-1 1.4.

25-2 12%.

25-3 16.2%; 45.9%.

25-4 a. $r_i = r_{RF} + (r_M - r_{RF}) \frac{\rho_{iM}\sigma_i}{\sigma_M}$

25-5 a. b = 0.56.
b. X: 10.6%; 13.1%.
M: 12.1%; 22.6%.
c. 8.6%.

25-6 a. b = 0.62.

26-1 a. \$1.074 million.
b. \$2.96 million.

26-2 a. \$4.6795 million.
b. \$3.208 million.

26-3 a. −\$19 million.
b. \$9.0981 million.

26-4 a. −\$2.113 million.
b. \$1.973 million.
c. −\$70,222.
d. \$565,090.
e. \$1.116 million.

26-5 a. \$2,562.
b. E[NPV] = \$9,786; Value of growth option = \$7,224.

26-6 P = \$18.646 million;
X = \$20 million; t = 1;
$r_{RF} = 0.08$; $\sigma^2 = 0.0687$;
V = \$2.028 million.

26-7 P = \$10.479 million;
X = \$9 million; t = 2;
$r_{RF} = 0.06$; $\sigma^2 = 0.0111$;
V = \$2.514 million.

26-8 P = \$18,646;
X = \$20,000; t = 2;
V = \$5,009.

© lulu/fotolia.com

Appendix C

Selected Equations

CHAPTER 1

$$\text{Value} = \frac{FCF_1}{(1+WACC)^1} + \frac{FCF_2}{(1+WACC)^2} + \frac{FCF_3}{(1+WACC)^3} + \cdots + \frac{FCF_\infty}{(1+WACC)^\infty}$$

CHAPTER 2

$$\text{EBIT} = \text{Earnings before interest and taxes} = \text{Sales revenues} - \text{Operating costs}$$

$$\begin{aligned}\text{EBITDA} &= \text{Earnings before interest, taxes, depreciation, and amortization} \\ &= \text{EBIT} + \text{Depreciation} + \text{Amortization}\end{aligned}$$

$$\text{Net cash flow} = \text{Net income} + \text{Depreciation and amortization}$$

$$\begin{aligned}\text{NOWC} &= \text{Net operating working capital} \\ &= \text{Operating current assets} - \text{Operating current liabilities} \\ &= \begin{pmatrix}\text{Cash} + \text{Accounts receivable} \\ + \text{Inventories}\end{pmatrix} - \begin{pmatrix}\text{Accounts payable} \\ + \text{Accruals}\end{pmatrix}\end{aligned}$$

$$\text{Total net operating capital} = \text{Net operating working capital} + \text{Operating long-term assets}$$

$$\text{NOPAT} = \text{Net operating profit after taxes} = \text{EBIT}(1 - \text{Tax rate})$$

$$\begin{aligned}\text{Free cash flow (FCF)} &= \text{NOPAT} - \text{Net investment in operating capital} \\ &= \text{NOPAT} - \begin{pmatrix}\text{CashCurrent year's total} & - & \text{Previous year's total} \\ \text{net operating capital} & & \text{net operating capital}\end{pmatrix}\end{aligned}$$

$$\text{FCF} = \text{Operating cash flow} - \begin{matrix}\text{Gross investment} \\ \text{in operating capital}\end{matrix}$$

$$\text{Return on invested capital (ROIC)} = \frac{\text{NOPAT}}{\text{Total net operating capital}}$$

$$\begin{aligned}\text{MVA} &= \text{Market value of stock} - \text{Equity capital supplied by shareholders} \\ &= (\text{Shares outstanding})(\text{Stock price}) - \text{Total common equity}\end{aligned}$$

$$\begin{aligned}\text{MVA} &= \text{Total market value} - \text{Total investor-supplied capital} \\ &= \begin{pmatrix}\text{Market value of stock} \\ + \text{Market value of debt}\end{pmatrix} - \text{Total investor-supplied capital}\end{aligned}$$

$$\text{EVA} = \begin{pmatrix}\text{Net operating profit}\\ \text{after taxes (NOPAT)}\end{pmatrix} - \begin{pmatrix}\text{After-tax dollar cost of capital}\\ \text{used to support operations}\end{pmatrix}$$

$$= \text{EBIT}(1 - \text{Tax rate}) - (\text{Total net operating capital})(\text{WACC})$$

$$\text{EVA} = (\text{Total net operating capital})(\text{ROIC} - \text{WACC})$$

CHAPTER 3

$$\text{Current ratio} = \frac{\text{Current assets}}{\text{Current liabilities}}$$

$$\text{Quick, or acid test, ratio} = \frac{\text{Current assets} - \text{Inventories}}{\text{Current liabilities}}$$

$$\text{Inventory turnover ratio} = \frac{\text{Cost of Goods Sold}}{\text{Inventories}}$$

$$\text{DSO} = \text{Days sales outstanding} = \frac{\text{Receivables}}{\text{Average sales per day}} = \frac{\text{Receivables}}{\text{Annual sales}/365}$$

$$\text{Fixed assets turnover ratio} = \frac{\text{Sales}}{\text{Net fixed assets}}$$

$$\text{Total assets turnover ratio} = \frac{\text{Sales}}{\text{Total assets}}$$

$$\text{Debt ratio} = \frac{\text{Total debt}}{\text{Total assets}}$$

$$\text{Liabilities-to-assets ratio} = \frac{\text{Total liabilities}}{\text{Total assets}}$$

$$\text{Market debt ratio} = \frac{\text{Total debt}}{\text{Total debt} + \text{Market value of equity}}$$

$$\text{Debt-to-equity ratio} = \frac{\text{Total debt}}{\text{Total common equity}}$$

$$\text{Equity multiplier} = \frac{\text{Total assets}}{\text{Common equity}}$$

$$\text{Times-interest-earned (TIE) ratio} = \frac{\text{EBIT}}{\text{Interest charges}}$$

$$\text{EBITDA coverage ratio} = \frac{\text{EBITDA} + \text{Lease payments}}{\text{Interest} + \text{Principal payments} + \text{Lease payments}}$$

$$\text{Net profit margin} = \frac{\text{Net income available to common stockholders}}{\text{Sales}}$$

$$\text{Operating profit margin} = \frac{\text{EBIT}}{\text{Sales}}$$

$$\text{Gross profit margin} = \frac{\text{Sales} - \text{Cost of goods sold}}{\text{Sales}}$$

$$\text{Return on total assets (ROA)} = \frac{\text{Net income available to common stockholders}}{\text{Total assets}}$$

$$\text{Basic earning power (BEP) ratio} = \frac{\text{EBIT}}{\text{Total assets}}$$

$$\text{ROA} = \text{Profit margin} \times \text{Total assets turnover} = \frac{\text{Net income}}{\text{Sales}} \times \frac{\text{Sales}}{\text{Total assets}}$$

$$\text{Return on common equity (ROE)} = \frac{\text{Net income available to common stockholders}}{\text{Common equity}}$$

$$\text{ROE} = \text{ROA} \times \text{Equity multiplier}$$

$$= \text{Profit margin} \times \text{Total assets turnover} \times \text{Equity multiplier}$$

$$= \frac{\text{Net income}}{\text{Sales}} \times \frac{\text{Sales}}{\text{Total assets}} \times \frac{\text{Total assets}}{\text{Common equity}}$$

$$\text{Price/earnings (P/E) ratio} = \frac{\text{Price per share}}{\text{Earnings per share}}$$

$$\text{Price/cash flow ratio} = \frac{\text{Price per share}}{\text{Cash flow per share}}$$

$$\text{Book value per share} = \frac{\text{Common equity}}{\text{Shares outstanding}}$$

$$\text{Market/book (M/B) ratio} = \frac{\text{Market price per share}}{\text{Book value per share}}$$

CHAPTER 4

$$FV_N = PV(1 + I)^N$$

$$PV = \frac{FV_N}{(1 + I)^N}$$

$$FVA_N = PMT\left[\frac{(1 + I)^N}{I} - \frac{1}{I}\right] = PMT\left[\frac{(1 + I)^N - 1}{I}\right]$$

$$FVA_{due} = FVA_{ordinary}(1 + I)$$

$$PVA_N = PMT\left[\frac{1}{I} - \frac{1}{I(1 + I)^N}\right] = PMT\left[\frac{1 - \frac{1}{(1 + I)^N}}{I}\right]$$

$$PVA_{Due} = PVA_{Ordinary}(1 + I)$$

$$\text{PV of a perpetuity} = \frac{PMT}{I}$$

$$PV_{\text{Uneven stream}} = \sum_{t=1}^{N} \frac{CF_t}{(1 + I)^t}$$

$$FV_{\text{Uneven stream}} = \sum_{t=1}^{N} CF_t(1 + I)^{N-t}$$

$$I_{PER} = \frac{I_{NOM}}{M}$$

$$APR = (I_{PER})M$$

$$\text{Number of periods} = NM$$

$$FV_N = PV(1 + I_{PER})^{\text{Number of periods}} = PV\left(1 + \frac{I_{NOM}}{M}\right)^{MN}$$

$$EFF\% = \left(1 + \frac{I_{NOM}}{M}\right)^{M} - 1.0$$

CHAPTER 5

$$V_B = \sum_{t=1}^{N} \frac{INT}{(1 + r_d)^t} + \frac{M}{(1 + r_d)^N}$$

$$\text{Semiannual payments: } V_B = \sum_{t=1}^{2N} \frac{INT/2}{(1 + r_d/2)^t} + \frac{M}{(1 + r_d/2)^{2N}}$$

$$\text{Yield to maturity: Bond price} = \sum_{t=1}^{N} \frac{INT}{(1 + YTM)^t} + \frac{M}{(1 + YTM)^N}$$

$$\text{Price of callable bond (if called at N)} = \sum_{t=1}^{N} \frac{INT}{(1 + r_d)^t} + \frac{\text{Call price}}{(1 + r_d)^N}$$

$$\text{Current yield} = \frac{\text{Annual interest}}{\text{Bond's current price}}$$

$$\text{Current yield} + \text{Capital gains yield} = \text{Yield to maturity}$$

$$r_d = r^* + IP + DRP + LP + MRP$$

$$r_{RF} = r^* + IP$$

$$r_d = r_{RF} + DRP + LP + MRP$$

$$IP_N = \frac{I_1 + I_2 + \cdots + I_N}{N}$$

CHAPTER 6

$$\text{Expected rate of return} = \hat{r} = \sum_{i=1}^{n} P_i r_i$$

$$\text{Historical average, } \bar{r}_{Avg} = \frac{\sum_{t=1}^{T} \bar{r}_t}{T}$$

$$\text{Variance} = \sigma^2 = \sum_{i=1}^{n} (r_i - \hat{r})^2 P_i$$

$$\text{Standard deviation} = \sigma = \sqrt{\sum_{i=1}^{n} (r_i - \hat{r})^2 P_i}$$

$$\text{Historical estimated } \sigma = S = \sqrt{\frac{\sum_{t=1}^{T}(\bar{r}_t - \bar{r}_{Avg})^2}{T-1}}$$

$$\hat{r}_p = \sum_{i=1}^{n} w_i \hat{r}_i$$

$$\sigma_p = \sqrt{\sum_{i=1}^{n}(r_{pi} - \hat{r}_p)^2 P_i}$$

$$\text{Estimated } \rho = R = \frac{\sum_{t=1}^{T}(\bar{r}_{i,j} - \bar{r}_{i,Avg})(\bar{r}_{j,t} - \bar{r}_{j,Avg})}{\sqrt{\sum_{t=1}^{T}(\bar{r}_{i,t} - \bar{r}_{i,Avg})^2 \sum_{t=1}^{T}(\bar{r}_{j,t} - \bar{r}_{j,Avg})^2}}$$

$$COV_{iM} = \rho_{iM}\sigma_i\sigma_M$$

$$b_i = \left(\frac{\sigma_i}{\sigma_M}\right)\rho_{iM} = \frac{COV_{iM}}{\sigma_M^2}$$

$$b_p = \sum_{i=1}^{n} w_i b_i$$

Required return on stock market = r_M

Market risk premium = $RP_M = r_M - r_{RF}$

$RP_i = (r_M - r_{RF})b_i = (RP_M)b_i$

$SML = r_i = r_{RF} + (r_M - r_{RF})b_i = r_{RF} + RP_M b_i$

CHAPTER 7

$$\hat{P}_0 = \text{PV of expected future dividends} = \sum_{t=1}^{\infty} \frac{D_t}{(1 + r_s)^t}$$

$$\text{Constant growth: } \hat{P}_0 = \frac{D_0(1+g)}{r_s - g} = \frac{D_1}{r_s - g}$$

$$\hat{r}_s = \frac{D_1}{P_0} + g$$

$$\text{Capital gains yield} = \frac{\hat{P}_1 - P_0}{P_0}$$

$$\text{Dividend yield} = \frac{D_1}{P_0}$$

$$\text{For a zero growth stock, } \hat{P}_0 = \frac{D}{r_s}$$

$$\text{Horizon value of stock} = \text{Terminal value} = \hat{P}_N = \frac{D_{N+1}}{r_s - g_L} = \frac{D_N(1+g_L)}{r_s - g_L}$$

$$V_{ps} = \frac{D_{ps}}{r_{ps}}$$

$$\hat{r}_{ps} = \frac{D_{ps}}{V_{ps}}$$

$\bar{r}_s$ = Actual dividend yield + Actual capital gains yield

$$\begin{aligned} V_{op} &= \text{Value of operations} \\ &= \text{PV of expected future free cash flows} \\ &= \sum_{t=1}^{\infty} \frac{FCF_1}{(1+WACC)^t} \end{aligned}$$

Horizon value of operations: $V_{op(\text{at time N})} = \dfrac{FCF_{N+1}}{WACC - g_L} = \dfrac{FCF_N(1 + g_L)}{WACC - g_L}$

Total entity value = V_{op} + Value of nonoperating assets

Value of equity = Total entity value − Preferred stock − Debt

CHAPTER 8

Exercise value = MAX[Current price of stock − Strike price, 0]

Number of stock shares in hedged portfolio = $N = \dfrac{C_u - C_d}{P_u - P_d}$

$$V_C = P[N(d_1)] - Xe^{-r_{RF}t}[N(d_2)]$$

$$d_1 = \frac{\ln(P/X) + [r_{RF} + (\sigma^2/2)]t}{\sigma\sqrt{t}}$$

$$d_2 = d_1 - \sigma\sqrt{t}$$

Put–call parity: Put option = $V_C - P + Xe^{-r_{RF}t}$

V of put = $P[N(d_1) - 1] - Xe^{-r_{RF}t}[N(d_2) - 1]$

CHAPTER 9

After-tax component cost of debt = $r_d(1 - T)$

$$M(1-F) = \sum_{t=1}^{N} \frac{INT(1 - T)}{[1 + r_d(1 - T)]^t} + \frac{M}{[1 + r_d(1 - T)]^N}$$

$$r_{ps} = \frac{D_{ps}}{P_{ps}(1 - F)}$$

Market equilibrium: $\begin{matrix}\text{Expected} \\ \text{rate of return}\end{matrix} = \hat{r}_M = \dfrac{D_1}{P_0} + g = r_{RF} + RP_M = r_M = \begin{matrix}\text{Required} \\ \text{rate of return}\end{matrix}$

Note: D_1, P_0, and g are for the market, not an individual company.

$$r_M = \hat{r}_M = \frac{D_1}{P_0} + g$$

Note: g is long-term growth rate in total dividends for the market and $D_1$and P_0 are for the market, not an individual company.

$$\text{CAPM: } r_s = r_{RF} + b_i(RP_M)$$

$$\text{DCF: } r_s = \hat{r}_s = \frac{D_1}{P_0} + \text{Expected g in dividends per share}$$

$$\text{Own-bond yield-plus-judgmental-risk-premium: } r_s = \begin{matrix}\text{Company's own} \\ \text{bond yield}\end{matrix} + \begin{matrix}\text{Judgemental} \\ \text{risk premium}\end{matrix}$$

$$g = (\text{Retention rate})(\text{ROE}) = (1.0 - \text{Payout rate})(\text{ROE})$$

$$r_e = \hat{r}_e = \frac{D_1}{P_0(1-F)} + g$$

$$\text{WACC} = w_d r_d(1 - T) + w_{ps} r_{ps} + w_s r_s$$

CHAPTER 10

$$\text{NPV} = CF_0 + \frac{CF_1}{(1+r)^1} + \frac{CF_2}{(1+r)^2} + \cdots + \frac{CF_N}{(1+r)^N} = \sum_{t=0}^{N} \frac{CF_t}{(1+r)^t}$$

$$\text{IRR: } CF_0 + \frac{CF_1}{(1+\text{IRR})^1} + \frac{CF_2}{(1+\text{IRR})^2} + \cdots + \frac{CF_N}{(1+\text{IRR})^N} = 0$$

$$\text{NPV} = \sum_{t=0}^{N} \frac{CF_t}{(1+\text{IRR})^t} = 0$$

MIRR: PV of costs = PV of terminal value

$$\sum_{t=0}^{N} \frac{COF_t}{(1+r)^t} = \frac{\sum_{t=0}^{N} CIF_t(1+r)^{N-t}}{(1+\text{MIRR})^N}$$

$$\text{PV of costs} = \frac{\text{Terminal value}}{(1+\text{MIRR})^N}$$

$$\text{PI} = \frac{\text{PV of future cash flows}}{\text{initial cost}} = \frac{\sum_{t=1}^{N} \frac{CF_t}{(1+r)^t}}{CF_0}$$

$$\text{Payback} = \begin{matrix}\text{Number of} \\ \text{years prior to} \\ \text{full recovery}\end{matrix} + \frac{\begin{matrix}\text{Uncovered cost} \\ \text{at start of year}\end{matrix}}{\begin{matrix}\text{Cash flow during} \\ \text{full recovery year}\end{matrix}}$$

CHAPTER 11

$$\text{Project cash flow} = \text{FCF} = \frac{\text{Investment outlay}}{\text{cash flow}} + \frac{\text{Operating}}{\text{cash flow}} + \frac{\text{NOWC}}{\text{cash flow}} + \frac{\text{Salvage}}{\text{cash flow}}$$

$$\text{Expected NPV} = \sum_{i=1}^{n} P_i\,(\text{NPV}_i)$$

$$\sigma_{NPV} = \sqrt{\sum_{i=1}^{n} P_i\,(\text{NPV}_i - \text{Expected NPV})^2}$$

$$CV_{NPV} = \frac{\sigma_{NPV}}{E(\text{NPV})}$$

CHAPTER 12

$$\begin{matrix}\text{Additional} \\ \text{funds} \\ \text{needed}\end{matrix} = \begin{matrix}\text{Required} \\ \text{asset} \\ \text{increase}\end{matrix} - \begin{matrix}\text{Spontaneous} \\ \text{liability} \\ \text{increase}\end{matrix} - \begin{matrix}\text{Increase in} \\ \text{retained} \\ \text{earnings}\end{matrix}$$

$$\text{AFN} = (A^*/S_0)\Delta S - (L^*/S_0)\Delta S - MS_1(1 - \text{Payout ratio})$$

$$\begin{matrix}\text{Full} \\ \text{capacity} \\ \text{sales}\end{matrix} = \frac{\text{Actual sales}}{\begin{matrix}\text{Percentage of capacity} \\ \text{at which fixed assets} \\ \text{were operated}\end{matrix}}$$

$$\text{Target fixed assets/Sales} = \frac{\text{Actual fixed assets}}{\text{Full capacity sales}}$$

$$\begin{matrix}\text{Required level} \\ \text{of fixed assets}\end{matrix} = (\text{Target fixed assets/Sales})(\text{Projected sales})$$

CHAPTER 14

$$\text{Residual distribution} = \text{Net income} - [(\text{Target equity ratio})(\text{Total capital budget})]$$

$$\text{Number of shares repurchased} = n_{Prior} - n_{Post} = \frac{\text{Cash}_{Rep}}{P_{Prior}}$$

$$n_{Post} = n_{Prior} - \frac{\text{Cash}_{Rep}}{P_{Prior}} = n_{Prior} - \frac{\text{Cash}_{Rep}}{S_{Prior}/n_{Prior}} = n_{Prior}\left(1 - \frac{\text{Cash}_{Rep}}{S_{Prior}}\right)$$

CHAPTER 15

$$V_{op} = \sum_{t=1}^{\infty} \frac{\text{FCF}_t}{(1 + \text{WACC})^t}$$

$$\text{WACC} = w_d(1 - T)r_d + w_s r_s$$

$$\text{ROIC} = \frac{\text{NOPAT}}{\text{Capital}} = \frac{\text{EBIT}(1 - T)}{\text{Capital}}$$

$$\text{EBIT} = PQ - VQ - F$$

$$Q_{BE} = \frac{F}{P - V}$$

$$V_L = S_L + D$$

MM, no taxes: $V_L = V_U$

MM, corporate taxes: $V_L = V_U + TD$

$$\text{Miller, corporate and personal taxes: } V_L = V_U + \left[1 - \frac{(1 - T_c)(1 - T_s)}{(1 - T_d)}\right]D$$

$$b = b_U[1 + (1 - T)(D/S)] = b_U[1 + (1 - T)(w_d/w_s)]$$

$$b_U = b/[1 + (1 - T)(D/S)] = b/[1 + (1 - T)(w_d/w_s)]$$

$$r_s = r_{RF} + RP_M(b)$$

$r_s = r_{RF}$ + Premium for business risk + Premium for financial risk

$$\text{If } g = 0\text{: } V_{op} = \frac{FCF}{WACC} = \frac{NOPAT}{WACC} = \frac{EBIT(1 - T)}{WACC}$$

Total corporate value = V_{op} + Value of short-term investments

S = Total corporate value − Value of all debt

$$D = w_d V_{op}$$

$$S = (1 - w_d)V_{op}$$

Cash raised by issuing debt = $D - D_0$

$$P_{Prior} = S_{Prior}/n_{Prior}$$

$$P_{Post} = P_{Prior}$$

$$n_{Post} = n_{Prior}\left[\frac{V_{opNew} - D_{New}}{V_{opNew} - D_{Old}}\right]$$

$$n_{Post} = n_{Prior} - (D_{New} - D_{Old})/P_{Prior}$$

$$P_{Post} = \frac{V_{opNew} - D_{Old}}{n_{Prior}}$$

$$NI = (EBIT - r_d D)(1 - T)$$

$$EPS = NI/n$$

CHAPTER 16

$$\text{Inventory conversion period} = \frac{\text{Inventory}}{(\text{Cost of goods sold})/365}$$

$$\text{Receivables collection period} = DSO = \frac{\text{Receivables}}{\text{Sales}/365}$$

$$\text{Payables deferral period} = \frac{\text{Payables}}{(\text{Cost of goods sold})/365}$$

$$\begin{matrix}\text{Cash} & & \text{Inventory} & & \text{Average} & & \text{Payables} \\ \text{conversion} & = & \text{conversion} & + & \text{collection} & - & \text{deferral} \\ \text{cycle} & & \text{period} & & \text{period} & & \text{period}\end{matrix}$$

$$\text{Accounts receivable} = \text{Credit sales per day} \times \text{Length of collection period}$$

$$\text{ADS} = \frac{(\text{Units sold})(\text{Sales price})}{365} = \frac{\text{Annual sales}}{365}$$

$$\text{Receivables} = (\text{ADS})(\text{DSO})$$

$$\text{Nominal annual cost of trade credit} = \frac{\text{Discount percentage}}{100 - \text{Discount percentage}} \times \frac{365}{\text{Days credit is outstanding} - \text{Discount period}}$$

CHAPTER 17

$$\text{Single-period interest rate parity}: \frac{\text{Forward exchange rate}}{\text{Spot exchange rate}} = \frac{1 + r_h}{1 + r_f}$$

$$\text{Expected t-year forward exchange rate} = (\text{Spot rate})\left(\frac{1 + r_h}{1 + r_f}\right)^t$$

$$P_h = (P_f)(\text{Spot rate})$$

$$\text{Spot rate} = \frac{P_h}{P_f}$$

CHAPTER 18

$$\text{Amount left on table} = (\text{Closing price} - \text{Offer price})(\text{Number of shares})$$

CHAPTER 19

$$\text{NAL} = \text{PV of leasing} - \text{PV of owning}$$

CHAPTER 20

$$\text{Price paid for bond with warrants} = \text{Straight-debt value of bond} + \text{Value of warrants}$$

$$\text{Conversion price} = P_c = \frac{\text{Par value of bond given up}}{\text{Shares received}} = \frac{\text{Par value of bond given up}}{\text{CR}}$$

$$\text{Conversion ratio} = \text{CR} = \frac{\text{Par value of bond given up}}{P_c}$$

CHAPTER 21

MM, no taxes (T = 0 and g = 0):

$$V_L = V_U = \frac{\text{EBIT}}{\text{WACC}} = \frac{\text{EBIT}}{r_{sU}}$$

$$r_{sL} = r_{sU} + \text{Risk premium} = r_{sU} + (r_{sU} - r_d)(D/S)$$

MM, corporate taxes (r_{TS} = rd and g = 0):

$$V_L = V_U + TD$$

$$V_U = S = \frac{\text{EBIT}(1 - T)}{r_{sU}}$$

$$r_{sL} = r_{sU} + (r_{sU} - r_d)(1 - T)(D/S)$$

Miller, personal taxes taxes (r_{TS} = rd and g = 0):

$$V_U = \frac{\text{EBIT}(1 - T_c)}{r_{sU}} = \frac{\text{EBIT}(1 - T_c)(1 - T_s)}{r_{sU}(1 - T_s)}$$

$$CF_L = (\text{EBIT} - I)(1 - T_c)(1 - T_s) + I(1 - T_d)$$

$$V_L = V_U + \left[1 - \frac{(1 - T_c)(1 - T_s)}{(1 - T_d)}\right]D$$

Adjusted present value approach (g = constant):

Tax savings = (Interest expense)(Tax rate)

Value of operations = $V_{op} = V_{\text{Unlevered}} + V_{\text{Tax shield}}$

$$V_L = V_U + V_{\text{Tax shield}}$$

$$V_{\text{Tax shield}} = \frac{r_d TD}{r_{TS} - g}$$

$$V_L = V_U + \left(\frac{r_d}{r_{TS} - g}\right)TD$$

Compressed adjusted present value approach ($r_{TS} = r_{sU}$ and g = constant):

$$V_L = V_U + \left(\frac{r_d TD}{r_{sU} - g}\right)$$

$$r_{sL} = r_{sU} + (r_{sU} - r_d)\frac{D}{S}$$

$$b = b_U + (b_U - b_D)\frac{D}{S}$$

$$r_{sU} = w_s r_{sL} + w_d r_d$$

Compressed adjusted present value approach ($r_{TS} = r_{sU}$):

$$\text{Horizon value of unlevered firm} = HV_{U,N} = \frac{FCF_{N+1}}{r_{sU} - g} = \frac{FCF_N(1+g)}{r_{sU} - g}$$

$$\text{Horizon value of tax shield} = HV_{TS,N} = \frac{TS_{N+1}}{r_{sU} - g} = \frac{TS_N(1+g)}{r_{sU} - g}$$

$$V_{Unlevered} = \sum_{t=1}^{N} \frac{FCF_t}{(1+r_{sU})^t} + \frac{HV_{U,N}}{(1+r_{sU})^N}$$

$$V_{Tax\ shield} = \sum_{t=1}^{N} \frac{TS_t}{(1+r_{sU})^t} + \frac{HV_{TS,N}}{(1+r_{sU})^N}$$

CHAPTER 22

$$FCFE = \text{Free cash flow} - \text{After-tax interest expense} - \text{Principal payments} + \text{Newly issued debt}$$

$$= \text{Free cash flow} - \text{Interest expense} + \text{Interest tax shield} + \text{Net change in debt}$$

$$FCFE = \text{Net income} - \text{Net investment in operating capital} + \text{Net change in debt}$$

$$HV_{FCFE,N} = \frac{FCFE_{N+1}}{r_{sL} - g} = \frac{FCFE_N(1+g)}{r_{sL} - g}$$

$$V_{FCFE} = \sum_{t=1}^{N} \frac{FCFE_t}{(1+r_{sL})^t} + \frac{HV_{FCFE,N}}{(1+r_{sL})^N}$$

$S = V_{FCFE} + \text{Nonoperating assets}$

$$\frac{\text{Total value of shares to target shareholders}}{\text{Total post-merger value of equity}} = \text{Percent required by target stockholders} = \frac{n_{New}}{n_{New} + n_{Old}}$$

CHAPTER 25

$\hat{r}_p = w_A\hat{r}_A + (1 - w_A)\hat{r}_B$

$$\text{Portfolio SD} = \sigma_p = \sqrt{w_A^2\sigma_A^2 + (1-w_A)^2\sigma_B^2 + 2w_A(1-w_A)\rho_{AB}\sigma_A\sigma_B}$$

$$\text{Minimum-risk portfolio: } w_A = \frac{\sigma_B(\sigma_B - \rho_{AB}\sigma_A)}{\sigma_A^2 + \sigma_B^2 - 2\rho_{AB}\sigma_A\sigma_B}$$

$$\hat{r}_p = \sum_{i=1}^{N}(w_i\hat{r}_i)$$

$$\sigma_p^2 = \sum_{i=1}^{N}\sum_{j=1}^{N}(w_i\, w_j\, \sigma_i\, \sigma_j\, \rho_{ij})$$

$$\sigma_p^2 = \sum_{i=1}^{N} w_i^2\, \sigma_i^2 + \sum_{i=1}^{N}\sum_{\substack{j=1\\ j\neq i}}^{N} w_i\, \sigma_i\, w_j\, \sigma_j\, \rho_{ij}$$

$$\sigma_p = \sqrt{(1 - w_{RF})^2\, \sigma_M^2} = (1 - w_{RF})\sigma_M$$

$$\text{CML: } \hat{r}_p = r_{RF} + \left(\frac{\hat{r}_M - r_{RF}}{\sigma_M}\right)\sigma_p$$

$$r_i = r_{RF} + \frac{(r_M - r_{RF})}{\sigma_M}\left(\frac{\text{Cov}(r_i, r_M)}{\sigma_M}\right) = r_{RF} + (r_M - r_{RF})\left(\frac{\text{Cov}(r_i, r_M)}{\sigma_M^2}\right)$$

$$b_i = \frac{\text{Covariance between stock i and the market}}{\text{Variance of market returns}} = \frac{\text{Cov}(r_i, r_M)}{\sigma_M^2} = \frac{\rho_{iM}\sigma_i\sigma_M}{\sigma_M^2} = \rho_{iM}\left(\frac{\sigma_i}{\sigma_M}\right)$$

$$\text{SML} = r_i = r_{RF} + (r_M - r_{RF})b_i = r_{RF} + (RP_M)b_i$$

$$\sigma_i^2 = b_i^2\sigma_M^2 + {\sigma_{e_i}}^2$$

$$\text{APT: } r_i = r_{RF} + (r_1 - r_{RF})b_{i1} + \cdots + (r_j - r_{RF})b_{ij}$$

CHAPTER 26

$$CV = \frac{\sigma\ (\text{PV of future CF})}{E\ (\text{PV of future CF})}$$

$$\text{Variance of project's rate of return: } \sigma^2 = \frac{\ln\,(CV^2 + 1)}{t}$$

© lulu/fotolia.com

Glossary

A

abandonment option Allows a company to reduce the capacity of its output in response to changing market conditions. This includes the option to contract production or abandon a project if market conditions deteriorate too much.

absolute priority doctrine States that claims must be paid in strict accordance with the priority of each claim, regardless of the consequence to other claimants.

account receivable Created when a good is shipped or a service is performed, and payment for that good is made on a credit basis, not on a cash basis.

accounting income Income as defined by Generally Accepted Accounting Principles (GAAP).

accounting profit A firm's net income as reported on its income statement.

acquiring company A company that seeks to acquire another firm.

actual, or realized, rate of return, $\bar{r}_s$ The rate of return that was actually realized at the end of some holding period.

additional funds needed (AFN) Those funds required from external sources to increase the firm's assets to support a sales increase. A sales increase will normally require an increase in assets. However, some of this increase is usually offset by a spontaneous increase in liabilities as well as by earnings retained in the firm. Those funds that are required but not generated internally must be obtained from external sources.

add-on basis installment loan Interest is calculated over the life of the loan and then added on to the loan amount. This total amount is paid in equal installments. This raises the effective cost of the loan.

agency cost or problem An expense, either direct or indirect, that is borne by a principal as a result of having delegated authority to an agent. An example is the costs borne by shareholders to encourage managers to maximize a firm's stock price rather than act in their own self-interests. These costs may also arise from lost efficiency and the expense of monitoring management to ensure that debtholders' rights are protected.

agency debt Debt issued by federal agencies. Agency debt is not officially backed by the full faith and credit of the U.S. government, but investors assume that the government implicitly guarantees this debt, so these bonds carry interest rates only slightly higher than Treasury bonds.

aggressive short-term financing policy Refers to a policy in which a firm finances all of its fixed assets with long-term capital but part of its permanent current assets with short-term, nonspontaneous credit.

aging schedule Breaks down accounts receivable according to how long they have been outstanding. This gives the firm a more complete picture of the structure of accounts receivable than that provided by days sales outstanding.

alternative minimum tax (AMT) A provision of the U.S. Tax Code that requires profitable firms to pay at least some taxes if such taxes are greater than the amount due under standard tax accounting.

amortization A noncash charge against intangible assets, such as goodwill.

amortization schedule A table that breaks down the periodic fixed payment of an installment loan into its principal and interest components.

amortized loan A loan that is repaid in equal periodic amounts (or "killed off") over time.

anchoring bias Occurs when predictions of future events are influenced too heavily by recent events.

annual report A report issued annually by a corporation to its stockholders. It contains basic financial statements as well as management's opinion of the past year's operations and the firm's future prospects.

annual vesting A certain percentage of the options in a grant vest each year. For example, one-third of the options in the grant might vest each year.

annuity A series of payments of a fixed amount for a specified number of periods.

annuity due An annuity with payments occurring at the beginning of each period.

APR The nominal annual interest rate is also called the annual percentage rate, or APR.

arbitrage The simultaneous buying and selling of the same commodity or security in two different markets at different prices, thus yielding a risk-free return.

Arbitrage Pricing Theory (APT) An approach to measuring the equilibrium risk–return relationship for a given stock as a function of multiple factors, rather than the single factor (the market return) used by the CAPM. The APT is based on complex mathematical and statistical theory, and it can account for several factors (such as GNP and the level of inflation) in determining the required return for a particular stock.

arrearages Preferred dividends that have not been paid and hence are "in arrears."

asset management ratios A set of ratios that measure how effectively a firm is managing its assets.

assignment An informal procedure for liquidating debts that transfers title to a debtor's assets to a third person, known as an assignee or trustee.

asymmetric information theory Assumes managers have more complete information than investors and leads to a preferred "pecking order" of financing: (1) retained earnings, followed by (2) debt, and then (3) new common stock. Also known as signaling theory.

average tax rate Calculated by taking the total amount of tax paid divided by taxable income.

B

balance sheet A statement of the firm's financial position at a specific point in time. The firm's assets are listed on the left-hand side of the balance sheet; the right-hand side shows its liabilities and equity, or the claims against these assets.

banker's acceptance Created when an importer's bank promises to accept a postdated check written to an exporter even if there are insufficient funds in the importer's account. If the bank is strong, then this financial instrument virtually eliminates credit risk.

Bankruptcy Reform Act of 1978 Enacted to speed up and streamline bankruptcy proceedings. This law represented a shift to a relative priority doctrine of creditors' claims.

basic earning power (BEP) ratio Calculated by dividing earnings before interest and taxes by total assets. This ratio shows the raw earning power of the firm's assets before the influence of taxes and leverage.

behavioral finance A field of study that analyzes investor behavior as a result of psychological traits. It does not assume that investors necessarily behave rationally.

benchmarking When a firm compares its ratios to other leading companies in the same industry.

best efforts arrangement A type of contract with an investment banker when issuing stock. In a best efforts sale, the investment banker is only committed to making every effort to sell the stock at the offering price. In this case, the issuing firm bears the risk that the new issue will not be fully subscribed.

beta coefficient, b A measure of the amount of risk that an individual stock contributes to a well-diversified portfolio.

bird-in-the-hand theory Assumes that investors value a dollar of dividends more highly than a dollar of expected capital gains, because a certain dividend is less risky than a possible capital gain. This theory implies that a high-dividend stock has a higher price and lower required return, all else held equal.

Black-Scholes option pricing model A model to estimate the value of a call option. It is widely used by options traders.

bond A promissory note issued by a business or a governmental unit.

bond insurance Protects investors against default by the issuer and provides credit enhancement to the bond issue.

book value per share Common equity divided by the number of shares outstanding.

break-even point The level of unit sales at which costs equal revenues.

breakup value A firm's value if its assets are sold off in pieces.

business risk The risk inherent in the operations of the firm, prior to the financing decision. Thus, business risk is the uncertainty inherent in future operating income or earnings before interest and taxes. Business risk is caused by many factors; two of the most important are sales variability and operating leverage.

C

call option An option that allows the holder to buy the asset at some predetermined price within a specified period of time.

call provision Gives the issuing corporation the right to call the bonds for redemption. The call provision generally states that if the bonds are called then the company must pay the bondholders an amount greater than the par value, or a call premium. Most bonds contain a call provision.

capacity option Allows a company to change the capacity of its output in response to changing market conditions. This includes the option to contract or expand production. It also includes the option to abandon a project if market conditions deteriorate too much.

Capital Asset Pricing Model (CAPM) A model based on the proposition that any stock's required rate of return is equal to the risk-free rate of return plus a risk premium reflecting only the risk remaining after diversification. The CAPM equation is $r_i = r_{RF} + b_i(r_M - r_{RF})$.

capital budget Outlines the planned expenditures on fixed assets.

capital budgeting The whole process of analyzing projects and deciding whether they should be included in the capital budget.

capital gain (loss) The profit (loss) from the sale of a capital asset for more (less) than its purchase price.

capital gains yield Results from changing prices and is calculated as $(P_1 - P_0)/P_0$, where P_0 is the beginning-of-period price and P_1 is the end-of-period price.

capital intensity ratio The dollar amount of assets required to produce a dollar of sales. The capital intensity ratio is the reciprocal of the total assets turnover ratio.

capital market Capital markets are the financial markets for long-term debt and corporate stocks. The New York Stock Exchange is an example of a capital market.

capital rationing Occurs when management places a constraint on the size of the firm's capital budget during a particular period.

capital structure The manner in which a firm's assets are financed; that is, the right side of the balance sheet. Capital structure is normally expressed as the percentage of each type of capital used by the firm such as debt, preferred stock, and common equity.

capitalizing Incorporating the lease provisions into the balance sheet by reporting the leased asset under fixed assets and reporting the present value of future lease payments as debt.

cash budget A schedule showing cash flows (receipts, disbursements, and cash balances) for a firm over a specified period.

cash conversion cycle The length of time between the firm's actual cash expenditures on productive resources (materials and labor) and its own cash receipts from the sale of products (that is, the length of time between paying for labor and materials and collecting on receivables). Thus, the cash conversion cycle equals the length of time the firm has funds tied up in current assets.

cash discounts The amount by which a seller is willing to reduce the invoice price in order to be paid immediately, rather than in the future. A cash discount might be 2/10, net 30, which means a 2% discount if the bill is paid within 10 days and otherwise the entire amount is due within 30 days.

CDO, collateralized debt obligation Created when large numbers of mortgages are bundled into pools to create new securities that are then sliced into tranches; the tranches are recombined and re-divided into securities called CDOs.

CDS, credit default swap Derivative in which a counterparty pays if a specified debt instrument goes into default; similar to insurance on a bond.

Chapter 11 bankruptcy The 11th chapter of the bankruptcy statutes, regulates reorganization in a bankruptcy.

Chapter 7 bankruptcy The 7th chapter of the bankruptcy statutes, regulates liquidation in a bankruptcy.

characteristic line Obtained by regressing the historical returns on a particular stock against the historical returns on the general stock market. The slope of the characteristic line is the stock's beta, which measures the amount by which the stock's expected return increases for a given increase in the expected return on the market.

charter The legal document that is filed with the state to incorporate a company.

check-clearing process When a customer's check is written upon one bank and a company deposits the check in its own bank, the company's bank must verify that the check is valid before the company can use those funds. Checks are generally cleared through the Federal Reserve System or through a clearinghouse set up by the banks in a particular city.

classified boards A board of directors with staggered terms. For example, a board with one-third of the seats filled each year and directors serving three-year terms.

classified stock Sometimes created by a firm to meet special needs and circumstances. Generally, when special classifications of stock are used, one type is designated "Class A," another as "Class B," and so on. For example, Class A might be entitled to receive dividends before dividends can be paid on Class B stock. Class B might have the exclusive right to vote.

cleanup clause A clause in a line of credit that requires the borrower to reduce the loan balance to zero at least once a year.

clientele effect The attraction of companies with specific dividend policies to those investors whose needs are best served by those policies. Thus, companies with high dividends will have a clientele of investors with low marginal tax rates and strong desires for current income. Conversely, companies with low dividends will have a clientele of investors with high marginal tax rates and little need for current income.

cliff vesting All the options in a grant vest on the same date.

closely held corporation Refers to companies that are so small that their common stocks are not actively traded; they are owned by only a few people, usually the companies' managers.

coefficient of variation, CV Equal to the standard deviation divided by the expected return; it is a standardized risk measure that allows comparisons between investments having different expected returns and standard deviations.

collection policy The procedure for collecting accounts receivable. A change in collection policy will affect sales, days sales outstanding, bad debt losses, and the percentage of customers taking discounts.

collections float Float created while funds from customers' checks are being deposited and cleared through the check collection process.

combination lease Combines some aspects of both operating and financial leases. For example, a financial lease that contains a cancellation clause—normally associated with operating leases—is a combination lease.

commercial paper Unsecured, short-term promissory notes of large firms, usually issued in denominations of $100,000 or more and having an interest rate somewhat below the prime rate.

commodity futures Futures contracts that involve the sale or purchase of various commodities, including grains, oilseeds, livestock, meats, fiber, metals, and wood.

common stockholders' equity (net worth) The capital supplied by common stockholders—capital stock, paid-in capital, retained earnings, and (occasionally) certain reserves. Paid-in capital is the difference between the stock's par value and what stockholders paid when they bought newly issued shares.

comparative ratio analysis Compares a firm's own ratios to other leading companies in the same industry. This technique is also known as benchmarking.

compensating balance (CB) A minimum checking account balance that a firm must maintain with a bank to compensate the bank for services rendered or for making a loan; generally equal to 10%–20% of the loans outstanding.

composition Creditors voluntarily reduce their fixed claims on the debtor by accepting a lower principal amount, reducing the interest rate on the debt, accepting equity in place of debt, or some combination of these changes.

compounding The process of finding the future value of a single payment or series of payments.

computer/telephone network A computer/telephone network, such as NASDAQ, consists of all the facilities that provide for security transactions not conducted at a physical location exchange. These facilities are, basically, the communications networks that link buyers and sellers.

conditional value at risk (CVaR) The average portfolio value (or loss) conditional upon the portfolio value being less than a specified threshold value (or threshold percentile). It can also be defined as the average NPV conditional upon the NPV being less than a specified threshold value (or threshold percentile). It is also called the expected shortfall (ES).

congeneric merger Involves firms that are interrelated but do not have identical lines of business. One example is Prudential's acquisition of Bache & Company.

conglomerate merger Occurs when unrelated enterprises combine, such as Mobil Oil and Montgomery Ward.

conservative short-term financing policy Refers to using permanent capital to finance all permanent asset requirements as well as to meet some or all of the seasonal demands.

consol A type of perpetuity. Consols were originally bonds issued by England in the mid-1700s to consolidate past debt.

continuous probability distribution Contains an infinite number of outcomes and is graphed from $-\infty$ and $+\infty$.

conversion price The effective price per share of stock if conversion occurs; the par value of the convertible security divided by the conversion ratio.

conversion ratio The number of shares of common stock received upon conversion of one convertible security.

conversion value The value of the stock that the investor would receive if conversion occurred; the market price per share times the conversion ratio.

convertible bond Security that is convertible into shares of common stock, at a fixed price, at the option of the bondholder.

convertible currency A currency that can be traded in the currency markets and can be redeemed at current market rates.

convertible security Bonds or preferred stocks that can be exchanged for (converted into) common stock, under specific terms, at the option of the holder. Unlike the exercise of warrants, conversion of a convertible security does not provide additional capital to the issuer.

corporate alliance A cooperative deal that stops short of a merger; also called a strategic alliance.

corporate bond Debt issued by corporations and exposed to default risk. Different corporate bonds have different levels of default risk, depending on the issuing company's characteristics and on the terms of the specific bond.

corporate governance The set of rules that controls a company's behavior toward its directors, managers, employees, shareholders, creditors, customers, competitors, and community.

corporate valuation model Defines the total value of a company as the present value of its expected free cash flows discounted at the weighted average cost of capital (i.e., the value of operations) plus the value of nonoperating assets such as T-bills.

corporation A corporation is a legal entity created by a state. The corporation is separate and distinct from its owners and managers.

correlation The tendency of two variables to move together.

correlation coefficient, ρ (rho) A standardized measure of how two random variables covary. A correlation coefficient (ρ) of +1.0 means that the two variables move up and down in perfect synchronization, whereas a coefficient of −1.0 means the variables always move in opposite directions. A correlation coefficient of zero suggests that the two variables are not related to one another; that is, they are independent.

cost of common stock, r_s The return required by the firm's common stockholders. It is usually calculated using Capital Asset Pricing Model or the dividend growth model.

cost of new external common equity, r_e A project financed with external equity must earn a higher rate of return because it must cover the flotation costs. Thus, the cost of new common equity is higher than that of common equity raised internally by reinvesting earnings.

cost of preferred stock, r_{ps} The return required by the firm's preferred stockholders. The cost of preferred stock, r_{ps}, is the cost to the firm of issuing new preferred stock. For perpetual preferred, it is the preferred dividend, D_{ps}, divided by the net issuing price, P_n.

costly trade credit Credit taken (in excess of free trade credit) whose cost is equal to the discount lost.

coupon interest rate Stated rate of interest on a bond; defined as the coupon payment divided by the par value.

coupon payment Dollar amount of interest paid to each bondholder on the interest payment dates.

coverage ratio Similar to the times-interest-earned ratio, but it recognizes that many firms lease assets and also must make sinking fund payments. It is found by adding earnings before interest, taxes, depreciation, amortization (EBITDA), and lease payments and then dividing this total by interest charges, lease payments, and sinking fund payments over 1 − T (where T is the tax rate).

cramdown Reorganization plans that are mandated by the bankruptcy court and binding on all parties.

credit period The length of time for which credit is extended. If the credit period is lengthened, then sales will generally increase, as will accounts receivable. This will increase the firm's financing needs and possibly increase bad debt losses. A shortening of the credit period will have the opposite effect.

credit policy The firm's policy on granting and collecting credit. There are four elements of credit policy, or credit policy variables: credit period, credit standards, collection policy, and discounts.

credit standards The financial strength and creditworthiness that qualifies a customer for a firm's regular credit terms.

credit terms Statements of the credit period and any discounts offered—for example, 2/10, net 30.

cross rate The exchange rate between two non-U.S. currencies.

crossover rate The cost of capital at which the NPV profiles for two projects intersect.

cumulative preferred dividends A protective feature on preferred stock that requires all past preferred dividends to be paid before any common dividends can be paid.

currency appreciation Occurs to a particular currency when it increases in value relative to another particular currency. For example, if the exchange rate of 1.0 dollar per euro changes to 1.1 dollars per euro, then euro has appreciated against the dollar by 10%.

currency depreciation Occurs to a particular currency when it decreases in value relative to another particular currency. For example, if the exchange rate of 1.0 dollar per euro changes to 0.9 dollars per euro, then euro has depreciated against the dollar by 10%.

current ratio Indicates the extent to which current liabilities are covered by those assets expected to be converted to cash in the near future; it is found by dividing current assets by current liabilities.

current yield (on a bond) The annual coupon payment divided by the current market price.

D

days sales outstanding (DSO) Used to appraise accounts receivable and indicates the length of time the firm must wait after making a sale before receiving cash. It is found by dividing receivables by average sales per day.

DCF (discounted cash flow) techniques The net present value (NPV) and internal rate of return (IRR) techniques are discounted cash flow (DCF) evaluation techniques. These are called DCF methods because they explicitly recognize the time value of money.

dealer market In a dealer market, a dealer holds an inventory of the security and makes a market by offering to buy or sell. Others who wish to buy or sell can see the offers made by the dealers and can contact the dealer of their choice to arrange a transaction.

debenture An unsecured bond; as such, it provides no lien against specific property as security for the obligation. Debenture holders are therefore general creditors whose claims are protected by property not otherwise pledged.

debt ratio The ratio of total debt to total assets, it measures the percentage of funds provided by investors other than preferred or common shareholders.

debt-to-equity ratio Ratio of debt divided by equity.

decision trees A form of scenario analysis in which different actions are taken in different scenarios.

declaration date The date on which a firm's directors issue a statement declaring a dividend.

default risk The risk that a borrower may not pay the interest and/or principal on a loan when it becomes due. If the issuer defaults, investors receive less than the promised return on the bond. Default risk is influenced by the financial strength of the issuer and also by the terms of the bond contract, especially whether collateral has been pledged to secure the bond. The greater the default risk, the higher the bond's yield to maturity.

default risk premium (DRP) The premium added to the real risk-free rate to compensate investors for the risk that a borrower may fail to pay the interest and/or principal on a loan when they become due.

defensive merger Occurs when one company acquires another to help ward off a hostile merger attempt.

depreciation A noncash charge against tangible assets, such as buildings or machines. It is taken for the purpose of showing an asset's estimated dollar cost of the capital equipment used up in the production process.

derivatives Claims whose value depends on what happens to the value of some other asset. Futures and options are two important types of derivatives, and their values depend on what happens to the prices of other assets. Therefore, the value of a derivative security is derived from the value of an underlying real asset or other security.

detachable warrant A warrant that can be detached and traded separately from the underlying security. Most warrants are detachable.

devaluation The lowering, by governmental action, of the price of its currency relative to another currency. For example, in 1967 the British pound was devalued from $2.80 per pound to $2.50 per pound.

development bond A tax-exempt bond sold by state and local governments whose proceeds are made available to corporations for specific uses deemed (by Congress) to be in the public interest.

direct quotation When discussing exchange rates, the number of units of home currency required to purchase one unit of a foreign currency.

disbursement float Float created before checks written by a firm have cleared and been deducted from the firm's account; disbursement float causes the firm's own checkbook balance to be smaller than the balance on the bank's records.

discount bond Bond prices and interest rates are inversely related; that is, they tend to move in the opposite direction from one another. A fixed-rate bond will sell at par when its coupon interest rate is equal to the going rate of interest, r_d. When the going rate of interest is above the coupon rate, a fixed-rate bond will sell at a "discount" below its par value. If current interest rates are below the coupon rate, a fixed-rate bond will sell at a "premium" above its par value.

discount interest Interest that is calculated on the face amount of a loan but is paid in advance.

discount on forward rate Occurs when the forward exchange rate differs from the spot rate. When the forward rate is below the spot rate, the forward rate is said to be at a discount.

discounted cash flow (DCF) method A method of valuing a business that involves the application of capital budgeting procedures to an entire firm rather than to a single project.

discounted payback period The number of years it takes a firm to recover its project investment based on discounted cash flows.

discounting The process of finding the present value of a single payment or series of payments.

distribution policy The policy that sets the level of distributions and the form of the distributions (dividends and stock repurchases).

diversifiable risk Refers to that part of a security's total risk associated with random events not affecting the market as a whole. This risk can be eliminated by proper diversification. Also known as company-specific risk.

divestiture The opposite of an acquisition. That is, a company sells a portion of its assets—often a whole division—to another firm or individual.

dividend irrelevance theory Holds that dividend policy has no effect on either the price of a firm's stock or its cost of capital.

dividend reinvestment plan (DRIP) Allows stockholders to automatically purchase shares of common stock of the paying corporation in lieu of receiving cash dividends. There are two types of plans: one involves only stock that is already outstanding; the other involves newly issued stock. In the first type, the dividends of all participants are pooled and the stock is purchased on the open market. Participants benefit from lower transaction costs. In the second type, the company issues new shares to the participants. Thus, the company issues stock in lieu of the cash dividend.

dividend yield Defined as either the end-of-period dividend divided by the beginning-of-period price or as the ratio of the current dividend to the current price. Valuation formulas use the former definition.

DuPont chart A chart designed to show the relationships among return on investment, asset turnover, the profit margin, and leverage.

DuPont equation A formula showing that the rate of return on equity can be found as the profit margin multiplied by the product of total assets turnover and the equity multiplier.

E

EBITDA Earnings before interest, taxes, depreciation, and amortization.

ECN In an ECN (electronic communications network), orders from potential buyers and sellers are automatically matched and the transaction is automatically completed.

economic life The number of years a project should be operated to maximize its net present value; often less than the maximum potential life.

Economic Value Added (EVA) A method used to measure a firm's true profitability. EVA is found by taking the firm's after-tax operating profit and subtracting the annual cost of all the capital a firm uses. If the firm generates a positive EVA, its management has created value for its shareholders. If the EVA is negative, management has destroyed shareholder value.

effective (or equivalent) annual rate (EAR or EFF%) The effective annual rate is the rate that, under annual compounding, would have produced the same future value at the end of 1 year as was produced by more frequent compounding, say quarterly. If the compounding occurs annually, then the effective annual rate and the nominal rate are the same. If compounding occurs more frequently, then the effective annual rate is greater than the nominal rate.

efficient frontier The set of efficient portfolios out of the full set of potential portfolios. On a graph, the efficient frontier constitutes the boundary line of the set of potential portfolios.

Efficient Markets Hypothesis (EMH) States (1) that stocks are always in equilibrium and (2) that it is impossible for an investor to consistently "beat the market." The EMH assumes that all important information regarding a stock is reflected in the price of that stock.

efficient portfolio Provides the highest expected return for any degree of risk. The efficient portfolio also provides the lowest degree of risk for any expected return.

embedded options Options that are a part of another project. Also called real options, managerial options, and strategic options.

enterprise risk management (ERM) A process that includes risk identification, risk assessment, and risk responses. ERM requires the participation of all levels within an organization.

entrenchment Occurs when a company has such a weak board of directors and has such strong anti-takeover provisions in its corporate charter that senior managers feel there is little chance of being removed.

equilibrium The condition under which the intrinsic value of a security is equal to its price; also, when a security's expected return is equal to its required return.

equity risk premium RP_M; Expected market return minus the risk-free rate; also called market risk premium or equity premium

ESOP (employee stock ownership plan) A type of retirement plan in which employees own stock in the company.

euro The currency used by nations in the European Monetary Union.

Eurobond Any bond sold in some country other than the one in whose currency the bond is denominated. Thus, a U.S. firm selling dollar bonds in Switzerland is selling Eurobonds.

Eurodollar A U.S. dollar on deposit in a foreign bank or a foreign branch of a U.S. bank. Eurodollars are used to conduct transactions throughout Europe and the rest of the world.

exchange rate Specifies the number of units of a given currency that can be purchased for one unit of another currency.

exchange rate risk Refers to the fluctuation in exchange rates between currencies over time.

ex-dividend date The date when the right to the dividend leaves the stock. This date was established by stockbrokers to avoid confusion, and it is four business days prior to the holder-of-record date. If the stock sale is made prior to the ex-dividend date, then the dividend is paid to the buyer; if the stock is bought on or after the ex-dividend date, the dividend is paid to the seller.

exercise price The price stated in the option contract at which the security can be bought (or sold). Also called the strike price.

exercise value Equal to the current price of the stock (underlying the option) minus the strike price of the option.

expectations theory States that the slope of the yield curve depends on expectations about future inflation rates and interest rates. Thus, if the annual rate of inflation and future interest rates are expected to increase, then the yield curve will be upward sloping; the curve will be downward sloping if the annual rates are expected to decrease.

expected rate of return, $\hat{r}_s$ The rate of return expected on a stock given its current price and expected future cash flows. If the stock is in equilibrium, the required rate of return will equal the expected rate of return.

expected shortfall (ES) The average portfolio value conditional upon the portfolio value being less than a specified threshold value (or threshold percentile). It can also be defined as the average NPV conditional upon the NPV being less than a specified threshold value (or threshold percentile). It is also called the conditional value at risk (CVaR).

extension A form of debt restructuring in which creditors postpone the dates of required interest or principal payments, or both.

extra dividend A dividend paid, in addition to the regular dividend, when earnings permit. Firms with volatile earnings may have a low regular dividend that can be maintained even in years of low profit (or high capital investment) but is supplemented by an extra dividend when excess funds are available.

F

fairness The standard of fairness states that claims must be recognized in the order of their legal and contractual priority. In simpler terms, the reorganization must be fair to all parties.

Fama-French three-factor model Includes one factor for the excess market return (the market return minus the risk-free rate), a second factor for size (defined as the return on a portfolio of small firms minus the return on a portfolio of big firms), and a third factor for the book-to-market effect (defined as the return on a portfolio of firms with a high book-to-market ratio minus the return on a portfolio of firms with a low book-to-market ratio).

FASB Financial Accounting Standards Board.

FASB Statement 13 The Financial Accounting Standards Board statement that spells out the conditions under which a lease must be capitalized and the specific procedures to follow.

feasibility The standard of feasibility states that there must be a reasonably high probability of successful rehabilitation and profitable future operations.

feasible set Represents all portfolios that can be constructed from a given set of stocks; also known as the attainable set.

financial distress costs Incurred when a leveraged firm facing a decline in earnings is forced to take actions to avoid bankruptcy. These costs may be the result of delays in the liquidation of assets, legal fees, the effects on product quality from cutting costs, and evasive actions by suppliers and customers.

financial futures Provide for the purchase or sale of a financial asset at some time in the future, but at a price that is established today. Financial futures exist for Treasury bills, Treasury notes and bonds, certificates of deposit, Eurodollar deposits, foreign currencies, and stock indexes.

financial intermediary Intermediary that buys securities with funds that it obtains by issuing its own securities. An example is a common stock mutual fund that buys common stocks with funds obtained by issuing shares in the mutual fund.

financial lease Covers the entire expected life of the equipment; does not provide for maintenance service, is not cancellable, and is fully amortized.

financial leverage The extent to which fixed-income securities (debt and preferred stock) are used in a firm's capital structure. If a high percentage of a firm's capital structure is in the form of debt and preferred stock, then the firm is said to have a high degree of financial leverage.

financial merger A merger in which the companies will not be operated as a single unit and for which no operating economies are expected.

financial risk The risk added by the use of debt financing. Debt financing increases the variability of earnings before taxes (but after interest); thus, along with business risk, it contributes to the uncertainty of net income and earnings per share. Business risk plus financial risk equals total corporate risk.

financial service corporation A corporation that offers a wide range of financial services such as brokerage operations, insurance, and commercial banking.

financing deficit The shortfall of spontaneous liabilities, planned change in external financing (total changes of debt, preferred stock, and common stock from the preliminary financing plan), and internal funds (net income less planned dividends) relative to additional assets required by the operating plan.

financing feedback Circularity created when additional debt causes additional interest expense, which reduces the addition to retained earnings, which in turn requires a higher level of debt, which causes still more interest expense, causing the cycle to be repeated.

financing surplus The excess of spontaneous liabilities, planned change in external financing (total changes of debt, preferred stock, and common stock from the preliminary financing plan), and internal funds (net income less planned dividends) relative to additional assets required by the operating plan.

fixed assets turnover ratio The ratio of sales to net fixed assets; it measures how effectively the firm uses its plant and equipment.

fixed exchange rate system The system in effect from the end of World War II until August 1971. Under the system, the U.S. dollar was linked to gold at the rate of $35 per ounce, and other currencies were then tied to the dollar.

floating exchange rates The system currently in effect, where the forces of supply and demand are allowed to determine currency prices with little government intervention.

floating-rate bond A bond whose coupon payment may vary over time. The coupon rate is usually linked to the rate on some other security, such as a Treasury security, or to some other rate, such as the prime rate or LIBOR.

flotation cost, F Those costs occurring when a company issues a new security, including fees to an investment banker and legal fees.

forecasted financial statements approach A method of forecasting financial statements to determine the additional funds needed. Many items on the income statement and balance sheets are assumed to increase proportionally with sales. As sales increase, these items that are tied to sales also increase, and the values of these items for a particular year are estimated as percentages of the forecasted sales for that year.

foreign bond A bond sold by a foreign borrower but denominated in the currency of the country in which the issue is sold. Thus, a U.S. firm selling bonds denominated in Swiss francs in Switzerland is selling foreign bonds.

foreign exchange (FX) risk The risk that a change in a currency exchange rate might adversely affect a company.

foreign trade deficit A deficit that occurs when businesses and individuals in the United States import more goods from foreign countries than are exported.

forward contract A contract to buy or sell some item at some time in the future at a price established when the contract is entered into.

forward exchange rate The prevailing exchange rate for exchange (delivery) at some agreed-upon future date, which is usually 30, 90, or 180 days from the day the transaction is negotiated.

founders' shares Stock owned by the firm's founders that have sole voting rights but restricted dividends for a specified number of years.

free cash flow (FCF) The cash flow actually available for distribution to all investors after the company has made all investments in fixed assets and working capital necessary to sustain ongoing operations.

free cash flow valuation model Defines the total value of a company as the present value of its expected free cash flows discounted at the weighted average cost of capital (i.e., the value of operations) plus the value of nonoperating assets such as T-bills.

free trade credit Credit received during the discount period.

friendly merger Occurs when the target company's management agrees to the merger and recommends that shareholders approve the deal.

fundamental value or price Value or price that incorporates all relevant information regarding expected future cash flows and risk.

FVA_N The future value of a stream of annuity payments, where N is the number of payments of the annuity.

$FVIFA_{I,N}$ The future value interest factor for an ordinary annuity of N periodic payments paying I percent interest per period.

$FVIF_{I,N}$ The future value interest factor for a lump sum left in an account for N periods paying I percent interest per period.

FV_N The future value of an initial single cash flow, where N is the number of periods the initial cash flow is compounded.

G

GAAP, Generally Accepted Accounting Principles. A set of standards for financial reporting established by the accounting profession.

going public The act of selling stock to the public at large by a closely held corporation or its principal stockholders.

golden parachute A payment made to executives who are forced out when a merger takes place.

greenmail Targeted share repurchases that occur when a company buys back stock from a potential acquirer at a higher than fair-market price. In return, the potential acquirer agrees not to attempt to take over the company.

gross profit margin Ratio of gross profit (sales minus cost of goods sold) divided by sales.

growth option Occurs if an investment creates the opportunity to make other potentially profitable investments that would not otherwise be possible, including options to expand output, to enter a new geographical market, and to introduce complementary products or successive generations of products.

GSE (government-sponsored entity) debt Debt issued by government-sponsored entities (GSEs) such as the Tennessee Valley Authority or the Small Business Administration; not officially backed by the full faith and credit of the U.S. government.

guideline lease Meets all of the Internal Revenue Service (IRS) requirements for a genuine lease. If a lease meets the IRS guidelines, the IRS allows the lessor to deduct the asset's depreciation and allows the lessee to deduct the lease payments. Also called a tax-oriented lease.

H

Hamada equation Shows the effect of debt on the beta coefficient—increases in debt increase beta, and decreases in debt reduce beta.

hard currencies Currencies considered to be convertible because the nation that issues them allows them to be traded in the currency markets and is willing to redeem them at market rates.

hedging A transaction that lowers a firm's risk of damage due to fluctuating commodity prices, interest rates, and exchange rates.

herding instinct When one group of investors does well, other investors begin to emulate them, acting like a herd of sheep.

holder-of-record date If a company lists the stockholder as an owner on the holder-of-record date, then the stockholder receives the dividend.

holding company A corporation formed for the sole purpose of owning stocks in other companies. A holding company differs from a stock mutual fund in that holding companies own sufficient stock in their operating companies to exercise effective working control.

holdout A problematic characteristic of informal reorganizations whereby all of the involved parties do not agree to the voluntary plan. Holdouts are usually made by creditors in an effort to receive full payment on claims.

horizon value of operations The value of operations at the end of the explicit forecast period. It is equal to the present value of all free cash flows beyond the forecast period, discounted back to the end of the forecast period at the weighted average cost of capital.

horizontal merger A merger between two companies in the same line of business.

hostile merger Occurs when the management of the target company resists the offer.

hurdle rate The project cost of capital, or discount rate. It is the rate used to discount future cash flows in the net present value method or to compare with the internal rate of return.

I

improper accumulation The retention of earnings by a business for the purpose of enabling stockholders to avoid personal income taxes on dividends.

income bond Pays interest only if the interest is earned. These securities cannot bankrupt a company, but from an investor's standpoint, they are riskier than "regular" bonds.

income statement Summarizes the firm's revenues and expenses over an accounting period. Net sales are shown at the top of each statement, after which various costs, including income taxes, are subtracted to obtain the net income available to common stockholders. The bottom of the statement reports earnings and dividends per share.

incremental cash flow Those cash flows that arise solely from the asset that is being evaluated.

indentures A legal document that spells out the rights of both bondholders and the issuing corporation.

independent projects Projects that can be accepted or rejected individually.

indexed, or purchasing power, bond The interest rate of such a bond is based on an inflation index such as the consumer price index (CPI), so the interest paid rises automatically when the inflation rate rises, thus protecting the bondholders against inflation.

indifference curve The risk–return trade-off function for a particular investor; reflects that investor's attitude toward risk. An investor would be indifferent between any pair of assets on the same indifference curve. In risk–return space, the greater the slope of the indifference curve, the greater is the investor's risk aversion.

indirect quotation When discussing exchange rates, the number of units of foreign currency that can be purchased for one unit of home currency.

inflation premium (IP) The premium added to the real risk-free rate of interest to compensate for the expected loss of purchasing power. The inflation premium is the average rate of inflation expected over the life of the security.

informal debt restructuring An agreement between a troubled firm and its creditors to change existing debt terms. An extension postpones the required payment date; a composition is a reduction in creditor claims.

information content, or signaling, hypothesis A theory that holds that investors regard dividend changes as "signals" of management forecasts. Thus, when dividends are raised, this is viewed by investors as recognition by management of future earnings increases. Therefore, if a firm's stock price increases with a dividend increase, the reason may not be investor preference for dividends but rather expectations of higher future earnings. Conversely, a dividend reduction may signal that management is forecasting poor earnings in the future.

initial public offering (IPO) Occurs when a closely held corporation or its principal stockholders sell stock to the public at large.

initial public offering (IPO) market Going public is the act of selling stock to the public at large by a closely held corporation or its principal stockholders, and this market is often termed the initial public offering market.

I_{NOM} The nominal, or quoted, interest rate.

insiders The officers, directors, and major stockholders of a firm.

interest coverage ratio Also called the times-interest-earned (TIE) ratio; determined by dividing earnings before interest and taxes by the interest expense.

interest rate parity Holds that investors should expect to earn the same return in all countries after adjusting for risk.

interest rate risk Arises from the fact that bond prices decline when interest rates rise. Under these circumstances, selling a bond prior to maturity will result in a capital loss; the longer the term to maturity, the larger the loss.

interlocking boards of directors Occur when the CEO of Company A sits on the board of Company B while B's CEO sits on A's board.

internal rate of return (IRR) method The discount rate that equates the present value of the expected future cash inflows and outflows. IRR measures the rate of return on a project, but it assumes that all cash flows can be reinvested at the IRR rate.

international bond Any bond sold outside of the country of the borrower. There are two types of international bonds: Eurobonds and foreign bonds.

intrinsic value or price Value or price that incorporates all relevant information regarding expected future cash flows and risk.

inventory conversion period The average length of time to convert materials into finished goods and then to sell them; calculated by dividing total inventory by daily costs of goods sold.

inventory turnover ratio Cost of goods sold divided by inventories.

inverted (abnormal) yield curve A downward-sloping yield curve.

investment bank A firm that assists in the design of an issuing firm's corporate securities and in the sale of the new securities to investors in the primary market.

investment grade bond Securities with ratings of Baa/BBB or above.

investment timing option Gives companies the option to delay a project rather than implement it immediately. This option to wait allows a company to reduce the uncertainty of market conditions before it decides to implement the project.

investor-supplied capital Total amount of short-term debt, long-term debt, preferred stock, and total common equity shown on a balance sheet. It is the amount of financing that investors have provided to a company. It also called total investor-supplied capital.

investor-supplied operating capital The total amount of short-term debt, long-term debt, preferred stock, and total common equity shown on a balance sheet, less the amount of short-term investments shown on the balance sheet. It is the amount of financing used in operations that investors have provided to a company. It also called total investor-supplied operating capital.

J

Jensen's alpha Measures the vertical distance of a portfolio's return above or below the Security Market Line; first suggested by Professor Michael Jensen, it became popular because of its ease of calculation.

joint venture Involves the joining together of parts of companies to accomplish specific, limited objectives. Joint ventures are controlled by the combined management of the two (or more) parent companies.

junk bond High-risk, high-yield bond issued to finance leveraged buyouts, mergers, or troubled companies.

L

lessee The party leasing the property.

lessee's analysis Involves determining whether leasing an asset is less costly than buying the asset. The lessee will compare the present value cost of leasing the asset with the present value cost of purchasing the asset (assuming the funds to purchase the asset are obtained through a loan). If the present value cost of the lease is less than the present value cost of purchasing, then the asset should be leased. The lessee can also analyze the lease using the IRR approach or the equivalent loan method.

lessor The party receiving the payments from the lease (that is, the owner of the property).

lessor's analysis Involves determining the rate of return on the proposed lease. If the internal rate of return of the lease cash flows exceeds the lessor's opportunity cost of capital, then the lease is a good investment. This is equivalent to analyzing whether the net present value of the lease is positive.

leveraged buyout (LBO) A transaction in which a firm's publicly owned stock is acquired in a mostly debt-financed tender offer, resulting in a privately owned, highly leveraged firm. Often, the firm's own management initiates the LBO.

leveraged lease The lessor borrows a portion of the funds needed to buy the equipment to be leased.

liabilities to assets ratio The ratio of total liabilities to total assets, it measures the percentage of funds provided by creditors.

LIBOR London Interbank Offered Rate; the rate that U.K. banks charge one another.

limited liability partnership A limited liability partnership (LLP), sometimes called a limited liability company (LLC), combines the limited liability advantage of a corporation with the tax advantages of a partnership.

limited partnership A partnership in which limited partners' liabilities, investment returns, and control are limited; general partners have unlimited liability and control.

line of credit An arrangement in which a bank agrees to lend up to a specified maximum amount of funds during a designated period.

liquidation in bankruptcy The sale of the assets of a firm and the distribution of the proceeds to the creditors and owners in a specific priority.

liquidity Liquidity refers to a firm's cash and marketable securities position and to its ability to meet maturing obligations. A liquid asset is any asset that can be quickly sold and converted to cash at its "fair" value. Active markets provide liquidity.

liquidity premium (LP) A liquidity premium is added to the real risk-free rate of interest, in addition to other premiums, if a security is not liquid.

liquidity ratio A ratio that shows the relationship of a firm's cash and other current assets to its current liabilities.

lockbox plan A cash management tool in which incoming checks for a firm are sent to post office boxes rather than to corporate headquarters. Several times a day, a local bank will collect the contents of the lockbox and deposit the checks into the company's local account.

long hedges Occur when futures contracts are bought in anticipation of (or to guard against) price increases.

low-regular-dividend-plus-extras policy Dividend policy in which a company announces a low regular dividend that it is sure can be maintained; if extra funds are available, the company pays a specially designated extra dividend or repurchases shares of stock.

lumpy assets Those assets that cannot be acquired smoothly and instead require large, discrete additions. For example, an electric utility that is operating at full capacity cannot add a small amount of generating capacity, at least not economically.

M

managerial options Options that give opportunities to managers to respond to changing market conditions. Also called real options.

margin requirement The margin is the percentage of a stock's price that an investor has borrowed in order to purchase the stock. The Securities and Exchange Commission sets margin requirements, which is the maximum percentage of debt that can be used to purchase a stock.

marginal tax rate The tax rate on the last unit of income.

market multiple method Multiplies a market-determined ratio (called a multiple) to some value of the target firm to estimate the target's value. The market multiple can be based on net income, earnings per share, sales, book value, or number of subscribers.

market portfolio A portfolio consisting of all stocks.

market risk That part of a security's total risk that cannot be eliminated by diversification; measured by the beta coefficient.

market risk premium, RP_M The difference between the expected return on the market and the risk-free rate.

Market Value Added (MVA) The difference between the market value of the firm (that is, the sum of the market value of common equity, the market value of debt, and the market value of preferred stock) and the book value of the firm's common equity, debt, and preferred stock. If the book values of debt and preferred stock are equal to their market values, then MVA is also equal to the difference between the market value of equity and the amount of equity capital that investors supplied.

market value ratios Relate the firm's stock price to its earnings and book value per share.

marketable securities Can be converted to cash on very short notice and provide at least a modest return.

maturity date The date when the bond's par value is repaid to the bondholder. Maturity dates generally range from 10 to 40 years from the time of issue.

maturity matching short-term financing policy A policy that matches asset and liability maturities. It is also referred to as the moderate, or self-liquidating, approach.

maturity risk premium (MRP) The premium that must be added to the real risk-free rate of interest to compensate for interest rate risk, which depends on a bond's maturity. Interest rate risk arises from the fact that bond prices decline when interest rates rise. Under these circumstances, selling a bond prior to maturity will result in a capital loss; the longer the term to maturity, the larger the loss.

merger The joining of two firms to form a single firm.

Miller model Introduces the effect of personal taxes into the valuation of a levered firm, which reduces the advantage of corporate debt financing.

MM Proposition I with corporate taxes $V_L = V_U + TD$. Thus, firm value increases with leverage and the optimal capital structure is virtually all debt.

MM Proposition I without taxes $V_L = V_U = EBIT/r_{sU}$. Since both EBIT and r_{sU} are constant, firm value is also constant and capital structure is irrelevant.

MM Proposition II with corporate taxes $r_{sL} = r_{sU} + (r_{sU} - r_d)(1 - T)(D/S)$. Here the increase in equity costs is less than the zero-tax case, and the increasing use of lower-cost debt causes the firm's cost of capital to decrease. In this case, the optimal capital structure is virtually all debt.

MM Proposition II without taxes $r_{sL} = r_{sU} + (r_{sU} - r_d)(D/S)$. Thus, r_s increases in a precise way as leverage increases. In fact, this increase is just sufficient to offset the increased use of lower-cost debt.

moderate net operating working capital policy A policy that matches asset and liability maturities. It is also referred to as maturity matching or the self-liquidating approach.

Modified Internal Rate of Return (MIRR) method Assumes that cash flows from all projects are reinvested at the cost of capital, not at the project's own IRR. This makes the modified internal rate of return a better indicator of a project's true profitability.

money market A financial market for debt securities with maturities of less than 1 year (short-term). The New York money market is the world's largest.

money market fund A mutual fund that invests in short-term debt instruments and offers investors check-writing privileges; thus, it amounts to an interest-bearing checking account.

Monte Carlo simulation analysis A risk analysis technique in which a computer is used to simulate probable future events and thus to estimate the likely profitability and risk of a project.

mortgage bond A bond for which a corporation pledges certain assets as security. All such bonds are written subject to an indenture.

multinational (or global) corporation A corporation that operates in two or more countries.

municipal bond Issued by state and local governments. The interest earned on most municipal bonds is exempt from federal taxes and also from state taxes if the holder is a resident of the issuing state.

municipal bond insurance An insurance company guarantees to pay the coupon and principal payments should the issuer of the bond (the municipality) default. This reduces the risk to investors who are willing to accept a lower coupon rate for an insured bond issue compared to an uninsured issue.

mutual fund A corporation that sells shares in the fund and uses the proceeds to buy stocks, long-term bonds, or short-term debt instruments. The resulting dividends, interest, and capital gains are distributed to the fund's shareholders after the deduction of operating expenses. Some funds specialize in certain types of securities, such as growth stocks, international stocks, or municipal bonds.

mutually exclusive projects Projects that cannot be performed at the same time. A company could choose either Project 1 or Project 2, or it can reject both, but it cannot accept both projects.

N

National Association of Securities Dealers (NASD) An industry group primarily concerned with the operation of the over-the-counter (OTC) market.

natural hedge A transaction between two counterparties where both parties' risks are reduced.

net advantage to leasing (NAL) The dollar value of the lease to the lessee. It is the net present value of leasing minus the net present value of owning.

net cash flow The sum of net income plus noncash adjustments.

net float The difference between a firm's disbursement float and collections float.

net operating working capital (NOWC) Operating current assets minus operating current liabilities. Operating current assets are the current assets used to support operations, such as cash, accounts receivable, and inventory. They do not include short-term investments. Operating current liabilities are the current liabilities that are a natural consequence of the firm's operations, such as accounts payable and accruals. They do not include notes payable or any other short-term debt that charges interest.

net present value (NPV) method The present value of the project's expected future cash flows, discounted at the appropriate cost of capital. NPV is a direct measure of the value of the project to shareholders.

net working capital Current assets minus current liabilities.

new issue market The market for stock of companies that go public.

nominal (quoted) interest rate, I_{NOM} The rate of interest stated in a contract. If the compounding occurs annually, the effective annual rate and the nominal rate are the same. If compounding occurs more frequently, the effective annual rate is greater than the nominal rate. The nominal annual interest rate is also called the annual percentage rate, or APR.

nominal rate of return, r_n Includes an inflation adjustment (premium). Thus, if nominal rates of return are used in the capital budgeting process, then the net cash flows must also be nominal.

nominal risk-free rate of interest, r_{RF} The real risk-free rate plus a premium for expected inflation. The short-term nominal risk-free rate is usually approximated by the U.S. Treasury bill rate, and the long-term nominal risk-free rate is approximated by the rate on U.S. Treasury bonds.

nonnormal cash flow projects Projects with a large cash outflow either sometime during or at the end of their lives. A common problem encountered when evaluating projects with nonnormal cash flows is multiple internal rates of return.

nonoperating assets Include investments in marketable securities and noncontrolling interests in the stock of other companies.

nonpecuniary benefits Perks that are not actual cash payments, such as lavish offices, memberships at country clubs, corporate jets, and excessively large staffs.

NOPAT (net operating profit after taxes) The amount of profit a company would generate if it had no debt and no financial assets.

normal cash flow project A project with one or more cash outflows (costs) followed by a series of cash inflows.

normal yield curve When the yield curve slopes upward it is said to be "normal," because it is like this most of the time.

O

off-balance sheet financing A financing technique in which a firm uses partnerships and other arrangements to (in effect) borrow money while not reporting the liability on its balance sheet. For example, for many years neither leased assets nor the liabilities under lease contracts appeared on the lessees' balance sheets. To correct this problem, the Financial Accounting Standards Board issued FASB Statement 13.

open outcry auction A method of matching buyers and sellers in which the buyers and sellers are face to face, all stating a price at which they will buy or sell.

operating capital The sum of net operating working capital and operating long-term assets, such as net plant and equipment. Operating capital also is equal to the net amount of capital raised from investors. This is the amount of interest-bearing debt plus preferred stock plus common equity minus short-term investments. Also called total net operating capital, net operating capital, or net operating assets.

operating company A company controlled by a holding company.

operating current assets The current assets used to support operations, such as cash, accounts receivable, and inventory. It does not include short-term investments.

operating current liabilities The current liabilities that are a natural consequence of the firm's operations, such as accounts payable and accruals. It does not include notes payable or any other short-term debt that charges interest.

operating lease Provides for both financing and maintenance. Generally, the operating lease contract is written for a period considerably shorter than the expected life of the leased equipment and contains a cancellation clause; sometimes called a service lease.

operating leverage The extent to which fixed costs are used in a firm's operations. If a high percentage of a firm's total costs are fixed costs, then the firm is said to have a high degree of operating leverage. Operating leverage is a measure of one element of business risk but does not include the second major element, sales variability.

operating merger Occurs when the operations of two companies are integrated with the expectation of obtaining synergistic gains. These may occur in response to economies of scale, management efficiency, or a host of other factors.

operating profit margin Ratio of earnings before interest and taxes divided by sales.

opportunity cost A cash flow that a firm must forgo in order to accept a project. For example, if the project requires the use of a building that could otherwise be sold, then the market value of the building is an opportunity cost of the project.

opportunity cost rate The rate of return available on the best alternative investment of similar risk.

optimal distribution policy The distribution policy that maximizes the value of the firm by choosing the optimal level and form of distributions (dividends and stock repurchases).

optimal dividend policy The dividend policy that strikes a balance between current dividends and future growth and maximizes the firm's stock price.

optimal portfolio The point at which the efficient set of portfolios—the efficient frontier—is just tangent to the investor's indifference curve. This point marks the highest level of satisfaction an investor can attain given the set of potential portfolios.

option A contract that gives its holder the right to buy or sell an asset at some predetermined price within a specified period of time.

ordinary (deferred) annuity An annuity with a fixed number of equal payments occurring at the end of each period.

original issue discount (OID) bond In general, any bond originally offered at a price that is significantly below its par value.

P

par value The nominal or face value of a stock or bond. The par value of a bond generally represents the amount of money that the firm borrows and promises to repay at some future date. The par value of a bond is often $1,000, but it can be $5,000 or more.

parent company Another name for a holding company. A parent company will often have control over many subsidiaries.

partnership A partnership exists when two or more persons associate to conduct a business.

payables deferral period The average length of time between a firm's purchase of materials and labor and the payment of cash for them. It is calculated by dividing accounts payable by credit purchases per day (i.e., cost of goods sold ÷ 365).

payback period The number of years it takes a firm to recover its project investment. Payback does not capture a project's entire cash flow stream and is thus not the preferred evaluation method. Note, however, that the payback does measure a project's liquidity, so many firms use it as a risk measure.

payment date The date on which a firm actually mails dividend checks.

payment, PMT Equal to the dollar amount of an equal or constant cash flow (an annuity).

pegged exchange rates Rates that are fixed against a major currency such as the U.S. dollar. Consequently, the values of the pegged currencies move together over time.

perfect hedge A hedge in which the gain or loss on the hedged transaction exactly offsets the loss or gain on the unhedged position.

periodic rate, I_{PER} The rate charged by a lender or paid by a borrower each period. It can be a rate per year, per 6-month period, per quarter, per month, per day, or per any other time interval (usually 1 year or less).

permanent net operating working capital The NOWC required when the economy is weak and seasonal sales are at their low point. Thus, this level of NOWC always requires financing and can be regarded as permanent.

perpetuity A series of payments of a fixed amount that continue indefinitely.

physical location exchanges Exchanges, such as the New York Stock Exchange, that facilitate trading of securities at a particular location.

plug technique Technique used in financial forecasting to "plug" in enough new liabilities or assets to make the balance sheets balance.

poison pills Shareholder rights provisions that allow existing shareholders in a company to purchase additional shares of stock at a lower-than-market value if a potential acquirer purchases a controlling stake in the company.

political risk Refers to the possibility of expropriation and the unanticipated restriction of cash flows to the parent by a foreign government.

pooling of interests A method of accounting for a merger in which the consolidated balance sheet is constructed by simply adding together the balance sheets of the merged companies. This is no longer allowed.

portfolio A group of individual assets held in combination. An asset that would be relatively risky if held in isolation may have little or no risk if held in a well-diversified portfolio.

post-audit The final aspect of the capital budgeting process. The post-audit is a feedback process in which the actual results are compared with those predicted in the original capital budgeting analysis. The post-audit has several purposes, of which the most important are to improve forecasts and operations.

precautionary balance A cash balance held in reserve for random, unforeseen fluctuations in cash inflows and outflows.

preemptive right Gives the current shareholders the right to purchase any new shares issued in proportion to their current holdings. The preemptive right enables current owners to maintain their proportionate share of ownership and control of the business.

preferred stock A hybrid security that is similar to bonds in some respects and to common stock in other respects. Preferred dividends are similar to interest payments on bonds in that they are fixed in amount and generally must be paid before common stock dividends can be paid. If the preferred dividend is not earned, the directors can omit it without throwing the company into bankruptcy.

premium bond Bond prices and interest rates are inversely related; that is, they tend to move in the opposite direction from one another. A fixed-rate bond will sell at par when its coupon interest rate is equal to the going rate of interest, r_d. When the going rate of interest is above the coupon rate, a fixed-rate bond will sell at a "discount" below its par value. If current interest rates are below the coupon rate, a fixed-rate bond will sell at a "premium" above its par value.

premium on forward rate Occurs when the forward exchange rate differs from the spot rate. When the forward rate is above the spot rate, it is said to be at a premium.

prepackaged bankruptcy (or pre-pack) A type of reorganization that combines the advantages of informal workouts and formal Chapter 11 reorganization.

pre-tax earnings or income The amount of earnings (or income) that is subject to taxes. It is also equal to earnings before interest and taxes (EBIT) less the interest expense. It is sometimes called earnings before taxes (EBT)

price/cash flow ratio Calculated by dividing price per share by cash flow per share. This shows how much investors are willing to pay per dollar of cash flow.

price/earnings (P/E) ratio Calculated by dividing price per share by earnings per share. This shows how much investors are willing to pay per dollar of reported profits.

price/EBITDA ratio The ratio of price per share divided by per share earnings before interest, depreciation, and amortization.

primary market Markets in which newly issued securities are sold for the first time.

priority of claims in liquidation Established in Chapter 7 of the Bankruptcy Act. It specifies the order in which the debtor's assets are distributed among the creditors.

private markets Markets in which transactions are worked out directly between two parties and structured in any manner that appeals to them. Bank loans and private placements of debt with insurance companies are examples of private market transactions.

private placement The sale of stock to only one or a few investors, usually institutional investors. The advantages of private placements are lower flotation costs and greater speed, since the shares issued are not subject to Securities and Exchange Commission registration.

probability distribution A listing, chart, or graph of all possible outcomes, such as expected rates of return, with a probability assigned to each outcome.

professional corporation (PC) Has most of the benefits of incorporation but the participants are not relieved of professional (malpractice) liability; known in some states as a professional association (PA).

profit margin on sales Calculated by dividing net income by sales; gives the profit per dollar of sales.

profitability index Found by dividing the project's present value of future cash flows by its initial cost. A profitability index greater than 1 is equivalent to a project's having positive net present value.

profitability ratios Ratios that show the combined effects of liquidity, asset management, and debt on operations.

progressive tax A tax system in which the higher one's income, the larger the percentage paid in taxes.

project cash flows The incremental cash flows of a proposed project.

project cost of capital The risk-adjusted discount rate for that project.

project financing Financing method in which the project's creditors do not have full recourse against the borrowers; the lenders and lessors must be paid from the project's cash flows and equity.

projected (pro forma) financial statement Shows how an actual statement would look if certain assumptions are realized.

promissory note A document specifying the terms and conditions of a loan, including the amount, interest rate, and repayment schedule.

proprietorship A business owned by one individual.

prospectus Summarizes information about a new security issue and the issuing company.

proxy A document giving one person the authority to act for another, typically the power to vote shares of common stock.

proxy fight An attempt to take over a company in which an outside group solicits existing shareholders' proxies, which are authorizations to vote shares in a shareholders' meeting, in an effort to overthrow management and take control of the business.

public markets Markets in which standardized contracts are traded on organized exchanges. Securities that are issued in public markets, such as common stock and corporate bonds, are ultimately held by a large number of individuals.

public offering An offer of new common stock to the general public.

publicly owned corporation Corporation in which the stock is owned by a large number of investors, most of whom are not active in management.

purchase accounting A method of accounting for a merger in which the merger is handled as a purchase. In this method, the acquiring firm is assumed to have "bought" the acquired company in much the same way it would buy any capital asset.

purchasing power parity Implies that the level of exchange rates adjusts so that identical goods cost the same in different countries. Sometimes referred to as the "law of one price."

put option Allows the holder to sell the asset at some predetermined price within a specified period of time.

PV The value today of a future payment, or stream of payments, discounted at the appropriate rate of interest. PV is also the beginning amount that will grow to some future value.

PVA_N The value today of a future stream of N equal payments at the end of each period (an ordinary annuity).

$PVIFA_{I,N}$ The present value interest factor for an ordinary annuity of N periodic payments discounted at I percent interest per period.

$PVIF_{I,N}$ The present value interest factor for a lump sum received N periods in the future discounted at I percent per period.

Q

quick, or acid test, ratio Found by taking current assets less inventories and then dividing by current liabilities.

R

real options Occur when managers can influence the size and risk of a project's cash flows by taking different actions during the project's life. They are referred to as real options because they deal with real as opposed to financial assets. They are also called managerial options because they give opportunities to managers to respond to changing market conditions. Sometimes they are called strategic options because they often deal with strategic issues. Finally, they are also called embedded options because they are a part of another project.

real rate of return, r_r Contains no adjustment for expected inflation. If net cash flows from a project do not include inflation adjustments, then the cash flows should be discounted at the real cost of capital. In a similar manner, the internal rate of return resulting from real net cash flows should be compared with the real cost of capital.

real risk-free rate of interest, r^* The interest rate on a risk-free security in an economy with zero inflation. The real risk-free rate could also be called the pure rate of interest since it is the rate of interest that would exist on very short-term, default-free U.S. Treasury securities if the expected rate of inflation were zero.

realized rate of return, $\bar{r}$ The actual return an investor receives on his or her investment. It can be quite different from the expected return.

receivables collection period The average length of time required to convert a firm's receivables into cash. It is calculated by dividing accounts receivable by sales per day.

red herring (preliminary) prospectus A preliminary prospectus that may be distributed to potential buyers prior to approval of the registration statement by the Securities and Exchange Commission. After the registration has become effective, the securities—accompanied by the prospectus—may be offered for sale.

redeemable bond Gives investors the right to sell the bonds back to the corporation at a price that is usually close to the par value. If interest rates rise, then investors can redeem the bonds and reinvest at the higher rates.

refunding Occurs when a company issues debt at current low rates and uses the proceeds to repurchase one of its existing high-coupon rate debt issues. Often these are callable issues, which means the company can purchase the debt at a call price lower than the market price.

registration statement Required by the Securities and Exchange Commission before a company's securities can be offered to the public. This statement is used to summarize various financial and legal information about the company.

reinvestment rate risk Occurs when a short-term debt security must be "rolled over." If interest rates have fallen then the reinvestment of principal will be at a lower rate, with correspondingly lower interest payments and ending value.

relative priority doctrine More flexible than absolute priority. Gives a more balanced consideration to all claimants in a bankruptcy reorganization than does the absolute priority doctrine.

relaxed net operating working capital policy A policy under which relatively large amounts of cash, marketable securities, and inventories are carried and under which sales are stimulated by a liberal credit policy, resulting in a high level of receivables.

reorganization in bankruptcy A court-approved attempt to keep a company alive by changing its capital structure in lieu of liquidation. A reorganization must adhere to the standards of fairness and feasibility.

repatriation of earnings The cash flow, usually in the form of dividends or royalties, from the foreign branch or subsidiary to the parent company. These cash flows must be converted to the currency of the parent and thus are subject to future exchange rate changes. A foreign government may restrict the amount of cash that may be repatriated.

replacement chain (common life) approach A method of comparing mutually exclusive projects that have unequal lives. Each project is replicated so that they will both terminate in a common year. If projects with lives of 3 years and 5 years are being evaluated, then the 3-year project would be replicated 5 times and the 5-year project replicated 3 times; thus, both projects would terminate in 15 years.

required rate of return, r_s The minimum acceptable rate of return, considering both its risk and the returns available on other investments.

reserve borrowing capacity Exists when a firm uses less debt under "normal" conditions than called for by the trade-off theory. This allows the firm some flexibility to use debt in the future when additional capital is needed.

residual distribution model In this model, firms should pay dividends only when more earnings are available than needed to support the optimal capital budget.

residual value The market value of the leased property at the expiration of the lease. The estimate of the residual value is one of the key elements in lease analysis.

restricted net operating working capital policy A policy under which holdings of cash, securities, inventories, and receivables are minimized.

restricted voting rights A provision that automatically deprives a shareholder of voting rights if the shareholder owns more than a specified amount of stock.

retained earnings The portion of the firm's earnings that have been saved rather than paid out as dividends.

retiree health benefits A major issue for employers because of the escalating costs of health care and a recent FASB ruling forcing companies to accrue the retiree health care liability rather than expensing the cash flows as they occur.

return on common equity (ROE) Found by dividing net income by common equity.

return on invested capital (ROIC) Net operating profit after taxes divided by the operating capital.

return on total assets (ROA) The ratio of net income to total assets.

revaluation Occurs when the relative price of a currency is increased. It is the opposite of devaluation.

revenue bonds Type of municipal bonds that are secured by the revenues derived from projects such as roads and bridges, airports, water and sewage systems, and not-for-profit health care facilities.

reverse split Situation in which shareholders exchange a particular number of shares of stock for a smaller number of new shares.

revolving credit agreement A formal, committed line of credit extended by a bank or other lending institution.

rights offering Occurs when a corporation sells a new issue of common stock to its existing stockholders. Each stockholder receives a certificate, called a stock purchase right, giving the stockholder the option to purchase a specified number of the new shares. The rights are issued in proportion to the amount of stock that each shareholder currently owns.

risk arbitrage The practice of purchasing stock in companies (in the context of mergers) that may become takeover targets.

risk aversion A risk-averse investor dislikes risk and requires a higher rate of return as an inducement to buy riskier securities.

risk premium for Stock i, RP_i The extra return that an investor requires to hold risky Stock i instead of a risk-free asset.

risk-adjusted discount rate Incorporates the risk of the project's cash flows. The cost of capital to the firm reflects the average risk of the firm's existing projects. Thus, new projects that are riskier than existing projects should have a higher risk-adjusted discount rate. Conversely, projects with less risk should have a lower risk-adjusted discount rate.

risky event An uncertain outcome that adversely affects a company's objectives.

roadshow Before an IPO, the senior management team and the investment banker make presentations to potential investors. They make three to five presentations daily over a 2-week period in 10 to 20 cities.

S

S corporation A small corporation that, under Subchapter S of the Internal Revenue Code, elects to be taxed as a proprietorship or a partnership yet retains limited liability and other benefits of the corporate form of organization.

safety stock Inventory held to guard against larger-than-normal sales and/or shipping delays.

sale-and-leaseback A type of financial lease in which the firm owning the property sells it to another firm, often a financial institution, while simultaneously entering into an agreement to lease the property back from the firm.

salvage value The market value of an asset after its useful life.

scenario analysis A shorter version of simulation analysis that uses only a few outcomes. Often the outcomes are for three scenarios: optimistic, pessimistic, and most likely.

seasonal effects on ratios Seasonal factors can distort ratio analysis. At certain times of the year, a firm may have excessive inventories in preparation of a "season" of high demand. Therefore, an inventory turnover ratio taken at this time will be radically different than one taken after the season.

secondary market Markets in which securities are resold after initial issue in the primary market. The New York Stock Exchange is an example.

secured loan A loan backed by collateral, which is often in the form of inventories or receivables.

Securities and Exchange Commission (SEC) A government agency that regulates the sales of new securities and the operations of securities exchanges. The SEC, along with other government agencies and self-regulation, helps ensure stable markets, sound brokerage firms, and the absence of stock manipulation.

securitization The process whereby financial instruments that were previously thinly traded are converted to a form that creates greater liquidity. Securitization also applies to the situation where specific assets are pledged as collateral for securities, thus creating asset-backed securities. One example of the former is junk bonds; an example of the latter is mortgage-backed securities.

Security Market Line (SML) Represents, in a graphical form, the relationship between the risk of an asset as measured by its beta and the required rates of return for individual securities. The SML equation is one of the key results of the CAPM: $r_i = r_{RF} + b_i(r_M - r_{RF})$.

semistrong form of market efficiency States that current market prices reflect all publicly available information. Therefore, the only way to gain abnormal returns on a stock is to possess inside information about the company's stock.

sensitivity analysis Indicates exactly how much net present value will change in response to a given change in an input variable, other things held constant. Sensitivity analysis is sometimes called "what if" analysis because it answers this type of question.

shareholder rights provision Also known as a poison pill, it allows existing shareholders to purchase additional shares of stock at a price that is lower than the market value if a potential acquirer purchases a controlling stake in the company.

shelf registration Frequently, companies will file a master registration statement and then update it with a short-form statement just before an offering. This procedure is termed shelf registration because companies put new securities "on the shelf" and then later sell them when the market is right.

short hedges Occur when futures contracts are sold to guard against price declines.

simple interest The situation when interest is not compounded; that is, interest is not earned on interest. Also called regular interest. Divide the nominal interest rate by 365 and multiply by the number of days the funds are borrowed to find the interest for the term borrowed.

sinking fund Facilitates the orderly retirement of a bond issue. This can be achieved in one of two ways: (1) the company can call in for redemption (at par value) a certain percentage of bonds each year, or (2) the company may buy the required amount of bonds on the open market.

social value Projects of not-for-profit businesses are expected to provide a social value in addition to an economic value.

soft currencies Currencies of countries that set the exchange rate but do not allow their currencies to be traded on world markets.

special dividend A dividend paid, in addition to the regular dividend, when earnings permit. Firms with volatile earnings may have a low regular dividend that can be maintained even in years of low profit (or high capital investment) but is supplemented by an extra dividend when excess funds are available.

speculative balances Funds held by a firm in order to have cash for taking advantage of bargain purchases or growth opportunities.

spin-off Occurs when a holding company distributes the stock of one of the operating companies to its shareholders, thus passing control from the holding company to the shareholders directly.

spontaneous liabilities Liabilities which grow with sales, such as accounts payable and accruals.

spot rate The exchange rate that applies to "on the spot" trades or, more precisely, to exchanges that occur two days following the day of trade (in other words, current exchanges).

spread, underwriting The difference between the price at which an underwriter sells the stock in an initial public offering and the proceeds that the underwriter passes on to the issuing firm; the fee collected by the underwriter. It is often about 7% of the offering price.

spread, yield The difference between the yield of a bond relative to another bond with less risk.

stakeholders All parties that have an interest, financial or otherwise, in a not-for-profit business.

stand-alone risk The risk an investor takes by holding only one asset.

standard deviation, σ A statistical measure of the variability of a set of observations. It is the square root of the variance.

statement of cash flows Reports the impact of a firm's operating, investing, and financing activities on cash flows over an accounting period.

statement of stockholders' equity Statement showing the beginning stockholders' equity, any changes due to stock issues/repurchases, the amount of net income that is retained, and the ending stockholders' equity.

stepped-up strike (or exercise) price A provision in a warrant that increases the strike price over time. This provision is included to encourage owners to exercise their warrants.

stock dividend Increases the number of shares outstanding but at a slower rate than splits. Current shareholders receive additional shares on some proportional basis. Thus, a holder of 100 shares would receive 5 additional shares at no cost if a 5% stock dividend were declared.

stock option Allows its owner to purchase a share of stock at a fixed price, called the strike price or the exercise price, no matter what the actual price of the stock is. Stock options always have an expiration date, after which they cannot be exercised.

stock repurchase Occurs when a firm repurchases its own stock. These shares of stock are then referred to as treasury stock.

stock split Current shareholders are given some number (or fraction) of shares for each stock share owned. Thus, in a 3-for-1 split, each shareholder would receive three new shares in exchange for each old share, thereby tripling the number of shares outstanding. Stock splits usually occur when the stock price is outside of the optimal trading range.

strategic options Options that often deal with strategic issues. Also called real options, embedded options, and managerial options.

stretching accounts payable The practice of deliberately paying accounts late.

strike (or exercise) price The price stated in the option contract at which the security can be bought (or sold).

strong form of market efficiency Assumes that all information pertaining to a stock, whether public or inside information, is reflected in current market prices. Thus, no investors would be able to earn abnormal returns in the stock market.

structured note A debt obligation derived from another debt obligation. Permits a partitioning of risks to give investors what they want.

subordinated debenture Debentures that have claims on assets, in the event of bankruptcy, only after senior debt (as named in the subordinated debt's indenture) has been paid off. Subordinated debentures may be subordinated to designated notes payable or to all other debt.

sunk cost A cost that has already occurred and is not affected by the capital project decision. Sunk costs are not relevant to capital budgeting decisions.

swap An exchange of cash payment obligations. Usually occurs because the parties involved prefer someone else's payment pattern or type.

sweetener A feature that makes a security more attractive to some investors, thereby inducing them to accept a lower current yield. Convertible features and warrants are examples of sweeteners.

synchronization of cash flows Occurs when firms are able to time cash receipts to coincide with cash requirements.

synergy Occurs when the whole is greater than the sum of its parts. When applied to mergers, a synergistic merger occurs when the post-merger earnings exceed the sum of the separate companies' pre-merger earnings.

T

takeover An action whereby a person or group succeeds in ousting a firm's management and taking control of the company.

target capital structure The relative amount of debt, preferred stock, and common equity that the firm desires. The weighted average cost of capital should be based on these target weights.

target cash balance The desired cash balance that a firm plans to maintain in order to conduct business.

target company A firm that another company seeks to acquire.

target distribution ratio Percentage of net income distributed to shareholders through cash dividends or stock repurchases.

target payout ratio Percentage of net income paid as a cash dividend.

targeted share repurchases Also known as greenmail, occurs when a company buys back stock from a potential acquirer at a price that is higher than the market price. In return, the potential acquirer agrees not to attempt to take over the company.

tax loss carryback and carryforward Ordinary corporate operating losses can be carried backward for 2 years or forward for 20 years to offset taxable income in a given year.

tax preference theory Proposes that investors prefer capital gains over dividends, because capital gains taxes can be deferred into the future but taxes on dividends must be paid as the dividends are received.

taxable income Gross income less a set of exemptions and deductions that are spelled out in the instructions to the tax forms that individuals must file.

technical analysts Stock analysts who believe that past trends or patterns in stock prices can be used to predict future stock prices.

TED spread The 3-month LIBOR rate minus the 3-month T-bill rate. It is a measure of risk aversion and measures the extra compensation that banks require to induce them to lend to one another.

temporary net operating working capital The NOWC required above the permanent level when the economy is strong and/or seasonal sales are high.

tender offer The offer of one firm to buy the stock of another by going directly to the stockholders, frequently over the opposition of the target company's management.

term structure of interest rates The relationship between yield to maturity and term to maturity for bonds of a single risk class.

terminal value Value of operations at the end of the explicit forecast period; equal to the present value of all free cash flows beyond the forecast period, discounted back to the end of the forecast period at the weighted average cost of capital.

time line A graphical representation used to show the timing of cash flows.

times-interest-earned (TIE) ratio Determined by dividing earnings before interest and taxes by the interest charges. This ratio measures the extent to which operating income can decline before the firm is unable to meet its annual interest costs.

total assets turnover ratio Measures the turnover of all the firm's assets; it is calculated by dividing sales by total assets.

trade credit Debt arising from credit sales and recorded as an account receivable by the seller and as an account payable by the buyer.

trade deficit Occurs when a country imports more goods from abroad than it exports.

trade discounts Price reductions that suppliers offer customers for early payment of bills.

trade-off model The addition of financial distress and agency costs to either the MM tax model or the Miller model. In this model, the optimal capital structure can be visualized as a trade-off between the benefit of debt (the interest tax shelter) and the costs of debt (financial distress and agency costs).

transactions balance The cash balance associated with payments and collections; the balance necessary for day-to-day operations.

Treasury bond Bonds issued by the federal government; sometimes called T-bonds or government bonds. Treasury bonds have no default risk.

trend analysis An analysis of a firm's financial ratios over time. It is used to estimate the likelihood of improvement or deterioration in its financial situation.

U

underinvestment problem A type of agency problem in which high debt can cause managers to forgo positive NPV projects unless they are extremely safe.

underwritten arrangement Contract between a firm and an investment banker when stock is issued. An investment banker agrees to buy the entire issue at a set price and then resells the stock at the offering price. Thus, the risk of selling the issue rests with the investment banker.

V

value at risk (VaR) The dollar value that defines a specified percentile in the probability distribution of portfolio's loss or a project's NPV. For example, if the specified percentile is 5%, a VaR of −$1 million means that there is a 5% probability that the portfolio will lose $1 million or more.

value of operations (V_{op}) The present value of all expected future free cash flows when discounted at the weighted average cost of capital.

variance, σ^2 A measure of the distribution's variability. It is the sum of the squared deviations about the expected value.

venture capitalist The manager of a venture capital fund. The fund raises most of its capital from institutional investors and invests in start-up companies in exchange for equity.

vertical merger Occurs when a company acquires another firm that is "upstream" or "downstream"; for example, an automobile manufacturer acquires a steel producer.

vesting If employees have the rights to receive pension benefits even if they leave the company prior to retirement, their rights are said to be vested.

vesting period Period during which employee stock options cannot be exercised.

W

warrant A call option, issued by a company, that allows the holder to buy a stated number of shares of stock from the company at a specified price. Warrants are generally distributed with debt, or preferred stock, to induce investors to buy those securities at lower cost.

weak form of market efficiency Assumes that all information contained in past price movements is fully reflected in current market prices. Thus, information about recent trends in a stock's price is of no use in selecting a stock.

weighted average cost of capital (WACC) The weighted average of the after-tax component costs of capital—debt, preferred stock, and common equity. Each weighting factor is the proportion of that type of capital in the optimal, or target, capital structure.

white knight A friendly competing bidder that a target management likes better than the company making a hostile offer; the target solicits a merger with the white knight as a preferable alternative.

window dressing Techniques employed by firms to make their financial statements look better than they really are.

working capital A firm's investment in short-term assets—cash, marketable securities, inventory, and accounts receivable.

workout Voluntary reorganization plans arranged between creditors and generally sound companies experiencing temporary financial difficulties. Workouts typically require some restructuring of the firm's debt.

Y

Yankee bonds Bond issued by a foreign borrower denominated in dollars and sold in the United States under SEC regulations.

yield curve The curve that results when yield to maturity is plotted on the y-axis with term to maturity on the x-axis.

yield to call (YTC) The rate of interest earned on a bond if it is called. If current interest rates are well below an outstanding callable bond's coupon rate, then the YTC may be a more relevant estimate of expected return than the YTM because the bond is likely to be called.

yield to maturity (YTM) The rate of interest earned on a bond if it is held to maturity.

Z

zero coupon bond Pays no coupons at all but is offered at a substantial discount below its par value and hence provides capital appreciation rather than interest income.

© lulu/fotolia.com

Name Index

A

Abreo, Leslie, 760
Adams, Paul D., 654n
Aeppel, Timothy, 357n
Agrawal, A., 533
Ainina, M. Fall, 875n
Alderson, Michael J., 802n
Allen, Jeffrey W., 899n
Allen, Samuel R., 397
Allen, Woody, 141
Altman, Edward I., 944n, 950n
Amram, Martha, 466n, 1029n
Anderson, Kenneth E., 889n
Andrade, Gregor, 606n
Appleton, Elaine L., 653
Ashcraft, Adam B., 43n
Asquith, Paul, 557n, 817n

B

Baker, H. Kent, 578n, 741n, 875n
Baker, Malcolm, 604n, 606n
Bansal, Vipul K., 932n
Barberis, Nicholas, 274
Barclay, Michael J., 604n
Bauguess, Scott, 744n
Benartzi, Shlomo, 558n
Beranek, William, 952n
Berger, Philip, 869n
Berk, Jonathan, 276n
Bernanke, Ben, 603
Berra, Yogi, 598
Bertrand, Marianne, 171
Betker, Brian L., 957n
Bhagwat, Yatin, 384n
Bielinski, Daniel W., 875n
Billingsley, Randall S., 817n
Black, Fischer, 345
Blake, Marshall, 910n
Blume, Marshall, 997, 997n, 999, 999n
Bodnar, Gordon M., 911n
Boehmer, Robert, 952n
Bonaparte, Napoleon, 963
Born, Jeffrey A., 558n
Branson, Richard (Sir), 771
Brav, Alon, 576n
Brennan, Michael, 1029n
Brick, I. E., 530
Brook, Yaron, 558n
Brooks, Robert, 294n
Brown, Keith C., 932n
Bruner, Robert E., 371
Bubnys, Edward L., 1004n
Buffett, Warren, 41, 578n, 867
Bunge, Jacob, 30, 729
Burman, Leonard, 555n, 599n

C

Cameron, Doug, 30
Campbell, John Y., 249n, 273n
Carbaugh, Robert, 692
Carell, Steve, 771
Cassidy, John, 43n
Castelino, Mark G., 928n
Chadha, S., 533
Chan, Louis K.C., 249n
Chance, Don, 346, 347n
Chang, Rosita P., 555n, 709n
Chapman, Brandyn, 357
Charlton, William, Jr., 558n
Chatterjee, Sris, 957n
Cherney, Mike, 748
Chiang, Raymond C., 762n
Clements, Jonathan, 269n
Colbert, Stephen, 659
Constantinides, George, 274n, 744n
Cook, Timothy, 547
Cooley, Philip L., 852n
Cooney, John W., 744n
Copeland, Thomas E., 1003n
Cruise, Tom, 37
Crum, Roy, 681
Cyr, Billy, 357

D

Daleo, Bob, 631
Daniel, Kent, 275n

Daniels, Joseph P., 692
Daouk, Hazem, 536
Darby, Joseph B., III, 712
Daves, P., 66n, 310n, 807n
Daves, Phillip R., 832n
DeAngelo, Harry, 552, 554n, 575, 606n
DeAngelo, Linda, 552, 554n, 575, 606n
DeBondt, W.F. M., 269n
DeFond, M., 537
De La Garza, Jesus M., 658n
Del Guercio, Diane, 529
Denis, David J., 571n, 746n
Dexember, Ryan, 729
Dhillon, Upinder S., 957n
Dichev, Illia D., 273n
Dimon, Jamie, 909
Dixit, Avinash K., 1012n
Dolde, Walter, 910n
Donne, John, 681
Dravid, Ajay, 578n
Drucker, Jesse, 712
Durfee, Don, 487, 709
Dyl, Edward, 557n

E

Eades, Kenneth M., 371
Eadie, Alexandra, 573
Easterwood, John C., 596n
Ebbers, Bernie, 742
Eberhart, Allan C., 952n
Eckbo, B. Espen, 871n
Edelman, Richard B., 741n
Ehrbar, Al, 533
Ehrhardt, Michael C., 310n, 384n, 807n, 809n, 832
Einzig, Robert, 932n
Emery, Douglas r., 817n
Esty, Benjamin C., 763n

F

Fabozzi, Frank J., 762n
Fama, Eugene, 270–273, 552
Farber, D. B., 537
Fastow, Andy, 774n
Faulkender, Michael, 605n
Fauver, Larry, 706n
Fee, T., 537
Fernandez, Fernando, 368
Fernández, Pablo, 368n
Ferris, Stephen P., 537
Finucane, Thomas J., 791n
Flannery, Mark, 605n
Followill, Richard A., 653n
Foroohar, Kambiz, 30
Francis, Jack C., 928n
Frank, Murray Z., 606n
Frankel, Jeffrey A., 709n
Franklin, Benjamin, 144, 913
Fraser, Donald R., 802n
French, Kenneth, 270–273, 552
Friedman, Thomas L., 6
Frieswick, Kris, 653
Frigo, Mark L., 919n, 935n
Froot, Kenneth A., 910n, 920n

G

Galai, D., 848n
Gale, William, 555n, 599n
Gardner, Matthew, 79
Garlappi, Lorenzo, 273n
Garvey, Gerald T., 596n
Gay, Gerald D., 571n, 912, 912n
Gentry, James A., 643n, 658n
George, Thomas J., 273n
Gervais, Simon, 274n
Geske, R., 1029n
Geske, Robert, 848n
Ghosh, Chinmoy, 558n
Gillan, Stuart L., 528
Gilson, Stuart C., 950n, 952n
Gitman, Lawrence J., 372n, 649n
Glick, Reuven, 618
Glickman, E. J., 774n
Goldenberg, David H., 1004n
Gonedes, N., 558n
Goodman, Laurie S., 932n
Gordon, Myron J., 296–297, 554n
Goyal, Vidhan K., 606n
Graham, John, 368, 368n, 372n, 607n
Graham, John H., 604, 605n, 609n
Graham, John R., 418, 576n, 1029n
Green, Lee, 598
Green, Richard C., 276n
Greenwood, Robin, 606n
Grullon, Gustavo, 552
Guerrera, Francesco, 523
Guffey, Daryl M., 959n
Gup, Benton, 551n

H

Hadlock, C., 537
Hamada, Robert, 858
Hamada, Robert S., 610n
Hammer, Jerry A., 690n
Hankins, Kristine, 605n
Hanouna, P., 533
Harikumar, T., 817n
Harris, Milt, 274n
Harris, Milton, 596n, 744n
Harris, Robert, 371, 875n, 1001n
Harvey, Campbell, 368, 368n, 372n, 607n, 418, 576n, 1029n
Hayt, Gregory S., 911n
Healy, P., 557n
Heck, J. Louis, 852n
Hei Wai Lee, 643n
Helms, Billy, 294n
Hendershott, Robert J., 558n
Henry, David, 897
Herbst, Anthony F., 932n
Higgins, Robert C., 371
Hilscher, Jens, 273n
Hirshleifer, David, 275n
Holden, Jonathan, 144
Hotchkiss, Edith, 944n
Houston, Arthur L., Jr., 802n
Houston, Carol Olson, 802n
Hsuen-Chi Chen, 706n
Hull, John, 346, 347n, 806n, 1029n
Hunt, Bob, 437
Hunter, William C., 690n
Hyun-Han Shin, 643n

I

Ibbotson, Roger G., 740
Ikenberry, David, 552
Impson, C. Michael, 558n
Irvine, Steven, 202
Iskandor-Datta, Mai E., 817n
Israel, Ronen, 596n
Ivanov, Vlad, 744n

J

Jackson, Thomas H., 950n
Jagannathan, Ravi, 276n
Jahera, John S. Jr., 571n
Jandik, Tomas, 537
Jegadeesh, N., 269in
Jensen, Michael, 525, 986n
Jobs, Steve, 547
John, Kose, 952n
Johnson, H., 1029n
Johnson, Sarah, 108
Johnson, Shane A., 899n
Jong-Chul Rhim, 817n
Jongmoo Jay Choi, 690n

K

Kadapakkam, P., 596n, 817n
Kahneman, Daniel, 275
Kai-Chong Tsui, 709n
Kaiser, Kevin M. J., 950n
Kale, Jayant R., 571n
Kalotay, Andrew, 760, 762n
Kamath, Ravindra R., 607n
Kapadia, Nishad, 273n
Kaplan, Steven, 538, 606n, 752n, 834n, 875n, 899n
Karafiath, Imre, 558n
Karceski, Jason, 249n
Karpoff, Jonathan M., 536
Karutis, Kayleigh, 703
Kasa, Kenneth, 256
Katz, David, 108, 631
Kaufman, Daniel, 875n
Keillor, Garrison, 274
Kensinger, John W., 898n
Keown, Arthur J., 898n
Kersnar, Janet, 703
Kester, George W., 709n
Kim, Dongcheol, 273n
Kiymaz, Halil, 875n
Klein, Daniel P., 899n
Klier, Thomas H., 964n
Knez, Peter J., 273n
Kolb, Robert W., 999n
Korteweg, Arthur, 604, 605n
Kramer, John L., 889n
Kravis, Henry, 222
Krishnan, V. sivarama, 817n
Kulatilaka, N., 466n, 1029n

L

Læssøe, Hans, 919n, 935, 935n
Lakonishok, Josef, 249n
Lane, William R, 571n
Lang, Larry, 869n, 952n
Lange, Bruce, 932n

Lansing, Kevin J., 618
La Porta, R., 536
Laufman, Gary, 539
Lauterbach, Beni, 809n
Lawless, Robert M., 537
Lease, Ronald C., 785n, 957n
Lee, Charles M. C., 536
Lee, D. Scott, 536
Lee, Insup, 709n
Lehn, Kenneth, 885n
Leiserson, Greg, 555n, 599n
Lemaster, Kelsey, 712
Leonard, David C., 809n
Lettau, Martin, 249n
Levine, Dan, 729
Levy, Robert, 999, 999n
Lewis, Craig M., 817n
Li Jin, 536
Lincoln, Abraham, 12
Linebaugh, Kate, 1011
Lintner, John, 554n
Loderer, Claudio, 744n
Long, Michael, 606n
Long, Michael S., 817n
Lopez-de-Silanes, F., 536
Loughran, Tim, 273n, 739n
Luehrman, Timothy A., 1016n
Lummer, Scott L., 899n

M

Madoff, Bernie, 265
Madura, Jeff, 692
Mahady, Nelda, 910n
Mahajan, Arvind, 710n
Makhija, Anil, 537
Malitz, Ileen, 606n
Malkiel, Burton, 249n, 992
Malmendier, U., 537
Malmendier, Ulrike, 275
Maltus, Jonathan, 202
Marchard, Patrick H., 653n
Margrabe, W., 1029n
Markowitz, Harry, 249, 984n
Marshall, John F., 932n
Marston, Felicia, 1001n
Marston, Richard C., 911n
Martin, Gerald S., 536
Martin, John D., 898n
Masulis, R., 848n
Mauer, David C., 762n
Maxwell, Charles E., 649n
McCafferty, J., 487
McConnell, John J., 785n, 899n, 957n
McIntyre, Robert S., 79
McMahan, John, 487
McNichols, Maureen, 578n
Meckling, William, 525
Mehotra, V., 605n
Mercurio, Vincent, 372n
Merton, Robert, 345
Mian, Shehzad L., 654n
Michaely, Roni, 552, 576n, 558n, 743n
Mikkelson, W., 605n
Milken, Michael, 222
Miller, Merton H., 596–599, 848n, 852n
Mitchell, Mark L., 571n, 885n, 889n
Modigliani, Franco, 596–597, 852n
Mohan, Nancy, 875n
Moore, William T., 809n, 952n, 959n
Morck, Randall, 870n
Morse, Adair, 171
Moser, William J., 557n
Moses, E. A., 649n
Mudd, Daniel, 532
Mukherjee, Tarun, 786n, 875n
Mulherin, Harold, 889n
Mullins, D., 557n
Mullins, David W., Jr., 817n
Muscarella, Chris J., 740
Myers, Stewart C., 536

N

Naik, Vasant, 276n
Nam, Doowoo, 551n
Nam, Jouahn, 912, 912n
Naranjo, A., 555n
Narayanan, m. P., 762n
Netter, Jeffry M., 571n
Ng, David, 536
Nimalendran, N., 555n
Nocco, Brian, 910n
Noe, Thomas H., 571n
Norton, Edgar, 607n

O

Odean, Terrance, 274n, 275n
Ofek, Eli, 869n
Opler, Tim, 648

P

Palepu, K., 557n
Palmateer, Jake, 144
Palmon, O., 530
Pandit, Vikram, 523
Park, C., 537
Parrino, R., 537
Partch, M., 605n
Pei-Ching Yang, 706n
Peterson, David R., 533, 578n
Peterson, Pamela P., 533, 578n
Pettit, R. Richardson, 557n
Phelps, Katherine L., 809n
Phillips, Aaron L., 578n
Phillips, Richard, 79
Pickens, T. Boone, 222
Pindyck, Robert S., 1012n
Pinkowitz, L., 555n, 648
Pleven, Liam, 157
Poff, Jared, 656
Pollert, W. R., 774n
Ponzi, Charles, 265
Pope, Thomas R., 889n
Powell, Gary E., 578n
Prasad, Anita Mehra, 690n
Prowse, Stephen D., 752n
Puckett, Andy, 557n
Pugh, William, 571n
Puri, Manju, 418

R

Raice, Shayndi, 729
Rajan, Raghuram, 714–715
Ramirez, Gabriel G., 957n
Ramirez, Steven A., 913n
Rangan, Kasturi, 605n
Rao, Ramesh P., 817n
Raviv, Artur, 596n
Ready, Mark J., 273n
Reed, Debra K., 899n
Re-Jin Guo, 276n
Rhee, S. Ghon, 555n
Ritchken, P., 1029n
Ritter, Jay, 30, 604n, 738, 739n, 740, 744n
Robin, Ashok J., 1004n
Rodriguez, Ricardo J., 999n
Roenfeldt, Rodney, 809n, 952n
Rogalski, Richard J., 817n
Rogers, Celina, 919n
Rohaly, Jeffrey, 555n, 599n
Roll, Richard, 1001n
Ross, Stephen A., 1002, 1002n
Ruback, Richard S., 834n, 875n
Rubenstein, James, 964n
Ryngaert, M., 555n

S

Sankarasubramanian, L., 1029n
Sarin, A., 533
Sarkar, Salil, 571n
Schalheim, James S., 772n, 785n
Schall, Lawrence D., 791n
Scharfstein, David S., 910n, 920n
Schellenger, Michael, 653n
Scholes, Myron, 345
Schuermann, Til, 43n
Schultz, Paul, 809n
Schwartz, Eduardo, 1029n
Scism, Leslie, 157
Seery, Laura, 529
Sefcik, Stephen F., 817n
Servaes, Henri, 912n, 919n, 957n
Seward, James K., 817n
Shakespeare, William, 13
Sharpe, William F., 249, 986n, 991
Shastri, Kuldeep, 1003n
Shaw, Wayne H., 743n
Shilling, James D., 558n
Shimko, David C., 1021n
Shleifer, A., 536
Shleifer, Andrei, 276n, 870n
Shrieves, R., 66n, 310n
Shrieves, Ronald E., 809n
Shukla, Ravi, 1004n
Shumwya, Tyler, 273n
Silverblatt, Howard, 559
Simkins, Betty, 913n
Sindelar, Jody L., 740
Singer, Ronald F., 817n
Sirmans, C. F., 558n
Skinner, Douglas J., 552
Smit, H., 466n
Smit, Han T. J., 1029n
Smith, Brooke, 952n
Smith, Clifford W., 604n, 654n
Smith, David M., 817n
Smith, Donald J., 932n
Smith, Jason, 605n
Smith, Stephanie A. M., 649n

Soenen, Luc, 643n
Solt, Michael E., 809n
Spitznagel, Mark, 267
Stein, Jeremy, 910n, 920n
Stempel, Jonathan, 729
Stephens, Clifford, 552
Stern, Joel, 74n
Stewart, Bennett, 74n, 75n
Stulz, René, 274n, 555n, 575, 648, 744n, 869n, 910n, 1029n
Subrahmanyam, Avanidhar, 275n
Su Han Chan, 898n
Summers, Bruce J., 649n
Szilagyi, Jan, 273n

T

Taggart, Robert A., Jr., 610n
Talmor, Eli, 555n
Tamayo, Ane, 912n, 919n
Tashjian, Elizabeth, 957n
Tate, Geoffrey, 275, 537
Thaler, R. H., 269n, 274, 276n, 558n
Thatcher, Janet S., 762n
Thatcher, John G., 762n
Thibodeaux, Verne L., 899n
Timme, Stephen G., 690n
Tita, Bob, 397
Titman, S., 269n, 555n
Trigeorgis, Lenos, 466n, 1029n
Tucker, Alan L., 932n
Tufano, Peter, 912n, 919n
Tversky, Amos, 275

V

Vaidyanathan, R., 643n
Van Binsbergen, Jules H., 604, 605n, 609n
Van Drunen, Leonard D., 744n
Van Hoose, David D., 692
Venkataraman, Subu, 681
Vetsuypens, Michael R., 740
Vijh, A. M., 1029n
Vijh, Anand, 743n
Vishny, R., 536
Vishny, Robert W., 870n
Volcker, Paul, 44–45

W

Wagoner, Rick, 532, 964
Wald, J., 530
Wansley, James W., 558n, 571n
Warther, Vincent A., 273n
Watts, R., 558n
Weaver, Samuel C., 875n
Weigand, Robert, 557n
Weisbach, Michael, 552, 899n
Weiss, Lawrence A., 952n
Weston, J. Fred, 889n, 950n, 1003n
White, I. T., 649n
Whited, Toni, 606n
Whitehouse, Tammy, 772n
Wilkins, Rebecca J., 79
Williams, George O., 762n
Williamson, R., 555n, 648
Wind, Serge, 44n
Winger, Bernard J., 875n
Woidtke, Tracie, 529
Wolf, Avner, 928n
Woolridge, J. Randall, 558n
Wurgler, Jeffrey, 604n, 606n
Wyatt, Steve B., 654n, 709n

Y

Yan, Hong, 273n
Yang, Deane, 762n
Yang, Jie, 604, 605n, 609n
Yehning Chen, 950n
Yermack, David, 538
Yexiao Xu, 249n
Yong H. Kim, 654n
Young-jin Lee, 558n

Z

Zhi Da, 276n
Zingales, Luigi, 714–715

© lulu/fotolia.com

Subject Index

A

AAA-rated companies, 217
Abandonment options, 464
ABB, 872
Abbott Labs, 217
Abercrombie & Fitch, 518
AB InBev, 659
Abnormal curve, 222
Abnormal returns, 897
  Absolute priority doctrine, 952
Accelerated Cost Recovery system (ACRS), 481
Accelerated depreciation, 481
  straight-line depreciation *vs.*, 449–450
Accounting
  accrual, 55n
  global, 108. *See also* International Accounting Standards Board (IASB)
  for mergers, 893*t*
  purchase, 892
  See also Generally accepted accounting principles; Financial Accounting Standards Board
Accounting beta method, 384
Accounting betas, 384
Accounting cost, 75
Accounting profit, 58
Accounting regulations, standardizing global, 779
Accounting return on assets, 384
Account receivable, 654
  as asset item, 654n
  equation for, 655
Accounts payable, 654n, 659
Accredited investors, 730
Accrual accounting, 55n
Accruals, 658–659
Acid test ratio, 99–100
ACP. *See* Average collection period
Acquiring company, 872
Actual rate of return, 295
Additional funds needed (AFN) equation, 504, 505
  addition to retained earnings, 505
  calculating additionals funds needed, 505
  key factors in, 506–507
  required increase in assets, 504
  self-supporting growth rate and, 507
  spontaneous liabilities, 504–505
  using MicroDrive's data to implement, 505
Additional Paid-in Capital, 58n
Add-on interest, 667
Adelphia, 12
Adjustable rate mortgages (ARMs), 38–39, 174
Adjustable rate preferred stock (ARPs), 803
Adjusted betas, 997
Adjusted present value (APV) model, 834–835
  dynamic capital structures and, 840–843
  hi-growth and lo-growth, 839–840
  levered value of operations, 843
  merger valuation using, 881–883
  overview of, 841
  unlevered value of operations, 842–843
  value of tax shield, 843
Adjustment bureau, 947
ADRs. *See* American Depository Receipts
ADS. *See* Average daily sales
AerCap Holdings NV, 771
Aeropostale, 28
AFN. *See* Additional funds needed (AFN) equation
After-tax cost of debt, 363–364
After-the-fact rate of return, 295
Agency conflicts, 524–527
  inside owners/managers *vs.* outside owners, 526
  managers *vs.* shareholders, 526–527
  stockholders *vs.* creditors, 525–526
Agency costs, 525
  convertible securities and, 815–817
Agency debt, 189
Agency problem, 9
Agency relationship, 524
Agent, 524
Aging schedule, 657–658, 657*f*
AIG, 40, 42, 532, 799, 847, 945
Airbus, 771
Alcan Aluminum, 705
Alcoa, 14–15, 801, 923
Alt-A mortgages, 38–41
Alternative Minimum Tax (AMT), 79, 345, 555n, 599n, 789
Amazon, 3, 254*t*, 644, 738

American Association of Individual Investors (AAII), 119–120
American Depository Receipts (ADRs), 706
American Eagle Outfitters, 534
American Finance Association, 848
American option, 327
American put option, 347n
American Recovery and Reinvestment Act of 2009, 44
American Stock Exchange (AMEX), 29, 552, 740
Amortization, lease financing and, 772
Amortization schedule, 172
Amortized loans, 170–171
  growing annuities, 174
  income, finding constant real, 174–176
  initial deposit to accumulate future sum, 176
  mortgage interest payments, 173
  payments, 171–172
  schedules, 172
AMT. *See* Alternative Minimum Tax
Anaconda Copper, 710
Analysis
  duration, 219
  financial statements, 96
  merger and acquisitions (M&A), 23
  multiple market, 311
  statement of cash flows, 97
  trend, common size, percentage change, 113–115
Analysts' forecasts, discounted cash flow (DCF) approach, 374
Anchoring bias, 274
Angel investors, 730
Anheuser-Busch, 659
Annual compounding periods, 165
Annual dividend, 550
Annual percentage rate (APR), 168
Annual report, 52
  statement of cash flows and, 61–64
Annual Statement Studies, 117
Annual unit sales, projections for expansion project, 444
Annual vesting, 532
Annuity, 150
  future value of ordinary, 151–153
  growing, 174
  plus additional final payment, 161
  present value of ordinary, 155–156
  variable, 157
Annuity due, 150
  future value of, 154
  present value of, 156–157
Annuity payments (PMT), finding, 158
Antron Corporation, 929–931
AOL, 868, 899
AOL Time Warner, 56n
Apple Computer, 3, 5, 51, 66, 117, 118*t,* 254*t,* 441–442, 547, 549, 631, 633, 717–718, 741
APV. *See* Adjusted present value model
Arbitrage, 334, 852, 896
  investment bankers and, 896
  with short sales, 856
Arbitrage pricing theory (APT), 1002–1004
Arbitrage proof, 854
Arbitrageurs, 896
Arca, 30, 32
Archer Daniels Midland, 923
Archipelago, 31
Arithmetic average, 367n
Armbrister Pyrotechnics, 424
ARPs. *See* Adjustable rate preferred stock
Arrearages, 800
Arthur Andersen, 10, 70, 914
Asia, bank representatives on boards in, 528
Asset-backed securities, 748
Asset management, investment banking and, 750
Asset management ratios, 100
  days sales outstanding, 101–102
  fixed assets turnover ratio, 101
  inventory turnover ratio, 102
  total assets, evaluate, 100
Assets
  balance sheet, 54–55
  depreciating, for tax purposes, 481–483
  N-asset case, portfolio theory, 982–983
  opportunity costs of owned, 441
  purchase and disposition of projections for expansion project, 447–448
  purchase below replacement cost, as merger rationale, 869
  required increase in, additional funds needed equation method, 504
  risk-free, combining with market portfolio, 987*f*
  risky, selecting optimal portfolio of, 985*f*
  risky *vs.* risk-free, 988
  two-asset case, portfolio theory, 979–982
Asset securitization, 748
Asset substitution, as potential agency conflict, 815
Asset valuation, 103
Assignee, 949
Assignment, 949
Asymmetric hedge, 924
Asymmetric information, 574–575, 600, 607, 755

AT&T, 579
Attachmate, 872
Auchen, 709
Auction, 29
Auction market, 32
Auction-rate preferred stock, 803n
Automatic debit, payment by, 651
Automatic stay, 951
Average collection period (ACP), 101, 639, 656
Average daily sales (ADS), 656
Average tax rate, 77
Average value at risk (AVaR), 935

B

Bahamas, as tax haven, 712
Bahrain, 705
Bain Capital, 752
Bait and switch
  investing in risky assets as, 846–847
  as potential agency conflict, 815–816
Balance sheet, 53–54
  assets on, 54–55
  before and after ESOP, 539–540
  income statements, 56–58
  lease financing and, 777*t*
  liabilities on, 55
  projected, 498–499
Baldor Electric Company, 872
Banker's acceptance, 16*t*, 716
Bank loans, short-term, 664–667
Bank of America, 23, 27, 32, 42, 235, 325, 532, 799, 869, 945
Bank of America Merrill Lynch, 750, 751
Bank of England, 692
Bankruptcy
  anatomy of (GM example), 963–965
  criticisms of laws, 966
  economic *vs.* legal, 589
  federal law, 949–950
  liquidation in, 777n, 959–963
  other motivations for, 965–966
  personal, 963
  reorganization in, 223, 950–959. *See also* Bankruptcy reorganization
  ten largest since 1980, 945*t*
  threat of, 600
  trade-off between tax benefits and costs of, 604–605
Bankruptcy Act, 223, 946, 950
Bankruptcy costs, 599
Bankruptcy reorganization, 223
  balance sheet, 955*f*
  illustration of, 954–957
  prepackaged bankruptcies, 957–958
  reorganization plan, 956*f*
  time and expense, 598–599
Banks
  interest charges, 666–667
  "too-big-to-fail," 45
Barclays, 704, 734, 930
Barclays Capital, 750
Base-case inputs, 443–444
Base-case scenario
  preliminary evaluation of, 448
  in scenario analysis, 455
Basel Committee, 915, 936
Basic earning power (BEP) ratio, 108
Basic EPS, 818–819
Baskin-Robbins, 618
BBB debt, 222
Bear Stearns, 40, 41, 42, 751, 945
Behavioral finance
  applications of, 275–276
  market bubbles and, 274–275
BellSouth, 217
Benchmark companies, 117
Benchmarking, 117
Berkshire Hathaway, 3, 578n, 801, 966
Best efforts basis, 733
Beta, 251–253
  effect on individual stocks, 252*f*
  estimating, 253–254, 371
  interpreting estimated, 254–257
  levered *vs.* unlevered, 840
  measuring divisional, 383–384
Beta coefficients, 991–999
  for actual companies, 254*t*
  advanced issues in calculating, 997–999
  calculating for portfolio (Magellan Fund), 995–996, 996*f*
  calculating for single stock (GE), 992–994, 993*f*
  changes in, common stock and, 261
  performance measures, 996–997
  tests of the stability of, 999
Beta risk, 384, 450
Bias, estimation, 424
Bid price, 884–887
Bigger fool theory (of investment), 295n
Big Lots, 656
Binomial approach, 331

Binomial lattice, 338, 339*f*
Bird in the hand theory, 554
Black & Decker, 589
Black-Scholes option pricing model (OPM), 335–336, 340
  application to call option, 342–343
  assumptions and results, 340–341
  factors affecting call option prices, 343–346
  valuing equity, 844–845
  valuing growth option, 1024–1028
  valuing investment timing option, 1018–1021
  valuing warrants, 805–806
Blackstone Capital Partners, 753
Blackstone Group, 26, 747, 753
Block ownership patterns, 536–537
Bloomberg, 221
Bloomberg Markets, 30
Blowout bid, 873
"Blue sky" laws, 730n
BMW, 464, 624
Board of directors
  compensation for board members, 530
  corporate governance and, 528–530
  interlocking, 529
  staggered, 529
Board of Governors of the Federal Reserve System, 19
Boeing, 79, 771
Bolivia, 710
Bombay Stock Exchange (BSE), 708
Bond, 188
  as financial instrument, 16*t*
  callable, 813
  comparing risk, 220
  convertible, 193, 811
  coupon interest rate, 190
  debentures/subordinated debentures, 211–212
  development, 212
  discount, 198
  financing with junk, 222–223
  floating-rate, 191
  floor price of, 813
  government, 189
  income, 193
  indentures, 211
  index, 193
  indexed, 193, 208
  investment-grade, 213
  junk, 213
  liquidity premium, 216
  markets, 194
  maturity date, 191
  maturity risk premium (MRP), 217–220
  mortgage, 211
  municipal, 16*t*, 81, 189
  number of years, 195
  original issue discount (OID), 191
  par value, 190
  payment-in-kind (PIK), 191
  pollution control, 212
  premium, 198
  provisions to call or redeem, 192
  purchasing power, 193
  ratings, 212–213
  ratings, subprime mortgage crisis, 40
  required rate of return, 195
  semiannual coupons, 202–203
  sinking funds, 192–193
  tax exempt, 212
  time path of value, 201*f*
  U.S. Treasury bonds. *See* Treasury bonds
  U.S. Treasury default swaps, 190
  U.S. Treasury STRIP, 191
  value, changes in over time, 199–201
  warrants, 193
  who issues, 188–189
  with warrants, 805–809
  zero coupon, 191
Bond contract
  bond indentures, 211
  bond ratings, 213–214
  development bonds, 212
  mortgage bonds, 211
  municipal bond insurance, 212
Bond indentures, 211, 573
Bond markets, international, 704–705
Bond ratings
  default risk premium and, 214–215
  financial ratios, 213
  qualitative factors, 214
Bond spread, 214, 216*f*
Bond the cash flow, 603
Bond valuation
  interest rate changes/bond prices, 198
  price, solving for, 195–198
  time line, cash flows, and formulas, 194–195
Bond yields
  cost of debt, intrinsic value and, 206
  current, 205–206
  yield to call, 204–205
  yield to maturity, 203–204

Bonus depreciation rate, 788
Book-building, 735
Book values, 54
  debt ratio, 829
  WACC and, 376
Borders Group, 577
Borrowing capacity, reserve, 606
Borrowing costs, risk management and, 912
Bosnia, 696n
BP, 710
Break-even quantity, 593
Breakup value, 870
Bretton Woods fixed exchange rate system, 692
Bribery, international regulation of, 703
BRIC countries, 397
Bristol-Myers, 744
Brokerage costs
  clientele effect and, 556
  dividend reinvestment plans and, 579
Brokerage departments, 32
BSE. *See* Bombay Stock Exchange
Budget, 398
  deficits/surplus, cost of money and, 20
  federal deficits/surplus, trade balances and, 20*f*
  See also Capital budgeting
Budgeting
  demand-pull, 487
  See also Capital budgeting
Burger King, 752
Business activity, cost of money and, 21
Business failure
  cases of, 944
  record of, 944–945
Business risk, operating leverage and, 592
BusinessWeek, 897
Buy orders, 32
Bylaws, 8

C

Cadbury, 873
Cadbury Schweppes, 899
CAEMC. *See* Central African Economic and Monetary Community
Callable bond, 813
Call option, 327, 805
  Black-Scholes formula option pricing model (OPM) and, 342–343
  five factors that affect prices of, 343–346
  with strike price, 343*f*
Call premium, 192
Call protection, 192
Call provision, 192
Canada, 705, 715, 943
Cancellation clause, in operating lease, 772
Cannibalization, 441
Capital
  alternative sources, 574
  divisional costs of, 382–383
  total investor-supplied, 68
  weighted average cost of. *See* Weighted average cost of capital (WACC)
Capital, raising
  preliminary decisions, 744–745
  private placements, 747
  seasoned equity offering, 745–746
  securitization, 748–479
  shelf registrations, 746–747
  See also Initial public offering (IPO)
Capital allocation, 13–14*f*
Capital Asset Pricing Model (CAPM), 250, 878, 986
  analyze common stock with, 370–372
  beta coefficient of, 991–999
  capital market line and security market line, 987–991
  current status of, 1001
  empirical tests of the, 999–1001, 1000*f*
  to estimate cost of equity, 608
  insights into risk and return and, 997
  market efficiency and, 276–277
  relevant stock risk and, 251–257
  unlevered cost of equity and, 882
Capital budgeting
  cash flow evaluation, 397–436
  comparison of methods for, 416–417
  corporate valuation and, 398
  decision criteria in practice, 418–419, 419*f*
  economic *vs.* physical life, 421
  equivalent annual annuities (EAA), 420
  first step in project analysis, 400–401
  formula for, 563
  internal rate of return (IRR) and, 403–410
  modified internal rate of return (MIRR), 410–413
  multinational, 708–714
  mutually exclusive projects with unequal lives, 419–425
  net present value and, 401–403
  optimal capital budget, 421–425
  overview, 398–400
  payback period, 414–416
  profitability index (PI), 413–414

replacement chains, 420
risk analysis in, 450–451
source of project's NPV, 417–418
unequal lives, 420–421
Capital budgeting, 398
Capital budgeting decisions, 846–847
Capital components, 359
Capital gains, 82
corporate, 78
as preferred, 554–555
Capital gains yield, 200, 294
Capital intensity, 506
Capital intensity ratio, 506
Capitalizing the lease, 776
Capital leases, 773
Capital loss, 82
Capital Market Line (CML), 989, 990*f*
Capital markets, 28
Capital market security, 15
Capital rationing, 421, 424–425
Capital structure, 590
analysis when permanent change in, 886–888
constant, valuation models for, 878–887
corporate governance and, 534–535
corporate valuation and, 590
dynamic. *See* Dynamic capital structures
effects on cost of capital, 612*f*
effects on stock prices and EPS, 617*f*
estimating optimal, 608–614, 610*f*
international, 714–715
overview, 590–591
Capital structure data, 361*f*
Capital structure decisions, 589–628
managers and, 607
Capital structure decisions, 590
option pricing and, 349–350
Capital structure policy, 381–382
Capital structure theory, 596–604
empirical evidence, 604–607
investment opportunity set and reserve borrowing capacity, 603–604
market timing theory, 604
Modigliani and Miller (MM) model and, 596–598
pecking order hypothesis, 602
reserve borrowing capacity, 602
signaling theory, 600–602
trade-off theory, 599–600
using debt financing to constrain managers, 602–306
CAPM. *See* Capital Asset Pricing Model
Career in finance, 5
Carlyle Group, 26, 753
Carryback, 79–80
Carryforward, 79–80
Cash balance, target, 648–649
Cash budget, 645*f*
daily, 647–648
income statements and free cash flows *vs.*, 647
monthly, 645–647
Cash conversion cycle (CCC), 638–644, 639*f*
benefits of reducing, 642–643, 643*f*
calculating, 638–641
international, 716
summary, 642*f*
Cash distributions
clientele effect, 556–557
constraints to, 573–574
dividend irrelevance theory, 554
dividend preference theory, 554
as dividends, 564*f*, 567–568
dividends *vs.* stock repurchases, 562–571
empirical evidence on policies for, 555–556
firm value and, 553–556
intrinsic value and, 565–571
policy decision on, 574–575
procedures for. *See* Cash distributions procedures
as repurchases, 570–571
setting target level, 559–561
sources of cash, 548–549
as stock repurchases, 565*f*
target level, 572
tax effect theory: capital gains, 554–555
uses of cash, 549–550
value of operations under different methods of, 566*f*
Cash distributions procedures
dividend payments, 550–551
patterns of cash distributions, 552
stock repurchase, 551–552
Cash flow (CF)
accounting income *vs.*, 439–440
asset purchases and, 439
bonding, 603
bond value and, 194–195
calculating, 398
depreciation and, 439
estimating. *See* Cash flow estimation
in project analysis, 401*f*
incremental, 438, 461
net, 439n
normal *vs.* nonnormal, 405

projecting, 438, 440
projecting post-merger, 879–884
projecting expansion project, 444–446
summary of approaches, 878*t*
synchronizing, 649–650
uneven or irregular, 160–163
Cash flow estimation
expansion projects, 440, 443–450
externalities and, 441–442
identify relevant cash flows, 438–443
for multinational capital budgeting, 710–711
opportunity costs of owned assets, 441
replacement projects, 440
sunk costs and, 440–441
timing of cash flows, 440
Cash inflows (CIFt), 412
Cash management
international, 715–716
target cash balance and, 648–649
Cash management techniques, 649–651
speeding up check-clearing process, 650
speeding up collections, 651
using float, 650
Cash outflows (COFt), 412
CBOE. *See* Chicago Board Options Exchange
CCC. *See* Cash conversion cycle
C corporation, 890n
CDS. *See* Credit default swaps
Celanese AG, 753
Celler Act (1950), 868n
Central African Economic and Monetary Community (CAEMC), 696
CEO, as board chairman, 528
Cerberus Capital, 26, 943
Certificates of deposits, 662
CF. *See* Cash flow
CFO Magazine, 631
CFO's model of financial planning, 503–504
Chapter 7 bankruptcy, 223, 949
Chapter 9 bankruptcy, 223
Chapter 11 bankruptcy, 949, 952, 966
Chapter 13 bankruptcy, 963
Characteristic line, 991
Charter, 8
Chartists, 266
Chase Bank, 25
Chateau Teyssier, 202
Check-clearing process, 650
Chesapeake Energy, 534
Chevron, 710
Chicago Board of Trade (CBOT), 29, 327n, 342, 922, 923
Chicago Board Options Exchange (CBOE), 329
Chicago Mercantile Exchange (CME), 923
Chile, 710
China
consumer finance in, 709
exchange rate policy, 691
U.S. debt ownership, 706
Chinese banks, 709
Chiquita Brands International, 534
Chrysler, 26, 44, 532, 589, 799, 943, 944, 945, 964
CIA World Factbook, 706, 707*t*
CIFt, 412
Cigigroup, 799
Circuit City, 589
Cisco Systems, 33, 741
CIT Group, 749
Citi, 750
Citibank, 25, 27, 703
Citicorp, 25
Citigroup, 27, 523, 530, 532, 534, 709, 734
Class A common stocks, 291–292
Class B common stocks, 291–292
Classified boards, 529
Classified stock, 291–292
Class life, 481
Clayton Act (1914), 868n
Clayton Dubilier & Rice, 26
Cleanup clause, 666
Clientele effect, 556–557
Cliff vesting, 531
CME. *See* Chicago Mercantile Exchange
CML. *See* Capital Market Line
CNN Financial, 221
Coca-Cola, 3, 11, 74–75, 81, 191n, 254*t*, 705
Coefficient of variation (CV), 456
COFt, 412
Colbert Report, 659
Collateral, maturity structure of debt and, 756
Collateralized debt obligations (CDOs), 37
Collection policy, 654
Collections float, 650
Combination leases, 773
Commercial banks, 24–25
Commercial paper, 16*t*, 662, 668
Committee of Sponsoring Organizations (COSO), 914–918
Commodity Futures Trading Commission (CFTC), 937
Commodity price risk, 921–924

futures contracts to reduce, 923
futures market overview, 921–923
options on futures, 923–924
Common pool problem, 950
Common size analysis, 113–115
Common stock, 16*t*
changes in beta coefficient of, 261
cost of, market risk premium and, 367–369
maximize price of, 9
types of, 291–292
use CAPM to estimate cost of, 370–372
valuing, 293–295
Common stockholders, 290–291
Companies
corporations, 7–8
key attributes of, 4–5
life cycle of, 5–6
partnerships, 6–7
proprietorships, 6
stockholder control of, 290–291
Comparative ratios, 117, 118*t*
Compensating balances, 649, 665
Compensation
executive, 534, 538
managerial, 12, 538
managerial-shareholder interests and, 531–533
plans, 350
risk management and, 912
Competition, in product markets, 537
Competitive bids, 745
Compliance objectives, 916
Component cost of preferred stock, 366
Composition, 947
Compounding, 135
Compounding periods
annual/semiannual, 165
frequent, 168–169*f*
interest rates, 166–168. *See also* Interest rates
Compound interest, 153
Compound options, 848
Comprehensive income, 58n
Compressed adjusted present value model (APV), 834–835
Computer/telephone network, 29
ConAgra, 899
Conditional value at risk (CVaR), 935
Congeneric merger, 871
Conglomerate merger, 871
Congressional Budget Office, 209n, 364n
ConocoPhillips, 710
Consolidated corporate tax returns, 80–81
Consolidated Tools, 754
Constant growth stock
constant growth model, 296–297
expected rate of return of, 300–301
illustration of, 297–298
long-term or short-term events, prices and, 298–299
volatility of price, 299–300
Constant payment, 160
Constant ratios, 508*f*
Constant real income, finding, 174–176
Consumer credit loans, 16*t*
Consumer credit markets, 28
Consumer Credit Protection Act, 168
Consumer Financial Protection Bureau, 44
Consumer Protection Act, 27, 44–45
Consumers, stock price maximization and, 11
Contingent value right (CVR), 873
Continuous compounding, 168
Contraction decisions, capital budgeting for, 399
Control systems, corporate governance and, 534–535
Conversion price, 810
Conversion ratio (CR), 810
Conversion value, 813
Convertible bonds, 193, 811
model, 812*f*
Convertible currencies, 695
Convertible securities, 810–817
agency costs and, 815–817
component cost of, 811–814
conversion ratio and price, 810–811
reporting earnings with outstanding, 818–819
use in financing, 814–815
warrants *vs.*, 817–818
Cooperative Regions of Organic Producer Pools (CROPP) markets, 803
Cooperatives, hybrid financing for, 803
Corporate alliances, 898
Corporate bonds, 16*t*, 189
Corporate FCF valuation model, 880–881
Corporate finance, option pricing in
capital structure decisions, 349–350
compensation plans, 350
real options, 348–349
risk management, 349
Corporate governance, 9, 524, 528–537
board of directors and, 528–530
capital structure and internal control systems, 534–535

compensation to align manager-shareholder interests, 531–533
corporate valuation and, 524
hostile takeovers and, 530–531
international, 538–539
noncontrollable environmental factors, 536–537
Sarbanes-Oxley Act and, 535
Corporate growth
by internal expansion, 868
See also Growth; Growth option
Corporate income taxes
capital gains, 78
consolidated tax returns, 80–81
improper accumulation, 80
interest and dividend income, 77–78
interest and dividends paid, 78
loss carryback/carryforward, 79–80
overseas income and, 81
Corporate life cycle, 5
corporations, 7–8
managers, shareholder wealth maximization and, 11–13
managing a corporation, 8–9
partnership, 6–7
proprietorship, 6
Corporate raiders, 222
Corporate risk, 384, 450
Corporate scandals, 12, 914
Corporate valuation
capital budgeting and, 398
capital structure and, 590
capital structure decisions and, 830
corporate governance and, 524
cost of capital, 358
financial planning and, 488
free cash flows and, 71–72
in global context, 682
risk management and, 910
stock prices and, 290
time value of money, 134
working capital management and, 632
Corporations, 7
advantages, 7
disadvantages, 8
growing and managing, 8–9
intrinsic stock value, 10–11
multinational, 682. *See also* Multinational corporations
tax rate of, 363n, 364
value maximization, 9
Correlation, 247–249
Correlation coefficient, 247–249
Corruption Perceptions Index (CPI), 711*t*
COSO. *See* Committee of Sponsoring Organizations
Cost
of common stock, 367–372
of debt, 188
of money. *See* Money, cost of
of preferred stock, 366
unit, projections for expansion project, 444
Costly trade credit, 662
Cost of capital
corporate valuation and, 358
divisional, 382–383
effects of capital structure on, 612*f*
estimating for individual projects, 384–385
global variations in, 377
managerial issues and, 381–385
risk-adjusted. *See also* Weighted average cost of capital, 401–402
small businesses/private firms, 379–380
weighted average (WACC). *See* Weighted average cost of capital (WACC)
Cost of debt
estimating, 609–610
intrinsic value and, 206
Cost of equity, 18, 608, 610–611
Cost of goods sold (COGS), 57, 102
Cost of new common equity, 378
Counterparty risk, 921
Country risk, 22
Countrywide Financial, 27, 40
Coupon debt, equity with risky, 847
Coupon interest rate, 190
Coupon payment, 190
Covenants, 638
Covered options, 329
CR. *See* Conversion ratio
Cramdown, 952
Credit, lease financing and, 786–787
Credit crisis, managerial decisions, cost of capital and, 381
Credit default swaps (CDS), 41, 212, 751, 936–937, 938*f*
Credit management, international, 716–717
Creditors
bankruptcy and. *See* Bankruptcy
informal reorganization and, 946–948
Credit policy, 654, 660
Credit risks
financial institutions, 936–937

nonfinancial companies, 936
Credit Suisse Securities, 734, 779
Credit terms, 645, 654, 660–662
and associated costs, 661*t*
for small businesses, 659
Credit unions, 24
Cross-default provisions, 950
Crossover rate, 407–408
Cross rate, 687, 689
Cuba, 710
Culture, multinational corporations and, 684
Cumulative issues, 800
Cumulative net cash flow, 646
Cumulative voting, 291n
Currencies
convertible *vs.* nonconvertible, 695–696
converting, 686–690
devaluation and revaluation, 695
hard, 695
ISO labels for, 685
key cross rates, 689
multinational corporations and, 683
no local currency, 696
U.S. dollar index *vs.* major, 693*f*
Currency appreciation, 693
Currency depreciation, 694
Currency swaps, 931
Current assets, operating. *See* Operating current assets
Current ratio, 97–99
Current yield, 200, 205–206
Curvilinear relationship (inventory/sales), 508*f*
CV. *See* Coefficient of variation
CVR. *See* Contingent value right

D

Data
gather for financial analysis, 96–97
using historical to estimate risk, 242–245. *See also* Estimate risk, historical data
Days of working capital (DWC), 631
Days sales outstanding (DSO), 101–102, 656, 639, 655–657
DCF. *See* Discounted cash flow
Dealer market, 29
Debentures (bonds), 211–212
Debt
after-tax cost of, 363–364
cost of, 188. *See* Cost of debt
estimating cost of after tax, 361–365
financial securities, 14–15
flotation costs, and cost of, 364–365, 378*t*
issuing new, 615
junk bonds and, 222
long-term, 362–363
managing maturity structure of, 754–756
managing risk structure of, 763–764
as negative use of FCF, 549
pre-tax cost of, 206–207
private placements of, 747
risky, 844–851
short-term, 361–362, 638
yield on, 845
Debt capacity, risk management and, 912
Debt capital, 78
Debt financing, using, to constrain managers, 602–603
Debt management ratios
defined, 103–104
EBIDTA coverage ratio, 106
leverage ratios, 104–105
times-interest-earned ratio, 105–106
Debtor-in-possession (DIP) financing, 952, 964
Debt ratio, 104–105
Debt-to-assets ratio, 104–105
Debt-to-equity ratios, long-term, 591*t*
Debt tranches, 43
Decision Making Under Uncertainty (DMUU), 437
Decision node, 466
Decision tree
abandoning project in work-case scenario, 465*f*
basic, 465–466
for investment timing option, 1015–1058, 1016*f*
with multiple decision points, 466*f*
staged, 466–467
Declaration date, 550
Declining ratios, 508*f*
Deere & Co., 397
Default risk premium (DRP), 207, 211–215
Deferred annuity, 150
Deferred call, 192
Defined benefit (DB), 133
Defined contribution (DC), 133
Deleveraging, 618
Dell Computer, 11, 418, 442, 644, 659
Delta Air Lines, 944
Demand-pull budgeting, 487
Denmark, 710, 717
Depository Trust and Clearing Corporation (DTCC), 33n
Depreciation
accelerated methods of, 481

accelerated *vs.* straight-line, 449–450
bonus rate, 788
double-declining balance method of, 481
projections for expansion project, 446–447
straight-line method, 481
sum-of-years'-digits method of, 481
tax, 481–483
Derivatives, 14–15, 910
Determinants of intrinsic value, 46*f*
Deutsche Bank AG, 750
Deutsche Bank Securities, 734
Deutsche Bõrse, 30
Deutscher Aktienindex, 708
Devaluation, 695
Development bonds, 212
Differentials, incremental cash flows as, 461
Diluted EPS, 818–819
DIP. *See* Debtor-in-possession financing
Direct investments, 703
Direct quote, 686
Disbursement float, 650
Discount
forward currency selling at, 697
with credit terms, 654
Discount bond, 198
Discounted cash flow (DCF), 134–135
Discounted cash flow (DCF) analysis
abandonment option and, 464
considering the timing option, 1014–1015
ignoring the timing option, 1014
for investment timing option, 1016*f*
limitations of, 1012
for merger valuation, 875–876
real options and, 1013
Discounted cash flow (DCF) approach, 373
about, 372–373
analysts forecasts, 374
estimating inputs for, 373–374
historical growth rates, 373
illustration of, 374
retention growth model, 373
Discounted payback, 415, 415*f*
Discounting, 144
future value to find present, 143–146
graphic view of process, 146–147
Discount rate, lease financing and, 778n
Discrete distributions, measuring risk for, 238–241
Discrete probabilities, 239*f*, 241*f*
Distribution
discrete. *See* Discrete distributions
normal, 241
risk in continuous, 241–242
Diversifiable risk, 249
Diversification
benefits of foreign, 256
multi-stock portfolios and, 249–250*f*
as rationale for merger, 869–870
Divestitures, 898–899
Dividend
annual, 550
of preferred stock, 800
regular quarterly, 550
Dividend growth, at different rates, 302*f*
Dividend growth models, comparing FCF with, 310
Dividend irrelevance theory, 554
Dividend payment procedures, 550–551
Dividend policy, managerial decisions, cost of capital and, 382
Dividend preference theory, 554
Dividend reinvestment plans (DRIPS), 579
Dividends
cash distributions as, 564*f*, 567–568, 568*f*
expected, stock value and, 295
from financially engineered preferred stock, 802n
global economic crisis and, 559
information content of, 557–558
payouts (selected companies), 553*t*
pros and cons of, 571–573
stable *vs.* volatile, 558
as "sticky," 571
stock repurchases *vs.*, 562–571
as use of cash, 550
yields worldwide, 573
See also Stock dividends
Dividends payable, 563n
Dividend yield, 294
Dividend-yield-plus-growth-rate. *See* Discounted cash flow (DCF)
DJIA. *See* Dow Jones Industrial Average
DMUU. *See* Decision Making Under Uncertainty
Dodd-Frank Act (Wall Street Reform), 27, 44–45, 534, 937
Dollar General, 222, 223
Dot-com boom, 345
Double-declining balance method of depreciation, 481
"Double Irish" and "Dutch Sandwich" tax havens, 712
Douglas Aircraft, 945
Dow Chemical Company, 801
Dow Jones Global Stock Indexes, 36*t*
Dow Jones Industrial Average (DJIA), 33, 215, 708, 992

Downgrade, U.S. Treasury bonds, 215
Drexel Burnham, 872
Drexel Burnham Lambert, 222
DRIPS. *See* Dividend reinvestment plans
Due diligence
  investment banks and, 745
  merger analysis, 880
Dumping, 717n
Dun and Bradstreet (D&B), 117
Dunkin' Brands Group, 618
Dunkin' Donuts, 618
Du Pont equation, 115–117, 634
Duration analysis, 219
DWC. *See* Days of working capital
Dynamic capital structures
  APV model and, 840–843
  arbitrage proofs of MM theorems, 852–858
  compressed adjusted present value model (APV), 834–835
  impact of growth and tax shields on value, 830–833
  Modigliani and Miller models and, 833–834
  personal taxes: the Miller model, 848–851
  risky debt and equity, 844–851
Dynamic trade-off theory, 605
Dynegy, 530, 577

E

EAA. *See* Equivalent annual annuity (EAA) method
EADS. *See* European Aeronautic Defence and Space Company
EAR. *See* Equivalent annual rate
Earnings, 58
Earnings per share (EPS)
  basic *vs.* diluted, 818–819
  effects of capital structure on, 617*f*
Eastern Caribbean Currency Union, 696
EBIT (earnings before interest and taxes), 446, 593
  Modigliani and Miller model and, 596
  operating income and, 494
EBITDA (earnings before interest, taxes, depreciation, and amortization), 57–58
EBITDA coverage ratio, 106
Economic bankruptcy, 589
Economic crisis, global, 4. *See also* Global economic crisis
Economic factors, cost of money and, 19–20
Economic life, 421
  physical life *vs.*, 421, 422*f*
Economic Ordering Quantity (EOQ) model, 509
Economic value added (EVA), 75–76
Economies of scale, 508–509, 508*f*
Economist, The, 702
Ecuador, 696
Edward Jones, 32
EFF. *See* Effective annual rate
Effective annual rate (interest), 167–168
Effective corporate tax rate, 364
Effective interest rate, 667
Efficient frontier, 984
Efficient markets hypothesis (EMH), 265–266
  market bubbles, 267–268
  semistrong form, 267, 269
  strong-form, 267, 269
  weak-form efficiency, 266, 269
Efficient portfolio, 990
Egypt, 913
Electronic communications network (ECN), 29
Eli Lilly, 712, 872
Embedded options, 463
Embedded rate, 362
Emergency Economic Stabilization Act of 2008 (EESA), 43–44
EMH. *See* Efficient markets hypothesis
Empire District Electric (EDE), 254*t*, 553*t*
Employees
  protect ethical, 10
  stock price maximization and, 11
Employees' Retirement Income Security Act of 1974 (ERISA), 960n
Employee Stock Ownership Plans (ESOPs), 539–542
EMU. *See* European Monetary Union
Energen Corp., 254*t*
Engineering life, 421
Enron Corporation, 10, 12, 526, 710, 774n, 847, 914, 944
Enterprise risk management (ERM), 909–942, 914
  commodity price risk, 921–924
  credit risks, 936–937
  foreign exchange (FX) risk, 920–921
  framework for, 915–918
  human safety, 938
  overview of, 913–915
  project selection risks, 933–936
  reasons to manage risk, 910–913
  risk event categories, 918–920
Environmental projects, capital budgeting for, 399
EOQ. *See* Economic Ordering Quantity (EOQ) model
EPS. *See* Earnings per share
Equifax, 936
Equipment Leasing Association, 772

Equity
  adjusting cost of for flotation costs, 377–379
  balance sheet and, 55
  Black-Scholes option pricing model to value, 844–845
  cost of (*See* Cost of equity)
  financial securities, 14–15
  levered cost of, 832
  private placements of, 747
  with risky coupon debt, 847
Equity capital, 78
Equity carve-out, 743–744
Equity instruments, 15
Equity premium, 367
Equity residual model, 876
Equity risk premium, 367
Equivalent annual annuity (EAA) method, 420
Equivalent annual rate (interest), 167–168
e-Resources, 46
ERISA. *See* Employees' Retirement Income Security Act of 1974
ESOPs. *See* Employee Stock Ownership Plans
Estimation
  beta, 253–257, 371
  cost of capital, 384–385
  cost of common stock, 370–372
  cost of debt, 361–365, 609–610
  cost of equity, 608
  market risk premium, 371
  optimal capital structure, 608–614
  price per share, 309–310
  risk, using historical data, 242–245
  risk-free rate of interest, 370–371
  value of operations, 306–308, 613–614
  See also Cash flow estimation
Estimation bias, controlling, 424
ETF. *See* Exchange traded fund
Ethics
  for individuals and businesses, dilemmas, 10
  whistleblowers, ethics and, 10
Eurex, 30
Euro
  currency appreciation and, 693
  exchange rate and, 685–690
Eurobond, 705
Eurodollar, 703–704
Eurodollar market time deposits, 16*t*
Euronext, 32
Europe, bank representatives on boards in, 528
European Aeronautic Defence and Space Company (EADS), 771
European bankruptcy laws, 950n
European call option, 845
European Monetary Union (EMU), 707
European option, 327, 343, 347n
European Union, 108
EVA (Economic Value Added), 533
Event risk, 192
Ex ante beta, 999, 1000
Ex ante model, CAPM as, 253
Excel
  finding NPV using, 404
  Scenario Manager, 448–449
  See also Spreadsheets
Excess capacity, 509
Exchange rate risk, 22, 36, 694, 709
Exchange rates, 685
  Bretton Woods fixed system, 692
  converting currencies, 686–690
  floating, 692–694
  foreign exchange notation, 685–686
  forward, 697
  inflation, interest rates and, 701–702
  international monetary system and, 691–696
  international trade and, 690–691
  inventory policy and, 717
  managed floating, 694
  pegged, 695
  selected, 687*t*
Exchange traded fund (ETFs), 25, 33, 977
Ex-dividend date, 551
Exercise price, 327, 531
Exercise value (options), 327
Expansion project, 440
Expansion project analysis
  base case inputs and key results, 443, 444*f*
  capital budgeting and, 399
  cash flow evaluation, 446, 448–450
  cash flow projections, 444–446
  cash flows and performance measures, 445*f*
  net operating profit after taxes (NOPAT), 446
Expectations theory, 222
Expected beta, 999
Expected dividends, stock value and, 295
Expected portfolio returns, 980
Expected rate of return, 294
  constant growth stock, 300–301
  discrete distributions, 239–240
Expected return on a portfolio, 262–263
Expected ROIC, 502
Expected shortfall, 935

Expected tail loss (ETL), 935
Experian, 936
Expiration date, 532
Expiration date (option), 327
Extension, 947
External equity, 378
Externalities, 441, 448
  environmental, 442
  negative within-firm, 441–442
  positive within-firm, 442
ExxonMobil, 217, 320, 579, 710, 717, 894

F

Facebook, 712
  IPO, 729, 731, 733–735, 737–738
  S-1 filing, 735
  underwriting and sales syndicate, 734
Fair market value, 103
Fairness (of bankruptcy reorganization), 953
Fair price, 144
Fama-French three-factor model, 270–273
Family Dollar Stores, 631
Fannie Mae. *See* Federal National Mortgage Association
FA/S. *See* Fixed assets to sales (FA/S) ratio
FASB. *See* Financial Accounting Standards Board
FCF. *See* Free cash flow
FCFE. *See* Free cash flow to equity (FCFE) approach
FCPA. *See* Foreign Corrupt Practices Act
FDIC. *See* Federal Deposit Insurance Corporation
Feasibility (of bankruptcy reorganization), 953
Federal agencies, bonds an, 189
Federal Bankruptcy Reform Act (1978), 959
Federal budget surplus/deficit, 20*f*
Federal Deposit Insurance Corporation (FDIC), 24–25, 42, 799, 943
Federal Home Loan Bank System, 189
Federal Home Loan Mortgage Corporation (Freddie Mac), 17, 42, 43, 189, 532
Federal Housing Finance Agency, 42, 43
Federal income tax system, 76
  corporate income taxes, 77–81
  personal taxes, 81–82
  S corporations, 81
Federal National Mortgage Association (Fannie Mae), 17–18, 42, 43, 189, 532
Federal Reserve Bank, 187, 216, 370, 799
  financial bailouts, 44
  pre-Bretton Woods, 692
  subprime mortgage meltdown and, 38
Federal Reserve Board, 221
Federal Reserve Bulletin, 221
Federal Reserve Economic Data (FRED), 14
Federal reserve policy, cost of money and, 19–20
Federal Reserve Statistical Release, 16*t*
Federal Trade Commission, 868n
FedEx, 3
Ferragamo, 731
Fiat, 26, 943
FICO score, 936
Fidelity, Magellan Fund, 991, 995–996, 996*f*
FIFO (first-in, first-out), 54
Final scenario, forecasted financial statements, 502*f*
Finance
  behavioral, 274–276. *See also* Behavioral finance
  MBA, career and, 5
Financial Accounting Standards Board (FASB), 108, 330
  FSP APD 14-1, 818n
  Statement 13, 776–778
  Statement 128, 818n
  Statement 141, 892n
  Statement 142 (impairment test), 889
Financial analysis
  beyond numbers, 119–120
  gather data for, 96–97
  financial statement, 96
  ratio, 97
  return on invested capital, 97
  statement of cash flows, 97
Financial asset markets, 27
Financial calculators
  time value, 137–138
  using, 167n
Financial distress
  bankruptcy and. *See* Bankruptcy
  business failure and, 944–945
  issues facing firm in, 946
  settlements without formal bankruptcy, 946–948
  stages of, 912
Financial engineering, 1021–1022
Financial fraud, Sarbanes-Oxley Act and, 70
Financial Industry Regulatory Authority (FINRA), 190, 194
Financial institutions, 23–26
  commercial banks, 24–25
  credit unions, 24
  deposit taking, 24–25
  investment banks/brokerage activities, 23–24
  investment funds, 25–26. *See also* Investment funds

life insurance companies/pension funds, 26
managing credit risk at, 936–937
savings and loan associations (S&Ls), 24
Financial instruments, 16*t*, 27
Financial intermediary, 13, 14*f*
deposit taking, 24–25
Financial leases, 773
Financial leverage, 103–104, 593*f*, 594*f*, 595
effect on value, 601*f*
financial risk and, 594–595
Financial management
multinational. *See* Multinational financial management
risk events related to, 919
Financial markets, 27
money markets, 28
mortgage markets, 28
physical asset markets, 27
primary markets, 28
private markets, 28
spot markets, 27
trading procedures, 29–30
world, national, regional, and local, 28
Financial options, overview, 326–329
Financial plan, 489
projected financial statements as output of, 496
Financial planning
additional funds needed (AFN) equation method, 504–507
analysis and revision of preliminary plan, 500–504
CFO's Model, 503–504
corporate valuation and, 488
financial plan, 489
forecasted financial statements (FFS) method, 491
forecasting operations, 491–495
forecasting when ratios change, 507–511
Internet and, 16o
at MicroDrive, Inc. (example), 490–491
operating plan, 489
paradox regarding, 487
Financial ratios
bond ratings, 213
summary of, 111*t*
Financial risk, 594–595
Financial securities, 14–15
Financial statements
analysis of, 96
balance sheets, 53–58. *See also* Balance sheets
calculating cash conversion cycle from, 640–641
cash flow, 59–64. *See also* Statement of cash flows
distributions as dividends, 564*f*
dividends *vs.* stock repurchases and, 562–563
intrinsic value, free cash flow and, 52
lease financing and, 776–778
liabilities and equity, 55
MicroDrive (example), 490*f*
net cash flow, 64
projected (pro forma), 488
reports and, 52–53
stockholders' equity, 58–59
Financial statements, projecting (MicroDrive example), 497*f*
forecast accounts from operating plan, 496
forecast items re: short-term financial policy, 498
projected balance sheets, 498–499
Financing
activities, statement of cash flows and, 61
short-term, 663–664
junk bonds, 222–223
Financing feedback, 503
Finland, 710
FINRA. *See* Financial Industry Regulatory Authority
First Chicago Trust, 579
First-mortgage bonds, 211
First Union, 873
First Union–Wachovia, 894
Fitch Ratings, 212–215, 217
Five-minute MBA, 4–5
Fixed assets to sales (FA/S) ratio, 509
Fixed assets turnover ratio, 101
Fixed exchange rate system, 692
Flexibility options, 464
Float
secondary securities market and, 740
using, 650
Floating exchange rates, 692, 694
Floating-rate bonds, 191
Floor price, of bond, 813
Flotation costs
adjusting cost of equity for, 377–378
with bond refunding, 758–759
cost of debt and, 364–365
on new refunding issue, 756
of short- *vs.* long-term debt, 664
Follow-on offering, 745
Ford Motor Company, 26, 127, 212, 306, 325, 530, 624, 705, 964
Forecasted financial statements (FFS) method, 491
Forecasting operations, 491–495
estimated intrinsic value, 495

free cash flow (FCF), 494–495
operating assets, 492–494
operating income, 494
operating liabilities, 494
sales revenues, 492
status quo scenario, 493*f*
Foreign bonds, 189, 704–705
Foreign Corrupt Practices Act (FCPA), 914
Foreign cost of capital, 377
Foreign exchange, trading in, 697–698
Foreign exchange notation, 685–686
Foreign exchange (FX) risk, 920–921
Foreign investment, benefits of, 256
Foreign stocks, exchange-rate risk, 36
Foreign trade deficit, 21
Formula, binomial option pricing, 335–336
Formula approach, time value and, 137
Fortune magazine, 3
Forty-Year-Old Virgin, 771
Forward contract, 920
Forward exchange rate, 697
interest rate parity and, 699
selected, units per U.S. dollar, 698*t*
Forward-looking risk premiums, 368–369
Founders' shares, 292
401(k) plans, 26
Fractional time periods, 169–170
France, 937
Fraud
financial, Sarbanes-Oxley Act and, 70
See also Insider trading
Fraudulent conveyance, 951
Freddie Mac. *See* Federal Home Loan Mortgage Corporation
Frederick's of Hollywood, 577
Free cash flows (FCF), 11, 65
analysis, 97
calculating, 65*f*, 69
cash budget and income statements *vs*., 647
cash distributions and, 566
corporate value and, 71–72, 290
cost of capital and, 358
distributions to shareholders, 548
expected future, 488, 590
forecasting operations and, 494–495
intrinsic value, financial statements and, 52
net investment in operating capital, 68
net operating profit after taxes (NOPAT), 65–66
net operating working capital, 66–67
return on invested capital, 72–74
total net operating capital, 67–68
uses of, 69–71
value of company and, 489
value of unlevered firm and, 831
weighted average cost of capital (WACC) and, 359–360
Free cash flows (FCF), valuation model, 304–305
comparing with dividend growth models, 310
estimating value of operations, 306–308
price per share, estimating, 309–310
sources/claims on value, 306
Free cash flow to equity (FCFE) approach, 876–877, 883
Free trade credit, 662
French Civil Law, 684
Frequent compounding, result of, 168–169*f*
FriendFinder, 31
Friendly merger, 873
Frist family, 752
FT-SE 100 Index, 708
Full capacity sales, 510
Fundamental beta, 998
Fundamental price, 9
Furr's/Bishop, 536
Futures contract, 922
hedging with Treasury bond, 926–928
to manage risk of debt issuances, 925–928
options on, 923–924
as risk management tool, 913
Futures dealers, 922
Futures market, 27, 921
Future value of the annuity, 151–153, 163
Future values (FVs), 135
compare procedures, 141–142
discounting to find present value, 143–146
financial calculators, 137–138
formula approach, 137
graphs, of compounding process, 142
simple interest *vs*. compound, 143
spreadsheets, 138–141
step-by-step approach, 136–137
FX. *See* Foreign exchange (FX) risk

G

Gain from leverage, 857
Gap, 530
GE Capital, 763, 787
GE Money, 709
General Electric (GE), 79, 217, 254*t*, 293*f*, 559, 649, 712, 776, 784, 991

calculating beta coefficient for, 992–995
General Electric Capital, 784
General Growth Properties, 747
Generally accepted accounting principles (GAAP), 63, 70
General Motors (GM), 44, 532, 589, 784, 799, 943, 944, 945, 949
bankruptcy of, 963–965
General partners, 7
Genzyme, 873
Geographic markets, expand into new, 463–464
Geometric average, 367n
Germany, 681, 703, 937
corporate governance in, 538
debt to total assets in, 714–715
Deutscher Aktienindex, 708
Frankfurt stock exchange, 705
Gillette, 867
Glass-Steagall Act (1999), 27, 42, 749
Glencore International, 31
Global accounting, IFRS *vs.* FASB, 108
Global corporations, 682. *See also* Multinational corporations
Global economic crisis, 4
adjustable rate mortgages and, 174
asset valuation and, 103
bankruptcies during, 943–945
Citigroup CEO and, 523
counterparty risk and, 921
credit crunch and, 273
credit default swaps, 190, 212
deleveraging and, 618
dividend policies and, 559
globalization of mortgage market and, 36–38
Hi-Yield spread and TED spread, 218
investment banking activities and, 749–751
liquidity and economic crisis, 42–43
mortgage-backed securities and, 103
option reset adjustable rate mortgages (ARMs), 174
preventing next, 44–45
sources of funding during, 809
structured investment vehicles (SIVs) and, 56
subprime mortgage meltdown and, 38–41
Sun Microsystems and, 577
toxic assets and, 43
Treasury bond credit default swaps, 190
U.S. government's response to, 43–44, 449n, 532, 788, 799
U.S. Treasury bonds downgraded, 215
Global Economic Watch (GEW) Resource Center, 4
Global Finance Magazine, 27
GMAC, 964
Going private, 752
Going public, 30–31, 731
advantages, 731
costs of, 739–740
process of. *See* Initial public offering
disadvantages, 732
Goldman Sachs, 13, 43, 45, 532, 709, 734, 745, 751, 867
Goodwill, 890
Google, 3, 28, 254*t*, 268, 738
Google Finance, 685
Google Inc., 712
Gordon model, 296–297
Government, multinational corporations and, 684
Government bonds, 189
Government debt, as percentage of GDP (selected countries), 707*t*
Government-sponsored entities (GSEs), 189
Gramm-Leach-Bliley Act, 27
Great Britain
Common Law of, 684
FT-SE 100 Index in, 708
See also United Kingdom
Great Depression, 23, 44
Great Fire of London, 913
Greece, 681, 707
Greenmail, 530
"Green shoe" agreement, 735n
Gross domestic product (GDP), 215
public debt as percentage of, 707*t*
government debt and, 706
Gross profit margin, 107–108
Gross working capital, 634
Growing annuity, 174
Growth
impact on value, 830–833
See also Corporate growth; Growth option
Growth options, 463–464, 1023–1028
DCF analysis ignoring, 1023
DCF analysis with qualitative consideration of, 1023–1024
decision-tree analysis of, 1024, 1025*f*, 1026*f*
estimating input for stock price in, 1026*f*
estimating input for stock return variance in, 1027*f*
estimating value of, using standard financial option, 1028*f*
scenario analysis of, 1025*f*
valuing with Black-Scholes option pricing model, 1024–1028

Growth rate, 294
GSAMP TRUST 2006-NC2, 43
GSE debt, 189
Guideline lease, 775
Gulf Oil, 710
Guyton Products Company, 400–401
Gymboree Corp, 752

H

Haas Family Trusts, 801
Hackett Group, 487
Half-year convention, 482, 483*t*
Hamada equation, 610–611, 882
Hang Seng Bank, 709
Hang Seng stock index, 708
Hard currencies, 695
Harley-Davidson Inc., 553*t*
Hartford Financial Services Group, 157
HCA Holdings, 31, 731, 752
Hedge
  asymmetric, 924
  symmetric, 924
Hedge funds, 25–26, 977
Hedge portfolio, 331–332
  number of shares in, 332
  option value, 333–334
  payoff, 332
  present value of payoff, 332–333
  replicating portfolios and, 334–335
Hedging
  risk management and, 912
  spot rates and, 697
  with Treasury bond futures contracts, 926–928
Heinz, 254*t*
Herding behavior, 274
Herman Miller Inc., 653
Hertz, 26
Herzegovina, 696n
Hewlett-Packard, 5, 7, 51, 442, 530, 578, 649, 712, 829
Hibernia Atlantic, 30
High frequency trading (HFT), 30
Historical betas, 997, 999
Historical data, estimate risk using, 242–245
Historical rate, 362
Historical risk premium, 246n, 367
Hi-Yield spread, 218
Holder-of-record date, 551
Holding companies, 868, 899–901
Holdout problem, 951
Home Depot, 15, 78, 440–441, 530
Home purchase, 37
Homogeneous expectations, 852
Homogeneous risk class, 852
Honda Motor Company, 1011
Hong Kong, 708, 709
Horizon date, 303
Horizontal merger, 871
Horizon value, 163, 303
Hospitals, per procedure leases and, 791
Hostile merger, 873
Hostile takeovers, 530–531, 874–875
Hot, Flat, and Crowded (Friedman), 6
Human resources, as risk event category, 919
Human safety, enterprise risk management and, 938
Humped (yield curve), 221
Hybrid financing, 799–819
  convertible securities, 810–817
  for cooperatives, 803
  preferred stock, 800–804
  reporting earnings with outstanding warrants or convertibles, 818–819
  warrants, 805–810
  warrants *vs.* convertibles, 817–818
Hybrid stock, 312–313

I

IASB. *See* International Accounting Standards Board
Ibbotson Associates, 367
IBM, 29, 81, 442, 649, 772, 784, 875
IESE Business School, 368
IIFRS. *See* International Financial Reporting Standards
ImClone Systems, 12, 872
IMF. *See* International Monetary Fund
Impairment of capital rule, 574
Improper accumulation, 80
Incentive Stock Option, 345
Income
  constant real, 174–176
  operating, 494
Income bond, 193
Income statement, 56–58
  merger's affect on, 893–894
  cash budget and free cash flows *vs.*, 647
Incremental cash flows, 438, 461–462
Indenture (bond), 211
Independent projects, NPV *vs.* MIRR evaluation, 412
Independent projects, 403
Indexed bonds, 193, 208
Index funds, 977
India, 913

Bombay Stock Exchange (BSE), 708
Indifference curve, 984–986
Indirect quote, 686
Industrial development agencies, 212
IndyMac, 42
INET, 30
Inflation
business activity, interest rates and, 21*f*
cost of money and, 18–19
currency exchange and, 691
fixed assets turnover ratio and, 101
interest rates, exchange rates and, 701–702
projections for expansion project, 444, 449
relative rates of, 702
Inflation premium (IP), 208–210
Infomatics Corporation, 805, 807, 809n
Informal liquidation, 949
Information content of dividends, 557–558
ING Group, 709
Ingles Markets Inc., 553*t*
Initial deposit, to accumulate future sum, 176
Initial public offering (IPO), 8
costs of going public, 739–740
equity carve-outs, 743–744
Facebook, 729, 731, 733–735, 737–738
first day of trading, 738
going public in, 731–732
highest first-day returns in 2011, 738*t*
questionable practices, 742–743
regulation of securities sales, 734–735
roadshow and book-building, 735–736
secondary market and, 740–742
selecting an investment bank, 733
setting offer price, 736–738
underwriting syndicate, 733–734
Initial public offering (IPO) market, 28
Insider trading, 329n, 741
Insolvent, 223, 954
Institute for Social Research, 209n
Insurance, subprime mortgage crisis and, 40–41
Intel, 33, 34, 741
Interest
compound, 153
dividends and, corporate earned/paid, 77–78
mortgage payments and, 173
paid, bonds, 195
paying, as use of cash, 549
simple, 170
Interest charge
bank's, 666–667
project cash flows and, 440
Interest coverage ratio, 105–106
Interest rate, 18
adjustable rate mortgages (ARMs), 174
annual percentage, 168
business activity, inflation and, 21*f*
changes, bond prices and, 198
cost of debt, determinants of market, 206–207
effective annual, 167–168
equivalent annual, 167–168
finding, 147–148, 159
inflation, exchange rates and, 701–702
inflation premium and, 208–210
irregular cash flows, 164–165
managerial decisions, cost of capital and, 381
maturity structure of debt and, 754–755
nominal (quoted), 166
nominal (quoted), risk-free, 210
periodic, 166–167
risk-free, 207
term structure of, 221–222
U.S. Treasury bond, 221*f*
variables, defined, 207
Interest rate futures, 925–926
Interest rate parity, 698–700
Interest rate risk, 217–219
comparing, 220
futures contracts to manage risk of debt issuances, 925–928
inverse floaters, 932
Interest rate swaps, 928–932
anatomy of, 931*t*
flowchart, 931*f*
Interlocking boards of directors, 529
Internal rate of return (IRR)
applying as evaluation measure, 409–410
calculating, 404–405
capital budgeting and, 403–410
evaluating mutually exclusive projects with, 407–409
finding, 405*f*
multiple, as potential problem, 405–406
Internal rate of return (IRR), 404
Internal Revenue Service (IRS), 345
on consolidated returns for holding companies, 900
consult publications of, 481
on deducting lease payments, 775
on stock merger, 889
International Accounting Standards Board (IASB), 63, 108, 779
International bond markets, 704–705

International capital structures, 714–715
International cash conversion cycle, 716
International corporate governance, 538
International Financial Reporting Standards (IFRS), 63, 108
International Game Technology, 534
International Harvester, 948
International investment, net present value of, 714*t*
International Monetary Fund (IMF), 692
International monetary system, exchange rate policies and, 691–696
International money and capital markets
  Eurodollar market, 703–704
  international bond markets, 704–705
  international stock markets, 705–706
  sovereign debt, 706–707
International Organization for Standardization (ISO), 685, 916n
International Swaps and Derivatives Association, 41
International trade
  exchange rates and, 690–691
  deficits/surpluses and, 21–22
Internet, financial planning on, 160
Interstate public offering, 734
In-the-money (option), 327
Intrinsic price, 9
Intrinsic stock price
  distributions as dividends, 567–568
  distributions as repurchases, 570–571
Intrinsic value, 76
  analysis of financial statements, 96
  cash distributions and, 565–571
  cost of debt and, 188, 206
  determinants of, 46*f*, 264*f*
  estimated, 495
  free cash flow, financial statements and, 52
  market price and, 263–265
  risk and return and, 236, 978
  of stock options, 326
Inventory conversion period, 639, 640
Inventory management, 652–653
  multinational, 717–718
Inventory turnover ratio, 102
Inverse floater, 932
Inverted curve, 222
Investing activities, statement of cash flows and, 61
Investment bank, 733
  conflict between company and, in IPO, 738–739
  global economic crisis and, 749–751
  refunding operations and, 756
  roadshow and book-building activities, 735–736
Investment banking
  asset management and, 751–752
  role in mergers, 895–896
  securitization and, 750
  trading operations, 751
Investment banking houses, 13, 23–24
Investment Company Institute, 10
Investment funds
  hedge funds, 25–26
  mutual funds, 25
  private equity funds, 26
Investment-grade bonds, 213
Investment opportunity schedule (IOS), 423*f*
Investment opportunity set, 603–604
Investment policy, managerial decisions, cost of capital and, 382
Investments
  direct *vs.* portfolio, 703
  efficient set of, 983*f*
  returns on, 237
Investment tax credit (ITC), 788
Investment timing options, 463, 1013–1022
  DCF analysis ignoring, 1014
  DCF analysis with qualitative consideration of, 1014–1015
  estimating input for stock price, 1019*f*
  estimating input for variance, 1020*f*
  estimating value of, 1022*f*
  financial engineering and, 1021–1022
  scenario analysis, decision trees and, 1015–1018
  valuing with Black-Scholes option pricing model, 1018–1021
Investor equilibrium, combining risk-free asset with market portfolio, 987*f*
Investors
  CAPM, market efficiency and, 276–277
  mortgages, 37–38
  optimal portfolio for, 986
Investor-supplied capital, 68
Involuntary bankruptcy, 949
IOS. *See* Investment opportunity schedule
IPO. *See* Initial public offering
Iran, 710
Iraq, 710, 717
Ireland, tax havens and, 712
Irregular cash flows, 160–165
IRS. *See* Internal Revenue Service
ISO. *See* International Organization for Standardization

Israel, 913
Italy, 681, 937
ITC. *See* Investment tax credit

J

Jackson Hewitt Tax Service, 577
Japan
  corporate governance in, 538
  debt to total assets in, 714
  Nikkei 225 Index in, 708
Japanese Ministry of International Trade and Industry (MITI), 717
J Crew, 752
Jensen's alpha, 996
Jerry Maguire, 37
Jo-Ann Stores, 752
Job Creation and Worker Assistance Act of 2002, 482n
Jobs and Growth Act (2003), 554
Johnson & Johnson, 217
Joint International Tax Shelter Information Centre, 703
Joint probability, with staged decision tree, 467
Joint venture, 898
Journal of Financial Economics, 418
JP Morgan, 750, 751
JPMorgan, 937
JPMorgan Chase, 532, 559, 799, 909, 943, 945
JP Morgan Chase & Co., 23, 25, 27, 42
Junior mortgages, 211
Junk bonds, 213, 222–223
Just-in-time inventory system, 652

K

Keiretsus, 538
Kellogg, 591
Klondike Paper Company, 800
Kohlberg Kravis Roberts & Company (KKR), 222, 752, 753
Kraft, 873
Kuwait, 717
Kuwait Investment Authority, 801

L

Language, multinational corporations and, 683
Laws
  bankruptcy, 949–950, 966
  "blue sky," 730n
  as noncontrollable factor, 536
  multinational corporations and, 684
  tax, lease financing and, 788–789
  tax, legal systems and, 684
  See also U.S. Congress
LBO. *See* Leveraged buyout
Lead underwriter, 734
LEAPS (Long-Term Equity AnticiPation Security), 329
Lease financing, 16*t*, 771–798
  balance sheet effects, 777*t*
  combination leases, 773
  discount rate and, 778n
  estimated residual value, 786
  evaluation by lessee, 778–783
  evaluation by lessor, 784–786, 785*f*
  evaluation of lease-*vs.*-buy decision, 780*f*
  financial (capital) leases, 773
  financial statement effects, 776–778
  high-technology items and, 790
  increased credit availability, 786–787
  lease analysis (example), 782*f*
  operating leases, 772
  per procedure lease, 791
  real estate leases, 787
  reducing risks by, airlines and, 790
  sale-and-leaseback arrangements, 773
  setting lease payment, 785–786
  synthetic leases, 774
  tax effects of, 775–776
  tax laws and, 788–789
  uncertain demand for products and, 790–791
  vehicle leases, 788
Lease securitization, 789
Leeds Castle Group, 703
Legal bankruptcy, 589
LEGO Group, 935, 936
Lehman Brothers, 23, 24, 40, 42, 45, 212, 589, 751, 847, 921, 943, 944, 963
Letter of credit, 716
Leverage
  effects of, 837*f*
  gain from, 857
Leveraged buyout (LBO), 222, 603, 752
Leveraged lease, 786
Leverage ratios, 104–105
Levered cost of equity, 832
Liabilities
  balance sheet and, 55
  current, 67
  operating, 494
  spontaneous, 504–505
Liabilities-to-assets ratio, 105
Liar loans, 40
Liberty Capital Group, 292

Liberty Media Corporation, 292
LIBOR (London Interbank Offered Rate), 16*t*, 191, 666, 704, 929n, 930
Libya, 710
Life-cycle theory, dividend policies and, 575
Life insurance companies, 26
LIFO (last-in, first-out), 54
Limited liability, 7
Limited liability company (LLC), 7
Limited liability partnership (LLP), 7
Limited partners, 7
Limited partnership (LP), 7, 750
Linear programming, 424
Line of credit, 665
LinkedIn, 31
  decision to go public, 731
  IPO, 738
Liquid asset, 99–100
Liquidate, 949
Liquidating dividends, 574
Liquidation, 223, 899
  informal, 949
Liquidation in bankruptcy, 959–963
  balance sheet at liquidation, 961*t*
  distribution of liquidation proceeds, 962*f*
Liquidity, 34
  information from payback methods about, 416–417
  premium, 207
Liquidity crisis, 42–43, 589
Liquidity premium (LP), 216
Liquidity ratios, 97
  current ratio, 97–99
  quick/acid test ratio, 99–100
Listed Options Quotations, 327*t*
Litigation, corporate governance coverage and, 537
Loans
  amortized, 170–176. *See also* Amortized loans
  payday, 171
  truth in lending, 168
Local markets, 28
Lockbox system, 651
Lockheed, 945
London SEAQ, 29
Long hedges, 922
Long Island Lighting, 763n
Long-term debt-to-equity ratios, 591*t*
Long-Term Equity AnticiPation Security (LEAPS), 329
Low-regular-dividend-plus-extras policy, 562
LP. *See* Limited partnership; Liquidity premium
Lumpy assets, 508*f*, 509

M

MACRS. *See* Modified Accelerated Cost Recovery System
Macy's, 95
Magellan Fund, 991, 992, 995–996, 996*f*
Make-whole call provision, 192
Managed floating rate system, 694
Managerial options, 463
Managers
  capital budgeting and investment decisions, 846
  capital structure decisions and, 607
  CAPM, market efficiency and, 276–277
  cost of capital and, 381–387
  personal incentives as merger rationale, 870
  senior, board of directors and, 527
  stock price maximization and, 11–13
  using debt financing to constrain, 602–603
Managing underwriter, 734
Mannesmann AG, 873
Manville asbestos case, 965–966
Marginal cost of capital (MCC) schedule, 423*f*
Marginal rates *vs.* historical rates, WACC and, 375–376
Marginal tax rate, 77
Margin calls, 742
Margin requirement, 741, 922
Market added value (MVA), 74–75
Market auction preferred stock, 803–804
Market/book (M/B) ratio, 111
Market bubbles, 267–268, 274–275
Market cap, 293
Market efficiency, CAPM and, 276–277
Market equilibrium, 264
  required *vs.* expected returns and, 263–265
Market multiple analysis, 875
Market portfolio, 249
Market price, 9, 294
Market risk, 384, 450
Market risk premium, 258, 371, 989
  cost of common stock and, 367–369
  estimating, 371
  managerial decisions, cost of capital and, 381
Markets, geographic, expand into new, 463–464
Market timing, capital structure and, 605–606
Market value, 54
  debt ratios and, 105
  WACC and, 376
Market value debt ratio, 829
Market value of equity (MVE), 270

Market value ratios, 109
market/book ratio, 111
price/cash flow, 110–111
price/earnings (P/E), 110
Mark to market, 103
Massachusetts Institute of Technology (MIT), 217
Matchmaking, 749
Matrix Securities, 202
Maturity
of bonds, 195
of short-term bank loans, 664
Maturity date (bonds), 191
Maturity matching approach, 635, 754
Maturity risk premium (MRP), 217
comparing risks, 220
interest rate risk, 217–219
reinvestment rate risk, 219–220
as variable, 207
Maturity structure of debt
amount of financing required, 755–756
availability of collateral, 756
information asymmetries, 755
interest rate levels and forecasts, 754–755
maturity matching, 754
MBA program, five-minute MBA, 4–5
MCC. *See* Marginal cost of capital (MCC) schedule
McDonald's, 3, 235
MCI, 870
MDA. *See* Multiple discriminant analysis
Mead Johnson, 744
Media, corporate governance coverage in, 537
Medicare, 238
Mergers, 868
accounting for, 893*t*
analysis for "true consolidation," 894–895
analysis when permanent change in capital structure, 886–888
capital budgeting for, 399
cash *vs.* stock offers, 885–886
common mistakes, 897
financial reporting for, 892–894
free cash flow to equity approach, 876–877
friendly, 873
hostile *vs.* friendly takeovers, 872–873
income statement effects, 893–894
largest completed, 872*t*
level of activity, 871–872
rationale for, 868–870
regulation of, 874–875
role of investment bankers, 895–896
setting bid price, 884–886
tax effects, 891*t*
taxes and takeover bid structure, 888–891
types of, 871
use of term, 868n
valuation models for constant capital structure, 878–887
who wins?, 896–898
Mergers and acquisitions (M&As), 23, 749–750
Merrill Lynch, 23, 24, 27, 32, 37, 40, 42, 734, 751, 774n, 867, 869, 945
Merrill Lynch Global Private Equity, 26
Merrill Lynch Ready Assets Trust, 16*t*
Methuselah Trust, 144
Mexico, 701, 705
MF Global Holdings, 944
Microsoft Corp., 3, 7, 33, 34, 81, 217, 254*t*, 417, 549, 553*t*, 578, 585, 633, 741
Microwave Telecommunications Inc. (MTI), 745
Miller model, 848–851, 850
application of, 850–851
derivation of, 849–850
Minnesota Mining & Manufacturing, 394–395
MIPS (Modified Income Preferred Securities), 802n
Misrepresentations, 735
MITI. *See* Japanese Ministry of International Trade and Industry
Moderate policy (of holding current assets), 634
Modified Accelerated Cost Recovery System (MACRS), 481
five 5-year life, 783
lease terms and, 775
major classes and asset lives for, 482*t*
Modified IRR, 410–413, 411*f*
Modigliani and Miller (MM) model, 554
arbitrage proofs of, 852–858
arbitrage with short sales, 856
corporate taxes, 833–834, 837–839, 857–858
no taxes, 833, 836–837, 853
effect of corporate taxes, 597–598
no taxes, 596–597
Money, cost of
about, 18
economic factors and conditions, 19–20
factors affecting, 18–19
Money market mutual funds, 25, 16*t*
Money markets, 28
Money market security, 15
Monte Carlo simulation, 457–460

applied to project analysis, 934*f*
financing risks and, 935
inputs and key results for current trial, 459*f*
project selection risks and, 933–935
simulation results summary, 460*f*
Moody's, 37, 40, 43, 215, 217, 607
Moody's Investors Service, 212–213
Morgan Stanley, 45, 618, 681, 734, 745
Mortgage(s), 16*t*
securitization, 17, 18
subprime meltdown, 38–41
Mortgage-backed securities (MBS), 43, 212
Mortgage bond, 211
Mortgage crisis, 589
Mortgage interest payments, 173
Mortgage market, 28
globalization of, 36–37
home purchase, 37
investors, 37–38
mortgage origination, 37
securitization and resecuritization, 37
sub-prime mortgage meltdown, 38–41
Mortgage origination, 37
Motley Fool, 298
Multinational capital budgeting, 708–714
cash flow estimation, 710–711
project analysis, 711–714
risk exposure, 709–710
Multinational corporation, 682–683
cash management goals in, 715–716
U.S., employment by, 684*f*
Multinational financial management, 681–726
domestic financial management *vs.*, 683–684
exchange rates, 685–691
inflation, interest rates, and exchange rates, 701–702
interest rate parity, 698–700
international capital structures, 714–715
international monetary system and exchange rate policies, 691–696
international money and capital markets, 703–708
multinational capital budgeting, 708–714
purchasing power parity, 700–701
trading in foreign exchange, 697–698
working capital management, 715–718
Multi-period binomial option pricing model, 337–340
Multiple discriminant analysis (MDA), 944
Multiple IRRs, 405–406, 406*f*
Multiple market analysis, 311
Municipal bond insurance, 212
Municipal bonds, 16*t*, 81, 189
Munis, 81, 189
Mutual funds, 25
Mutually exclusive projects, 403
analyzing, 407–409
NPV *vs.* MIRR evaluation, 412
with unequal lives, 419–425, 419*f*
Mutual savings banks (MSBs), 24
MVA. *See* Market Value Added, 398

N

Naked options, 329
NAL. *See* Net advantage to leasing
NASA models, 1012
NASCAR, 79
NASD. *See* National Association of Securities Dealers
NASDAQ, 29, 32–33, 573, 741
Facebook IPO and, 729
firms paying dividends, 552
National Market, 741
secondary market, 32–33
SmallCap Market, 741
NASDAQ Composite Index, 33
NASDAQ OTC Bulletin Board, 33
NASDAQ Small-Cap Markets, 33
NASD Automated Quotation System (NASDAQ), 32–33. *See also* NASDAQ
National Association of Credit Management, 947n
National Association of Securities Dealers (NASD), 32–33, 742
National Bureau of Economics Research, 4
National markets, 28
Natural hedge, 922
Negotiable certificates of deposit (CDs), 16*t*
Negotiated deals, 745
Nestlé's, 937
Net advantage to leasing (NAL), 781
Net asset value, 892
Net cash flow, 64, 439n
Netherlands, tax havens and, 712
Net income, 58
Net investment in operating capital, 68
Net lenders, 13
Net operating capital (NOWC), 494–495
Net operating profit after taxes (NOPAT), 65–66, 489
operating income and, 494
post-merger cash flows and, 879–880
projections for expansion project, 446
Net operating working capital (NOWC), 67, 633
changes in, 439
projections for expansion project, 445–448

Net present value (NPV), 401
analyzing mutually exclusive projects with, 407–409
as best project analysis measure, 400
calculating, 401–403
as evaluation measure, 403
Monte Carlo simulation and, 457–458
multiple IRRs and, 406
project analysis, 402*f*
projections for expansion project, 444
of refunding operations, 760–761
source of project's, 417–418
Net present value profile, 407, 408*f*
Net profit margin, 107–108
Net sales, 56
Net working capital, 634
Net worth, 55
Newbridge Capital, 709
New Century Mortgage, 40, 42, 43
New debt, 362
New issue (bond), 199
New stock, cost of selling, 574
New York Commodity Exchange, 923
New York Stock Exchange (NYSE), 28, 29, 31–32, 194, 243, 249, 552, 705, 740
New York Stock Exchange Composite Index, 998
New York Yankees, 598
New Zealand, 573, 710
Nike, 690
Nikkei 225 Index, 708
Nominal rate (interest), 166, 210
Noncash adjustments, operating activities, statement of cash flows, 60–61
Nonconstant growth firms, 302
Nonconstant growth stock, valuing, 301–304, 305*f*
Nonconvertible currency, 696
Nonconvertible preferred stock, 802
Nonfinancial companies, managing credit risk at, 936
Nonlinear relationships, 509
Nonmonetary resources, constraints on, 424
Nonoperating assets, 66
Nonpecuniary benefits, 526
Nontaxable offer, 889
Non-tax-oriented lease, 776
NOPAT. *See* Net operating profit after taxes
Normal distribution, 241–242
Normal yield curve, 221–222
Northern Rock (U.K. bank), 25
Norway, 702, 703
Notational principal, 930
Novell, 872
NOWC. *See* Net operating capital; Net operating working capital
N periods, 303
NPV. *See* Net present value
NPV break-even analysis, 453, 454*f*
NYSE. *See* New York Stock Exchange
NYSE Composite Index, 33
NYSE Euronext, 30, 32
NYSE Group Inc., 31–32

O

Obama administration, TARP and, 964
Objectives, risk management, 916
Occidental Petroleum, 710
Occupational Safety and Health Administration (OSHA), 10
Off-balance sheet financing, 776
OID. *See* Original issue discount
Olivetti, 873
Omissions, 735
OMX Nordic exchange, 34
OPEC, 913
OpenIPO, 739
Operating activities, statement of cash flows
noncash adjustments, 60–61
working capital, changes in, 61
Operating assets, forecast for, 492–494
Operating companies, 900
Operating current assets, 66
alternative financing policies, 636*f*
efficient use of, 634
financing, 635–638
Operating current assets financing policy, 635
Operating current liabilities, 67
Operating leases, 772
Operating leverage, 593*f*, 594*f*
Operating merger, 879
Operating objectives, 916
Operating plan, 489
forecast accounts from, 496
Operating profit margin, 107–108
Operating transactions, routine (but uncertain), 648
Operations
estimating value of, 306–308
forecasting, 491–495
as risk event category, 919
value of. *See* Value of operations
OPIC. *See* Overseas Private Investment Corporation
OPIC insurance, 710
OPM. *See* Black-Scholes formula option pricing model

Opportunity cost, 75, 143, 370, 441
  projections for expansion project, 448
Optimal capital budget, 421–425
  capital rationing and, 424–425
  increasing cost of capital and, 422–423
Optimal capital structure, 375
Optimal distribution policy, 553
Option pricing model. *See* Black-Scholes option pricing model
Options, 326
  on futures, 923–924
  investment timing, 1013–1022
  multi-period binomial pricing model, 337–340
  overview of financial, 326–329
  pricing in corporate finance, 348–350
  pricing model, 333n
  put, valuation of, 346–348
  real. *See* Real options
  single-period binomial pricing approach, 330–335
  taxes and stock, 345
Option to delay, 463
Option values, positive, 1012
Oracle Corp., 712
Ordinary annuity, 150. *See also* Annuity
Ordinary income, 81
Organic Prairie, 803
Organic Valley, 803
Organization for Economic Cooperation and Development (OECD), 706, 714
  Anti-Bribery Convention, 703
Original issue discount (OID) bond, 191, 809n
Original maturities, 191
OTC. *See* Over-the-counter (OTC) market
OTC trading, 33n
Out-of-the-money (option), 327
Outstanding bond, 199
Overallotment option, 735n
Overseas income, taxes on, 81
Overseas Private Investment Corporation (OPIC), 710
Oversubscribed, 735
Over-the-counter (OTC) market, 33n, 706
Own-bond-yield-plus judgmental-risk premium approach, 378–380

P

Pacific Exchange, 31
Palisade Corporation, 437
Par, of bonds, 195
Parent company, 900
PARRS. *See* Putable Automatic Rate Reset Securities
Partial multiple taxation, 900
Partial public offering, 743
Partnerships, 6–7
Par value (bonds), 190
Paulson & Company, 801
Payables deferral period, 639
Payback period, 414–416
  example project, 414*f*
Payday lending, 171
Payment date, 551
Payment-in-kind bonds, 191
Payoff matrix, 239
Payout ratio, 373, 507
Payroll checks, issuing, 651
PE. *See* Private equity (PE) fund
Pecking order, 602, 606
Pegged exchange rate, 695
Pension funds, 26
Pension plan liabilities, bankruptcy settlements and, 960n
Pentagon, Sept. 11 attacks on, 917
Pepisco, 872
Percentage change analysis, 113–115
Percentage flotation costs, 365
Perfect capital markets, 852
Performance measures, ROI, FCF and, 72–74
Periodic rate (interest), 166–167
Periods
  finding number of (N), 158–159
  fractional time, 169–170
Permanent operating current assets, 635
Perpetuity, 149–150
  cash flows as, 852
Pershing Square Capital Management, 747
Personal bankruptcies, 963
Personal property, recovery allowance percentage for, 483*t*
Personal taxes, Miller model and, 848
Peru, 705, 710
Pfizer, 325, 417, 530, 712
Pharmasset, 235
Philip Morris, 776
Phoenix Stamping Group LLC, 357
Physical asset markets, 27
Physical life, 421
  economic life *vs.*, 421, 422*f*
Physical location exchange, 29
PIK bonds, 191
Pilgrim's Pride, 589

PIPE. *See* Private investment in public equity
Pizza Hut, 696
Poison pill, 531
Policy, cost of money and, 19–20
Political risk, 684, 710
  multinational corporations and
Pollution control agencies, 212
Pollution control bonds, 212
Ponzi scheme, 265
Pooling accounting, 892n
Porter Electronic Controls Inc., 576, 923
Portfolio
  efficient, 978–983
  hedge. *See* Hedge portfolio approach
  payoffs, put-call parity, 346*t*
  returns and evaluation, 262–263
  risk *vs.* stand-alone, 237
Portfolio companies, 731
Portfolio risk
  correlation and risk for two-stock, 247–249
  creating a portfolio, 246–247
  diversification, multi-stock portfolios and, 249–250*f*
Portfolio investments, 703
Portfolio theory
  choosing the optimal portfolio, 983–986, 985*f*
  efficient frontier, 984
  efficient portfolios, 978–983
  minimum risk portfolio, 982
  N-asset case, 982–983
  returns, risk and attainable set, 981*f*
  risk–return indifference curves, 984–986
  two-asset case, 979–982
Portugal, 937
PPP. *See* Purchasing power parity
Prada, 731
Precautionary balances, 648
Preemptive bid, 873
Preemptive right, 291
Preferred stock, 15, 16*t*, 55, 800
  adjustable rate (ARPs), 803
  advantages and disadvantages, 804
  basic features of, 800–803
  cost of, 366
  dividends on, 312–313
  financial risk and, 594n
  as hybrid financing, 800–804
  market auction, 803–804
  nonconvertible, 802
  restrictions to, 573
  risk and, 801
  U.S. treasury purchase of, 799
Preliminary prospectuses, 735
Premier Pay Cards, 651
Premium, 697
  option market price, 328
Premium bond, 198, 199
Prepackaged bankruptcy (pre-pack), 957–958
Present values (PV), 135
  annuities due, 156–157
  discounting future value, to find, 143–146
  ordinary annuity, 155–156
Present value of a nonconstant growth stock, 314
Price(s)
  applications of option, in corporate finance, 348–350
  asset valuation and, 103
  binomial option pricing, 335–336
  bond, interest rate changes and, 198
  estimating price per share, 309–310
  five factors that affect call option, 343–346
  multi-period binomial option model for, 337–340
  option pricing model, 333n
  single-period binomial option, 330–335
  solving for bond, 195–198
  stock, corporate valuation and, 290
  stock, reflect long- short-term events, 298–299
  unit, projections for expansion project, 444
  volatility, 299–300
Price/cash flow ratio, 110–111
Price/earnings (P/E) ratio, 110
Price EBITDA ratio, 110
Primary EPS, 818n
Primary markets, 28
Primary market transactions, 13
Prime rate, 637n, 666
PrimeRevenue network, 656
Primitive securities, binomial option pricing formula and, 336–337
Princeton University, 217
Private equity (PE) fund, 26, 752
Private firms
  adjusting for lack of liquidity, 380
  estimating consistent weights in capital structure, 380
  estimating cost of stock by comparison approach, 378
  own-bond-yield-plus judgmental-risk premium approach, 378–380
Private investment in public equity (PIPE), 747
Private markets, 28
Private placements, 730, 747

Probability distribution, 238–239
Probability ranges, normal distribution, 242*f*
Procter & Gamble, 3, 32, 51, 254*t*, 437, 829, 867
Production opportunities, 18–19
Product line, increase capacity of existing, 463
Product markets, competition in, 537
Products, add new, 464
Professional association (PA), 8
Professional corporation (PC), 8
Profit, 58
Profitability index (PI), 413, 413*f*
Profitability ratios, 107
  basic earning power (BEP), 108
  net profit margin, 107–108
  return on common equity, 109
  return on total assets, 109
Profit margin, 506
Profit margin on sales, 107–108
Pro forma financial statements, 488
Pro forma income, 58n
Progressive tax, 81
Project analysis
  capital budgeting and, 398–399
  first step in, 400–401
  Monte Carlo simulation applied to, 934*f*
  multinational capital budgeting, 711–714
  mutually exclusive projects, using IRR, 407–409
  valuation, cash flows, and risk analysis, 438
  See also Project selection risks
Project cash flows, 438
Projected financial statements, 488
Project financing, 365, 763–764
Project selection risks, 933–936
Promissory notes, 665
Property, depreciation of residential rental, 483*t*
Proprietorship, 6
Prospectus, 734
  preliminary or "red herring," 735
Proxy, 291
Proxy ballot, 529
Proxy fight, 291, 874
Proxy statements, SEC and, 741
Public markets, 28
Purchase accounting, 892
Purchasing power bonds, 193
Purchasing power parity (PPP), 700–702
Pure expectation theory, 222
Pure financial merger, 879
Pure play method, 384, 384n
Putable Automatic Rate Reset Securities (PARRS), 760
Put-call parity relationships, 346–347
Put option, 327
  five factors affecting prices of, 347–348
  put-call parity, 346–347

Q

Qualcomm, 631
Qualitative factors, bond ratings, 214
Quantitative easing, 44
Quick ratio, 99–100
QUIDS (Quarterly Income Debt Securities), 802n
Quiet period, 735
QUIPS (Quarterly Income Preferred Securities), 802n
Quoted interest rate, 207, 210
Quoted rate (interest), 166
Qwest, 870

R

Ralcorp Holdings, 899
Random Walk Down Wall Street (Malkiel), 992
Ratings agencies
  AAA-rated companies, 217
  bonds, 212–213
  subprime mortgages and, 40
  U.S. Treasury bonds downgrade, 215
Ratio analysis, 97
  asset management, 100–103. *See also* Asset management
  comparative/benchmarking, 117
  current ratio, 97–99
  debt management, 103–107. *See also* Debt management ratio
  Du Pont equation, 115–117
  market value, 110–112
  profitability, 107–109. *See also* Profitability ratio
  quick/acid test, 99–100
  uses and limitations of, 118–119
  on the web, 119
Ratio relationships, 508*f*
Rayonier Inc., 553*t*
Real estate
  appraisers, liar loans and, 40
  boom, housing prices/mortgage rates, 39*f*
Real estate leases, 787
Realized rate of return, 242–243, 295
Real options, 463, 1011–1034
  abandonment options, 464
  concluding thoughts on, 1028–1029
  flexibility options, 464
  growth options, 463–464, 1023–1028

pricing, 348–349
valuing, 464–465, 1012–1013
Real Options: Managing Strategic Investment in an Uncertain World (Amram and Kulatilaka), 466n
Real risk-free rate of interest, 207–208
Recap, 614. *See also* Recapitalization
Recapitalization, 614–618, 614*f*
deleveraging and, 618
issuing new debt, 615
stock repurchases, 615–617
Receivables conversion period, 639
Receivables management, 654–658
accumulation of receivables, 654–655
credit policy, 654
monitoring the receivables position, 655–658
Recovery period, 481
Redeemable at par, 192
"Red herring" prospectuses, 735
Refunding operations, 192, 756–762
annual interest savings, 759
flotation costs and, 758–759
now *vs.* later, 761–762
NPV of, 760–761
required investment outlay, 757–758
spreadsheet for bond refunding decision, 757*f*
Regional markets, 28
Regions Financial Corp., 553*t*
Registration statement, 734
Regular interest, 666–667
Regular quarterly dividend, 550
Regulation D, 747n
Regulation Fair Disclosure, 95
Regulation S, 747n
Regulations, as noncontrollable factor, 536
Reinvestment rate risk, 219–220
Relative priority doctrine, 953
Relaxed policy (of holding current assets), 634
Relevant risk, 249
Renaissance Capital, Global IPO Report, 744n
Reorganization
bankruptcy. *See* Bankruptcy reorganization
informal, 946–948
Repatriated, 710
Repatriation taxes, 547
Replacement analysis, 461–462, 462*f*
Replacement chains, 420
Replacement projects, 399, 440
Replicating portfolios, 334–335
Reporting
annual reports, 52, 61–64
for employee stock options, 330
stock market, 292–293
Reporting objectives, 916
Required level of fixed assets, 510
Required rate of return, 294, 612*f*
Required return on a portfolio, 262–265
Reserve borrowing capacity, 602–604, 606
Reserve Primary Fund, 42
Residual distribution model, 560
financial statements and, 563, 565
in practice, 561–562
Residual value, 781
estimated, of lease, 786
Restricted policy (of holding current assets), 634
Restricted voting rights, 531
Restrictive covenants, 211, 213–214
Restructuring, 947
Retention growth equation, 373–374
Retirement plans, self-directed, 26
Return on assets, 109
Return on common equity (ROE), 109
efficient use of operating current assets and, 634
financial leverage and, 595
Return on invested capital (ROIC), 72, 495
analysis, 97
expected, 502
free cash flows and, 72–74
Return on total assets (ROA), 109
operating leverage and, 594
Returns, 237
actual/expected, 241
required/expected portfolio, SML and, 262–263
trade-off between risk and, 246
Reuters, 117, 685
Revaluation, 695
Reverse split, 577
Revolving credit agreement, 665–666
Reynolds American Inc., 553*t*
Rho, 247
Right of offset, 960n
Risk, 237, 243
Bernie Madoff, 265
commodity price, 921–924
in continuous distribution, 241–242
cost of money and, 18–19
country, 22
diversifiable, 249
exchange rate, 22
financial, 594–595
foreign exchange, 920–921

historical data to estimate, 242–245
information from payback methods about, 416–417
interest rate, 925–932
interest rate, reinvestment rate, and maturity risk premium, 220
investment return and, 236
market, 249, 251–253
measuring for discrete distribution, 238–241
mortgages and, 37
in portfolio context, 246–250
relevant of stock, CAPM and, 250–257
security market line and, 257–259
stand-alone *vs.* portfolio, 237
trade-off between return and, 246
types of, 450
using historical data to estimate, 242–245
intrinsic value, return and, 978
Risk-adjusted cost of capital, 385, 398, 401–402, 451. *See also* Weighted average cost of capital
Risk analysis
in capital budgeting, 450–451
measuring stand-alone risk, 451
Monte Carlo simulation, 457–460
phased decisions and decision trees, 465–466
project risk conclusions, 460–461
project valuation, cash flows and, 438
real options, 463–465
replacement analysis, 461–462
scenario analysis, 455–457
sensitivity analysis, 451–454
Risk appetite, 916
Risk arbitrage, 896
Risk averse, 985
Risk aversion, 236, 260–261, 261*f*
Risk events
dimensions of risk, 919–920
major categories, 919
Risk-free rate of interest, 210, 258
estimate using CAPM, 370–371
impact of changes in, 259–260
option prices and, 345
Risk management
corporate finance, option pricing in, 349
corporate valuation and, 910
See also Enterprise risk management
Risk Management Associates, 117
Risk-neutral valuation, 1022
Risk premium, 985
forward-looking, 368–369
Risk premium for an individual stock, 258–259
Risk–return indifference curves, 984–986, 984*f*
Risky assets, selecting optimal portfolio of, 985*f*
Risky event, 916
ROA. *See* Return on total assets
Roadshow, 735
Robert's Online Option Pricer, 341
ROE. *See* Return on common equity
Rohm & Haas, 801
ROI. *See* Return on investment
ROIC. *See* Return on invested capital
Rojacks Food Stores, 787
Rolling forecast, 487
Royal Bank of Scotland, 709
Rule 144A, 747, 747n

S

S-1 form, 734n
Saddleback Valley Community Church, 217
Safety projects, capital budgeting for, 399
Saint Emilion Grand Cru., 202
Sales
annual unit, projections for, 444
under GAAP, 63
Sale to another firm, 898
Sales growth, 506
Sanofi, 873
Sarbanes-Oxley Act (SOX), 10, 30, 70, 535, 914
Savings and loan associations (S&Ls), 15, 17–18, 24
Scenario analysis, 455
expected NPV and its risk, 457*f*
inputs and key results for each scenario, 455*f*
for investment timing option, 1015–1018, 1016*f*, 1017*f*
SCF. *See* Supply chain finance techniques
SCM. *See* Supply chain management
S corporation, 8, 81, 890n
Seasoned equity offering, 30–31, 745–746
Seasoned issue (bond), 199
SEC. *See* Securities and Exchange Commission
Secondary offering, 745
Secondary stock market, 28, 31
competition in, 34
NASDAQ, 32–33
New York Stock exchange, 31–32
regulating, 741–742
Securities
asset-backed, 748
financial intermediaries and, 13
regulation of sales, 734–735
securitization process, 15–18

structured investment vehicles (SIVs0, 56
See also Financial securities
Securities Act (1933), 730, 747
Securities and Exchange Commission (SEC), 30, 33, 42, 53, 95, 108, 211, 730, 741
bankruptcy reorganization plan and, 954n
on basic and diluted EPS, 819
Dodd-Frank Act and, 937
Sarbanes-Oxley Act (SOX) and, 535
SEC oversight of new security issuance, 891
Securities Industry and Financial Markets Association, 977
Securitization, 748–749
investment banking and, 750
lease, 789
Securitization process, 15–18
mortgage securities, globalization and, 37
subprime meltdown and, 42
Securitize, 748
Security
in short-term financing, 668–669
use of term, 748
Security Market Line (SML), 257–258, 991
Capital Asset Pricing Model (CAPM) and, 987–991
changes in beta coefficient, common stock and, 261
figures, 260, 261
impact of changes in risk free rate, 259–260
portfolio returns and performance evaluation, 262–263
risk aversion, changes in, 260–261, 262*f*
risk-free rate, 258
risk premium for individual stock, 258–259
tests of CAPM based on slope of, 1000–1001
Self-insure, 917
Self-liquidating approach, 635
Self-supporting growth rate, 507
Selling group, 734
Sell orders, 32
Semiannual compounding periods, 165
Semiannual coupons, bonds with, 202–203
Semiannual payments, 202–203
Semistrong-form efficiency, 267, 269
Senior mortgages, 211
Sensitivity analysis, 451
extensions of, 453–454
NPV break-even analysis, 453, 454*f*
sensitivity graph, 452–453, 452*f*
Tornado diagrams, 453, 454*f*
Sensitivity graph, 452–453, 452*f*
September 11, 2001, attacks, 917
SETS, stock exchange, 30
Settlement price, 925
Seven Country Working Group, 703
Shareholder rights provision, 531
Sharpe's reward-to-variability ratio, 996
Shelf registration, 746
Shenzhen Development Bank, 709
Sherman Act (1890), 868n
Short hedges, 922
Short sales, arbitrage with, 856
Short-term bank loans, 664–667
Short-term debt, flexibility of, 638
Short-term financing, 663–664
use of security in, 668–669
Short-term investments
managing, 662–663
purchase or sell, 549–550
Siemens, 703
Sigma, 240
Signal, 602
Signaling, 557, 606
Simon Property Group, 534
Simple interest, 143, 170, 666–667
Simulation analysis, probability distribution in, 457–458
Singapore, 705
Singapore Airlines, 771
Single-period binomial option pricing approach, 330
hedge portfolio approach, 331–334. *See also* Hedge portfolio approach
formula, 335–336
payoff in, 331
primitive securities and, 336–337
Sinking fund, 106
Sinking fund provision, 192–193
SIX Swiss Exchange, 30
Small Business Administration, 189
Small businesses
adjusting for lack of liquidity, 380
estimating consistent weights in capital structure, 380
estimating cost of stock by comparison approach, 378
own-bond-yield-plus judgmental-risk premium approach, 378–380
SMG Fairfax, 789
Smith Barney, 27
SML. *See* Security market line
Social Security, 238, 369
Social Security Trust fund, 706

Social welfare, stock value maximization and, 10–11
Soft currency, 696
Somalia, 710
Sony, 442
South America, 701
Southwest Airlines, 3, 631
Sovereign debt, 706–707
Soviet Union, Pizza Hut in, 696
SOX. *See* Sarbanes-Oxley Act
S&P 500 Index, 33
  performance of, 35*f*
Spain, 937
Special purpose entity (SPE), 774
Speculation, 922
Spinning, 742
Spin-off, 898
Spontaneous liabilities, 494, 504–505
Spontaneous liabilities-to-sales ratio, 506
Spot exchange rate
  interest rate parity and, 699
  purchasing power parity and, 700
  selected, units per U.S. dollar, 698*t*
Spot exchange rate, 697
Spot markets, 27
Spread, 739
Spreadsheets
  time value and, 138–141
  uneven cash flows, 162–163
Sprint Nextel, 530
Sprint-Nextel merger, 871
Staged decision tree, 466
Stand-alone risk, 237, 384, 450
  measuring, 240, 451
  quantitative analysis of, 451
  portfolio risk vs., 237
Standard deviation, 240
  calculating historical, 243–244
Standard & Poor's (S&P), 37, 43, 212–213, 215, 217, 559, 607
Standard & Poor's depository receipt (SPDR), 33
Starbucks, 90, 591, 712
Start-up company, financial life cycle of, 730–731
Starz Entertainment Group, 292
Statement of cash flows, 52, 59
  analyze, 97
  annual reports and, 61–64
  financing activities, 61
  investing activities, 61
  operating activities, 60–61
Statement of stockholders' equity, 52
Statoil, 703
Status quo scenario, forecasted financial statements, 495, 500*f*
Step-by-step approach, future value, 136–137
Stock
  intrinsic value, maximize, 10–11
  issue new, as use of cash, 550
  reluctance to issue new, 424
  repurchase, as use of cash, 550
  tracking, 292
  types of common, 291–292
  valuing constant growth, 296–301
  valuing nonconstant growth, 301–304
Stock dividends, 577, 578. *See also* Dividends
Stock exchanges, SEC and, 741
Stockholders
  choices with stock repurchases, 571
  claims, 54
  clientele effect, 556–557
  common, legal rights/privileges of, 290–291
  wealth maximization, 9
Stockholders' equity statement, 58–59
Stock index, 33
Stock market
  bubbles in, 267–268
  manipulation of, 741, 742n
  measuring, 33
  reporting, 292–293
  returns, 34–36
  secondary, 31–34. *See also* Secondary stock markets
  social welfare and, 10–11
  trading, 33
  types of transactions on, 30–31
Stock market indices, worldwide, 708
Stock option compensation plan, 531
Stock options
  intrinsic value of, 326
  reporting for employee, 330
  taxes and, 345
Stock price maximization, 11–13
Stock prices, effects of capital structure on, 617*f*
Stock quote, 293*f*
Stock repurchases, 615–617
  cash distributions as, 565*f*, 570–571
  disadvantages of, 572
  procedures, 551–552
  pros and cons of, 571–573
Stock splits, 576–578
Stonyfield, 803
Straight-line method of depreciation, 481

accelerated depreciation *vs.*, 449–450
Strategic alliances, 898
Strategic Investments: Real Options and Games (Smit and Trigeorgis), 466n
Strategic objectives, 916
Strategic options, 463
Strategy, as risk event category, 919
Stretching accounts payable, 661
Strike price, 327, 807, 1018, 1019*f*
Strong-form efficiency, 267, 269
Structured investment vehicles (SIVs), 56
Subordinated debentures (bonds), 211–212
Subprime mortgage meltdown, 38–41
Sum-of-years'-digits method of depreciation, 481
Sunbeam, 12
Sunk costs, 440–441, 448
Sun Microsystems, 577
Sunny Delight Beverage Co., 357
SunTrust, 873
Supernormal growth firms, 302
Super poison put, 192
Supply chain finance (SCF) techniques, 656
Supply chain management (SCM), 653
Surplus cash, 646
Swap, 928
cash flows under, 929*f*
See also Credit default swaps; Currency swaps
Switzerland, 701, 702, 705
Symmetric hedge, 924
Symmetric information, 600
Synchronization of cash flows, 650
Synergistic benefits, 884
Synergy, 868
Synthetic lease, 774

T

Taiwan, 573
TALF. *See* Term Asset-Backed Securities Loan Facility
Target capital structure, 360, 375, 503–504, 590
Target cash distribution, 572
Target company, 872
Target distribution ratio, 553
Targeted share repurchases, 530
Target fixed assets/Sales, 510
Target payout ratio, 553, 561
Target stock, 292
TARP. *See* Troubled Asset Relief Program
Taxable offer, 889
Tax Code, 80
interest payments as expense, 597
surtax on improperly accumulated income, 574
Tax depreciation, 481–483
Tax effect theory, 554–555
Taxes
after-tax cost of debt, 361–365
corporate, Modigliani and Miller model and, 597–598
corporate and personal, Miller model and, 598–599
corporate evasion of, 79
double taxation, 8
federal rate for corporations, 363n, 364
federal system. *See* Federal income tax system
long-term debt, before-tax cost of, 362–363
managerial decisions, cost of capital and, 381
net operating profit after (NOPAT), 65–66
noncash adjustments, 60–61
overseas income, corporate, 81
personal, 81–82
as rationale for merger, 869
repatriation, 547
risk management and, 912
short-term debt, before-tax cost, of t, 361–362
stock options and, 345
takeover bid structure and, 888–891
Tax-exempt bonds, 212
Tax havens
"Double Irish" and "Dutch Sandwich," 712
See also Tax shelters
Tax Increase Prevention and Reconciliation Act (2005), 555n
Tax laws
lease financing and, 788–789
legal systems and, 684
See also Internal Revenue Service
Tax-oriented lease, 775
Tax-qualifying grant, 345
Tax Reform Act (1986), 79, 481
Tax shelters
international regulation of, 703
See also Tax havens
Tax shield
capital structure and, 886–887
impact on value, 830–833
present value of, 598
value of, 843, 857
Technical analysts, 266
Technology, as risk event category, 919
TED spread, 218
Telecom Italia, 873
Telefonica SA, 937
Temporary operating current assets, 635

Tender, 873
Tender offer, 873
Tennessee Valley Authority, 189
Term Asset-Backed Securities Loan Facility (TALF), 759
Terminal date, 303
Terminal value, 163, 303, 411
Term structure of interest rates, 221–222
Terrorism Risk Insurance Act (TRIA), 917–918
Terrorist attacks, risk management and, 917
Texas and Western (T&W) Transport Company, 560–561
Thales Group, 437
Thomson Reuters, 631, 930
3M, 217, 394–395, 417
TIAA-CREF, 536
Ticker tape, 292–293
Tiffany and Company, 553*t*
Time deposits, as short-term investment, 662
Time lines
  bond value and, 194–195
  time value of money analysis, 135
Time preferences for consumption, 18–19
Times-interest-earned ratio (TIE), 105–106
Time value of money (TVM), 134–135
  amortized loans, 170–176. *See also* Amortized loans
  annuities, 150
  annuity payments, periods, interest rates, finding, 158–159
  corporate valuation, 134
  fractional time periods, 169–170
  future value of annuity, 151–153
  future value of uneven cash flow, 163
  future values, 135–143. *See also* Future values, of money
  interest rate (I), finding, 147–148, 164–165
  perpetuities, 149–150
  present values, 143–147, 155–157. *See also* Present value
  semiannual/other compounding periods, 165–170. *See also* Compounding periods
  time lines, 135
  years, finding number of, N, 148
Time Warner, 292, 325, 868, 889, 899
Tobacco bonds, 748
Tommy Hilfiger, 690
Too-big-to-fail banks, 45
TOPrS (Trust Originated Preferred Stock), 802n
Tornado diagrams, 453, 454*f*
Total assets turnover ratio, 100
Total investor-supplied capital, 68
Total investor-supplied operating capital, 68
Total net operating capital, 67–68
Total returns, 34
Total Revenue (GAAP), 63
Toxic assets, 43
Toyota, 624
Tracking stock, 292
Trade
  high-frequency, 30
  international, deficits/surpluses, 21–22
Trade balances, federal budget surplus/deficits and, 20*f*
Trade credit, 659–662. *See also* Accounts payable
Trade deficit, 690
Trade discounts, 648
Trade-off theory, 599–600
  dynamic, 605
  effect of financial leverage on value, 601*f*
Trading
  in financial markets, 29–30
  insider, 329n
Trading-day returns, 342n
Trailing twelve months, 293
Tranches, 37, 43, 789
Trane Corporation, 652
Transactions balances, 648
Transfer price, 711
Transfers, 13, 14*f*
Transnational corporations, 682. *See also* Multinational corporations
Transparency, in markets, 45
Transparency International (TI), 710
  Corruption Perceptions Index (CPI), 711*t*
TransUnion, 936
Travelers insurance, 27
Treasury bills, 16*t*, 246
Treasury bonds, 189, 760
  credit default swaps, 190
  futures contracts, hedging with, 926–928
  futures prices, 925*t*
  interest rate futures and, 925
  interest rates, 221*f*
Treasury Inflation-Protected Securities (TIPS), 193, 208
Treasury stock, 551n
Trend analysis, 113–115
Treynor's reward-to-volatility ratio, 996
Trial, in Monte Carlo simulation, 458
Triple taxation, 78

Troubled Asset Relief Program (TARP), 43–44, 799, 964
investment banks and, 751
TARP funds, 532
Trustee, 211
bankruptcy, 949
Truth in Lending Act, 168
Turnover ratio, inventory, 102
TVA, 760
Two-period binomial lattice and option valuation, 339*f*
Tyco, 12, 914

U

UAW. *See* United Auto Workers
UBS, 729, 867
Ukraine, Big Macs in, 702
Underinvestment problem, 534
Underwrite, 733
Underwriters, 13, 733
Underwriting, mergers & acquisitions and, 749
Underwriting syndicate, 733–734
Unequal lives, conclusions about, 420–421
Uneven cash flows, 160–163
Unilever, 437
Union Carbide, 579
Union Fire Company, 913
Unit costs, projections for expansion project, 444
United Auto Workers (UAW), 964
United Kingdom, 715. *See also* Great Britain
United Parcel Service (UPS), 217
United States
board of director's duty toward managers in, 528
corporate governance in, 538
dividend yields in, 573
merger waves in, 871–872
OECD Anti-Bribery Convention and, 703
ranking as honest country, 710
runaway inflation in (1970s), 913
stockholder protection, 292
trade deficits, 22n
use of futures contracts in, 913
Unit prices, projections for expansion project, 444
University of Chicago, 171, 714
University of Florida, 738
University of Michigan, 209n
Unlevered beta, 611
Unlevered cost of equity, 882
Unsyndicated stock offering, 734
U.S. agency securities, as short-term investment, 662
U.S. Bankruptcy Court, 223
U.S. Bankruptcy Trustee, 598
U.S. Congress
antitrust acts, 868n
Bankruptcy Act, 946, 950
bankruptcy law and, 949–950
bonus depreciation rate, 788
Foreign Corrupt Practices Act (FCPA), 914
Job Creation and Worker Assistance Act of 2002, 482n
Sarbanes-Oxley (SOX) Act, 914
Securities Act (1933), 730, 747
on tax shelters, 712
temporary "bonus" depreciation (2008-09), 449n
Terrorism Risk Insurance Act (TRIA), 917–918
Williams Act (1968), 874
U.S. Department of Justice, 868n, 871
U.S. dollar
currency appreciation and, 693
currency depreciation and, 694
foreign bonds denominated in, 705–706
foreign currency depreciating or appreciating against, 701
index, *vs.* major currencies, 693*f*
as leading currency, 704
spot and forward exchange rates per, 698*t*
U.S. Export-import Bank, 717
U.S. Financial Accounting Standards Board (FASB), 63
U.S. firms, debt to total assets in, 714–715
U.S. government
as board of director, 532
as Chrysler owner, 943
response to global economic crisis, 799
U.S. Justice Department, 10, 930
U.S. Supreme Court, 874–875
U.S. Treasury, 25n, 103, 189n
U.S. Treasury bills, 16*t*, 246
U.S. Treasury bond. *See* Treasury bonds
U.S. Treasury Department, 799
U.S. Treasury securities
notes and bonds, 16*t*
as short-term investment, 662
STRIP bonds, 191
See also U.S. Treasury bills; Treasury bonds

V

Valuation
of constant growth stock, 296–301
corporate, cost of capital, 358
corporate, stock prices and, 290
estimating operations, 306–308

free cash flows (FCF) model, 304–311
nonconstant growth stocks, 301–304
preferred stock, 312–313
of put options, 346–348. *See also* Put options, valuation
Valuation formulas, bonds, 194–195
Value, estimated intrinsic, 495
Value at risk (VaR), 934
Value Line, 117, 253, 254, 371, 997, 998
Value maximization, corporate, 9
Value of operations
cash distributions and, 566–567
under different distribution methods, 566*f*
effects of capital structure on, 613*f*
estimating, 613–614
levered, APV model and, 843
Variable annuities, 157
Variance, 240
VCs. *See* Venture capitalists
VEBA. *See* Voluntary employee's beneficiary association
Vehicle leases, 788
Venezuela, 710
Venture capital fund, 730
Venture capitalists (VCs), 731
Verizon, 870
Vertical merger, 871
Vesting period, 531
Vetco International, 703
Vietnam War, 17
Virco Manufacturing, 791
Virgin Atlantic, 771
Virgin Group, 771
Vodafone AirTouch, 873
Volatility, call options and, 344
Volker Rule, 44–45
Volume, trading, 34
Voluntary bankruptcy, 949
Voluntary employee's beneficiary association (VEBA), 964
Voluntary settlements, 948
Vote, stockholder, 290–291

W

W. R. Hambrecht & Co., 739
WACC. *See* Weighted average cost of capital
Wachovia, 530, 873, 945
Wachovia–Wells Fargo merger, 871
WAEMU. *See* West African Economic and Monetary Union
Walgreens, 51
Wall Street Journal, The, 16*t*, 30, 160, 194, 221, 292, 342, 397, 685
cross rate reports in, 689
Investment Dartboard Contest, 992
Wall Street Journal Online, 750, 925*t*
Walmart, 578, 659
Walmart credit card, in China, 709
Walt Disney Co., 191n
Warrants, 193, 805–810
component cost of bond with, 807–809
convertibles *vs.*, 817–818
initial market price of bond with, 805–806
reporting earnings with outstanding, 818–819
strike price on, 807
use in financing, 806–807
valuation analysis after exercise of, 809*t*
Washington Mutual, 589, 943
WD-40 Company, 553*t*
Weak-form efficiency, 266, 269
Wealth management, investment banks and, 750
Weighted average cost of capital (WACC), 12, 359–360, 375, 400, 444
book values *vs.* market values *vs.* targets, 376
choosing weights for, 360–361
at different debt levels, 611
estimating for different debt levels, 609–612
estimated target, 495
financing choices and, 590–591
marginal rates *vs.* historical rates, 375–376
project cash flow and, 440
risk and, 525
risk-adjusted, 398
target weights *vs.* annual financing choices, 376
value of unlevered firm and, 831
Well known seasoned issuers (WKSIs), 746n
Wells Fargo, 532, 618, 734, 873, 945
West African Economic and Monetary Union (WAEMU), 696
What-if analysis, with operating plans, 489
Whistleblowers, ethics and, 10
White knight, 895
White squire, 895
Williams Act (1968), 874
Williamson Scientific Company, 807
Wimm-Bill-Dann Foods, 872
Window dressing techniques, 119
Wire, payment by, 651
Within-firm risk, 384, 450
WKSIs. *See* Well known seasoned issuers

Working capital, 634
  changes in, 61
  negative, 644
  net operating, 439
  origination of term, 634n
  projections for expansion project, 447–448
  use of term, 633–634
Working capital management
  corporate valuation and, 632
  efficient use of operating current assets, 634
  overview, 633–634
  using and financing operating current assets, 634–638
  multinational, 715–718
Workouts, 947
WorldCom, 10, 12, 70, 526, 742, 914
World is Flat, The (Friedman), 6
World markets, 28
World Trade Center, Sept. 11 attacks on, 917
WPP, 534
Writing (option), 328

X

XTO Energy, 217

Y

Yahoo! Finance, 33, 74, 221, 253, 291, 293*f*, 685, 998
Yankee bond, 705
Years, finding number of, time value of money, 148, 195
Yield curve, 221
Yield on debt, 845
Yields to maturity (YTM), bonds, 203–204, 410
Yield to call (YTC), 204–205
Yom Kippur War, 913
YRC Worldwide, 235

Z

Zacks.com, 95, 96–97
Zero coupon bonds, 191